Freud's
Self-Analysis

FREUD'S SELF-ANALYSIS

DIDIER ANZIEU

Translated from the French by
PETER GRAHAM

With a Preface by
M. MASUD R. KHAN

International Universities Press, Inc.
Madison•Connecticut

French title: L'auto-analyse de Freud
et la découverte de la psychanalyse
(originally published in two volumes by
Presses Universitaires de France, 1975)

Library of Congress Cataloging-in-Publication Data

Anzieu, Didier.
Freud's self-analysis.

Translation of: L'auto-analyse de Freud et la découverte de la psychanalyse.
Includes bibliographies and indexes.
1. Freud, Sigmund, 1856-1939. 2. Psychoanalysts—
Austria—Biography. 3. Psychoanalyses—History.
I. Title. II. Series.
BF173.F85A5913 1986 150.19'52 86-14924
ISBN 0-8236-2045-X

Manufactured in the United States of America

Contents

Abbreviations viii

Preface by M. Masud R. Khan ix

Introduction xv

1 FREUD UP TO 1895 1

Childhood 1
Engagement and marriage (1882–86) 21
Biological and medical education 32
Freud and Charcot 45
Freud and Breuer 56
Freud and his time 84
Freud and Fliess 108

2 THE DISCOVERY OF THE MEANING OF DREAMS 122

Freud's progress by July 1895 122
The dream of 'Irma's injection' (July 24, 1895) 131
From the Irma dream to the death of Freud's father (July 1895–October 1896) 156

3 THE DISCOVERY OF THE OEDIPUS COMPLEX 175

The notion of the 'psychical apparatus' 175
The 'Rome' dreams (January 1897) 182
Prelude to systematic self-analysis (February–May 1897) 213
Dreams: 'Uncle with the yellow beard', 'Villa Secerno', 'Hella', 'Running up stairs undressed'
Systematic self-analysis (June–November 1897) 231
Dreams: 'Sheep's head', 'One-eyed doctor and schoolmaster'; screen memory of the 'wardrobe' scene; the discovery of the Oedipus myth and the blunder in the old woman's injection

4 THE DISCOVERY OF THE PRIMAL SCENE AND THE FIRST VERSION OF *The Interpretation of Dreams* 252

Freud's first attempt to break away from Fliess (December 1897–February 1898) 252
Dream: 'My son, the Myops'

Work on *The Interpretation of Dreams* gets under way (February–July 1898) 265
Dream: 'Otto was looking ill'
Dreams dreamt by Freud while writing the first version of *The Interpretation of Dreams* 278
Dreams: 'Botanical monograph', 'My mother and the bird-beaked figures', 'Goethe's attack on Herr M.', 'Castle by the sea', 'Hall with machines', 'Phantasies during sleep'
The important dreams of the summer of 1898 324
'Hollthurn', 'Open-air closet', 'Count Thun'

5 THE DISCOVERY OF CASTRATION ANXIETY AND THE SECOND VERSION OF *The Interpretation of Dreams* 354
Two disguised autobiographical dreams (August 1898?) 354
'Yellow lion', 'Nansen's sciatica'
First analyses of name-forgetting 358
The forgetting of the names 'Julius Mosen' and 'Signorelli' (August–September 1898)
The working over of anxiety about death (September–October 1898) 362
*Dreams: 'Three Fates', 'Riding on a horse', and '*Non vixit*'*
The discovery of the condensation of words (autumn 1898) 388
*Dreams: 'Hearsing', '*Norekdal*', '*Autodidasker*', and 'Frau Doni'*
Confrontation with the difference between the sexes 404
Screen memory: 'Green meadow with yellow flowers' (December 1898–January 1899)
Further theoretical progress (January–May 1899) 411
Dreams: 'Father on his death-bed like Garibaldi', 'Famous speakers', 'Dissecting my own pelvis', and 'Etruscan cinerary urn'
The writing of the second version of *The Interpretation of Dreams* (May–September 1899) 431
Dreams: 'Being in the sixth form', '1851 and 1856', and 'Stopping a runaway horse' (daydream)

6 FREUD'S THEORY OF THE PSYCHICAL APPARATUS IN *The Interpretation of Dreams* AND HIS FURTHER DISCOVERIES 456
The structure of *The Interpretation of Dreams* 456
Occasional self-analysis and continued work 513
The writing of The Psychopathology of Everyday Life *(November 1899–February 1901); the end of E.'s treatment and the elimination of Freud's 'transference' on to Fliess (December 1899–August 1900); a second book on dreams,* Über den Traum*; the '*Trottoir roulant*', 'Glass top-hat', 'Swimming-pool', and 'Company at table d'hôte' dreams, and the beginning of the Dora case (October–December 1900); Freud in 1901 and 1902; self-analysis in Freud's later life and work*

CONCLUSION 561

APPENDICES

Freud bibliography 586

Bibliography excluding Freud 590

Name index 597

Subject index 608

TABLES

1. Chronology of psychological notions acquired by Freud between 1892 and 1895, before his self-analysis 79
2. Alphabetical list of the main notions used by Freud in 1895 125
3. Sigmund Freud's family tree 248
4. The first and second versions of *The Interpretation of Dreams:* a comparison 270
5. The various stages of Freud's gathering of scientific data on sexuality 477
6. Alphabetical list of psychoanalytic notions acquired by Freud during his self-analysis (1895–1901) 564

Abbreviations

SE — *The Standard Edition of the Complete Psychological Works of Sigmund Freud* (1953–74), translated from the German under the general editorship of James Strachey, in collaboration with Anna Freud, assisted by Alix Strachey and Alan Tyson; published in twenty-four volumes by The Hogarth Press (London) and W. W. Norton (New York).

ID — *The Interpretation of Dreams* (1900*a*), *SE* 4 and 5.

OD — *On Dreams* (1901*a*), *SE* 5.

PEL — *The Psychopathology of Everyday Life* (1901*b*), *SE* 6.

F — *The Complete Letters of Sigmund Freud to Wilhelm Fliess, 1887–1904* (1985), translated and edited by Jeffrey Moussaieff Masson; published by The Belknap Press of Harvard University Press (Cambridge, Massachusetts, and London, England).

L — *Letters of Sigmund Freud, 1873–1939* (1961), edited by Ernst L. Freud, translated by Tania and James Stern; published by The Hogarth Press (London) and Basic Books (New York).

J — Ernest Jones, *Sigmund Freud: Life and Work*, 3 volumes, published by The Hogarth Press (London) and, with different pagination, Basic Books (New York). Volume 1 (1953) 'The Young Freud, 1856–1900'; Volume 2 (1955) 'The Years of Maturity, 1901–1919'; Volume 3 (1957) 'The Last Phase, 1919–1939'.

G — Alexander Grinstein, *Sigmund Freud's Dreams* (1980), published by International Universities Press (New York).

E — Henri F. Ellenberger, *The Discovery of the Unconscious* (1970), Basic Books (New York) and Allen Lane, The Penguin Press (London).

S — Max Schur, *Freud: Living and Dying* (1972), International Universities Press (New York) and The Hogarth Press (London).

Preface

M. MASUD R. KHAN

> O God! I could be bounded in a nut-shell, and count myself a king of infinite space, were it not that I have bad dreams.
>
> Shakespeare, *Hamlet*, Act 2, Scene 2

THE *HOW* OF IT

Professor Didier Anzieu, in this immense book, sets himself one, and only one, labyrinthine task: to chart *how* Sigmund Freud conducted his self-analysis, which became a life-long preoccupation with him. As he puts it himself (p. 557 below), 'Freud lived in an atmosphere of permanent self-analysis'. He assiduously describes (pp. 568–9) what were the functions of Freud's self-analysis in his own experience, and *how* all of Freud's discoveries and doctrines resulted from it:

> There was certainly a large narcissistic element in Freud's self-analysis, but it never became its only element. It resulted in his experiencing moments of regression which were very far-reaching but always under the control of the ego. In all the aspects I have just mentioned, his self-analysis proceeded in exactly the opposite way to that attempted by his imitators. His main aim was knowledge not so much of the self as of general, normal psychical processes. There can be no denying that Freud withdrew into himself – though subsequently, as we have seen, he greatly exaggerated the extent of his isolation: scientifically he was indeed isolated, but socially, professionally and emotionally he was not.

Professor Anzieu's method in accomplishing this task he has clearly stated himself (p. 572, and see his Introduction):

> As I have attempted to show throughout this book, ideas presented themselves to Freud in three strands – experience of psychoneuroses, experience of himself, and experience of the unconscious with which various civilisations have invested their cultural products; it was the interweaving of those three strands which gave rise to his discovery, and their unravelling which provided him with proof.

There was, however, a fourth source, which Freud stated in a letter to Fliess dated 14 November 1897:

My self-analysis is still interrupted, I have now seen why. I can only analyse myself with objectively acquired knowledge (as if I were a stranger). . . .' (Freud, 1950*a*, p. 234).

Freud had always needed an *interlocutor*, present, imaginary or absent, to eventuate his self-analysis, and Professor Anzieu spells out this *need*, and *desire*, in Freud with tact and thoroughness. This brings me to state the true virtues and merits of Professor Anzieu's '*le travail de l'oeuvre*' (to use his own concept, p. 514). He has collated and rearranged the relevant data from its randomised scatter, above all:

(a) Freud's correspondence, the most important in this context being his letters to Fliess (which Professor Anzieu had to cull from several different sources, but which have now been published in English in a complete edition, hereafter referred to as *F* – see Abbreviations, p. viii).
(b) Freud's overt and covert, at times devious and evasive, autobiographical writings.
(c) Freud's 'confidences' in his interviews, with anyone who sought him out, which were 'recorded' by them later, according to their bias of sensibility, and often to his chagrin.
(d) The retrospective reportage by his patients, his family, friends, even his 'femme de ménage', Paula, etc. Some of these were 'interviewed', after his death, by journalists from all over the world, who made up their own 'tales', and versions, to publish for an ever-growing public, which had a voracious curiosity for such 'discoveries' about the Professor's private life.

Professor Anzieu navigates discreetly through these accretions, always retaining his lambent and insightful perspective, as the narrator, almost never letting himself become the 'as-if analyst' of Freud; a temptation that nobody else has escaped, and largely due to Freud's own '*complicity*' with them. Freud would, through his *écriture* abreactively 'confide' in *others*, and then retreat into himself. He left 'residues' of his *vécu* in the memory of everyone whom he had encountered. Yet, in all innocence, he could write to Romain Rolland (13 May 1926, *L* 371): 'It seems to me a surprising accident that apart from my doctrines my person should attract attention at all.' Freud had made sure it should, and would. To Ferenczi he wrote (2 October 1910, *L* 291: 'Your letter reminded me that I am the same person who picked papyrus in Syracuse, had a scuffle with the railway staff in Naples, and bought antiques in Rome. The identity has been reestablished. It is strange how easily one gives in to the tendency to isolate parts of one's personality.' To make matters worse, from adolescence onwards, Freud hovered from *telling* himself to others, *needing* them to know the enormity of his suffering in achieving the great *aim* he had set for himself, namely, to give us a new and a revolutionary psychology of the human being, to a hide-and-seek ploy, not only with the interlocutors, in his life-time, but with us, of posterity, as well. He did it with a conscious glee. Freud had a sense of his destiny from childhood and adolescence; otherwise, he would not have written to his young friend Emil Fluss (16 June 1873, *L* 22):

> Incidentally, my professor told me – and he is the first person who has dared to tell me this – that I possess what Herder so nicely calls an *idiotic* style – i.e., a style at once correct and characteristic. I was suitably impressed by this amazing fact and don't hesitate to disseminate the happy event, the first of its kind, as widely as possible – to you, for instance, who until now have probably remained unaware that you have been exchanging letters with a German stylist. And now I advise you as a friend, not as an interested party, to preserve them – have them bound – take good care of them – one never knows.

Yet, he was to announce, with a tone of malice almost, to his fiancée, Martha Bernays, from Vienna on 28 April 1885 (*L* 152–3):

> One intention as a matter of fact I have almost finished carrying out, an intention which a number of as yet unborn and unfortunate people will one day resent. Since you won't guess what kind of people I am referring to, I will tell you at once: they are my biographers. I have destroyed all my notes of the past fourteen years, as well as letters, scientific excerpts and the manuscripts of my papers. . . . As for the biographers, let them worry, we have no desire to make it too easy for them. Each one of them will be right in his opinion of 'The Development of the Hero', and I am already looking forward to seeing them go astray.

One of his close and celebrated pupils, Theodor Reik, was to write about him: 'Freud was a confessor . . . but at the same time he kept certain secrets to himself. He was a self-revealer and a self-concealer' (quoted by Clark, 1980). To his former colleague, Fritz Wittels, and perhaps his first biographer, he wrote on 18 December 1923: 'It seems to me that the public has no concern with my personality, and can learn nothing from an account of it, so long as my case (for manifold reasons) cannot be expounded without any reserves whatever' (quoted by Clark, 1980, p. 64).

Freud was to write to Arnold Zweig on 31 May 1936 (*L* 426):

> Anyone turning biographer commits himself to lies, to concealment, to hypocrisy, to flattery, and even hiding his own lack of understanding, for biographical truth is not to be had, and even if it were it couldn't be used. Truth is unobtainable; humanity does not deserve it, and incidentally, wasn't our Prince Hamlet right when he asked whether anyone would escape a whipping if he got what he deserves.

Freud had more in common with Prince Hamlet than he was aware of, even if he would change Hamlet's statement 'readiness is all', and say 'cheerfulness is all'. Alas! it was not so with Freud. His amplitudes of mood were awesome and frightening, to himself and for others. He could easily have 'a fit of gloom', faint from suppressed anguish or rage (Clark, 1980, pp. 326–7), be 'so dreadfully tired', yet bounce back to his creative productive self, and thus leave us the vast heritage of his knowledge, and his researches into the human nature. But Freud, after his crisis in adolescence, became melancholic in temperament, with its accompanying symptom of 'acedy', against both of which he battled heroically, all his life (cf. Starobinski, 1985). He would flaunt his isolation: 'It was a beautiful, heroic period, the splendid isolation was not devoid of advantages and charm' (Freud, 1914*d*). He could be as self-contradictory, *naive*, and equally suspended in indecision, for long periods of time about one venture or another, as Prince Hamlet. About his being self-contradictory, this cannot be better exemplified than by his own prying into other famous lives – real persons (such as Leonardo da Vinci [Freud, 1910*c*] or Dostoevsky [Freud, 1928*b*]) or a mythic figure of the stature of Moses (Freud, 1939*a*). And how he prevaricated with himself; was undecided for years about finishing his treatise on Moses (cf. Clark, 1980).

If I have claimed for Professor Anzieu an objectivity and lack of prurient curiosity about Freud's private life as such, the reader should not misunderstand me, and think that Professor Anzieu is not aware of Freud's perturbed and tormented soul, and its role (always beneficial, miraculously enough) in his total life-work, which in English we are privileged to have, in the magnificent annotated translations by James Strachey and others, in twenty-three volumes of the *Standard Edition* (*SE*, see Abbreviations, p. viii). Professor Anzieu candidly states (p. 562):

> Yet Freud, who was so talented, so intellectually and physically energetic, so apparently calm and reasonable, was gnawed by suffering. He easily gave into resentment, remorse, self-doubt, and dependence on others. He was not easily discouraged, but became depressed. He tended to wallow in failure. He attributed his moodiness to the vicissitudes of life, and in particular to health problems following a recent and distressing cardiac episode. In fact Freud, then nearly 40, was simply in the throes of the mid-life crisis that ushers in maturity.

It is not my wish to stand between Professor Anzieu's monumental narrative and the reader, who must study it with a patience matching the author's impeccable documentations and labours in accomplishing his *task*.

It only remains for me to state a few facts to complete what I had to tell. In 1975, as the then editor of The International Psycho-Analytical Library of the British Psycho-Analytical Society, I received the book in its enlarged two-volume French edition. I read it and was astonished that someone could achieve such a task. Freud's correspondence with Wilhelm Fliess had been published (with most prejudicial cautions, as well as discretions) in 1950, and had been followed soon after by the first volume of Ernest Jones's 'official' biography, *Sigmund Freud: Life and Work* (1953), which includes a selection of Freud's letters to his fiancée, Martha Bernays, almost exclusively from the period of his betrothal to her. With these publications a whole 'industry' of *analysing* Freud, the private person, had begun. It had escalated, in two decades, to a point where few seemed to have as much interest in reading Freud's works as in learning about his private life. This prurient, exogenous infringement on Freud's privacy became a veritable cult in the United States. Even Freud's personal physician from Vienna, Dr Max Schur, does not spare us unnecessary 'prurient' details from Freud's life, during his last days (S 526–7). So it was a relief to read a scholarly account of Freud's life that helped one to grasp and understand more deeply, as well as profoundly, what constituted Freud's doctrines and his clinical practices (I use the latter noun in the plural because, unlike his self-appointed guardian-angels, amongst his followers, Freud himself varied in the clinical handling of his patients from person to person). I had heard such different accounts of his modes of clinical relating and interpreting, from James and Alix Strachey, John Rickman, and a few others, that I still wonder where the so-called 'classical technique' of analysis has accrued from.

Anyway, I called on Miss Anna Freud, to ask what she thought of Professor Anzieu's book. She had received it, she said, but had not read it, as yet. I told her I had. She asked me, with a wry smile, knowing my way of doing things, what I had decided as the editor. I told her that I knew of no other study that did such justice to the roles of Professor Freud's life-experiences, self-analysis and 'autobiographical' 'give-aways' as Professor Anzieu's; and that I considered it to have a merit and value comparable with that of Laplanche and Pontalis's *The Language of Psychoanalysis* (1967/1973). Miss Freud gave me her blessings to go ahead and write to Professor Didier Anzieu, which I immediately did; and received by return of post a most genial and courteous acceptance of my offer to publish *L'auto-analyse de Freud* in The International Psycho-Analytical Library in an English translation.

Now we ran into two problems: one purely commercial and social, the other more vexing and complex. The commercial and social one was that, in my experience as an editor, across some twenty years, in one capacity or another, a two-volume edition of any book, no matter what its quality and merit, rarely sells well. A one-volume edition in English would, however, be feasible only if we could cut out the four 'annexes' from the original French edition. We proposed that to Professor Anzieu, and he agreed. It is however, a pity that we had to delete Annexe 2, 'Chronologie générale des événements et des oeuvres (1850–1901)'. The material from the rest is readily available in English, in the *Standard Edition*.

The second problem turned out to be a real nightmare for us; that is, for me, as the editor, and for the publishers both in Britain and America. Not just once but twice our translators let us down, for the most macabre reasons on the first occasion. Time was passing, and all the while the American 'industry' of Freudiana was churning out books by the month. In the end we were lucky enough to find Mr Peter Graham, who was not only an experienced translator, but also had the advantage of living in France, so could consult Professor Anzieu whenever necessary. Even though the process of translation has taken so long, I am sure Professor Anzieu will be gratified by the result, because Mr Graham has taken the most commendable care in his work, and has been faithful throughout to the spirit and the scholarly detail of the original French texts.

I can say, with both relief and joy, that fortunately, as a result of the publication in 1985 of the complete letters of Freud to Fliess, edited by J. M. Masson, Professor Anzieu's book has benefited from the time-lag between the French edition of 1975 and its English version published now, in 1986. I am, however, most grateful to Professor Anzieu for his gracious patience during this decade, and for his unstinting availability to Mr Graham.

To crown it all, Professor Anzieu has written a new introduction for the English edition, telling us how this monumental task was organised and achieved.

London December 1985 M. MASUD R. KHAN

Introduction

This book was originally published in French in two successive versions. The first version, which consisted of one volume, appeared in 1959 and was entitled *L'auto-analyse. Son rôle dans la découverte de la psychanalyse par Freud. Sa fonction en psychanalyse* (*Self-analysis. Its role in Freud's discovery of psychoanalysis. Its function in psychoanalysis*). The theme of the book had been suggested to me by my teacher Daniel Lagache.

The second version, which filled two volumes, came out in 1975 under the title of *L'auto-analyse de Freud et la découverte de la psychanalyse* (*Freud's self-analysis and the discovery of psychoanalysis*). In it, Chapter I of the first version, which discussed Freud's self-analysis, was considerably enlarged; but Chapters II and III, entitled 'Self-Analysis since Freud' and 'Self-Analysis and Psychoanalysis' respectively, were dropped. The second French version, then, focussed more particularly on what constituted the most singular aspect of the discovery of psychoanalysis (and consequently lent my book its originality) – the self-analysis carried out by Freud between 1895 and 1902 on the basis of his dreams and other products of his unconscious.

It is this second version which has been translated into English. It occupies only one volume because it was felt that the many appendices contained in the French original were not essential to English readers and could therefore be left out. They were: a chronological account of Freud's life up until 1902 (which duplicated information contained in the many biographies of Freud that have come out since Ernest Jones' three-volume life of Freud (1952–55)); a general chronology of historical events and contemporary dramatic and literary works from 1850 to 1901; a chronological table of Freud's dreams and other material used in his self-analysis (day-dreams, parapraxes, childhood memories) and mentioned or published by him between 1895 and 1902; alphabetical tables of that same material; an alphabetical table of dreams and day-dreams by Freud's patients or friends; an alphabetical table of dreams found by Freud in the scientific literature (similar alphabetical tables are to be found in volumes 5, 6 and 24 of the *Standard Edition*); a complete bibliography of Freud's writings up until 1902 (which duplicated the bibliography in the *Standard*

Edition); a bibliography of Freud's writings that have been translated into French; and, lastly, an iconography consisting of illustrations that are now too well-known to need reproducing once again. As far as the Freud-Fliess correspondence is concerned, the present volume quotes from the recently published *Complete Letters of Sigmund Freud to Wilhelm Fliess, 1887–1904*, translated and edited by J. M. Masson (1985).

What chiefly mobilised my energies and my interest in writing the two versions of my book was the chance to reconstruct the creative psychical work that resulted in the discovery of psychoanalysis. This was made possible by the fact that the creator himself, Sigmund Freud, made available to posterity – often intentionally, but sometimes without realising it – an exceptionally large number of documents with a close bearing on the unconscious. My task was to bring together fragments of the same dream found in several different published works by Freud; to compare the text of the dreams with accounts of past or contemporary events described in Freud's correspondence or revealed by his biographers; to date the dreams and other material connected with his self-analysis; and finally, by placing them in chronological order, to assess their role as milestones (which sometimes helped and sometimes hindered him) in a process of personal crisis, epistemological revolution, and hitherto unparalleled conceptual innovation. In my view, it is that process which resulted in the foundation of psychoanalysis in its triple function as a clinical practice, a science of the unconscious, and a school to train people for that practice and that science.

As regards the importance of Freud's self-analysis in the process that led to the discovery of psychoanalysis, I have been guided by the work of several predecessors in this field. In an impressive series of papers, Siegfried and Suzanne Cassirer Bernfeld (1944*a*, 1944*b*, 1946, 1949, 1951, 1952 and 1953) were the first to cast a historian's eye on Freud's childhood and education, mainly by referring to published fragments relating to his self-analysis, and to realise that the central passage of Freud's paper on screen memories, *Über Deckerinnerungen* (1899*a*), was in fact a disguised autobiographical account. A paper by Edith Buxbaum (1951) set out to reinterpret certain of Freud's dreams in the light of his correspondence with Fliess, and aroused considerable debate (C. van der Heide, 1952; Jones, 1952; S. C. Bernfeld, 1952).

In his book *On Sigmund Freud's Dreams* (1968) – since republished in an enlarged second edition under the title of *Sigmund Freud's Dreams* – Alexander Grinstein applied considerable erudition to a study of eighteen of Freud's own dreams described in *The Interpretation of Dreams*. I am indebted to him for numerous factual details concerning, for example, dates, identities of figures that appear in the dreams, extracts from newspapers and official documents, contemporary events, and so on, as well as for his exhaustive analyses of books read by Freud. But Grinstein confines himself to rather less than half the forty-three of Freud's dreams published in *The Interpretation of Dreams* (1900*a*); what is more, he overlooks the four dreams, one of them crucial, which subsequently appeared in *On Dreams* (1901*a*), as well as the three dreams we know of only from Freud's letters to Fliess. Moreover, while he succeeds in dating sixteen dreams, it did not occur to him to examine them in chronological order. Had he done so, his book would have had greater unity; and he might have been put on the track of other fruitful insights. Finally, in his analysis, Grinstein lays far too much emphasis on the importance of the day's residues for an understanding of Freud's dreams, at the expense of unconscious wishes, defensive conflicts, and various mechanisms other than that of symbolic representation.

I have striven as far as possible to take into account subsequent published work on Freud's childhood and youth, his earliest psychoanalytic writings, and various of his dreams. But it is so voluminous that I am bound to have overlooked some of it. I trust that readers will be good enough to correct for themselves any mistakes or omissions they may encounter.

The documents central to Freud's self-analysis are as follows: – fifty dreams up to 1902; of these, forty-three are described in *The Interpretation of Dreams* and four in *On Dreams* ('Swimming-pool', '*Trottoir roulant*', 'Glass top-hat', and 'Company at table d'hôte'), while three are only to be found in letters to Fliess ('Sheep's head', 'Being in the sixth form', and 'Hella'); two day-dreams described in *The Psychopathology of Everyday Life* (1901*b*) should also be mentioned ('Stopping a runaway horse', and 'Revenge when "coincidentally" meeting parents who had not had confidence in his professional capacities'); – forty-eight childhood memories, screen memories, parapraxes and acts of forgetfulness up to 1907; of these, forty-three are described in *The Psychopathology of Everyday Life*, three only in letters to Fliess ('The forgetting of Julius Mosen', 'Memories from his third year', and 'Memory of his fear in Breslau station'), one in his paper on 'Screen Memories' (1899*a*) ('Green meadow with yellow flowers snatched from Pauline'), and one mentioned both in that paper, in the Fliess letters, and in the 1919 edition of *The Interpretation of Dreams* ('Injury to his face with a lasting scar', which occurred during his third year but of which he had no conscious memory).

As far as Freud's most important dreams are concerned, I have succeeded in giving a precise date to most of them and an approximate one to the rest. Only a few minor dreams remain impossible to date ('Communication from Social Democrats', 'Keeping a woman waiting', 'Cliff in Böcklin style', 'Mother and daughter', and 'Funeral oration by young doctor').

I should add a few words about my working methods. The second version of this book was the result of group work. All members of the group were psychoanalysts or apprentice psychoanalysts. Several of them, excellent German-speakers, clarified textual points or translation difficulties. One participant from a Viennese background similar to Freud's, by drawing on his personal memories or consulting members of his family, provided information about everyday life, practices, beliefs, ideals, and dialects prevalent at that time. Another member, a historian, complemented, corrected and generally shed light on Freud's allusions to certain events and works. Others, who were training to become psychoanalysts, discovered for the first time the young Freud and his earliest psychoanalytic work, *The Interpretation of Dreams*: their ingenuous questions, unpredictable responses and spontaneous criticism helped to counterbalance the academic and sophisticated turn sometimes taken by the discussion and provided food for thought.

The seminar took place over a period of two years at the rate of one evening every fortnight. Each session was devoted to one of Freud's dreams; a completely new translation of the dream was usually sent out to the participants in advance, sometimes with additional documentation prepared by myself and by Eva Rosenblum, who led the seminar with me. Members of the seminar freely communicated the results of their preparatory work and, usually at the end of each session, mentioned any flashes of insight that may have occurred to them during the evening.

With experience, we gradually adopted a very productive working method, that of literal interpretation: after sorting out all the linguistic, biographical, sociological and literary questions, we would read out the text of the dream one sentence at a time, and try to pin down the specific meaning (or even double or triple meaning) of each sentence or important clause considered in isolation. When we had finished, we read through the dream again, trying to see it this time as a whole and identify its unity. As a result of this technique, instead of restricting ourselves to such well-worn themes as Freud's 'transference' on to Fliess, his recollection of childhood memories, his ambivalence towards the paternal imago, his personal 'neurosis', his discovery of the Oedipus complex, or his countertransference on to his patients (especially those of the female sex), we were able to grasp many other dimensions. These included: Freud's anticipation, in the form of thought pictures, of the whole theory of the psychical apparatus; the increasingly obvious recurrence of an anxiety that Freud ended up vaguely identifying as castration anxiety – though he did not yet call it that; the deployment of body images with their attendant succession of erotogenic zones and visual, auditory, tactile, olfactory, gustatory, kinaesthetic and coenaesthetic sensations, set against an imaginary spatial background; and, lastly, the constantly reiterated need for references to cultural works, which in Freud's view provided a symbolic endorsement for the truths he had glimpsed.

Lastly, I would like to thank all the members of the seminar – Alain Besançon, Hélène Bourgeau, Guy Cauquil, Nicole Enriquez-Coupère, Michel Gribinski, Elsa Hawelka and above all Eva Rosenblum. I am also deeply grateful to Prince Masud Khan, whose idea it was to have the present work translated into English.

November 1985 DIDIER ANZIEU

CHAPTER I

Freud up to 1895

'As for the biographers, let them worry, we have no desire to make it too easy for them. Each one of them will be right in his opinion of "The Development of the Hero", and I am already looking forward to seeing them go astray.' (Letter from Sigmund Freud to his fiancée, Martha Bernays, dated April 28, 1885 (*L* 153), in which he tells her he has destroyed many of his papers.)

Childhood

FREUD THE CREATOR

Sigmund Freud was fortunate in more than one way. First, his father was a Jew who had no talent for trade, although he made it his calling; he was, on the other hand, a self-taught man and an unbeliever who professed liberal and modern ideas. Sigmund's half-brothers, from his father's previous marriage to Sally Kanner, and another, younger brother chose respectively to engage in business or to teach its skills, succeeding where their father had failed. Sigmund himself, after receiving a comprehensive education and becoming a man of science, achieved success on an intellectual plane: it was the kind of success which his father had always desired, and the desire for which he had transmitted to Sigmund.

Freud's second good fortune was to have been conceived by a vivacious, cheerful and gentle young woman who had just married a widower twenty years her senior, and whose proud, loving passion for her first-born son gave him early stimulation, a strong sense of security and faith in life, great familiarity with incestuous desire, and the degree of masochism vital to any creator.

His third stroke of luck was to have spent three blissful years of freedom in the country, surrounded by a kind of 'primal horde' and a multitude of languages, creeds, cultures and social classes.

Freud's first misfortune – premature exile at the age of about three and a half – turned out in fact to be yet another boon: a person creates not by continuing to mourn for what he has lost, and what he knows to be irretrievable, but by replacing it with a work of the kind that enables him, in the process of constructing it, to reconstruct himself.

His second misfortune was again a blessing. From the end of his fourth year he lived in Vienna, where he experienced poverty and constant house-moving in an urban milieu: he came to resent the city, which intensified his masochism and, by way of reaction, his determination to succeed. In Vienna, he learned to write a language that existed in two forms of characters (Roman and Gothic), a language of reference by which his parents set great store, and a code that arranged, but did not destroy, previously existing structures. He read the Bible in an illustrated translation, then Shakespeare in the original. He studied classics with great success. He attended one of the oldest universities in the world, where he acquired scientific exactitude and encountered – then repudiated – all the teachers that he needed to admire, imitate and reject. In other words, Vienna was an ideal medium for his conquering identifications (those of a dashing young romantic hero), his fierce ambition to make a spectacular discovery, and his need to be put to the test by himself alone – a need that was the positive counterpart of his narcissism.

The rest – that is to say, how psychoanalysis came to be invented – is the story this book sets out to piece together, and it cannot be grasped unless Freud's background is kept in mind. It is the story of an internal venture which drew sustenance from the whole range of psychical processes resulting from Freud's recurrent good fortune, and which implemented them before, finally, representing them in the work itself. But it is also a story closely tied up with a particular social, cultural and family background, which fostered, both in Freud and in many of his contemporaries and patients, psychological problems of a certain type and a certain functioning of the psychical apparatus.

This explains the double theme that runs like a guiding thread throughout this book: the relationship between the discovery of psychoanalysis and the man who made it, and between that discovery and the milieu which produced it.

Over the last century, western society has undergone a profound transformation. Relations between nations, classes and races have changed; attitudes towards children, sex and science are no longer the same as before; mythological terms of reference tend to be replaced by ideological ones; education now engenders new types of nervous disorders, or at least causes those that have always existed to occur more frequently. Mental pathology, the organisation of the psychical apparatus, and psychoanalytical techniques are all in the process of changing. Freud's message is still relevant to us; but if we wish to grasp the full meaning of psychoanalysis today, that message must be put in perspective – for Freud was both addressing himself to and writing about his own period. The present work will conclude with further discussion of this topic, to which I intend to devote a subsequent book.

Freud invented psychoanalysis when he was between 40 and 45, by personally embarking on the study of his own dreams. Here we have two characteristics – the mid-life crisis and an interest in dreams and day-dreams – commonly found in creative people. But why it should be that an individual innovates, that the forties are a critical phase in his life, and that dreams provide him with an ideal channel for creation, is a question that has never received a comprehensive explanation. The present book, while striving to give as precise and accurate an account as possible of Freud's discovery, will never lose sight of this second set of problems. And it may well help to propose an answer to them: for it is only rarely that researchers in this field have at their disposal documents as consistent, reliable and revealing about the innermost recesses of the creative process as those bequeathed by Freud.

Why, then, does a man feel the urge to create something new? Is it, as Freud suggested in his own case, due both to the sublimation of pre-genital component instincts and to the displacement of the Oedipal object? It is true that possession of an unknown territory which derives doubly – both metaphorically and metonymically – from the body of the mother would make possible a creative substitution for that object. Is creation, as Melanie Klein subsequently maintained, an attempt to repair the earliest damage caused to the psychical apparatus by destructive instincts and primal anxieties? Or is it, as Balint has suggested, a way, once certain conditions are fulfilled, of opening up a third avenue in order to come to terms with the basic fault that lies behind all mental pathology – an avenue between neurotic evolution and psychotic evolution?

What is it that makes a man on the brink of the second half of his life – when he has run through the whole gamut of identifications, when his sexual activity has begun to wane, and when death first looms perceptibly on the horizon instead of being seen as something lost in the mists of the indefinite future – call into question the direction his life has taken and, if he is already a creator, his sources of inspiration and his style? Why does he feel the need to create something directly out of himself, instead of out of other people? Why does he give the impression, as he struggles to turn back the tide of ebbing pleasure and approaching death, of making the supreme gamble of allowing fresh certitudes to germinate and take root, then of trying to communicate them?

Such was the new direction taken by James Joyce (1882–1941) at the age of 40 (he was to live another nineteen years), after the publication of *Ulysses* (1922) and before putting *Finnegans Wake* (1939) in hand (cf. H. Cixous, 1968). Similarly, Marcel Proust (1871–1922) was 33 – and still had eighteen years to live – when, following the deaths first of his father, then of his mother, and at the time he began to see Albertine, he underwent the experience of rediscovering the past, eventually constructing a whole work around that experience, whereas during the first half of his literary life he had merely dabbled in criticism and pastiche (cf. G. D. Painter, 1965). Blaise Pascal (1623–62) also suffered an internal crisis: it began when his father died (1651) and his youngest sister, Jacqueline, became a nun (1652), continued during his journey to the province of Poitou with Antoine Gombaud, chevalier de Méré (1652), and came to a head, when Pascal was 31 and still had eight years to live, with his so-called 'mystic night' of November 23, 1654 (described in his *Mémorial*). The crisis turned the mathematician and man of the world into the author of *Les provinciales* and *Les pensées* (cf. D. Anzieu, 1960).

In these three cases, the mid-life crisis was at once a break and a continuation: what Joyce was tentatively trying to do in the last chapter of *Ulysses* he extended to the whole of *Finnegans Wake*; *A la recherche du temps perdu* contains some admirable imitations of the Goncourts' style; and when Pascal turned philosopher, not only did he continue his mathematical work, but he introduced the 'argument of the wager'[1] into his projected *Apologie de la religion chrétienne*.

Classical psychiatry and modern psychosomatic medicine have described the various endocrinian disorders and psychical repercussions that attend climacteric periods. Elliott Jaques (1965) opts for a Kleinian approach when he identifies the dynamics of this process as a re-working over of the depressive position – a reorganisation caused by the certainty, at last, of one's own eventual death. It should also be remarked that in the case of many creative people (including, as we shall see, Freud) this reorganisation is set in train by the work of mourning, usually after the death of the father.

But if the process of the creative crisis is to be properly understood, account must be taken not only of the Kleinian approach, but of the specific characteristics of mourning as later described by Freud himself (1917*e*, 'Mourning and Melancholia'). The survivor can, through a process of revival, master both the conflict of ambivalence towards the image of his father and the dependence or counter-dependence that goes with

1. The argument was that there was everything to be gained, and nothing to be lost, by wagering on the existence of God.

authority, and thereby, if he has the makings of a creator, cease to consider himself solely as someone's child and assert himself as the father of his own works. A considerable amount of psychical energy that had been absorbed by that conflict and had remained fixated on that image is liberated, thus becoming available for new cathexes – in this instance, for cultural products of a new type. Lastly, regression to narcissism plays an important role: overcome by grief, the mourner loses interest in the outside world and hypercathects memories connected with the dead person, until a point is reached when 'the ego, confronted as it were with the question whether it shall share this fate, is persuaded by the sum of the narcissistic satisfactions it derives from being alive to sever its attachment to the object that has been abolished' (*ibid.*, *SE* 14, 255). In other words, the work you are about to create takes the place of the loved and lost object that created you. By composing it, the ego not only re-establishes its personal identity and value, but derives from the renewal of its internal life, i.e. of its own psychical reality, the guiding insights of the work in question. The latter then functions for the author as a mirror image of the regression to narcissism. The now waning anaclitic object-choice of the loved object is replaced by a narcissistic object-choice – the creator's relationship with his creation.

I would now like to turn for a moment to the relationship between dreams and creativity. Here again, Freud had his precursors and his successors. The composer Tartini wrote a sonata, the beginning of which was apparently dictated to him, in a dream, by the devil. Coleridge composed his poem *Kubla Khan* while asleep. There have been famous hypnagogic dreams, such as those which enabled Voltaire to write one canto of *La Henriade*, and Richard Wagner the prelude to his opera *The Rhine Gold.* Kekulé von Stradonitz, an Austrian physicist of Czech origin, found a solution, while day-dreaming, to the problem with which he was then grappling – the structure of benzene (C_6H_6): when he saw atoms whirl in the air and come together to form a regular hexagon, he realised he had just discovered the hexagonal structure in which each carbon atom is attached to a hydrogen atom, forming the new compound and its three disubstituted derivatives.

Since Freud, writers have no longer merely been content to jot down some of their dreams and attribute them to one of the characters in their books, or even, like the first surrealists (cf. S. Alexandrian's 1974 study of the surrealists' attitude to dreams), to assemble a series of their own dreams, and add a commentary, thus making a work of literature. Several writers – among them Julien Gracq, Alain Robbe-Grillet, and indeed a contemporary of Freud, Robert Louis Stevenson – have based a chapter or even a whole novel on one of their dreams. The dream is no longer presented as such, though it provides the chapter or novel with its plot, characters and atmosphere. In the preface to his collection of short stories, *Doctor Brodie's Report* (1970), Jorge Luis Borges writes: 'I owe to a dream of Hugo Rodríguez Moroni the general outline of the story – perhaps the best of this collection – called "The Gospel according to Mark". [. . .] But after all, writing is nothing more than a guided dream.'

Freud's distinctive achievement was no doubt his ability to exploit his dreams and their processing in both a scientific and a literary way. Like Kekulé, he sometimes saw figurative representations in them that foreshadowed aspects of his later theory of the psychical apparatus. And like a modern novelist, not only did he centre several chapters or subsections of *The Interpretation of Dreams* on his own dreams interspersed with those of relatives, friends and patients, but he used material in his dreams to make immediate the psychical realities which he had discovered, and whose existence and nature he wished to make known, in particular the Oedipal organisation of the instincts. While awake, Freud discovered the meaning of dreams; and while dreaming he visualised his discoveries as they came into being and anticipated new ones. Dreams in themselves are not creative. They can prepare and prolong the conscious mental activity inherent in creativity, though that function can be performed separately or jointly by various other kinds of mental products such as day-dreaming, self-communion, dialogue with someone in sympathy with one's own way of thinking, and any activity that could be described as 'projective' or 'automatic', in the sense understood by the surrealists when they talked of automatic writing.

But the advantage of dreams is that they supply a more detailed, intelligible and convincing form of evidence than that produced by conscious mental activity, one that has a more direct bearing on the psychical work of creation, particularly at the three levels on which dreams operate: that of the borderline between the unconscious and the pre-conscious, where drives are given their figurative form in representations and their expression in affects; that of the transformation of mental images into words and vice versa; and, lastly, that of the secondary revision of pre-conscious thoughts through the perceptual-conscious system.

The scientific scope of the present book will be restricted to the areas of study just enumerated. Let me turn now to the extraordinary figure who is the central character of this work, at the precise moment when he embarked on the creative adventure that I shall endeavour to document in detail: who was Sigmund Freud in 1895?

THE FREIBERG YEARS
(FROM FREUD'S BIRTH, IN 1856, TO 1859)

In 1895, Sigmund Freud (1856–1939) was 39, an age when a man begins to lose his mathematical powers, but is often capable of making major discoveries in natural and human sciences. Sigmund came into the world in 1856, in all probability on May 6, the date that he and his parents always took to be accurate, even though the local civil register records March 6 (J I, 1 n.1; recent research by Gicklhorn and Sajner (1969) has confirmed May 6). He was born in Freiberg, a small town of about 5,000 inhabitants in Moravia, which at that time formed part of the Austro-Hungarian Empire. It lay between the kingdom of Prussia and another Austro-Hungarian province, Galicia, of which his father, Jacob, was a native. Today, Freiberg is called Příbor and is located in Czechoslovakia near the border with Poland. The main town in the vicinity, where the Freud family went to make important purchases, was Neu-Titschein (now Nový-Jičín). Most of the citizens of Freiberg were Czech-speaking Catholics, while the Freud family was Jewish and spoke Yiddish and German. It could well be that Sigmund Freud became accustomed at an early age to the minority status he was destined to endure throughout his life both as a Jew and as a doctor interested in psychology and sexuality. Freiberg lies in wooded, rolling country near the source of the Oder. Freud's earliest memories include playing in steep meadows lined with cottages, and walking in the nearby woods with his father.

Sigmund was circumcised, though neither he himself – at least in his published papers and letters – nor his biographers specifically mention the fact. Indeed, there was little need to do so, as all boys born to Jewish families at that time and in that region would automatically be circumcised. He was given two first names. One of them was, as then stipulated by law, a Christian name – Sigismund. His childhood friends made a diminutive (Sigi) out of it, and he himself shortened Sigismund to Sigmund at about the age of 19. Sigismund was a name once lent a certain celebrity by the Polish kings, but by the nineteenth century there was a dated and pretentious ring to it. It is understandable, then, that in his desire for social acceptance Freud turned Sigismund into the much commoner German form, Sigmund. But in the process he eliminated the letters 'is', which must, at a more unconscious level, have seemed superfluous to him; G. Rosolato (1969, p. 107) puts forward the theory that the 'is' represented the 'beginning of Israel, which was his father Jacob's other name. [. . .] Here again, [Freud] was abandoning the particularism common to all religions in order to assert himself through the universality of his own truth.' There was another, and possibly more important, unconscious echo in Freud's mind. The legendary hero, Siegfried, who became well-known to the public through two operas by Richard Wagner (1848 and 1876), was 'pure' because he was the son of twins (Siegmund and Sieglinde) – in other words, the issue of a 'super-incest' between brother and sister.

Freud was also given a Jewish first name, Schlomo, in memory of his paternal grandfather Schlomo Freud, who died on February 21, 1856, between the time Sigmund was conceived and the date of his birth: his was the first of many deaths that were to occur at regular intervals throughout Freud's infancy and youth, leaving their symbolic mark on his inner life. In the Bible, King Sh'lōmōh (in the correct Hebrew spelling) succeeded King David; the book of *Wisdom* and part of the book of *Proverbs* are ascribed to him. According to Eva Rosenblum, the name contains the root Sh-l-m, which means 'to make complete'. It was Latinised as Solomon.

The great freedom of Freud's infancy in the country town of Freiberg left him with a heightened sensoriality and a love of nature, plants and flowers – he liked nothing more than going for walks in hilly country, admiring the scenery, and picking wild strawberries and mushrooms. Freud was, in my view, an exemplary empiricist: nothing entered his mind without first passing through his senses. He is a good illustration of how sensorial stimulation at an early age can, as Phyllis Greenacre was later to show (1953), cause a predisposition to creative work.

Freud's parents were still alive in 1895. They, too, had been living in Vienna since their move there in 1860. Sigmund respected, loved and helped them. He gave them as large an annuity as he could afford, though he was also very quick to show his independence from them. For instance, when his father upbraided his extravagance in buying expensive scientific monographs instead of standard manuals, Sigmund paid not the slightest attention.

His father Jacob Kelemen (Kallamon) Freud (1815–96), who was a draper and possibly also a grain merchant, had decided in 1844 to leave his native town[1] of Tysmenitz (now Tysmenica) in eastern Galicia, near Lemberg (now Lvov, and part of the Soviet Union), on the border between Poland and Ukraine, and to accept a proposition from his maternal grandfather, who lived in the small town of Klogsdorf, to join him in opening a business in nearby Freiberg. Like many Jewish traders of the period, Jacob Freud spent much of his time in the role of the Wandering Jew (*Wanderjude*) of legend, travelling incessantly for the next eight years

1. Jacob Freud was born on December 18, 1815. When he married Sigmund's mother he decided to switch from the Jewish to the Gregorian calendar, and chose April 1 as his date of birth.

between Klogsdorf, Freiberg, Tysmenitz (where his wife and children lived), and the great cities of the Austro-Hungarian Empire, Vienna and Budapest. He bore a passport issued by the government of Lemberg, capital of Galicia.

This is a convenient point at which to say something about Galicia, which was at that time an Austro-Hungarian province, and which had long been, and was to continue to be, the subject of a dispute between Austria, Poland and Russia. Its considerable Jewish population, having been among the first both willing and able to live outside the ghettoes, were issued with permanent trading licences, whereas in the neighbouring province of Moravia, for instance, where Freiberg was situated, such licences had to be renewed every six months. Ellenberger devotes several pages (E 419–27) to a description of the daily lives of Jewish minorities in nineteenth-century central and eastern Europe.

Leopold Ritter von Sacher-Masoch (1836–95) was Freud's senior by twenty years. Born in Lemberg, he worked as a history teacher before making his name as the author of such works as *Venus in Furs*. In his *Galizische Geschichten 1846* (*A Galician Story 1846*) (1876), he gives a remarkable description of the class struggle and rivalry between Poles, Ruthenians and Jews in Galicia, where Freud's mother and father were born. Sacher-Masoch's whole life was strongly marked first by his affection for Handscha, a Russian peasant woman who had been entrusted by his mother with the task of bringing him up, and who taught him Ruthenian (Freud, too, was brought up by a woman other than his mother – a nurse, who was both a Czech and a Catholic – but only for the first three years of his life), then, unlike Freud, by the spectacle of local women committing acts of perverse cruelty during the Poles' rebellion against their Austrian overlords in 1848. It was after that, when his father was appointed chief of police in Prague, that Sacher-Masoch learned German.

Many of the Jewish families in Vienna at the end of the nineteenth century who counted among their number wealthy traders or intellectuals of repute had originally come from Galicia. It is widely recognised that new ideas, changing mores, and the emergence of men and women of genius are phenomena found more particularly at those points in time and place where different cultures and languages are brought into confrontation, then coalesce.

Jacob Freud belonged to a rising generation of central and eastern European Jews who could read and write Hebrew, but who also aspired to a thorough knowledge of the German language and of European culture; they no longer believed much in God or religion, but greatly respected education and the rabbi as institutions; and they had succeeded in emerging strengthened from a background of internal dissension between different Jewish factions – the ritualistically-minded orthodox Jews, the liberal Jews who followed the philosopher Mendelssohn in seeking social assimilation, and the Hasidic Jews, who were much addicted to logical, verbal and numerological games and skilled at coded interpretation of the Talmud.

It would appear that Jacob Freud's business thrived. After remarrying, he brought his family to Freiberg, where they lived comfortably, according to Sigmund's own screen memory of the 'Green meadow with yellow flowers' (1899*a*). Then, perhaps through mismanagement, perhaps as a result of ill luck, Jacob ceased to be successful in business. An initial economic crisis caused by mechanisation forced him to leave Freiberg in 1859, when Sigismund was three-and-a-half. He apparently did not start up a business in Vienna (there is no record of his name on the trade register). He probably made a living from temporary expedients, perhaps working for other Jewish traders. He may also have had some kind of private income. The slump of 1872, however, ruined him for good, and he was able to keep his head above water only with the assistance of his wife's family. Sigmund was enabled to complete his education by numerous 'loans' – more often than not, they ended up as gifts – from distant relatives, family friends, teachers and colleagues who very quickly recognised his abilities. At the same time, Sigmund himself worked in temporary jobs, wrote book reviews, did translations, gave lessons and carried out research for pharmaceutical laboratories; but he always shared any earnings from such activities with his family, fiancée, and friends in need. Sigmund remained somewhat ashamed of his father's improvidence and haunted by the poverty he experienced during the second part of his childhood.

Sigmund knew that, before marrying his mother Amalie, Jacob (who was 80 in 1895) had had a previous wife, Sally Kanner, when he was still only about 16. Marriage at such an early age strongly suggests that she became unexpectedly pregnant. Whatever the case, Jacob had two sons by his first marriage, Emanuel in 1833, and Philipp one year later. Ernest Jones says that according to Sigmund's younger brother, Alexander, Sally died in 1852; but no official record has so far confirmed the fact. Research that J. Sajner was able to carry out into local registers during the short-lived Prague springtime of 1968 shows that by 1852, the year he decided to settle with his family in Freiberg, Jacob, then 37, had married a 32-year-old woman by the name of Rebekka. She disappears from the register in 1854; whether she, too, died or was repudiated remains a mystery.

Now Sigmund Freud either never knew of, or chose never to refer to, his father's second wife. He probably suspected the existence of Jacob's curious secret even if he was not told of it; and if he did in fact know, he quickly put it out of his mind. The secret of Rebekka's disappearance must have been all the more acutely felt by Sigmund because his nurse (or nannie) also disappeared subsequently, probably when he was about three. However that may be, in July 1855, when he was 40, Jacob Freud married Amalie Nathansohn (1835–1930), a woman twenty years his junior, in the city of Vienna where she was then living. Amalie was born in Brody in northern Galicia, on the Russian frontier (the town is now in the Soviet Union), and brought up in Odessa. She was of the same generation as Emanuel and Philipp. This was a situation familiar to us from Greek mythology, where Hippolytus is faced with a young and attractive step-mother in the person of Phaedra, his father's second wife. Thus, Freud's parents, whose age difference could be said both to separate and to unite them, created, through their choice of love-objects, an implicitly Oedipal situation.

About nine months after his parents' marriage, Sigmund was born. As we shall see, he himself later stressed how important it was to him – and how decisive an effect it has on any individual's confidence in his own lucky star – that he was a cherished, first-born child and much wanted son of a young and vivacious mother. In my view, he acquired even more than that from the happy relationship between his own body and his mother's – a sturdy constitution, a love of physical exercise (as expressed in swimming or in long walks that used to leave his friends exhausted), and the desire to communicate to other people the invigorating joy procured by such activities.[1]

As so often happens, this great happiness was short-lived. The circumstances that led to Sigmund being faced with the equally fundamental contrary experience of separation and loss occurred in the following way. A brother, Julius, was born. The exact date of his birth remains unknown, though it has been established, from the death certificate discovered by Grinstein (G 279) that he died on April 15, 1858, at the age of six months. So, between the age of two and two-and-a-half, Sigmund had a younger brother. Freud's infancy was thus bounded on either side by two deaths, that of his paternal grandfather, after whom he was named, and that of a younger brother, hated because he had deprived Sigmund of his status as an only child. Anna, the first of a series of sisters, was born shortly afterwards on December 31, 1858. Sigmund never liked her.

Jones' biography shows a photograph of the house where Freud was

1. In German poetry and in South German colloquial speech, the word for 'joy' is *die Freud* (as opposed to the official form *die Freude*) [Translator's note].

born, at 117 Schlossergasse (now Freudova Ulice) in Freiberg (J I, 4). The name of its owner, Zajíc, can be seen on its façade. Investigations by Sajner (1968) have established that the Zajícs, a family of locksmiths, had been living and working in the building for four generations, and that they had let half of it off to the Freuds. On one side of the ground floor was the locksmith's workshop (Zajíc's son, Johann (1850–1924) later described to his own daughter how Sigmund liked to drop in there and build little toys for himself out of scraps of metal). On the other side was Jacob Freud's shop, where he worked with his two grown-up sons, Emanuel and Philipp, his wife, Amalie, and Emanuel's wife, Maria. The first floor was made up of two apparently quite large bedrooms (in the photograph, each has two windows); one was occupied by the locksmith and his family, the other by Jacob, Amalie, Sigmund and, once they were born, Julius and Anna. Philipp (1834–1912) lived on the other side of the street. Emanuel (1833–1915), Maria, who was three years younger than him, and their children, John (born in 1854 or 1855), Pauline (born in 1856), and Berta (born on February 22, 1859), had lodgings in another street not far away.

While their mothers were making up parcels in the shop, all the children were looked after by an unmarried woman of about 40, whom Freud referred to simply as his nurse or nannie. Her actual name was Monika, and she was a member of the Zajíc family – in other words, a very close neighbour.[1] Monika, who was a Czech and a Catholic, used to sing the children lullabies in her own language and take them off secretly to mass. It is hardly surprising that in 1895 Freud imagined Rome as some kind of inaccessible city, both alluring because of its very ancient associations, and dangerous because it was the seat of a church that persecuted the Jews. Equally, one can see why, in *Studies on Hysteria* (1895*d*), the book he had just written with Breuer, Freud likened the unconscious to a foreign language.

This, then, was the 'primal horde' – an expression Freud used in *Totem and Taboo* (1912–13) – whose leader was Jacob and within which Sigmund made his debut in life. The idea that the psychical apparatus could be conceived as something similar to the proto-group of his childhood, in which psychical forces and systems of different types, each using its own language, cohabited in a continual process of conflict, alliance and subordination, came to Freud only well after the period of his earliest discoveries forming the subject of the present book. It dates from a later phase of his thought, when he reorganised his previous theoretical model and produced a second topography of the psychical apparatus (id, ego and super-ego) and a second theory of instincts (Eros and Thanatos). Much of

1. All this information was discovered by Sajner (1968) after questioning the living members of the Zajíc family, who still occupied the same house.

the energy that Freud, in 1895, began to devote to the exploration of the psychical apparatus was sustained by a key idea in the back of his mind – an echo of his experience of the primal group: the need to reconcile the unity of that apparatus with its diversity, which, Freud thought, was the purpose of psychical health, in contrast with the alienated unity of neurosis; and the need to find a transcription system between the various languages spoken by each of the psychical apparatus' subsystems, in order to prevent the eclipse of one of them and a 'babelisation' of the whole.

The proto-group that embraced the infant Sigismund consisted of three families, headed respectively by the locksmith, Jacob, and Emanuel. Philipp's closest ties were with the last-mentioned of the three families, while the nurse was part of all three. We should therefore expect notions of unity and of the triad to play some part in Freud's self-analysis: they do, appearing in the formula of trimethylamin that occurs at the end of the dream about Irma's injection. The only member of the Zajíc family specifically mentioned by Freud was Monika, but he must obviously have visited them when, at the age of 16, he spent the summer holidays of 1872 in Freiberg (it was to be the only time he returned there); and according to Sajner (1968), Johann Zajíc, who was six years older than Freud, made a point of calling on him every time he went to Vienna. Freud does not mention the name Zajíc in his self-analysis, doubtless because apart from his nurse nothing connected with them had taken a hold on his unconscious. But the same reasoning cannot be used to explain the fact that of all Emanuel's children the one he never mentions is Berta. It is almost as though only John and Pauline, with whom he preferred to play and, on occasion, to fight, had really existed for him. Obviously, when Sigmund was old enough to run around the nearby woods and fields, he must have done so with children of at least the same age as himself – Johann Zajíc, the three Fluss brothers and their sister, Gisela, a rough *concierge*'s son whom Freud remembered during his prepuberty in an anxiety dream ('His mother and the bird-beaked figures'), probably a few other neighbours' children as well, and of course his nephew John, who was almost a year and a half older than Sigmund, and his niece Pauline, who was the same age as him. When the Freuds moved from Freiberg, no doubt in the autumn of 1859, his sister Anna and his other niece Berta were still only about eight and ten months old, and could not yet walk.

But Freud's memory of this period is distorted: he thought he left Freiberg when almost two-and-a-half years old, whereas he in fact did so at about the age of three and a half. The year he conjured away in his mind was precisely the one when the two youngest girls in the family were born. Further evidence of this is to be found in the fact that his first memory of

Anna, which he retrieved in the course of his self-analysis, dated from the Vienna, not the Freiberg, years. So what 'departure' occurred when Freud was two-and-a-half? Surely, as I have already suggested, Julius' death. Thus, this primal period in Freiberg came to an end, in Freud's conscious memory, with the death of a younger brother, or, in the eyes of a hitherto only child, of a rival; and, paradoxically, the period was chiefly characterised, again according to Freud's recollection, by memories of games and fights that would have been unlikely to take place until he was older, probably between two-and-a-half and three-and-a-half, in other words precisely *after* the period marked by Julius' death.

John, the son of Sigmund's half-brother Emanuel, was older than his uncle, and lost no opportunity of showing that he was also stronger than him. Sigmund already had to face the problem of his father's several marriages and his parents' age difference, so life can only have been made more complicated for him by the fact that his nephew was bigger than him and his niece a kind of twin sister. Yet another difficulty was that throughout this period Sigmund slept in the same room as his parents (though the practice was, of course, less unusual then than now). Freud's recollection of the room apparently came back to him only during his self-analysis. But he always remembered the meadow near Freiberg, a sloping green carpet dotted with yellow flowers and with a cottage at the top: it was a landscape whose image came to represent his longing for a beloved and long-lost childhood home. As the French literary critic, Bertrand Poirot-Delpech, has so rightly pointed out:[1] 'Exile in one form or another has incited a very great number of creators to live in an imaginary world and to share their dreams with others.'

One other person should be mentioned before I move on from the Freiberg period, the Freuds' 'one-eyed and obliging' family doctor. His name, finally unearthed by Sajner (1968), was Dr Josef Pur: this is the first appearance of the name Joseph, whose recurrence was very important to Freud throughout his life, and whose symbolic meaning (the biblical Joseph, whose father, too, was called Jacob, interpreted the Pharaoh's dreams) was to take on a new significance, in 1895, for the future author of *The Interpretation of Dreams*.

Quite apart from the problems of origin and kinship I have just described, another experience lived through by Freud while in the protogroup of his Freiberg years had an equally crucial bearing on what he was to become – his twofold contact with the fierce rivalry that exists between contemporaries and with the strength that emanates from a united group.

1. *Le Monde*, January 4, 1973.

In 1895, it was chiefly at a scientific and professional level that Freud experienced this rivalry most keenly. His household, on the other hand, was beginning to resemble, in size and composition, something approaching the 'primal horde': by the end of 1896 it had attained its final number of ten – four adults (Freud, his wife, his sister-in-law, and a devoted maid, Marie) and six children.

THE MOVE TO VIENNA IN 1860 AND FREUD'S SECONDARY EDUCATION (1866–73)

In the second half of 1859, 'the ancient march of the family – Palestine, Rome, Cologne, Lithuania, Galicia, Moravia – was resumed, as he himself had to resume it once more nearly eighty years later. He remembered the long ride in the horse-drawn vehicle and his first sight of a railway' (J I, 14). This painful experience of departure and separation left Freud, in 1895, with a phobic anxiety about travelling by train.

It would seem that in the summer of 1859 the three adult male members of the family emigrated to Leipzig, where they were joined by the women and children in October, and that they spent the next six to twelve months looking into the possibilities of working in Germany. At that point the proto-group, which was already smaller than it had been, split in two. Emanuel moved, with his wife, three children, and brother Philipp to Manchester, where he proved successful in the same line of business as his father. Sigismund, who had been greatly affected by his father's failure as a wool merchant, continued to hold his half-brothers in admiration – an admiration he extended to England as a whole, to its culture and to its highly tolerant policy towards Jews. He went to stay with them in 1875, when he was 19. Emanuel went on quite frequent business trips to Europe, either alone or accompanied by certain members of his family; when he did so, he made a point of visiting his relatives in Vienna.

Jacob, his young wife and their children settled in Vienna in 1860. Jones does no more than mention that they lived first in the Weissgärberstrasse, in the heart of the Jewish quarter near the Prater gardens, and then, when the family had grown larger, in the Kaiser Josefstrasse, where they were to live from 1875 to 1885. There, Sigmund, who by then was doing as brilliantly at university as he had done at school, was given a small independent 'cabinet' (study-cum-bedroom). He was the only one of the children to be given this special treatment. It probably had the effect for him of compensating for the loss of status as an only child, providing him with the privilege of being a boy in relation to his many sisters, and with the possibility of asserting his own individuality and autonomy vis-à-vis the proto-group from which he had originally been almost indistinguishable.

But it should be remembered that Sigmund was 19 and already a medical student when he first occupied his 'cabinet', and that he was soon to have his own room in the hospital. So it is perhaps a trifle hasty to jump from 1860 to 1875 without further ado. If for a long time Freud's biographers had difficulty in unravelling this period in his life, it was because it remained hazy for Freud himself.

Research in Vienna itself by Professor Renée Gicklhorn (1965) has thrown light on the matter. The Freuds apparently settled there in about February 1860, when Sigmund was three-and-three-quarter years old, and moved several times between 1860 and 1865.[1] Thus, the move to Vienna, which involved all the restrictions of an urban milieu, continual changes of address, living conditions that became increasingly cramped as a succession of sisters came into the world, and, finally, indigence,[2] eventually snuffed out any hankering Sigmund may have had to return to the blissful life of a village boy in Freiberg. Jones was quite clear in his own mind on this point: 'The early years in Vienna were evidently very unpleasant. Freud said later that he remembered very little of the early period between the ages of three and seven: "They were hard times and not worth remembering." He greatly missed the freedom and enjoyments of the countryside' (J I, 17). Freud's dislike of Vienna dated from then and remained with him to the end of his life. His surname became the subject of incessant jokes, which caused him considerable distress (there were allusions, which recurred in his dreams, to *die Freude*, joy, and prostitutes).

What Freud hypercathected on the other hand – as a compensation, a sublimation, a way of preserving and intensifying his parents' love and admiration for the child who was for a long time their only son – were his studies. It is very likely that he was taught to read and write German by his mother; when Sigmund was probably about seven, responsibility for his education was taken over by his father. At least that is what apparently emerges from the somewhat hazy recollections of Anna Freud-Bernays, as recorded by Jones: 'After the first lessons with his mother, Freud's father took charge of his education before sending him to a private school.

1. Renée Gicklhorn unearthed the following information from the city records: the Freuds lived in 1860 at 114 Weissgärberstrasse; in 1864 at 5 Pillersdorfgasse; in 1865 at 1 Pfeffergasse; and in 1872 a few yards down the same street at No. 5; the date at which they moved to Kaiser Josefstrasse has not been established.

2. Sigmund often referred to his father's poverty in his letters to Martha Bernays. It is not known how Jacob Freud managed to support his family. Renée Gicklhorn (1965) found no record of him in either the trade or tax registers of the city. Nevertheless, Jacob always paid for Sigmund's full school fees without ever applying for a grant.

Though self-taught, he was evidently a man of parts, above the average in intelligence and outlook' (J I, 20).

It was in any case at the age of seven, when he could read fluently and showed a marked appetite for learning, that Sigismund first had an opportunity to set eyes on Philippson's illustrated bilingual (Hebrew/German) edition of the Bible. The book opened up unknown territories for the young boy: the twofold medium of words and pictures revealed bird-headed Egyptian gods, the early history of God's chosen people, the Jews, Moses' Tables of the Law, the interpretation of dreams, and a wide spectrum of human behaviour, the actual existence of which he had probably not suspected till then, and the narration of which must have stirred him deeply, alluding as it did to 1) fratricide, parricide and filicide, 2) alliances, rivalries and betrayals, and 3) abduction, rape, concubinage, and incest. Philippson's Bible in any case gave substance to an anxiety dream, 'My mother and the bird-beaked figures', which Freud had when nearly nine-and-a-half years old, following the death of his maternal grandfather on October 3, 1865, and which he was later to recall and interpret in the course of his self-analysis.

Freud learned English not long after learning German, but it is not known where or from whom he did so, or whether his half-brothers had mastered the language before emigrating to Manchester. We can in any case be sure that Sigmund was incited to do so by his identification with the English branch of his family, and by his desire to communicate with them in their own language. According to Jones: 'He was especially fond of English and he told me once that for ten years he read nothing but English books. Shakespeare, in particular, whom he started reading at the age of eight, he read over and over again and was always ready with an apt quotation from his plays' (J I, 24). Freud, then, became acquainted with the Bible at the age of seven and with Shakespeare at the age of eight. When nine, he passed the entrance examination to the high school (*Gymnasium*) a year early. He was ten and already attending the *Gymnasium* when his brother Alexander was born. Far from feeling rivalry for this youngest member of the family, Sigmund saw to his education just as first his mother, then his father, had seen to his own.

When Sigismund was 13, he began to accompany his father on excursions into the countryside surrounding Vienna, combining the exhilaration of long walks with the enjoyment of an almost Socratic dialogue with his father, a self-taught man as I have already said, who liked to share with his son his knowledge and moral values expressed in the form of concrete examples. This is a pattern often encountered in the lives of men of genius: Etienne Pascal devoted himself, when his wife died, to the task of educating

Blaise; and both Leonardo da Vinci and John Stuart Mill, both of whom interested Freud, were taken care of by their fathers after an initial happy period with their mothers.

But let me go back a little in time. Freud's sister Anna was born in Freiberg. His next four sisters came into the world in Vienna: Regine (Rosa) – whom Freud always adored as much as he disliked Anna, and whom he felt to be 'neurasthenic' like himself; Maria (Mitzi); Adolfine (Dolfi), whom he loved very much and who, until his marriage, was his walking and even travelling companion; and Pauline (Pauli). The last of the Freud children, Alexander (Schani) was born in 1866; his first name was suggested by Sigmund, in honour of Alexander the Great, about whom he daydreamed much during his tenth year.

What had become of Freud's sisters and brother by 1895? In 1883, Anna (1858–1955) had married a businessman, Eli Bernays (1860–1922), whose sister, Martha, later married Freud. Relations between the two men were very strained for a time: Sigmund accused Eli of being slow to hand over part of Martha's dowry, which had been placed in his keeping and which he had invested. The Bernays and their children, Judith, Lucia and Edward, had settled permanently in New York in 1892, at which time Sigmund lent them moral and financial support.[1]

His other sisters and his brother had continued to live in Vienna. In 1895, Rosa (1860–1942), after recovering from an unhappy love affair, was about to marry Dr Heinrich Graf. Maria (1861–1942) had married her cousin Moritz Freud in 1887 and borne him three daughters, Margarethe, Lilly and Martha. Pauline (1864–1942) had also taken a husband, Valentin Winternitz. Only Adolfine (1862–1942) had remained single and was living with her mother. Alexander (1866–1943), with whom Sigmund got on very well, was still at business school and doing well.[2]

Sigmund had given financial and psychological support to his sisters, and in particular to Rosa and Adolfine. They quite soon found employment as lady's companions – one of them worked for a time as a maid in Paris – in order to provide for their own needs and for those of their parents.

1. In an article entitled 'My brother, Sigmund Freud', which she contributed to the *American Mercury* (November 1940), Anna Freud-Bernays gave her version (unfortunately a distorted one) of Sigmund's childhood and adolescence as she recalled it.

2. Something should be said about what became of Freud's sisters and brother. Anna died in New York at the age of 96. The four other sisters, who stayed in Vienna in 1939, were exterminated in concentration camps in 1942. Alexander ended up by finding a wife in 1909 (his celibacy was for long a cause of concern to Sigmund); he had a son, Harry, and emigrated to England, then Switzerland, and finally to Toronto, Canada, where he died. Rosa's life was particularly tragic: her husband met an early death in 1908, her son was killed in the First World War, and her daughter, unmarried and pregnant, committed suicide.

Sigmund also took it upon himself, on occasion, to lecture them on the moral unsuitability of their reading matter.

Although very careful to preserve his independence, Sigmund had remained on good terms with his father's and his mother's relations. He invariably visited either family whenever in the course of his travels he found himself in their vicinity.

Of all Jacob's brothers it was 'Uncle' Joseph who counted most in Sigmund's life, not only because his first name had strong semantic associations and because, living in Vienna, he naturally saw a lot of Sigmund, but also because his son's brush with the law was a cause of concern to the whole family, and because he himself died of epilepsy. Furthermore, another of Sigmund's paternal uncles, who lived in Breslau, had several insane or mentally deficient children (J I, 4; and letter to Martha, February 10, 1886, *L* 222–3). So in 1895, Freud, like many of his contemporaries, at a time when nervous disorders were generally explained by the theory of degeneracy, and when chemotherapy was as yet unknown, continued to fear that he may have inherited a pathological tendency from his father's side of the family, and that he might pass it on to his descendants. The fact that Freud gradually came to specialise in psychiatry probably reflected his need to reassure himself that he was normal and to cure the victims of such disorders by treating them before it was too late and by inventing specific remedies for them. The fact that this supposed phantasied deterioration was thought to arise on his father's side – his mother and her family were, on the other hand, imagined to be purely benign – indicates that he harboured vague feelings of ambivalence and guilt towards his father.

In 1866, when he was 10, Freud entered the Leopoldstädter Communal Realgymnasium, the school also known colloquially as the Sperlgymnasium or Sperlaeum, which was reputed for its high academic standards. A rich and vivid imagination filled his prepubertal daydreams with feats of war: his heroes were Hannibal the Semite, who made Rome tremble, Napoleon's general André Masséna, who was believed to be Jewish, and Oliver Cromwell, protector of the Jews in England, while his bedside book was Adolphe Thiers' *Consulate and Empire*. Then, in early adolescence, Freud's fondness for philosophical speculation suddenly asserted itself, and, inspired by Goethe, he imbued himself with the 'philosophy of nature' professed by Friedrich Schelling and his followers.

At the Sperlgymnasium, Freud did only moderately well at the exact sciences (mathematics, physics and chemistry). But he proved equally gifted both at natural science, the study of which he eventually decided to pursue after passing the *Matura* (his final school examinations), and at political and moral sciences, which he had originally thought of taking up. He warmly welcomed recent legislation which had allowed Jews to accede to positions of responsibility in society and politics, and was keen to take an active part in this process. His friends were republicans, liberals and socialists. At school, his closest ties were with the future German socialist politician Heinrich Braun (1854–1927); Braun introduced him to Fritz Adler, later secretary of the Third International, and Viktor Adler (1852–1918), who subsequently married Braun's sister and became leader of the Austrian Social Democratic Party, and with whom Freud, when still a student, was involved in a quarrel that almost ended in a duel (letter to Julie Braun-Vogelstein, October 30, 1927, *L* 378–80).

But Freud's ambitions at that time, his friendships, and his passion for history books were to be shortlived, and by 1895 they had been almost completely abandoned. One influence that was destined to endure, on the other hand, was that of the classics. As I have already pointed out, Freud's Jewish contemporaries and elders regarded the classics as a means of obtaining universal culture, which was seen as the main source of spiritual fulfilment. Freud learned Greek and Latin at school, and in extracurricular lessons was taught Hebrew by Samuel Hammerschlag (who died in 1904), a very poor man of great dignity and spirituality, who, along with his wife and his relatives, gave Sigmund constant support; their youngest son Albert became a doctor, and their only daughter Anna unexpectedly lost her husband Rudolf Lichtheim in 1886 only one year after their marriage.

Freud also spoke four foreign living languages by 1895 – English, the language spoken by his much-envied relatives in Manchester; French, which he had mastered during his stay in Paris; Spanish, learned together with a school friend, Silberstein, with whom he had developed a private mythology derived from Cervantes, and who lost favour in Freud's eyes because he became a banker (letter to Martha, February 7, 1884, *L* 113); and lastly a little Italian, which he gradually improved on each of his many enthusiastic trips to Italy. Freud had a very thorough knowledge of the major German writers; indeed it was such that his first biographer Fritz Wittels (1924 and 1931) saw the key to Freud's genius in his identification with Goethe.

Freud was always top of his class at school (this piece of information, supplied by Freud himself, was verified in the school archives by the Gicklhorns (1960) and shown to be correct), and he passed his end-of-school *Matura* examinations in 1873 with flying colours. In the Latin unseen translation, he was given a passage from Virgil 'which I happened to have read on my own account some time ago', and in Greek thirty-three lines from *Oedipus Rex* (an extraordinarily prophetic coincidence!); and for his German essay on the subject 'On the Considerations in the Choice of a Profession', he was complimented on his style (letter to Emil Fluss, June 16, 1873, *L* 21–2).

Freud was as at home with mythological thought as he was with scientific observation, and his experience of it was longer-standing. He was very familiar with Mediterranean mythologies – particularly the Greco-Roman mythology of Homer, Sophocles, and Virgil's *Aeneid.* But he had read, and was to read, an increasing number of general works on Greek civilisation and Roman history, as well as specific studies of certain myths and folk traditions. He was also interested not only in Semite, Egyptian, Germanic, Scandinavian and Hindu mythologies, and in mediaeval superstitions, but in the major Italian and Spanish (i.e. Mediterranean) works that fulfil an almost mythological function for the modern world – Ariosto's *Orlando Furioso*, Dante's *Divine Comedy*, and Cervantes' *Don Quixote.*

Engagement and marriage (1882–86)

By 1895, Freud was a family man with five children. He had married at the age of 30, on September 14, 1886, at Wandsbek near Hamburg, where Martha Bernays (1861–1951), his fiancée, was living at the time. Martha was born on July 26, 1861, in Hamburg, and was five years younger than Freud. When she was eight, her family, like that of Freud's mother Amalie, had moved to Vienna. Martha and Sigmund's marriage was the culmination of a great love, to which neither of them referred during their lifetime; it was brought to light by Ernest Jones, who was able to consult their correspondence after Martha's death in 1951, and by the publication of parts of it (*L*).

The Bernays and the Freuds knew each other. Martha and her sister Minna (1865–1941) saw Sigmund's sisters often, and Sigmund was friendly with Eli, Martha's brother and fiancé-to-be of his sister Anna Freud, and with Ignaz Schönberg, who was later engaged to Minna. One evening in April 1882, Sigmund, then almost 26, came home to find Martha chatting with other members of his family. Instead of retiring as he usually did to his study, he joined them. He was attracted by the young woman's gaiety, which probably reminded him unconsciously of the playfulness so characteristic of his own mother Amalie. Moreover, Martha was 21, as was Amalie when Sigmund was born.

It was the second time Freud had fallen in love at first sight. The first occasion was in 1872, when he made his one and only return visit to his birthplace, Freiberg, and fell in love with Gisela Fluss, a childhood playmate of his who was still living there and with whose parents he was staying. Her brothers had kept in regular touch with Sigmund by letter, and subsequently became friends when they moved much later to Vienna. But the shy 16-year-old Freud said nothing to the girl with whom he was fleetingly in love, and she guessed nothing. Sigmund described the episode to his fiancée in an unpublished letter of October 28, 1883, quoted by Jones (J I, 36).

In his comments on the dream I shall examine later, 'Company at table d'hôte', Freud gave inaccurate details about the circumstances of his engagement. Jones (J I, 115–20), who had access to the diary then kept by Sigmund (but which has remained unpublished), was able to piece together the following chain of events.

After an 'incubation period' of several weeks, involving meetings, little gifts, and increasingly elated conversations, and with the encouragement of Martha, who, when invited to dinner at the Freuds on June 13, had pressed his hand under the table, Sigmund declared his love on the 15th in a letter passed on to Martha by Eli. Her response was surreptitiously to give him a ring two days later, on June 17, 1882. It was from that date that they considered themselves engaged, and wrote to each other almost every day for four years while scraping together enough money to get married. This correspondence, which took over from Freud's private diary, was a kind of dress rehearsal for his later correspondence with Fliess, and represented not only a process of disengagement from the introspection peculiar to adolescence, but the beginnings of self-analysis in a relationship with a special interlocutor. The letters were of course love letters, in which Freud comes across as passionate, constant, jealous, and – as was only to be expected in someone from a background so strictly governed by moral and religious precepts – chaste. He discovered that 'it makes one unspeakably happy to feel oneself loved' (letter to Martha, August 23, 1883, *L* 59). He likened their first meeting alone after their official engagement, in a little wood at Wandsbek, to paradise before the Fall, when Adam and Eve, at the dawn of the world, surrounded by animals, tall trees, and kindly onlookers, exchanged kisses: 'Nowhere to be seen [was] an angel with a flaming sword' (letter to Martha, August 14, 1882, *L* 41). Freud bared his soul in his second letter to Martha, telling her 'how exclusive' he was when he loved (letter to Martha, June 19, 1882, *L* 27). He described the immediate effects that love had on him: 'The sweet girl [. . .] came towards me [and] strengthened the faith in my own value and gave me new hope and energy to work when I needed it most' (*ibid.*, *L* 25).

Freud showed himself so jealous of the various men – an uncle, then a cousin of Martha, and lastly a friend in common – who paid court to her, and so demanding in his relationship with her that it came close to breaking point on more than one occasion. True, to start with at least, Martha seemed but moderately in love, and it was only later that she was won over by Freud's rich and lively personality, whose image gradually came across to her with each new letter or secret visit. Moreover, Martha, by frequently sticking to her own point of view with considerable firmness and independence of mind, caused Freud much bitterness; but she also answered his need to be able to exchange views with another person on equal terms, and their disagreements, as was also to be the case later on with Fliess, enabled him to progress. 'I found you so fully matured and every corner in you occupied, and you were hard and reserved and I had no power over you. This resistance of yours only made you the more precious to me, but at the same time I was very unhappy' (letter to Martha, June 30, 1884, *L* 133).

But other obstacles of a non-emotional nature stood in the way of their love: shortage of money meant that their marriage plans were frowned upon by many relatives and friends, and in particular by Martha's mother, Emmeline, who had long been a widow. Emmeline suddenly decided, just as her three children were about to get engaged (Eli to Anna Freud, Minna to Ignaz Schönberg, and Martha to Sigmund), that she wanted to go back and live in Wandsbek, near Hamburg, where she was born. She also insisted on taking her daughters with her, much to the despair of their suitors. The separation proved costly for Sigmund in emotional frustration and, indeed, in railway fares; but it paid in the end because his love emerged stronger than ever from the ordeal. He behaved towards his future mother-in-law as he had always done towards his own parents – in other words, he was deferential and affectionate, but quite unbending when it came to doing what he wanted to do. For instance, a strongly worded letter from Frau Bernays, enjoining Freud to postpone his marriage because he was not yet earning a sufficient income (letter of June 27, 1886, quoted in J I, 161–2), fell on deaf ears.

The exchange of correspondence between the engaged couple provides an account of their occupations, the books they were reading, their travels, their friendships, events that occurred in their entourage, their frequent attempts to extract money from usual or potential sources, and their dreams (which are described, but not commented upon or interpreted). Freud refers in the letters to many figures and scenes that he was later to recall in the course of his self-analysis. Conversations with his teacher Hermann Nothnagel (professor of medicine and head of one of the Faculty's medical departments), Josef Breuer and Jean-Martin Charcot are vividly recounted, often in the form of a dialogue. Freud describes the suicide of a colleague, Nathan Weiss (1851–83), who hanged himself shortly after returning from his honeymoon, with a mixture of emotion, precision and intelligence, and goes on to offer an extremely subtle psychological analysis of the motives that lay behind his act (letter to Martha, September 16, 1883, *L* 73–80). Weiss seemed destined for a brilliant future as a neurologist; and his death, combined with Breuer's advice, convinced Freud to take his place in that speciality and to stay in Vienna in the hope of making a career there.

Later on, Minna's fiancé, suffering from incurable tuberculosis, released her from their engagement in 1885 and died the following year. This misfortune elicited much concern on the part of Freud, who did what he could for the couple and showed them great sympathy. More specifically Freudian, perhaps, were Sigmund's exhortations that the inevitable, however painful, should be accepted with lucidity and resignation.

Freud's letters also contain lively descriptions of Sarah Bernhardt's acting in Sardou's *Théodora*, at the Théâtre de la Porte-Saint-Martin in Paris, and of a visit to Dresden Museum with his half-brothers Emanuel and Philipp (letters to Martha, November 8, 1885, *L* 190–3; December 20, 1883, *L* 96–8). There are remarkably spirited portraits of Don Quixote, a copy of whose adventures Sigmund sent Martha to read (letter to Martha, August 23, 1883, *L* 60–1) – she confessed to being surprised at the daring nature of certain passages! – and of Ernst Fleischl von Marxow, one of Brücke's two assistants at the Institute of Physiology, a rich and cultivated bachelor interested in Sanskrit and the game of Go, but at the same time a morphine addict (letter to Martha, June 27, 1882, *L* 29–30). The name of one of Martha's friends, Bertha Pappenheim, who had been treated not long before by Breuer, recurs several times (unpublished letter to Martha, November 19, 1882, quoted in J I, 248; and letter to Martha, July 13, 1883, *L* 56). (Her case history was published under the pseudonym of Anna O. in *Studies on Hysteria* (1895*d*) shortly before Freud began his self-analysis.) Sigmund conducted a lengthy exchange of views with Martha, who was a pernickety reader and sometimes scathing letter-writer, on John Stuart Mill's *Enfranchisement of Women*, which he translated (1880*a*): while readily accepting that women were the equals of men and capable of sharing their preoccupations, he found them at the same time to be different from men and chiefly suited to the domestic life and to the raising of progeny (letter to Martha, November 15, 1883, *L* 90–1).

With the same candour – a quality which Freud retained throughout his life and which earned him much hostility – he expressed a low opinion of the bourgeoisie, which, he said, prevented individuals from expending their vital energies: 'To average bourgeois common sense, I have been lost long ago' (letter to Martha, June 19, 1884, *L* 128). He repeated this view to Breuer, informing him in highly cavalier fashion that he had turned down a fee of 1,000 florins to accompany one of Breuer's wealthy patients on a journey: Freud preferred, even though it involved a financial sacrifice, to use his holidays to go and visit his fiancée: 'The journey to my Martha belongs to a certain rash, frivolous life-plan inconsiderate of others, including yourself. This plan I was willing to sacrifice for a while in order to live according to bourgeois timidity and caution. But for lack of talent for this mode of life I abandoned this course' (letter to Breuer, June 23, 1884, *L* 130).

Freud expressed equally vigorous criticism of the populace, for the converse reason that they were in no position either to control those same vital energies or to exploit them: 'The mob gives vent to its appetites, and we deprive ourselves. [. . .] And this habit of constant suppression of natural instincts gives us the quality of refinement. [. . .] The poor people, the masses, could not survive without their thick skins and their easy-going ways. Why should they take their relationships seriously when all the misfortune nature and society have in store threaten those they love? [. . .] The poor are too helpless, too exposed, to behave like us' (letter to Martha, August 29, 1883, *L* 65–6). A sociologist would say that Freud here was thinking and behaving like a typical representative of the middle classes: he aimed to rise in society by exploiting his intellectual gifts. But equally worthy of note is the fact that terms like repression and instinct flowed easily from his pen, and that this last quote describes nothing less than the process of sublimation.

Other passages in the letters constitute a defence and illustration of a certain form of Bohemian life: they show lack of concern for the future, for social proprieties, or for established ideas, and espouse the ethos of lending when you have money, borrowing when you have not, and trying to get what you want. Freud obviously knew nothing of erotic libertinage, but was very familiar with what might justifiably be called intellectual libertinage.

Sigmund also devoted much of his energy to group activities with fellow students and the sons of his parents' friends. He mentions in particular the *Bund* (union), which he formed with Ignaz Schönberg, Eli Bernays, the three Wahle brothers, and his former neighbours and friends from early childhood, the three Fluss brothers, who had moved from Freiberg to Vienna in 1878 (letter to Martha, August 14, 1882, *L* 40): all the members of the *Bund* were Jewish. This group life, which was quite common among young men of that age, especially in the Germanic countries, not only counterbalanced in Freud's case another of his characteristic traits – individualism and contempt for superficial social relationships – but, in conjunction with the games he played when still an infant with his nephew, niece and young neighbours, prepared him fully for the problems of collective relationships that were to arise with the institutionalisation of psychoanalysis, and in particular the running of 'the Committee', which controlled the development of the psychoanalytic movement from 1912 to the death of Karl Abraham in 1925. But this takes us outside the period under examination here, one that saw the culmination of Freud's scientific isolation; but, even then, a small and loyal group of friends, whose pastimes and professional or everyday worries he shared, was to give him unfailing support.

The letters to Martha Bernays also reveal some interesting facts about Freud's Judaism. By that time, he was no longer a practising Jew, and he induced his fiancée to give up all forms of religious practice herself. He had already succeeded in asserting his self-respect when standing up to the kind of anti-Semitic abuse that was common at the time (e.g. when on a night-train, he was called 'a dirty Jew' after he had opened a window of the carriage) (letter to Martha, December 16, 1883, *L* 93). But in his letters he stated very clearly – and was never to change his stance – that he belonged to Judaism spiritually: 'And as for us, this is what I believe: even if the form wherein the old Jews were happy no longer offers us any shelter, something of the core, of the essence of this meaningful and life-affirming Judaism will not be absent from our home' (letter to Martha, July 23, 1882, *L* 39–40). In the same letter, Freud mentions Martha's grandfather, Rabbi Isaac Bernays (1792–1849), a cultivated and liberal-minded man who had been leader of the Jewish community in Hamburg. His three sons were Jakob Bernays (1824–81), who taught classical philology in Breslau, then in Bonn; Martha's father Berman (1826–79), who worked with a talented economist in Vienna; and Michaël (1834–97), who was Professor of Modern Languages at the University of Munich (or of Vienna – biographers disagree on this point), a post from which Jews were debarred at that time, and which he obtained only by renouncing his faith, much to the distress of his family.

A Jewish shopkeeper in Hamburg, from whom Freud bought a gift for his fiancée, had a clear recollection of Rabbi Isaac Bernays: 'Religion was no longer treated as a rigid dogma, it became an object of reflection for the satisfaction of cultivated artistic taste and of intensified logical efforts, and the teacher of Hamburg recommended it finally not because it happened to exist and had been declared holy, but because he was pleased by the deeper meaning which he found in it or which he projected into it' (*ibid.*, *L* 38–9).

While Plato defined philosophy as the love of truth, and Heidegger saw it as the truth of love, Freud could be said to have embarked, between the ages of 26 and 30, on a third course: truth in love. Part of it was of course scientific truth: from the start, Sigmund told Martha exactly what his conditions were on this point. She accepted them all the more willingly, one imagines, because her grandfather, father and uncles were cultivated men who had broken new ground. Freud repeatedly told her and wrote to her that only pure science interested him, and that patients were an unfortunate necessity if he were to earn a living; a degree of poverty was bearable to someone driven by a passion that has since been termed epistemophilic. The making of an important discovery was for Sigmund an ambition indistinguishable from that of making a success of his love for Martha: both ambitions sustained and nourished each other, and by 1895 they were still very much alive and complementary. Sigmund's letters to Martha recount in detail two discoveries which he thought he had made – a method of staining nervous tissue, and the anaesthetising properties of cocaine – but which both eventually misfired. Freud's scientific ambitions were, in my opinion, chiefly responsible for the fact that although it was difficult for any doctor without private means to earn a living in Vienna, which was full of many eminent specialists, although latent and sometimes official anti-Semitism was rife there, and although his ideas later met with indifference or hostility, Freud always lived in Vienna, moving only when his life was in danger.

The University of Vienna was at the time one of the most distinguished in the world; its biological and medical research departments were particularly active and productive, and Freud was always able to find the teacher, adviser or collaborator he needed. That is why he lent only half an ear to suggestions from well-wishing medical teachers that he should take up a job in a provincial clinic, or set up as a country doctor, or even emigrate to America. In 1895, then, his most ardent desire in the professional sphere was to follow in the footsteps of many men he admired in a wide variety of fields and become a professor at the University of Vienna. But, although a non-believer, Freud had by no means resolved to renounce his Judaism, as Martha's uncle had done, in order to obtain the appointment.

In any case, under the rich and intellectually fertile Austro-Hungarian Empire of the nineteenth century, some Jews from Prussia and the recently unified Germany had emerged from their business milieux and from their hermetic spiritual world, and had begun to embrace not only politics (Eduard Lasker was one of the leaders of the German National Liberal Party, and Ferdinand Lassalle a founder of the German Social Democratic Movement: they appear in the dream '*Autodidasker*'), but the liberal professions and a whole scientific, literary and artistic heritage that was at once non-religious and common to all. Alain Besançon has pointed out that the frequent references to universal culture in Freud's dreams between 1895 and 1900 – references that were already common in his letters to Martha and in hers to him – were perceived by him as a symbolic guarantee of truth in the sphere of human sciences and as proof that the discoveries he was making not only were valid for his own people, but formed part of the corpus of man's knowledge about himself.

But general truth was for Freud only one panel of the diptych: its symmetrically opposite panel was personal truth. In his letters to Martha, Freud was lucid and far from lenient with himself. But had he been otherwise, his fiancée, who, as we have seen, was very independent-minded, would certainly have called him to order. 'All that has happened and is happening will, by the interest you take in it, become an added interest for me. [. . .] You will be able to read me like an open book, it will make us so happy to understand and support each other' (letter to Martha, October 23, 1883, *L* 86).

The wish to seduce was a feeling unknown to Freud throughout his life. The price he had to pay for it was social and professional isolation. But there was a reward, too, as we shall see later on – the discovery of counter-transference. Freud's letter of August 22, 1883, contains the rough outlines of a self-portrait: 'I am afraid I do have a tendency towards tyranny, as someone recently told me, and added to this is the fact that I am all too gay nowadays; I let myself go in a kind of youthful high spirits of immaturity, which used to be quite alien to me. I also have the capacity, in other respects praiseworthy, of hating someone on intellectual grounds, just because he is a fool' (*L* 58). This last remark shows that Freud was already confident of belonging to the intellectual aristocracy. Throughout his school and student days, he was given moral and financial support by parents, relatives and colleagues, who sensed that he possessed a powerful and original mind. Freud himself began to winnow the people with whom he had professional dealings according to two criteria: intellectual superiority and openness to new ideas. In retaining the same attitude right up to his death, Freud exacerbated the hostility of second-rate minds, who sensed they were being judged for what they were; but at the same time, through this judicious process of selection and rejection, he enabled psychoanalysis to establish itself more or less permanently as a science and a practice within less than a third of a century.

Freud's almost Nietzschean contempt for the blinkered petty-mindedness of the masses and for the *idées reçues* of the Establishment may surprise modern readers, accustomed as they are to hearing his name used in support of egalitarian ideologies. In a letter of June 19, 1884, Sigmund tells Martha he has finished his article on coca and continues as follows: 'You know the key to my life, that I can work only when spurred on by great hopes for things uppermost in my mind. Before I met you I didn't know the joy of living, and now that "in principle" you are mine, to have you completely is the one condition I make to life, which I otherwise don't set any great store by. I am very stubborn and very reckless and need great challenges, I have done a number of things which any sensible person would be bound to consider very rash. For example, to take up science as a poverty-stricken man, then as a poverty-stricken man to capture a poor girl – but this must continue to be my way of life: risking a lot, hoping a lot, working a lot' (*L* 128). Nearly two years later, he wrote: 'You know what Breuer told me one evening? I was so moved by what he said that in return I disclosed to him the secret of our engagement. He told me he had discovered that hidden under the surface of timidity there lay in me an extremely daring and fearless human being. I had always thought so, but never dared tell anyone. I have often felt as though I had inherited all the defiance and all the passions with which our ancestors defended their Temple and could gladly sacrifice my life for one great moment in history' (letter to Martha, February 2, 1886, *L* 215).

Sigmund spoke with equal frankness of what he felt to be his own psychopathology: 'Now and again I have something like attacks of despondency and faintheartedness . . .' (letter to Martha, October 23, 1883, *L* 85). Or again: 'For my tiredness is a sort of minor illness; neurasthenia it is called; produced by the toils, the worries and excitements of these last years, and whenever I have been with you it has always left me as though touched by a magic wand' (letter to Martha, February 2, 1886, *L* 213). In the same letter he lists his personal problems: 'Poverty, long struggle for success, little favour amongst men, over-sensitiveness, nervousness and worries' (*ibid.*, *L* 214). Cocaine, which for a time he took quite regularly in small doses, interested him because of the observable dynamogenic effects it had not only on other people but on himself.

Freud's long period of engagement, then, led to the setting up of a relationship with his wife that was lastingly happy, fertile and stable, and, temporarily at least, in harmony with his professional life (for many years, Sigmund used to discuss his cases with Martha in the evening). But it did more than that. It brought to maturity within him a process that was to prove vital later on: the interaction of self-knowledge and knowledge of others, and the reciprocity between the knowledge one obtains of others and the knowledge others obtain of oneself. Freud's engagement also trained him to use an alert, clear and precise writing style that could shift effortlessly from ideological issues to concrete observations and references of a more general cultural nature. In other words, it constituted, in the best German tradition to which he had already so often referred in his writings, Sigmund Freud's 'years of apprenticeship'. This was the comparison used by Freud himself, in his first letter to Martha after their engagement: 'And all the while I kept thinking that somewhere I had read about a man who carried his sweetheart about with him in a little box, and having racked my brain for a long time I realised that it must be "The New Melusina", the fairy tale in Goethe's *Wilhelm Meister's Wanderings*, which I remembered only vaguely. For the first time in years I took down the book and found my suspicion confirmed. But I found more than I was looking for' (letter to Martha, June 19, 1882, *L* 26).

In the nine years between his marriage and his self-analysis, Freud had fathered five children (three boys and two girls), and in the middle of 1895 Martha was pregnant with a sixth. This was in Freud's opinion his finest achievement to date: 'Three and three: they are my pride and my treasure' (*ID* 301). Following his own suggestion to his parents on the birth of his younger brother Alexander, he gave symbolic overtones to all his children's names. His first daughter, Mathilde, born in 1887, was called after the wife of Breuer, his senior, his scientific mentor, and his main source of financial support: for more than fifteen years up to 1895, Sigmund had constantly confided in and received encouragement and friendship from Mathilde and Josef Breuer. By calling his second child Jean Martin (born in 1889), Freud had wished to pay homage to Jean-Martin Charcot, in whose department in Paris, during the winter of 1885–86 he had spent the most fruitful study course of his medical career. Oliver (born in 1891) was named after Oliver Cromwell, protector of the Jews, and citizen of a country where Sigmund's half-brothers were then living happily and prosperously. The name given to Ernst (born in 1892) was a token of Freud's respect and gratitude towards the much admired and feared Ernst Brücke, professor of physiology in the laboratory where Freud received the best part of his training as a research scientist.

Sophie (1893–1920) was called after an unfortunate widow whose tragic life I shall describe, as it throws light on later episodes in this book. The Schwabs were, after the Breuers, Freud's main source of financial support. Frau Schwab was a rich sister of Frau Hammerschlag, wife of the penniless teacher of Hebrew whom Sigmund always worshipped. The Hammerschlags had been (and were still in 1895) Freud's longest-standing helpers and confidants. In 1884, one of the Schwab daughters, Sophie, married Joseph Paneth (1857–90), a wealthy fellow-student of Sigmund's, whom he replaced as Demonstrator in Brücke's Institute of Physiology in 1882.

Once he had married, he set aside a donation for Freud, the interest on which paid for the latter's annual trip to see his fiancée in Wandsbek, then in 1889 took over the post of Assistant formerly occupied by Ernst Fleischl von Marxow, who was to die from cocaine addiction in 1891. But Paneth held down this unhoped-for job, which Freud had once coveted, for only a year before succumbing to tuberculosis. Sophie Freud's first name was a kind of tribute to Sophie Schwab-Paneth. These two deaths were followed, tragically, by a third and a fourth in the same branch of Freud's family: Sophie Freud, who became Frau Halberstadt in 1913, died of pneumonia at the age of 27 in Hamburg, where she was living, and left two orphans, the younger of whom, Heinz-Rudolf, died of tuberculosis three years later. His elder brother, Ernst, was looked after by his grandparents and maternal uncles and aunts in Vienna.[1]

The education of Freud's five children had gone smoothly. Sigmund, while making no secret of the fact that he was a free thinker as far as religious matters were concerned, gave them a solid moral grounding. Although Martha enjoyed appreciable – and much appreciated – domestic help (she had the knack of holding on to her staff), her successive pregnancies had drained her energies. Much of her attention was taken up with her children; but although Sigmund had with regret stopped sharing with her his intellectual development, which had in any case become increasingly esoteric and no doubt too audacious for her to follow, he could still rely on her to encourage his progress at all times and applaud the signs of his success.

1. Here are some details of what became of Freud's other children. Mathilde married Robert Hollitscher (1875–1959) in 1909; they had no children. They emigrated to England with Sigmund and Martha in 1938, and initially looked after their house in London. Jean Martin, who was generally known as Martin, married Esti Drucker in 1919, by whom he had a son, Anton Walter, in 1921, and a daughter, Miriam Sophie, in 1924; after obtaining a law degree, he became director of the publishing house Internationale Psychoanalytischer Verlag from 1932 until it was confiscated by the Nazis in 1938, at which time he and his family also emigrated to London. Oliver became a chemical engineer and worked in Berlin until 1933; after a failed first marriage, he married Henny Fuchs in 1923; she bore him a daughter, Eva Mathilde (1924–44). Ernst (1892–1970) married Lucie Brasch (known as Lux) in 1920; they had three sons, all called after painters: Stefan (later Stephen) Gabriel (b. 1921), Lucian Michael (b. 1922) and Clemens (later Clement) Raphael (b. 1924). Ernst, who was an architect, settled in Berlin, then, from 1933 on, in London, where he prepared for his parents' move in 1938. He was Sigmund Freud's executor, along with Anna Freud, after his death, prepared the various editions of Freud's correspondence, and supervised the translation of his works. Thus Freud had eight grandchildren in all (six boys and two girls). After the Anschluss in 1938, Sigmund and his wife moved from Vienna to London (where they died) via Paris, thanks to the intervention of Princess Marie Bonaparte. They were accompanied not only by the Hollitschers and by Martin Freud and his family (see above), but also by Anna Freud (who set up as a psychoanalyst in London, where she died in 1982; she never married), by the young Ernst Halberstadt, by Minna Bernays, by Paula Fichtl their maid, and by Freud's doctor, Max Schur, who brought his wife and two children with him.

Biological and medical education

FREUD'S MEDICAL STUDIES AND FIRST ANATOMICAL AND PHYSIOLOGICAL RESEARCH (1873–81)

By 1895, Freud had already been practising for fourteen years as a doctor. He first began to study medicine, in October 1873, not because he wanted to treat patients, but in order to be able to carry out biological research in a laboratory. I shall later discuss the circumstances that lay behind his choice. Freud enthusiastically attended more lectures than he was required to, at the expense of his clinical work. 'I have moved into another laboratory, where I am preparing myself for my real profession: "flaying of animals or torturing of human beings", and I find myself more and more in favour of the former' (letter to Wilhelm Knöpfmacher, August 6, 1878, *L* 24).

By 1875, when he was 19, and after only two years' study, Freud had not only attended the philosopher Franz Brentano's lectures on Aristotle, but worked at the Institute of Comparative Anatomy under Professor Carl Claus (1835–99) and, with the help of a travel grant, at its extension, the Zoological Experiment Station in Trieste (the Trieste peninsula was, it should be remembered, Austrian at the time). It was in Trieste that Freud confirmed Syrski's identification of a small lobed organ as the so far undetected immature testes of the eel. This was the first piece of research work carried out by Freud, though it came second in order of publication (1877*b*): thus sexuality, by a curious coincidence, was in evidence from the very start of Freud's scientific research. Claus was a disciple of Ernst Haeckel, who had discovered the celebrated biogenetic law whereby 'ontogeny recapitulates phylogeny'. Under Claus's influence, Freud became a keen follower of Darwin.

But, after a disagreement with Claus, Freud moved to Brücke's Institute of Physiology at the beginning of the 1876 university year. Professor Ernst Wilhelm Brücke (1819–92) enjoyed a considerable reputation as a scientist, and was greatly admired by Freud, who remained his pupil for six years, first as a *Famulus* (research student), then once he had graduated as a doctor (on March 31, 1881), as a Demonstrator, posts for which he received no remuneration. Freud was very happy under Brücke, who was at once strict and encouraging, and who, like Freud's father, was forty years his senior. Brücke asked him to study the histology of nerve cells, which was little known at the time. Very soon Freud published promising papers on the spinal cord of a fish, the Petromyzon, or lamprey (1878*a*), and of its larva the Ammacoetes (1877*a*), on the nervous system of the crayfish (1882*a*), on a modification of the Reichert formula facilitating the preparation of nervous tissue for microscopical examination (1879*a*). Freud had the satisfaction of receiving modest royalties for these works. He contributed an argument in favour of extending the evolutionist theory to the nervous system, as he found in the Petromyzon all sorts of intermediate nerve cells between the bipolar cell, typical of the spinal ganglion of fish, and the unipolar cell, typical of higher vertebrates.

Let me say something about the Petromyzon, which is a rare example of a surviving species belonging to an otherwise long-extinct class of living organisms. It is one of the cyclostomes, whose characteristic feature, as the etymology of their name indicates, is a round jawless mouth adapted to sucking. It is also an anadromous fish, in other words like the eel it feeds in the sea and spawns in fresh water. Often it is carried by another fish – salmon, for example – to which it adheres, digging into its flesh and sucking its blood. The Petromyzon reproduces only once in its lifetime and dies from wounds received during copulation.

Study of such a strange creature as the Petromyzon not only strengthened Freud's belief in the evolutionary process, but also, no doubt, confirmed his feeling that instincts affecting the psychical apparatus were deeply rooted in the realm of biology. I would even go so far as to hazard the opinion that the petromyzon's life, habits and structure were to constitute an equivalent of the 'day's residues' from which Freud was later to elaborate the myth of parricide in *Totem and Taboo* (1912–13).

When working for Brücke, Freud was also the first to establish that the axis cylinders of the nerve fibres in crayfish are without exception fibrillary in structure, and that the nerve cells are composed of two substances, one of which is net-like, and is the origin of the nerve process. This conclusion led him to conceive of the neurone theory, of which he gave an early hint in a lecture, in 1882 or 1883, on the structure of the elements of the nervous system (1884*b*). But the specialists paid no attention to his remarks. Freud may also have been over-anxious to restrict himself to his own field, that of anatomy, without extrapolating from physiology. He would have gained by such an extrapolation, but at the same time risked shocking Brücke and his other researchers, who had not ventured in that direction. Freud repeated his theory, without adducing further evidence for it, in the chapter on the nervous system he later wrote for a collective work (1887*f*). But in the end it was Waldeyer who in 1891 took the credit for the discovery that nerve cells and fibres connect to form what he called the 'neurone'. This discovery, which in retrospect proved Freud to have been correct and which was to form the basis of neurology, was still uppermost in his mind in

1895 and occupied a central position in 'Project for a Scientific Psychology' (1950*a*), the manuscript of which he sent Fliess in October of that year.[1]

Brücke had a decisive influence on Freud's elaboration of a system of scientific theories about the living organism, which marked a reaction away from his adolescent enthusiasm for the *Naturphilosophie* and vitalist romanticism as propounded by Goethe and Schelling. Hermann Helmholtz (1821–94) had founded a school of thought which was based on the application of strict determinist principles to biology and which made possible the magnificent flowering of the science of psychophysiology in the Germanic countries during the latter half of the nineteenth century. Helmholtz and his three colleagues, Emil Du Bois-Reymond (1818–96), Karl Ludwig (1816–95) and Ernst Brücke, the group's representative in Vienna, were united by a friendship and a common crusading spirit that no doubt provided Freud with a model for his own subsequent efforts to engineer the development and triumph of psychoanalysis. Partially attached to this school was Gustav Theodor Fechner (1801–87), who was the first person to try to apply the recently discovered principle of the conservation of energy to neurology and psychology.

The best definition of the Helmholtz school, which was purely physicalist, is to be found in the following section of a letter from Du Bois-Reymond to Ludwig in 1842, discovered by Bernfeld (1944*a*): 'Brücke and I pledge a solemn oath to put into effect this truth: "No forces other than the common physical and chemical ones are active in the organism. In those cases which cannot at the time be explained by these forces, one has either to find the specific way or form of their action by using the physical-mathematical method or to assume new forces equal in dignity to the chemical-physical forces inherent in matter, reducible to the force of attraction and repulsion."' The four scientists' conception of physiology was *antivitalist*: there is nothing in a living organism that is not reducible to physical and chemical forces. It was *dynamic*: the functioning of the living organism is explained by the interaction of physical and chemical forces. It was also *evolutionist*: the very same interaction takes account of the evolution of living beings. And lastly, although *materialist* in its explanation of life, it was not necessarily so in its explanation of the mind – an area where the views of most followers of the school coincided with the intellectualist concepts of Johann Friedrich Herbart, which I shall examine in a moment.

1. There have been many studies of Freud's neurological work as a young man: Brun (1936), Jelliffe (1937), Bernfeld (1944*a*, 1949, 1951, 1953), Spehlmann (1953). Jones repeats some of their findings in the first volume of his biography of Freud (J I). Ellenberger (1956) traces the influence of Fechner on Freud. Amacher (1965) re-examines the whole question. More recently, Freud's biologism formed the subject of a work by Jean Laplanche (1970), *Vie et mort en psychanalyse*.

By 1895, these pioneers of psychophysiology were either already dead or shortly to die. Freud had assimilated their spirit, methods and theories sufficiently well to be able both to apply it to psychical life, an area to which they had refrained from directing their attentions, and to feel free, in doing so, to introduce a number of insights dating from the romanticism of his adolescence.

As far as psychology was concerned, Freud's readings, by 1895, had not extended much beyond the work of Johann Friedrich Herbart (1776–1841). The admiration in which this psychologist was held by Freud's physiology teacher, Brücke, and by his psychiatry teacher, Meynert, served only to confirm what he had already learned. Gustaf Adolf Lindner's manual, *Lehrbuch der empirischen Psychologie nach genetischer Methode* (1858), which Freud had used during his final year at school (according to Bernfeld, who is quoted by Jones, J I, 410), was a compendium of Herbartian psychology. As a disciple of Kant, Herbart naturally preached the anteriority, and therefore the primacy, of ideas over affects. At the same time, like Spinoza, he asserted the existence of a psychical determinism: we believe ourselves to be free because we do not know the reasons for our actions. That determinism consisted, in his view, of an interaction of representations containing the specific forces of psychical life.

It was from Herbart that Freud derived his first notion of several concepts which, in *Studies on Hysteria*, he had just, in 1895, transposed with minor alterations into the psychopathology of neuroses: psychical conflict, the dynamic unconscious, repression, and even (although not yet very clear-cut) the return of the repressed. Other Herbartian notions had been, or were about to be, adopted by Freud under other names. Herbart's two thresholds (the 'static threshold' and the 'mechanistic threshold') became Freud's 'two censorships'; his 'physiological resonance' foreshadowed his follower's 'somatic compliance'. And the 'striving for equilibrium', which Herbart saw as a characteristic of mental processes, the notion that 'ideas are indestructible', and his project for a 'mathematic psychology' are all found in Freud expressed in the form of the Fechnerian principle of constancy, the indestructibility of instincts, and the hope of a possible quantification of mental energies.[1]

Herbart's influence was relayed and boosted by his disciples, with whose works Freud was more directly familiar: Fechner, who confirmed the importance of thresholds, the striving for constancy, unconscious dynamics and the quantification of psychical phenomena (he believed even

1. It was Maria Dorer (1932) who first pointed to Herbart's influence on Freud. Her comparisons, which range from the useful to the debatable, were rectified and complemented by Jones (J I, 407–15).

the phenomena of pleasure-unpleasure to be capable of quantitative treatment); the celebrated Berlin psychiatrist Wilhelm Griesinger; and, in Vienna, Meynert and Breuer.

But by 1895 Freud's psychological grounding was not exclusively Herbartian. I shall have occasion later on to mention the influence of Brentano and Mill. What is more, the English empiricist school, which had defined mental processes as 'the association of ideas', was all the more familiar to Freud because he greatly admired everything that emerged from that country. According to Gregory Zilboorg (1952), it is likely that Freud knew of experimental work on free associations carried out by Francis Galton (1822–1911) in 1879. But it was Helmholtz's and Brücke's approach which had retained the greatest immediacy and relevance for Freud (as it was to continue to do so throughout his life), and which led him to see mental processes – just as they had seen organic processes – from both a dynamic and an economic viewpoint, i.e. as a system of interacting or opposing forces. It was not, however, until Freud had completed his histological work and shifted the focus of his scientific interest from the living organism to the psyche that he was able to take that further important step.

CLINICAL STUDY COURSES AND NEUROLOGICAL RESEARCH (1882–86)

It was Freud's engagement to Martha Bernays in 1882 that caused him reluctantly to resign his position in Brücke's laboratory, which he appreciated so much for its pioneering scientific spirit and warm human atmosphere. Brücke had left him in no doubt: one or other of his two assistants, Sigmund Ritter von Exner (1846–1926) or Ernst Fleischl von Marxow (1847–1891), would in due course succeed him, at which point Freud would himself become an Assistant. But Freud was aware that it might be a very long time before the post of Professor, occupied by someone only ten years his senior, would be vacated. As it turned out, Fleischl died in 1891, and after Brücke's death the following year Exner, who discovered among other things the reaction time and how to measure it, succeeded unhindered to the vacant Chair at the age of 46.

So on July 31, 1882, Freud entered the General Hospital of Vienna in order to gain experience with patients and prepare himself to earn a living as a doctor partly in private practice and partly in hospital. At the same time he steadily continued his research, which he saw as his main aim in life. To that end, and also in the hope of gaining the qualifications and the reputation that would attract patients on the competitive Viennese medical market, Freud persevered with his initial plan to take up a university career. But it was some time before he found his bearings. He spent six months (from October 1882 to April 1883) in the Division of Internal Medicine headed by the celebrated Hermann Nothnagel (1841–1905), first as an *Aspirant* (Clinical Assistant) with a nominal salary, then as a *Sekundararzt* (House Physician), a post that provided lodging and therefore enabled Freud to leave his parents' home for good at the age of 27. Then he occupied the same position first, from May to October 1883, in the Psychiatric Clinic of Theodor Meynert (1833–92), the famous brain anatomist with whom he also continued to do research work until leaving for Paris, then in the Departments of Dermatology (the last quarter of 1883), Neurology, with the slapdash Franz Scholz (from January 1884 to February 1885), Ophthalmology (from March to May 1885), and then again Dermatology until the end of August 1885.

At that point, things began to move fast. Freud had spent three well-paid weeks acting as a locum tenens in a mental hospital run by Professor Heinrich Obersteiner just outside Vienna. He was taken on by Professor Max Kassowitz (1842–1913) to run the neurological department of his Children's Clinic – paediatrics was a new speciality at the time. He was elected to the purely honorary but highly prized position of *Privat Dozent* (Lecturer) in neuropathology; lastly, he obtained a travel grant to go to Paris and study under Charcot. Freud then left the field of general medicine.

The period from 1882 to 1885 was fruitful for Freud as far as his clinical training was concerned, but at a scientific level it was hyperactive and rather lacking in direction. He did best at the anatomopathology of the nervous system. When working under Scholz, Freud succeeded in producing a brilliant diagnosis, corroborated by autopsy, of several cerebral lesions (cerebral haemorrhage, syringomyelia, and endocarditis with acute multiple neuritis; 1884*a*, 1885*c*, 1886*a*) – thus confirming the wisdom of his decision in September 1883, after Nathan Weiss's suicide and a talk with Breuer, to specialise in neurology. And there were also other clinical studies, which he mentions in letters to his fiancée, but which were never published.

In Meynert's laboratory he had done even better: such was the esteem in which his ageing teacher held him that he suggested to Freud that he replace him as Lecturer, on condition that he definitively devote himself to brain anatomy. Freud refused. After having concentrated his research on the rachidian bulb of kittens, puppies, embryos and babies, he made three minor discoveries: the roots of the auditory nerve, the relation of restiform body to the posterior column, and the homology between certain cranial sensory nerves with three roots and the ganglions of the posterior root of the medulla (1885*d*, 1886*b*, 1886*c*). His governing idea had been to reveal the persistence of early structures in the development of the nervous system.

This idea, to which Freud remained faithful throughout his life, of the intrication of ontogeny and phylogeny, began to take on a new significance for him when he read the work of the English neurologist, John Hughlings Jackson (1835–1911), in whom Freud was one of the first people in Vienna to take an interest. In a series of memoranda published from 1868 on, and in his Croonian Lectures of 1884, Jackson argued that disorders of the nervous system are reversals of evolution; in other words, dissolutions, some of them general, others local; in his view, dissolution moves in the opposite direction from evolution; evolution as regards the nervous system, is a passage from the earliest, lowest, simplest and most automatic centres, which are also the most resistant, to the most recent, highest, most complex, most voluntary, but also most fragile, centres; dissolution not only removes the more recent dominance of the latest developed centres, but liberates, in anarchic fashion, hitherto subordinate centres; of the latter, those with the highest level of evolution remaining take control of the system, and replace the new arrangement with an old arrangement which has been restored to their advantage.

Freud did not systematically apply Jackson's theories in his neurological work, partly because they were too revolutionary, and partly because Meynert and the other researchers in his laboratory were not interested in them: in other words, Freud might yet again have found himself in the position of a maverick. He was happy merely to repeat them a little later in his book *On Aphasia* (1891*b*), whose lack of success confirmed, in Freud's mind, the persistent indifference of Germanic neurologists towards this English theory. Nevertheless, in 1895, the theory was as relevant to Freud as that of the Helmholtz school, and he was quite prepared to see the relationship between consciousness and the unconscious in terms of an evolutive, integrative emergence of the latter from the former, and to see neurotic symptomatology as the result partly of a decrease in the regulating activity of consciousness, i.e. as a regression, and partly of a freeing of early or repressed mental processes and contents.

But from about 1884 to 1886 Freud remained under the influence of Meynert, who, like his equal and rival in Berlin, Griesinger, saw himself mainly as a follower of Herbart. Meynert (J I, 400–12) had convinced Freud not only of the illusory nature of free will and of the universality of natural laws, but of the specificity of the psyche and of its irreducibility to any materialistic explanation of a physical or chemical kind. In his view, the brain and thought are without doubt closely correlated (at no time in his life did Freud believe in the immortality of the soul), and psychical processes are conditioned by physical and physiological processes, but they are not caused by them (on this point, Freud followed Fechner's theory of a parallelism between the two chains – a theory that Jackson later adopted and made more specific: the psychical is a process parallel to the physiological, or 'a dependent concomitant').

Other, more original ideas of Meynert's also influenced Freud: the analogy between the psychical apparatus and an optical system (the cortex is a dark-room in which impressions from various sources gather before being 'projected' into consciousness); the two directions of energy in terms of 'attack' and 'defence'; the notions of the 'unpleasure principle' and the 'summation of excitations'; and the distinction between a 'primary ego', which belongs to the earliest period of life and is unconscious, and a 'secondary ego', whose function is to 'inhibit' and to 'press back'.

Griesinger, whose work was closely followed in Meynert's laboratory, also influenced Freud. Here are three characteristic statements by him. The first two are quoted by Jones (J I, 412–3): ideas 'absent from consciousness' are of greater importance than those present in it; 'how a material, physical process in the nerve fibres or ganglion cells can become an idea, an act of consciousness, is wholly incomprehensible'; the third, which dates from 1861, was quoted several times in condensed form by Freud: 'Ideas in dreams and in psychoses have in common the characteristic of being *fulfilments of wishes*' (*ID* 91; cf. *ID* 134, 230).

THE COCAINE EPISODE (1884–85) AND THE QUESTION OF FREUD'S 'ADDICTION'

Freud's experiments, unlike his clinical observations, were failures. From the start he proved to be an unrivalled observer and a poor experimenter. This was shown at the Laboratory of Experimental Physiology, headed by Professor Salomon Stricker (1834–98), where, in 1878 and again in 1884, Freud did some unsuccessful research into the function of glands in relation to the circulatory system. And between those dates, with the encouragement of his friend Sigmund Lustgarten (1857–1911), he worked on the analysis of gases at Professor Ludwig's Chemical Institute. But success again eluded him. A similar fate eventually befell a technique developed by Freud at Meynert's laboratory, which made practicable Paul Flechsig's suggestion in 1876 that nervous tissue could be stained with gold chloride: Freud himself, his teacher and his colleagues all believed that a remarkable discovery had been made, and it was immediately published in German and English (1884*b*, *c*, and *d*). But the hopes it raised in scientific circles were soon dashed by the irregularity of the results it produced. Yet another failure – which came within an inch of success – lay in store for a further discovery by Freud: the anaesthetising properties of cocaine (1884*e*, 1885*a*, 1885*b*, 1885*e*).

This last failure requires some explanation. By about this time, Freud had noticed that he was dealing with two types of patient in his medical practice – the neurological, where the main difficulty was one of diagnosis, and the neurotic, where the basic problem was one of therapy. He then looked into the various therapeutic possibilities then available. Breuer had told him about hypnosis, but also about the unfortunate effects it had had on a patient of his, Anna O. For a time Freud pinned his hopes on electrotherapy and conducted several experiments with his colleagues using an expensive piece of apparatus, which had been bought through the generosity of Fleischl; but nothing came of them. Then it gradually dawned on Freud that he might be able to discover a new method, and he carried out a therapeutic test with cocaine (letter to Martha, April 21, 1884, *L* 122–3), whose beneficial effects on Bavarian soldiers during manoeuvres had been noted by a German army doctor. Freud tested its stimulating and analgesic properties on himself, on Fleischl, whose terrible nerve pain could no longer be held at bay by morphine, on colleagues, on their patients, and on his sisters. He conducted summary experiments, whose methods and findings he subjected to no critical examination, on the increase of muscular strength resulting from the direct ingestion of cocaine. Finally, he and Carl Koller (1858–1944), a House Doctor in the Department of Ophthalmology and colleague from Freud's early student days,[1] whom he had just treated privately for a neurotic affection (unpublished letter to Martha, April 4, 1885, quoted in J I, 96), experimented with cocaine on themselves.

Freud felt convinced by their results and became a keen supporter of the drug. He saw it as an effective panacea for digestive disorders, fatigue, depression and morphine addiction. He took particular interest in those of its effects which, though minor, he felt to be personally important to him. The whole episode represented a pleasant but eventually wearying digression from his serious neurological work, and in mid-June 1884 he hastily finished his first article, 'Über Coca' ('On Coca', 1884*e*), in which he referred to anaesthetic properties that might one day be discovered in the substance, but into which he did not himself wish to research. He entrusted his older friend, the ophthalmologist Leopold Königstein (1850–1924) with the task of establishing whether the pain of trachoma and other eye complaints could also be alleviated by the marvellous drug; Königstein

1. The German edition of Freud's correspondence (1968) contains seven previously unpublished letters to Koller written between 1880 and 1887.

showed that it could, though he took his time in doing so. But when it occurred to Freud in October 1884 to use cocaine for surgical anaesthesia he learned that the discovery he thought was his own had already been made in early September by Koller when experimenting, with the help of the Assistant, Gärtner, on animals and then on themselves at Stricker's Institute of Pathological Anatomy: cocaine did indeed have the power to anaesthetise the eye.

In *An Autobiographical Study* (1925*d*), Freud put his failure down to his eagerness to seize the opportunity of going to Wandsbek and joining his fiancée, whom, he says, he had not seen for two years. In fact, she had left Vienna only a year before; they had always planned to spend the summer holidays of 1884 together; and once he had written his article Freud stayed in Vienna doing nothing and getting bored for another month before leaving for Wandsbek. But the reasons for his failure lay elsewhere: he had centred his attention on one isolated fact while ignoring its related facts, allowed his enthusiasm to get the better of his critical faculties, and been guilty of amateurishness in his conduct of experiments. For a time Freud was delighted with Koller's discovery because it confirmed the validity of his interest in cocaine, and proved Koller right in his fight for priority with Königstein.

There was, however, a reconciliation between the three men, who met in April 1885 to treat Freud's father, Jacob, who was suffering from glaucoma. Königstein operated, while Koller, with Freud's help, administered the local anaesthetic. Then Freud's luck changed. Koller's find (the anaesthetising properties of cocaine) was highly successful, whereas that of Freud (the use of cocaine as a stimulant and analgesic) earned him unwelcome notoriety as soon as the first cases of cocaine addiction became known (Fleischl's was one of the first). Freud had rashly gone into print saying that the substance presented no risk of addiction. He answered his critics tardily and only partially (1887*d*), arguing, quite rightly as it happened, that he had advocated only the oral ingestion of cocaine, whereas addiction had resulted from hypodermic injection. Freud was doubly self-reproachful after the episode, because he had contributed to Fleischl's distress and because, like a one-eyed or myopic person (cf. the future dream, 'My son, the Myops'), he had spotted the bad side of the discovery and overlooked the good. He had been too unilateral. The words 'Injections of that sort ought not to be made so thoughtlessly' were to conclude the dream known as 'Irma's injection' (July 1895), which can be said to have given birth to psychoanalysis.

The cocaine episode prompts two observations. First, one is constantly startled, when reading Freud, at the insistence with which the inventor of psychoanalysis, a purely psychological therapy, hoped throughout his life – and even up to *An Outline of Psycho-Analysis* (1940*a*) – that advances would be made in chemotherapy which would enable neurosis to be treated more quickly and more radically, particularly when one remembers that today's psychotropic medicines, which have resulted precisely from progress in that direction, have been shown to eliminate symptoms temporarily without affecting their causes, and have brought into being new forms of drug addiction among the young, among people who tend, through the nature of their jobs, to overwork, and even in the medical profession itself. The vocation that Freud discovered in himself during his not very successful encounter with cocaine was that of curing neurotic suffering by any means available, and it was a vocation that remained with him all his life. The failure of cocaine was an anticipatory symbol of the failure of all drugs and the sign of the long, difficult and inevitable detour that Freud had to accomplish for himself and his patients via the dissection of unconscious psychical processes. Hypnotherapy and mental concentration – solutions, as we shall see, with which he contented himself in 1895 – constituted an intermediate phase: although they were, at last, purely psychological techniques they did still aim to eliminate the symptoms. They were informed with the same phantasy of therapeutic omnipotence which led to the notion of a chemotherapeutic Utopia, and which was caricatured by Aldous Huxley in *Brave New World*. Freud never completely shook off this phantasy: and I am tempted to see the residual form of it that remained with him all his life as something that can never be totally absent in anyone who has devoted himself or herself to the practice of psychoanalysis (however loudly some may protest to the contrary): the desire to cure. Indeed, it is difficult to see how a neurotic patient could embark fruitfully on the difficult task of psychoanalysis unless he or she sensed that the therapist possessed not only a reliable technique but some desire of that kind.

My second observation is that while Freud gradually extended psychoanalytic understanding to cover most psychopathological manifestations, drug addiction remained an unexplored area for him – the sign of a 'resistance' based on a personal flaw. Although Freud's childhood seems to have passed without any notable somatic incident (apart from a fall at an early age which he no longer thought of, and the circumstances of which came back to him during his self-analysis), his health gave cause for moderate, varying but frequent concern from adolescence right up to his death from cancer. The symptoms he complains of in the letters to Martha often have psychosomatic overtones: he refers to a light 'typhoid' (i.e. gastrointestinal disorders) in 1882, a 'sciatica' in 1884, and a mild attack of 'small pox' in 1885. As I have already pointed out, Freud admitted to his fiancée his propensity for hypochondria, neurasthenia and fatigue. His correspondence with Fliess later refers more than once to headaches, nose complaints (probably chronic sinusitis), and yet more gastrointestinal disorders, all symptoms that may be interpreted, as Jones has done, as further manifestations of Freud's 'neurosis'.

A more complicated episode occurred in 1893 (letter to Fliess, October 18, 1893, quoted in S 41; see also *F*60 n.5), which Jones again puts down to Freud's neurosis, and which Max Schur sees rather as the intrication of an actual organic disease and drug addiction. It involved heart trouble (tachycardia, arrhythmia and anginal pains), which had become so acute by the spring of 1894 that for the first time in his correspondence with Fliess Freud expressed an intense fear of death (April 19, 1894, *F*67–8). By 1895, the symptoms had almost disappeared. Fliess was in no doubt that Freud was suffering from nicotine poisoning and would have to stop smoking. Since the age of 24, and like his father before him (two facts mentioned in 1929 by Freud in his answer to a questionnaire sent to important figures inquiring about their smoking habits, and quoted in S), Freud had been a heavy smoker, progressing from just a few cigarettes at first to an average of twenty cigars a day (cf. J II, 430). On more than one occasion, Freud went through the agonies of trying to stop smoking, but failed. Breuer on the other hand diagnosed myocarditis (following a bad bout of influenza in 1889); this boded ill for the future, but caused Freud less immediate inconvenience as it required him to stop smoking only temporarily. The *a posteriori* diagnosis made by Max Schur, the doctor who treated Freud in his last years, was coronary thrombosis of a small artery, with temporary allergy to nicotine. Freud's cardiac symptoms disappeared with treatment, and from June 1895 on he began to smoke again for a period of many years (S, Chapter 2, 'Freud's cardiac episode. The battle against nicotine addiction').

So according to this version of events there was no neurosis underlying the episode, but Freud's organic lesion served to reveal what one can only call, following Jones (J II, *ibid.*), drug addiction. Freud needed tobacco in order to be able to concentrate his thoughts, attain a state of intellectual excitement, and combat his tendency to depression. Abstinence was extremely unpleasant for him, as he was to discover again during the latter years of the First World War. He was not worried about or, right up to his death, afraid of organic disease. What did consciously worry him, though, as can be seen from its very frequent mention in his correspondence with Fliess, was the problem he had to face whenever deprived of tobacco. He was also concerned about what would happen to his family if he were to die prematurely.

I myself am tempted to piece together the episode as follows. In about 1880, when working with Brücke, Freud began to smoke cigarettes. In 1884–85, his research into cocaine led him to experience its stimulating and mood-elevating effects, and he began to take the drug fairly regularly. This he ceased to do as soon as various cases of cocaine addiction came to his attention. It was then only by smoking a large number of cigars a day that Freud was able to counterbalance, in large part, his neurotic symptomatology, which was of a psychosomatic nature. It would seem that from then on, apart from an allusion to drug addiction as a substitute for masturbation, in a letter to Fliess of December 22, 1897,[1] and his theory of an erotogenic fixation in the labial region among drinkers and smokers in his *Three Essays on the Theory of Sexuality*,[2] he took no further interest, in a scientific sense, in this form of psychopathology.

This cardiac episode had a considerable bearing on Freud's later discoveries. It was the first time that the 'young' Freud became aware of the inevitability of his future death, that he felt limits being set on his temporal horizon, and that there suddenly seemed to be a certain urgency to achieve his life's work. In 1895, he was grappling with the crisis of entering middle age. He had to find a new balance between the two lines of force arising from oral erotism – the 'normal' tendency characterised by the daydreams accompanying first thumbsucking, then masturbation, and the 'toxic' tendency illustrated by the abuse first of cocaine, then of tobacco. At the same time that Freud began smoking again, he was preparing to carry out – complementarily and, so to speak, contrapuntally – his self-analysis. In other words, he was to embark on a new form of auto-erotic mental activity: an exploration of his dreams.

What was at issue, from the point of view of the unconscious? That Freud's addiction to tobacco was probably a struggle not only against depression but also against internal persecution is suggested by the fact

1. 'The insight has dawned on me that masturbation is the one major habit, the "primary addiction", and it is only as a substitute and replacement for it that the other addictions – to alcohol, morphine, tobacco, and the like – come into existence. The role played by this addiction in hysteria is enormous; and it is perhaps there that my major, still outstanding obstacle is to be found, wholly or in part. And here, of course, doubt arises about whether an addiction of this kind is curable, or whether analysis and therapy must come to a halt at this point and content themselves with transforming hysteria into neurasthenia' (*F* 287).

2. 'It is not every child who sucks in this way. It may be assumed that those children do so in whom there is a constitutional intensification of the erotogenic significance of the labial region. If that significance persists, these same children when they are grown up will become epicures in kissing, will be inclined to perverse kissing, or, if males, will have a powerful motive for drinking and smoking. If, however, repression ensues, they will feel disgust at food and will produce hysterical vomiting' (*SE* 7, 182).

that he shows some of the characteristics which Herbert Rosenfeld (1960) later identified in drug addicts: these include idealisation of the breast, with which the subject experiences the need to feel united or identified (Freud became partly aware of this), the search for a way of artificially producing a hallucination of that ideal breast, the transformation of a good and restorative drug into a bad and harmful substance (Freud came close to recognising this process when he discovered ambivalence), the disavowal of frustration and persecutory anxiety (Freud never became aware either of that anxiety or of his defence against it), and identification with a sick or dead object (in this case, Freud's grandfather Schlomo, then his younger brother Julius). On the other hand, the orgy of destruction and weakness of the ego are not present in Freud's case: their absence explains why his was never more than a mild form of drug addiction. Whenever the psychical working over of an early unconscious process proves impossible for a given subject, one solution is recourse to biochemical methods such as drugs, tobacco or alcohol. As we shall see, Freud's self-analysis was no more and no less than a mental working over of depressive anxiety. Persecutory anxiety led him to seek a solution of a second kind – a biochemical solution.

Freud and Charcot

THE STUDY COURSE AT THE SALPÊTRIÈRE (1885–86)

Coming in timely fashion after the cocaine episode, Freud's four-month stay, from mid-October 1885 to the end of February 1886,[1] in the Neurological Department of the Salpêtrière in Paris, marked a fresh turning point in his scientific career. On a previous occasion – to which I shall return later on – a public reading of the *Essay on Nature*, attributed to Goethe, and the internal maturation specific to adolescence had incited Freud to give up the study of political and social science in favour of biology. And on a second occasion, the engagement to his fiancée and the continuation of an obscure internal process led him to abandon the patronage of Brücke and switch from fundamental research to medical practice, and from physiological anatomy to neurology. Jean-Martin Charcot (1825–93) was a world-renowned neurologist, brilliant teacher, influential scientist, and

1. Sigmund spent the late summer of 1885 with Martha in Wandsbek. From there he travelled to Paris, with two stops on the way, in Cologne and Brussels. He made a return trip to Wandsbek to spend Christmas week there. When he finally left Paris he went straight to Berlin to study at Adolf Baginsky's Clinic. While in Paris he stayed at the Hôtel de la Paix, rue Royer-Collard, then at the Hôtel du Brésil, rue Le Goff.

researcher at the clinic's own teaching unit. (Once, when interrupted by someone who said: 'That cannot possibly be so, it contradicts the theory of Young-Helmholtz,' Charcot retorted: 'Theory is all very well, but it can't stop things existing!') Charcot weaned Freud from Meynert's influence. He made him understand the importance of the psychical factor in nervous diseases and the need to complement neurology, which was the speciality of the head of the clinic (and Charcot's successor), Pierre Marie (1853–1940), with psychopathology, the province of an assistant, Joseph-François Babinski (1857–1932), with whom Freud collaborated closely and efficiently throughout his Paris stay.[1]

Freud's early days in Paris were difficult: he could not understand French well, and was forced to count his pennies in a city renowned for its easy pleasures. He felt so lonely and unhappy that he almost returned to Vienna (unpublished letter to Martha, December 9, 1885, quoted in J I, 228). Jones regards Freud's desire to return as a defence against the fierce attraction for psychopathology that Charcot had implanted in him. Chertok (1969 and 1973) sees 'a mixture of attraction and repulsion' experienced by Freud when faced with the clearly erotic nature of the hysterical fits he witnessed – in some cases, reactions as extreme as orgasm were triggered off when the doctor touched certain parts of the body. I myself prefer to interpret Freud's homesickness, in the light of his future 'Rome' dreams and of the subsequent analysis (1936*a*) of his disturbance of memory on the Acropolis, and coming at a moment of depression, as one of the first manifestations of a Freudian constant: the realisation of any very highly cathected desire (as was the case of his desire to go to Paris and work with Charcot) filled him with intense anxiety.

However that may be, Freud eventually fitted into his new milieu and earned the esteem of his colleagues. Charcot asked him to translate his next book (1886*f*), invited him round to his home on two occasions, and suggested that he make an observation of a hemiplegia. Freud later published this observation in the monograph he wrote with Oscar Rie, entitled 'Klinische Studie über die halbseitige Cerebrallähmung der Kinder' ('Clinical Study of the Unilateral Cerebral Paralysis of Children') (1891*a*). He realised that a lively and warm interest in patients with nervous disorders produced better results than the 'serene superficiality' of Viennese doctors. He learned that the functional disorders of hysterics, such as paralysis or paraesthesia, were psychogenic (they can in fact be

1. Pierre Janet (1859–1947) worked in the department at a later date, and Freud never heard his name mentioned there. In any case, his earliest publications came later on. Chapter 6 of Ellenberger (1970), 'Pierre Janet and Psychological Analysis', throws useful light on his published work and on the priority claim which he subsequently disputed with Freud.

artificially induced in such patients by hypnotic suggestion) and reversible (produced by an idea, they can also be abolished by an idea). This led to the technique, which was specific to the Paris school, of 'counter-suggestion' under hypnosis, and to the observation that since such complaints were psychical in origin and had nothing to do with anatomy – or more precisely, with the sexual anatomy of women as it had long been understood (the word hysteria derives etymologically, and in accordance with phantasy, from the Greek word for womb) – they could affect men and women alike. Charcot professed the theory that hysteria had two causes. He said that the main one was neurological (with predisposition probably caused by nervous degeneracy), but that little was known about it; for these two reasons, no action could be taken against hysteria itself. On the other hand, the 'idea', usually a psychical trauma, if it were merely the cause of the symptom, was a mechanism that could be elucidated and dominated; it was therefore possible to cure not hysteria, but its symptoms. This was a point of view that Freud still broadly supported in 1895.

In his subsequent obituary of Charcot (1893*f*), Freud, likening him to Philippe Pinel who a century earlier, also at the Salpêtrière, had freed insane patients from their chains, saw him as some kind of hero who freed hysteria from the anatomical and moral prejudices that were then hindering its study. Any ordinary doctor of the Victorian era would undoubtedly have jeopardised his respectability by taking seriously the ravings and the grotesque and equivocal contortions of girls and women who made an exhibition of their bodies. Their symptoms were thought to be the result of simulation, imaginary illness, or a disorder of the womb, which had deranged them and which could sometimes be cured by extirpation of the clitoris. Had it not been for Charcot's stature, his authority, and the intelligence he displayed in establishing and unravelling facts, Freud would probably never have approached the diagnosis and the psychotherapy of neuroses in a scientific manner.

But Freud's assessment of Charcot seems exaggerated for two reasons. First, it was a personal judgment that was not shared by very many: in France, Charcot's successors not only did not develop his theories, but were already beginning to question them by 1895; outside France, the theatricality of the Salpêtrière and the suspicion that Charcot's use of hypnosis was merely a form of *dressage* on suggestible subjects tended to arouse disbelief or pity. The second reason is that from 1895 on no further trace of Charcot's influence on Freud can be detected. Indeed, none of Freud's dreams during his self-analysis evokes Charcot, whereas Brücke, Meynert, Fleischl, Breuer and Fliess appear in them often. *The Interpretation of Dreams* contains no reference to any of Charcot's writings or ideas. This fact calls for some explanation. Charcot was 'a visual'. His look was peculiarly fascinating because he suffered from a squint. In a letter to Martha of October 21, 1885 (*L* 187), Freud describes his 'dark, strangely soft eyes (or rather one is, the other is expressionless and has an inward cast)'. In his obituary of Charcot, there are constant references to sight. Charcot the visual was unconsciously a voyeur, in whose presence the hysterics of the Salpêtrière gave free rein to their exhibitionism. His presentations of patients were veritable shows, attended by the cream of Parisian high society. The coordinates of Charcot's scientific and therapeutic method were corporal space and scenic space. Distance and listening, on the other hand, were what Freud strove for. The methods he later employed to organise psychoanalytic space were quite different from those on which demonstrations of hypnosis were based: the analyst sat out of sight behind the patient, who reclined on a couch and was invited, without the presence of any other spectators, to describe his or her sexual desires and to recognise their subject matter, rather than miming their various forms in the mechanical and impersonal manner that Charcot aimed to achieve. As J.-B. Pontalis has rightly observed (1974), Charcot's full, theatrical space – which is in fact the spontaneous space of the hysteric – was replaced by Freud with an empty, purely mental space. The discovery of psychoanalysis and the theory of the psychical apparatus were to be born as a direct result of this change of perspective. But it should be noted in passing that inevitably psychoanalytic theory and technique are still marked by the circumstances in which they came into being: Freud stamped them with his hysterophobic tendencies. The progress currently being made by psychoanalysis in the understanding of psychotics, psychosomatic cases and borderline states is slow and laborious because, on top of the difficulties inherent in such types of psychical organisation, psychoanalysis is unwilling to break away from its original moorings.[1]

When he got back to Vienna, Freud saw for himself how strong and deep-rooted the prejudice against hypnosis was in medical circles. It was identified with mesmerism, in other words with charlatanism. This prejudice was all the keener in Vienna because it was there that Franz Anton Mesmer had announced his discovery before being driven out of the city. It was a prejudice that Moritz Benedikt, who had introduced Freud to Charcot, had already experienced on his own return from Paris in 1878, and that Albert Moll, some of whose ideas influenced Freud, also encountered, one year after the latter's Paris visit, when he described his own

1. Anyone interested in a detailed study of Charcot's influence on Freud and in Freud's development in relation to Charcot's ideas should consult Chapters 2 and 4 of Andersson's book (1962).

studies at the Salpêtrière and at Nancy to a conference of the Berlin Society of Medicine on October 28, 1887 (cf. L. Chertok, R. de Saussure, 1973, 149–50). In April 1886, Freud enthusiastically wrote his 'Report on My Studies in Paris and Berlin' (which was published posthumously, 1956*a*), and in the course of the next two months gave a large number of lectures to various learned societies on his visit and on hypnotism (which Meynert abhorred). On October 15, 1886, Freud spoke on a more risqué subject, male hysteria, before the Kaiserliche Gesellschaft der Ärzte in Wien (Imperial Society of Physicians of Vienna). Certain members of the audience – reports on the debate that followed Freud's address have survived (cf. E 439–41) – minimised Charcot's contribution by pointing out that male hysteria was a well-known phenomenon. Meynert, on the other hand, regarded the disorders in males described by Charcot as epileptoid and challenged Freud to come up with such a case among his hospital patients. Freud found several, but the senior physicians in each department refused to allow him to show them. Eventually Freud was able, on November 26, 1886, to demonstrate, once again before the Society, a serious case of hemi-anaesthesia in a hysterical male (1886*d*), who had been given an ophthalmological examination by Freud's friend Königstein. Later, in his book *An Autobiographical Study* (1925*d*, *SE* 20, 15–16), Freud gave a somewhat embittered version of the events that ensued. He complained that although politely applauded he was permanently ostracised by the 'high authorities' (this was true of some but not all of them), excluded from Meynert's laboratory of cerebral anatomy (this indeed happened, but only six months later; in any case, Freud had no wish to stay), and deprived of a room in which he could deliver his lectures (this is unlikely, as his university lectures continued almost uninterruptedly up to 1895, as indeed they probably did until 1917). He claimed that for 'a whole generation' he never set foot in the Society of Physicians and withdrew from 'academic life': yet Jones found evidence that he attended meetings of the Society on fairly frequent occasions (he had no difficulty in getting elected a member of it on March 18, 1887), and lectured to other bodies (J I, 255)!

Notwithstanding this, it is obvious that Freud was the victim of threefold prejudice – that of the narrowly rationalist and materialist neurophysiologists who challenged psychical facts in their most specific form, that of doctors, who so hotly denied feeling any possible attraction for their female patients that they refused to take into account their imaginative phantasies and private emotions in relation to them, and lastly – and more generally – that of his age and milieu (a wealthy *petite bourgeoisie* or middle class of Puritan morality), which held sexuality to be something which should never be allowed to emerge from specific institutional structures or depart from a restricted number of licit practices, any other outlet being bound to result in shame or hypocrisy. This prejudice was at that time reinforced by a reaction of defence, anger and contempt against increasing permissiveness in aristocratic and working-class milieux. It was frequent in Vienna, as indeed it was in other large cities at that period, for female domestic staff to be forced to prostitute themselves to their employers, for men to have fun with women of a lower social position but never marry them, and for them to refuse to accept that their wives and daughters might have sexual desires or needs. Incest[1] was relatively common, as was sexual unhappiness among many members of the most powerful families.

Against this background it is easy to see why Freud waited five years before publishing 'Some Points for a Comparative Study of Organic and Hysterical Motor Paralyses' (1893*c*), which he wrote in 1888, and which summarises Charcot's contribution to the subject. And it was Charcot himself who, a few days before his death, published the study in French in *Archives de neurologie*.

The autumn of 1886, when regarded in historical perspective, looks very much like a private dress rehearsal for what was to become, from 1900 on, a public drama – by which time psychoanalysis had already been invented, the moving forces of sexual psychology were beginning to be revealed, the secrets of people's private lives were no longer restricted to the confessional (where absolution was sought), to those playing an active part in them, or to the purveyors of salacious gossip, but had become the subject of an explanatory general science, and, lastly, it was accepted that neurosis could not be cured without the innermost secrets of the patient's life and thoughts being shared.

Prejudices of that kind, whose form and content vary from one country and one period to another, but whose roots are inherent in the very organisation of the psychical apparatus, caused, in Freud's case, a good deal of bitterness. But, although not as great as he obviously liked to think in retrospect, his bitterness cannot be explained solely by socio-cultural factors. I would argue that two psychological phenomena operated within him. The first was yet another trait he owed to the spirit of his age, German romanticism, which advocated the equal development of enthusiasm and discipline in every individual. Brücke provided an example of such a

1. This frequency was such that it encouraged Freud to suppose, towards the end of 1895, that hysteria was always primarily caused by an actual seduction of the child by the parent. The fact that *A Man without Qualities* (1930–42), the first great modern novel to treat the subject of incest (between adult brother and sister), was written by an Austrian, Robert Musil (1880–1942), seems to be of some relevance.

model, and Freud, who already showed a temperamental predisposition, cast himself in the same mould. Such romantic notions as 'the young prodigy' and 'the unrecognised genius' would seem to have been underlying influences during this episode in his life. The University of Vienna, one of the most highly reputed in the world, had opened up its laboratories and prepared him to take up a career within its walls. While Freud was still very young, it had sent him on study courses to Trieste, Paris and Berlin, preferring him to his rivals because of the promise held out by his already budding talents. He felt confident of making great achievements in his life. He would be a Brücke, a Griesinger, a Charcot. Now, after offering up the poisoned gift of cocaine to his university, he brought back great tidings from the Salpêtrière in Paris – the psychical aetiology of certain mental disorders.

Here, a second phenomenon took over from the first. The prodigal son discovered on his return home that, far from being fêted by his colleagues as he had expected, he was assailed by the criticism with which society brands those who are too far ahead of their time or have worked too unfamiliar a seam – *poètes maudits*, original thinkers, scientists who overthrow accepted ideas. Freud then adopted an attitude of haughty isolation, except for a single friend – first Breuer, then Fliess – to whom he confided the full force of the secret fire that continued to consume him; he imposed a new asceticism on himself with the aim of braving all opposition and making a discovery that would burst like a bombshell on a shamefaced and shocked society: that was precisely what could be expected of a romantic hero. The personal causes of Freud's behaviour should obviously be put down both to a megalomaniac defence against depression and above all against internal persecution, and to an unstable position of attacker-attacked in which he had probably been fixated since the death of his younger brother and rival, Julius. For does not each of us choose an answer to our own set of personal problems in our surrounding culture?

The second phenomenon is easier to define, but more difficult to understand. Freud approached sexuality in a different way from many of his male contemporaries. While libertine in their acts, they were inhibited in thought and speech. Freud, on the other hand, was reserved when it came to doing, and transgressive when it came to knowing. What economy of the psyche can have supported him in this position?

Two factors seem to have played a role here. First, there was a certain relationship in Freud between the ego-ideal and the super-ego: the super-ego simply forbade him to act, and the ego-ideal encouraged him to think. The rigour of the former was tempered by the liberality of the latter. When the super-ego accepts from the ego the possibility of being challenged and allows the ego to free itself from a position where it would be subjected to the super-ego's destructive aggressiveness, that aggressiveness can then be directed at parts of the external world on to which the super-ego is projected, such as taboos, stupidity, other individuals and established ideas. This, I feel, explains why Freud felt the need to attack everything which, in society, in scientific circles, and in the entourage of any person, constricts the intellectual and emotional freedom of that person.

The other factor involves the relationship between sublimation and somatisation. In Freud's case, the sexual instinct, except in relation to his wife, with whom he fully satisfied that instinct, was suspended as regards its aim with other objects, but not inhibited. He did not need to resort to neurotic repression in order to control it; it was enough for him to represent it to himself and to identify it. In circumstances such as these, the instinct becomes available not only for tasks of sublimation, but for a particular type of sublimation, i.e. knowledge of its workings as an instinct. But a sublimation of that kind, which I would call reflexive as opposed to the more common sublimations, which are expressive, produces quantitatively only a partial and insufficient discharge of instinctual energy. There remains an appreciable instinctual residue which is bound neither in thought by reflexive work, nor by repression into a neurotic symptomatology. The residue tends to discharge itself in the body, in the form of more or less hypochondriac disorders, fatigues, and mobile, highly variable functional disorders never affecting the same organ for a very great length of time. We have already seen, and shall see again, that this was precisely Freud's case.

FREUD'S BEGINNINGS IN PRIVATE PRACTICE AND HIS FINAL NEUROLOGICAL RESEARCH (1885–91)

Apart from coping with the aftermath of his trip to Paris, which I have just described, Freud spent most of 1886 settling into his new life. He was 30. After spending the whole of March in Berlin, on a study course at the clinic for children's diseases run by Adolf Baginsky (1843–1918), he returned to Vienna and began working three times a week at the public Institute for Children's Diseases which had just been founded and was directed by Professor Max Kassowitz (1842–1913). On Easter Sunday, Freud opened a private practice at 7 Rathausstrasse. Without waiting to find out whether he would have enough patients to support him, he married on September 13 at Wandsbek. As the civil ceremony, which was sufficient for Germany, was not valid in Austria, Freud had to accept a Jewish religious ceremony (reduced, however, to its barest essentials) at the home of Mamma Bernays. When the newly-wed couple returned to Vienna, it was to a new rented four-room apartment, in which Freud also held his practice, at 8 Maria Theresienstrasse.

Freud devoted most of the next five years to family life and to building up a practice. The first children were born. The Freuds had to move in 1891 to 19 Berggasse, where they were to live until finally emigrating to London in 1938. Their flat on the first floor was supplemented in 1892 by three rented rooms on the mezzanine, which Freud put to professional use. They overlooked a small garden. Freud had unconsciously reconstituted the arrangement of the house where he was born in Freiberg, with its bedroom on the first floor, its shop downstairs, and its nearby meadow.

Freud met Fliess in 1887. Throughout this period (up to 1891), Freud ceased publishing original papers, except for an observation of hemianopsia in two infants, a hitherto unknown occurrence (1888*a*), and various articles already described, which were connected with his previous research into cocaine (1887*d*) and the structure of the elements of the nervous system (1887*f*). In order to maintain his scientific reputation and round out his income, Freud also wrote a large number of book reviews (1887*a*, *b*, *c*, *e*, *g*, *h*, *i*, 1889*a*). He successfully completed his translation into German (1886*f*) of Charcot's *Lectures on the Diseases of the Nervous System*, which appeared in French only a year later, and then (1888–89) that of *Suggestion and its Therapeutic Effects*, an earlier work by Hippolyte Bernheim, Charcot's great rival in Nancy in the field of hypnotism and hysteria – a translation which Freud furnished with an important preface on the controversy that had arisen between the Nancy and Salpêtrière schools. He also wrote five articles ('Aphasia', 'Brain', 'Hysteria', 'Infantile Paralysis' and 'Paralysis') for Villaret's medical encyclopaedia, *Handwörterbuch der gesamten Medizin* (1888*b*, 1891*c*).

As Freud stated in letters (in 1887 and 1888) to Fliess, with whom he had entered into an increasingly regular correspondence, his ambition was to produce a monograph – perhaps a general survey of existing knowledge – on brain anatomy. This project, a relic from an earlier phase in his life, was never completed, but it did result in several publications pertaining no longer to pure neurology, but to neuropathology; they were in fact to be Freud's last contributions to that field. The initial and more considerable series of such papers, which was prompted by his work at Kassowitz's Institute for Children's Diseases, concerned infantile paralyses. Written in conjunction with a paediatrist, Freud's assistant, friend, and future family doctor, Oscar Rie (later 'my friend Otto' in the dream of 'Irma's injection'), the first of the series was a large monograph on hemiplegia in children (1891*a*), which was subsequently summarised in three papers in a medical journal. It was followed by another monograph, this time on central cerebral diplegias (1893*b*); a summarised version of it appeared in France in the *Revue neurologique* (1893*e*) at the request of Pierre Marie, and was complemented by an observation of two brothers who both suffered from the same hereditary diplegia (1893*d*). The series ended with several studies of specific symptoms: hypertonia of the lower extremities, which often accompanies *enuresis nocturna* (1893*g*), an affection of a nerve in the upper thigh which he had himself experienced and described, and to which Bernhardt, unaware of his predecessor's work, had attached his name (1895*e*). Freud the neurologist, then, had got into the habit of observing dysfunctions in himself and of corroborating them with his own case observations. And once again, through a mixture of bad luck and lackadaisicalness in backing up his hunches and making known his findings, one of Freud's minor discoveries was pinched, so to speak, from under his nose.

The same remarks could apply to the other form of neuropathological work in which Freud was simultaneously engaged, and which resulted in his first book, *Zur Auffassung der Aphasien. Eine kritische Studie* (*On Aphasia. A Critical Study*) (1891*b*), which he dedicated to Breuer. As I have already mentioned, Freud quotes in it Hughlings Jackson's brand-new doctrine of 'dissolution', and backs it up with numerous examples. Freud's two monographs on infantile cerebral paralyses brought him fame in European medical circles: for a long time they were cited in specialised works on the subject. Nothnagel, a rare example of a teacher of Freud's who did not turn against his pupil, asked him to cover the same ground in more concise form for one section of his great encyclopaedia of medicine, *Handbuch der specielle Pathologie und Therapie* (1897*a*); and for the next three years Freud wrote abstracts and reviews on the subject of infantile cerebral paralysis for a year-book (1898*c*, 1899*b*, 1900*b*). His book on aphasia, on the other hand, was a complete flop: sales were extremely sluggish, all unsold copies – about two-thirds of the print run – were pulped by the publishers in 1900, and no later authorities on the subject, except Goldstein in 1910, refer to it at all. It is not enough to argue that Freud's 'functionalist' explanation of aphasia was too far ahead of its time. There can be no denying that he felt a certain unconscious attraction for the plight of the *poète maudit*, the unrecognised genius, the prophet cast out by his own people, a man to whom justice would be rendered only after his death. This explains the scathing tone that his book, aptly subtitled *A Critical Study*, adopts towards established authorities and towards the generally accepted doctrine that each form of aphasia was the result of a localised lesion of a different part of the brain. Freud demolished the reigning Wernicke–Lichtheim theory. He no doubt revelled in being able to announce that the theory dear to the heart of his now repudiated former teacher, Meynert (that the cortex contains a topographical 'projection' of the various parts of the body), had been shown by histological analysis to be totally unfounded: 'In a few weeks, I shall afford myself the pleasure of sending you a small book on aphasia for which I myself have a great deal of warm feeling. In it I am very impudent, cross swords with your friend Wernicke, with Lichtheim and Grashey, and even scratch the high and mighty idol Meynert' (May 2, 1891, *F* 28).

Revolutionary views, without which there can be no scientific progress, have never contributed to that progress when it is their revolutionary nature, rather than their logical cogency, that is proclaimed with uncompromising passion. This is what happened to Freud: the revolution caused a storm in a teacup – and foundered in it. The new idea was not examined on its own merits, because those that it aimed to provoke could only reject it out of hand before even examining it properly. Many years later, a plagiarist would rescue it from oblivion and cunningly pass it off as his own, or some less venomous researcher who had made the same discovery would believe, and sincerely have others believe, that he was first past the post. The quarrel that Freud had been constantly picking with Meynert ever since his visit to Charcot had not been a purely intellectual one. Meynert was well-known for being 'a very erratic and neurotic person and a heavy drinker' (J I, 253n.). On his death bed, in 1892, he confessed in one final moment of honesty that he had himself been a classical case of the male hysteria whose existence he had always so vehemently challenged (*ID* 438). During his lifetime, Meynert, a man to whom dissimulation was second nature, and whose moral calibre was dubious, acted as a father figure to Freud, who reacted to him with a clearly Oedipal defiance. On his death, Freud must have thought, with a twinge of exultation: '*Non vixit*' ('He did not live'), a theme that recurs in one of the dreams of his self-analysis.

In any case, there is no reason why we, in the second half of the twentieth century, should have any regrets about Freud's failure in this field: old bonds have to be broken before a person can feel free enough to contract new ones. It could even be that the little voice of the inner demon to which, in 1895, Freud increasingly enjoyed listening, had nudged events in this direction. In his book on aphasia, Freud was so to speak playing at double your money when he called his scientific contemporaries to account. Had he won his wager, he would have pursued a career in neuropathology, probably rising to ever more brilliant heights. Having lost, as he may secretly have desired, he felt that he had squared his account and was free to change course. Jones believes that Freud's obituary of Charcot (1893*f*) represented a twin farewell – to his teacher before he had had occasion to repudiate him, and to the discipline Charcot had rendered illustrious by renewing it (J I, 240). Thus the young Freud, as he grew older, no longer felt the desire – or need – to imitate models: if he wished to create, he had now to do so from his own resources, even if this meant that nothing came of it. The sudden change of course was agonising for Freud, and the stakes were high; but driven by inner necessity, Freud had no choice but to move on to new pastures.

Freud and Breuer

THE THERAPY OF HYSTERICS BY HYPNOSIS (1889–93)[1]

Freud's private patients increasingly brought home to him a fact that he had begun to deduce from his hospital work: between one third and half of all cases suffering from nervous disorders were not neurologically sick at all. For these patients, whose sickness was one of ideas, or affects, he had to find not only the diagnosis but the appropriate therapy. After his first period of trial and error with cocaine and electrotherapy, Freud pinned his hopes on hypnosis. While still a student, Freud had attended a public exhibition given by the celebrated 'magnetist' Carl Hansen, which convinced him that hypnotic phenomena were genuine. When Assistant in hospital, he witnessed hypnotherapy sessions conducted no doubt by Breuer and by the neurology professor Moritz Benedikt (1835–1920), who later gave him a letter of introduction to Charcot. There was great international solidarity between hypnotists at the time, because of the already described virulent prejudice of the medical profession against a science that was regarded as a mystification, if not a cause of physical deterioration.

Breuer, whom Freud met at Brücke's laboratory in about 1880, and who became his protector, financial supporter, family doctor and friend, had often told him about the fascinating case history of Anna O., its unhappy outcome, and the discovery he made in the course of the case – the so-called cathartic method. Joseph Breuer (1842–1925) treated Bertha Pappenheim (1859–1936) – as I have already mentioned, this was her real name (J I, 245–8) – from December 1880 to June 1882. The young woman, who combined personal charm with extraordinary intelligence, had been ill since the beginning of her father's fatal illness. She came from one of the

1. For a fuller description, see Chapter 3 of Andersson (1962).

wealthiest Jewish merchant families in Austria. There is a very fine photograph of her in Ellenberger's book (1970). Breuer had been called to her bedside to treat her for a nervous cough, a symptom which was in fact a shield for a dual personality. She was able, through auto-hypnosis, to shift from the twilight state of an unruly and unbearable child to that of a normal self-aware young lady. She also suffered from various paralyses, anorexia, fits of rage, and disturbances of sight (strabismus) and of speech (dumbness, agrammatism). She had forgotten German, her mother tongue, though she could still understand it, and spoke only in English. She was also able to read French and Italian.

Breuer, who saw her often, sometimes twice daily, got into the habit of making her the last patient of the day and became extremely interested in her case. Under hypnosis she would tell him what she had suffered from during the day – unpleasant incidents, 'negative' hallucinations, frights. One day she described to him, with considerable precision and emotion, how one symptom (hydrophobia) had first appeared: her English lady's companion got her dog to drink from a glass of water in her presence – and much to her (Anna O.'s) disgust. Once related in this way, the symptom disappeared completely. Anna O. was herself aware of the effectiveness of the process, and called it (in English, as she spoke only English at the time) 'the talking cure', or 'chimney sweeping'. With Breuer's help, she applied it to her other symptoms, with considerable success. From November 18, 1882 (unpublished letter to Martha of November 19, 1882, quoted in J I, 248), Breuer began to mention to Freud certain details of the case history which he refrained from including in his subsequent publication of it (*Studies on Hysteria*, 1895*d*), and which were later communicated to Jones (Freud's own confidences were confirmed when Jones consulted the letters, some of which remained unpublished, from Sigmund to Martha, who was an old friend of Bertha Pappenheim): just as Anna O. made spectacular progress thanks to her doctor's increasing interest in her case and person, so Breuer's wife, Mathilde, began, for the same reason (only Breuer himself remained unaware of the implications), to feel mounting jealousy, and eventually summoned him to stop visiting his patient. When Anna O. learned that her treatment was being curtailed, she reacted by experiencing the throes of an imaginary childbirth at the termination of a phantom pregnancy resulting from Breuer's 'ministrations' – but unperceived by him, as the notion of being the father of an immaculate conception was quite unthinkable to him. 'Though profoundly shocked, he managed to calm her down by hypnotising her, and then fled the house in a cold sweat. The next day he and his wife left for Venice to spend a second honeymoon, which resulted in the conception of a daughter' (J I, 247). It is interesting to learn, as a result of Ellenberger's researches (E 483) that the Breuer daughter in question had in fact already come into the world on March 11, 1882, and was called, of all things, Dora! She eventually (in 1942) committed suicide in Vienna to escape deportation by the Nazis.

The version of the story published by Breuer in *Studies on Hysteria* (1895*d*) was very different: the 'talking cure' culminated, according to him, in a session where the patient was able to reproduce the hallucinations which she had had at the bedside of her seriously ill father (that of a black snake trying to bite her on the right arm), and which had set off the whole chain reaction of symptoms; as the patient was cured, Breuer ended his treatment.[1] Breuer was 40 at the time, and Bertha 23 – exactly the same age as Jacob, and almost the same age (within three years) as Amalie, when they conceived Sigmund Freud.

By 1895, Bertha Pappenheim had only with difficulty recovered from the relapses to which she had been doomed by this 'brutal' termination of her treatment. She was looked after in Frankfurt by her mother ('somewhat of a dragon', according to Jones). She was unmarried, and was to remain so. Right up until her death, she held the post of social worker in an orphanage (she was the first social worker in Germany). It will come as no surprise to learn that she was also a keen supporter of women's emancipation.[2] She also occasionally saw Martha, to whom she became related by marriage.

Breuer, on the other hand, remained traumatised by this specimen case of the cathartic method. He again took flight when Freud showed him a female hysteric who was experiencing a phantom pregnancy. Freud only partially – and much later, probably in June 1892 (cf. p. 63) – reassured Breuer when he described how a female patient of his own had one day leapt into his arms; he pointed out that the hysteric was suffering from sexual repression, and that her act was a phenomenon of transference.

Breuer accepted Freud's reasoning intellectually, and even shared responsibility for committing it to print in *Studies on Hysteria*, which he wrote with Freud. Despite the latter's impatience, the book took two years to write and came out only in 1895. It was scarcely more successful than Freud's work on aphasia: in thirteen years, only 626 of the 800 copies printed were sold. The mere idea that there could be some sort of sexual interchange between a slightly unhinged woman and her doctor, especially

1. The diagnosis of hysteria has since been challenged. Some authors believe it to have been a case of schizophrenia. Schur (S 38) sees it as a borderline state (cf. Chertok and de Saussure, 1973, 167–8).

2. Bertha Pappenheim and her historical role were important enough to merit an obituary in the *Blätter des Jüdischen Frauenbundes* (*Journal of the League of Jewish Women*) and a book by Dora Edinger (1963). Ellenberger (1970) summarises the essential facts of her life.

when he was the same age as her father, who had just died, was something that Breuer was deeply reluctant to admit. In all the observations published on Anna O. he did not write a single line relating to sexuality. He then refused to follow Freud any further along that avenue, and while maintaining his friendship and esteem for the younger man put an end to their collaboration. Freud was able more easily to keep a cool head because of his deep-rooted Puritanism, the moderation of his sexual needs, the passion which he had displaced on to Fliess, and his histological eye. He was to continue, alone, to use the body of the hysteric as a tool for deciphering the great book of sexual metaphor.

In 1871, Josef Breuer had given up the university career for which his gifts and his teachers had destined him, and devoted himself to his private practice, which was to become one of the finest in Vienna, while at the same time pursuing research along the lines of the Helmholtz school. As a Jew who had become a wealthy doctor and a renowned researcher, Breuer had, in Freud's eyes, achieved the ideal kind of success to which a member of that community could aspire. Conversely, Breuer found in Freud first a younger man as gifted as himself, whom he could encourage and help, and then someone with whom he could get together to discuss their respective ideas, case histories, and a phenomenon later known as counter-transference. Freud mentioned Breuer's cathartic method to Charcot, who attached no importance to it. But Charcot convinced Freud of the specific merits of hypnosis in the treatment of hysterics. Freud was beginning to use hypnosis, in conjunction with baths, massage and rest, at the time he opened his private practice, and persuaded Breuer to use hypnosis again in collaboration with him. They did not use the cathartic method straight away, but as a precaution began in 1889 merely with the counter-suggestion technique commonly used at the Salpêtrière, under which the symptom is forbidden, under hypnosis, to reappear. Pierre Janet was using the same method, which he described, also in 1889, in his *L'automatisme psychologique* (*Psychological Automatism*), but he had also tried the cathartic method (in the Lucie case history, published in 1886, and the Marie case history, published in 1889): it is impossible to establish whether Freud knew of these publications at the time (cf. E 358–74 and 485). The case history of Frau Emmy von N., whose treatment, according to Freud, began on May 1, 1889[1] and who formed the subject of the first of the four

1. The editors of the *Standard Edition* (*SE* 2, Appendix A) assume that Freud changed the dates of treatment in his publication of the case history, and that it in fact began in May 1888; this assumption is wrong, as the Sigmund Freud Archives contain the autobiography of Frau M. M., Frau Emmy's daughter, which confirms that her mother's treatment started in May 1889 (Andersson, 1962, 74 n.2). As in the preceding case, the diagnosis of hysteria may here seem debatable.

observations written by Freud for *Studies on Hysteria*, shows what difficulty he had in choosing between the two techniques.

The patient (1848–1925), a 40-year-old widow with two adolescent daughters, whom Freud separated from their mother during her seven-week course of treatment, had been suffering from various symptoms since the illness and premature death of her husband fourteen years before, including tics, a clacking of the tongue (similar, Freud said, to the call of the capercaillie) (1895*d*, *SE* 2, 49n.), stammering, anorexia, neck-cramps, and above all zoophobias.

What Freud failed to mention in his published case history, but which Andersson (1962) discovered from the autobiography of Frau Emmy's daughter, was that she was rumoured to have poisoned her husband, who left her a considerable fortune. The inquest into his death resulted in there being no ground for prosecution. 'Psychical chimney-sweeping' enabled Freud to find the cause of her phobia of mice and rats in a first traumatic childhood memory: her brothers and sisters often threw dead animals at her. Instead of allowing catharsis to operate, he interrupted those digressions he felt to be of no use to the patient and wiped out the symptom with active counter-suggestion. But instead she experienced a sudden series of phobias – of snakes, a toad and a lizard, whose symbolism was at no time considered. Similarly subtle yet taxing bouts of shadow-boxing between the therapist's counter-suggestions and the Protean metamorphoses of the patient's symptoms recurred with each new symptom. The twin satisfactions experienced by Frau Emmy at being separated from her daughters, who were an obstacle to possible remarriage, and at having attracted the attention of a man in the person of a doctor, escaped Freud for a time: this explains why swift improvements were followed by repeated relapses, which coincided with the absence of those two favourable conditions.

As regards his theory of the psychical processes, the case of Frau Emmy caused Freud – though probably only when he actually came to write it up in about 1893 for publication in *Studies on Hysteria* – to use for the first time the concept of cathexis (*Besetzung*) to describe the dominant abulia of that patient: referring to his first article in French (1893*c*), in which he had used the term '*muni d'une valeur affective*' ('provided with a large quota of affect'), Freud wrote: 'I showed from examples from ordinary life that a cathexis such as this of an idea whose affect is unresolved always involves a certain amount of associative inaccessibility and of incompatibility with new cathexes' (1895*d*, *SE* 2, 89).

Freud drew two lessons from the case. The first set him on the track of free association: Frau Emmy complained that his counter-suggestions were too hasty and that they interrupted her train of thought: 'When, three days ago, she had first complained about her fear of asylums, I had interrupted her [. . .]. I now saw that I had gained nothing by this interruption and that I cannot evade listening to her stories in every detail to the very end' (1895*d*, *SE* 2, 61). The second lesson was that the often spectacular disappearance of symptoms lasted only as long as the physician gave the patient assiduous care. When this was the case, the patient was cured because she wanted to please the physician. The cessation of treatment frequently caused a relapse. Freud realised this when in May 1890 Frau Emmy underwent a further brief and equally ineffectual course of treatment. But, ever faithful to Charcot, he continued to hold that traumatic experiences could produce hysteria only when a hereditary neurophysiological predisposition (degeneracy) was present.

Meanwhile, Freud had travelled to Nancy in July 1889 to study the methods of Hippolyte Bernheim and of the elderly Auguste Liébeault (1823–1904), which were different in technique from those of Charcot. He took with him a woman patient on whom hypnotism had had little effect: he wished to find out what to do with such patients, who were quite common in his practice. Bernheim, alas, was no more successful than Freud had been (cf. *An Autobiographical Study*, 1925*d*, *SE* 20, 17–18). It was no doubt at this point that the notion of 'resistance' began to gain ground in his mind. When studying with Bernheim, Freud also saw a patient awaken in the hospital ward and suddenly hold an open umbrella over the doctor's head, as he had been instructed to do while under hypnosis. The patient attempted to justify his senseless behaviour by lamely pleading that he thought it was raining outside and that the doctor would want to open his umbrella before going out. This put Freud on the track of another concept, that of rationalisation. The incident was described first by Fritz Wittels (1924) in his biography of Freud, then by Freud himself in 1938, in his last and unfinished work, 'Some Elementary Lessons in Psycho-analysis' (1940*b*). In a note to *Studies on Hysteria*, Freud refers to other similar incidents he observed when with Bernheim (1895*d*, *SE* 2, 67). Later (*ID* 570n.), he says he borrowed from Liébeault's book *Le sommeil provoqué et les états analogues*, which appeared the same year (1889), the idea that dreams are the realisation of the wish to sleep. Oddly enough, however, no trace of this idea is to be found anywhere in the works of Liébeault (E 493). Freud went from Nancy to Paris in August to attend the First International Congress on Hypnotism.[1] He returned to Vienna with renewed enthusiasm for hypnotherapy; his enthusiasm led him definitively

1. The year 1889, the centenary of the French Revolution, was marked by many internationally important events in Paris: the opening of the Eiffel Tower offered the occasion for the International Congress on Hypnotism.

to abandon electrotherapy, but he gradually grew weary with the tedium of having constantly to repeat the same suggestions.

The year 1892 marked a vital turning point. Freud began to make progress at a theoretical level. This progress was only modest in his first article on hypnotic treatment, entitled 'A Case of Successful Treatment by Hypnotism, with Some Remarks on the Origin of Hysterical Symptoms through "Counter-will"' (1892–93), a case which he did not consider worthy of inclusion in *Studies on Hysteria*. The case concerned a woman who was prevented by vomiting, insomnia, agitation and *anorexia nervosa* from breast-feeding her first, second, and third babies despite her desire to do so. In each case, she was cured of her symptoms after a few sessions of hypnotic suggestion with Freud. Freud then posited the existence of 'antithetic ideas' which run against conscious intentions and produce, in the case of hysteria, physiological disorders, and in the case of neurasthenia, weakness of will. But Freud continued to believe in the theory that neurotic symptoms are the result of a particular predisposition. In Charcot's view, that predisposition was organic: it was the neurological degeneracy observed in neuropathic families. Janet, on the other hand, held that it was psychical – an innate weakness in the capacity for synthesis and a narrowing of the field of consciousness.

At about the same time (1892–93), Breuer worked out the concept of a 'hypnoid state', which he later explained in *Studies on Hysteria* and which immediately won the conviction of Freud: it is a 'vacancy of consciousness' similar to that produced artificially by hypnosis, and in which any representation can impose itself without resistance. Such a 'twilight state' is encouraged by feelings of love, or by anxiety when a person is watching at the sick bed of someone dear to him or her. It is triggered off either by fright or by the transformation of a daydream into auto-hypnosis.

Freud wanted to jog Breuer into collaborating with him on a book, which was to be their 'Preliminary Communication' (1893*a*). In a letter of June 28, 1892, Freud told Fliess he had just obtained Breuer's agreement. To that end, he then sent Breuer three short memoranda, which were published posthumously. His letter of June 29, 1892 (1941*a*) enunciates 'the theorem concerning the constancy of the sum of excitation', puts forward the idea that symptoms result from the 'displacement' of sums of excitation which have not been released, and proposes 'the pathological formula of hysteria: [. . .] the magnitude of the sum of excitation, the concept of trauma, the second state of consciousness' (this last idea is the direct precursor of the psychoanalytic notion of the unconscious) (*SE* 1, 147–8). Note 'III' (1941*b*) gives further details: in hysteria, 'the content of consciousness easily becomes temporarily dissociated and certain complexes of ideas which are not associatively connected easily fly apart'; the 'hypnoid state' predisposes the subject to such a '*condition seconde*', similar to the dream; but sexual life can provide non-disposed subjects with the content of traumas likely to produce a dissociation in them (it is worth noting, in passing, the deftness with which Freud tries to strike a balance between Breuer's theory of the hypnoid state and his own theory of the sexual aetiology of neuroses); lastly, it is necessary to put an end to this dissociation and its pathogenic effects 'either by reviving the trauma in a state of somnambulism and then abreacting and correcting it, or by bringing it into normal consciousness under comparatively light hypnosis' (*SE* I, 149–50). This formed the basis for the note entitled 'On the Theory of Hysterical Attacks' (1940*d*), which Freud wrote with Breuer. It, too, contains its fair share of new notions: the 'splitting of consciousness', the 'return of a memory' (the hysterical attack is the return of the memory of a psychical trauma), the 'unconscious' nature of the memory when the patient is in a state of *condition seconde*, and the idea that repression (the process is described though not yet given that name) is responsible for the rejection of certain ideas into the second state of consciousness. The principle of constancy is formulated: health is the result of the nervous system 'disposing associatively of every sensible accretion of excitation or [. . .] discharging it by an appropriate motor reaction' (*SE* I, 151–4). These three texts, then, contain in virtually its final form the whole approach that Freud was later to term 'economic'. They tie up with the notion of 'cathexis', which I mentioned in connection with Frau Emmy von N., and which was probably elaborated by Freud at about the same time.

Freud's and Breuer's decision to go ahead with a joint publication was possibly the result of an important event which, according to Chertok (1968 and 1973) occurred shortly before the month of June, 1892, when Freud told Breuer about it: a patient (a nurse) threw herself into Freud's arms during a hypnosis session. It was this event that finally brought home to him the sexual aetiology of neuroses – a discovery which Jones (J I, 298) says 'greatly excited' Freud, and which bore the hallmark of all Freud's later discoveries in that it was both subjectively experienced and objectively formulated.

During the same period, Freud also carried out one last technical improvement. Repeated suggestion under hypnosis wearied Freud because it was monotonous and not very effective. Moreover, he began to have doubts as to whether this technique was consistent with the theory of the psychical functioning which he was then working out. In 1892, he eventually concluded that it was not, in a note appended to his second translation of a work by Charcot: 'In the long run neither the doctor nor the patient can tolerate the contradiction between the decided denial of the ailment in the suggestion and the necessary recognition of it outside the suggestion' (1892–94, 286n., *SE* 1, 141).

In the autumn of 1892, Freud agreed to treat Fräulein Elisabeth von R. (Ritter) for abasia, even though she showed herself to be refractory to hypnosis. He remembered Bernheim telling him that memories of events during hypnosis were only apparently forgotten and that the doctor could, if he insisted hard enough, revive them when the patient was awake. Freud then proceeded to invent the technique of mental concentration. The patient was put in a reclining position as for hypnosis, but did not keep her eyes open: from then on, it was a case of 'You are requested to close the eyes', as on the placard that later appeared in one of Freud's dreams. (This twofold procedure was adhered to by Freud throughout the period of systematic self-analysis; and it was not until 1904 (1904*a*) that he stopped asking his patients to keep their eyes closed, though they had to remain in a reclining position.) Freud asked the patient to concentrate successively on a particular symptom and try to recall anything that might throw light on its origin: this was the method of 'psychical analysis' which in 1895 Freud was about to transpose from the symptom to the dream by the successive analysis of each fragment of the latter. If nothing came to the patient, Freud would repeat his question with one hand on her forehead, usually with success. This procedure, which Freud continued to use until 1896, and this technique[1] enabled him over a period of six months to unravel the whole thread of Elisabeth's story.[2] He learned of the 24-year-old girl's repressed and guilt-ridden love for the husband of one of her sisters, and of her wild hopes of marrying him when the sister in question, while giving birth to a second child, died of a heart attack, as her father had done several years before. She had suffered from contracture of the right thigh ever since looking after her sick father. The pains had extended to the left leg following a delightful walk alone with her brother-in-law during his wife's illness. For the first time, Freud realised that the pathogenic idea was of an 'erotic' nature: 'The erotic idea was repressed from association and the affect attaching to that idea was used to intensify or revive a physical pain which was present simultaneously or shortly before' (1895*d*, *SE* 2, 146–7). This led him to extend the notion of the 'hysterogenic zone', which

1. Although Freud developed the procedure and technique with Elisabeth von R., he described them in his observation on Fräulein Lucy R. (*SE* 2, 107–12).

2. The case history later formed the subject of *The Red Thread*, a three-act play by Henry Denker, which was itself turned into a film of the same name. Curt Jurgens played Freud in both the stage and screen versions.

Charcot had defined as a painful zone whose stimulation could bring about a hysterical attack. When the painful zone of her thigh was stimulated, 'she cried out – and I could not help thinking that it was as though she was having a voluptuous tickling sensation' (*ibid.*, 137). Moreover, the patient ended up by recalling the reasons for the conversion: 'It was in this place that her father used to rest his leg every morning, while she renewed the bandage round it, for it was badly swollen' (*ibid.*, 148). It was only later (1905*d*, 1909*a*) that Freud identified 'hysterogenic zone' with 'erotogenic zone' and saw the hysterical attack as the equivalent of coition. The repercussions of that observation remained limited, however, for two reasons: Freud denied the existence of a symbolic link between the young woman's abasia and her attraction towards her brother-in-law; it was, he says, purely a case of association through proximity; moreover, Freud regarded pathogenic sexual emotion as belonging solely to the field of adult sexuality. He also noticed that his work of psychical analysis made progress only when the symptom 'began to "join in the conversation"' during the actual sessions (*ibid.*, 148). The case confirmed what Freud had already sensed after the nurse had thrown herself into his arms: on December 18, 1892, in a letter to Fliess, he referred for the first time to the notion of the sexual aetiology of neuroses.

Simultaneously, over a period of nine weeks from the end of 1892 to the beginning of 1893, Freud treated Fräulein Lucy R., a 30-year-old English governess with a Viennese family, who had lost her sense of smell after suppurative rhinitis. The case, which he also later included among his observations in *Studies on Hysteria*, enabled him to make an important theoretical step forward: he had his first inkling of two basic mechanisms which he later clearly described and definitively named when writing his commentaries on himself. They were intentional 'repression' (*Verdrängung*) by the governess of her secret love for her employer, then a widower (a repression that occurred when the latter's violence proved to her that he did not love her), and the 'somatic conversion' of an unacceptable and repressed idea. As in the previous case, and for the same reason (the patient's resistance), Freud contented himself with light hypnosis and successfully used the technique of mental concentration. Its results confirmed for him the validity of the assumptions on which the technique was based: '– "But if you knew you loved your employer why didn't you tell me?" – "I didn't know – or rather I didn't want to know. I wanted to drive it out of my head and not think of it again; and I believe latterly I have succeeded"' (*ibid.*, 117). Freud then remarked in a note: 'I have never managed to give a better description than this of the strange state of mind in which one knows and does not know a thing at the same time.' Here again, it was to an emotion of adult sexuality that he attributed the aetiology of the hysterical symptom.

The case history of Fräulein Katharina, the last of the four important cases included in *Studies on Hysteria* along with those of Frau Emmy von N., Fräulein Elisabeth von R., and Fräulein Lucy R. (1895*d*), also proved very fruitful as regards both procedure and theory. Freud met Katharina while on holiday, possibly also in 1892 (E 487), possibly again during the summer of 1894, though the actual year has not been established.[1] The daughter of the landlady of a country inn, she asked to speak to him when he was out walking (she had learned that he was a doctor). She complained of breathlessness and said she feared she would suffocate. In the course of a single conversation with Freud, who did not resort to hypnosis or place his hand on her forehead, she recalled the two incidents that had been pathogenic for her: first, the witnessing, when she was 16, of sexual intercourse between her father – Freud calls him her uncle, but later admitted the truth in a note of 1924 (*ibid.*, 134 n.2) – and her sister; and secondly, the advances of the same person to herself when she was 14, advances that she did not immediately recognise as being sexual. This realisation, which came later when she saw her father and sister making love, produced an initial attack with loss of breath. One evening, when drunk, her father had lain on her sleeping body; when she woke up, she experienced breathlessness, and could feel the contact of his erect penis through her clothes.

Freud, who was under the impression that the symptoms had vanished after this one and only session, felt unequivocally encouraged to go against Charcot's teaching and make the two following assertions: that hysteria may occur without there being any hereditary predisposition (he immediately said as much in a note he added to the translation of Charcot's *Tuesday Lectures* he was completing at the time) (1892–94, 224 n., *SE* 1, 139); and that the pathogenic factor is not the initial trauma, but the memory of it, a notion he also made clear in another note to the same translation (1892–94, 107n., *SE* 1, 137–8). Thus Freud had given the first description of the phenomena of *deferred action* (the traumatising event, which is often apparently banal, has a pathogenic force only when

1. According to Jones (J I, 365–66), in 1892 and 1893, Freud spent only brief holidays in Austria; he did, however, do a lot of travelling during the summer of 1894, particularly on the confines of the Italian Alps. It was in the mountains that Freud met Fräulein Katharina, whose conversation was peppered with Italian dialect, and whose real name (Katharina was a pseudonym) would seem to have been Italian. That being the case, Freud must have included this case history in place of another one, presumably on the grounds that it was more interesting, since he seems to have already written four case histories *before* the summer of 1894 (cf. letter to Fliess, June 22, 1894). The pseudonym Katharina, by the way, cannot but recall the celebrated case of 'Saint' Anna Katharina Emmerich who relived the Passion (cf. p. 84).

associated with a previous psychical reality which at the time had no traumatising effect) and of *regression* (the neurotic reacts to a fairly recent situation according to a pattern that has previously formed within him). He was also led to the conclusion that sexual trauma occurred at around the age of puberty. Moreover, it seemed clear to him that trauma was not merely an erotic idea, but a sexual act, or attempted act, carried out by an adult on a preadolescent. Sexuality, then, was well and truly responsible for psychical disorders even in virginal individuals. The case of Katharina seemed to Freud a perfect example of 'virginal anxiety' about sexual relations. The symbolism of the symptom in it also struck him as exemplary: 'We [Breuer and I] had often compared the symptomatology of hysteria with a pictographic script which has become intelligible after the discovery of a few bilingual inscriptions. In that alphabet being sick means disgust' (1895*d*, *SE* 2, 129). It is perhaps worth noting, incidentally, a small error: the deciphering of cuneiform script and hieroglyphs was made possible thanks to trilingual – not bilingual as Freud says – inscriptions (cf. p. 201–02); it was not until 1909 that Freud used the comparison with hieroglyphs (cf. p. 331).

When he came to publish this case history, Freud, as I have mentioned, decided – whether out of personal embarrassment or following Breuer's instructions we do not know – to drop the reference to the role played by Katharina's father and attribute it to an uncle instead. In 1895 Freud admitted incest in the form of acts between uncle and niece (Katharina) and in the form of thoughts between sister and brother-in-law (Fräulein Elisabeth von R.). But he still resisted the notion that fathers could harbour incestuous feelings towards their daughters. And he naturally did not yet have the slighest suspicion that such desires might exist in the young girls themselves. When one rereads today Freud's observations in *Studies on Hysteria* one is struck by their obviously Oedipal content, even to the extent of being surprised that Freud could fail to see what was in fact staring him in the face. But then we have the benefit of hindsight, whereas Freud, in 1895, was still on the brink of his great discovery. If one were to describe his situation in the very terms of the theory he was about to work out, it would read something like this: he no longer represses into his unconscious his perception of the existence of incestuous desires of an Oedipal nature in hysterics (repression continued in Breuer's case); this perception has overcome an initial censorship at the expense of a distortion (it is the adult, not the child, that experiences the desire), is now present in his preconscious, and controls, unknown to him, the gathering of his clinical material; but recognition of it, and its rectification by consciousness, both of them conditions without which it cannot be conceptualised and fitted into a theory, remain blocked by the second censorship. The intuition, although present, is waiting, along with many others, in the 'entrance hall' (a recurring metaphor in Freud's dreams).

The same story recurs in the case of Fräulein Rosalia H., a 23-year-old singing student who suffered from constriction in her throat when singing certain parts of her register (1895*d*, *SE* 2, 169–73). Psychical analysis revealed the pathogenic trauma: her tyrannical widowed father (again Freud describes him as an uncle, re-establishing the truth in a note to the 1924 edition), who was suffering from rheumatism, asked her to massage his back. Suddenly he sprang out of bed and tried to catch hold of her.

Of even greater interest is another note by Freud, in which he sums up the first case history that provided him with material pointing unmistakably to the theory of the sexual aetiology of neuroses: 'I was treating a young married woman who was suffering from a complicated neurosis and, once again, was unwilling to admit that her illness arose from her married life. She objected that while she was still a girl she had had attacks of anxiety, ending in fainting fits. [. . .] She suddenly said to me one day: "I'll tell you now how I came by my attacks of anxiety when I was a girl. At that time I used to sleep in a room next to my parents'; the door was left open and a night-light used to burn on the table. So more than once I saw my father get into bed with my mother and heard sounds that greatly excited me. It was then that my attacks came on"' (*ibid.*, 127n.). Thus it was through a phantasy of the primal scene that sexuality first impressed itself on Freud's mind as being the cause of hysteria. The fact that he relegated this fact to a footnote and never mentioned it again in any of his later works is all the more understandable because he himself slept in his parents' bedroom during the three and a half years he lived in Freiberg. This case history probably dates from the spring of 1894: in a letter to Fliess at that time, Freud makes his first reference to 'two cases of this kind; it was a *presentient dread* of sexuality, and behind it things they had seen or heard and half-understood – thus, the aetiology is purely emotional but nevertheless of a sexual nature' (*F*, May 30, 1893, 49). Whereas this description contained a remarkable anticipation of the notion of phantasy, Freud sought its explanation in real events: it is the sexual scene that is traumatic, whether the individual is a spectator of it or is one of the participants enduring it. He did on the other hand remark on the great diversity of guises such scenes could take: an attempted heterosexual double rape of two sisters (1895*d*, *SE* 2, 276), for instance, or a homosexual relationship between a governess and the small girl in her care (*ibid.*, 274–5).

It was an earlier case history, that of Frau Cäcilie M., who was treated with hypnosis by Freud and Breuer together, possibly from 1890 to 1893, that finally decided Breuer to agree to their joint publication, the 'Preliminary Communication' (1893*a*). For reasons of professional discretion, the case is not described systematically in *Studies on Hysteria*, but discussed in three separate passages. The first of these contains the expression, which was later to become famous, describing the work of catharsis as 'the payment of old debts' (1895*d*, *SE* 2, 69–70 n.1). The second describes for the first time the mechanism of negation (*ibid.*, 76 n.1). The third passage relates the discovery of 'symbolisation' (*ibid.*, 176–81): Frau Cäcilie's violent facial neuralgia was the result of an insulting remark by her husband, to which she reacted as though she had been given 'a slap in the face'; a penetrating pain in her forehead was caused by the fact that her grandmother had given her a suspicious and 'piercing' look; one incident had 'stabbed [her] to the heart'; another had constricted her throat when she thought 'I shall have to swallow this'. She was even troubled by a hallucination that her two doctors, Breuer and Freud, were hanging on two trees next to each other in the garden after they had both refused to give her the drug she had asked for. 'There's nothing to choose between the two of them; one's the *pendant* [match] of the other.' However, the future idea that the symptom is a mnemic symbol of trauma was still restricted by Freud to conversion hysteria; only much later did he assert that symptom and symbol were broadly equivalent (1916*c*).

The first joint publication by Breuer and Freud, entitled 'On the Psychical Mechanism of Hysterical Phenomena: Preliminary Communication' (1893*a*), which appeared on January 1 and 15, 1893, in the *Neurologisches Zentralblatt*[1] and was subsequently reprinted, with changes, as the first chapter of *Studies on Hysteria* (1895*d*), contains both a word and a sentence that were destined to become famous: they were 'repression' and 'hysterics suffer mainly from reminiscences'. The mechanism of overdetermination is also described in it (though it is not called by that name until *Studies on Hysteria*). The notion of trauma, now reworked, has become either the impossibility of expressing an emotion for social reasons, or 'fright', shame or moral suffering connected with a distressing event in the individual's private life. As well as these specific contributions from Freud, the article also contained two views close to Breuer's heart – the idea that as the profound causes of hysteria cannot be known the psychotherapy of the hysteric should be restricted to symptoms alone, and the theory that

1. On January 11, 1893, Freud gave a good summary of the 'Preliminary Communication' in the form of a lecture to the 'Wiener medizinischer Club', entitled 'On the Psychical Mechanism of Hysterical Phenomena'; a shorthand report of the lecture revised by the author then appeared in the *Wiener medizinische Presse* on January 22 and 29 (1893*h*).

the pathogenic trauma of hysteria occurs during a 'hypnoid state', i.e. during deep daydreaming.

In the final chapter of *Studies on Hysteria* (1895*d*), however, which was written one and a half years later, Freud advanced the qualification that such a state was always preceded by an act of repression. It was only after his complete break with Breuer that Freud was able, from 1896 on, to forget about the cumbersome notion of the 'hypnoid state' – which he described in 1901, when writing his case history of Dora, as a 'superfluous and misleading term' (1905*e*, *SE* 7, 27 n.1) – and to claim, as early as the autumn of 1895, that he was capable of curing not only the symptoms of hysteria, but the predisposition to it (letter to Fliess, October 16, 1895, *F* 145).

As regards the effectiveness of the 'talking cure', Breuer and Freud insisted in their 'Preliminary Communication' (1893*a*) on the fact that revival of a traumatic memory is curative only if it is emotional, and not merely intellectual: thus, the 'cathartic effect' resides in an 'affective abreaction' (both expressions make their first appearance here), i.e. in a discharge of excess excitation that has remained in potential form within the patient since the traumatic event. This economic conception of the power of the cure squared fully with the principles of the Helmholtz school.

But where did the neologisms 'cathartic effect' and 'cathartic method' come from? The phenomenon was of course discovered by Breuer when he was treating Anna O., although the word 'catharsis' was probably suggested to him by her, and although, unaware of the importance of his discovery, he became confident enough to apply it to other cases only after lengthy discussion and joint practice of it with Freud. It was very like Freud to derive scientific notions from Ancient Greek tragedy. He did the same in 1897 when seeking a name to describe a psychopathological phenomenon he had discovered, this time on his own, and chose the term 'myth of Oedipus' after Sophocles' play. It was Aristotle who used the noun catharsis (purification or deliverance) to describe the effect of tragedy on the spectator: 'Tragedy is an imitation of an action that is serious, complete, and of a certain magnitude, effecting through pity and fear the proper catharsis, or purgation of emotions' (*Poetics*, 1449*b*, 27). The notion of *abreaction*, which from an economic point of view was strictly faithful to the German school of neurophysiology, would seem to have been largely the invention of Breuer; the notion of *cathartic* effect, on the other hand, is doubly Freudian because it regards psychical conflict as a personal drama similar to that presented by the novelist or playwright, and its treatment as a liberation, along lines posited by Hughlings Jackson, of old emotions blocked in the lower neuropsychical formations on account of excessive control by the higher neuropsychical formations. Further evidence in support of these hypotheses was supplied by Juan Dalma (1963): Jakob Bernays, one of Martha's uncles, whom I have already mentioned (p. 26), published in 1880 *Zwei Abhandlungen über die Aristotelische Theorie des Drama* (*Two Essays on the Aristotelian Theory of Drama*), a work that can hardly have failed to attract Freud's attention because after its publication catharsis became a talking point among students and in society *salons*. Ellenberger (E 484) even goes so far as to suppose that Anna O. adopted this fashionable word as a kind of device for her cure, adding: 'It is ironic that Anna O.'s unsuccessful treatment should have become, for posterity, the prototype of a cathartic cure.'

The 'Preliminary Communication' was very well received – unlike Freud's immediately subsequent psychoanalytic publications – and this encouraged him to keep going along the same lines. Janet, among others, gave it a long and laudatory review, as Freud reported to Fliess in a letter of July 10, 1893, and even used his paper as the final chapter of his book *L'état mental des hystériques*[1] (1894).

Freud's reputation was such by 1893 that he appeared in the local version of *Who's Who, Das geistige Wien*.

FREUD'S NEW PSYCHOPATHOLOGICAL CONCEPTIONS (1893–95)

No sooner had the 'Preliminary Communication' been written than Freud forged ahead on new work. He had a character trait apparently found only in men of genius: he advanced at such a pace that none of his former teachers, none of his current collaborators, and none of his future followers was able to keep up with him. Similarly, when he embarked on the strenuous daily hikes that formed the basis of all his holidays spent away from Vienna, a friend or relation would keep him company for a day or two, then fall by the wayside. I myself must confess that while writing the present book I experienced acute difficulty in encompassing the wide range of Freud's scientific skills and in circumscribing the man in the fullness of his culture and the wealth of his clinical experience, such was the prodigious ease and masterly accuracy with which he could read, assimilate, compare, synthesise, conceptualise, recall, write and engage in a process of self-renewal. Men such as he, however banal other areas of their lives may be, wear their fellow human beings into the ground. Only a few of Freud's

1. Up until 1895, Janet and Freud were complimentary about each other's work. Relations cooled, however, with the publication of *Studies on Hysteria*, in which Breuer strongly attacked Janet's theory that 'psychological weakness' constituted the predisposition to hysteria. Later, Janet could no longer tolerate Freud's sexualism or his notoriety, and in 1913 began to attack psychoanalysis openly, claiming among other things that he had used the cathartic method before Freud (cf. n.2 in *SE* 2, xii).

contemporaries – Nietzsche, Marx, and Einstein (a more recent example was André Malraux) – possessed such a formidable arsenal of thought and expression.

While Freud was writing the works I have just passed in review, his attention in 1893 and 1894 was intently focussed on two new notions, as can be judged from his correspondence with Fliess. The first idea was that the 'trauma', or rather 'conflict' of defence, as Freud was beginning to call it (*F*, May 21, 1894, 75), which was the cause of hysteria, involved sexuality. The second idea was that what held true for hysteria – repression, recollection, anxiety, difficulty of discharge, sexual shock – was also probably valid, *mutatis mutandis*, for other nervous disorders. In 'On the History of the Psycho-Analytic Movement' (1914*d*), Freud recalled three casual conversations that encouraged him to identify as sexual something he already believed to be more and more manifestly so (while we are alone in seeing what we see, there is a lurking fear that our sight or our subjective belief may have played a trick on us). In 1881–82, Breuer told Freud (he later denied having done so), referring to the neurotic behaviour of a patient, that such behaviour was always connected with the 'marriage bed'; he even used the French expression '*secrets d'alcôve*' – at that time, the French were credited with enjoying not only the practice but also the discussion of such pursuits. In Paris, during the winter of 1885–86, Freud had heard Charcot tell an assistant that certain neurotic disorders could always be put down to '*la chose génitale*' ('a question of the genitals'). And in 1886 the great Viennese gynaecologist, Rudolf Chrobak (1843–1910), after passing on to Freud one of his women patients who was suffering from anxiety, and whose husband was totally impotent, added in Latin – though he, too, later denied having done so – that the only prescription for such a malady was 'repeated doses of normal penis' (1914*d*, *SE* 14, 13–15).

Unlike the afore-mentioned authorities, who were quick to retract their theories, Freud was logical with himself and began to include in the anamnesis of patients who consulted him questions about their sexual life since puberty. He paid ever closer attention to the nature of intense emotions, whether it was hypnosis or mental concentration that had caused them to re-emerge: they usually consisted of a fright, followed by a sudden repression and, subsequently, the appearance of certain symptoms. Such emotions included the emotions of adolescents of both sexes on witnessing or hearing a sexual scene,[1] and the emotions of adults faced with

1. 'I believe I understand the anxiety neuroses of young persons who must be presumed to be virgins and who have not been submitted to abuse. I have analysed two cases of this kind; it was a *presentient dread* of sexuality, and behind it things they had seen or heard and half-understood – thus, the aetiology is purely emotional but nevertheless of a sexual nature' (*F*, May 30, 1893, 49).

a sexual approach, sexual temptation, or sexual failure. Sexual failure was the problem of Herr K., who developed an anxiety neurosis after failing to seduce a young woman with whom he had fallen in love (*F*, Draft F, August 18, 1894, 90). It seemed increasingly to Freud that the chief characteristic of the neurotic was that he lacked a happy sex life, since he believed that sexual satisfaction, achieved without too many practical obstacles, with a partner who was good company, was one of the conditions of a happy life. This idea, which broke the taboos of Freud's period and virtually all the reigning ideologies, alarmed most of his colleagues with whom he broached the subject, and even those patients he advised to strive for a satisfying sex life. In July 1895, for example, Irma, one of his young women friends in whom a chaste widowhood had produced hysterical symptoms, had just decided to call off Freud's treatment of her by psychical analysis because she rejected precisely such a 'solution', which he had doubtless prescribed for her disorder. In Freud's view, prolonged continence was neither natural nor healthy, and masturbation, male contraceptives, techniques whereby sexual intercourse was cut short before the orgasm of both partners, and recourse to prostitutes were no more than temporary and unsatisfactory expedients. As early as the beginning of 1893, in a letter to Fliess, Freud made a suggestion that was fifty years ahead of its time and would have caused a scandal had it been made public: 'The only alternative would be free sexual intercourse between young men and unattached young women, but this could only be adopted if there were innocuous methods of preventing conception. Otherwise, the alternatives are masturbation, neurasthenia in the male, hystero-neurasthenia in the female, or syphilis in the male, syphilis in the next generation, gonorrhoea in the male, gonorrhoea and sterility in the female' (*F*, Draft B, February 8, 1893, 44).

Statements of this kind mark the demise of a distinction that had gradually, over two or three centuries, come to be taken for granted by European culture, fascinated as it was by the virtues and illusions of individualism – the distinction between public and private life. With Freud, man is no longer defined by what he does: thus did he demystify the cult of the hero, for so long fostered by political and military history and by moral codes with action as their foundation. Equally, man ceases to be defined by what he thinks or believes, for thoughts and beliefs are but the visible tip of the iceberg – psychical analysis had shown that the significance of our ideas, when they have any, derives from a vast, invisible and constantly shifting bedrock: thus did Freud demystify religion and philosophy. Thanks to Freud, man is pinned down in those areas where he tries to escape and uncovered in what he hides (what he hides from other people does not always coincide with what he hides from himself); he is circumscribed both in what he denies and in what he expresses, at the same time, in a roundabout way, through digression or dissimulation; man is to be found in what he externalises when he cannot internalise it, and in what he internalises when he cannot externalise it. The barrier of private life, instead of acting as a guardian of happiness (a role that would have been, and still is, its sole justification), is criticised by Freud for being used as a psychical Bastille, a dungeon of suffering. The fallaciousness and over-simplification of setting in opposition to each other the internal and the external, the individual and society, body and mind, and thought and action, were revealed for all to see. By 1895, Freud had progressed no further than a limited theory of symbolisation: as far as he was concerned, man was an apparatus for producing symptoms. A little later, he was able to say something that was, in a sense, the same thing: that man was an apparatus for producing dreams, screen memories, and jokes. This is what I would venture to term his theory of generalised symbolisation. Before he could make the step from one to the other, he had first to carry out his self-analysis.

The general remarks I have just made are relevant to the progress Freud had achieved not only by recognising sexuality as a fundamental psychical phenomenon, but also by extending the problems that hysteria led him to examine to the whole field of neuroses.

Draft A, which Freud sent to Fliess at the end of 1892 or the beginning of 1893, raises the following questions: what causal connection is there between anxiety neuroses and 'abnormal' sexual practices such as onanism and infantile masturbation by nurses, or incomplete sexual practices such as *coitus reservatus* (involving the use of a condom), impotence and frigidity? The same draft proposes a number of 'theses' by way of an answer, e.g.: 'No neurasthenia or analogous neurosis exists without a disturbance of the sexual function', or again: 'Anxiety neurosis is in part a consequence of inhibition of the sexual function'.

Drafts B (February 8, 1893) and C (May/June 1893) developed these themes and moved towards the realisation that tension not discharged during coition turns into anxiety.

On August 16, 1893, Jean-Martin Charcot died. Freud wrote an obituary of him (see p. 55), which although full of admiration for the great man's genius, fame and influence, concluded by criticising the doctrine of the 'neuropathic family' (Charcot believed predisposition to hysteria could be caused by congenital nervous degeneracy): in other words, Freud was not only bidding Charcot farewell but also, in a way, casting off his moorings.

Freud's article 'Die Abwehr-Neuropsychosen' ('The Neuro-Psychoses of Defence'), which appeared in May and June 1894 (1894*a*), proposed a general theory of neuroses by classifying them according to three defence mechanisms:[1] transformation of affect in conversion hysteria, displacement of affect in obsessions (an idea Freud took up separately in an article he wrote in French for the *Revue neurologique* entitled 'Obsessions et phobies'; 1895*c*), and exchange of affect in anxiety neuroses and melancholia. He also draws a distinction, depending on the pathogeny, between 'hypnoid' hysteria (a tribute to Breuer; but Freud believed it was due not so much to a twilight state as to a state of excessive fatigue), 'retention' hysteria (where abreaction is impossible for social reasons), and Freud's own contribution, 'defence' hysteria (where abreaction is impossible because of defence on the part of the subject). Only this third category was to survive, after Freud dropped the second, then the first. A letter to Fliess dated May 21, 1894 (*F* 74–5) complemented these classifications by taking into account four aetiological categories: innate 'degeneration', 'senility' or degeneration acquired in old age, 'conflict' or acquired defence against sexuality, and lastly 'conflagration' or a non-sexual serious trauma. The first two aetiologies were an act of allegiance to the prevailing theory of the time. The last was an idea that Freud plucked out of the air but never mentioned again. His whole scientific future lay in the manner he was later to develop the third aetiology.

Draft D, which was probably written at the same time as the letter of May 21, was an attempt to give consistency to the explanation of various neuroses by basing it on Fechner's principle of constancy.

Draft E, which probably dates from June 1894, states that in the case of anxiety neurosis it is an accumulation of *physical* sexual tension, and in hysteria an accumulation of *psychical* sexual tension, which are discharged in the form of somatic symptoms. Freud later returned to and justified this idea in a paper entitled 'On the Grounds for Detaching a Particular Syndrome from Neurasthenia under the Description "Anxiety Neurosis"' (1895*b*). Draft E also contains the first use, by Freud, of the term libido: 'in anxiety neurosis there must be a deficit to be noted in sexual affect, in psychic libido' (*F* 81). The term was subsequently published in the paper just mentioned, where Freud distinguishes between 'somatic sexual excitation' and 'sexual libido', which he defines as 'psychical desire', without, however, expressly describing that psychical desire as unconscious (1895*b*, *SE* 3, 107).

It is worth looking a little more closely at Freud's use of the term libido.

1. Chapter 5 of Andersson (1962) deals with Freud's introduction of the concepts of defence and sexual aetiology.

Although not found in 'Project for a Scientific Psychology' (1950*a*), written at the end of 1895, it appears in most of Freud's subsequent essays (1895*f*, 1896*b*, 1896*c*, 1898*a*), and in *The Interpretation of Dreams* (1900*a*), as well as forming the essential concept of *Three Essays on the Theory of Sexuality* (1905*d*). Yet, surprisingly, in a much later encyclopaedia article entitled 'The "Libido" Theory' (1923*a*, *SE* 18, 255), Freud attributes the first use of the term to Albert Moll (in *Untersuchungen über die Libido Sexualis*, published in 1898), while in *Civilization and its Discontents* (1930*a*, *SE* 21, 117) he says that he himself first introduced the word.

It has emerged from research by Ellenberger (E 328) that the word libido was not in fact introduced by either Moll or Freud, since Benedikt (1868) and Krafft-Ebing (1889) had used it on more than one occasion. However, it should be remembered that libido was by no means a novel term: it was commonly used in Christian moral theology to denote concupiscence; the Jansenists frequently referred to it; and Blaise Pascal, drawing on a passage in the epistles of St John, made libido one of the key concepts in his picture of man's unhappiness without God and in his *Apologie de la religion chrétienne* (*Apologia for Christian Religion*) on the basis of human psychology ('Tout ce qui est au monde est concupiscence de la chair ou concupiscence des yeux ou orgueil de la vie: *libido sentiendi, libido sciendi, libido dominandi*'[1]). Although Freud did not have a Christian background, his very thorough classical education and the intellectual circles in which he moved were such that he must have known, if only indirectly, of the word libido and its connotations. Like many scientists and doctors of his time, Freud used Latin to describe notions that might have seemed too crude in his 'mother' tongue. Libido expressed desire, with all the overtones of lust, force and tension that it injects into psychical life.

As I have already said, it was probably during the summer of 1894 that Freud became acquainted with the case of Katharina. When he returned from Vienna, he included it in the manuscript of *Studies on Hysteria*, whose final chapter, entitled 'The Psychotherapy of Hysteria', he had completed a few months earlier in March 1895 (cf. letter to Fliess of March 4, 1895).

Draft G, doubtless written at the beginning of 1895, pointed to a

1. Literally: desire of the senses, desire to know, desire to dominate. The passage in the English Authorised Version reads: 'For all that is in the world, the lust of the flesh, and the lust of the eyes, and the pride of life, is not of the Father, but is of the world' (I. John 2, 16). The spiritual father of Jansenism, St Augustine, may be regarded, on the evidence of his *Confessions* and his insistence on the search for inner truth, as an early precursor of Freud's self-analysis: 'Noli foras ire, in teipsum redi; in interiore homine habitat veritas' ('Do not search without, turn within yourself; truth inhabits the inner man') (*De Vera Religione*, Book 39, §72).

connection between melancholy (a term that Freud used to describe various states of depression, even when mild) and frigidity, masturbation and anorexia. He suggested that melancholia consisted of 'mourning over the loss of libido'. Because of a 'psychical inhibition', libido is diverted from sexual realisation, resulting in 'instinctual impoverishment' and 'pain'.

Enclosed with a letter of January 24, 1895, Draft H deals with paranoia and sees in it a new defence mechanism, 'projection' – the projection of hatred into delusions of persecution and of self-love into megalomania. Freud also refers to a case where the actual sexual seduction of an 'aging spinster (about thirty)' caused neurosis (in this case, paranoia). In Draft I, Freud explained migraine by the 'summation' of excitation and, in order to please Fliess, stressed its 'periodicity' (Freud had already emphasised the periodicity of melancholia); he also attempted to describe the localisation of migraine in terms of the anatomo-physiology of the nervous system.

Lastly, in a letter to Fliess of April 27, 1895 (*F* 127), Freud announces a new plan, which 'consumes' him and leaves him feeling 'overworked' – a plan for a 'Psychology for Neurologists'. Thus, after labouring to bring together the various neuroses, Freud was now, in the middle of 1895, striving to unify pathological psychology and normal psychology. As he wrote in his next letter: 'A man like me cannot live without a hobbyhorse, without a consuming passion, without – in Schiller's words – a tyrant. I have found one. In its service I know no limits. It is psychology, which has always been my distant, beckoning goal, and which now, since I have come upon the problem of neuroses, has drawn so much nearer. I am tormented by two aims: to examine what shape the theory of mental functioning takes if one introduces quantitative considerations, a sort of economics of nerve forces; and, second, to peel off from psychopathology a gain for normal psychology. Actually, a satisfactory general conception of neuropsychotic disturbances is impossible if one cannot link it with clear assumptions about normal mental processes' (*F*, May 25, 1895, 129). Freud's intellectual exhilaration at such a heady prospect became so intense that shortly afterwards he broke an important piece of news to his friend: after fourteen months of abstinence following the cardiac episode already described (pp. 43–4), he began smoking again (*F*, June 12, 1895, 132). He felt he had progressed far enough to deserve such a treat, and needed a physical stimulant in order to be able to keep going.

Breuer was by now out of his depth, and could not make up his mind whether his former protégé was a madman or a genius. But he did realise that something very important was gestating in Freud. He wrote to Fliess:

'Freud's intellect is soaring at its highest. I gaze after him as a hen at a hawk' (letter of August 5, 1895, quoted in J I, 266).

Studies on Hysteria (1895*d*) consists of the 'Preliminary Communication' (Chapter I), the case histories of Fräulein Anna O., Frau Emmy von N., Miss Lucy R., Katharina, and Fräulein Elisabeth von R. (Chapter II), Breuer's 'Theoretical' (Chapter III), and Freud's 'Psychotherapy of Hysteria' (Chapter IV). On February 7, 1894, Freud wrote to Fliess that the book was 'half-finished', as almost all the case histories had already been done. By May 21, 1894 (*F* 73), he was writing the last case history. After a long hold-up, Freud returned to his task, and on March 4, 1895, he was working on the final chapter, 'The Psychotherapy of Hysteria'; he finished it on March 13 (*F* 119), and the book was published in May 1895. Reviews were unfavourable in Germany. The book was better treated in Britain, and was ignored in France. This mixed reception speeded up Freud's rupture with Breuer.

In the explanation of hysteria in his theoretical chapter, Breuer adheres closely to the principles of the Helmholtz school. He stresses the 'ideogenic' nature of hysteria. He posits the existence of an 'intra-cerebral tonic excitation' which flows actively in waking life, and which during sleep is reduced to a state of 'nervous tension', on the analogy of electric tension (this parallel between the central nervous system and an electric appliance is drawn repeatedly throughout the chapter): it was this that subsequently led Freud to draw the fundamental distinction between free energy (during sleep) and bound energy (during waking life). To this intracerebral tension Breuer applies the principle of constancy, a notion he attributes to Freud: the principle works less and less effectively when the 'increase of excitation' comes not from organic needs any more, but from the 'sexual instinct' or the 'aggressive' instinct as a result of the 'affects' they cause. If those affects can find no motor discharge either directly (through shouting, sobbing or gesticulations) or through a transfer to other acts (breaking things, aimless agitation), there is a 'short-circuit'. This is what happens in the case of a 'psychical trauma': it causes 'the hysterical conversion of psychical excitation' (Breuer gives Freud the credit for the idea of conversion). 'The affective idea is withdrawn from "associative contact"', while at the same time retaining its whole 'quota of affect': this produces the symptom. There are two reasons for this exclusion of affective ideas from association: the subject either instigates a 'defence' against the idea (Freud) or goes into a 'hypnoid' state (Breuer). Breuer goes on to assert that hysterics are subject to 'unconscious ideas' and a 'splitting of the mind'. He criticises Janet's explanation of disposition to hysteria (caused, he argued, by 'psychological weakness'; cf. p. 71, n.1), and attributes any such disposition to three causes: 1) the concentration of energy in some part of the body in subjects whose nervous system releases, when at rest, a surplus of 'floating' excitation; 2) sexual traumas; and 3) the tendency to auto-hypnosis (hypnoid state).

We do not know exactly when Freud discovered other notions such as censorship, resistance (which he correlated to the notion of defence – discarding, in the process, retention hysteria and hypnoid hysteria, and retaining only defence hysteria), and the process, as yet only vaguely defined, whereby a patient displaces feelings on to his or her psychotherapist. These notions, implicit in several of the case histories I have just mentioned, were published for the first time in the final chapter of *Studies on Hysteria*, which was devoted to psychotherapy and written by Freud alone. According to Ellenberger (E 490), the corresponding ideas, if not the terms themselves, were familiar to magnetizers and hypnotists: Forel had related that the closer he came to memories that were painful to the patient under hypnosis, the more difficult it was to get him to recall them; 'rapport' with the magnetizer and Janet's notion of 'somnambulic influence' were the precursors of transference. The final sentences of *Studies on Hysteria* are, however, indicative of Freud's continuing dependence on neurophysiology in formulating his theories: 'But you will be able to convince yourself that much will be gained if we succeed in transforming your hysterical misery[1] into common unhappiness. With a nervous system that has been restored to health you will be better armed against that unhappiness' (1895*d*, *SE* 2, 305). It was only in 1925 that Freud replaced the words 'nervous system' by 'mental life'.

TABLE 1. *Chronology of psychological notions acquired by Freud between 1892 and 1895, before his self-analysis*

1892–93

Abreaction (*Abreagieren*) and *Cathartic effect*

a) *Abreagieren*, a neologism coined by Breuer and Freud, first appears in a letter to Fliess of June 28, 1892 (*F* 31).

b) The term reappears in the 'Preliminary Communication' (1893*a*), written, mostly by Freud, in December 1892 and published jointly with Breuer on January 1 and 15, 1893 (*SE* 2, 8–9). 'Cathartic effect' is used in that paper as a synonym of 'abreaction'. Abreaction is defined as being one of the ways in which the affect is normally discharged after a psychical trauma. It is a 'reaction, whether in deeds or

1. I am tempted to interpret this phrase as an allusion to the notion of 'psychological misery' popularised by Janet.

words, or in the mildest cases in tears'. Other normal manners of discharge include the rectification of the memory of the traumatic event through its integration into other associative chains and the effacement of impressions through forgetting.

c) The term is defined as being 'the abreaction of accretions of stimulus' (*Das Abreagieren der Reizzuwächse*) at the end of Freud's paper on 'Organic and Hysterical Motor Paralyses' (1893*c*, *SE* 1, 172).

Analysis (*Analyse*)

a) 1893*a* contains the term 'to analyse'.

b) 1894*a* contains the terms 'psychical analysis', 'clinico-psychological analysis', 'hypnotic analysis' and 'psychological analysis'.

c) 1896*a* contains the term 'psychoanalysis'.

Complex (*Komplex*)

a) 'Complex of ideas' in the sense of a group of repressed ideas appears in 1941*b* (a note written in November 1892 for inclusion in 1893*a*): 'In hysteria [. . .] the content of consciousness easily becomes temporarily dissociated and certain complexes of ideas which are not associatively connected easily fly apart' (*SE* 1, 149; it is used with the same meaning in 'Project for a Scientific Psychology' of October 1895 (1950*a*, *SE* 1, 355).

b) Following Jung's definition of a complex as 'an emotionally coloured ideational content', Freud's 1906*c* paper notes that 'it has become customary to speak of an ideational content, [. . .] which is able to influence the reaction to the stimulus-word, as a "complex" ' (without making it clear whether or not the complex is unconscious and whether or not it is the result of repression) (*SE* 9, 104); following the same line of thought, the 1907 edition of *PEL* identifies the 'family complex' and the 'professional complex' as causes of the forgetting of names.

c) Freud's 1908*c* paper says that psychical conflict in general can turn into a 'psychical dissociation' and bring into being the 'nuclear complex of a neurosis': this 'complex' is 'suppressed and "unconscious" '; the case histories of 'Little Hans' (1909*b*) and the 'Rat Man' (1909*d*) specify that such nuclear complexes are connected with children's sexual desires for their parents.

d) Freud's 1910*h* paper contains the first use of the term 'Oedipus complex'. *N.B.* The Oedipus legend was already referred to as applying to neurotic conflict in a letter to Fliess of October 15, 1897, in *The Interpretation of Dreams* (1900*a*) and in the 'Dora' case history (1905*e*), which was written in January 1901.

Displacement (*Verschiebung*)

a) The French term *transfert* appears in Freud's encyclopaedia article on 'Hysteria' (1888*b*) and in the preface to his translation of Bernheim's *Suggestion* (1888–89): a hysterical symptom can, under certain influences, be transferred to the symmetrical area in the other half of the body.

b) 'The chronic symptoms would seem to correspond to a normal mechanism; they are displacements' (letter to Breuer of June 29, 1892, 1941*a*, *SE* 1, 148).

c) The term 'displacement' recurs in 1894*a* (see quotation under *Quota of affect*, *b*)), alternating with the verbal forms 'dislodged' (*disloziert*) and 'transposed' (*transponiert*) (*SE* 3, 54); it is at once an explanation of the 'false connections' that are responsible for obsessional ideas, and a general mechanism governing the circulation of the 'quota of affect'.

d) 'Project for a Scientific Psychology' (1950*a*), written in October 1895, explains the displacement of the quantity of one idea to another – total displacement in the case of primary processes, limited in the case of secondary processes – and sees displacement as the basis of symptom-, symbol- and dream-formation.

Fixation (*Fixierung*)

a) Freud first uses this term in the sense in which it was employed by hypnotists, i.e. a concentrated stare (preface to the translation of Bernheim's *Suggestion*, 1888–89, etc.).

b) Then he uses it in the sense of the establishment of a symptom as a result of 'counter-will' or, as he says a little later on, of 'repression' (1892–93, *SE* 1, 125, etc.; other references are given in a note in the *SE*).

c) Fixation may possibly be used in its true psychoanalytic sense – namely, the attachment of the libido to infantile experiences peculiar to one of its stages of development – in Draft L, which Freud sent Fliess on May 2, 1897, and is certainly used in that sense in the 'Dora' case ([1901] 1905*e*) and *Three Essays on the Theory of Sexuality* (1905*d*).

Principle of constancy (*Konstanzprinzip*)

a) This is described in Freud's letter to Breuer of June 29, 1892 ([1892] 1941*a*): 'The theorem concerning the constancy of the sum of excitation' (*SE* 1, 147; in 1893*h*: 'In every individual there exists a tendency to diminish this sum of excitation once more, in order to preserve his health' (lecture of January 11, 1893, *SE* 3, 36); in *Studies on Hysteria* (1895*d*), Chapter 3, written by Breuer, who nonetheless gives the idea as Freud's: 'There exists in the organism a "*tendency to keep intracerebral excitation constant*" (Freud)' (*SE* 2, 197).

b) It is called the 'principle of inertia' in 'Project for a Scientific Psychology' ([1895] 1950*a*, *SE* 1, 296–8).

c) It is called the 'principle of constancy' and also the 'Nirvana principle' in *Beyond the Pleasure Principle* (1920*g*).

Quota of affect (*Affektbetrag*)

a) Freud translated this term as '*valeur affective*' in the paper he published in French on 'Organic and Hysterical Motor Paralyses' (1893*c*, *SE* 1, 170–71).

b) Quota of affect is used at the end of 'The Neuro-Psychoses of Defence' (1894*a*, *SE* 3, 60) as a synonym of 'sum of excitation': 'In mental functions something is to be distinguished – a quota of affect or sum of excitation – which possesses all the characteristics of a quantity (though we have no means of measuring it), which is capable of increase, diminution, displacement and discharge, and which is spread over the memory-traces of ideas somewhat as an electric charge is spread over the surface of a body.' The quota of affect is therefore psychical excitation of external origin, but above all of internal origin insofar as it is detached from the idea.

c) The editors of the *SE* (*SE* 3, Appendix, 61–8) suggest that a distinction should be made between the 'quota of affect' and the 'sum of excitation'. Laplanche (1973) holds that the contrast between Freud's use of the terms 'affect' and 'quota of affect' corresponds to that between quality and quantity.

Repression

a) The notion of hysterical 'counter-will' is explained in 'A Case of Successful Treatment by Hypnotism' (1892–93).

b) Repression is described but not named in 1940*d* (a draft written by Breuer and Freud in November 1892 in preparation for 1893*a*): '*If a hysterical subject seeks intentionally to forget an experience or forcibly repudiates, inhibits and suppresses an intention or an idea, these psychical acts, as a consequence, enter the second state of consciousness*' (*SE* 1, 153).

c) The term 'repressed' (*verdrängt*) appears in the 'Preliminary Communication' (1893*a*), but it still refers to voluntary repression where there has been an irreparable loss of a loved one, where a reaction is made impossible by social circumstances, or where the person wishes to forget something (*SE* 2, 10).

d) The term 'repression' (*Verdrängung*) appears in Freud's paper on 'Anxiety Neurosis' (1895*b*), which was written at the end of 1894 (*SE* 3, 111): it is used to describe the intentional repression of sexual ideas by abstinent women – widows and ageing women at the time of the menopause.

e) Repression is defined as a synonym of 'defence' and as an 'unconscious' mechanism at the beginning of 'Further Remarks on the Neuro-Psychoses of Defence', and used in that sense throughout the paper (1896*b*, *SE* 3, 162ff.).

f) Freud draws a distinction between 'repression' and 'defence' in 1926*d*.

Return of a memory, Return of the repressed

a) The content of a major hysterical attack is 'the return of a memory' of an experience that has been excluded from consciousness: draft written jointly with Breuer in November 1892 (1940*d*, *SE* 1, 152).

b) The expression 'return of the repressed' appears in Draft K, which Freud sent Fliess on January 1, 1896, and in 'Further Remarks on the Neuro-Psychoses of Defence' (1896*b*, *SE* 3, 169ff.).

Sum of excitation (*Erregungssumme*)

a) This term appears in Freud's letter to Breuer of June 29, 1892 (1941*a*, *SE* 1, 148) and in the 1940*d* draft, written in 1892 (*SE* 1, 153–4).

b) It makes its first published appearance in 'The Neuro-Psychoses of Defence' (1894*a*, *SE* 3, 48), where it is used as a synonym of 'quota of affect' (see under that term).

c) The term 'summation' (*Summation*), which Freud borrowed from Sigmund Exner, appears in Draft I on migraine (letter to Fliess, March 4, 1895; *SE* 1, 213) and in 'Project for a Scientific Psychology' of October 1895 (1950*a*, *SE* 1, 316); the accumulation of endogenous stimuli has to exceed a certain threshold before the latter can become psychical stimuli moving around the psychical apparatus.

Symbolisation

a) Certain hysterical symptoms (such as pain between the eyebrows) are symbolisations, that is to say they literally represent certain common linguistic expressions used to formulate the repressed idea – in this case, to be given a piercing look (the case of Frau Cäcilie M. in 1893*h* and again in *Studies on Hysteria*, 1895*d*).

b) Freud subsequently develops a wider parallel between symptoms and symbols; for example, he suggests the symbolic equivalence of money and faeces in a letter to Fliess of January 24, 1897.

1894

Conversion (*Konversion*)

The term appears in 'The Neuro-Psychoses of Defence' (1894*a*), which Freud wrote in January 1894 (*SE* 3, 49).

Defence (*Abwehr*)

a) The mechanism is described by Freud when defining the term 'repressed' in 1893*a* (see *Repression, b*)).

b) The term appears in the title and content of 'The Neuro-Psychoses of Defence' (1894*a*), written in January 1894.

Flight into illness (*Flucht in die Krankheit*)

a) It is described as 'flight into psychosis' in 'The Neuro-Psychoses of Defence' (1894*a*), written in January 1894 (*SE* 3, 59).

b) The term 'flight into illness' first appears as such in 1909*a*.

Libido

This term appears in manuscript form in Draft E (undated, probably June 1894) and in Draft F, which was sent to Fliess on August 18, 1894; its first published appearance is in 'On the Grounds for Detaching a Particular Syndrome from Neurasthenia under the Description "Anxiety Neurosis"' (1895*b*), which appeared on January 15, 1895 (*SE* 3, 102): in it, Freud distinguishes between 'somatic sexual excitation' on the one hand, and 'sexual libido, or psychical desire' on the other; he later summarised the main idea of that paper as follows: '*Neurotic anxiety is transformed sexual libido*' (1897*b*, *SE* 3, 251).

1895

Cathexis (*Besetzung*)

a) It is described by Freud as 'displacements of the excitability in the nervous system' in the preface to his translation of Bernheim (1888–89) and as 'provided with a quota of affect' ('*munie d'une valeur affective*') in his 1893*c* paper, which was written in French.

b) The term first appears as such in *Studies on Hysteria* (1895*d*), in the case history of Frau Emmy von N., probably written in 1893 (*SE* 2, 89).

Censorship (*Zensur*)

The term appears in *Studies on Hysteria* (1895*d*), Chapter 4, which Freud wrote in March 1895 (*SE* 2, 269).

Projection (*Projektion*)

The first use of this term in manuscript form is in Draft H, which Freud sent Fliess on January 24, 1895, and in published form in 'Further Remarks on the Neuro-Psychoses of Defence' (1896*b*).

Resistance

This term first appears in *Studies on Hysteria* (1895*d*) in the case history of Fräulein Elisabeth von R., written in about 1893, and in Chapter 4 of the same work, written in March 1895 (*SE* 2, 154 and 268ff.).

Transference (*Übertragung*) (in the psychoanalytic sense)

This term first appears in *Studies on Hysteria* (1895*d*), Chapter 4, written by Freud in March 1895 (*SE* 2, 302).

Freud and his time

MAGNETISM AND HYPNOTISM IN THE NINETEENTH CENTURY

The psychopathological culture of the nineteenth century was marked, successively, by magnetism, hypnotism and the first catalogues of sexual aberrations. Against that background, as Ellenberger shows (1970), it was scarcely surprising that Freud should be very much a child of his time.

Magnetism first took root in France at the end of the eighteenth century as a result of the activities of two people – first, the German Franz Anton Mesmer (1734–1815), who had studied medicine in Vienna, and who found favour in the entourage of Louis XVI, and then Amand-Marie-Jacques de Chastenet, Marquis de Puységur (1751–1825), who practised on his estate in the village of Buzancy. Magnetism captured the imagination of the general public. A magnetizer called Abbé Faria served as a model for one of the characters in Alexandre Dumas' *The Count of Monte Cristo*. The German Romantics enthusiastically adopted a theory that postulated the existence of a universal 'fluid' and a technique that enabled a supposed sixth sense to communicate with the world of the mind. Two accounts of specific cases, both penned by writers of considerable talent, were to become famous. In 1829, the poet-physician Justinus Kerner (whose *Klecksographien* gave Hermann Rorschach the idea for his inkblot tests) published *Die Seherin von Prevorst* (*The Seeress of Prevorst*). The woman in question was one Friedericke Hauffe (1801–29), a game-keeper's daughter who had already had visions and premonitions at a very early age. Kerner treated her with 'magnetic passes'; she then led a 'bodiless life', in a regularly repeated magnetic sleep, during which she received messages, made prophecies, moved objects without touching them, spoke in a beautiful and sonorous unknown language which, she said, was the original language of mankind.

The second case was that of a nun, Anna Katharina Emmerich (1774–1824), a 'saint' who, in her cataleptic states, had visions of the Passion, bore its stigmata, and suffered greatly. At night her dreams showed scenes from the life of Christ and the Blessed Virgin according to the cycle of the liturgical year. The poet Clemens Brentano settled in her village and lived there for four years until her death. With the material he gathered from her dictation, he published two books, in 1837 and in 1852.

Other nineteenth-century writers who found inspiration in magnetism include Ernst Theodor Amadeus Hoffmann, whose tales written between 1815 and 1820 form a virtual handbook on the subject, Honoré de Balzac in *Louis Lambert* (1832) and *Ursule Mirouet* (1841), Alexandre Dumas in his portrait of Cagliostro in *Mémoires d'un médicin, Joseph Balsamo* (1846–48), Frédéric Soulié in his best-seller, *Le magnétiseur* (1834), Edgar Allan Poe in *The Facts in the Case of Mr. Valdemar* (1845), and Robert Browning in his poem *Mesmerism* (1855).

The interest in cases of double or multiple personality aroused by the books on the seeress of Prevorst and Saint Anna Katharina continued unabated throughout the nineteenth century. In its final decades, new observations on the subject were published by Théodule Ribot, Alfred Binet and Pierre Janet in France, by Frederick Myers in Britain, and by Morton Prince and Silas Weir Mitchell in the United States. Writers of fiction took up the theme with gusto and illustrated its three forms – the *Doppelgänger*, or 'double', the multiple personality, and a milder form of the dual personality which might be called the split personality.

One of the first writers to portray the 'double' was Hoffmann (once again), in *Die Elixire des Teufels* (*The Devil's Elixir*, 1816), which Freud discusses in 'The "Uncanny"' (1919*h*). He was followed by Poe (*William Wilson*, 1839), Fyodor Dostoevsky (*The Double*, 1846), and Oscar Wilde (*The Picture of Dorian Gray*, 1891). The second form, dual personality, makes its appearance in Léon Gozlan's three-volume best-selling novel, *Le médecin de Pecq* (1839). It tells the story of a neurotic young man who, while in a somnambulic state, makes a young woman pregnant, but has no recollection of the episode in his waking state. The genre was enriched by Robert Louis Stevenson, whose *Strange Case of Dr. Jekyll and Mr. Hyde* (1886) proved immensely popular and inspired many other writers. *Soeur Marthe* (*Sister Martha*), a novella written in 1889 by Charles Richet (under the pen name of Charles Epheyre), describes how a young physician is asked to treat the nervous disorders of Marthe, who is about to become a nun. Under hypnosis, she takes on another personality, that of a rich heiress, Angèle. Angèle falls in love with the doctor, who agrees to elope with her. But at the railway station, Marthe's personality reappears: she abandons her lover, takes her final vows, enters a convent and dies.

In *Le somnambule* (1880), William Mintorn portrays a respectable Protestant minister, good husband and father, who, in his somnambulic state, rapes women and murders children. In 1893, Paul Lindau wrote a highly successful play, *Der Andere* (*The Other*), in which a judge discovers that the crime he is investigating was in fact committed by his second personality. These themes show the keenness of interest at the time in theories about mental processes which Freud was later to describe in such scientific terms as transference-love for the analyst, the Oedipus complex, and fusion of desire and defence. Some of Auguste Villiers de L'Isle-Adam's short stories, in *Contes cruels* (1883) and *Histoires insolites* (1889), are written in the same vein.

The third form of the theme, split personality, involves the existence of very different – but less dramatically manifested – facets within a single personality: the heroines of Paul Bourget's *L'irréparable* (1883) and Marcel Prévost's *Le jardin secret* (1897) undergo marked character changes when they marry. Only this third form of the theme survived into the early twentieth century, when it was treated by such celebrated writers as Luigi Pirandello, Italo Svevo, Marcel Proust, James Joyce and Virginia Woolf.

At the same time, it became customary for literary critics to explain genius as a splitting of the personality, inspiration as a kind of trance, and the unconscious use, by the creator, of precursors' ideas as an effect of cryptomnesia as popularised by Théodor Flournoy with his investigation of the medium Helen Smith, published in 1900 under the title of *Des Indes à la planète Mars*.

Interest in magnetism had begun to wane by about 1840; but spiritism, 'invented' in the United States by one John Fox in 1848, swiftly took its place, spreading to Europe in 1852 and causing an extraordinary proliferation of mediums. In 1857, Hippolyte Rivail, a Paris schoolteacher who had been a disciple of Pestalozzi, published, under the pen name of Allan Kardec, *Le livre des esprits, contenant des principes de la doctrine spirite*. This work became, according to Janet, 'a guide not only for the spiritists, but also for the spirits'. Both Victor Hugo (while in exile on the isle of Jersey), the astronomer Camille Flammarion, and Henri Bergson (when still a young teacher in Clermont-Ferrand) held frequent table-turning sessions with their friends and published accounts of them. In the 1850s, Michel Chevreul repeated his celebrated experiments of 1833, in which he had demonstrated that the movements of the divining rod and the pendulum were unconsciously influenced by the performer's hidden thoughts.

Between 1860 and 1880, both hypnotism and magnetism fell into such disrepute that any physician resorting to them ran the risk of jeopardising his professional career and losing his practice. Then, from 1880 on, the tide turned. Demonstrations given by the French magnetizer Charles Lafontaine much impressed the English physician James Braid. He decided to repeat the Frenchman's experiments and, after rejecting the mysterious fluid theory (which lent itself too easily to fraud), proposed a new neurophysiological theory of artificial sleep, which he called 'hypnosis'.

Similarly, demonstrations by hypnotizers such as Carl Hansen in

Germany (as we have already seen, Freud attended one of them when still a student) and Alfred Donato in Belgium, France and Italy prompted renewed interest among physicians in Europe and the United States: Krafft-Ebing, Benedikt and Breuer (the last two were Jewish) in Vienna; Charles Richet (who was to win the Nobel Prize in 1913 for his discovery of anaphylaxis) and Charcot in Paris; Liébeault and Bernheim in Nancy; August Forel at the Burghölzli Hospital in Zurich, where Bleuler, Jung and Rorschach later studied; Albert Moll in Germany; Vladimir Bechterev in Russia; and Morton Prince in the United States.

Charcot enjoyed a considerable international reputation: luminaries came from all over the world for consultations with him, while he himself travelled the length and breadth of Europe in order to visit his illustrious patients. Scathing portraits of Charcot and descriptions of his spectacular demonstrations of hysteria at La Salpêtrière, which were attended by physicians, artists, politicians and members of high society alike, can be found in Léon Daudet's *Les Morticoles* (his father, Alphonse Daudet, was a close friend of Charcot's), in Edmond and Jules de Goncourt's *Journal*, and in Axel Munthe's *The Story of San Michele*. Charcot's literary friendships, his books on art, written in collaboration with Paul Richer, such as *Les démoniaques dans l'art* (1887) and *Les difformes et les malades dans l'art* (1889), and his demonstrations at La Salpêtrière resulted in a whole generation of novelists being inspired by psychiatry – the Daudets father and son, Emile Zola, Guy de Maupassant, Joris Karl Huysmans, Paul Bourget, Jules Claretie, and later Pirandello, Proust and the Surrealists. In 1928, Louis Aragon and André Breton celebrated the fiftieth anniversary of Charcot's discovery of hysteria as 'the greatest poetic discovery of the end of the nineteenth century'.

By about 1880, it became fashionable to adduce hypnotism and suggestion as explanations for a great number of historical, ethnological and sociological events such as miracles, wars, and the origins of religions. In his *Psychologie des foules* (1895), Gustave Le Bon compared the relationship between a crowd and its leader with that between a hypnotised mind and its hypnotist. Great interest was shown in subjects who, under hypnosis, played theatrical roles, painted or sang. Teaching systems were founded on the concept of suggestion.

Novelists exploited the theme of hypnotism. A crime committed in a normal state might be confessed to under hypnosis or under the effect of a suggestion by the dying victim upon his murderer. Or else a criminal might hypnotise an innocent person to make him commit a crime in his place, forgetting that the psychiatrist in charge of examining the performer of the crime could hypnotise him too and thus discover the truth. Similarly in *Le*

Horla (1886), a short story written by Maupassant just as he was about to be struck down with general paresis of the insane, a man is terror-stricken by strange happenings in his house, as if it had been invaded by mysterious forces. After travelling to Paris, he attends a hypnotic session, during which a woman is given an order; next day, in his presence, she carries out that order without knowing why. To his consternation, he then realises that the same thing is happening to him – someone is in possession of his mind and governs his actions and thoughts.

George du Maurier's best-selling novel, *Trilby* (1894), tells the story of a young woman who is hypnotised by her perfidious music teacher and turned into a brilliant singer. He subsequently marries her. But she can sing only when kept in a hypnotic trance by her husband, who watches her constantly from his box in the theatre. One evening, he dies of a heart attack at the beginning of a performance. Triby can no longer sing and her career ends disastrously. Hypnotism also fitted in with the dynamic psychological theories of Herbart in Germany and Pierre Laromiguière in France, one of the founders of the ideodynamic school, which postulated the existence of a force peculiar to ideas themselves and capable of causing acts.

In conjunction with the influence of Romanticism, hypnotism also provided support for the notion of the subconscious, or unconscious, which was becoming increasingly well-established during the second half of the nineteenth century. I need only mention here the writer whose views were closest to Freud's, Friedrich Nietzsche (1844–1900). In Nietzsche's view (cf. E 271–8), the unconscious is the realm of the wild instincts, which come from the dawn of mankind and find expression in passion, dreams, and mental illness. It was Nietzsche who invented the term *das Es* (the id). He had some understanding of the economic point of view, which comprises notions of mental energy, quanta of inhibited or latent energy, discharge, and transfer of energy from one drive to another. But he believed that aggression and self-destruction were stronger than sexuality. On several occasions he used the word sublimation (applying it to both the aggressive and the sexual instincts). He described repression, but called it inhibition; he talked of the super-ego and of guilt feelings, but called them resentment, bad conscience and false morality. Nietzsche also described, without giving them a name, the turning of drives against oneself, the paternal imago, the maternal imago, and the renunciation imposed by civilisation on the gratification of our instincts. The 'superman' was the individual who succeeded in transcending this conflict between established values and his instinctual urges, thus achieving inner freedom and establishing his own personal morality and scale of values: in other words,

Nietzsche foreshadowed what was to be one of the major aims of psychoanalytic treatment.

THE ATTITUDE OF FREUD'S CONTEMPORARIES TO SEX

One of the features of the period between Freud's twentieth and fortieth birthdays (i.e. roughly between 1875 and 1895) was the growing tension caused by sexual problems in his cultural milieu. The sexual repression typical of Victorian puritanism was still very much the rule, but it was being met, in Europe, by ever more numerous and more insistent attempts to rid science of sexual taboos. This explains why Freud's contemporaries – and indeed Freud himself – were torn between two different feelings of outrage: one directed at the indiscriminate, unfair, hypocritical and pathogenic pattern of repression then in force, and the other at the rise of licentiousness and pornography, and at the decline of moral values. It also helps to explain why Freud's contribution to science has been assessed in such contradictory fashion.

Ellenberger, after reviewing the flood of literature on sexual psychopathology that swept over late nineteenth-century Europe, expresses surprise at the precautions consistently taken by Freud when publishing his works on sexuality (despite the fact that they were always of a strictly scientific nature). And he shows that almost all Freud's discoveries in that field belonged to the *Zeitgeist* and had already been described, and sometimes even named, by this or that physician or writer. Ellenberger takes a totally opposing view from that of Stefan Zweig, who, in his portrait of Freud (1930), praises the courage, daring and intelligence with which he succeeded, at last, in putting an end to the puritanism of the Victorian age. I myself see the truth as lying somewhere between the two points of view. First, there have always been, and there always will be, feuds between those who have inhibitions about mentioning sex, if not about indulging in it, and those who jump at any opportunity of discussing sex, endeavour to reveal its secrets, and are keen to initiate children and adolescents in its practice: the range of attitudes to be found between repression on the one hand and perverse desires to seduce on the other is governed less by social forces than by varying organisations of the libido. And secondly, every period believes itself to be the first to have discovered sexuality and to have dared to discuss it openly: in this respect, modern society is particularly vain and long-winded. Thus, some of our contemporaries are startled to learn that when a civilisation has a literature it automatically has a sexual literature too, and that, simply to take the case of Europe in recent times, the whole of the eighteenth and the end of the nineteenth centuries produced a wealth of such writings. Surely sexuality remains, for every child, the primal mystery that stimulates his intelligence and imagination while threatening his emotional balance? There will never be a culture where the individual, in the course of his emotional development, can remain unaffected by infantile sexual theories or by the actual discovery of sex after puberty. This is an area where the starting point is always square one.

I propose first of all to examine the most obvious and regular symptoms of sexual repression manifested by the nineteenth century. They include: the hypocritical manner in which sexual matters were broached – or, more usually, not broached; ignorance and strong disapproval of homosexuality; the non-circulation of contraceptive methods, except by word of mouth, or of contraceptive appliances, except clandestinely; dread of venereal disease, and fear of prostitutes, who usually suffered from it. In the nineteenth century, syphilis was still an incurable, lifelong disease that often ended in general paresis and produced certain hereditary effects (successful treatment of the disease began only in 1909 with Paul Ehrlich's discovery of Salvarsan, and, eight years later, Julius von Wagner-Jauregg's use of malaria to treat general paresis). The tragedies caused by syphilis were portrayed in plays and novels such as Henrik Ibsen's *Ghosts*, Oskar Panizza's *The Love Council*, and Brieux' *Les avariés*. The disease is known to have affected politicians (Eduard Lasker) and writers (Nietzsche, Alphonse Daudet, and probably Maupassant). So it should come as no surprise to discover from Freud's self-analysis that he felt most uneasy about his own contraceptive methods and his homosexual tendencies, and feared prostitutes, syphilis and general paresis.

Between 1880 and 1900, the feminist movements that had come into being in French revolutionary circles towards the end of the eighteenth century experienced a new lease of life. The notion that women were naturally inferior to men was still current, despite work by the Swiss sociologist Johann Jakob Bachofen showing the existence of matriarchy in earlier cultures and efforts by the socialist August Bebel to obtain equal rights for women. The notion that human beings are fundamentally bisexual became popular (though the actual term bisexual was not used) with the revival of the Romantic myth of the Androgyne, which was discussed by Jules Michelet. Similarly, the female imago (though, here again, the term imago was not used) was described by the Romantics as something at once alluring and formidable. It took various forms, from the *femme fatale* (Ibsen's plays, Rider Haggard's novels) and the mother-virgin (cf. Villiers de L'Isle-Adam's *L'Eve future*), to the muse, or what the French call the *femme inspiratrice*, who played an essential, and warmly acknowledged, role in the lives of writers, artists, philosophers and composers

(Lou Andreas-Salomé in the case of Nietzsche, Rainer Maria Rilke, and Freud; and Malwida von Meysenbug in the case of Alexander Herzen and Wagner).

Let us now examine the other side of the coin. What previous work, what precursors, and what cultural factors might have orientated, stimulated, or paved the way for Freud's discoveries (E 291–303, 502–10)? First, alongside the puritanism of certain milieux, there was a notorious relaxation of sexual mores in other circles, particularly in Vienna and Paris. In the Russian Empire, 'free-love leagues' proliferated among teenagers and students. Such issues as venereal diseases, contraceptive methods, and the sexual experiences of children began, especially from 1880 on, to be talked about widely. Writers like Maupassant in France and Arthur Schnitzler in Austria deliberately set out to portray every aspect of sexual life with increased outspokenness. Arthur Schopenhauer gave sexual desire a central position in his philosophy. Already in 1875, the Italian Paolo Mantegazza decided to supplement his modest teacher's income by publishing a semi-pornographic sexual manual for the general public. The book, *Fisiologia dell'Amore* (*Physiology of Love*), immediately became a best-seller and was translated into several languages. It was also, incidentally, the favourite reading of Freud's future patient, Dora. In 1890, the German dramatist and political satirist, Frank Wedekind (1864–1918) wrote *The Spring Awakening*, a play that portrays the sexual apprenticeship of boys and girls. Another best-seller of the period was Wilhelm Bölsche's three-volume *Das Liebesleben in der Natur (Love Life in Nature)*, which was published in Jena from 1898 to 1902, and which describes in detail the very varied processes of reproduction in the animal world. Otto Weininger's *Geschlecht und Charakter* (*Sex and Character*), which was published in Vienna in 1903, and played a part in the final rupture of Freud's friendship with Fliess because of its use of the idea of bisexuality (see p. 555), was also highly successful. In it, Weininger created a veritable sexual mystique by drawing on a vast amount of accurate and up-to-date information on the subject. Janet, Krafft-Ebing, Breuer, Freud, Fliess and all other sexologists both ancient and modern were cited in it (for a detailed summary of this book, see E 788–9).

Publications of this kind naturally – and inevitably – caused a storm of protest both in scientific circles and in 'respectable' society. So Freud must have been aware of the reception his own works on sexuality were likely to receive. Some scientific societies, for instance, had even toyed with the idea of excluding Krafft-Ebing.

Most of Freud's discoveries in the field of sexuality were not totally new. Erasmus Darwin, in 1801, saw the origins of aesthetic pleasure in the infant's pleasure at its mother's breast. In 1879, a Hungarian paediatrician, Lindner, described the pleasures of thumb-sucking. Krafft-Ebing believed that certain mothers and wet nurses experienced erotic gratification from breast-feeding. Charles Fourier noted how children enjoyed playing with mud and dirt. A compilation by Krauss and Ihm in 1913 passed in review the role of excrement among various peoples of the world, a theme well known to students of folklore. The notion of sexual symbolism in primitive religions and the importance of the phallic image had been stressed by religious historians since the beginning of the nineteenth century.

While child sexuality was still regarded as an extremely rare abnormality, priests and educators of the time recognised that masturbation among infants, sex play among children, and the seduction of children by servants were all very common. Bishop Félix-Antoine Dupanloup of Orleans stated that 'bad habits are contracted between the ages of one and two years' (*De l'éducation*, 1866). In his widely read book, *Nos fils* (*Our Sons*, 1869), Michelet listed the dangers facing educators, such as girls falling in love with their fathers, and boys with their mothers, jealousy between brothers, incestuous relationships between siblings, the seduction of children by servants, the habit indulged in by some mothers of taking their child to bed with them, the simulation of sleep by children in order to spy on their parents' sexual activities, and so on. This is clearly a far cry from the supposed 'angelic purity' of small children.

The investigation of sexual deviations, like that of child sexuality, had ceased to be a novelty by 1885 to 1890. Rémy de Gourmont noted discerningly that the study of sexual deviations had two sources: the Catholic church and pornographic literature. Thomas Sanchez' manual of moral theology, *De Sancto Matrimonii Sacramento* (*On the Holy Sacrament of Marriage*) and a similar treatise by Alfonso de Liguori in the eighteenth century were standard works of reference for the clergy and widely read. Sexual deviations, like other sins, were classified according to their gravity. Thus, Liguori distinguished between unconsummated acts (ranging from impure thoughts and obscene language to physical contact without actual consummation), consummated acts committed according to nature (such as rape, adultery and incest), and those committed contrary to nature (such as sodomy and bestiality).

New ground was broken by writers who began to treat sexuality objectively, adopting neither a moralising nor a pornographic tone. In his *Confessions*, Jean-Jacques Rousseau (1712–78) describes his childhood experiences of masturbation, exhibitionism, and what was later to be called moral masochism. Restif de la Bretonne (1734–1806) depicted what came to be known as fetishism. The Marquis de Sade (1740–1814) and Leopold Sacher-Masoch (1836–95) illustrated in their writings the practices which were subsequently named after them.

The tradition was carried on by physicians, the most celebrated of whom was Krafft-Ebing, professor at Vienna University's medical faculty: he was to encourage Freud as soon as the latter started publishing his studies of sexual psychology and actively supported his candidature for the position of professor. The first edition of *Psychopathia Sexualis* appeared in Germany in 1886. Its title was taken from a treatise in Latin by a Russian physician, Henricus Kaan, published in 1844. Krafft-Ebing's book, which he constantly enlarged and republished, was enormously successful. It contained not only many neologisms, such as Krafft-Ebing's own 'sadism' and 'masochism', and a term coined by one of Charcot's students, 'erotogenic zone', but also an impressive list of deviations such as fetishism (a coinage of Alfred Binet), exhibitionism, homosexuality, paedophilia, zoophilia, gerontophilia and auto-erotism. Such was the volume of studies published on the subject that a special yearbook called *Jahrbuch für sexuelle Zwischenstufen* began appearing in Germany from 1899 on, which popularised, among other things, the notion of transvestism. A mere 282 pages long in 1899, it had swollen to 1,368 pages by 1903. Havelock Ellis followed suit in Britain with his *Studies on the Psychology of Sex*, which first came out in 1899.

A number of important questions were frequently debated in the medical circles of the time. For instance, are sexual deviations innate or acquired? Believers in the degeneracy theory (such as Bénédict-Augustin Morel, Valentin Magnan, and Krafft-Ebing) held them to be of constitutional origin. Educators, on the other hand, were in no doubt that homosexuality, for instance, was encouraged by the living conditions of boys and young men in closed communities such as schools, prisons, the army and the navy. The notion that the origin of certain perversions could be traced to a particular event in childhood began to gain currency. Rousseau had shown how a spanking he had received from a young woman when he was eight had been the starting point of his abnormal sex life. In 1894, Charles Féré published the case histories of two women who had been subjected to sexual caresses by servants and who later, at a difficult time in their lives, showed homosexual tendencies. Theodor Meynert, one of the professors under whom Freud worked for a time, argued on the basis of his clinical experience that homosexuality was always acquired; he published the case history of a necrophile whose deviation occurred when he began working in a morgue and experienced his first sexual stimulation from the sight of naked female corpses.

Théodule Ribot, in *La psychologie des sentiments* (Paris, 1896), classified sexual deviations according to their various origins: a) anatomical and physiological causes; b) sociological causes (closed communities of men); c) unconscious psychological causes (sexual stimulations during childhood producing early and permanent fixations); and d) conscious psychological causes (erotic imagination).

The notion that sexual deviations might be of psychogenic origin naturally prompted attempts to treat them by what was later known as behaviour therapy. Thus, Charcot and Magnan, in 1882, showed a male homosexual the picture of a naked man in order to arouse him, then immediately replaced it with the picture of a naked woman. After a time, the latter picture alone produced sexual arousal; and the patient later enjoyed satisfactory heterosexual relations.[1]

The idea that neurasthenia could be caused by masturbation was commonly held by physicians at the time. There was even a growing feeling that the complaint might have other sexual causes, such as *coitus interruptus*: in 1890, for example, the Zurich physician, Alexander Peyer, quoted a dozen authorities in support of that theory. The notion that sexual frustration was the cause of hysteria had long and widely been held. It had been strongly disputed by Briquet's celebrated publication, *Traité de l'hystérie* (1859), which argued that the neurosis was caused by extreme susceptibility to strong emotions.

But in Vienna Moritz Benedikt maintained the traditional view that hysteria was related to disorders of what he called the libido. He published four cases of male hysteria and demonstrated that the subjects had been maltreated in childhood. He contended that in the case of women the obligation to keep their sexual life secret was pathogenic. He also advocated the use of electrotherapy in the psychotherapy of hysteria. The Austrian criminologist Hans Gross showed that frustration of the sexual instinct could be the starting point of certain crimes. According to Krafft-Ebing, sexual abstinence could result in agitation, insomnia and even hallucinations. Lastly, the important bearing of love life on creativity, the role of sexuality in men of genius, and the sexual origins of aesthetic feeling and a sense of beauty were all notions commonly propounded by a number of nineteenth-century writers.

FREUD AND JEWISH THOUGHT

I have discussed Freud's scientific training at some length, because of its

1. Twenty-one years later Magnan published the follow-up to that story: the patient married but became a homosexual again – precisely when his case history was published.

diversity and complexity. But chronologically speaking it came third in Freud's life: it was preceded first by his Jewish spiritual upbringing, then by his literary and philosophical education, both of which also need to be described. For it was their return, between 1895 and 1900, to a central position in Freud's thinking (which had become excessively 'scientific') that enabled psychoanalysis to be invented.

Freud, as I have pointed out, and as he repeatedly stressed throughout his life, was a freethinker. He had no religious faith and abhorred all forms of religious practice. At the same time, he fully accepted his Jewish heritage: he was perfectly capable of standing up to the petty antisemitic harassment he occasionally encountered in public places or in laboratories; he persisted in his hopes of a university career despite the handicap that his background was felt to be by some in the Ministry of Education; he showed solidarity with those in the same boat as himself. All his friends and many of his patients were Jewish. In 1895, Freud joined a kind of Jewish masonic lodge, B'nai B'rith, whose fortnightly meetings he attended scrupulously for much of his life. On his seventieth birthday, he sent a letter to the members of the B'nai B'rith lodge, in which he wrote: 'And before long there followed the realisation that it was only to my Jewish nature that I owed the two qualities that have become indispensable to me throughout my difficult life. Because I was a Jew I found myself free of many prejudices which restrict others in the use of the intellect: as a Jew I was prepared to be in the opposition and to renounce agreement with the "compact majority"' (letter to members of the B'nai B'rith lodge, May 6, 1926, 368).[1]

Sigmund inherited these attitudes from his father Jacob, an enlightened freethinker who, although proud of his Jewishness, had never been a strict observer of religious custom. The Jewish communities of Moravia and Galicia in the mid-nineteenth century spoke Yiddish and usually German as well. Moreover, all children were taught Hebrew, and the more talented of them – such as Jacob Freud, and later Sigmund – succeeded in reading passages of the Bible in that language. It was in Vienna that Sigmund learned to read; and, as I have already mentioned, he worshipped his Hebrew teacher, Samuel Hammerschlag.

But things were made much easier for Sigmund by his father, who decided that the best edition of the Bible for his young son would be that published by the Philippson brothers. Regarded as revolutionary at the time, it was a bilingual edition (Hebrew–German), containing not only lavish annotations relating to archaeology, linguistics, and the compara-

1. Freud had already used the expression 'compact majority' in *An Autobiographical Study* (1925*d*, *SE* 20, 9); it is a quotation from Ibsen's *An Enemy of the People*.

tive history of religions, but also – to the horror of orthodox Jews, for whom any visual representation of God was forbidden – lavish illustrations. It was the source of the Egyptian gods with falcon's heads which appeared in the anxiety dream dating from Freud's prepuberty, 'My mother and the bird-beaked figures', the only childhood dream which he remembered in 1895 and later analysed (see pp. 294–309). On Freud's 35th birthday, in 1891, Jacob gave him, as a souvenir, a copy of the second volume of the same edition; part of the dedication he wrote in Hebrew reads: 'It was in the seventh year of your age that the spirit of God began to move you to learning. I would say the spirit of God speaketh to you: "Read in My book; there will be opened to thee sources of knowledge of the intellect." It is the Book of Books; it is the well that wise men have digged and from which lawgivers have drawn the waters of their knowledge' (J I, 21–2). Freud's close knowledge of the Bible helped instil in him the idea that the world is governed by a secret logic and resembles a great book which needs to be deciphered.

Freud had two other marked characteristics that were typical of contemporary Jewish culture. One of them, which is well known, was his fondness for alluding, in his work, to Jewish humour and jokes. Freud also believed, as Schur has pointed out (S 25–6), in some old superstitions connected with names and numbers. For example, Monday was a 'bad' day of the week, because, according to Genesis, God did not state, after describing the second day of creation (the Jewish week begins on Sunday), that 'it was good'. Whereas Friday, the sixth day, when man was created and God announced that 'it was very good', was a 'very good' day. The number 17, which is spelt in Hebrew the same way as the Hebrew word for 'life', was a good number (for many years, Sigmund and Martha celebrated the 17th of the month, the day on which they became engaged), while the number 52, which is spelt the same way as 'dog', was a bad number; the 52nd birthday was regarded as a critical one, especially for men, and Freud, as we shall see, dreaded that year in his life. Thirty-six, which corresponded to the combination of the Hebrew letters Lamed and Vov, was another important number. According to Hasidic tradition, there are always 36 just people on earth. When one of them dies, God calls on another one, usually a poor young boy of humble origins: faced with the material problems of his adolescence, Sigmund must surely, at one time or another, have cherished the hope of being selected in that way.

David Bakan (1958) goes one step further and contends that Freud was influenced by the Jewish mystical tradition, and more particularly by the Cabalistic tradition, from which he derived his fondness for playing with numbers and seeking hidden meanings. How plausible is this theory?

Quite apart from the fact that it has not been generally accepted by people well grounded in both psychoanalysis and Jewish culture, it seems to me that any attempt to explain Freud's discovery in sociological terms must be highly debatable. Although Jewish superstitions, esoteric traditions and folklore remained in the forefont of Freud's mind, they were, so to speak, like the 'day's residues'. They were just one of several sources of material that Freud's preconscious used for the psychical work whose main results were to be the reform of himself and the psychoanalytic theory of the psychical apparatus. The fact that Freud borrowed the substance of his numerological, onomastic and cryptographical games from Jewish tradition fails to answer the (to my mind) more important question: what inner need did those games satisfy?

In my view, a similar predilection for such games in the Argentine short-story writer, Jorge Luis Borges, who was brought up a Roman Catholic, and whom I have studied (Anzieu, 1971*a*), constitutes a transposition, at the level of symbolic exchanges made possible by speech and its rules, of the games played by infants as they discover the various parts of their mothers' and their own bodies. Such a transposition enables the subject to recover, in his internal reality, the initial power of discovery inherent in such infantile games and to put it to creative use, while at the same time avoiding the proscription that terminated them in external reality. I would suggest that this hypothesis fits Freud's case equally well.

A final word on the rise of Judaism in the nineteenth century, particularly in central Europe. At the beginning of that century, the textile and grain trades were controlled by Jews. Such Jews, who were obliged by the nature of their business to travel, began to emerge from the ghettoes and adopted, like Jacob Freud, freethinking attitudes. Some of their children carried on their father's businesses; others became scientists, professors, politicians or members of the liberal professions. At the University of Vienna, to mention only those men with whom Freud worked, Professors Benedikt, Kassowitz, Stricker and the Zuckerkandl brothers, Assistant Fleischl von Marxow, and *Privat-Dozent* Breuer were all Jewish – proof enough that although antisemitism undoubtedly existed in Vienna it could hardly be described as virulent. In 1867, Jews were granted equal political rights in Austria. They already enjoyed civil rights (which had meant that they were forced to comply with dual civil registration and have two first names, one Hebrew, the other non-Hebrew). And they began to pour into Vienna, rising in number to 72,000 by 1880, 118,000 by 1890, and 147,000 by 1900, out of a total population of one million (cf. E 423). This rapid influx was one of the reasons for an upsurge of anti-Semitism.[1] Freud's social life and scientific career must be seen against the background I have just described.

FREUD AND GENERAL CULTURE

In 1895, the main features of Freud's conscious cast of mind were his talent for the systematic organisation of data and his exclusive belief in the primacy of rational thought. In this, he had not changed since the mid-1870s, when he entered the medical faculty and conducted his first laboratory experiments. But a longer-standing character trait, which he had temporarily, so to speak, put into abeyance, continued indirectly to affect his scientific work, sometimes for the better and sometimes for the worse: his imagination.

In *An Autobiographical Study* (1925*d*, *SE* 20, 8), Freud says that he decided to become a medical student after hearing Goethe's beautiful essay on Nature read aloud at a popular lecture just before he left school. The fact that the essay in question is now generally agreed to have been written by Goethe's Swiss friend, Tobler, is of little importance. Nor does it matter whether Freud did or did not write a review of the lecture (which was on comparative anatomy) for a daily newspaper, as was claimed by an old friend of his, Fritz Eckstein (J I, 31 n.1). The first of Professor Carl Brühl's series of Sunday lectures on the 'Bodystructure of man and animals', which began on February 9th, 1873, was entitled 'The University education of women viewed from the vantage points of anatomy, experience, natural law and social need'. It is possible that Freud confused that series of lectures with other popular lectures on Goethe also given during March 1873 (G 262–5). However that may be, the essay on Nature is remarkable for its dithyrambic tone and its constant use of the Romantic metaphor whereby Nature is seen as a bountiful, omniscient and omnipotent Mother, who grants her favourite children – a Faustian echo – the exclusive right to seek out her secrets. It may be assumed that the essay satisfied, in the adolescent Freud, a new manifest content – 'to understand something of the riddles of the world in which we live' ('Postscript to *The Question of Lay Analysis*', *SE* 20, 253), and more particularly the riddle of how living organisms work – and a latent content from early childhood –

1. 'If anti-Semitism existed in Vienna towards the turn of the century, it did so almost exclusively in the middle classes; they [Ticho and Ticho, 1972] observe that the aristocracy and the intelligentsia were hardly antisemitic at all – and that there were only very rare cases in academic circles. They conclude that the main reason why Freud's career was slow to take off was not so much racialism as, simply, the scandalous and revolutionary nature of his theories. They resulted in his becoming isolated to a certain degree (as they would have in any other country). [Ticho and Ticho] argue that not only was Freud quite happy working alone, but his genius was probably spurred on as a result' (Chertok, de Saussure, 1973, p. 146n.).

the desire to become once again the cherished son of a good mother, to compare male and female anatomy, and to understand how babies are made. So in choosing to specialise in biology, Freud was guided not so much by Goethe himself, a learned and inventive man with an encyclopaedic mind, as by a mythology of Nature, which, although only a pastiche of Goethe, struck a chord in his personal 'phantasmatic'. Thus, for the first but not the last time, an important turning point in Freud's intellectual life occurred as a result of interaction between mythology and phantasy.

Freud was always a voracious reader. Thanks to his extraordinary powers of concentration and assimilation, he always found time, however busy he might be, working in the laboratory, visiting patients or looking after his family, to follow his teachers' example and cultivate his mind with books unconnected with his speciality. His reading included literary masterpieces in German, English or French – at least those which were thought at the time to be masterpieces, and on which he held his own very individual opinions – as well as general works on philosophy, religion and history. Although the following checklist dates from a later period than the one under examination here, I include it because it accurately reflects Freud's unflagging interest in literature and human sciences. When asked by a Viennese newspaper editor in 1907 to list 'ten good books' (*L* 278), Freud selected the following:

- three English-language writers: Rudyard Kipling (1865–1936): *The Jungle Book* (1894); Thomas Macaulay (1800–1859): *Essays* (1825–43); and Mark Twain (1835–1910): *Sketches*;
- two French novelists: Anatole France (1844–1924): *Sur la pierre blanche* (1905); and Emile Zola (1840–1902): either *Fécondité* (1899) or *Le docteur Pascal* (1893);
- three German-language writers: two Swiss novelists, Gottfried Keller (1819–90): *Die Leute von Seldwyla* (*People of Seldwyla*) (1856), and Conrad Ferdinand Meyer (1825–1898): *Huttens letzte Tage* (*Hutten's Last Days*) (1871); and the celebrated Viennese Hellenist, Theodor Gomperz, who came from a wealthy Jewish family (1832–1912): *Grieschische Denker* (*Greek Thinkers*);
- the German translation of a book by a Dutch author, Multatuli: *Briefe und Werke* (*Letters and Works*);[1]

1. The pseudonym, from the Latin *multa tuli* (which can mean both 'I have borne much' and 'I have related much'), chosen by Edward Doyweac Dekker (1820–87); his novel *Max Havelaar* (1860), an indictment of Dutch colonial administration in Indonesia, made him famous in Austria, where he was regarded as a revolutionary.

– and lastly, another German translation, of the Russian historian and essayist Dmitri Merezhkovsky (1865–1941): *Leonardo da Vinci* (1903).

Without aiming to be exhaustive, I collated the literary references in Freud's letters to Martha and to Fliess and in his works up to 1901 – either published or still at the manuscript stage – in the hope of producing a more representative sample of his general culture. The result was as follows.

As might have been expected, the writers Freud quotes most frequently are German, with Goethe easily in first place and Schiller second. After them come the following: the mediaeval period: the anonymous legends of the *Nibelungenlied*; the eighteenth century: poets, novelists and playwrights such as Gottfried Bürger, Christian Fürchtegott Gellert, Johann von Herder, Karl Kortum, Gotthold Lessing, Georg Lichtenberg, and the archaeologist Johann Winckelmann; the nineteenth century: Heinrich Heine (a Jew, rebel and exile, to whose grave in Paris Freud made a pilgrimage, and who was for long his favourite reading), closely followed by the well-known fairy tales compiled by the Grimm brothers; but the novels and short stories of the Swiss author Conrad Ferdinand Meyer began to fascinate Freud more than any other contemporary literature. However, his considerable intellectual curiosity also led him to take an interest in such widely differing writers as Fritz Reuter, a regionalist writer from Mecklenburg, who elevated Low German (*Plattdeutsch*) to a literary level, and four dramatists – Heinrich von Kleist and Franz Grillparzer, who were the national glories of Germany and Austria respectively, the Hungarian Theodor Herzl, who founded the Zionist movement, and Oskar Panizza, who scandalised his contemporaries with his anti-Catholic and libertine excesses. The Romantic writers Jean Paul and Novalis are alluded to only fleetingly. Freud also quotes from many other German, Austrian and Swiss novelists and storytellers (Wilhelm Busch, Jakob Julius David, Theodor Fontane, Gottfried Keller, Otto Ludwig, Joseph von Scheffel and Friedrich Theodor Vischer), playwrights (Arthur Schnitzler, Ludwig Fulda, Louis Schneider and Adolf Wilbrandt), poets (Anastasius Grün, Nicolaus Lenau and Johann Ludwig Uhland), and numerous authorities on Graeco-Roman history, mythology and archaeology.

The German philosophers with whom Freud was acquainted included Franz Brentano, Friedrich von Schelling, Eduard von Hartmann and Immanuel Kant. It is not until *The Interpretation of Dreams* that Freud first mentions Schopenhauer, quoting his definition of dreams ('Dreams [are] a brief madness and madness a long dream') and summarising his important theory of representation (*ID* 90 and 36). He also quotes Nietzsche's phrase 'transvaluation of all psychical values' (without mentioning Nietzsche) and applies it to dreams (*ID* 330 and *OD* 655). Freud ignored, and continued to ignore, both Marx and Hegel, and seems to have shared Heine's opinion of the latter, which he quotes with relish: 'With his nightcaps and the tatters of his dressing-gown/He patches up the gaps in the structure of the universe' (letter to Martha of October 31, 1883, quoted in J I, 214).

Both intellectually and emotionally Freud's next preference was English literature. He read English fluently, and idealised the country to which his half-brothers had decided to emigrate. The works he mentions most often are Shakespeare's tragedies (almost all of them). He also refers to Thomas Hobbes' *Leviathan*, Jonathan Swift's *Gulliver's Travels*, John Milton's *Paradise Lost*, Adam Smith's *The Wealth of Nations*, and, among his contemporaries, the philosophers John Stuart Mill and Herbert Spencer, the biologist Charles Darwin, the novelists George Eliot, Rudyard Kipling, Charles Kingsley, and Rider Haggard, the poets Algernon Swinburne and Alfred Lord Tennyson, and the Orientalist Max Müller. The psychologists in whom Freud was interested included the Englishman Sir Francis Galton and the American James Mark Baldwin, though not William James.

As for French culture, we find no reference in Freud either to its poetry, probably because he did not feel as at home with French as with English, or to its philosophy, because, as he later admitted, he had no sympathy for Latin rationalism. He liked François Rabelais' *Gargantua* in the edition illustrated by Jules Garnier, Molière's *Le malade imaginaire* (when in Paris, Freud saw, and had some difficulty in following, the same author's *Le mariage forcé*, *Tartuffe* and *Les précieuses ridicules*), Voltaire's *Candide*, Rousseau's *Confessions*, Pierre Beaumarchais' *Le mariage de Figaro* and Victor Hugo's *Notre-Dame de Paris*. Freud's only allusion to Pascal comes at the beginning of the article he wrote in French, 'Obsessions et phobies' (1895*c*), where he refers to the philosopher's obsession with seeing an abyss on his left hand – an obsession whose existence is vouched for only by late and untrustworthy sources. Contemporaries that interested Freud included, as well as the historian Thiers, who has already been mentioned, the playwright Victorien Sardou (whose *Théodora* Freud saw in Paris) and Alexandre Dumas *fils* (author of the celebrated *La dame aux camélias*), the novelists Alphonse Daudet, France, Maupassant, Zola and, possibly, Paul Bourget, and the psychologists Alfred Binet and Hippolyte Taine.

Freud also took an interest in the literature of other countries. It is not certain that by 1895 he had already begun to read Dostoevsky, on whom he later wrote an essay (1928*b*). He was fascinated by two Norwegians, the playwright Ibsen and the explorer Fridtjof Nansen, and by two Danish authors, the storyteller Hans Christian Andersen and the novelist Jens Peter Jacobsen (Martha's mother could still remember Swedish, which she learnt as a child; and both Martha and her sister Minna showed a keen interest, which they got Freud to share, in Scandinavian literature and mythology). Lastly, Freud was interested in both Arab literature (the *Maqāmāt* by al-Hariri) and the Sanskrit *Hitopadesa* by Narayana.

Freud loved classical painting. He had read Giorgio Vasari's contemporary account of the Renaissance art world, *Lives of the Most Excellent Italian Architects, Painters and Sculptors*. The artists whose works most struck him when he visited Dresden's picture gallery were Van Dyck, Veronese and above all Holbein (*Madonna*) and Titian (*Maundy Money*). He liked etchings (Jacques Callot's *Miseries of War*, Gustave Doré's illustrations of *Orlando Furioso* and *Don Quixote*, and Garnier's already mentioned Rabelais). Freud was particularly fond of Arnold Böcklin, a contemporary Swiss artist whose powerful, tortured paintings were very highly regarded at the time. Three of them, evocatively entitled *Island of the Dead*, *A Castle in Ruins*, and *Roman Villa*, were referred to specifically by Freud between 1897 and 1901.

Lastly, the frequently made claim that Freud's blind spot was music is untrue. Like any self-respecting Viennese gentleman of the last half of the nineteenth century, he loved opera, both light and serious. We know for a fact that he was particularly fond of the following works: Wolfgang Amadeus Mozart's *The Magic Flute*, *Don Giovanni*, and *The Marriage of Figaro*, Franz Schubert's *Die schöne Müllerin*, based on poems by Wilhelm Müller, Ludwig van Beethoven's *Fidelio* and *Hymn to Joy*, Carl Maria von Weber's *Der Freischütz*, Jacques Offenbach's *La belle Hélène*, George Bizet's *Carmen*, and Wagner's *Die Meistersinger von Nürnberg* (which he heard in 1898) and *Tannhäuser*.

Such a voracious cultural appetite suggests that Freud quite literally espoused as his motto the well-known line from Terence: '*Homo sum; humani nil a me alienum puto*' ('I am a man; I count nothing human foreign to me'). But in 1895 his considerable culture remained latent – or rather was kept separate from his scientific research. There are only about half a dozen literary references to be found in all his published work up to that date, other than *Studies on Hysteria*, which contains about ten. Things had changed by 1900, however: there are some hundred literary allusions in *The Interpretation of Dreams*, and almost as many again in *The Psychopathology of Everyday Life*, which came out in 1901 (though it should be noted that many were later added to successive enlarged editions of the latter work at the suggestion of Freud's followers). It was his self-analysis that enabled him to reconcile his scientific experience with his cultural knowledge.

There are two further points I feel ought to be made in order to complete the picture. First, the literary culture of the various great doctors on whom Freud modelled himself during his studies is significant: they were either friends of writers or writers themselves, and regarded their scientific work as indissociable from a thorough knowledge of contemporary literature. Brücke wrote about the scientific principles of the fine arts and about the physiological basis of German poetry, as well as inventing a universal writing system which he called Pasigraphia, or universal writing (E 431). Breuer, Meynert and Charcot all had many friends in the literary world. Their undoubted common denominator was curiosity about all that was new, combined with a high regard for creative work. It is hardly surprising that some of those who grew up in that kind of atmosphere themselves became pioneers in their own fields. In 1895, Charcot's son, Jean-Baptiste Charcot (1867–1936), was shortly to give up medicine and embark on the career of polar explorer. The boat with which he achieved many of his exploits, and which eventually sank with him aboard, was called, significantly enough, the *Pourquoi pas?* (*Why not?*).

My second point concerns the originality of the intellectual stands taken by some of the great minds on whom Freud also modelled himself in Vienna. I have already mentioned Krafft-Ebing's audacity in drawing up a nomenclature and a description of sexual perversions. More needs to be said about Franz Brentano (E 541–2). A Dominican priest and professor of philosophy at Würzburg, Brentano came from a family that had already produced a famous poet and a noted economist. When the dogma of the infallibility of the Pope was promulgated, he left the Catholic church and settled in Vienna (whatever Freud was later to claim, Vienna was a veritable haven for people who had opted out of sexual or social normalcy). He taught philosophy there as a *Privat Dozent* – a most unusual example of a university career going into reverse. Brentano, a brilliant man with great personal charisma, was once described as resembling a Byzantine Christ. Among those who attended his lectures were several men who later became famous, such as Edmund Husserl, Thomas Masaryk, Franz Kafka, Rudolf Steiner, and Freud. Brentano combined gifts that were quite often found in men and women nurtured on nineteenth-century culture, particularly in the Germanic countries – erudition, a gift for logic and for languages, and wit. He thought up a new kind of riddle based on complicated puns, which he called 'dal-dal-dal' and became all the rage in Vienna. His philosophical teaching, which paved the way for phenomenology, was contained in his *Psychology from the Empirical Standpoint* (1874), and was founded on the concept of intentionality – in other words, on a dynamic and non-conscious internal attitude. Brentano, a somewhat unorthodox figure who was not only accepted but loved by the Viennese, had many qualities that must have seemed exemplary to Freud – philosophical intransigence, rigorous reasoning, interdisciplinarity, spontaneous wit and a passionate desire to communicate – though whether he actually influenced Freud, (who attended his lectures for three semesters) as Merlan has argued (1945 and 1949), is open to doubt.

Freud's immense culture was mirrored by a genuine talent for writing. The limpidity of his style, which distinguished most of his scientific publications up to 1895, is also evident in his elegant German translations of five works. I have already mentioned four of these, two by Charcot (1886*f*, 1892–94) and two by Bernheim (1888–89, 1892*a*), because their subject matter was medical. Freud's first translation, however, which kept him busy during his military service, was of various essays by the English philosopher, John Stuart Mill (1806–73). The essays, originally entitled 'Enfranchisement of Women', 'Plato', 'Thornton on Labour and its Claims', and 'Chapters on Socialism', made up the twelfth and last volume of Mill's *Gesammelte Werke* (collected works) in the German edition (1880*a*). The German translator of the other volumes had just died, and Freud's name was put forward by Brentano to Theodor Gomperz (the editor of the German version). Freud was undoubtedly influenced by Mill, to judge from the lengthy and enthusiastic passage he later devoted to him in a letter to his fiancée (letter to Martha, November 15, 1883, *L* 90–91). Mill's essay on the emancipation of women provided Freud with examples of 'woman's hostile bitterness against the man', which he later analysed in his work on female psychology. Along with Gomperz's book, *Grieschische Denker*, which, as we have seen, Freud mentioned in his list of 'ten good books', Mill's second essay was his main source of information about Plato: he was particularly impressed by Plato's theory of reminiscence, and saw a concrete illustration of it in Breuer's cathartic method (whereby memories repressed by traumas are recalled under hypnosis). Lastly, the pleasure principle, which lies at the basis of Mill's utilitarianism, was a familiar notion to Freud because of his predilection for British empiricist psychology. The aim of human behaviour is to seek pleasure and avoid pain: in 1895 Freud was prepared to regard that principle as an explanation for the workings of what he was later to call the psychical apparatus.

As far as more recent philosophical ideas were concerned, Freud allowed himself to be influenced by them only when they squared with his line of research. To anyone with a German cultural background, the notion of the unconscious was far from outlandish. It had started with Leibniz's 'unclear perceptions', been developed by Herbart, gathered momentum with the Romantic movement and Schopenhauer's philosophy, and finally, in 1869, come to maturity in a celebrated book, which Freud had read, *Philosophie des Unbewussten*, by Eduard von Hartmann.

On May 25, 1895, Freud told Fliess in a letter (*F* 129) that he had been 'greatly advanced' by a book that had just come out, Jerusalem's *Urteilsfunktion*; the author, who was familiar with the latest work on hypnosis, maintained that there was justification for 'belief in unconscious mental phenomena'. It is obvious that what all these thinkers meant by the unconscious was in fact what we have called, since Freud, the preconscious. In 1895, the unconscious, in its proper psychoanalytical sense, had yet to be invented. Here I beg to differ with Ellenberger, who in *The Discovery of the Unconscious* (1970) argues that Freud merely repeated the theories of his countless precursors. Up until Freud, the notion of the unconscious had remained a limited concept, used solely according to the dynamic and economic points of view. But the idea of linking the unconscious with the erotogenic body and with sexuality, the idea of giving it specific phantasy contents, the idea that its development depended on a series of infantile experiences, the idea of seeing, in dreams or symptoms, a manifestation of those contents produced by the interaction of mechanisms of defence and processes of representation – all these notions were Freud's alone.

Moreover, in 1895, Freud was by no means acquainted with *all* the work of his predecessors, as he is now credited with being: indeed, it was precisely because he knew relatively little that he did not feel too cramped by those of their theories that were superficial, defensive and contradictory. He made his discoveries by separating the wheat from the chaff in what he assimilated from books and by heeding what his patients and his own self told him. Freud never showed any curiosity about his contemporary, Pierre Janet, who was working with the same sort of patients in Paris as was Freud in Vienna, and who used a comparable method of hypnosis. Janet only half-reached his goal: although his work was highly individual and clinically very valuable, it did not go far enough to establish a method or form a school. Freud, on the other hand, achieved both those objectives because he saw his enterprise right through to the end. True, he needed encouragement and reassurance. He found them in certain insights and felicitous turns of phrase hit upon by other investigators using various different approaches – doctors, psychologists, poets and philosophers. But Freud realised that while such insights and turns of phrase were useful they alone were not capable of producing a scientific achievement in the true sense. What he needed as well were a technique and a theory that were properly attuned to the phenomena he was studying.

The technique was free association. Literature was responsible not for providing Freud with the technique itself but for giving him confidence in its validity. He had been put on the right track by his patients, first, as I described on p. 60–1, by Frau Emmy von N., and then by those on whom he began to apply the technique of mental concentration: the less he pressed them, the more they began to forget their mute resistance and to digress, and the more their digressions, which he had initially interpreted as being a form of resistance, proved to be the most natural manner of circumventing that resistance and of gaining access to the repressed, yet still vivid, painful memory. In psychology, the shortest way from A to B is not a straight line. Long before Wolfgang Köhler investigated experimentally 'detour problem-solving' in monkeys and saw it as the stage in the lengthy evolution of species at which practical intelligence begins to emerge, Freud had realised that detour behaviour was a vital element of human thought processes, whereas before him it had been relegated to the rank of rhetoric, military strategy, or courtship: digression enables progress to be made in transgression, in other words, it provides knowledge about an individual's psychical life and his inner conflicts.

But an insight does not become a concept unless it can be slotted into a symbolic system that guarantees its validity. For Freud, that system was at once scientific and literary. Brücke and the Helmholtz school had instilled in him absolute confidence in the universality of causality and determinism. But he derived his confidence in the creative power of free association from literature, and more particularly from Schiller, whose works he knew well. So it is no surprise to find, for instance, in the second edition of *The Interpretation of Dreams* (1909) that he inserts a phrase from Schiller into a passage on his technique: 'Nevertheless, what Schiller describes as *a relaxation of the watch upon the gates of Reason* [my italics], the adoption of an attitude of uncritical self-observation, is by no means difficult. Most of my patients achieve it after their first instructions. I myself can do so very completely, by the help of writing down my ideas as they occur to me' (*ID* 103). This is an allusion to a letter written by Schiller to Karl Theodor Körner on December 1, 1788, and unearthed by Otto Rank (as Freud points out in the previous paragraph, also added in 1909).

It should be noted, incidentally, that the encouragement to write freely was later presented by Freud as a kind of self-analytical transposition of the basic requirement to talk freely. According to Zilboorg (1952), Freud had read the works of the English psychologist Sir Francis Galton, who, among other things, was interested in the psychology of men of genius, devised word-association tests and, more particularly, stressed the creative powers of such free association. Much later (1920*b*), Freud said that when he put his trust in the validity of free association he was following 'an obscure intuition', the source of which turns out to be his first favourite author, Karl Ludwig Börne (1786–1837). This Jewish journalist, an idealist and fervent champion of freedom, justice and sincerity, became the propagandist for the Germans' liberation struggle against Napoleon and subsequently fought all forms of oppression. When Freud was in Paris, he went to see Börne's tomb, as he did Heine's. Börne's collected works, which he was given as a present on his fourteenth birthday, were in 1895 the only books dating from his adolescence which were still in his possession. He was startled, when adult, to discover that he had apparently quite forgotten one of Börne's essays, written in 1823 and resoundingly entitled 'The Art of Becoming an Original Writer in Three Days', while he clearly remembered other passages from the volume containing the essay in question. The essay concluded as follows: 'Here follows the practical prescription I promised. Take a few sheets of paper and for three days in succession write down, without any falsification or hypocrisy, everything that comes into your head. Write what you think of yourself, of your women, of the Turkish war, of Goethe, of the Fonk criminal case, of the Last Judgment, of those senior to you in authority – and when the three days are over you will be amazed at what novel and startling thoughts have welled up in you. That is the art of becoming an original writer in three days.'

I do not agree with Jones' contention that Freud adopted the free association technique because of his 'unusual capacity for patience' and 'something passive in his nature' (J I, 269). On many occasions in his life. Freud showed extreme impatience (had this not been so he would often have been slowed down by teachers, colleagues and followers unable to keep pace with his intellect). Impatience came naturally to him. The only time we find him patiently resigned is when he is faced with the necessities and realities of life – and then only after he had reached 40, when his libido, as is normal, decreased and he already had the satisfaction of knowing he had succeeded in his professional and family life. Face to face with his patients – he had not yet adopted the technique of sitting behind them – Freud was not at all passive. On the one hand, he kept deliberately aloof as required by medical deontology and, even more so, by 'psychical analysis'; and on the other he engaged in continuous and intense mental activity, which involved moving to and fro between the three levels – the unconscious, the preconscious, and consciousness. If one were to employ purely psychological and moral terms, it would be more accurate to talk of

Freud's humanity, empathy and concern. He himself mentions this last quality as one of the vital attributes of the psychotherapist: 'The procedure [the cathartic method] is laborious and time-consuming for the physician. It presupposes great interest in psychological happenings, but personal concern for the patients as well. I cannot imagine bringing myself to delve into the psychical mechanism of a hysteria in anyone who struck me as low-minded and repellent, and who, on closer acquaintance, would not be capable of arousing human sympathy; whereas I can keep the treatment of a tabetic or rheumatic patient apart from personal approval of this kind' (*Studies on Hysteria*, *SE* 2, 265).

I feel it would be more useful here to formulate a theory of a psychoanalytical nature that takes into account one result of his self-analysis: what we see in Freud's case is a mentally active position faced with the primal scene. That scene, which Freud must have witnessed as a child, filled him with anxiety, yet he was keen to watch it and made no attempt to stop himself doing so; later, he cast his mind back to the scene in order better to understand it, both recalling and phantasising what he had seen and heard. In my view, what we have here is one of the roots of the creative imagination, one of the sources of the abundance of free associations that the subject will later draw upon during adolescence or adulthood.

Let us go back for a moment to the relationship between literary creation and the discovery of psychoanalysis. Freud spotted it as early as 1895, in *Studies on Hysteria*: '. . . and it still strikes me myself as strange that the case histories I write should read like short stories and that, as one might say, they lack the serious stamp of science. I must console myself with the reflection that the nature of the subject is evidently responsible for this, rather than any preference of my own. The fact is that local diagnosis and electrical reactions lead nowhere in the study of hysteria, whereas a detailed description of mental processes such as we are accustomed to find in the works of imaginative writers enables me [. . .] to obtain at least some kind of insight into the course of that affection' (*ibid.*, 160–1). Later Freud often expressed envy at the way poets were able to 'plug in' directly to psychical processes, whereas the scientific investigator could ascertain them only after much laborious effort.

Freud and Fliess

There is one aspect of Freud's life up to 1895 that requires examination. In 1887, he made the acquaintance of Wilhelm Fliess (1858–1928), an ear, nose and throat specialist who had come to Vienna from Berlin to do some post-graduate study. They were brought together by Breuer, immediately took to each other, and began to correspond. Fliess's marriage, five years later, to a wealthy Viennese client of Breuer's, Ida Bondy, and the growing similarity of Freud's and Fliess's scientific ambitions and interest in sexuality brought the two men increasingly close together. They talked of writing a book together and decided to hold regular 'congresses'. The first of these two-men meetings took place in Salzburg in August 1890, and was followed by others in Berlin (1893), Munich (August 1894) and Vienna (February 1895), to mention just a few (not all the dates are known). Fliess often came to Vienna with his wife to visit his family-in-law, and naturally saw Freud on each occasion.

Fliess had an attractive personality. He was a brilliant talker, inquisitive about a wide range of topics, and fond of throwing light on his own speciality by drawing comparisons with other fields of study. In Jones' words, his outstanding characteristics were 'an unrestrained fondess for speculation and a correspondingly self-confident belief in his imaginative ideas' (J I, 318). Moreover, at a time when Freud's home city of Vienna had a notoriously antisemitic mayor, Karl Lueger, the dynamic and liberal atmosphere that flourished in Berlin under Kaiser Wilhelm II somehow gave Fliess a special charisma. The correspondence between the two men gradually became, for Freud, a substitute for his love letters to his fiancée. The passion manifested by their correspondence, rendez-vous and exchanges of gifts remained on a purely intellectual plane, but, as Freud was later to admit (J I, 348), it was quite clearly fired by latent homosexual tendencies. The narcissistic nature of the object-choice should also be noted. Freud could see himself in Fliess (who was two years his junior) as in a mirror: they both came from the same middle-class Jewish background, worked in the same profession, and were equally keen to establish a practice in their respective specialities and provide for their young families. Both of them had received the same kind of general education, were eager to see psychology in physiological terms, and physiology in physical and mathematical terms, and nursed ambitions of making a great discovery.

Fliess had two theories which, he hoped, might help him achieve that aim. The first was that all human beings were subject to 'sexual periods', much like menstruation in women, whose length and periodicity had yet to be established, and which, he claimed, determined the sex and the date of birth of babies, the development of adults, and the dates of their illnesses and their death. Freud was enthusiastic about this idea for two reasons. One was theoretical: the notion that human psychology, human life, could be reduced to a mathematical formula was very much in line with the teachings of the Helmholtz school (in 1898, Fliess sent Freud two volumes of Helmholtz's lectures as a Christmas present). The other reason was purely practical: 'Now if conception, like all vital processes, was determined by Fliess's periodic law, then surely it should be possible to discover the dates in the menstrual cycle when intercourse was safe from that risk' (J I, 330). By 1893, Freud was writing to Fliess in the following terms: 'I still look to you as the messiah who, by an improvement in technique, will solve the problem I have pointed out' (*F*, July 10, 1893, 51). And in the spring of 1895: 'If you really have solved the problem of conception, just make up your mind immediately which kind of marble is most likely to meet with your approval' (*F*, May 25, 1895, 129). Note the ambiguity of Freud's phrase: which kind of marble did he mean? That of a statue – or a grave?

Fliess's second theory was that there was a relationship between the mucous membrane of the nose and genital activity. He was convinced that dysmenorrhoea had a nasal origin. In his first publication, in 1893, he described a 'nasal reflex neurosis', whose symptoms (headaches, disturbances of the circulation, respiration and digestion, and pains in the cardiac, lumbar and stomach regions) could always be relieved by applying cocaine to the nose. These symptoms were the same as those of neurasthenia, one of the 'actual neuroses' then being investigated by Freud; and the therapeutic properties of cocaine – the source of such disappointment to Freud in the past – now seemed worth exploring once again. Here, too, theory and practice merged: Freud, who had been suffering from empyema, had already been operated on by Fliess in February 1895 (cauterisation of the sinus), and planned to return to Berlin for a second operation after the summer holidays of 1895.

Already during the summer of 1894, while he was busy writing *Studies on Hysteria*, Freud had complained to Fliess of his isolation: 'since the scientific contact with Breuer has stopped, I have to rely solely upon myself, which is why progress is so slow' (*F*, June 22, 1894, 86). Breuer had refused to venture with Freud into the field of sexuality. Fliess, on the other hand, had no qualms about doing so, and his daring and determination helped Freud to muster the courage he needed to overcome his own internal taboos and the opprobrium of society.

It is worth pausing for a moment to look at this feature of the relationship between Freud and Fliess, as it illustrates rather well one of the processes involved in creativity. Two resistances have to be overcome by anyone who makes a new discovery or breaks new ground in art or literature. First there is an epistemological resistance, as has been clearly shown by Bachelard (1938): our existing knowledge acts as a kind of inertia which numbs awareness of anything new we may discover. To invent is to contradict; it requires us to forget knowledge acquired relatively late in life and shared with many others, to delve, alone, into some very early stratum of our psyche, to recall a personal image that is stored there, and to make that image blossom into a discovery of a work of art. At this point, the second resistance intervenes – a resistance which has parallels with what Freud termed, towards the end of his life in 'Analysis Terminable and Interminable' (1937*c*), the 'negative therapeutic reaction'. This resistance consists of a searing and demoralising doubt as to the value of what we are in the process of discovering and as to our own ability to carry through the next stage – demonstration, writing up, composition. We are negating the work we are about to produce outside ourselves, negating the self as a potential father/mother of the work with which we are pregnant. The nature of the underlying anxieties is easily guessed: a guilt feeling, according to the 'Freudians', about a child conceived by the imagination with one of the two parents; a phantasy which, in Kleinian theory, returns to the individual and consists of entering the mother's womb to destroy the father's penis and the infants in gestation. Whichever route it takes, it is the death instinct which is operating here, quick as always to nip in the bud any burgeoning creativity and, in the words of Paul Valéry, in *Le cimetière marin*:

'. . . Rendre la lumière
Suppose d'ombre une morne moitié.'

The first resistance can be overcome by isolation, which enables us to withdraw into ourselves, to renounce generally accepted opinion, and, by finding our real selves, to discover what we were looking for. But with the second resistance, succour can come only from other people. Recently, some light has been thrown on the nature of this relationship. The other person, for instance, may be the one with whom the potential creator 'shares his secret', according to B. C. Meyer, quoted in Kligerman's report (1972) on a psychoanalytical panel on 'creativity'. Thus, the novelist Joseph Conrad produced his best work and achieved considerable fame as long as he remained on friendly terms with Ford Madox Ford (then Ford Madox Hueffer); the sudden end of that friendship in 1910 resulted in a fall in his artistic output and a serious decompensation.

M. Masud R. Khan (1970) has studied Freud's and Fliess's relationship in the light of the relationship between Montaigne and La Boétie, which, after the death of the latter, was internalised by the former and thus enabled him to conceive his *Essays*. Khan compares this case with that of Jean-Jacques Rousseau, who needed a whole series of constantly renewed male and female friendships in order to complete his *Confessions*, a work in which self-criticism alternates with self-praise without producing, as it did in Montaigne's case, an awareness of universal mental processes. Khan talks of a 'catalytic' function that is fulfilled by intellectual and emotional exchanges in a crucial friendship.

That role is indisputable – and vital to almost all major creative work. The partner (B) may or may not be of the same sex as the potential creator (A). A's relationship with B, although always of an erotic nature, may or may not find satisfaction in sexual activity. These are merely associated factors. The essential part of the relationship resides in what one might call the immediacy of understanding with which B reacts to the mental ideas that A draws from within himself and tries to communicate to him. With B – and with B alone – A no longer has to struggle, as he used to with a blank sheet of paper or with his other contemporaries, in order to express himself or make himself understood. B is immediately able to grasp, as though at the touch of a wand, the idiosyncrasies in the organisation of A's sensations, images and affects; occasionally, B finds parallels with his own experience in them; at other times – and this is what is of great value to A – he is addressed in an area of his being he was not previously aware of, an area where he reverberates actively, intensely and favourably to A's ideas and reflects back to him an amplified and encouraging echo of the little voice of creative genius that has begun, still only gingerly and falteringly, to nudge A towards some genuine discovery. B is, so to speak, A's pole of least resistance, and the regulating feedback that returns from B diminishes A's internal resistance, which then soars to its peak level whenever it is a question of creating.

The problem is: how can this phenomenon be described in psychoanalytic terms? The expression 'resonance of phantasies', which some psychoanalysts who use group techniques have applied to the strong bond that suddenly springs up between two people in a collective situation, is no more than descriptive. The phenomenon obviously involves a reciprocal interplay of identifications and projections, but various questions remain unanswered, such as: what identification, what projections, and what kind of interplay? The notion of projective identification does not, in my view, go far enough, though it does come close to describing the phenomenon. The mechanism known as transitional phenomena, a term introduced by Winnicott, seems to me best to fill the bill in this case. A feels directly understood by B just as the suckling child is, intuitively, by its mother. A has difficulty in dissociating a reality principle (without which he would not be inventive) from the pleasure principle and needs to leave the task of reality-testing to someone he can trust; so he sets up B as an intermediary between that reality and himself, while at the same time ensuring that the omnipotent force of phantasy is subject to a to-ing and fro-ing in a kind of narcissistic commutativity. If a creator is to succeed in his creation when he is ravaged by doubt, he surely needs to regain his early illusion, made possible by an affectionate mother, that he is omnipotent? Between the author and the friend, the work that is born is like a transitional space.

By 1895, the resonance of phantasies between Freud and Fliess had reached its peak. They shared a secret that was none other than the mysterious secret of sex. Fliess approached the subject from the angle of biological cycles, the nose, and what was later called endocrinology. Freud was interested in its other aspects – the affects, repression, anxieties, 'hiccups' in the discharge of psychical energy. Fliess's encouragement increasingly fulfilled a catalytic role for Freud, as can be judged from two extracts from his letters. One of them dates from 1890: 'Otherwise quite content, happy if you will, I still feel quite isolated, scientifically dulled, lazy and resigned. When I talked with you and saw that you thought well of me, I even used to think something of myself, and the picture of absolutely convincing energy that you offered was not without its effect on me. [. . .] for many years now I have been without a teacher . . .' (*F*, August 1, 1890, 27). The second passage was written four years later: 'Your praise is nectar and ambrosia for me' (*F*, July 14, 1894, 87).

Fliess represented many things in Freud's imaginary: a mentor who preceded and guided him in breaking new ground in the field of sexual knowledge; an ever-willing and, what is more, favourably disposed audience for Freud's ideas; a man who was critical of the content of those ideas, but kindly in his manner; a colleague who could treat him when he was ill; and a twin, an idealised double of himself. When Freud later realised that Fliess by no means lived up to those imagined characteristics (indeed, who could have?), a rift gradually opened up between them. A revealing detail gives an idea of their complementarity in 1895. At the end of spring, Freud announced that Martha was expecting a sixth child. Four weeks later, he learned that Ida Fliess, after three years of marriage, was pregnant for the first time. He reacted to the news with some sarcasm – Fliess had told him he was on the point of discovering a foolproof method of contraception (see the letters quoted in S 85–6).

Each of the two friends expected the other to recognise his own greatness. But a minor detail suggests a fundamental difference between them. Their correspondence, and especially the part of it discussed by Schur, consists of lengthy descriptions of their respective health problems. As we have already seen, Freud was extremely worried about his cardiac symptoms and by Fliess's peremptory insistence that in view of them he should give up smoking (Breuer, who was not such a good friend but a better physician, inclined to believe that Freud was suffering from post-infectious myocarditis, not nicotine poisoning). Fliess, on the other hand, complained of headaches and, as a friendly gesture, Freud devoted Draft I to the subject of migraine. But here again the sufferer did not take kindly to the diagnosis offered by his colleague: the more Freud hinted that the migraine might be caused by anxiety, the more Fliess stressed its strictly anatomo-physiological nature. Each said to the other: 'Cure me' (projecting on to him the much-desired power to heal), and then offered the other the part of himself that was ailing. Thus, at Berchtesgaden station, after their first 'congress' in 1890, Freud flaunted to Fliess his phobia of railway journeys, which took the form of fear of arriving late for the train and worry about departing. (It should be noted that this anxiety never prevented Freud from travelling extensively.) What the two men were exhibiting to each other in 1895 were two parts of the body that were very different not only physiologically but, even more so, from the viewpoint of phantasied anatomy. Fliess's pains were in his head, Freud's in his heart. The images of the body that they tried to exchange with each other did not correspond any more than did their idea of the correct treatment, Fliess increasingly favouring chemotherapy, and Freud psychical analysis. Fliess's head complaint was in fact an unconscious resistance, which was something he refused to admit. Freud's heart complaint was in fact a neurosis, and he would have liked Fliess to help him get to the 'heart' of that neurosis. Their theoretical opinions and assessments of their own personalities were so enormously discrepant that there could only be one outcome in the middle term: conflict. But until that happened, Fliess played the role of friend, supporter, confidant, sounding-board and amplifier that is vital to any genius embarking, as Freud was, upon a great creative venture. Had it not been for Fliess, psychoanalysis would probably not have been discovered. When this is remembered, the contempt with which Jones constantly refers to Fliess in the relevant chapter ('The Fliess Period') of his biography of Freud seems distinctly unfair.

FREUD'S ENTRY INTO THE MID-LIFE CRISIS

Elliott Jaques (1965), following Melanie Klein, has postulated the existence of two major crises in human life outside childhood. In his view, the crisis of adolescence, which prepares children for adult life, hinges on the paranoid-schizoid position; the mid-life crisis, on the other hand, which marks the beginning of middle age, consists of a renewed working through of the depressive position. The second crisis occurs at about the age of 40, in the case of both ordinary individuals and creators (though Jaques studied male subjects only). Taking a sample of 310 well-known writers, painters, sculptors and musicians, Jaques worked out that the average age at which important changes took place in their lives was 37: some of them, who had never before produced creative work, suddenly became creators; those whose creative life had started early lost their dynamism, and sometimes died young (e.g. Mozart, Raphael, Chopin, Rimbaud, Purcell and Watteau, who all died between the ages of 35 and 39); the greatest of them continued to create, but their sources of inspiration and style changed.

Although it is well known that the Romanticism of youth is usually succeeded by the classicism of maturity, it is not always realised that working methods change too. The ideal of the young creator is to succeed at the first attempt, without pausing for a moment during execution (an ideal that closely matches sexual behaviour at that age). The creativity of the young is swift, spontaneous, brilliant and feverish.

As the artist or scientist matures, inspiration comes more slowly. Creative work procures him less frequent but also, no doubt, more prolonged and better organised pleasures. The first type of creator advocates the letting loose of emotions and passions, the second believes in controlling them. The first is satisfied merely with creative output. The second, engrossed with form as much as with content, is constantly occupied and preoccupied with the task of licking his work into shape. The first draft is no longer an end in itself, but the point of departure for a process of elaboration that usually takes years.

But diminished sexual energy, which is characteristic of the climacteric, is not the only symptom of the mid-life crisis. There is also a change in the attitude to death that brings about a new conception of life. Young people do not think about death; they are therefore idealistic and optimistic, impatient and revolutionary; they tend to believe in the goodness of human nature and in the evil character of nature or society; this is because they split both the life instincts, whose internalised object they idealise, and the death instincts, which they project.

As a person enters maturity, he becomes aware of the inevitability of his own death and tolerant towards manifestations of evil. He recognises that the forces of love and destruction coexist in man, and realises that their coexistence is the true source of human misery and tragedy. Hence his dispassionate pessimism, liberal conservatism, and constructive resignation. Hence his new ability to adopt what Goldmann (1955) calls a 'tragic vision of the world' – a vision that originated with Racine and Pascal and was elaborated into a theory by Hegel. Hence, too, the risk, for anyone undergoing the crisis of entering maturity, of depression and the bringing into play of manic, obsessional or hypochondriac defences against depressive anxiety. The adolescent's illusions of immortality are swept away, as soon as he enters middle age if not before, by the certitude of death. He thinks of death as a personal experience, sees it looming on the horizon of his life, realises for the first time that his future is not unbounded, and feels an urgent need to fulfil himself before that inevitable final hour. For the creator, the work is experienced almost like a mother's friendly breast, capable of replacing the life that is slipping away. More generally, a person who during childhood has been able to internalise a sufficiently friendly object can, if he successfully weathers the mid-life crisis, begin to mourn his own future death instead of feeling persecuted by it. As a result, he acquires a greater ability to show courage, to love, to understand other people, and to sublimate, and achieves a greater freedom of interaction between his internal objects and those of the external world. But the mid-life crisis is a difficult period, and not everyone gets over it: Jaques compares it to Aeneas' descent to the underworld.

It was in 1895 that Freud began to enter his mid-life crisis. He was 39. He was aware of the diminution in his sexual activity (a point I shall return to; see pp. 282–4). That diminution, which is physically normal in men of about 40, was more marked in Freud's case for the following reason: his wife, worn out by a succession of pregnancies and by the demands of looking after five children between the ages of two and eight, was both surprised and unhappy to learn that she was expecting another baby. So Sigmund and Martha decided that this was to be their last child. Freud realised that the precautions he had been taking (*coitus reservatus*, *coitus interruptus*) were ineffective as well as being unpleasant and a cause of anxiety. The hope that Fliess's original research into sexual cycles would solve that problem of contraconception and make sexual pleasure easier to obtain was one of the factors that led Freud to overrate his friend. It was all the easier for Freud to resign himself to a less active sex life because it meant he no longer had to face the discomfort of *coitus reservatus* or the risk of conception. Moreover, he always enjoyed a highly satisfactory sexual relationship with his wife; and this, combined with his very strict personal morals, discouraged him from indulging in extra-marital sex. Freud's feeling of resignation was quite serene, and relatively unmarked by bitterness, aggressiveness towards others, or self-deprecation, precisely because he was interested in sexuality in a different, scientific way. It gradually dawned on him that his patients' neurotic problems were produced either by neurotic defence mechanisms against sexual desires (although hysterical repression was his model, he sought a specific mechanism for each psychoneurosis), or by practices resulting in an incomplete sexual discharge and a transformation of excess libido into anxiety (actual neurosis). He felt he *had* to take an interest in sexuality if he wished to cure his patients (and not just calm them down); and he felt he was *able* to take such an interest because it was a field in which, on a personal level, he had achieved a blend of internal tranquillity and constructive pessimism, and a sufficient degree of self-observation, to perceive within himself a dim echo of those mechanisms, and therefore to verify the way they worked.

At the same time Freud was beginning to think about death, as is inevitable at an age when we realise we have entered the second half of our lives. The first time he thought of his own death was when he suffered cardiac symptoms caused either by a post-infectious myocarditis or by a coronary thrombosis (mild in either case); these attacks reached their peak in 1894. Since that time, he had been worried, though not obsessed, by the thought that he might die before being able to bring up all six of his children (when the child about to be born in 1895 reached the age of 21 he would be 60).

Freud always took a realistic view of death. In his view, it was the inevitable event par excellence, a necessity in the sense of the Greek ἀνάγκη, and had to be accepted as such. That was the attitude he adopted when close friends, such as Minna's fiancé Schönberg, died. He never experienced the defensive need to believe in some kind of immortality of the soul. Deep down he knew that when the time came he would agree to die. But up to then, like any normal young man who felt he still had his whole life to live, he had refrained from pondering his own death. The thought, when it comes, inevitably causes considerable personal turmoil and a harrowing reassessment of plans and attitudes.

As far as sexuality was concerned, Freud was increasingly prepared to bring his imagination and intelligence to bear on what his patients had been telling him in ever-greater detail since his suggestion that they use the technique of free association; but where death was involved his attitude was very different. He accepted it, but could not imagine it. And he was shortly to come up with a highly debatable theory to justify that fact: the unconscious, he said, contained no representation of death. Freud's self-analysis involved him in a lengthy and difficult process of working over, which led him to recognise that bound up with sexuality there was a different dimension connected in some way with death; but his self-analysis took him no further than the discovery of the Oedipus complex, and enabled him to overcome his mid-life crisis. It was not until his next crisis, at the age of 60, which was characterised by feelings that his own death was imminent, that Freud resumed that process of working over and pursued it until he discovered the concept of the Death instinct.

By 1895 Freud had already published a good deal and gained quite a reputation as both an investigator and a practitioner. But his output – magazine and encyclopaedia articles, chapters in collective publications, and a couple of monographs on cocaine and aphasia – could hardly be described as works in the proper sense of the word. This is not to say he was short of ideas. But he achieved only limited success because of his very immature method of working: he staked all on enthusiasm and the inspired guess instead of taking the necessary time and care to check his facts thoroughly (cocaine), to draw the proper conclusions (the basic structure of the nervous system), or to exploit his most important findings (aphasia). He could write as he could think; but he made little use of that rare gift, for no sooner had he written down his thoughts than he lost interest in them and moved on to something else. Up to 1895 he was quite happy with that way of working. He knew that he had great abilities and that they were not being stretched to the full. So far, he had had all the time in the world; tomorrow would do just as well as today.

Suddenly the future looked very different. He had completed his years of apprenticeship. The time he had ahead of him no longer seemed infinite: it stopped on the horizon – a horizon that would from now on move inexorably ever closer to him. If ever there was a time to create, it was then. But to do so he would have to change a lot of things – his style, his theoretical references, and the very nature of the subject of his study. He would have to work in a different way, probe himself at another level, painstakingly marshal the material he found there, get a feeling for it, systematise it, react to his treatment of it and, in giving it a construction, reconstruct himself.

For a creative regression of this kind to take place, there has to be, among other things, an identificatory reliance on a creator, who acts as a guide. After the failure of his earlier identifications with Brücke, Meynert, Breuer and Charcot, Freud returned to an identification of his adolescence, Goethe. The parallels between the two men are striking. Goethe (1749–1832) studied law; Freud had originally intended to take up law, and if he opted for medicine at the last moment it was because he had heard a reading of extracts from an essay on Nature attributed to Goethe. Alongside his literary activities, Goethe took a keen interest in various scientific fields (such as optics, botany, geology, and osteology), where on more than one occasion he made discoveries which, although of minor importance, were deemed interesting by his contemporaries (Helmholtz, for instance, who influenced Freud, paid tribute to Goethe's theory of colours).

Freud, following the example of Brücke, conceived what he was to term the psychical apparatus on the analogy of optical apparatus; he enjoyed reading botanical monographs; he was beginning to picture the unconscious as a succession of superimposed geological layers dating from different periods and organised in different ways; as for osteology, Freud's identification with Goethe is in this case patently obvious, as we shall see, in the 'Sheep's head' dream (see pp. 236–9). One of the women whom Goethe loved, Minna Herzlieb (she appears under a different name in *Elective Affinities*), had the same first name as Freud's sister-in-law, Minna Bernays, whom he was coming to like more and more. The Brentano family (a contemporary member of which, the philosophy professor Franz Brentano, had a considerable influence on Freud) had been made famous by the great romantic poet, Clemens Brentano and his sister Bettina, who, although married to the novelist Achim von Arnim, engaged in a passionate correspondence with Goethe; another member of the family, Maximiliane, the sad young wife taken by the widowed grocer Brentano, appears in *Werther*. Finally, once Goethe had reached maturity, he experienced between 1794 and 1805 a period of renewed creativity – distinguished chiefly by *Wilhelm Meister* – that coincided with his very close friendship with Schiller. Fliess was called upon by Freud to occupy the same position and play the same role. One last coincidence: Freud, like Goethe, died at the age of 83.

But these are only minor similarities. More significantly, Goethe wrote, in fragmented form, an account of his childhood and youth entitled *Dichtung und Wahrheit* (*Poetry and Truth*). The characters from his works who appear in it so resemble Goethe himself that he succeeds in constantly switching from the actual world of his autobiography to the poetic universe of his creations. True, Goethe does adapt some autobiographical details so as to lend the memory of his life the same perfect form he always strove to give his literary creations. But unlike Saint Augustine or Jean-Jacques Rousseau he was not motivated by humility, pride, exhibitionism or the desire to set an example. His aim was to show to others, and to himself, the *Bildung* or inner structure of his personality – first its ἐντελέχεια (the Aristotelian term he liked to use), then its various metamorphoses. So far, that side of Goethe had not influenced Freud, but it was to serve as an identificatory model for him as he progressed in his self-analysis. Freud never lost interest in Goethe's autobiographical sketch, and later wrote an essay entitled 'A Childhood Recollection from *Dichtung und Wahrheit*' (1917*b*).

Meanwhile, another important event in Goethe's life was exercising Freud's mind in the middle of 1895. Every German schoolboy, including Freud, knew that Goethe's voyage to Italy marked a vital turning point in his development. Up to the age of 37, he had published a number of rather brief easy, romantic pieces – half a dozen plays, including *Götz von*

Berlichingen, and a novel, *Werther*, which brought him fame. He had also started work on his first version of *Faust*. Then, from 1786 to 1788, he stayed in Rome, Naples, and again in Rome. In Naples, he experienced a tragic vision of mankind for the first time: 'The Neapolitans are caught between the paradise of the sea and the hell of Vesuvius' (which was erupting at the time). During his second stay in Rome, he first began to enjoy the personal equilibrium he had hankered after, and, from that point on, his sources of inspiration changed. His new models were the classical ideal, Greek tragedy, the Renaissance. He then began to produce his great works of drama, tragedy, and lyric or elegiac poetry. When subsequently writing batches of his *Voyage to Italy* (in 1788–89, 1813, 1817 and 1829), Goethe showed himself to be perfectly aware of the change that had taken place within him.

Freud had long dreamed of going to Italy and visiting Rome and Naples. But lack of money, probably combined with the feeling that he was not yet mature enough to follow Goethe's example and undergo a metamorphosis there, had caused him constantly to put off his voyage. Now the time was ripe. At Easter, 1895, he made a lightning trip to Abbazia, in Istria (then part of Austria), which reminded him of the very happy times he had spent in Trieste as a student. He then made up his mind: that same summer, he would visit Italy for the first time. In July, he spent the holidays with his family at Bellevue, on a wooded hill overlooking Vienna, and had the dream of 'Irma's injection'. In August, he visited Venice with his younger brother Alexander (Goethe always travelled with a companion). In a short letter to Martha (*L*, letter to Martha, August 27, 1895, 241), Freud describes himself as being in 'a trance'. Fliess had expressed the hope that Freud would find a skull on the Lido to enlighten him. Goethe, it will be remembered, arrived at his theory of the cranial vertebrae after picking up the remains of a sheep's skull on that beach. In September, still accompanied by Alexander, Freud stopped off in Berlin, on the way home, to see Fliess and have another nose operation. It was during the return journey to Vienna that Freud began to write 'Project for a Scientific Psychology'.

In *A la recherche du temps perdu*, when describing the early career of the novelist Bergotte, Proust strives to pinpoint the moment when he 'took off'. Proust's phrase applies perfectly to Freud (who, incidentally, was both a contemporary and an admirer of Anatole France, one of Proust's models for the character of Bergotte). During his three-part voyage to Bellevue, Venice and Berlin, Freud was indeed preparing to 'take off'.

But my narrative has begun to spill over into the next chapter. Let us pause a moment and take our bearings. The ideas, people, events, situations and references which I believe to be essential to any understanding of Freud's development from July 1895 on have been passed in review. The scene has been set; the actors, the prompter and the stagehands are all ready; the curtain is about to rise. The play we shall see takes place on Freud's internal stage. In many ways, it will seem familiar to those who like modern theatre: every performance will rely on improvisation; the sets will have the incongruity of a dream; the lighting will focus on accessories and walk-on characters rather than on what is essential; and the producer of the play will conduct a rehearsal quite openly in front of the audience until the point is reached when they understand that the rehearsal is in fact the play they have come to see. Characters in search of an author will fleetingly appear in the course of this controlled improvisation. Recorded sound and projected pictures will be superimposed on the performance. From time to time, a halt will be called while the foreground is filled with placards bearing ambiguous messages. Through this interplay of mirrors, the stage – a representation of the unconscious – will sometimes give the illusion of having various degrees of depth, and sometimes provide an opportunity for actions to take place simultaneously on distinctly separate levels. It was not until the age of psychoanalysis that theatre of this kind became possible; so it is hardly surprising that in retrospect its prototype would now seem to be the actual discovery of psychoanalysis itself.

In the course of the game that Freud was about to play with, within and against himself, from July 1895 until October 1900, his achievement was to be not so much the discovery of a technique for treating neuroses as a self-initiation into a creative approach in the field of individual mental processes. Right up to his death, he showed himself capable of playing other games and pursuing his discovery even further. But he no longer felt the need to pass on to his readers and correspondents the same quantity of personal details, the same number of glimpses of the interaction between the outer shell and the core of his subjectivity. That need was largely made redundant by the countless conversations he had with those of his original followers he held in the greatest affection or esteem. In other words, Freud's self-analysis was succeeded by inter-analysis, a process which psychoanalysts specialising in group techniques have recently described as playing an essential role in their discipline (see D. Anzieu and others, 1972).

Now let us follow, scene by scene, the five-act play where Freud is one moment the producer, the next the leader of the chorus, the next the audience, and sometimes all the protagonists rolled up in one.

CHAPTER 2

The discovery of the meaning of dreams

'Do you suppose that some day one will read
on a marble tablet on this house:

HERE, ON JULY 24, 1895,
THE SECRET OF THE DREAM REVEALED
ITSELF TO DR. SIGM. FREUD'

(letter to Fliess, June 12, 1900, *F* 417)

Freud's progress by July 1895

By this stage, Freud had already, under the indirect influence of Herbart, partly arrived at the dynamic point of view (he and Breuer often referred to 'psychical conflicts') and, under the direct influence of the Helmholtz school, almost completely arrived at the economic point of view. He had already formulated the theory that psychical life is endowed with its own energy, one which is, to quote Emil Du Bois-Reymond, 'equal in dignity to the physico-chemical forces inherent in matter'. He called it libido and put forward the hypothesis that it turns into anxiety if not discharged. We have already examined (see Table 1, pp. 79–84) the main concepts worked out by Freud within this economic framework (it should be noted, however, that he did not use the terms 'dynamic', 'economic' or 'topographical' until much later): a psychical 'trauma' produces a 'fright' which becomes and remains pathogenic unless it is discharged in an 'abreaction' (a discharge of the 'affect' that has a 'cathartic' effect); the organism is governed by the principle of 'constancy', which strives to keep constant the 'sum of excitation' or 'quota of affect'; for the organism to function normally, 'energy' has to be 'bound' in 'cathexes'.

The influence of Darwin and Haeckel had familiarised Freud with the concepts of phylogeny and ontogeny in the field of biology; but he had not yet perceived their specific relevance to psychology. Only later would he discover the topographical point of view, for which he had no precursor, and which he derived – as I hope to demonstrate – from the very substance of his dreams. As regards two other lines of thought which he was pursuing at the time, he had only half-reached his goal. He modelled his conception of what he was soon to call the psychical apparatus on the nervous system, which he had discovered in the course of his anatomo-physiological work, but persisted in seeking exact, term-for-term parallels between the two systems. He believed that adult neurosis was caused before puberty – though not in infancy – by sexual emotions whose consequences were catastrophic for the subject, but thought that such emotions were always caused by adults, usually parents.

The same was true of Freud's clinical observations. He was able, not only by their symptoms but by some of their psychical mechanisms, to differentiate between a) 'neuro-psychoses of defence' (his own term, which includes hysteria, phobia and 'obsessional neurosis', and another term invented by him), b) actual neuroses (which in his view consisted of neurasthenia and, more particularly, anxiety neurosis – another term coined by Freud), and c) mental states of a psychotic nature (such as melancholy and paranoia – the distinction between neurosis and psychosis was common in German psychiatry towards the end of the nineteenth century). The sexual aetiology of many of these disorders seemed increasingly clear to Freud. He believed them to be caused, in the case of hysteria, by scenes of real sexual seduction by adults during puberty and, in the case of actual neuroses, by sexual abstinence or frustration due to the use of certain contraceptive techniques. But he had yet to discover what lay behind those symptoms and mechanisms, i.e. the organisation of desire and defence in the scenario of the phantasy, and single it out as the keystone of all specifically psychical disorders. Like Breuer, he thought phantasy to be just a conscious daydream, but he knew of the existence of Anna O.'s phantasy of pregnancy.

Freud thought he had discovered different defence mechanisms for each disorder – conversion and symbolisation in the case of hysteria (in this particular area he had realised that signs and symbols were the same), displacement, substitution, and self-accusation in the case of obsessions, and projection in the case of paranoia. And he had already understood that what all these defence mechanisms had in common was repression, which resulted in the formation, outside consciousness, of 'groups of ideas' he called 'complexes' or 'pathogenic unconscious ideas', and whose correlative was the 'return of the memory' (he had not yet used the term 'return of the repressed').

Similarly, Freud had already used the expression 'flight into psychosis', which anticipated his subsequent notion of 'flight into illness', and was gradually working towards concepts such as negation, isolation and splitting. He had also realised that the 'hysterogenic zones', so called by Charcot because of the pain they caused, were in fact areas of sexual excitation. But he continued to cling partly to the scientific belief that degeneracy (cf. Charcot's notion of the 'neuropathic family') and the hypnoid state (Breuer) constituted the invariable organic basis of hysteria, even though he was beginning to question those ideas.

As far as therapeutic techniques were concerned, Freud was gradually giving up hypnosis and mental concentration, but had not yet finally adopted the free association method. He had already identified censorship, resistance and transference, but had only a vague idea of what was involved in the last concept and had not yet recognised the operational role of counter-transference. He was using the terms 'analysis', 'psychical analysis' and 'psychological analysis', but not yet 'psychoanalysis'. He did, however, believe that the treatment of psychoneuroses necessarily required a 'psychical working out' (Charcot's concept) of the pathogenic trauma and its 'cathartic discharge' (Breuer's concept).

Table 2 shows the main theoretical and clinical notions used by Freud in 1895. Out of the sixty-four listed, over twenty were permanently retained by him; another score are merely early forms of psychoanalytic terms he subsequently adopted; ten were later discarded completely; and ten others were – and in most cases still are – commonly used psychological or psychiatric terms. Over half the expressions listed (thirty-five) were coined by Freud himself, and some thirty of these have survived. Other notions still in use today were derived by Freud, after a rigorous selection process, from Charcot and, more especially, Breuer.

Although the field of psychopathology itself was becoming increasingly familiar to Freud, he did not know to what extent it overlapped the field of normal, general psychology, or indeed if it overlapped at all (he had a hunch that it did). In order to clear up the problem, he needed to find a psychical phenomenon half way between the two fields which would enable him to establish how human beings move from a normal to a pathological state. He was becoming increasingly interested in a phenomenon that seemed to satisfy those requirements: the dream. The dream is at once a normal phenomenon (everyone has at least one dream every night) and a pathological phenomenon (the dream is a brief hallucination).

TABLE 2. *Alphabetical list of the main notions used by Freud in 1895*

Abreaction (Breuer and Fr.)
Affect (term used in German psychiatry and borrowed by Breuer and Fr.)
Analysis (Fr.)
Anxiety (general term)
Anxiety neurosis (Fr.)
Auto-hypnosis (Breuer)
Cathartic method (Breuer and Fr.)
Cathexis (Fr.)
Censorship (Fr.)
Complex (in its pre-psychoanalytic sense) (Breuer and Fr.)
Constancy principle (Fr.)
Conversion (Fr.)
Conversion hysteria (Fr.)
Defence (Fr.)
Defence hysteria (Fr.)
Deferred action (notion described but not yet formulated) (Fr.)
Displacement (Fr.)
Ego-consciousness (Breuer and Fr.)
Energy (free e., bound e.; notion described but not yet formulated) (Breuer)
Fixation (in its pre-psychoanalytic sense) (Fr.)
Flight into psychosis (Fr.)
Fright (Breuer and Fr.)
Hypnoid state (Moebius and Breuer)
Hypochondria (general term)
Hysterogenic zone (Charcot and Fr.)
Innervation (Fr.)
Isolation (notion described but not yet formulated) (Fr.)
Libido (Fr.)
Memory-trace (general psychological and physiological term)
Mixed neurosis (Fr.)
Mnemic symbol of the trauma (Symptom as) (Fr.)
Negation (half-formulated notion) (Fr.)
Neurasthenia (Beard, redefined by Fr.)
Neuropathic family (Charcot)
Neuro-psychosis of defence (Fr.)
Obsessional neurosis (Fr.)
Over-determination (Fr.)
Paranoia (term used in German psychiatry)
Pathogenic unconscious idea (Breuer and Fr.)
Phantasy of pregnancy (half-formulated notion) (Fr.)
Phantasies (in the sense of daydreams) (Breuer and Fr.)
Phobia (general term)
Projection (Fr.)
Psychical conflict (Fr.)
Psychical trauma (Breuer and Fr.)
Psychical working out (Charcot)
Psychosis (term used in German psychiatry)
Quota of affect (Fr.)
Regression (half-formulated notion) (Fr.)
Repression (Fr.)
Resistance (Fr.)
Retention hysteria (Fr.)
Return of the memory or of the repressed (Fr.)
Seduction (as cause of mental disorders) (Fr.)
Sexual abstinence (as cause of mental disorders) (Fr.)
Splitting of the ego, of the mind (Breuer and Fr.)
Subconscious (general term)
Substitute-formation (Fr.)
Suggestion (general term)
Summation (Exner and Fr.)
Sum of excitation (Fr.)
Symbolisation (hysterical) (Fr.)
Transference (Fr.)
Traumatic hysteria (Charcot)

FREUD'S INTEREST IN DREAMS

Freud had long been interested in his own dreams. Much evidence for this is provided by Jones (J I, chapter 16), who had access to Freud's unpublished letters to Martha. On June 30, 1882, a fortnight after their engagement, Freud wrote to her: 'I never dream about matters that have occupied me during the day, only of such themes as were touched on once in the course of the day and then broken off.' On July 19, 1883, he mentioned a blissful dream of a landscape, 'which according to the private note-book on dreams which I have composed from my experience indicates travelling.' On December 31 of the same year, he again dreamed of travelling. On another occasion, he dreamed he was dreaming. On January 13, 1886, he mentioned an anxiety dream he had had: 'Last night I dreamt I was fighting someone for your sake and had the disagreeable feeling of being paralysed just when I wanted to strike a blow. I often dream that and it comes at the place of the dream where I still have to pass my doctor's examination, a task which had tormented me for years.'

Then Freud became interested in the dreams of his neurotic patients, who, once he had given up using pressure or suggestion and allowed them to express themselves freely, began spontaneously to describe their dreams to him. He had a feeling that the dreams were significant and began to jot them down. In the spring of 1894, he told Breuer he had learned how to interpret them, by which he probably meant that he asked his patients to associate freely on the subject of their own dreams rather than that he had discovered the interpretation of their meaning. As with all his major discoveries, Freud was unconsciously guided by something he had read. As I have already mentioned, Griesinger, whose work Freud knew well, had published a book on pathology and therapy in 1861 in which he described dreams and psychoses as being fulfilments of wishes. Meynert had noted the same mechanism in a disorder he called amentia (acute hallucinatory confusion). Freud's observations led him to adopt the same view. In January 1895, he sent Fliess a paper on paranoia (*F*, Draft H, 107–12), which argued implicitly in favour of interpreting hallucinations in the same way. On March 4, he told him of a significant case: 'Rudi Kaufmann, a very intelligent nephew of Breuer's and also a medical man, is a late riser. He has his maidservant wake him, and then is very reluctant to obey her. One morning she woke him again and, since he did not want to listen to her, called him by his name, "Mr. Rudi." Thereupon the sleeper hallucinated a hospital chart (compare the Rudolfinerhaus) with the name "Rudolf Kaufmann" on it and said to himself: "So R.K. is already in the hospital; then I do not need to go there,'' and went on sleeping!' (*F* 114; cf. Pepi's dream, *ID* 125).

But Freud needed to check his theory, and the only way he could do so was on himself. This was nothing new for him – he had, after all, tested the effects of cocaine on himself. More recently, he had observed, also on himself, a particular disturbance of sensibility in the thigh (1895*e*). Moreover, in 1894 or at the beginning of 1895, he wrote, in a note to the case history of Frau Emmy von N. in *Studies on Hysteria* (1895*d*, *SE* 2, 69n.): 'For several weeks I found myself obliged to exchange my usual bed for a harder one, in which I had more numerous or more vivid dreams, or in which, it may be, I was unable to reach the normal depth of sleep. In the first quarter of an hour after waking I remembered all the dreams I had had during the night, and I took the trouble to write them down and try to solve them. I succeeded in tracing all these dreams back to two factors: (1) to the necessity for working out any ideas which I had only dwelt upon cursorily during the day – which had only been touched upon and not finally dealt with; and (2) to the compulsion to link together any ideas that might be present in the same state of consciousness. The senseless and contradictory character of the dreams could be traced back to the uncontrolled ascendancy of this latter factor.'

Freud was perhaps encouraged by the example of many well-known authors of the time who had written books on dreams that included descriptions of their own dreams – Karl Albert Scherner (1861), Johannes Volkelt (1875) and Hildebrandt (1875) in German, and Alfred Maury (1861), Joseph Delboeuf (1885), Marie-Jean-Léon Hervey de Saint-Denis (1867) and Simon (1888) in French. Freud was bound to have known of the existence of these books, though in 1895 he had not yet read them. This he did in 1898 and 1899 in order to be able to write the historical and critical first chapter of *The Interpretation of Dreams*. He even complained that he had been unable to get hold of the Marquis Hervey de Saint-Denis' book (for the simple reason that it had been published anonymously); the Marquis was reputed to have revealed many secrets of his own love life in it. Indeed, it was precisely because Freud had read nothing of his predecessors that he was able to pursue his own ideas more freely and discover the psychoanalytic technique of dream-interpretation.

Psychologists of the second half of the nineteenth century had shown considerable interest in dreams (for that very reason, Freud felt entitled to tackle the subject himself); but the results they achieved were meagre, as can be seen from Freud's survey of existing scientific literature at the beginning of *The Interpretation of Dreams* (a detailed summary of it will be found on pp. 460–3 of the present book). For the sake of thoroughness, I read

Maury's *Le sommeil et les rêves*. Three things struck me. Maury's dreams are on the whole jejune compared with the wealth of inspiration that typifies Freud's (this almost certainly has something to do with the fact that Maury strives to relate his dreams to minor details of everyday life, whereas Freud's quest for his own desire through the prism of his dreams results in dreams where the voice of desire can be heard). Maury suffers from moralising prejudice, and accordingly believes that only the dreams of madmen or those on the brink of madness realise man's basest instincts (rape, incest, murder); this contrasts strongly with Freud's great openness of mind. And Maury is also intellectually prejudiced: he holds that the psychological faculties function sometimes in a noble mode (when the intelligence is in action, for example), and sometimes in an enfeebled mode (as when dreams are taking place) – a prejudice later espoused, with variations, by Bergson and Janet. Freud, on the other hand, achieved an almost Copernican revolution by demonstrating that what was involved was not two levels of a single function but two different organisations of thought.[1]

When Freud began to investigate his own dreams, he did not work within the intellectualist or spiritualist parameters commonly used by psychologists at that time. His point of reference was Romanticism. As we saw in the last chapter, the German Romantics were fascinated by magnetism and multiple personality. Hand in hand with this went an interest in dreams, another channel for making contact with the spiritual world. But when scientific research into dreams began in about 1850 it dissociated itself from the literary and mystical exploitation of the theme by the Romantics (see E 303–11).

Volkelt (1875) argued that during dreaming the soul does not, as the Romantics believed, escape from the body, but depends more directly on it. Strümpell (1874) provided new answers – which seem obvious to us today – to several of the traditional questions about dreams. Here are a couple of examples. When we are awake, we are able to attribute events taking place in our mind either to the past or to the present. But we can no longer do so when dreaming, hence our tendency to see dreams as having some significance for the future. Why does the dreamer believe his dream to be real? Because he constructs a 'dream space' in which sensations and

1. Pathological dreams 'do not merely lay bare our vices and our hidden tendencies, but [. . .] stem from an excitement of tendencies which in the waking state remain very restrained.' (Maury, 1861, p. 28). When dreaming, man 'becomes the plaything of all the passions that are forbidden to him, in his waking state, by his conscience, sense of honour, and fear' (*ibid.*). Those interested in pursuing the matter further should compare Maury's comments on his dream about the death of his father with Freud's analysis of dreams he had when mourning his father, such as 'Close the eyes' and 'Father on his death-bed like Garibaldi'.

memories are projected, and which gives the impression of true perception because the sleeper cannot distinguish between objective and subjective reality.

The connection between dreams and the body was pursued in two directions. Speculation that sensations of organic origin affected dreams led Maury to devise the following experiment: while he was asleep his assistant would make a noise or sprinkle perfume; when Maury awoke, he recorded the effects of the stimulation on his dreams. Scherner, on the other hand, interpreted dream images as representations of the dreamer's mental state. He put forward the theory that light or dark in dreams was related to the degree of clarity or imprecision in thoughts and feelings. He believed there to be one basic dream symbol, the image of a house, which represented the whole body, and whose rooms corresponded to its various parts. The male and female sex organs both had their own sets of symbols. While Maury's book was a great success, running into several editions and triggering off a spate of experimental research into dreams, Scherner's work went unrecognised until Freud quite rightly acknowledged him as his precursor in the field of dream symbolism.[1] The results obtained by Scherner were too far ahead of their time, while the hazy, Romantic-cum-metaphysical trappings he gave them seemed old-fashioned (the dream, he wrote, speaks to the soul 'like a lover to his beloved'!).

A phenomenon cannot be established as a fact unless some method of studying it is available. The development of techniques to study one's own dreams was one of the great contributions of the second half of the 19th century. The French investigators, Maury and Hervey de Saint-Denis, played a decisive role in that achievement. They showed that, with training, and with a prepared sheet of paper at hand when one goes to sleep, it is possible to observe and remember dreams – and even to awake and write them down – whenever they occur. They also demonstrated that certain dreams can be triggered off either intentionally (Hervey de Saint-Denis) or as a result of stimulation activated by an assistant (Maury).[2]

The Marquis Hervey de Saint-Denis (1823–92) taught Chinese at the Collège de France in Paris. His book *Les rêves et les moyens de les diriger*, published anonymously in 1867, is entirely devoted to his own dreams. He had been systematically writing them down since the age of 13, filling

1. The immediate influence of Scherner's views was on theories of aesthetics, not on psychology: Robert and Friedrich Theodor Vischer drew a parallel between his symbolism of the body in dreams and architectural symbolism in ancient Egypt and India, and showed that temples were conceived by those civilisations as representations of the human body.

2. Maury and Hervey de Saint-Denis were later claimed by the surrealists to be the precursors of the dream's active involvement in literary creation. The two men are discussed by Alexandrian (1974) at the beginning of his book *Les surréalistes et le rêve*.

twenty-two notebooks with the visions of no less than 1,946 nights, and in some cases including drawings. His aim was to achieve complete mastery of his dreams (a dream of omnipotence over dreams – in other words, a classical obsessional defence mechanism against the upsurge of desire). Hervey de Saint-Denis describes the four stages he went through in order to master his dreams. First he became aware, while sleeping, that he was dreaming. Then he succeeded in waking up at will to jot down interesting dreams. After that, he acquired the ability, while dreaming, to concentrate on any part of the dream he wished to explore more deeply. Lastly, he managed to direct his dreams the way he wanted to, though there were certain limitations. For example, wishing to dream about his own death, he directed his dream to take him up a tower so he could throw himself off the top. But at that point the dream suddenly shifted, and he found himself among the crowd watching a man fall from the top of the tower.

Hervey de Saint-Denis' technique was used by Robert Louis Stevenson, who called upon characters from his dreams – he called them 'brownies' – to help him write his books. He got the idea for *Dr. Jekyll and Mr. Hyde* from a feverish dream that he had after suffering a haemorrhage. The technique also inspired other novels, such as *De Nachtbruid* (*The Bride of Dreams*) by the Dutch poet and psychiatrist Frederik van Eeden (1909), which describes how he meets demon personalities in his dreams, and George du Maurier's *Peter Ibbetson* (1891), in which two lovers, who are separated, manage to meet every night in their dreams and together explore their childhood, the world of their ancestors, and past centuries.

Hervey de Saint-Denis' conclusions frequently anticipate those of Freud (who, as has already been said, was unable to get hold of his book, though he did read accounts of it). He contends that, in dreams, *clichés-souvenirs* (snapshot memories) which the subject thinks he has forgotten are reproduced; that the creative imagination continues to function and even to solve problems; and that phenomena occur which he calls 'abstraction' and 'superimposition' (and which are similar to what Freud later termed displacement and condensation).

According to the German writer Hildebrandt (1876), dreams can fulfil four roles: they can comfort us with the beauty of their images, warn us of immoral tendencies, which are given a magnified image in dreams, give us clear insight into things we perceived only hazily the day before, and announce certain organic diseases at their outset. Another German, Robert (1886), showed that the aim of 'dream-work' (a term later borrowed by Freud) was to rid our mind of images that burden it.

Thus it can be seen that dreams were central to psychological, medical and literary investigations towards the end of the nineteenth century.

Although Freud had not made a thorough survey of existing literature on the subject, he must have been aware of its importance and known that it was possible to observe one's own dreams scientifically. At the same time, the great originality of Freud can be gauged from the way he reversed the existing epistemological approach, associating dreams with internal, not external, stimuli, and studying his own dreams not in order to master them, but to let them give voice to the wish.

In July 1895, Freud left with his family to spend the first part of his holidays in rented accommodation apparently adjoining the former Hotel Bellevue on a pleasantly verdant wooded hill near the Kahlenberg overlooking Vienna (today the Bellevue has been replaced by other buildings – an engraving showing how it originally looked is reproduced in Grinstein (G 64a) – but the location is still much sought after). Now that Freud had broken with Breuer and found a valuable confidant in the person of Fliess, he was anxious to plough ahead. He wanted to do further work on the notion of 'defence', which he saw as the unifying element of the neuropsychoses, and to complement his first paper on the subject (1894*a*) with a new publication (1896*b*). In April and May he had embarked on the more ambitious task of trying to work out a general psychological theory that would combine normal psychology, the dynamics of the nervous system, and neurotic mechanisms; but the difficulty of the subject, his swelling practice, and the demands of occasional publications (1895*e*, 1895*f*) prevented him from making headway. He longed for a little peace and quiet to sort out all those matters. And Freud's mind was also exercised by the question of dreams: were the dreams of normal subjects like himself any different from those of the sick? Were only the dreams of the sick wish-fulfilments? Or were his own as well? As often happens with someone who puts a lot of effort into questions that are as yet unsolved, the beginnings of an answer appeared to him one night in a dream.

The dream of 'Irma's injection' (July 24, 1895)

THE ANTECEDENTS OF THE DREAM

The day's residues on which this so-called 'specimen' dream was based were extremely diverse. Freud applied the technique of free associations to every sentence, and fragment of sentence, contained in it; he also described most of those associations, whereas his method in subsequent dreams was less systematic. There was another reason for this: the dream, which Freud hoped would help him bring into focus the scientific questions involved in dreams, normal psychology and neurosis, in fact exceeded his preconscious expectations and made him see himself in focus. It passed in review every area of his life and featured many of the personalities, events, situations and ideas I discussed in the first chapter. Freud, fragmented into disparate pieces, was searching for his true unity. The system of identifications that had governed him up to then crumbled away. So far, his life had been dominated by the wishes of others. During that night of July 23–24, 1895, his dream questioned him about his own wishes.

It should be remembered that Freud was not solely preoccupied by his scientific work. He was anxious about his health, his job and his family. His comments on the dream mainly highlight worries of a medical nature. In the days leading up to the dream he had received several unpleasant pieces of news. A patient whose swelling of the nasal mucous membrane he had treated – on Fliess's advice – with applications of cocaine had developed necrosis. A hysteric whom he had allowed to go off to Egypt had an attack there that was diagnosed by an ignorant doctor as dysentery. The news from his half-brother Emanuel in Manchester and from his friend Fliess in Berlin was no better: arthritis had given Emanuel a limp, and Fliess, though a nose specialist, was suffering from a suppurative nasal infection. The very day before Freud had the dream, yet more bad news arrived. He met the son of an old lady to whom he had been giving injections twice a day (she later played a role in the discovery of the Oedipus complex), and learned she had had an attack of phlebitis while on holiday, probably caused by a dirty syringe (she was being treated by another doctor at the time). Finally, he had been visited by his assistant and friend, Dr Oscar Rie (Otto in Freud's dream), who was also the family paediatrician. Otto, then a bachelor (he married one of Fliess's sisters in 1896), had the habit – which irritated Freud – of bringing presents. On this occasion, his choice of gift was particularly unfortunate: a bottle of pineapple liqueur, with the word 'Ananas' on it, which had gone off, smelled bad (of amyl) and had to be thrown away. Otto irritated Freud even more by telling him about a young hysteric whom Freud had recently treated (and whom he gave the pseudonym of Irma); when treatment had been broken off because of the summer holidays, the patient had disagreed with Freud over the solution he was offering her. Otto had seen her and thought her to be incompletely cured. Freud took the remark as a slight. That evening, he wrote a report on the case of Irma for Breuer (the Dr. M. of the dream) in order to vindicate himself. Working late, Freud suffered a fresh bout of the rheumatism that affected his left shoulder. To crown everything, Irma, as a friend of the family, was invited to the party the Freuds were to give three days later for Martha's 34th birthday. The rest of the day was taken up with preparations for the party.

Freud was aware of the complexities involved in the doctor–patient relationship and of the repercussions they can have on the doctor's state of mind: 'During the summer of 1895 I had been giving psychoanalytic treatment to a young lady [Irma] who was on very friendly terms with me and my family. It will be readily understood that a mixed relationship such as this may be a source of many disturbed feelings in a physician and particularly in a psychotherapist. While the physician's personal interest is greater, his authority is less; any failure would bring a threat to the old-established friendship with the patient's family' (*ID* 106).

Freud is less forthcoming on his family worries. He alludes, in a note (*ID* 110), to the fact that his wife suffered from pains in the abdomen, and he intentionally brings his analysis of the dream to a close at the point where he remembers the thrombosis that affected Martha during one of her pregnancies (*ID* 118). The correspondence with Fliess throws more light on the matter. As I have already pointed out, Martha was expecting her sixth child at the end of the year. Freud gave Fliess the news on May 25 (cf. p. 113). It will be remembered that Fliess had focussed his research on the sexual cycle – 23 days in males and 28 in females – and that he was hoping to use that observation to determine the periods when conception was unlikely. During their last meeting but one, in Munich (where Fliess was receiving treatment) in the summer of 1894, they had discussed sexual chemistry. Fliess had drawn Freud's attention to the important role he believed was played by a substance like trimethylamin. Moreover, Fliess, an ear, nose and throat specialist, was convinced that there was a connection between certain nose complaints and sexual dysfunctions. Freud often suffered from worrying sores on the turbinal bones of his nose, which Fliess had already cauterised in February 1895 in Vienna, and which Freud treated with local applications of cocaine, again on the advice of his friend. The fact remains that Freud was not exactly overjoyed at Martha's sixth pregnancy. Perhaps he felt that he had enough responsibilities as it was with five children, on top of parents and sisters, to look after (*F* 135). Or else he thought that another pregnancy would not be good for Martha, who, in addition to looking after a large household, was already tired after her many babies (*F* 86). And, as it turned out, the progress report of Martha's pregnancy that Freud gave Fliess during the coming months was not invariably good (August 16, September 23, October 31, and November 8).

Freud was also wondering what to call the child. In a letter dated October 20, 1895, he assumed that Fliess would have no objection to his calling it Wilhelm if it was a boy. 'If *he* turns out to be a girl, *she* will be called Anna' (*F* 147). The choice of the name Anna was in honour of one of Hammerschlag's daughters, who married Rudolf Lichtheim in 1885 – and was widowed a year later.[1] According to Jones (J I, 245), Anna Hammerschlag was 'a favourite patient of Freud's'. Like Irma, then, she was at once a family friend, a widow, and one of Freud's patients. So it is tempting to conjecture that the Irma of the dream was in fact Anna Hammerschlag-Lichtheim. This would seem to be confirmed by a note added by Freud (*ID* 115 n.1): 'The sound of the word "Ananas" bears a remarkable resemblance to that of my patient Irma's family name.' It would have been quite normal for Freud, in a case history, to cover his tracks by writing 'family name' instead of 'first name'. However that may be, the Irma dream reproduces the kind of atmosphere which surrounded the birth of Anna Freud and which, in my view, had a decisive effect on her development. Anna was also the first name of one of Freud's sisters, the first to be born after him, whom he did not like and who had since married Martha's brother, Eli Bernays, and emigrated to New York.

In Freud's very closely-knit Jewish milieu, doctor–patient relationships were frequently complicated by ties of friendship. For example, Ida Bondy, who married Wilhelm Fliess, was a former patient of Breuer's. Like Martha, she was pregnant – for the first time after three years of marriage. Fliess announced the news in reply to a letter in which Freud told him that his own wife was expecting a sixth – and unplanned – child. Unlike Martha, Ida came from a wealthy family. In his comments on the dream, Freud makes no mention of all this, nor does he make any reference to Anna O., though she was clearly present in his thoughts. As we have already seen, Mathilde Breuer became jealous, in 1882, of this young hysteric whom her husband had been visiting twice a day for many months. And when Anna made an indirect declaration of love to her doctor by displaying the symptoms of a phantom pregnancy and hysterical childbirth, Breuer took fright and broke off his treatment. Bertha Pappenheim (Anna O.'s real name) was an old friend of Martha's; in 1895 they still saw each other and were long to continue doing so. When describing

1. Was this the same Lichtheim as the professor of neurology in Breslau who, with Carl Wernicke (himself a professor at the Universities of Vienna and Breslau), put forward a theory of aphasia that was later criticised by Freud in his book on the subject (1891*b*)? A passage from one of his letters to Martha from Berlin (March 19, 1886) suggests that this might have been so: 'I had a letter from L. in Breslau asking me to look up his sister-in-law and a *Sanitätsrat* [member of the board of health] who is also related to him.' The editors add the following note: 'Presumably Rudolf Lichtheim, Hammerschlag's son-in-law' (*L* 225). I am not convinced of this. Lichtheim is rather a common German name, and there is no reason to doubt, unless more conclusive evidence emerges to the contrary, that Lichtheim the neurologist and Anna Hammerschlag's husband were simply two different people with the same name.

Freud's private life between 1901 and 1909, Jones writes that on Sunday afternoons 'Frau Professor had her visitors, Anna Lichtheim, Bertha Hammerschlag, Frau Professor Königstein, the Rosanes couple, etc., and if it was anyone in whom Freud was interested he would drop into the drawing-room for a few minutes' (J II, 429). Anna O. was possibly invited to Martha's birthday party, which Freud anticipated in his dream. In any case she knew Anna Lichtheim, who was certainly invited. Anna L. must have reminded Freud of Anna O: they were friends and both suffered from hysterical symptoms; the first name of one of them was the pseudonym of the other; and while Anna Lichtheim was a widow in real life, Anna O. was the symbolic widow of Breuer.

Freud's comments dwell particularly on an intimate friend of Irma's, who at one point in the dream replaces Irma, and who was examined by Breuer for false diphtheritic membranes. Freud suspected that she suffered from hysterical choking. He liked her very much and would have been pleased to have her as a patient. She was probably yet another of the young widows in Freud's immediate entourage.

The other characters in the dream are easy to identify. The dead friend who misused cocaine is Fleischl. The other friend, who mentions trimethylamin, is Fliess, whose name has a certain assonance with Fleischl. Otto and Leopold are two paediatricians, Oscar Rie and Ludwig Rosenberg, who were Freud's assistants at the Kassowitz Institute for Children's Diseases. The latter had married a sister of the former. Every Saturday evening, the three men went round to the home of the ophthalmologist Leopold Königstein for a game of tarot. It may even be surmised that when Otto visited the Freuds on July 23 he examined Martha, who did not wish to be treated by her husband, and found her in poor health.

The dream occurred, says Freud, in the early hours of July 24, 1895.

TEXT OF THE DREAM AND FIRST INTERPRETATION

'A large hall – numerous guests, whom we were receiving. – Among them was Irma. I at once took her on one side, as though to answer her letter and to reproach her for not having accepted my "solution" yet. I said to her: "If you still get pains, it's really only your fault." She replied: "If you only knew what pains I've got now in my throat and stomach and abdomen – it's choking me" – I was alarmed and looked at her. She looked pale and puffy. I thought to myself that after all I must be missing some organic trouble. I took her to the window and looked down her throat, and she showed signs of recalcitrance, like women with artificial dentures. I thought to myself that there was really no need for her to do that. – She then opened her mouth properly and on the right I found a big white patch; at another place I saw extensive whitish grey scabs upon some remarkable curly structures which were evidently modelled on the turbinal bones of the

nose. – I at once called in Dr. M., and he repeated the examination and confirmed it . . . Dr. M. looked quite different from usual; he was very pale, he walked with a limp and his chin was clean-shaven . . . My friend Otto was now standing beside her as well, and my friend Leopold was percussing her through her bodice and saying: "She has a dull area low down on the left." He also indicated that a portion of the skin on the left shoulder was infiltrated. (I noticed this, just as he did, in spite of her dress.) . . . M. said: "There's no doubt it's an infection, but no matter; dysentery will supervene and the toxin will be eliminated." . . . We were directly aware, too, of the origin of the infection. Not long before, when she was feeling unwell, my friend Otto had given her an injection of a preparation of propyl, propyls . . . propionic acid . . . trimethylamin (and I saw before me the formula for this printed in heavy type). . . . Injections of that sort ought not to be made so thoughtlessly. . . . And probably the syringe had not been clean' (*ID* 107).

Before carrying out a detailed examination of this dream, let me give my general impressions. The scenario of the dream seems to consist of two phases: first, a tête-à-tête conversation with Irma, where there is intense heterosexual attraction, and where the desire to observe – to observe the mystery of conception – is satisfied; then a discussion between men where the desire for knowledge is realised in the form of a search for causes. The unity of the dream resides in its description and explanation of sexuality. The 'hall' with its guests and Irma's 'throat' represent the female genital organs; it 'opened properly' and made 'receiving' possible – an image of coitus. A diagnosis of Irma's symptoms – she is 'choking', 'pale and puffy', suffering from 'pains' in her 'abdomen' and 'some organic trouble' – would strongly suggest pregnancy. The 'extensive whitish grey scabs' on 'some curly structures' are traces of sperm and represent impregnation. The phrase 'the toxin will be eliminated' contains an allusion to the miscarriage that Freud must have to some extent hoped for when he got the unexpected news that his wife was pregnant again. According to Fliess, 'trimethylamin' was a key ingredient of sexual chemistry; similarly, the examination of Irma's 'turbinal bones' was a kind of tribute paid by the dreamer to another of Fliess's theories, which postulated a connection between the nose and sex. As for the end of the dream and the moral of the tale – the 'injections' made 'so thoughtlessly' with a 'syringe' that 'had not been clean' – they refer to the need to resort to contraceptive techniques.

But this preliminary interpretation of the dream does not explain the discussion between Drs M., Otto and Leopold or the localisation of the 'dull area' on Irma's 'left shoulder'. What we have here is another medical examination, which actually took place sixteen months earlier: Freud was the patient, not the practitioner; he was suffering from heart trouble; and Breuer and Fliess made very different diagnoses. Thus the dreamer was doubly present in his dream, both as the theoretician of the sexual aetiology of neuroses and as a patient suffering from a possibly fatal cardiac complaint. He may even be said to have been triply present, for the investigation of sex and the auscultation of the heart represent rather accurately the self-analysis that Freud had been intending to carry out for some time using one of his dreams – in fact this very one.

FREUD'S COMMENTS AND INTERPRETATION

Few dreams have been the subject of so much comment. First there are Freud's own observations, which take up thirteen pages immediately following the text of the dream (*ID* 108–21), then fill eleven more pages at ten other points in the book (in Chapter 4, 'Distortion in Dreams': *ID* 136 and 140; in Chapter 5, Section A, 'Recent and Indifferent Material in Dreams': *ID* 165 and 173; in Chapter 6, Section A, 'The Work of Condensation': *ID* 292–5; in Section B, 'The Work of Displacement': *ID* 306; and in Section C, 'The Means of Representation': *ID* 314, 316 and 322; and finally in Chapter 7, Section A, 'The Forgetting of Dreams': *ID* 513). The dream has been examined by psychoanalysts such as Erik H. Erikson (1954), H. G. Leavitt (1956), and I. Berenstein (1974). Max Schur (1966, and in S, Chapter 3) throws light on one meaning of the dream by revealing the episode of Emma, who was being treated by both Freud and Fliess (I shall return to this episode later on). Alexander Grinstein (1980) devotes the first chapter of his book to the dream. His contribution to the subject focusses on Freud's likening of the Otto-Leopold pair to bailiff Bräsig and his friend Karl, two characters in Fritz Reuter's celebrated novel, *Ut mine Stromtid (An Old Story of My Farming Days)*, written in 1864 in Mecklenburg dialect.[1] A close reading of the novel by Grinstein leads him to the conclusion that it has an Oedipal structure; and he surmises that the dream has an underlying structure of the same nature. I find this extrapolation debatable, for it overlooks the long process of meditation and working-through that Freud needed to undergo, between July 1895 and October 1897, before he could succeed in recognising his own Oedipus complex. In any case, surely it must be possible, with a little determination, to detect an Oedipal problematic in virtually any dream?

Let me summarise the initial thirteen pages of Freud's comments. On first reading, the analysis of his dream seems a trifle untidy, probably because of the way it is fragmented by the systematic use of free associations. But it is in fact remarkably well structured, and unfolds like a play,

1. Fritz Reuter (1810–74) rose to fame by writing the first literary work in the Low German dialect, *Plattdeutsch*. Freud suggested to Martha that she read the book, in a letter of April 19, 1884 (*L* 122).

with the characters being introduced in the early acts and the dénouement coming in the last.

The female characters are the first to come on stage (*ID* 108–11). The most important among them are the three recalcitrant patients, Irma, her friend, and Martha, while the governess with false teeth plays only a minor role. Freud's feelings during this first act are embarrassment (at having to carry out a medical examination on a woman), annoyance (because they will not let him treat them), and fear. The second act brings on the male characters. First, there is a disturbing trio consisting of Fleischl, Breuer and Emanuel (*ID* 111–2). All of them Freud's seniors, they stand in permanent accusation against him: he had hastened the death of the first with cocaine; the second had witnessed his errors of diagnosis and treatment; as for his half-brother, about whom Freud says nothing here, a later part of the self-analysis reveals Freud's resentment of him. The act comes to an end with three other women bursting in on stage: the patient incorrectly treated with cocaine; another woman patient, called Mathilde, whom Freud had accidentally killed with sulphonal; and Freud's eldest daughter, also called Mathilde, who had almost died of diphtheria. At this point, Freud's feeling of anxiety turns into one of inescapable guilt. What is more, the human figures are no longer alone. Other elements – diseases, substances that cure or kill, and Death itself – have made their appearance.

The third act (*ID* 112–5) introduces two members of a new male trio, Otto and Leopold (the third person is being kept for the next act). This time they are Freud's alter egos, both up-and-coming physicians the same age as him. Berenstein (1974) points out that in the choice of the pseudonym Leopold there is a latent allusion to the Jewish quarter of Leopoldstadt, where Freud's parents settled on arriving in Vienna. He also stresses the way the dream contrasts the two characters: Otto is less prudent, less meticulous, and hastier than Leopold. They are accompanied by a minor trio made up of a child in the Kassowitz Institute, the patient in Egypt with dysentery, and a patient of Breuer's whose urine contained albumen. Here the drama reaches its climax, and there is a turning point in the trial – for trial it undoubtedly is. The first act begins with a defence speech by Freud ('It is not my fault, but Irma's') and ends with his feeling afraid. In the second act, Freud stands accused by overwhelming evidence. In the third, that evidence is demolished by witnesses and lawyers. The question that lies at the heart of the tragedy, or the investigation, is now openly posed: who is responsible? The next act (*ID* 115–7) provides the dénouement, at Fliess's instigation: everything can be accounted for by the injection of trimethylamin. Injections are always risky: they were responsible for Fleischl's poisoning; Otto gives too many injections, and had brought as a gift an evil-smelling pineapple liqueur. But a conclusive explanation is to be found in trimethylamin. Irma's complaint has been caused by her frustrated sex life. It is Freud who is right, despite his detractors, when he advocates the sexual aetiology of neuroses. The merry-go-round of cocaine, sulphonal, amyl and propyl has jolted to a halt: Freud has found the formula he was looking for. There remains the epilogue. As if following the rules of classical drama, it shows the main protagonists involved in the consequences of the solution. Fliess will treat Irma. We see the three men in whose eyes Freud has vindicated himself – Fleischl, Otto, and the son of the old lady with phlebitis. In none of these cases had Freud's syringe been responsible. The old lady reminds Freud of three women, Martha, Irma and Mathilde, who are connected by the theme of pregnancy. At this point, Freud breaks off his commentary, but adds: 'It will be understood that I have not reported everything that occurred to me during the process of interpretation' (*ID* 118 n.2). We can however infer its ending. Freud now feels fully responsible not only for his work but for the living being that Martha is about to bring into the world. This is not a case of a thoughtless trimethylamin injection. The furies who desire the death of that child as the price to be paid for the misdeeds of the father will not get the better of him. They have been warded off by the formula of life which Freud has discovered, and which he sees printed in bold type. The child will be Wilhelm or Anna.

This dream has a very precise meaning for Freud, which he passes on to us while at the same time hinting at other possible meanings: it shows that he is not responsible for Irma's continuing illness. He throws the accusation back at Otto, who irritated him with his remarks and his presents: as always, Otto has shown bias and thoughtlessness. In any case, there are many other plausible reasons for the persistence of her complaint: Irma has rejected the solution that Freud suggested to her; or maybe her present pains are organic and not hysterical; or maybe they have been caused by a lack of trimethylamin, i.e. sexual satisfaction, to which she has been condemned by widowhood; or maybe, yet again, Otto's unfortunate intervention was responsible for everything. The dream, then, is an arena where Freud pleads his cause to three understanding people (Leopold, Irma's friend, and Fliess) against three opponents (Otto, Irma and Breuer). This is the meaning of the dream if Irma's illness is regarded as its main content.

Freud hinted at other possible interpretations connected with his fear of death or his counter-transference. But he discarded them in favour of a more essential conclusion: 'For the moment I am satisfied with the achievement of this one piece of fresh knowledge. If we adopt the method of interpreting dreams which I have indicated here, we shall find that dreams really have a meaning and are far from being the expression of a fragmentary activity of the brain, as the authorities have claimed. *When the work of interpretation has been completed, we perceive that a dream is the fulfilment of a wish*' (*ID* 121). Here we yet again see the vital relationship between Freud and his work. Freud was wondering whether dreams were really wish fulfilments. The Irma dream confirmed that hypothesis for him. Furthermore, Freud noted subsequently that thoughts which follow on from dreams are still dream-thoughts. So the thought that dreams are wish fulfilments is an integral part of the dream content.

OTHER INTERPRETATIONS

1. *Relative to people in Freud's immediate milieu*

Freud's interpretation of his dream is by no means exhaustive. When offering that interpretation to his readers, he deliberately confines himself to his professional life. Moreover, the emphasis he puts on his own guilt feelings is important to him, for it constitutes his first self-analytic discovery about himself and is the common denominator of his counter-transference on to his patients, his embarrassment vis-à-vis his wife, his dependence on Fliess, his independence from Breuer, and his anxiety about being cardiac. But many other mutually complementary interpretations should also be taken into consideration. Let us first look briefly at those which involve Freud's relationship with important people in his professional and family milieu.

As regards Freud's counter-transference on to his young and hysterical female patients as symbolised by Irma, the wish fulfilled in the dream is the desire not to behave towards Anna L. (always supposing that my identification of Anna Lichtheim as Irma is correct) in the same way that Breuer behaved towards Anna O.: in other words, not to remain blind and therefore insensitive to the unconscious desire transferred on to the therapist by such young women or young widows – manifestly the desire to have a child by their own father; and not to let himself be swayed by that incestuous desire or by the temptation to satisfy it in real life (this is one of the few passages in the dream that hints at the imminent discovery of the Oedipus complex), when his patients relate how they were seduced, on reaching puberty, by their father or by his substitute. For in the dream Freud carries out a thorough examination of Irma's sexuality and sees in her an image – later he would have called it a phantasy – not only of coitus and pregnancy but, most of all, of conception; he also criticises a form of treatment that involves giving Irma just what she desires in her phantasy, a 'thoughtlessly' made 'injection'. Hence, too, the dream's criticism of Breuer: 'He [Dr. M.] was very pale, he walked with a limp and his chin was clean-shaven.' I interpret this to mean: he is lily-livered, his reasoning is unsound, and he is a greenhorn.

As regards his wife, Freud felt guilty about her new and unwanted pregnancy, which was bound to be an ordeal for her and might even endanger her health. He blamed himself for being careless in his application of contraceptive techniques ('The syringe had not been clean'). The dream brought back to him the conclusion he had eventually had to face three or four months earlier: Martha's symptoms were not hysterical but organic, they were symptoms of pregnancy. As André Berge has pointed out, the wish that is fulfilled in the dream is that of a miscarriage ('The toxin will be eliminated'), which would have brought the unfortunate pregnancy to a timely end.

As regards Fliess, the dream pays tribute to his ideas. It uses one of those ideas (that there is a connection between the nose and sex) as a framework in which to represent the latent content – a gynaecological examination – in a manifest content consisting of an examination of the nose and throat. The dream expresses Freud's wish to occupy as eminent a position in his speciality (the sexual aetiology of neuroses) as Fliess did in his own (the ear, nose and throat). Fliess's second major theory – that men and women are subject to different periodic phenomena regulated by the body's biochemistry – is introduced into the dream by trimethylamin, a substance which, Fliess believed, held the key to that system of regulation. Freud longed to make discoveries in psychology that could rank alongside those being made by Fliess in biology. He wanted to be Fliess and no one else but Fliess. The dream fulfils Freud's wish to espouse Fliess's views totally, to attribute great discoveries to him, and to identify with him.

At the same time, the dream is full of ambivalence – to use a term subsequently adopted by Freud – towards the very same Fliess. He had bungled his operation on Emma, one of Freud's patients (I shall describe the incident in detail later on). He had made his own wife pregnant, after claiming he was on the point of revolutionising contraceptive techniques by using his theory of periods to work out the days when women are fertile. It would seem likely that the examination of Irma is a disguise for Freud's latent desire to auscultate Ida Fliess, his friend's young wife and Breuer's former patient, whom he must have known before she got married. In this way Freud can get his revenge on the friend that made her pregnant; he has her as his patient, he is psychoanalysing her, he tries to see the child she is bearing in her womb – yet another hint of the Oedipal nature of Freud's 'transference' on to Fliess and an anticipation of his coming discovery. Both of Fliess's blunders, involving Emma and Ida respectively, are excused by Freud: his idealisation of Fliess must not be damaged by the intrusion of grievances.

Why should this be so? The dream reenacts another medical scene, which took place a few months earlier, in February, when Fliess visited Vienna. During that trip, not only did he perform his unfortunate operation on Emma, but he cauterised Freud's turbinal bones. Another cauterisation session was due to take place in Berlin when Freud returned from his planned tour of northern Italy. When looked at from that angle, the Irma of the dream becomes Freud himself: he fulfils his wish to be treated by his friend, an omnipotent healer. Here again, there are hints of ambivalence. Freud was by then of the opinion that Breuer's diagnosis of his cardiac episode the previous summer was more accurate than Fliess's; disregarding the latter's opinion, Freud had begun to smoke his much-loved cigars once again, and, far from suffering any harmful effects, found them a useful stimulant. But in the dream the correct diagnosis proposed by Dr M. (Breuer) – 'a dull area low down on the left' – is immediately counterbalanced by the appearance of Fliess's magic formula that explains the whole question of sexuality – the formula of trimethylamin. Freud's underlying infantile wish is to be cured by Fliess as though by an omnipotent, good mother. I shall now discuss a number of existing interpretations in more detail and suggest some new ones.

2. *Relative to Fliess and the Emma episode*

Freud and Fliess both had nose complaints, respectively empyema of the sinuses and suppurative rhinitis. In their letters they discussed the state of health of their noses at self-indulgent length. Thus on May 25, 1895, Freud wrote: 'Now, to my ideas about the nose. I discharged exceedingly ample amounts of pus and all the while felt splendid; now the secretion has nearly dried up and I am still feeling very well' (*F* 130). They were, so to speak, bound together by their noses, a bond made all the stronger by cocaine: Freud revealed the substance to medicine, and only just failed to discover its anaesthetic properties; Fliess urged his patients, Freud's patients and Freud himself to undergo treatment of the affected parts of the nose with a local application of cocaine. This came as sweet revenge to Freud, who had been so fiercely criticised for causing a new form of drug addiction. But strong admonishment, too, is contained in the penultimate sentence of the dream: 'Injections of that sort ought not to be made so thoughtlessly.' This is an allusion to the hypodermic injections of cocaine that turned Fleischl into a drug addict. Freud's nose, alas, did not heal, nor did Fliess's. Indeed,

Fliess was forced to cancel one of their 'congresses' so he could have an operation. No matter, Freud's trust in him remained undiminished.

The incident that first began to shake that trust was unearthed by Schur (1966 and 1972) in some of Freud's then still unpublished letters to Fliess. In February 1895, Freud started treating an apparently hysterical young woman called Emma.[1] He asked Fliess to examine her to see if her abdominal symptoms were of nasal origin. During a brief trip to Vienna, Fliess saw Emma, advised on surgery, and carried out the operation himself; he also took the opportunity to examine Freud's nose and cauterise his turbinal bones. Fliess learned subsequently, from Freud's letters to him during March, that Emma's operation had not been a success. Emma had suffered persistent pain, fetid secretions and some bleeding. Freud first attributed her complaints to hysteria, but changed his mind and called in a specialist, who tried without success to improve the drainage of the wound. A second specialist, examining Emma at her home, then discovered that Fliess had inadvertently left a half-metre strip of iodoform gauze in the cavity. The extraction of the gauze caused the patient to suffer a severe haemorrhage and to go into shock until a new packing was inserted. Freud felt badly shaken (out of shame rather than at the sight of blood) and recovered only after leaving the room and drinking a glass of cognac. He hesitated a whole day before writing to tell Fliess about his faulty action. Emma's condition remained serious for some considerable time (further haemorrhages, danger of infection, and so on). Instead of admitting his mistake, Fliess was furious that his Viennese colleagues had suspected him of professional negligence and demanded a retraction. Freud hastened to quell his friend's indignation: 'For me you remain the physician, the type of man into whose hands one confidently puts one's life and that of one's family' (*F*, April 20, 1895, 125).

The scenario of the Irma dream reenacts the Emma episode. A doctor (who is Freud this time, not Fliess) examines Irma's throat, but he in fact describes what Fliess saw in Emma's nose (in real life Freud no more examined his patients' noses than he looked at Irma's throat). The doctor is accused of making a professional error of judgment by one or two other colleagues. He defends himself, denies the charge, counterattacks and finally succeeds in shifting the blame on to a third party. In other words, Freud was assuming responsibility for Fliess's error: he (Freud) was

1. This is probably the same Emma as the one whose case history is described in 'Project for a Scientific Psychology' (1950*a*; *SE* 1, 353–6) as an example of the hysterical 'first lie': she was unable to go into shops alone, because some shop assistants had laughed at her clothes when she was aged about 12. Analysis brought to light an earlier incident which occurred when she was eight: a shopkeeper had grabbed at her genitals through her clothes. Her 'bad conscience' was due to the fact that she had gone to the shop a second time and provoked the same reaction.

primarily to blame for the Emma episode because he had failed to make a sufficiently clear distinction between a hysterical and an organic symptom. The Irma dream was a post-traumatic act of repetition aimed at reparation. It harks back to the Emma incident so that the matter can be closed once and for all and any lurking doubts about Fliess's professional competence and moral honesty can be scotched. Dreams do indeed have a meaning: wish fulfilment. The Irma dream does, as Freud realised, fulfil one of his wishes – a wish to exonerate – but not in the way suggested by Freud: as Schur was the first to point out, it fulfils Freud's wish to exonerate Fliess.

The dream's bearing on Freud's relationship with Fliess does not reside merely in the Emma episode. As I have already mentioned, Freud had already had his turbinal bones cauterised by his friend and was due to go to Berlin for a further operation after his tour of northern Italy. In the dream, Freud sees himself as a patient who is examined and treated by Fliess. And by identifying with a woman (the patient Irma), he offers himself as an object of Fliess's desire. Now it so happens that this wish, which the dream fulfils, has been frustrated in real life. The dream says: 'I at once took [Irma] on one side, as though to answer her letter and to reproach her for not having accepted my "solution" yet.' This sentence should be understood as follows: Fliess no longer confides in me; he has not answered my last letter; I must write and chide him for not having approved my solution. Fliess had not replied to Freud's letter of June 12, 1895, which announced that despite his friend's repeated advice to the contrary he had started smoking again (*F* 132).

Understandably then, Freud wrote to Fliess on July 24, the day after his dream, to complain that his earlier letter had not been answered; he did not breathe a word, however, about the dream or the original way in which he had just begun to analyse it: 'Daimonie [Demon],[1] why don't you write? How are you? Don't you care at all any more about what I am doing? What is happening to the nose, menstruation, labour pains, neuroses, your dear wife, and the budding little one?[2] [. . .] Are we friends only in misfortune? Or do we also want to share the experiences of calm times with each other? Where will you spend the month of August? We are living very contentedly in Himmel' (*F* 134). The Bellevue, where the Freuds were staying, was located on Himmelstrasse (literally 'Heaven Street').

As I have already pointed out, Ida Fliess, like Martha, was pregnant –

1. Freud used to employ this term in the Socratic sense of an attendant spirit and source of inspiration.
2. This sentence manifestly summarises the dream that Freud had just had about Irma's injection.

an event that her husband's subtle contraceptive calculations had failed to forestall. On June 22, 1895 (*F* 133), Freud greeted the news with enthusiasm, and also announced his plans to visit Berlin early in September. I have already stressed the close complementarity of phantasies that existed between the two men, which resulted in their making their wives pregnant at the same time. The double child about to be born is in a sense their shared child: it is as if they had made it themselves, each through the intermediary of the other's wife. As Green has remarked (1972, p. 169): 'The allusion to pregnancy can even be seen as a way of making Freud's future work the offspring of the relationship between the two men.' In real life, Otto examines Martha, the pregnant wife of his friend Freud. In the dream, Freud examines Ida, the pregnant wife of his friend Fliess. The underlying question, which is related to Freud's childhood, is: who is the father?

3. *Relative to infantile wishes*

Although Freud was to restrict himself, for some time to come, to the notion that dreams fulfil the wishes of the day preceding the dream, the Irma dream also needs to be examined from the angle of infantile wishes.

Freud was born on May 6, 1856. His parents had married on July 29, 1855. In other words, he was conceived almost immediately. The dream occurred on the morning of July 24, 1895. Its manifest content portrays Martha's 34th birthday, which is to be celebrated on July 26; its latent content represents, in my view, the 40th anniversary of Sigmund's conception. In the dream, Freud imagines the scene that resulted in his birth. This is suggested by the German word for 'birthday', *Geburtsfest*, which literally means 'festival of birth'. The first sentence of the description of the dream also fits in with this interpretation: the 'large hall' is the female sexual cavity, and it is there that 'we were receiving' (in German, the verb *empfangen* has two meanings, 'to receive socially' and 'to conceive'). What is more, the venue of the reception, the Bellevue, is a name that must have been full of significance for Freud, who had a good understanding of French. On the analogy of the title of a famous paper later written by Freud, '"Ein Kind wird geschlagen"' ('"A Child Is Being Beaten"'; 1919*e*), the dream could well be called 'Ein Kind wird empfangen' ('A Child Is Being Conceived'). Berenstein (1974) sees the metaphor in the following terms: Freud and his wife 'conceive' lots of children, patients, and ideas.

The examination of the nose and throat is a gynaecological examination in disguise, a substitute for it. In the folds of flesh, in the pink cavities of the mother's vagina and uterus (a Latin word from the same root as the Greek ὑστέρα, from which the term hysteria is derived), there is a big white patch, the father's sperm. It is the kind of scene that may one day be protected from the risk of impregnation by Fliess's clever calculations. Meanwhile, it has been responsible for Martha's present pregnancy (her sixth), Ida Fliess's present pregnancy (her first), and the first pregnancy, forty years ago, of Amalie, whose difference in age from her husband Jacob was the same as that between Fliess and Emma and between Freud and Irma. The scene is a 'maculate conception'.

The rest of the dream represents the rest of that scene. The dreamer moves from amyl (whose unpleasant smell is paralleled by that of the sexual secretions) to propyl (propylaea, in Greek architecture, are an entrance; it is also a word given to the labia majora surrounding the vaginal orifice – cf. the 'large hall' at the beginning of the dream), then to propionic acid (which, as Erikson (1954) has pointed out, has a certain assonance with the word 'priapic'), and lastly to trimethylamin and its formula 'printed in heavy type' (sexual secretions print such type on the bedsheets). I would suggest that the formula $N\begin{array}{l}\diagup CH_3\\ -CH_3\\ \diagdown CH_3\end{array}$ neatly fits Freud's childhood in Freiberg. The three CH_3s match the three families making up the protogroup in Freiberg – three couples (the Zajícs, Emanuel Freud and his wife, and, more recently, Jacob and Amalie Freud) and their respective children. A family consists of a husband and a wife who enact the scene and thus produce the third term, the child. The three families, which are themselves triadic, all have one member who is a common denominator – the nurse, Monika Zajíc. So the formula provides Freud, temporarily, with an explanation of his origins. The infantile wish of the dream is the wish to find out where children come from.

Why, you may ask, does that particular infantile wish provide the dream content rather than one of the many other repressed wishes of childhood? Surely because it is particularly relevant to Freud's current situation. He knows that he must study himself if he is to make any headway in the study of an uncharted land, the unconscious. He has cast off his moorings. He must rely not on Brücke, Meynert, Charcot or Breuer, but on himself and himself alone. He is, in a sense, about to be born again, with Fliess acting as midwife. Following the example of Goethe and his hero Wilhelm Meister, Freud will accomplish his own *Bildung*. This imminent second birth cannot fail to evoke for him his first birth, which brought him into the world. Something tells him, after his origins have appeared in the dream, that like Bergotte in Proust's novel he has just 'taken off'. Moreover, the propylaea are not only an entrance but a triumphal arch. Freud was well acquainted with those of the Acropolis (he saw them for himself in 1904), and he had visited the Propylaea in Munich while Fliess talked to him about trimethylamin. He saw himself as a hero walking through that portico, which symbolised both the power and the glory; he had 'penetrated' the secret; everything had gone rather smoothly, except for a twinge of bad conscience that he was doing his best to shake off.

The story of the kettle referred to by Freud in his comments on the dream should, I believe, be approached from this angle: 'The whole plea – for the dream was nothing else – reminded one vividly of the defence put forward by the man who was charged by one of his neighbours with having given him back a borrowed kettle in a damaged condition. The defendant asserted first, that he had given it back undamaged; secondly, that the kettle had a hole in it when he borrowed it; and thirdly, that he had never borrowed a kettle from his neighbour at all' (*ID* 119–20). The story takes on a particular piquancy if the kettle is replaced by an object that its shape suggests, i.e. a woman's belly. The man accused of having 'borrowed' his neighbour's wife or daughter and of having returned her 'in a damaged condition' defends himself in three ways: no, I returned her undamaged; she already 'had a hole' in her; I did not lay a finger on her. When someone is the first to examine a new subject, does he not deflower it?

4. *Relative to Freud's work*

The Irma dream contains the symbolic representation of several elements that will form part, or already form part, of Freud's discovery.

A large hall – numerous guests, whom we were receiving. This is a figurative representation of the notion of the preconscious, which is just beginning to take shape in Freud's mind; there is an implicit guardian of the threshold as well as many identifications/projections, which are contained in it and which Freud decides to 'receive', in other words to recognise as such. This part of the dream fulfils Freud's wish to 'conceive' a new science.

To reproach [Irma] for not having accepted my 'solution' yet. The solution referred to here is 'psychical analysis' and the taking into account of sexuality which it entails, and which Breuer, who, incidentally, knows Irma well, has refused to accept. In an already mentioned letter of June 12, 1895, which Fliess did not answer, Freud also revealed that he was 'overflowing with new ideas', and that his 'theories on defence have made an important advance' (*F* 131). The dream expresses a worry: Breuer did not accept Freud's solution to the problem of the aetiology of hysteria; would Fliess, in turn, pour cold water on the solution that Freud was moving towards in his attempt to elaborate a general theory of the psychical apparatus?

The laryngeal-cum-gynaecological examination of Irma's throat is not only a figurative representation of Freud's ideas on the aetiological role of sexuality in hysteria, but also a reenactment of the original scene – another 'primal' scene – between Joseph Breuer and Anna O. The symptoms displayed by Anna O. (the pseudonym Breuer gave to Bertha Pappenheim) were those of imaginary pregnancy followed by phantom childbirth; in the dream, the symptoms displayed by Irma (the pseudonym Freud subsequently gave to a patient who was probably called Anna) are those of coitus followed by pregnancy (pains, a choking sensation, a 'puffy' look). This is a further argument in support of my contention as to the identity of Irma. It would also explain more satisfactorily why Freud intended to call his sixth child Anna 'if *he* turns out to be a girl': the name would symbolise the first major discovery – that of the meaning of dreams – made by her father with the help of the Anna–Irma figure. It would also make it easier to understand why Anna Freud was the only one of his children who became a psychoanalyst.

The scene where Irma's throat is examined is a figurative representation of:

– the 'fertile' discovery which Freud feels he is carrying in him like a child, whose gestation is laborious, but which he is now confident of bringing into the world;
– the certitude that hysterics have repressed ideas not only, like Anna O., of pregnancy and childbirth, but of every phase of coitus (before, during, after);
– Chrobak's prescription for the hysterical wife of an impotent husband: '*Rx Penis normalis dosim repetatur*' (Prescribe repeated doses of normal penis) (*SE* 14, 15);
– the method of free associations, with artificial suggestion or the pressure technique, in other words acceptance of resistance ('She showed signs of recalcitrance') and an invitation to the patient to speak freely ('She then opened her mouth properly').

The concluding tableau of the dream is a printed inscription. This feature, which recurs in many subsequent dreams, is interesting in the light of a remark in *Studies on Hysteria* (1895*d*, *SE* 2, 288): 'It was as though we were examining a dossier that had been kept in good order.' Memories we believe to be forgotten are recorded somewhere and, if the right technique is used, they can be retrieved. In the Irma dream, the recorded inscription is the formula for trimethylamin. Its ternary structure, when looked at from this fresh angle, can be seen to match the three types of neurone that Freud was about to use as a basis for his formula of the nervous apparatus. The formula $\phi\psi\omega$ appeared for the first time in a letter to Fliess written three weeks after the dream (*F* 135). The dream had set Freud thinking again, after a pause of two months, about a general theory of normal and pathological psychology. There is a hint of this already in his letter of August 6: 'It is bold but beautiful, as you will see' (*F* 135).

Moreover, the theory – a triad expanding into other triads – matches the formal construction of the dream, where figures mostly appear in sets of three. In other words, the dream contains a symbolic representation of its own structure. It is instructive to set out this part of Freud's self-analysis in abstract, formal terms, by arranging the most important figures revealed by it in a table according to their order of appearance and, to a certain extent, their hierarchical importance. It looks like this:

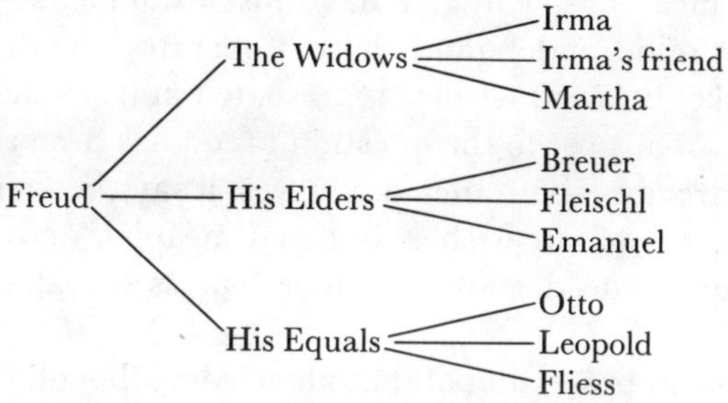

This arrangement produces the same pattern as the formula for trimethylamin when set out in full:[1]

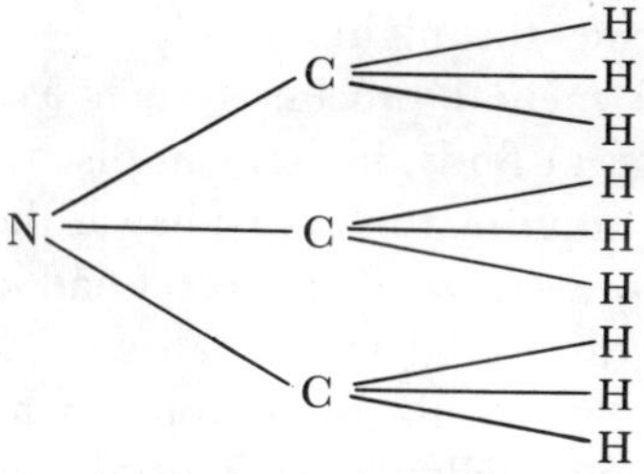

So it looks very much as though, in his dream, Freud realised that dreaming, far from being a disorganised activity as was generally believed, obeys a strict and secret pattern, of which the ternary structure is one illustration. Immediately before the mention of trimethylamin in the dream, there is an allusion to a common series in organic chemistry, in which each term is obtained from its predecessor according to a specific

1. Lacan first had the idea of comparing the ternary structures of the figures in the dream and of the formula for trimethylamin (Study Seminar on texts under the auspices of the Société Française de Psychanalyse, November 4, 1953, unpublished).

law of progression and whereby substitutions enable a transition to another series to be made. Here is the alcohol series:

Methyl	CH_3	CH_2	CH	
Ethyl	CH_3	CH_2	CH_2	OH
Propyl	CH_3	$(CH_2)_2$	CH_2	OH
Butyl	CH_3	$(CH_2)_3$	CH_2	OH
Amyl	CH_3	$(CH_2)_4$	CH_2	OH

A reaction between amyl and ammonia, NH_3, yields trimethylamin.

The dream's evocation of the other organic series (the acid series: propionic acid) and of the compounds obtainable from each term (the propylic compounds) can be interpreted as the symbolic transcription of its diversity of meanings, which I have just examined. As the dream unfolds, Freud's mind understands how it operates: the dream's formal processes are, like its latent wishes, represented in its content. The Irma dream provides an answer to the question Freud has been asking himself for months (do dreams have a meaning?): yes, it says, not only do dreams express the meaning of our wishes, but that meaning derives from their symbolic structure. Indeed, could a wish be expressed at all without fitting into that structure?

Freud was now in possession of that knowledge, though he was not yet conscious enough of it to express it explicitly. It was to be the fountainhead of the science that would shortly be known as psychoanalysis. In collaboration with Breuer, Freud had already discovered that hysterical symptoms have a meaning. During the night of July 23–24, 1895, he correctly surmised that normal mental processes such as dreams also have a meaning. Like many great finds, his crucial discovery came to him in a dream. But what was unique on this occasion was the fact that the secret of dreams was revealed by a dream. That secret had implications that went far beyond dreaming, as Freud soon realised. There exists in man a thought process – usually an unconscious one – whereby he strives to get his wishes recognised by his fellow men. The fact that the thought process is symbolic does not mean, as was believed by Jung and those of Freud's followers who were unfaithful to his basic thinking, that it can be reduced to a mere set of allegories and images.[1] This is spelled out to us by Freud's use of chemical concepts and the logical and mathematical framework of his commentary. But that is not all. Like any German schoolboy, Freud had been taught how Kekulé von Stradonitz, while day-dreaming, had

1. Binswanger (1957) is similarly confused in his criticism of the Freudian conception of dreams. He fails to see the difference, which is implicit in Freud's work, between the imaginary structure of dreams (related to latent wishes) and their symbolic structure (related to formal processes).

discovered the hexagonal structure of benzene C_6H_6 and its derivation in relation to carbon C. Freud dreamt that, like some latter-day Kekulé, in his dream he was making a discovery that showed a certain kinship with Kekulé's in its form (though it was triangular, not hexagonal), and, in its content, with Fliess's theories about sexual chemistry – a discovery involving not C, carbon, but N, the formula for the mystery of origins, and also, according to Rosolato (1969, p. 46), the secret cipher of Aleph, the alpha and omega of knowledge. I disagree, on the other hand, with those who see the formula as a forerunner of the Oedipal 'triangle'. In July 1895, Freud had no inkling yet of the Oedipal organisation of the instincts, and he was never to describe it in terms of a triangle.

Although Freud kept in his possession some of the results of his self-analytical work, he was certainly unaware of the full range of interpretations that seem plausible to us today in the light of the documentary evidence we possess and the various personal and scientific problems that he was known to be grappling with at the time. It was for that very reason that his internal development continued. In the following period, while Freud subjected his dreams, then his memories and parapraxes, to psychoanalytic examination, striving principally to identify processes (condensation, displacement, dramatisation, repression, regression and so on) and to establish where they take place (the unconscious, the preconscious, consciousness), a parallel and concomitant, but different and largely unconscious, mental activity continued to focus on the phantasy contents, identifications/projections, and defensive conflicts peculiar to them. Occasionally some element of that mental activity was picked up and exploited by the psychoanalytic process. Often the psychoanalytic process was represented figuratively in those especially important products of mental activity, dreams. It was precisely because Freud concentrated on the formal aspect of what is produced by the unconscious that he was able not only to understand how the psychical apparatus worked but also to give the unconscious dynamic the relatively discreet corner of his psyche, outside of which it would have fallen silent.

The many passages of *The Interpretation of Dreams* where the dream of 'Irma's injection' supplies examples of primary psychical processes cannot be dated, though we do know they were written long after July 1895. They nonetheless deserve examination. In the longest of those passages (*ID* 292–5), Freud emphasises the mechanism of condensation. Irma is a 'composite figure'. She represents both herself, the friend of hers that Freud wanted to treat, Freud's eldest daughter, a woman patient killed by Freud, a child from the Kassowitz Institute, a governess who tried to conceal her false teeth when examined by Freud, and lastly Martha. Dr M.

is composed of two people, himself (Breuer) and Emanuel. Finally, propylene is a kind of 'compromise' between amylene, which belongs to the Otto group, and Propylaea, which belongs to the opposite Fliess group; the Propylaea is a monument in Munich, where Freud had met Fliess a year earlier.

Further points revealed by the Irma dream are discussed in other, shorter passages of *The Interpretation of Dreams* (they are listed earlier on in this chapter). They include:

- the *distortion* of the wish fulfilled by the dream (the scene where the wish is fulfilled seems indifferent in the manifest content; the dreamer's perception of events does not reflect reality, but his wishes; Chapter 4);
- the importance of the *day's residues*: the wish hiding behind the plea: I am justified because I am a man of worth, so 'I may allow myself to do this' (Chapter 5, A);
- the absence of *displacement*, in contrast to subsequent dreams (Chapter 6, B);
- the lack of *logical representation*, particularly in the chronological sequence and in the impossibility of alternatives being expressed in dream images (Chapter 6, C);
- one of the meanings of *identification*, i.e. the attribution of a common element to two persons in the dream, or the wish to exchange one of those persons for the other (*ibid.*);
- the significance of *forgetting* to interpret any detail, however apparently trivial, that appears in the text of the dream (Chapter 7, A).

5. *Relative to the body image*

The final angle from which the dream can be interpreted is that of the body image. I have already pointed to the image of the penis in the dirty syringe and to that of the female genitals in the buccal or nasal cavity. These are metaphorical devices. In this connection, it is worth remembering that Anna O. had consulted Breuer about her severe cough (*tussis nervosa*). But the infantile sexual theory that children are conceived by the mouth and throat, although implicit in the dream, was something that Freud came to recognise only much later, with the case of Dora. It should be noted, too, that the architectural space in which the dream takes place (a 'large hall' with a 'window') or which the dream evokes (the Propylaea in Munich) is also a symbolic representation of the female sexual organs. The dream's setting, then, reduplicates the dream's central scene. This reduplication is not merely a repetition designed to emphasise the importance of the scene.

It is, at a more profound level, the regression to a very early interchangeability of the container and the contents, in other words to a mechanism of primary thought which in this case is a metonymical mechanism.

The dream also evokes a whole series of sensations, which range from the gustatory (the pineapple liqueur) and olfactory (the smell of amyl, the implicit stench of nasal suppuration) to the chromatic (the 'whitish grey scabs' and, no doubt, the reddish-violet turbinal bones), coenaesthetic ('It's choking me'), and tactile ('Leopold was percussing her' and 'I noticed this, just as he did, in spite of her dress'). This sensorial richness, which is fairly typical of Freud and ties in with what I have already said about his basic empiricism, contrasts with the fact that most ordinary dreams consist chiefly of visual sensations and secondarily of auditory sensations. It is true that vision plays an important part in the dream (he looks down Irma's throat) and that there are two snatches of dialogue (the exchange between Freud and Irma, and the discussions between Freud, Dr M., Otto and Leopold). But the final visual image is of a very special nature: it is the sight of an inscription (the formula for trimethylamin), in other words a reading, a decipherment.

The dream also alludes to excretory functions such as defecation ('dysentery') and urination ('the toxin will be eliminated'; Fliess had told Freud that trimethylamin is eliminated in the urine). Similarly, as Eva Rosenblum has pointed out, there is a play on the word Ananas, 'the sound [of which] bears a remarkable resemblance to that of my patient Irma's family name': Ananas is pronounced in German in exactly the same way as *Anna nass* (wet Anna); so she stinks.

She has a dull area low down on the left. In his comments, Freud connects this detail first with the painful rheumatism that had just affected his left shoulder once again, and secondly with memories of clinical examinations involving cases of pulmonary tuberculosis. The cases, which he does not mention by name, are easily deduced. Three great friends of Freud's – Minna Bernays' fiancé, Ignaz Schönberg, Sophie Schwab's young husband, Josef Paneth, and Anna Hammerschlag's young husband, Rudolf Lichtheim – had all died of tuberculosis, leaving behind them three inconsolable 'widows'. The latent content is probably as follows: if Martha, who was experiencing a difficult pregnancy, happened to die, if Freud became a widower, one or other of these desirable widows would be available to replace her. There is confirmation for this: with regard to Freud's daughter Mathilde, whom he mentions in his commentary, Eva Rosenblum tells me that there is a well-known joke in Germany about the widower who collapses on to his wife's brand-new grave exclaiming

'*Mathilde, Mathilde, so eine krieg' ich nicht wieder*' ('Mathilde, Mathilde, I'll never find another like her').

But let us return to the body image. What was Freud worried about on the left? Over the previous two years, heart trouble had caused him pain and concern, but matters had improved so much that he had just decided to start smoking again. The dream materialises both the threat issued by Fliess (Fliess had auscultated Freud – just as Leopold percusses Irma – and warned him that there would be a recurrence of his cardiac intolerance to nicotine) and Freud's determination to contravene that threat.

The last reference to the body concerns the navel, a visible sign of man's origin in his mother's body. The reference comes in a note that is difficult both to translate and to understand: 'There is at least one spot in every dream at which it is unplumbable – a navel [*Nabel*], as it were, that is its point of contact with the unknown [*Unerkannten*: literally the "ungraspable"].' Eva Rosenblum tells me that Freud did not write *Unbekannten* (the unknown), the word which one would expect in the context, and which appears, incorrectly, in most translations. If Freud preferred *Unerkannten* it was probably because the word recalled the biblical expression *ein Weib erkennen* (to know a woman). The overall meaning of the note is in any case hard to 'grasp', and, unconsciously and symbolically, Freud no doubt wished it to be so. If he meant that the psychoanalytic interpretation of dreams cannot be brought to a successful conclusion, it would contradict the work he had done on this dream and his definitive and oft-repeated discovery that the meaning of dreams, in the last account, is wish-fulfilment. A phantasy, then, has infiltrated both his thinking and its written expression, a phantasy that would have made him write, if he had used plain language: the woman we dream of is the woman to whom we were once connected by the umbilical cord, and who remains 'unknowable' by us in the biblical sense. Freud's feeling that it is impossible fully to interpret a dream or a symptom is much more an internal resistance caused by the barrier against incest than the consequence of any inadequacy in his theoretical and clinical equipment. This brief and obscure footnote is the only point in the whole dream and its extensive commentary – and I cannot say that this comes as a surprise to me – where an Oedipal emotion, which in any case goes no further than the incestuous dimension of the Oedipus complex, makes a fleeting appearance before being swiftly nipped in the bud. It would be an abuse of psychoanalytic ideology to go so far as to interpret the dream's half-avowed hostility towards Otto, Breuer and even Fliess as the expression of a specifically parricidal wish. It was only when his father died that Freud began to admit the possibility that such wishes might exist. For the time being, as I have already suggested, he was content to defend himself against his own ambivalence.

Thus, the Irma dream makes a kind of inventory of the body, with, in the background, the five external senses, the internal sensibility, and references to most of the major functions such as breathing, circulation, elimination, reproduction, phonation, the nervous system and, to a lesser extent, nutrition (represented only by an undrinkable liqueur). Highlighted in the foreground are sensitive points of an erotogenic or painful nature – facts, functions and areas that belong sometimes to the dreamer's own body, and sometimes to the body which constitutes the object of his wish. In this respect, the wish that the Irma dream fulfils is the paradisiacal wish to possess the mother's body and to merge the child's body into it. This may indeed be the deeper meaning of dreams in general, a hypothesis first outlined by Stein ('Dreams enable us to find paradise lost every night', 1968*a*, p. 87) and later fully formulated by Pontalis (1972). It does seem, however, that the hypothesis works better for men's dreams than for women's; no doubt the wish to possess the body of the father is equally important in women's dreams. But the Irma dream's euphoric inventory of a properly working body necessarily implies its opposite, an inventory of a sick body. The dream lists all the disorders from which Freud had suffered or was still suffering – intestinal symptoms (dysentery), the pharyngitis of 1881 that prevented him from swallowing or speaking, nasal suppuration, and heart trouble. Freud is the patient he himself examines in the dream. In other words, the dream expresses his wish to carry out self-analysis.

In this sense, the dream of 'Irma's injection' is a programme dream for the whole series of subsequent discoveries that were to constitute psychoanalysis. It spells out the identity of both the body of the dream and the dream of the body. Freud experiences the unconscious, whose corpus he has set out to establish, as the body of the crime from which he must exculpate himself, for it represents symbolically, and contains metonymically, the desired body of the unpossessed mother. But it was here, precisely, that in the early morning of July 24, 1895, his wish finally took shape: he was going to be able to regain possession, at a symbolic level, of the very thing whose possession, at a carnal level, he had been obliged to renounce.

From the Irma dream to the death of Freud's father (July 1895 – October 1896)

The year that followed the dream of 'Irma's injection' was one of progress. The new impetus expressed in the dream helped Freud to continue forging ahead with his work. He made a number of partial discoveries that grew out of previous insights. There were no radical changes in his life. His practice increased in fits and starts, though on the whole satisfactorily.

THE 'PROJECT FOR A SCIENTIFIC PSYCHOLOGY' (SEPTEMBER–OCTOBER 1895)[1]

A number of situations foreshadowed by the Irma dream actually occurred. After Freud had made a brief trip to northern Italy and Venice with his brother Alexander, the two men travelled to Berlin to see Fliess and consult him (in mid-September 1895). Freud had a nose operation there, thus becoming his friend's patient once again. He found their meeting highly stimulating, and while travelling home by train, and for three weeks after that, he enthusiastically wrote a long and untitled essay solely for Fliess's consumption. He never had it published; it was brought out posthumously with the Fliess letters in 1950, and given the title 'Project for a Scientific Psychology' (1950*a*; *SE* 1, 295–397). Freud enclosed the manuscript (of which he would seem not to have kept a copy) in his letter of October 8, 1895. It sketches out a new conception of psychical life. In it, Freud reconstructs the laws of the mind, in the fashion of the empiricist philosophers, but bases his argument on the neurone theory, which had just been discovered, and which he had himself come close to formulating in the past. His inspiration was a huge book published by his teacher, Exner, in 1894, *Entwurf zu einer physiologischen Erklärung der psychischen Erscheinungen* (Introduction to a physiological explanation of psychical processes). With the term 'contact-barriers' Freud anticipated the notion of 'synapse' (formulated by Charles Sherrington in 1897). He set forth not only the principle of constancy but the principle of inertia, which stated that neurones 'tend to divest themselves of *Q* (quantity)' – and which later became the pleasure-unpleasure principle. He gave prominence to the notion of the ego, relating it to inhibition and reality-testing; he also saw consciousness as forming only part of the psychical processes.

1. Chapter 6 of Andersson (1962) is devoted to the development of Freud's ideas during the autumn of 1895.

But the major and lasting contribution of the 'Project' was Freud's distinction between two forms of mental functioning, primary processes, which aim merely to discharge excitation and are exemplified in dreaming, and secondary processes, which move from attention to perception and intelligence, and allow a choice of several possibilities of discharge (an anticipation of the reality principle). Freud recognised the important contribution to the theory made by Breuer, whose notions of free energy and bound energy were characteristic of the primary and secondary processes respectively.

The 'Project' remains, however, a perfect example of a theoretical model with no experimental basis. Its insights into the mind are cramped by its rigid neuro-physiological foundations. Freud here regards psychical processes as quantitatively determined states of neurones. He postulates three classes of neurones, designated by the letters ϕ, ψ, and ω, which correspond respectively to external stimuli, internal stimuli, and the perception-consciousness system. Whereas the function of the first two categories is to discharge quantity, that of the ω neurones is to transform quantity into quality, i.e. to start with, into unpleasure and pleasure. The whole system constitutes an 'apparatus' (Freud does not yet call it 'psychical') that is capable of functioning by itself. The complex – and purely imaginary – interaction of these neurones does, however, enable Freud to make an observation that also proved to be of lasting value. A young infant screams in order to obtain, through external intervention, the discharge of an internal excitation in a 'specific action' – for example 'supply of nourishment, proximity of the sexual object' (note the link, which recurs often later on, between hunger, or desire for the breast, and sexual appetite). This constitutes an 'experience of satisfaction', which effects a 'lasting' and real discharge (unlike the purely hallucinatory discharge), establishes an 'association by simultaneity' (whereby the return of an analogous state of tension revives the memory of satisfaction and creates a desire for that satisfaction), and leads to the facilitation of a contact-barrier. Lastly, 'this path of discharge thus acquires a secondary function of the highest importance, that of communication, and the initial helplessness of human beings is the primal source of all moral motives' (*SE* I, 318).

Following the process further for this same baby, Freud supposes that 'the mnemic image wished for is an image of the mother's breast and a front view of its nipple' (*ibid.* 328), since the baby tries to find 'an object like this [which] was [the subject's] first satisfying object and further his first hostile object, as well as his first helping power' (*ibid.* 331). The first part of the 'Project', entitled 'General Scheme', is devoted to the distinction between primary and secondary processes. The prime examples of primary processes are sleep and dreams:

'The *essential precondition* of sleep may be clearly recognised in children. Children sleep so long as they are not tormented by any [physical] need or external stimulus (hunger or cold from wetting). They go to sleep after being satisfied (at the breast). Adults, too, fall asleep easily *post coenam et coitum* [after dining and copulating]. Accordingly, the precondition of sleep is a *lowering of the endogenous load in the ψ nucleus*, which makes the secondary function superfluous. In sleep an individual is in the ideal state of inertia, rid of his store of *Q*ή.

'In adults this store is collected in the 'ego'; we may assume that is *the unloading of the ego* which determines and characterises sleep. And here, as is immediately clear, we have the *precondition of psychical primary processes*' (*ibid.* 336).

The only clinical material mentioned in the whole of this first part of the 'Project' is the formula for trimethylamin from the dream of 'Irma's injection' – which is not otherwise alluded to in any way. The formula furnishes an example of an unconscious intermediate link between two conscious thoughts, one about a conversation with Fliess on sexual chemistry, the other about the possible sexual aetiology of Irma's illness: the existence of such unconscious links explains the apparent discontinuity of dreams. Moreover, the conclusion arrived at by Freud in his analysis of the Irma dream – that dreams are wish fulfilments – is here stated independently of that dream. As the analogy between symptoms and dreams is hinted at on two occasions in the 'Project', the reader may draw the conclusion that symptoms too are wish fulfilments; but that conclusion is not explicitly stated in the text.

The second part of the 'Project' is devoted to 'The Psychopathology of Hysteria'. The only case mentioned is that of Emma (cf. pp. 143–5). Freud gives an example of the *proton pseudos* (preceding falsity) at the origin of hysteria. A sexual incident during childhood becomes traumatic for the subject only *after the event*, at puberty, when a second incident causes an unconscious recollection of the first and when the sexual release aroused by the recollection turns into anxiety. Freud believed that 'sexual release' can occur only from puberty on, and that this very important mechanism of *deferred action* is the result of the 'retardation' of puberty compared with the rest of the individual's development (*ibid.* 356). Freud's subsequent discovery of the existence of infantile sexuality did not invalidate the mechanism of deferred action, and it was the prematuration of the infant that became the main cause of disposition to neurosis.

The third part, 'Attempt to Represent Normal ψ Processes', tries to give an explanation of secondary processes. These originate in psychical attention, whose operation is described in terms of 'mechanics', in other words psychical dynamics, and which lasts until it results in an 'identity' between the wishful idea and actual perception of reality. The terms 'perceptual identity' for the primary process, and 'thought identity' for the secondary process were used only later, in Chapter 7 of *The Interpretation of Dreams*. Another idea that Freud returned to and developed in the same chapter of *The Interpretation of Dreams* was the importance of 'speech associations', which create a mechanism for directing 'the ψ cathexis to the memories emerging during the passage of Qή. This is *conscious, observing thought*' (*ibid.* 365). Speech associations form a bridge between perception of a quality and discharge of a quantity. '*The indications of speech-discharge* [. . .] put thought-processes on a level with perceptual processes, lend them reality, and *make memory of them possible*' (*ibid.* 366).

The question that comes to mind is: what did the writing of the 'Project' mean exactly to Freud at that point in his life and thinking? James Strachey makes a number of pertinent remarks on the subject in his Introduction to the 'Project' in the *Standard Edition* (*SE* 1, 291–2)[1]. He emphasises the divorce between theoretical and clinical material. The theoretical system outlined by Freud is desexualised, except for an occasional allusion to endogenous stimuli or to instincts, where all the clinical progress he had made over the previous three years pointed to a sexual aetiology of neuroses. Strachey notes the negative and inhibiting nature attributed to the principle of psychical processes, which is governed by the avoidance of unpleasure – a notion still found in *The Interpretation of Dreams*. It was only later that the pleasure principle, i.e. the predominant need to strive after the production of pleasure, was set forth. For the time being, Freud restricted himself to the unpleasure principle (though he did not call it by that name). Finally, Strachey calls the 'Project' a 'defensive' description of the mind.

In my view, the 'Project' should be seen as a kind of farewell by Freud to familiar psychological conceptions that remain restricted to the ego's perspective on body and mind, before he embarked on the study of the id (as he later called it) for a period of twenty years, up until his theoretical revision of the 1920s. An important point often overlooked by commentators is the fact that Freud never thought of publishing the 'Project'. This was understandable: he quickly grew dissatisfied with it and found it

1. That volume contains all the extracts of letters and drafts sent to Fliess that have a bearing on Freud's theoretical work (but not on his private life). Strachey's notes and introductions are extremely valuable, and students researching into psychoanalytic theory are recommended to refer to this edition.

obsolete. True, it contains a number of insights in embryo, and uses for the first time several notions that eventually found their way into the psychoanalytic canon. In this respect, the essay is a compromise-formation. More specifically, because of his scientific turn of mind and even more, as we shall see later on, because of his own psychopathological organisation, which was hysterophobic, Freud needed to provide himself with a conceptual framework that would keep the phenomena he was studying at arm's length without however masking them. He could thus venture to see them as they really were, with both acuity and perspicacity – to see them while at the same time controlling them.

Strachey also points out that Freud's approach in the 'Project' contained a hint or two at the hypotheses of cybernetics and computer theory, as well as at behaviourist theory. There is nothing surprising in this, since those theories derived from neuropsychology, which set itself up as a science in the nineteenth century, and in whose development Freud played an active part before becoming a psychoanalyst. Epistemologically speaking, the situation is the same today as it was in 1895: the wishes, phantasies, repression, representability and creations of the unconscious cannot be apprehended unless a complete break is made with any schema modelled on man-made machines.[1]

A GREATER VOLUME OF SCIENTIFIC RESEARCH, A CLOSER RELATIONSHIP WITH FLIESS, AND GROWING ANXIETY

Immediately after sending his manuscript to Fliess, Freud felt elated: at last he was beginning to make serious headway in his investigations. But very soon he was assailed by doubts, and his morale plummeted. He wrote to Fliess: 'I have packed up the psychological manuscripts and thrown them into a drawer' (*F*, November 8, 1895, 150). He had finally abandoned writing the last chapter on the psychopathology of repression; and it would seem that he never again wrote any further essays on the theme of the 'Project'. During the first half of 1896, on the other hand, he wrote unusually long letters to Fliess in which he set out his constantly evolving ideas on the 'φψω apparatus', as he still called it. In his letter of January 1, 1896, he simplifies and emends his exposition, introducing changes that he later transposed directly to Chapter 7 of *The Interpretation of Dreams* after

1. The 'Project' is a difficult text; it is also very well-known and has been the subject of numerous commentaries. Those interested in investigating it more thoroughly should consult papers by André Green (1972), and Peter Amacher (1965), who revealed that Freud had been chiefly influenced by Brücke, Meynert and Exner in elaborating his schema, as well as Chapters 2 and 3 of Jean Laplanche's book (1970).

removing their neurological underpinnings: hallucination is no longer a backward movement of excitation to φ, but only to ω; the ψ neurones imply a state of consciousness only when linked with speech associations; the release of unpleasure is caused by the conflict between quantity of internal origin from ψ neurones, and the process of consciousness (in other words, both the conflict and the suffering it engenders arise from man's difficulty in facing up to his instincts, and in particular sexuality) (*F* 160). On May 30, 1896, Freud meditates on the process he calls 'becoming conscious': the process of becoming conscious depends on access to the associated word-presentations; it is a compromise between repression and the repressed, made possible by a 'freely displaceable *attention*'; and he states that 'symptoms are almost all *compromise* formations' (*F* 189).

Side by side with his investigations into the φψω apparatus, Freud's theory of the sexual aetiology of neuroses went one step further and, after hysteria, embraced obsessional neurosis. Hysteria is conditioned by 'a primary sexual experience (before puberty), accompanied by revulsion and fright'; and obsessional neurosis is conditioned by the same 'accompanied by *pleasure*' (*F*, October 8, 1895, 141). A few days later, Freud added: 'Have I revealed the great clinical secret to you, either orally or in writing? Hysteria is the consequence of a presexual *sexual shock*. Obsessional neurosis is the consequence of a presexual *sexual pleasure*, which is later transformed into [self-] *reproach*. [. . .] the relevant events become effective only as *memories*' (*F*, October 15, 1895, 144). The following day, he announced triumphantly: 'I am still all mixed up. I am almost certain that I have solved the riddles of hysteria and obsessional neurosis with the formulas of infantile sexual shock and sexual pleasure, and I am equally certain that both neuroses are, *in general*, curable – not just individual symptoms but the neurotic disposition itself' (*F*, October 16, 1895, 145). Shortly afterwards, a case of male hysteria confirmed to him that 'sexual shock' did indeed consist of 'infantile abuse' (*F*, November 2, 1895, 149). This is the first occasion that Freud uses the term, and (probably) his second allusion to the case of Herr E., described in the previous letter as 'my "bashful" case [who] developed hysteria in his youth and later showed delusions of reference' (*F*, October 31, 1895, 148). Freud continued to treat this case – the first male patient to be psychoanalysed by him – right up until April 1900, in other words throughout the period of his systematic self-analysis (see E. Rosenblum's paper (1973) on the case and the note on p. 190 of the present book which lists all references to it). Another insight implicit in the Irma dream – the simulation of orgasm by the symptom – began to take shape (the case of Mrs P.J.; *F*, Draft J, probably the end of 1895, 155–8). Freud then made other adjustments to his theory. He began to replace the notion of defence by the notion of repression, stated that the latter was actuated by the ego, made a distinction between secondary repression (involving conscious derivatives, such as self-reproach in obsessional neurosis) and primary repression (involving memories of traumatic sexual scenes), suggested that the symptom was a compromise, and anticipated the notion of the latency period (inspired by Fliess) in his paper 'Further Remarks on the Neuro-Psychoses of Defence' (1896*b*).

But in Freud's professional life, things were not going so smoothly. Breuer, who claimed in public that he had come round to the theory of sexual aetiology, attacked it in private. Freud, now no longer able to trust him, decided the time had come for a final parting of the ways. He summarised his own views on sexual aetiology at that time in an article which appeared in the *Revue neurologique* of March 30, 1896, 'L'hérédité et l'étiologie des névroses' ('Heredity and the Aetiology of the Neuroses') (1896*a*). The article mentions a number of cases where sexual trauma in childhood produced either hysteria or obsessional neurosis (respectively thirteen and six cases), and contains the first published appearance of the word 'psychoanalysis'. The word appears again, for the first time in German, in the already mentioned 'Further Remarks on the Neuro-Psychoses of Defence', which was written at the same time but appeared only on May 15, 1896. This change of terminology was clearly of little significance to Freud, as he did not even bother to tell Fliess about it in a letter referring to the two articles (*F*, February 6, 1896, 170). But it nevertheless had the value of a signature and a token: Freud now recognised that he had made a specific discovery by himself (though he also thought fit to indicate that psychoanalysis was Breuer's 'exploratory procedure') and was prepared to forge ahead on his own.

But it was no easy task: 'I am as isolated as you would wish me to be [. . .] for a void is forming all around me' (*F*, May 4, 1896, 185). His practice was dwindling. The paper entitled 'The Aetiology of Hysteria', which he gave in May 1896 to the Vienna Society for Psychiatry and Neurology (1896*c*), received an icy reception, which did not help matters. Referring this time to eighteen cases, Freud had the audacity to talk of prepubertal sexual emotions and – horror of horrors! – to argue that the attempted sexual seduction of children by adults, and even by close relatives, was a prime cause of hysteria. The only publication likely to bring him any public esteem, a treatise on children's paralyses commissioned by Nothnagel, failed to rouse his interest. He let it drag on (1897*a*) and complained that it was preventing him from doing his real work. On top of all that, the Liberals had lost the Vienna elections (September 1895), and the anti-

Semitic Lueger was on the point of becoming mayor. The future looked bleak for the Jewish community. Freud decided to join the B'nai B'rith, a masonic lodge of liberal Jews, whose Tuesday meetings he subsequently attended every fortnight. But intellectually he felt lonely. This led him to pin all his hopes on Fliess.

Freud never ceased to be amazed at the parallels between their lives and their scientific interests. Anna Freud was born on December 3, 1895. (At that point, Freud's sister-in-law Minna moved into the house to help out for a few months, and his practice suddenly grew.) Fliess's first son, Robert, was born a few days later. Both Fliess and Freud were pursuing a scientific ideal through medicine – the understanding of psychology, physiology, and even 'philosophy' (*F*, January 1, 1896, 159). Six weeks later, Freud changed his emphasis and coined a word that was to have a great future: 'I am continually occupied with psychology – really *meta*-psychology' (*F*, February 13, 1896, 172). Both men attributed a key role to sexuality in the phenomena they were investigating. They sent one another their drafts. There was much mutual praise, despite one or two criticisms, and encouragement to tackle greater fields of investigation. Freud got Fliess to develop his 'nasal reflex neurosis' theory into a treatise; Fliess sent Freud the manuscript of *Die Beziehungen zwischen Nase und weiblichen Geschlectsorganen: in ihrer biologischen Bedeutung dargestellt* (The relationship between the nose and the female sexual organs: presented from the point of view of its biological significance) in late February, 1896, and the book was published in 1897. Fliess got Freud to investigate migraine and submit his theory of periodicity to psycho-pathological verification. Freud had not worked with anyone on a project for quite some time, and hoped that this would be possible with Fliess. He said as much in a letter of January 1, 1896, while at the same time congratulating him on the birth of his son and enclosing as a Christmas present a draft on the neuroses of defence (*F*, Draft K, 162–9). The draft describes four 'pathological aberrations of normal psychic affective states: of *conflict* (hysteria), of *self-reproach* (obsessional neurosis), of *mortification* (paranoia), of *mourning* (acute hallucinatory amentia)'.

In 1896, Freud met Fliess twice, at Easter in Dresden, and at the end of August in Salzburg. These 'congresses' were occasions of wonderful self-renewal for Freud, who humbly placed enormous expectations in his friend. 'I feel a pall has been cast over me, and all I can say is that I am looking forward to our congress as to the slaking of hunger and thirst. I bring nothing but two open ears and one temporal lobe lubricated for reception' (*F*, June 30, 1896, 193). Such extraordinarily high hopes were bound to lead to disappointment: Fliess, resenting the fact that he had not obtained Freud's unqualified support for his theory of periodicity, failed to respond to the suggestion that they should collaborate.

Let us reexamine one aspect of the relationship between the two men that emerges from their correspondence. It was brought to light by Max Schur (1972), who had access to the then unpublished correspondence and whose interest was naturally aroused as he had been Freud's doctor during the closing years of his life. What I am referring to is the two friends' constant and reciprocal interest in their physical ailments (nasal suppurations and migraine, from which they both suffered, and Freud's occasional heart trouble and gastrointestinal symptoms), in their moods (elated enthusiasm alternating with sudden bouts of depression), and in their hypochondriacal worries (more or less vague feelings of ill-being). They exhibited, described and entrusted to one another their sick bodies, just as a child whose masochism has been keenly fostered believes that his mother can love him only when he is ill.[1]

Freud's letter of April 16, 1896 (*F* 180–1) is typical of this aspect of their relationship:

'My head full of dates and ideas about summations, proud of having received some recognition, and with a cocky feeling of independence, I returned to a sense of too much well-being and have since then been very lazy because the modicum of misery[2] essential for intensive work will not come back. I can record only a very few ideas arising from my daily work about the in-between realm[3], as a general reinforcement of the impression that *everything* is as I surmise it to be and thus that everything will be clarified. Among these, a completely surprising explanation of Eckstein's haemorrhages – which will give you much pleasure[4]. I have already figured out the story, but I shall wait to communicate it until the patient herself has caught up.

'In accordance with your request, I have started to isolate myself in every respect and find it easy to bear. I have one prior commitment, though – a lecture to be given at the psychiatric society on Tuesday. [. . .]

1. O. Mannoni (1967) makes two further points that help us to understand the relations between the two men: the relationship that Freud had built up with Breuer was anaclitic, while with Fliess it was narcissistic. Fliess had carefully avoided – unlike Freud – marrying a woman of slender means. I would add that Freud must have found his friend's young and wealthy wife commensurately more desirable.

2. Literally 'middle misery'. The German word *Mittelelend* is a pun by Freud on *Mittelschmerz*, the pain experienced by women at the time of ovulation, i.e. in the middle of the menstrual cycle.

3. *Zwischenreich* is a term coined by Freud, combining *zwischen* (in-between) and *Reich* (realm). It probably refers to the intermediate state between body and mind, which preoccupied both Freud and Fliess.

4. The original German (literally: 'You will have Your joy') puts both *Du* and *Deine* in capitals. Freud is making a pun: I am bringing you 'Your Joy' (the literal translation of *Freude*), in other words 'Your Freud'.

'As for me, I note migraine, nasal secretion, and attacks of fears of dying, such as today, although Tilgner's cardiac death is most likely more responsible for this than the date. You have helped me a great deal toward moderation in regard to tobacco, just as I feel more resolute and in better shape since our *entrevue*. It was very good for me and very necessary. I shall probably surprise you shortly with psychological scraps; right now I am exceedingly lazy about writing. By the way, any drop of alcohol makes me completely stupid.'

The problem facing both Freud and Fliess was how to explain scientifically their physical ailments and fluctuating moods. Temperamentally, each of them was attracted by a different type of explanation, biological in Fliess's case, and psychological in Freud's. And it was this divergence which eventually turned out to be insurmountable and precipitated their rupture. Fliess's explanation, which he communicated to Freud during their 'congresses' and in a paper he sent him at the end of February 1896, extends the periodical nature of women's menstruation to both sexes. Men have 'periods', too, but their cycle is shorter (23 days instead of 28). Nasal suppurations are the equivalent of menstrual bleeding. The well-known symptoms experienced by women during menstruation – headaches, fatigability, irritability and moroseness – are also found in men. So Freud made a point of jotting down the dates of all his ailments and noting the intervals between them, so that he could work out their chronological connection with major or minor events in his life. It is surprising that none of the psychoanalysts who have looked into this question (Jones, Kris, Schur) ventured to formulate an interpretation that seems to stare us in the face: in his theory of periods Fliess was expressing his phantasy of the suppression of sexual difference. But whereas this phantasy normally takes the form of a masculine-based claim that women are men's equals (in other words, an attempt to give women a phallic equivalent, if not a penis), the opposite occurs with Fliess (who is enthusiastically followed by Freud): the phantasy expresses itself in his attribution to men of characteristics that are equivalent to those of supposed feminine castration. Moreover, the sharing of this phantasy by the two men was bound to have satisfied their latent homosexuality.

Ever since the spring of 1894, when, as we have seen, Freud experienced heart trouble that was made more acute by nicotine poisoning, he had been familiar with the fear of dying and aware of the inevitability of his own death. Since then, his usual depressive and psychosomatic symptoms had become more marked, but he was not yet able to establish a clear connection between that fear and his symptoms. Just as he occasionally obeyed Fliess's orders to stop smoking or to smoke less, so he went along with his friend's theoretical explanation of the periodicity of male ailments, probably because of the latent phantasy I have just described: the castration anxiety which took the intellectual form of the period theory somehow enabled Freud to focus on his fear of death without either understanding or identifying it. At the same time, Fliess's biological and numerological explanation, one guided by external determinism, could hardly have satisfied Freud, who was becoming increasingly convinced of the existence of an internal determinism. The letter that I have just quoted at length shows clearly that Freud was hesitating between an explanation by periods, which he accepted intellectually while poking gentle fun at it, and a psychological explanation, hinted at in the sentence where Freud identifies with the well-known sculptor Victor Tilgner, who had just died, before being able to enjoy his ultimate artistic triumph.

Schur (S 100–4) quite rightly draws attention to the impact of Tilgner's death on Freud and provides data that helps us to understand it. Born into a poor family that moved to Vienna when he was 2, Tilgner (1844–96) was a brilliant student at the Academy of Arts. He then gradually developed a highly personal style, particularly after a trip to Italy made possible by a gift from a patron. His supreme success came when he competed for, and won, a commission to create a large statue of Mozart, Vienna's favourite son. By the time the statue had been completed and the date of its unveiling fixed, Tilgner was beset by premonitions: he feared he would never live to enjoy his day of glory. In the afternoon of April 15, 1896 (six days before the inauguration), he decided to have a few bars from Mozart's *Don Giovanni* engraved on the base of the monument (the scene in which the ghost of the Commendatore appears before Don Giovanni, who had murdered him after seducing his daughter, and strikes down the guilty man). Then Tilgner played tarot. During the night, he had a heart attack (coronary thrombosis), which responded to treatment. But on the morning of April 16 a second attack proved fatal. The same afternoon, *Neue freie Presse* published Tilgner's obituary, which Freud read after dinner. He immediately wrote Fliess the already quoted letter. It is easy to imagine the parallels that Freud spotted between Tilgner's life and his own, and the fears which the sculptor's death from a heart attack must have aroused in him. It is also easy to see why Freud suffered a fresh and more serious outbreak of symptoms, pondering, as he must have, that like Moses all great innovators are doomed to get only a distant view of the Promised Land and to die before success is theirs.

This episode both foreshadowed and paved the way for the psychical work that took place in January, 1896, with the Rome dreams. It shows that two well-known factors of creation were actively functioning within

Freud – identification with a submissive and fertile woman, and the fight against the fear of death.

DREAMS OF THIRST AND AWAKENING

But what of Freud's dreams, at a time when his moods were still oscillating between elation and depression, and the problem of smoking was beginning to worry him again? On September 21, 1895, while still in high spirits after his return from Berlin, Freud had a dream which provided 'the funniest confirmation of the conception that dreams are motivated by wish-fulfilment' (*F*, September 23, 1895, 140). In Chapter 3 of *The Interpretation of Dreams*, which follows the analysis of the Irma dream and is entitled 'A Dream Is the Fulfilment of a Wish', Freud discusses a category of his own dreams which he calls dreams of convenience. They are dreams about drinking. 'For instance, there is a dream that I can produce in myself as often as I like – experimentally, as it were. If I eat anchovies or olives or any other highly salted food in the evening, I develop thirst during the night which wakes me up. But my waking is preceded by a dream; and this always has the same content, namely, that I am drinking. I dream I am swallowing down water in great gulps, and it has the delicious taste that nothing can equal but a cool drink when one is parched with thirst' (*ID* 123). Now the context of the letter of September 23 suggests that the dream Freud had had two nights before was of an experimental nature.

As I have already said, the first part of 'Project for a Scientific Psychology' – a section that Freud had by then completed – concludes with a long passage on dreams. Freud states that 'the aim and sense' of dreams are wish-fulfilments, at least in the case of normal dreams. Using the example of the injection of trimethylamin, he illustrates the fact that conscious dream thoughts are connected by unconscious intermediate links, which are in this case the idea that Irma's illness is of a sexual nature, and the recollection of a discussion with Fliess about sexual chemistry. Freud points to a great similarity between dream-processes and pathological mechanisms (*SE* 1, 336) – a discovery he forgot about until he made it again in 1899 (*F*, February 19, 1899, 345). In other respects the explanation for dream mechanisms is abstractly deduced from the three-neurone theory.

The following year, Freud sought further confirmation for his theories in children's dreams, and more particularly those of his own children. During the summer holidays of 1896 on Lake Aussee, his eldest daughter Mathilde, who was 8½, dreamed that her mother had thrown big bars of chocolate, wrapped up in blue and green paper, into the bedroom – the very same bars which her mother had prevented the children from getting from a slot-machine the previous day. During the same night, Freud's son Oliver, who was five-and-a-quarter, dreamed he had reached the Simony hut on the Dachstein mountain, which to his great disappointment they had not walked up the previous day (*ID* 127–9). That same summer, Freud's daughter Sophie, who was three-and-a-quarter, fulfilled in a dream a longer trip across the Aussee than the disappointingly short one she had been taken on the day before (*ID* 129). The following summer, Freud's other daughter, Anna, then only nineteen months old, dreamed of 'stwawbewwies' she had not been allowed to eat the previous day (*ID* 130; *F*, October 31, 1897, 276).

It was probably at about the same time that Freud enlarged the field covered by his method of dream analysis. He discovered from his patients, and verified on himself, that it was possible to make a successful interpretation of a dream that occurred in the past, even in childhood. Chapter 3 of *The Interpretation of Dreams* describes a number of Freud's own dreams similar to the one dreamt by Rudolf Kaufmann (already mentioned on pp. 126–7): 'Dreams of convenience like these were very frequent in my youth. Having made it a practice as far back as I can remember to work late into the night, I always found it difficult to wake early. I used then to have a dream of being out of bed and standing by my washing-stand; after a while I was no longer able to disguise from myself the fact that I was really still in bed, but in the meantime I had had a little more sleep' (*ID* 125).

That same summer of 1896 was a happy period for Freud. He no longer had any financial problems, and took two months' holiday for the first time ever. He settled his family on Aussee, in Styria, which was rather far from Vienna, and joined them there in mid-July for a month. During the last week of August, Freud met Fliess in Salzburg, then went on a second tour of northern Italy with his brother Alexander. It was more extensive than their trip of the previous year: first they returned to Venice, then, for the next fortnight, visited Padua, Bologna, Ravenna, Faenza, and Florence, a city that impressed them so deeply they spent a whole week there.

In October, Martha left her family for the first time since her marriage to spend a fortnight with her mother in Hamburg, stopping in Berlin to see the Fliess family on both the outward and the return journeys. Her sister, Minna, had by then settled in for good with the Freuds. Intelligent, witty and receptive, she gradually took on the role, which Martha had played in the past, of a confidant with whom Freud could talk about his scientific projects and new ideas.

THE 'CLOSE THE EYES' DREAM
(OCTOBER 25–26, 1896)

On June 30, 1896, Freud wrote to Fliess: 'My old father (age 81) is in Baden in a most shaky state, with heart failure, paralysis of the bladder, and so forth. Eagerly waiting for news and travelling to see him were the only things of interest in these past two weeks' (*F*, June 30, 1896, 193). On October 26, a brief letter, couched in medical terms, describes Jacob Freud's death, which occurred on the 23rd (*F*, October 26, 201). But by November 2 Freud's emotions had got the better of him:

'By one of those dark pathways behind the official consciousness the old man's death has affected me deeply. I valued him highly, understood him very well, and with his peculiar mixture of deep wisdom and fantastic light-heartedness he had a significant effect on my life. By the time he died, his life had long been over, but in [my] inner self the whole past has been reawakened by this event. I now feel quite uprooted' (*F* 202). Then Freud describes a dream he had on the night after the funeral. This marked a turning point in Freud's inner life that was to have important repercussions on his work. It was responsible for his getting the idea of carrying out a self-analysis and writing a book on dreams – as he realised himself once he had completed that twofold task. In the preface to the second edition of *The Interpretation of Dreams* in 1909, he wrote: 'For this book has a further subjective significance for me personally – a significance which I only grasped after I had completed it. It was, I found, a portion of my own self-analysis, my reaction to my father's death – that is to say, to the most important event, the most poignant loss, of a man's life. Having discovered that this was so, I felt unable to obliterate the traces of the experience' (*ID* xxvi).

The dream of October 25–26, 1896, consisted of nothing more than a notice. The letter to Fliess and *The Interpretation of Dreams* give slightly differing versions of it. Here is how the letter describes the dream:

'I must tell you about a nice dream I had the night after the funeral. I was in a place where I read a sign:

You are requested
to close the eyes.

I immediately recognised the location as the barbershop I visit every day. On the day of the funeral I was kept waiting and therefore arrived a little late at the house of mourning. At that time my family was displeased with me because I had arranged for the funeral to be quiet and simple, which they later agreed was quite justified. They were also somewhat offended by my lateness. The sentence on the sign has a double meaning: one should do one's duty to the dead (an apology as though I had not done it and were in need of leniency), and the actual duty itself. The dream thus stems from the inclination to self-reproach that regularly sets in among the survivors' (*F* 202).

In *The Interpretation of Dreams*, the dream is described in Section C, 'The Means of Representation', of Chapter 6, 'The Dream-Work', as an example of the way an *alternative* is expressed:

'During the night before[1] my father's funeral I had a dream of a printed notice, placard or poster – rather like the notices forbidding one to smoke in railway waiting-rooms – on which appeared either

"You are requested to close the eyes"
or, "You are requested to close an eye."

I usually write this in the form:

"You are requested to close the/an eye(s)."

Each of these two versions had a meaning of its own and led in a different direction when the dream was interpreted. I had chosen the simplest possible ritual for the funeral, for I knew my father's own views on such ceremonies. But some other members of the family were not sympathetic to such puritanical simplicity and thought we should be disgraced in the eyes of those who attended the funeral. Hence one of the versions: 'You are requested to close an eye', to 'wink at' or 'overlook'. Here it is particularly easy to see the meaning of the vagueness expressed by the 'either – or'. The dream-work failed to establish a unified wording for the dream-thoughts which could at the same time be ambiguous, and the two main lines of thought consequently began to diverge even in the manifest content of the dream.

'In a few instances the difficulty of representing an alternative is got over by dividing the dream into two pieces of equal length.

'The way in which dreams treat the category of contraries and contradictories is highly remarkable. It is simply disregarded. "No" seems not to exist as far as dreams are concerned. They show a particular preference for combining contraries into a unity or for representing them as one and the same thing. Dreams feel themselves at liberty, moreover, to represent any element of its wishful contrary; so that there is no way of deciding at a first

1. If this second version is more accurate, the dream must then date from the night of October 24–25, 1896. I prefer to follow the more immediate version given in the letter to Fliess, which states that the dream took place during the night *after* the funeral, in other words that of October 25–26.

glance whether any element that admits of a contrary is present in the dream-thoughts as a positive or as a negative' (*ID* 317–18).

The notice has the same function as trimethylamin in the dream of 'Irma's injection', but does not use complicated chemical symbols. The symbol is provided by a double meaning taken from everyday language. It is a macabre joke, the first of the many plays on words to be found in Freud's dreams (cf. *Jokes and their Relation to the Unconscious*, 1905*c*). The placard looks rather like the NO SMOKING notices one finds in railway stations. Do not smoke, otherwise you will wear out your heart prematurely and die young. This is an allusion to the cardiac episode of April 1894 and Fliess's repeated injunctions since then not to smoke. The station waiting-room refers to another of Freud's anxieties, his phobia of railways.[1] 'You are requested to close the eyes' is the sacred duty that the living pay the dead, as Freud had indeed done vis-à-vis his father. But in the case of someone who arrived late at the house of mourning, and who 'had arranged for the funeral to be quiet and simple'[2] – thus doubly shocking the rest of his family – this is clearly a request for indulgence: close your eyes to Freud's dereliction of duty. In German, the expression 'to close the eyes' has only the concrete meaning of a physical act. It is used by the dreamer to represent the last respects he must pay as the son of the dead man. The expression 'to close an eye', on the other hand, is used in the figurative sense of moral indulgence. The two expressions, which look so apparently similar but have opposite meanings, are combined in the dream in what looks like a mathematical formula. The double meaning comes across more clearly in English, because the expression 'to close the eyes' has both a literal and a figurative meaning. It was not until Freud was plunged into the pain of mourning that he began to feel rising within him guilt feelings towards his father that had lain hidden since his earliest childhood.

With regard not only to Fliess but to Freud's waking wishes, the dream is a request for indulgence. Shut your eyes, it says, if I do not obey your prohibitions, or if, in my life as in my dreams, I fulfil my wishes. We learn later from Freud that Jacob was an indulgent father. Fliess is invited to replace him as both a stimulating ego ideal and a tolerant super-ego: this is the first time that Freud gives a written description of one of his own dreams to Fliess (the 'Project' had contained only passing references to the Irma dream).

1. Edith Buxbaum (1951) was the first to draw attention to the way Freud's two main neurotic symptoms are alluded to in this dream.

2. Jewish funerals consist of a single, straightforward and free service. By 'quiet' Freud probably meant that he had not announced the death in the newspapers.

With regard to infantile wishes, the ambivalence which the Irma dream sought to avoid, and which it located in figures of authority, begins here to become conscious, and the primal object at which it is directed – the father – is recognised. For the first time, the parricidal dimension of the Oedipal organisation is foreshadowed.

With regard to psychoanalytic procedure and to the representation of Freud's self-analysis in his own dreams, the injunction to 'close the eyes' was one of the instructions that Freud gave his patients when starting treatment. In the Irma dream, he followed his own instruction to associate freely in the course of an episodical session. This time, he applies the second instruction to himself: he undertakes a continuous psychoanalytic effort, shifting from fragmentary self-analysis to systematic self-analysis. To close both eyes is to sleep and to dream. To keep both eyes open is to be awake and to reason. To open one eye and close the other represents an intermediate stance – that of the work of analysis.

Analysis of the dream enabled Freud later on, when he was writing *The Interpretation of Dreams*, to make a discovery about a formal process whereby the *ambivalence* of latent thoughts can be expressed by the *double meaning* of the manifest text.

Lastly, as regards the body image, two organs are referred to. The heart, Freud's weak point, is implicitly present in the injunction not to smoke: now that my father is dead, it will be my turn to die – and to die of a heart complaint. The eyes move into a prominent position, anticipating later recollections of the one-eyed doctor (hence the ambivalence between one and two eyes) of his childhood and the operation for glaucoma undergone by the dead man. There is also a reference to the biblical law forbidding a son to look at his father's naked genitals, a law that Freud had transgressed when treating his dying father. Another important body theme is that of cleanliness – the barber who shaves Freud every day, and the laying out of the dead man in which, implicitly, Freud has taken part (this point becomes explicit in subsequent dreams). The dream establishes, though does not explain, the connection between cleanliness and guilt feelings.

Conrad Stein (1968*a*), in his lengthy discussion of this and subsequent dreams in which Freud's father appeared, came to the following conclusions. Jacob Freud's death from natural causes (he was old and ill) foiled his son's still strong infantile wish to kill his father: 'What was important for the dreamer was for himself to be the author of his father's death' (p. 81). He goes on: 'It is an obvious fact that the death of the father makes the mother available, at least according to infantile conceptions' (p. 86). In this respect, the death and the dream were, in my view, a necessary stage in Freud's discovery of the Oedipus complex. Returning to the earliest infantile wish – a wish for omnipotence – Stein interprets the 'Close the eyes' dream as a negation of the father's 'natural' death and as a reaffirmation, through feelings of guilt at having acted reprehensibly towards him, of the omnipotence of the son's wish to kill his father: 'The father died because he was destined to die: that is what must be denied by fulfilling, in a dream, one's own death wishes or by showing that one is reprehensible. The implication is that one is guilty, not of the misdemeanour with which one charges oneself, but of having caused the death of one's father. That implication must not be revealed' (p. 87).

I have already remarked that the decor of the Irma dream (a reception hall with a window) reproduced, in tableau form, the scene that was going to be enacted, according to its own dynamics, in the foreground (the examination of the inside of a woman's body through an orifice). In the dream about the death of Freud's father, the setting is again a hall (this time a hall in a station, in other words a departure hall), which contains connotations of separation anxiety as well as the symbolic representation, of which Freud was beginning to become aware, of death as a journey. This feature of the setting further intensifies one of the meanings of the writing on the placard: the son is requested to close the eyes – of his dead father, which he had in fact done one or two days before. But the setting is also a shop, the shop where the barber wields his razor, or maybe the workshop of Zajíc the locksmith, where the young Freud used to make little objects with scraps of metal, and the neighbouring warehouse where the two Freud families used to work. But the dream itself does not describe a setting anything like that: there is nothing to be seen, and instead of the scene it might have depicted (a razor in action, keys being cut, adults at work), there is a placard which says, precisely, that nothing *should* be seen ('Close the eyes'). Thus the infantile memory which motivated the dream, and whose recollection enabled Freud to make decisive progress in his discovery of psychoanalysis, is not actually present. The place where it should have been is indicated, and the conditions governing its content are listed. It is the memory of something, or rather someone, that Freud saw as a child on the occasion of a departure, separation, and/or railway journey – someone he saw in a situation which was bound to make his father take offence and firmly instruct him, when that person was in that situation, to close his eyes. Caught between his father's injunction and his own desire to look, the young Sigmund found a compromise solution that the dream expresses quite literally: he closed one eye, but opened the other.

The Irma dream and its interpretation had, to some extent, been no more than an intellectual exercise for Freud. In the 'Close the eyes' dream, on the other hand, the dreamer's own involvement in his dream and the self-questioning inherent in its interpretation assume greater importance. Up to then, Freud had regarded the fact that dreams had a meaning as a scientific truth. It now became a subjective truth that required him to commit himself to a sustained personal effort.

CHAPTER 3

The discovery of the Oedipus complex

'There is an unmistakable indication in the text of Sophocles' tragedy itself that the legend of Oedipus sprang from some primaeval dream-material which had as its content the distressing disturbance of a child's relation to his parents owing to the first stirrings of sexuality. At a point when Oedipus, though he is not yet enlightened, has begun to feel troubled by his recollection of the oracle, Jocasta consoles him by referring to a dream which people dream, though, as she thinks, it has no meaning:

> "Many a man ere now in dreams hath lain
> With her who bare him. He hath least annoy
> Who with such omens troubleth not his mind."[1]

(*ID* 263–4)

The notion of the 'psychical apparatus'

Mourning set in motion a process of intense psychical work in Freud. The Irma dream made him aware of his guilt feelings, but did not explain them to him. The 'Close the eyes' dream made him realise that those feelings involved his father. His new awareness had a liberating effect. For about six months after that, he stopped complaining of fatigue, moments of depression, or an intellectual block.

Yet he could not have been busier. He had a large practice. He was writing the treatise on *Die infantile Cerebrallähmung* (*Infantile Cerebral Paralysis*; 1897*a*) which he had promised Nothnagel (he grumbled about having to do it, as he had by then lost interest in the subject). And he had embarked upon a major work on neuroses – which was never to see the light of day. He had already selected the quotations he intended to use as epigraphs to each chapter. They were the only part of the book he told Fliess about:

1. *Oedipus Rex*, line 982ff., translated by Lewis Campbell.

'The psychology of hysteria will be preceded by the proud words: *Introite et hic dii sunt* [Enter – for here too are gods];[1]

the chapter on summation by:

Sie treiben's toll, ich fürcht' es breche,
Nicht jeden Wochenschluss macht Gott die Zeche
[They are exceeding all bounds, I fear a breakdown:
God does not present the reckoning at the end of every week].[2]

the symptom-formation by:

Flectere si nequeo superos, Acheronta movebo
[If I cannot bend the Higher Powers, I will move the Infernal Regions],[3]

and resistance by:

Mach es kurz!
Am jüngsten Tag ist's doch nur ein . . .'[4]
[Cut it short!
On doomsday it won't be worth a . . .]

(*F*, December 4, 1896, 205)

A month later, Freud told Fliess of other epigraphs he had chosen:

'The section on Therapy will be preceded by the quotation "*Flavit et dissipati sunt*" ["He blew and they were scattered"];[5] that on Sexuality by the motto "*Vom Himmel durch die Welt zur Hölle*" ["From heaven through the world to hell"]'[6] (*F*, January 3, 1897, 220).

This sudden flurry of epigraphs shows that Freud was beginning to see himself surrounded by a forest of symbols – a sign which has since been recognised as denoting that the creator has begun the process of discovery

1. This refers to a story about Heraclitus: he was talking to his disciples round the kitchen stove, when some visitors appeared at the door. He invited them in with these words. He was a pantheist philosopher and believed that the gods were everywhere, even in a kitchen.

2. The origin of this quotation remains obscure; it may come from Goethe. The 'Project for a Scientific Psychology', which Freud sent Fliess in October 1895, contained a chapter devoted to the notion of a 'summation' of the quantity of excitation (Part I, General Scheme; Chapter 10, 'The ψ Paths of Conduction', *SE* 1, 316). Neither the quotation nor the theories found in that chapter are found in any of Freud's later works.

3. Virgil, *Aeneid*, VII, 312. In a later note (1925), Freud remarked that 'this line of Virgil is intended to picture the efforts of the repressed instinctual impulses' (*ID* 608).

4. A quotation from Goethe's *Zahme Xenien*. The words are used by God the Father when interrupting Satan, who has launched into a diatribe against Napoleon. The quotation in full ('Cut it short! On doomsday, it won't be worth a fart') is used ironically by Freud to head Section III, devoted to a discussion of dissident views, of 'On the History of the Psycho-Analytic Movement' (1914*d*, *SE* 14, 42).

5. The inscription of the medal struck to commemorate the destruction in 1588 of the 'invincible' Spanish Armada, most of which was in fact lost in a storm. Freud alludes to the medal twice in *The Interpretation of Dreams* (*ID* 214 and 469) (see also pp. 333–4 and 347 of the present book).

6. The last line of the 'Prologue in the Theatre' from Goethe's *Faust*. Freud used the quotation again in connection with perversions in the first of his *Three Essays on the Theory of Sexuality* (1905*d*, *SE* 7, 162).

or that the patient has begun to explore his unconscious. As we have already seen, Freud had long been fascinated by Goethe, so his appearance here is no surprise. There is, however, a new reference which probably dates from Freud's two trips to Italy in the summers of 1895 and 1896: his identification with Aeneas. Virgil's hero is a Trojan prince who sets out to avenge the defeat of his forebears. He is a wanderer, like the Jews after him. In the course of his long journey, he has to overcome storms, monsters and sorceresses, all of them symbols of internal dangers. He constantly eschews the vain and dissipated pleasures of martial or amorous conquest and remains loyal to his father, his child, his comrades and his vocation. With the Sibyl as his guide, he proves himself brave enough to go down into the underworld, and prudent enough to return unscathed. Lastly, he is a founding hero, the ancestor of the people that builds Rome, and the father of a new civilisation that vanquishes those who sacked Troy, the Greeks. Like Aeneas, Freud has lost his father; and the work of mourning, which enables him to recover the image of the dead man deep within his psyche, no doubt reminds him that the reason Aeneas went down into the underworld was to consult his father, Anchises.

Anyone wishing better to understand the internal processes that were at work within Freud between November 1896 and Easter 1897 would be well advised to read Book VI of the *Aeneid* carefully. Let me mention just one or two parallels. For instance, the Sibyl pronounces ambiguous oracles, sometimes chanting them, sometimes writing them down on pieces of paper. We have already noted the role of ambiguity and writing in Freud's first two dreams; they recur in later dreams as well. Aeneas, terrified by the monsters he meets on his way down into the underworld, draws his sword. But he soon realises that they are empty shadows, mere ghosts. Tartarus is a part of the underworld where evildoers expiate their sins; one of them, the last mentioned by the Sibyl no doubt because his crime is the most horrible, is a father who 'forced a way to a forbidden marriage in his own daughter's chamber' (VI, 623). In the Elysian Fields, on the other hand, souls that have been cleansed of their sins prepare to drink the waters of the river Lethe, source of peace, sleep and forgetfulness, before being reincarnated. Forgetfulness caused by repression, the role of incest, and the need to confront terrifying, if imaginary, internal images must all have struck a chord in Freud's mind.

The quotation from Virgil chosen by Freud in 1896 and eventually used by him as an epigraph to *The Interpretation of Dreams* (*Flectere si nequeo superos, Acheronta movebo*) does not in fact come from Book VI. Were it indeed spoken by Aeneas, it would be easy to understand: Freud, identifying with his model, would be turning his back on conscious ideas and values in order better to examine their unconscious, infernal, and abyssal foundations. This is the interpretation given to the quotation by most commentators. But the line in fact comes from a passage in the following book where Juno, queen of the gods, curses Aeneas. Aeneas, after being told by his father in the underworld what the future holds in store for him, after landing at the mouth of the river Tiber, and after the pact with King Latinus, who has promised him his daughter and a land to settle on, now feels confident of his destiny: he will found a line in Italy, thus accomplishing his life's work. But Juno, protectress of the Greeks and enemy of the Trojans, will not allow him to succeed without 'wars, outbursting wrath, treachery and recriminations'. 'They now have their desire, and are finding refuge in Tiber's bed' (VII, 303–4), she exclaims in one of those turns of phrase where poetic genius reveals, with unwitting straightforwardness, the unconscious object of a conqueror's desire (they have found refuge in a 'bed'). Her husband Jupiter and the gods of Olympus, both reluctant and unable to change Fate, turn a deaf ear to her entreaties. So she decides to call on an evil genius to help her further the ends of her jealous hatred – a symbol of the destructiveness that dogs any creative enterprise. Juno unleashes on Aeneas the Fury Allecto, whose hair is twined with writhing serpents. She is one of the infernal powers that Aeneas thought he would be able to keep at a distance even if he went to look at them at close quarters. In other words, she represents the persecutory anxiety which in his own case Freud never succeeded fully in elucidating. The message is clear: no one can go down into the underworld of the mind without setting hidden forces in motion; it was at his own risk that Freud was beginning his self-analysis proper.

Political or military leaders (in his adolescence Freud dreamed of becoming one), people like Columbus, who tackled the Atlantic Ocean, or Nansen, who was braving the cold of the Arctic at that very time (the adult Freud admired them both), like to pit themselves against external dangers. This tendency – as I have often seen in those of my patients engaged in such activities – masks a flight from internal dangers. Being a psychoanalyst means, on the contrary, that one prefers to tackle those dangers head on, that one tolerates the inevitable anxiety caused by them, and that one also accepts one's own weakness when faced with some awesome external danger – which may vary, depending on the subject, from addressing a hostile crowd to climbing a mountain, driving a car or (in Freud's case) taking a train.

Ancient Italy had begun to have other symbolic repercussions for Freud. He showed a keen interest in the excavations that were in full swing at the time – an interest which represented in his case a generalisation of the search for vestiges of his or his patients' past. The process he had called 'psychoanalysis' for the first time a few months earlier (1896*a*) now seemed to be a kind of archaeology of the individual psyche. This metaphor, like all metaphors, is no more than an analogy: the past, as revealed by archaeology, is well and truly dead; and although, when brought to light, it enables us better to understand the way our collective history hangs together, it has no influence on current events, whereas the past with which psychoanalysis is concerned remains alive and active in each individual, and its revival can help to resolve current conflicts. But when a metaphor has greater significance for an individual than a mere rhetorical exercise, it serves as a vehicle for a phantasy. I do not intend to apply the notion of phantasy, which was invented later, to Freud's situation towards the end of 1896. But it is, I think, worth pointing to the thematic structure that was beginning to emerge: once his father had died, Freud was fascinated by an image whose meaning he did not for the moment grasp – that of a man who explores the ground thoroughly.

The first stirrings of Freud's unconscious phantasy were simultaneous with, and related to, a period of intense activity at a conscious level. In describing the subject of his study, he dropped the terms nervous system or φψω apparatus, and used 'psychical' apparatus for the first time. And in formulating it, he divided it up into three systems, which he did not see fit to modify for the next twenty-five years: the conscious, the preconscious, and the unconscious (*F* 207–14). Memory presents not one, but several registrations of events – a notion already hinted at in *On Aphasia* (1891*b*). The perception-consciousness system registers immediate perceptions and arranges them according to associations of simultaneity; but as it does not retain them, it becomes available for fresh perceptions – like the 'mystic writing-pad' to which Freud later compared the psychical apparatus (1925*a*). Unconsciousness represents 'the second registration, arranged according to other, perhaps causal, relations'. Preconsciousness is 'the third transcription, attached to word presentation and corresponding to our official ego'. Only preconscious traces can become conscious, since consciousness, it will be remembered, does not itself retain memory-traces. This was the first time that Freud looked at the mind not as a system of forces but as a system of transcription, the first time, as Derrida (1967, p. 307) has pointed out, that 'the metaphor of writing took over both the structure of the psychical apparatus and the fabric of the psychical text'.

The ideas expressed by Freud in the letter were to form the basis of Chapter 7 of *The Interpretation of Dreams* (1900*a*), 'The Psychology of the Dream Processes'. The passage where the expression 'psychic[al] apparatus' first appears concerns the aetiology of perversion – in other words

Freud also expresses for the first time another important idea, perversion, which he later developed fully in the first of his *Three Essays on the Theory of Sexuality* (1905*d*). Here is the passage: 'Another consequence of premature sexual experiences is perversion, of which the determinant seems to be that defence either does not occur before the psychic apparatus is completed or does not occur at all' (*F* 210). Freud goes on to suppose that it is the perversion of the parents that produces hysteria in children, to explain 'why the outcome is sometimes perversion and sometimes neurosis', to distinguish between normal defence and pathological defence, and to attempt a structural classification (in fact rather a jab in the dark) of psychical pathologies: repression takes place, he claims, in the perception-consciousness system in the case of hysteria, in the preconscious in the case of paranoia, and in the unconscious in the case of obsessional neurosis; it is 'impossible or not attempted' in the case of perversion.

The same letter also sets out the new notion of 'erotogenic zones' and contains a statement that runs directly counter to Freud's and Breuer's theory of abreaction or catharsis: 'A hysterical attack is not a discharge but an *action*; and it retains the original characteristic of every action – of being a means to the reproduction of pleasure'. It contains his first ontogenetic theory about the development of the psychical apparatus: 'I should like to emphasise the fact that the successive registrations represent the psychic achievement of successive epochs of life. At the boundary between two such epochs a translation of the psychic material must take place.' Patients who had something sexual done to them during sleep when they were children repeat the experience by bouts of somnolence or hypnotic giddiness: 'One of my patients still whimpers in his sleep as he did long ago (in order to be taken into bed by his mother, who died when he was 22 months old' (*F* 213). These attacks of giddiness, somnolence and sobbing, then, are aimed at 'the prehistoric, unforgettable other person'.

The most important aspect of this letter is, no doubt, the fact that it shows Freud to have discarded for good the neurophysiological foundations which were so vital to his 'Project for a Scientific Psychology' (October 1895), and which in his view encapsulated the essential ideas of his pre-psychoanalytic scientific work. The three levels of the pyschical apparatus no longer correspond to different types of neurones. Now that his father was dead and he was beginning to think in terms of taking Rome by storm Freud broke away from the model of the biological body and started to understand the phantasy body – the body that expresses itself in hysterical symptoms and is represented in dreams, the body of pleasure, desire and transgression.

Over the next three months, Freud made steady progress in his theories.

He had new explanations for phobias. Fear of throwing oneself out of the window, in the case of women, was a way of rejecting the anxiety-producing wish to beckon to a man to come up. Agoraphobia was 'the repression of the intention to take the first man one meets in the street: envy of prostitution and identification' (*F* 218). His explanation of hysteria, and later of other neuroses, by sexual trauma and subsequent repression was extended to psychoses (amentia and confusional states), epilepsy and perversions. Freud used for the first time his well-known formulation: hysteria is the negative of perversions (*F* 227). He also developed the notion of specific erotogenic zones, after studying perversions in the light of work by Meynert's successor, Krafft-Ebing, and investigating mediaeval witchcraft. But under Fliess's influence his conception of those zones remained highly organic. We shall shortly examine the evolution of this theory step by step when discussing the 'Rome' dreams (p. 189).

Freud used Fliess's beloved theory of bisexuality to explain the choice between perversion and neurosis. In a purely male subject, the original sexual incident produces pleasure and perversion; in a purely female subject it causes unpleasure and neurosis of defence. Freud even attempted to make Fliess's periods fit into his theory. That only strengthened his belief that seduction of a child by an adult is pathogenic: 'It seems to me more and more that the essential point of hysteria is that it results from *perversion* on the part of the seducer' (*F* 212). Heredity is involved solely insofar as a daughter is made neurotic by a perverted father.

At the same time, Freud complained to Fliess that he had not yet been able to carry out a full psychoanalysis. His patients were content merely with an improvement in their condition. That was not enough for Freud, who wanted to go back to the original cause of their troubles and corroborate the existence of an initial pathogenic situation. He pressed his patients to try to find people who might have witnessed or known about incidents in their childhood so that they could be completely reconstructed. This may have been the case with Herr E., if indeed it is he who is referred to in the following passage: 'This year I have had no further news from a patient with obsessional ideas whom I treated only for seven months. Yesterday I heard from Mrs. F. [. . .] that this man travelled to his hometown in order to ascertain the reality of the things he remembered and that he received full confirmation from his seducer, who is still alive (his nurse, now an old woman). He is said to be doing very well; he is obviously avoiding a complete cure, aided by this improvement' (*F* 219). Freud, then, was moving further and further back in time, from puberty to the second dentition, and then to the first three years of life.

Freud's choice of reading matter changed similarly. He now looked for parallels or transpositions of his fundamental research. From novelists, poets and archaeologists he obtained documents which complemented the rather too idiosyncratically individual evidence he obtained from his patients, and which he was soon to interpret much as he would a symptom or a dream. Freud even initiated himself in areas that were new to him, such as anthropology, folklore and witchcraft. He read *Malleus Maleficarum* (The Hammer of Evil-doing Women). He was struck by the similarities between his theory of hysteria and the mediaeval theory of possession. The devil, after taking possession of his victims, fornicated with them. Confessions extracted under torture resembled what his patients told him under psychoanalysis. The inquisitors' cruel ways could be found in the scene of seduction that later engendered hysteria (*F* 225). As for the flying of witches, the broomstick they straddled could be explained as 'the great Lord Penis' (*F* 227).

Theoretical activity on such an intense scale prompts two questions. First, what was it that Freud so needed to defend himself against through such a degree of intellectualisation? There can be only one answer: against the depressive anxiety caused by the death of his father. Secondly, what were the events taking place in his unconscious which he was striving to transcribe in the form of a theoretical formulation? His psyche was the theatre and the witness, but not the instigator, of a profound upheaval. The work of mourning has an advantage over dream-work: it takes place during the daytime as well as at night, is independent of any interest, or lack of interest, in the outside world, and can be monitored during the waking state instead of having to be reconstructed afterwards. It proves the existence of an internal reality of the mind which cannot be reduced either to the functioning of the brain or to conscious thought. If a specifically psychical work takes place within us in this way, at once against our will and with our assent, it must mean that a purely psychical apparatus exists in order to produce it.

The 'Rome' dreams (January 1897)

As I have already mentioned, Freud and his brother Alexander visited northern Italy during the summer of 1896 more extensively than they had done the year before. In the autumn, Freud began collecting antiques. On December 6, in the letter where he mentions many important concepts for the first time, such as the psychical apparatus and consciousness, the preconscious and the unconscious, he tells Fliess: 'I have now adorned my room with plaster casts of Florentine statues. It was a source of extraordinary invigoration for me' (*F* 214). The enthusiasm with which Freud followed the major archaeological discoveries of his time is an indication of the similarity he saw between psychoanalysis and archaeology (cf. S. C. Bernfeld, 1951). Italy, one of the cradles of world civilisation, held great fascination for a man like Freud, whose culture was Jewish and German. He was drawn to the Italian Renaissance, Etruscan art and, above all, Roman ruins. For several years in succession, he spent all his holidays in Italy. He would have liked to have held a 'congress' there with Fliess, in Naples or Pompeii (cf. the end of his important letter of December 6, 1896). Fliess, replying later that month, no doubt suggested they met instead in Prague at Easter, to judge from a remark by Freud in his letter of January 3, 1897.

It is highly probable that the four 'Rome' dreams described in *The Interpretation of Dreams* (*ID* 193–8) all date from this period (December 1896–January 1897). As it is quite impossible to establish their chronological sequence, I shall discuss them in the order in which they are described by Freud, dividing them into two groups of two dreams – the first, shorter dreams where the dreamer sees Rome from afar, and the second pair where he dreams he is in Rome. They are examined in Section B, 'Infantile Material as a Source of Dreams', of Chapter 5, 'Material and Sources of Dreams', after Freud has discussed two anonymous dreams, the 'Yellow lion' and 'Nansen's sciatica' (as we shall see, there is every reason to suppose they were dreamed by Freud himself), and completed his analysis of the 'Uncle with the yellow beard' dream and of his underlying ambition to become a professor. His wish to become a professor and his wish to go to Rome remained closely entwined for nearly five more years, before being resolved at virtually the same time. Grinstein devotes a chapter to the Rome dreams (G Chapter 3).

THE FIRST AND SECOND 'ROME' DREAMS

'In another instance it became apparent that, though the wish which instigated the dream was a present-day one, it had received a powerful reinforcement from memories that stretched far back into childhood. What I have in mind is a series of dreams which are based upon a longing to visit Rome. For a long time to come, no doubt, I shall have to continue to satisfy that longing in my dreams: for at the season of the year when it is possible for me to travel, residence in Rome must be avoided for reasons of health. For instance, I dreamt once that I was looking out of a railway-carriage window at the Tiber and the Ponte Sant'Angelo. The train began to move off, and it occurred to me that I had not so much as set foot in the city. The view that I had seen in my dream was taken from a well-known engraving which I had caught sight of for a moment the day before in the sitting-room of one of my patients. Another time someone led me to the top of a hill and showed me Rome half-shrouded in mist; it was so far away that I was surprised at my view of it being so clear. There was more in the content of this dream than I feel prepared to detail; but the theme of "the promised land seen from afar" was obvious in it. The town which I saw in this way for the first time, shrouded in mist, was – Lübeck, and the prototype [*Vorbild*] of the hill was – at Gleichenberg' (*ID* 193–4).

The very few associations provided by Freud to this dream mean that we can do no more than conjecture its meaning. The view over 'the Tiber and the Ponte Sant'Angelo' suggests the approach to the Vatican, seat of the papacy and symbol of the persecution of the Jews. This is enemy territory, whose menacing power is embodied in its prison, the castle of Sant'Angelo. The formidable Rome portrayed here, a city best not approached, contrasts with the image, in the second dream, of a desirable Rome, a 'promised land', which, however, can only be seen from afar. The wish that the two dreams have in common is that of seeing the 'promised one' – fiancée, sisters, niece and other playmates from childhood, and lastly mother.

Freud was being driven by the same wish in his epistemological quest. It involved trying to see how sexuality and the psychical apparatus work. But whereas seeing is libidinally hypercathected, approaching, touching and penetrating is forbidden. The Pope (the father) possesses the Urbs, the archetypal city (the mother). He allows the scene to be viewed from afar, but persecutes those who would like to enjoy a possession he has reserved for himself. When transposed to a conscious register, the conflict is revealed to Freud as follows: he is attracted by ancient Rome, but fears Catholic Rome. Goethe's famous line 'Eternal Woman draws us upward' was no doubt in the back of his mind, the Eternal Woman being replaced by the Eternal City.

This theme is complemented by various elements. The 'mist' shrouding Rome evokes the 'blank screen' since discovered by Bertram Lewin (the blank screen of the dream represents the mother's breast). Thus, as we have already remarked, the space providing the background of the dream duplicates its central signifier. Were the interpretation of the 'view' in the dream taken further, it would mean bringing to light the infantile memory underlying it (but which Freud has not yet retrieved) – the memory of having seen the naked body of a close female relative.

At the time when Freud had his 'Rome' dreams, the Pope was in conflict with the Italian government led by the anticlerical Crispi and had shut himself away in the Vatican. The persecutor, then, can in turn be persecuted. Hostile powers, when faced head on, become controllable. The signifier 'bridge' points in the same direction. A bridge represents the possibility of getting over a natural obstacle. Brücke (whose name means 'bridge' in German) fulfilled that role at the start of Freud's scientific career. Charcot took over from him in Paris, a city whose bridges, among other things, excited Freud's admiration, and whose proud motto, *Fluctuat nec mergitur* (It floats and does not sink), likening the Ile de la Cité to a ship afloat on the River Seine, remained impressed on his mind. After a success in Paris, why not a success in Rome?

The risks involved in crossing the bridge, in going forward, in other words in 'transgressing', are considerable. The train in the first dream 'begins to move off' before Freud can alight – an allusion, by inversion, to his fear of railways and anxiety about being unable to board trains. The train that suddenly moves off represents the instinctual impulse – desire for the mother – which may incite him to act or behave dangerously. What would happen to him if the train, which he is so afraid of taking in real life, and which he cannot get off in time in his dream, took him to the object aimed at by his desire? The argument put forward by Freud for not going, in real life, to Rome during the summer – 'for reasons of health' (no doubt an allusion to the scorching heat, malaria and noxious strench of the Pontine Marshes, which had not yet been drained) – was not merely the rationalisation of an unconscious inhibition: it should be taken quite literally.

The city in the second dream is Lübeck, where as both Jones (J I, 150) and Grinstein (G 70) have pointed out, Sigmund and Martha went on their honeymoon – in other words, where Freud first possessed the object of his desire. It was in Lübeck, too (as Eva Rosenblum has indicated to me), that Martha, a year earlier, had had a phantasy of being drowned while bathing with a girlfriend in the Baltic. We know from Jones (J I, 146) that she informed Freud of her phantasy somewhat callously in a letter. His rather tetchy reply begins with the words: 'Sieh da, Lübeck' ('Fancy, Lübeck!') (letter to Martha of August 12, 1885, *L* 179). Rome 'half-shrouded' – in other words, drowned – in mist represents a metonymical substitute for 'Martha drowned in the sea at Lübeck'. The latent thought is: Martha might have died before I possessed her. This is confirmed by the second place in the dream: Gleichenberg, as Grinstein has pointed out, is a small spa in Styria where Freud went in the summer of 1883 to see Ignaz Schönberg (J I, 181), Minna's fiancé, who was seriously ill. Two years later, Schönberg saw Minna for the last time, and, knowing that he was doomed, preferred to release her from their engagement. She refused.

Freud then wrote to Martha: 'And you wouldn't behave differently, wouldn't leave me before I died, if it looked as though I were going to die. And I certainly wouldn't give up what is most precious to me as long as I am alive' (letter to Martha of June 23, 1885, *L* 167). Schönberg died in February 1886.

The anxiety aroused in Freud by the sight of the Promised Land (in other words, of the scientific discovery he was in the process of making) was, therefore, separation anxiety: the first dream evoked the separation of travel, the second the separation caused by the death of a loved woman. In real life, however, the separation that Freud was then experiencing through the work of mourning was of a different kind: it was the separation of the father. Although in one sense painful, it also had a liberating effect. A dead father is less of a threat than a living one. Entrenched in his palace, the Pope can no longer call the tune.

An identification which, following D. Lagache (1961), I would describe as heroic can be detected in the second dream.

In *Deuteronomy* (Freud, as we have seen, knew the Bible well), God bids Moses to go up Mount Nebo and shows him the Land of Canaan, which has been promised to the children of Israel. But He tells him that he will never reach that land, but will die on the mountain. This is Moses' punishment for having disobeyed God when he twice smote the rock with his rod to bring forth water, instead of speaking to Him as He had bidden him. According to the exegetists, Moses was punished for his impatience to quench man's thirst, the thirst for the Messiah. Moses was the subject of Freud's last work, *Moses and Monotheism* (1939*a*), in which he quotes abundantly from the Bible.

The second 'Rome' dream takes Freud up the Gleichenberg – literally, according to Eva Rosenblum, up the mountain (*Berg*) which resembles (*gleichen*), in other words up the same mountain as Moses. This is the first time, though Freud does not explicitly say so, that he identifies with the man who was unable to take possession of the Promised Land because he had rebelled against his God, but who had had time, meanwhile, to draw up the Tables of the Law. Freud had a hunch that he was about to recognise the Law of the Father, the keystone of the psychical organisation, but he feared that the price of his triumph might be his own death.

Other elements in the two dreams also seem to represent the discovery which Freud was in the process of making. The first of them describes what the dreamer could see when looking 'out of a railway-carriage window'. A letter that Freud wrote to Fliess at about the same time explains, as we have already seen, why some women have a phobia of throwing themselves out of the window. The unconscious idea is that approaching the window is like beckoning to a man, as prostitutes do: 'Think of Guy de Maupassant's *faire de la fenêtre*,' Freud adds (*F* 217). In the dream, Freud, too, *fait de la fenêtre* – another case of his identification with his female patients which has already been noted in the Irma dream, and without which he would never have been able to understand the mechanisms of neurosis.

Another recurring feature that deserves mention is the twin presence in Freud's dreams of a visual image and a verbal, or more precisely onomastic, element. The first two Rome dreams both consist of a view that relates to proper names – Tiber and Sant'Angelo in the first, Lübeck and Gleichenberg in the second – which themselves relate to certain signifieds. The psychical apparatus is represented here by the twofold psychical content that characterises it: word-presentations (the preconscious) and thing-presentations (the unconscious). As Freud wrote in his important letter to Fliess of December 6, 1896, it is a system of multiple transcriptions. The meaning of a visual image can be transcribed into words, and words, in turn, open up new signifying chains: by experimenting on himself, Freud had discovered the very process of interpretation itself. But there is another point that needs to be made. Tiber, Sant'Angelo, Lübeck and Gleichenberg are all place names. This marks the appearance of toponymy in Freud's dreams, thus confirming my theory that the body image is a key dimension of his dreams. The letters to Fliess at that time are full of descriptions of erotogenic zones, which Freud makes a point of not only 'seeing' but naming. The first two 'Rome' dreams show Freud's disappointment vis-à-vis Fliess, who had turned down the idea of a 'congress' in Italy. At the very moment when Freud was ready to travel to Rome, on condition he was accompanied (like the agoraphobic women referred to in his letter of December 17, 1896), Fliess's counterproposal caused the train to move off in the direction of Prague before he had had time to set foot in the Eternal City.

THE THIRD 'ROME' DREAM

Here is the third dream with the complete text of Freud's comments on it:

'In a third dream I had at last got to Rome, as the dream itself informed me; but I was disappointed to find that the scenery was far from being of an urban character. *There was a narrow stream of dark water; on one side of it were black cliffs and on the other meadows with big white flowers. I noticed a Herr Zucker* [=sugar] (whom I knew slightly) *and determined to ask him the way to the city.* I was clearly making a vain attempt to see in my dream a city which I had never seen in my waking life. Breaking up the landscape in the dream into its elements, I found that the white flowers took me to Ravenna, which I have visited and which, for a time at least, superseded Rome as capital of

Italy. In the marshes round Ravenna we found the loveliest water-lilies growing in black water. Because we had such difficulty in picking them out of the water, the dream made them grow in meadows like the narcissi at our own Aussee. The dark cliff, so close to the water, reminded me vividly of the valley of the Tepl near Karlsbad. "*Karlsbad*" enabled me to explain the curious detail of my having asked Herr Zucker the way. The material out of which the dream was woven included at this point two of those facetious Jewish anecdotes which contain so much profound and often bitter worldly wisdom and which we so greatly enjoy quoting in our talk and letters. Here is the first one: the "*constitution*" story. An impecunious Jew had stowed himself away without a ticket in the fast train to *Karlsbad*. He was caught, and each time tickets were inspected he was taken out of the train and treated more and more severely. At one of the stations on his *via dolorosa* he met an acquaintance, who asked him where he was travelling to. "To Karlsbad," was his reply, "if my constitution can stand it." My memory then passed on to another story: of a Jew who could not speak French and had been recommended when he was in Paris to ask the way to the rue Richelieu. Paris itself had for many long years been another goal of my longings; and the blissful feelings [*Seligkeit*] with which I first set foot on its pavement seemed to me a guarantee that others of my wishes would be fulfilled as well. "Asking the way", moreover, was a direct allusion to *Rome*, since it is well known that all roads lead there. Again, the name *Zucker* [sugar] was once more an allusion to *Karlsbad*; for we are in the habit of prescribing treatment there for anyone suffering from the *constitutional* complaint of diabetes. The instigation to this dream had been a proposal made by my friend in Berlin that we should meet in Prague at Easter. What we were going to discuss there would have included something with a further connection with "sugar" and "diabetes"' (*ID* 194–5).

The structure of the dream is one with which we are now familiar. The first part of it is visual: it refers to scenery (a thing-presentation). The second consists of a word-presentation, made up of a name that is both a proper and a common name (Herr Zucker, or Mr Sugar) and of a question (what is the way to the City?). The dominant effect is disappointment ('I was disappointed . . .'), which was caused, as I have already pointed out, by Fliess's refusal to help Freud fulfil his wish to go to Rome. I shall analyse the two parts of the dream one after the other.

The scenery is divided by a 'narrow stream of dark water', similar to the Tiber, which separates the ancient City of Rome from the Vatican City. But there are other pairs of opposites in that division. One side is white, the other black. One side is mineral (the cliffs), the other vegetable (meadows and flowers). When we remember Freud's favourite reading matter, his recent quotation from Vergil and his idealisation of ancient Rome, it is easy to interpret this fantastic topography as a Graeco-Roman, not Christian, description of hell. It is the hell evoked by Dante, who, as it happened, died in Ravenna before being to taken to Florence for burial. We find the dark, stagnant waters of the Styx, the black rocks of Tartarus where evil-doers were tortured, and the flower-studded meadows of the Elysian Fields, dwelling place of the blessed. More specifically, the river in the dream is a compression of the Phlegethon, which was next to Tartarus, the Lethe, which came at the end of the Elysian Fields, and the Styx, across which dead souls had to be ferried before meeting the gigantic three-headed Cerberus at the entrance of hell itself – a symbol of the transgression that every creator needs to commit and its inherent dangers. Here we have a heroic identification with Aeneas, who sees this same scenery on his journey into the underworld in Book VI of the *Aeneid*.

While this scenery, in its symbolic, universally comprehensible aspect, represents Freud's search for an objective set of references in classical culture, it also reproduces, on the very different level of the individual infantile wish, the setting of a childhood memory which Freud has not yet retrieved. The signifiers that prepare the way for and foreshadow that recollection may be briefly mentioned here. *Fluss*, the German word for a stream, is an allusion to Gisela Fluss, Freud's childhood playmate and first adolescent love. The meadows with big white flowers recall the field in Freiberg where he played and fought with his nephew and niece. The difficulty in picking the water-lilies anticipates the central metaphor of the memory he was later to retreive: plucking the flower of a girl. I would simply emphasise here something which the Rome dreams brought home to Freud – the need for an infantile wish to tie up with a waking wish before a dream can occur, and the need, too, for personal memories to tie up with universal culture before the unconscious can be understood.

If we now relate the scenery of the dream to the pregenital erotogenic zones that Freud was beginning to investigate, we see that they are symbolically represented in it even though Freud does not yet have a clear conception of them: the oral zone (the 'meadows'), the anal zone (the 'black cliffs', and the name of the valley of the Tepl, a word which also means chamber-pot: G 72), and the urethral zone (the 'narrow stream of dark water'). Immediately afterwards, in his letter of January 11, 1897, Freud proposes to Fliess for the first time the notion of an 'oral sexual system' and the idea that 'as long as smell (or taste) is dominant, urine, faeces, and the whole surface of the body, also blood, have a sexually exciting effect' (*F* 223). The equivalence between gold and excrement is mentioned in his letter of January 24, 1897. Once again, Freud owes the discovery to the case of Herr E.:[1] E. suddenly told him that for Louise, his nurse, first love and seductress, 'money always was excrement'. In his letter of February 8, 1897, Freud asks Fliess about 'the eating of excrement' and the date 'when disgust first appears'. It will be remembered that in his letter of December 4, 1896 (see p. 176, n.4), Freud censored the word 'fart'. Once again, then, Freud happed on a discovery in a dream, and eventually became fully aware of what he had discovered only a few days later. One final case of opposition is alluded to – Ravenna's fleetingly successful bid to supersede Rome, as a son tries to outstrip his father. But as with Rome, seat of the Vatican, in the first dream, the reference is as much in the service of the wish as in that of the defences: Ravenna was taken even though it believed itself to be impregnable. Power may always, one day, change hands.

The second part of the dream, the meeting with Herr Zucker, no longer focusses on Freud's childhood, but concerns his relationship with Fliess at that time. It defines his position with regard not to the culture he used as a reference (Graeco-Roman culture), but to the culture into which he had been born (Judaism).

Fliess (whose name, by the way, suggests the German verb, *fliessen*, which means 'to flow'; cf. the 'narrow stream' at the beginning of the dream) is the guide Freud approaches to ask his way. The commentary on the dream ends with a mention of the 'proposal by my friend in Berlin that we should meet in Prague at Easter', but does not refer to Freud's own earlier suggestion that they hold their 'congress' in Italy. Freud has such confidence in his guide that he prefers to give in and accept his counter-proposal. He does so in his letter of January 3, 1897, though he does add the word 'maybe': 'At our next congress I hope there will be important things to talk about. I think by Easter at the latest, maybe in Prague' (*F* 219–20). At the beginning of the same letter we find a combination of two references, one alluding to the motto of Paris ('if we do not prematurely capsize [. . .] we shall arrive'), the other to one of the two Jewish anecdotes mentioned in Freud's comments on the dream ('if our constitutions can stand it'). These allusions suggest that Freud had the dream on January 3, 1897, or thereabouts.

1. This is the first time that Freud specifically mentions Herr E. He had probably already been alluded to in the letters of October 31 and November 2, 1895 (see p. 161), as well as that of January 3, 1987 (p. 181). Freud referred to his case on many subsequent occasions: Draft L of May 2, 1897 (*F* 242), December 29, 1897 (*F* 290), February 19, 1899 (*F* 345), December 21, 1899 (*F* 391), January 8, 1900 (*F* 395), January 26, 1900 (*F* 397), March 11, 1900 (*F* 403), and April 4 and 16, 1900 (*F* 408–9).

The two anecdotes, given in telegraphic form by Freud, need to be gone into in detail for a proper understanding of the dream. Karlsbad (today Karlovy Vary) was a celebrated spa in Bohemia. But the price of accommodation was high and the treatment gruelling (its waters are laxative). The Jews who stayed at Karlsbad were wealthy (hence the temerity of the impecunious Jew in the story, who tries to travel there without paying his fare – a reference to the straitened circumstances in which Freud's father and, indeed, Freud himself had lived). Visitors' 'constitutions' had to be able 'to stand it'. There are two allusions here. The Jew without a ticket has to stand the maltreatment of the ticket inspector. Curiously, the text talks of his successive stations in the sense of 'stations of the cross', or *Leidensstation* (one of the words for railway station in German is *Station*). Why did Freud compare that poor Jew with Jesus, another poor Jew, who had been delivered to the Romans by the rich Jews and was going up the Via Dolorosa? In the background, what we have here is a personal memory connected with Freud's discovery of antisemitism (he recalled it in the following dream). In this third dream, the emphasis is on the anal nature of the allusion. Cartoons of the period – I am told by Eva Rosenblum – commonly depict a patient in Karlsbad hurrying through the park or along a corridor on his way to the lavatory and being asked by a friend: 'Where on earth are you off to in such a rush?' Similarly, one of the variants of the story about the impecunious Jew without a ticket has the inspector kicking him off the train at each stop with a boot in the backside. What are the personal memories that converge on this cultural reference? The infantile memory was retreived only at a later stage, but we can already infer that it will be a memory of shame connected with anal or urethral loss of control. It is possible, on the other hand, to point to a day's residue that was already clearly present in Freud's mind, even though he mentioned it only in connection with a subsequent dream: Freud's father had died a few weeks before of heart failure and paralysis of the bladder, and had had a motion shortly after his death.

Thus, his father's constitution had been able to stand antisemitic harassment, as we shall see; but it could come to terms neither with the business failures that forced him to move from town to town (as though following the stations of the Cross), then end up in Vienna, a ruined man, nor with old age, illness and death: all this 'loss of control' was the cause of shame in his son. To return to the adult Freud, one of the meanings of the dream, suggested to me by Eva Rosenblum, would seem, in the light of the anecdote, to be as follows: he wants to get to Rome/Karlsbad to cure himself, even though he is a poor Jew who might want to hide the fact that he has no ticket, and who must at all times confront an implacable enemy.

The ticket is no doubt a reference to Heinrich Heine's celebrated remark: 'The act of baptism is the entrance ticket to European culture'. One might add that if self-analysis is henceforth intended by Freud to be curative, it has at the same time begun to be 'laxative'.

Freud assumes the second anecdote to be too well-known to need enlarging upon. It runs as follows: an impecunious Jew, who knows no French, emigrates to Paris. He has been told by a mischievous friend to ask his way by saying: 'Savez-vous où est la rue Richelieu?' (the suggestion is mischievous because – as I am told by Eva Rosenblum – the sound 'ieu' does not exist in Yiddish). So the Jew is bound to pronounce it 'Richelié' and give away his origins, which he wants to hide. The plot thickens when the freshly arrived Jew puts the question to a passer-by whom he believes to be 100% French, but who is in fact a wealthy, well-assimilated Jew with a perfect grasp of French. The latter quickly realises who he is dealing with, and answers, in excellent French: 'Oui, je sais où est la rue de Richelieu' ('Yes, I know where the rue Richelieu is'). The first Jew is struck by the mischievousness of the answer, which does not in fact answer the question at all, and realises the other man is also a Jew. To show that he knows, he answers ironically in Yiddish with a reference to a fundamental Jewish rite, the Sabbath: '*Man kann Schabbasmachen mit das*' (literally: 'Sabbath can be made with that'; which means both 'a fat lot of use your answer is to me' and 'you and I know perfectly well what is required for the ritual preparation of the Sabbath because we are both Jews').

But there is more to the story than that. As Alain Besançon has suggested to me, the choice of proper name is doubly ironic: 'Richelieu', as a signifier, cannot be properly pronounced by Jews and therefore shows up their poor accent; as a signified, the proper name becomes a common noun, '*riche lieu*' (rich place), which points to love of lucre, another characteristic imputed to the Jews. So despite all his efforts to disguise his origins, the Jew always ends up by being recognised at the level of both signifier and signified. The implicit message of the story is that the Jew's identity is ineffaceable.

Freud, when he arrived in Paris in 1885, was himself the impecunious Jew: he spoke halting French and must have had difficulty in asking the way. It should be noted that for him the rue de Richelieu – he told Martha, in a letter of October 19, 1885, that he had walked down it – must have meant cultural, not material, wealth because it was the street where the Bibliothèque Nationale and the Comédie Française were located. However that may be, the 'humiliation' of not mastering the language of the foreign country in which he was staying cannot have daunted Freud too much, for he became Charcot's friend and translator. He who has conquered Paris shall surely conquer Rome. For do not all roads lead to Rome (a proverb that Freud adapted to suit his own case)? Indeed, one of the other meanings of the third dream is an illustration of that proverb. The mechanism involved here is a mechanism of reassurance that Freud describes a little later in connection with examination dreams: the only examinations people dream of failing are those they have passed in real life. The manifest affect of the dream – disappointment at being in Rome and not seeing the City – reverses the latent affect 'the blissful feelings (*Freude!*) with which I first set foot on [a Parisian] pavement.' Stopping a passer-by – an idealised guide and a fully assimilated, mischievous compatriot: surely Fliess? – and asking him the way to Rome is in no way humiliating or anxiety-producing since the questioner already, and exultantly, knows the answer: all roads lead to Rome. This is the sort of commonsense answer that is often better than a sophisticated one. André Gide, in *Oedipe*, attributes a similar merit to his hero: if Oedipus found the right answer to the Sphinx's question it was because he already knew the answer – because 'man' is the answer to all questions. But a second proverb, with a different meaning, lurks behind the first: 'See Naples and die'. Had not Freud suggested to Fliess that they hold a 'congress' in Naples or in Pompeii, another city with strong associations of death because of the cataclysm that overwhelmed it? The idea is: you succeed, then you succumb to your success.

Once again we can see how important the relationship between the visual and the verbal was for Freud. In this case, the dream expresses a proverb visually; other dreams had sought the word, the proper name, the phrase that would describe a view, a setting, a landscape or a vignette. Here, the difficulty and necessity of translating one's mother tongue into a foreign language are affirmed. It is not only – the conscious manifest content – materially necessary for a Jew to speak the language of the country he lives in, and intellectually necessary for him to learn the major languages of European culture; he also has to do so – the preconscious latent content – because the unconscious is another transcription, and deciphering it is a way of finding out the vocabulary and syntax it uses. Lastly – the unconscious latent content – a certain maternal world was lost for ever when the Freuds moved from Freiberg, and the only creative way of recovering it was not to relive it in a repetitive and nostalgic way, but to formulate a coherent and accurate account of it.

One final signifier still needs elucidating – the name given to the guide-cum-passer-by, Herr Zucker (Mr Sugar), a proper name that is also a common noun, just as Richelieu becomes *riche lieu*. This signifier-signified is clearly overdetermined. The waters of Karlsbad were used in the treatment of diabetes, a disease (at that time virtually incurable) which is characterised by excess sugar in the blood. The German word for diabetes is *Zuckerkrankheit*. According to Eva Rosenblum, it used to be said jokingly in Jewish circles at that time that all elderly Jews had diabetes; people made fun of their saccharine pills just as the French nowadays claim flippantly that the whole French nation suffers from a bad liver. Herr Zucker is the Death figure of Germanic legend whom the lost traveller innocently and unwisely asks the way. Sugar and diabetes were also one of the questions on the agenda of Freud's imminent 'congress' in Prague with Fliess. Fliess is here Herr Zucker, just as in the dream of 'Irma's injection' he is to some extent Herr Trimethylamin, a man who knows what goes on inside the body and carries out chemical analysis, whereas Freud restricts himself to the surface and orifices of the skin and to psychical analysis. On the black rock of biology, which grows ever more solid thanks to Fliess, Freud will be able to plant the meadows and white flowers of psychology.

Who exactly was this Herr Zucker, whom Freud says he knew 'slightly'? The only connection I have found is with the two Zuckerkandl brothers, who are mentioned in a letter to Carl Koller included in the second, enlarged German edition of Freud's correspondence (1968). Emil Zuckerkandl had become a professor of anatomy. His younger brother, Otto, was specialising in urology. It was his meeting with Otto, a youthful, pleasant medical student preparing for his penultimate examination, that Freud described to Koller, who was later to discover the anaesthetising properties of cocaine. In that case, the themes underlying the dream must therefore be micturition, rivalry with a fellow discoverer, and the ambition to become a professor – a hypothesis borne out by the fact that, in the diagnosis of diabetes, urine analysis was used to establish the blood's sugar content.

A more important aspect of the dream is, to my mind, the fact that it focusses particularly on two mechanisms, the transformation of a proper name into a common noun, and reversal into the opposite. Both mechanisms can be applied to the proper name that is the sought-for object in this series of dreams: if we write that name in Latin, i.e. ROMA (for it was ancient Rome, the city founded by the descendants of Aeneas, that interested Freud), and spell it backwards, we get a common noun that is the key word of the dreams, AMOR (the Latin for love). There is nothing particularly original about the inversion. Like the proverb about all roads leading to Rome, it is well-known to present-day Latin scholars and was certainly familiar to schoolboys in Freud's time. (Incidentally, the surname of the modern Italian novelist, Alberto Moravia, is in fact a pen name consisting of a double anagram of VIA ROMA and VIA AMOR.)

Although it is only later that Freud mentions the story of the oracle given to the Tarquins, in the form of a quotation from Rank in the 1911 edition of *The Interpretation of Dreams* (*ID* 398 n.), surely he must have remembered it, if only vaguely, from his classical studies. Rank, and Freud after him, gives only an elliptical version of the story: 'The oracle given to the Tarquins is equally well known, which prophesied that the conquest of Rome would fall to that one of them who should first kiss his mother ("*osculum matri tulerit*") ["who shall have given his mother a kiss"]. This was interpreted by Brutus as referring to Mother Earth. ("*Terram osculo contigit, scilicet quod ea communis mater omnium mortalium esset*" ["He kissed the earth, saying it was the common mother of all mortals"] Livy, I 56.)' Here is the story in more detail. The aged tyrant Tarquinius, frightened by strange portents, sent two of his sons and his nephew, Brutus, an ambitious man who feigned idiocy, to consult the oracle at Delphi and find out which of them would succeed to the throne. His sons, who took the oracle literally, agreed to keep the matter secret from their other brother, who had remained in Rome. Brutus, on the other hand, decided to 'interpret' the oracle: falling to the ground as if by chance, he kissed the Mother-Earth. Marie Delcourt (1944, pp. 197–202), in her important work, *Oedipe ou la légende du conquérant*, puts the story in the context of the history of myths and religions and goes into a detailed discussion of the episode and of many others like it: in her view, they are evidence of a Graeco-Roman rite of entitlement to kingship through the symbolic possession of the mother either in a dream or by the actual kissing of the earth. At the beginning of 1897, Freud identified with the conquering hero of classical antiquity. He imagined himself as Oedipus – though had no idea yet of how true that would prove.

THE FOURTH 'ROME' DREAM

The last 'Rome' dream, not surprisingly, involves inscriptions: 'A fourth dream, which occurred soon after the last one, took me to Rome once more. I saw a street-corner before me and was surprised to find so many posters in German stuck up there. I had written to my friend with prophetic foresight the day before to say that I thought Prague might not be an agreeable place for a German to walk about in. Thus the dream expressed at the same time a wish to meet him in Rome instead of in a Bohemian town, and a desire, probably dating back to my student days, that the German language might be better tolerated in Prague. Incidentally, I must have understood Czech in my earliest childhood, for I was born in a small town in Moravia which has a Slav population. A Czech nursery rhyme, which I heard in my seventeenth year, printed itself on my memory so easily that I can repeat it to this day, though I have no notion what it means. Thus there was no lack of connections with my early childhood in these dreams either' (*ID* 195–6).

The dream has the same construction as Freud's dream about the death of his father. It is basically no more than a setting and an inscription. The setting is a street-corner, in other words we have an urban scene, not a country landscape. It is also a crossroads. Against this background, there are posters. We are not told what they say, though we know they are in German.

In his letter to Fliess of January 3, 1897, already referred to, Freud accepted, with just a touch of reluctance ('maybe'), the idea of a 'congress' in Prague. All reluctance disappears in the next letter (of February 8, 1897): 'I shall bring a lot of strange material with me to Prague' (*F* 231).

The national minorities belonging to the Austro-Hungarian Empire had frequently – and more especially after 1848 – carried out an organised struggle against the hegemony of the Germans and their language. Czech irredentism had always been vigorous. The governor of Bohemia, Count Thun, who appeared in one of Freud's dreams in 1898, had just stepped down from office after failing to reconcile the Czechs and the Germans. The University of Prague was one of the oldest in Europe. Lectures were originally given in Latin, then in German; Czech had been authorised only recently. Czech culture had already produced one genius, Kekulé, who was followed by Edmund Husserl and Franz Kafka. Freud was both sympathetic towards oppressed minorities in which creators flourish and keen that German should be recognised as a universal language that guaranteed the objectivity of science.

In the dream, Freud finds himself in Rome. To his great surprise (as in the second dream, where he was surprised that the view over the city was so clear), he sees not a Latin inscription, but posters in German. This Latin–German manifest content (Latin and German were the two key languages of his secondary education; they were also the two successive languages imposed on Czechs studying at the University of Prague) is matched, in the latent content, by Czech–German bilingualism (which left its mark on Freud's preschool period in Freiberg). For Freud, then, manifest bilingualism involves written languages, and latent bilingualism spoken languages. In the manifest content, Latin, a phylogenetically ancient language, replaces Czech, an ontogenetically ancient language for Freud. Just as Fliess the Berliner, when he changed the venue of their 'congress' from Rome to Prague, caused, in Freud's expectations of it, Latin to be obliterated by German, so Jacob Freud, when he moved from Freiberg to Vienna, caused Czech to be obliterated, in his son's case, by German, and German alone. The dream, then, combines a childhood memory with a day's residue. There was a halfway point between the age of three and a half and the 40th birthday Freud had just celebrated – the age of 17, when he went to spend his holidays in Freiberg, heard Czech spoken again, and fell in love with Gisela Fluss. At the same time, in his theory, Freud had by then adopted the view that pathogenic events occur not during adolescence or prepuberty, but at the age of three or earlier. As he says in the same letter of January 3, 1897: 'Everything [. . .] is converging more and more on the first period of life, up to three years'.

The dream reminded Freud of the Czech he used to hear as an infant and of a nursery rhyme he still knew by heart. The memory of the person who sang him the nursery rhyme and taught him the language came back to him later. When that happened, the duality of language turned out also to include a duality of religions (Catholic and Jewish) and a duality of the mother image (the real mother and the nurse). In the meantime, the idea in the dream of an obliterated ancient language showed that the process of recovering 'forgotten' childhood memories had begun to operate in Freud's self-analysis.

But a fourth language is missing. In A.D. 70, the future Roman Emperor, Titus, destroyed the Temple of Jerusalem. The Jews, finally defeated, were forced to embark on their destiny of eternal wandering: the Diaspora had begun. Latin had obliterated Hebrew, so speaking a foreign language became a necessity for them. In Freud's time, it was still forbidden for Jews to walk under the Arch of Titus in Rome. In the nineteenth century, Jews throughout central and even eastern Europe spoke Yiddish, which is a mixture of German and Hebrew. Those who wanted to succeed in their countries and cultures of adoption were obliged to speak German, and to speak it well. The young Freud fulfilled his parents' wish by speaking perfect German. It is very likely that the mother tongue of Freud's parents was Yiddish, that they subsequently learned German and, in Jacob's case no doubt, Hebrew, and that when they were still in Freiberg the young Sigismund heard them speak sometimes Yiddish and sometimes German.

But just as repressed memories are not totally forgotten, so obliterated languages do not disappear completely. They leave traces in the unconscious. The traces of 'ancient' languages 'forgotten' by the young Freud when he moved from Freiberg to Vienna connoted for him 'ancient' memories of the time when those languages were still living languages. Not only do words denote things, not only do word-presentations exist independently of thing-presentations, but word-presentations can denote thing-presentations with which they are associated by contiguity.

Let me now apply my interpretative method to the fourth 'Rome' dream more systematically than I have done for the three previous ones, i.e. by looking at it from several angles: a) Freud's relationship with Fliess (which here merges with his relationship with the waking wish), b) his infantile memory, c) the process of the discovery of psychoanalysis, and d) the body image.

Freud made no mention at all to Fliess of his first three 'Rome' dreams – at least not in writing. He referred to the fourth about a year later, in a letter he began on December 3, 1897, and completed two days later. During the intervening period, they had met some time around Easter (April 20, 1897) in Nuremberg (i.e. neither in Rome nor in Prague), Freud had discovered the Oedipus complex, and they had planned another 'congress' at Christmas 1897 in Breslau: 'All of this is only introductory to our meeting – in Breslau, as Ida proposed, if the train connections suit you. You do know that what happened in Prague proved I was right. When we decided on Prague last time, dreams played a big part. You did not want to come to Prague, and you still know why, and at the same time I dreamed that I was in Rome, walking about the streets, and feeling surprised at the large number of German street and shop signs. I awoke and immediately thought: so this was Prague (where such German signs, as is well known, are called for). Thus the dream had fulfilled my wish to meet you in Rome rather than in Prague. My longing for Rome is, by the way, deeply neurotic. It is connected with my schoolboy hero worship of the Semitic Hannibal, and this year in fact I did not reach Rome any more than he did from Lake Trasimeno' (*F*, December 3, 1897, 284–5). Thus it is a frustrated waking wish – the wish to go to Rome – that is fulfilled in this dream; and in the three preceding dreams Fliess represents a father image who prevents Freud's wish from being fulfilled. Here the dream tells us something important about Freud's creative dynamics: when in real life he was prevented from doing something by authority, he accomplished it nonetheless, despite that authority, in his dreams. This can probably be explained by the duality of the figures of authority in Freud's childhood. It was his two much older half-brothers, Emanuel and Philipp, who embodied the repressive father figure, while his father Jacob, who was of an older generation, was more of a grandfatherly figure, kindly, liberal, and keen to share his experience of life. No one can become a creator unless he or she has been able to identify with a permissive possessor of knowledge.

The infantile memories connected with the Rome series of dreams are known with some precision. What we do not know are the exact dates of their recollection by Freud. His interpretation of them took place in two phases – immediately afterwards, in January 1897, and almost a year later (as shown by the letter to Fliess of December 3, 1897), in other words after an intense process of retrieval of memories dating from Freiberg, a process that coincided with the discovery of the Oedipus complex.

Freud's discussion of the dreams in *The Interpretation of Dreams* refers to three categories of memories: the memory of rivalry, when he was about three, with his nephew John, who was older than him; memories dating from prepuberty and connected with imaginary heroes he had read about and conversations with his father about the philosophy of life; and the memory of the holidays he spent in Freiberg as an adolescent. These memories are interesting not only for what they say, but also for what they omit. For they are not continuous: there are blanks in the narrative. The lack of any reference to the intermediate period, between the ages of four and nine, seems to me particularly significant. I would argue that the memories which are essential for these dreams are not the conscious memories recalled at the time of the dreams, but others, belonging precisely to the missing period, which are unconsciously relived and repeated.

Memories of his rivalry with John and of the person who spoke Czech to him in Freiberg came back to Freud at the end of September or beginning of October 1897. Other memories of Freiberg were later elucidated in his analysis, at the end of December 1898 or beginning of January 1899, of his screen memory of a 'Green meadow with yellow flowers'. In my view, the only memory he had already recalled in January 1897 was the one which, at the end of his comments, he sees as the common source of the four 'Rome' dreams:

'I may have been ten or twelve years old, when my father began to take me with him on his walks and reveal to me in his talk his views upon things in the world we live in. Thus it was, on one such occasion, that he told me a story to show me how much better things were now than they had been in his days. "When I was a young man," he said, "I went for a walk one Saturday in the streets of your birthplace; I was well dressed, and had a new fur cap on my head. A Christian came up to me and with a single blow knocked off my cap into the mud and shouted: 'Jew! get off the pavement!'" "And what did you do?" I asked. "I went into the roadway and picked up my cap," was his quiet reply. This struck me as unheroic conduct on the part of the big, strong man who was holding the little boy by the hand. I contrasted this situation with another which fitted my feelings better: the scene in which Hannibal's father, Hasdrubal, made his boy swear before the household altar to take vengeance on the Romans. Ever since that time Hannibal had had a place in my phantasies' (*ID* 197). Just after *The Interpretation of Dreams* was published, Freud realised he had named Hannibal's father incorrectly, calling him Hasdrubal instead of Hamilcar Barca (cf. p. 516), and corrected his mistake in the second edition of 1909. The underlying theme of the memory has three facets: identification with the humiliated father and Jew; resentment at his humiliation, resulting in a certain disavowal of the weak and submissive father; and lastly freedom to forge ahead (if the father had encountered someone stronger than him – just as the Pope of the time had met his master – the son had no reason to feel threatened by him in attempting to satisfy his curiosity).

Identification with the victim is not manifest solely in this recollection. It is implicit in the list of heroes enumerated in Freud's final and complete commentary on the dream. They include: Johann Joachim Winckelmann, a German archaeologist who in the eighteenth century conducted the first important research into ancient Roman art; Hannibal, the Carthaginian (and therefore Semitic) hero who, when still only nine, swore eternal hatred against the Romans at the bidding of his father, Hamilcar Barca (whom Freud initially confused with Hannibal's brother, Hasdrubal), and who later surprised the Romans from the rear by crossing Spain and the Alps, defeating them at Lake Trasimeno, then at Cannae (Cannes); and André Masséna, one of Napoleon's most successful generals, whom the young Freud wrongly believed to be Jewish (no doubt because of the similarity of his name with the Jewish Manasseh). As Grinstein was the first to observe, they are all 'tragic heroes', in that after achieving glory through their exploits they all ultimately failed in life or met an unfortunate end (G 91).

Winckelmann (1717–68), who came from a poor background and was unable to complete his medical or theological studies, was converted to Catholicism and became librarian to a cardinal, a position that enabled him to carry out his investigations in Italy. His reputation as a scholar was such that in 1768 the Empress of Austria, Maria Theresa, received him at court and showered him with gifts. But a few days later Winckelmann was murdered in Trieste by a fellow traveller called Archangeli (cf. the exterminating angel), to whom he had unwisely shown some of the gifts (G 77). Hannibal (247–183 B.C.) failed to follow up the successes of the earlier part of his campaign, and decided not to try and take Rome. One of his lieutenants criticised him in the following terms: 'You know how to vanquish, Hannibal, but you do not know how to exploit victory.' His subsequent failure to withstand the Romans had serious consequences for himself and his people. His brother, Hasdrubal, when coming to his aid via Spain, was defeated and killed. Later, Hannibal was forced to retreat in order to save Carthage, which was being threatened by the Romans.

Traumatised by the relentless war Hannibal had waged against them, the Romans were quite relentless in seeking vengeance. They successively conquered the kings of Syria and of Bythnia, with whom Hannibal had taken refuge. In the end, he committed suicide rather than be handed over to the Romans, who went on to take Carthage and raze it to the ground. So it was that Hannibal, who wanted to destroy Rome, in fact brought down destruction on himself and his people.

Masséna (1759–1817), after a brilliant victory against the Austrians at the battle of Rivoli, was called '*l'enfant chéri de la victoire*' ('victory's beloved son'). He repeated his exploit in 1799 against the Russians at Zürich. He took part, on the whole successfully, in many other battles. But his campaign in Spain and Portugal in 1810 was affected by Napoleon's interference. The result was a disastrous failure to take Lisbon and a difficult retreat. That marked the moment when Napoleon's fortunes in war began to change. It is arguable that in causing indirectly Masséna's defeat Napoleon was anticipating the failure of his own Russian campaign, and his own eventual fall from power. Thus, we can begin to glimpse the significance of Freud's heroic identifications: they were also masochistic identifications. But he did not himself become aware of them until a few months later, when he found their prototype in another tragic destiny taken not from history, but from legend – that of a Greek tragic hero. And much later Freud wrote an essay entitled, significantly, 'Those Wrecked by Success' (1916*d*).

Let us now examine the fourth 'Rome' dream from the third angle, that of the representation of the discovery Freud was in the process of making. As we have already seen, the German–Latin bilingualism implicit in the 'posters' which appear in the dream in fact harks back to Freud's German –Czech–Yiddish trilingualism in Freiberg. It should be added that Freud's schooling in Vienna was characterised by a two-tiered trilingualism – the 'dead' languages, Latin, Greek and Hebrew, and the living foreign languages, English, Spanish and French (Freud had not learned Italian properly until his recent trips to Italy). This pattern of triple trilingualism matches the logic of the triply ternary formula for trimethylamin – $N(CH_3)_3$ – which features in the Irma dream. I have already pointed out (p. 67) that Freud shifted easily from bilingualism to trilingualism when, in the course of comparing hysterical symptoms with a pictographic script, he pointed out that such scripts had been deciphered with the help of a bilingual inscription. But the Rosetta Stone, which enabled Champollion to make his discovery about hieroglyphics was a trilingual inscription (hieratic Egyptian, demotic Egyptian, and Greek). Similarly, the decipherment of cuneiform script that was carried out at various times during the nineteenth century was made possible by the existence of trilingual inscriptions (if a language is completely unknown, it is impossible to find the key to it from a text consisting of only two languages). The discovery made by Champollion in 1822, when he was 32, fascinated the general public in the nineteenth century, as it still does today, purely because of its connection with Napoleonic legend. But people, like Freud, who were familiar with Mediterranean and Asian history, knew the true story of how cuneiform script was deciphered. Briefly, it was as follows.

A 27-year-old German, Georg Grotefend, noticing that the few cuneiform texts known at that time consisted not of one, but of three different forms of writing, began to decipher the first of them (Zend, or Old Persian) in 1802–3. Then an Englishman, Henry Rawlinson, after discovering a trilingual rock inscription at Behistun in which the same text was written in three cuneiform scripts, completed the decipherment of the first of them. Working on the same inscription, Edwin Norris deciphered the second (Scythian, Median or Elamite) between 1838 and 1851; and Rawlinson, with the help of other British scholars, cracked the third (Assyrian/Babylonian or Akkadian) between 1853 and 1857.

Champollion's discovery, which came after Grotefend's but before those of Rawlinson and Norris, unconsciously[1] provided Freud with a clue to the interpretation of dreams. The hieroglyphic signs used in religious Egyptian texts fall into three categories, as Champollion correctly surmised. Sometimes signs work as ideograms, in other words the signifier is a figurative drawing of the signified: thus, the sign for 'goose' is , and the sign for 'tree' 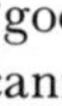. At other times a word, when it cannot be shown figuratively, is represented by another picture with the same sound; the sign is then phonetic. Thus, the word for 'son', which has the same consonants as the word for 'goose', is written in the same way (which corresponds to the Greek sound Z). Lastly, determinatives placed at the end of a word inform the reader, where more than one possible interpretation is possible, as to which family of meanings the word belongs. Thus, the sign  means '*the* house', while  means '*his* house', the snake  being added because its phonetic value, 'f', is also found in the word for 'his'. Hieroglyphic writing, then, helped Freud to see the preconscious as a system of associative chains that added verbal presentations (phonetic, toponymic, onomastic) to unconscious thing-presentations, and more generally to conceive of consciousness, the preconscious and the unconscious as three script systems which, although different, could be

1. I say unconsciously, because Freud did not draw an explicit parallel between the decoding of dreams and the decipherment of hieroglyphs until the second edition of *The Interpretation of Dreams* in 1909 (cf. p. 331).

transliterated from one system to the other and, eventually, deciphered.

The setting of the dream now becomes intelligible. A street corner is the place where two of those systems meet: 'At the boundary between two such epochs a translation of the psychic material must take place,' Freud wrote in the letter to Fliess where he describes how he has discovered the notion of the psychical apparatus (*F* 208).

When Lacan contends, on the basis of similar passages in Freud, that 'the unconscious is structured like a language', he is mistaken because his reading of those passages is superficial. In the fourth 'Rome' dream, the analogy between psychoanalysis and linguistics, coming after the analogy between psychical analysis and chemical analysis, is obviously used by Freud's psychical apparatus as a way of representing to himself not only the process of discovery in which he is engaged, but the ternary structure of the psychical apparatus, and the transcription in book form (and of course in the German language) of what he can see in the unconscious, in other words the transliteration of a personal insight into universal and communicable knowledge. This analogy should no more be taken literally than the previous analogy between associations of ideas and chemical compounds, or than the analogy with the classification of species that lies behind the later dream of the 'Botanical monograph'. It neither proves nor invalidates Lacan's theory: but further evidence is needed for that theory to become plausible.

It is clear, too, that Freud's polyglottism was of considerable help to him: it gave him the ability, at an early age, to understand ways of feeling, thinking and speaking that were different from those of his immediate circle. The fact that any Jew wishing to escape his material and moral isolation was forced, whether he liked it or not, to learn a foreign language turns out in Freud's case to have been a source of victory and revenge – the victory that the intellect, thus stimulated, wins over ignorance, and the revenge for the humiliation of the Jews that Freud, deep down, has promised his father Jacob, just as Hannibal swore to his father Hamilcar Barca that he would avenge the Carthaginians, and Anchises told his son Aeneas that one day he would exact revenge for the Trojans.

In the 'Rome' dreams, as in the dreams of 'Irma's injection' and the death of his father, the result is represented in advance in several guises – a formula, a notice, a rule, place names, a proper name that becomes a common noun, and, lastly, posters. Scientific work does indeed result in formulae and formulations, diagrams, laws, designations and neologisms. Later on, Oedipus, Eros and Narcissus were examples of how proper names could be turned into both common nouns and scientific terms. But why posters? The key is to be found in the third 'Rome' dream: like Moses guided by God, Freud, secretly guided by his dead father in the work of mourning, goes up on to the hill and sees Rome, i.e. the twofold original love he received from a young German mother and another woman, who spoke Czech. He will never in his lifetime be able to repossess that love; he will, however, manage to recall it and to understand the role and meaning of the traces he still has of his infantile experiences; above all, he will, before he dies, find the time, strength, and acuity of mind to make his mark, like Moses, as a lawgiver. The German posters will turn out to be the Tables of the Law of the unconscious.

Let us now look at the dream from one last angle, that of the body image. The way the fourth dream succeeds the third corresponds to the transition from the earliest image of the body to the constitution of an abstract mental space, a transition which also implies a shift in the object-relationship to the mother. The hypothesis which I now intend to test was first put forward in a paper by Besdine (1968). Studying the special kind of relationship that the mothers of geniuses-to-be have with their children, he discovered that Michelangelo, Shakespeare, Goethe, Heine, Balzac, Proust, Sartre, Dostoevsky and, of course, Freud all had mothers who developed a veritable Jocasta complex towards their sons, mothering them to an extreme degree – in other words, not only transferring their incestuous love on to them but doing so in a deeply symbiotic relationship, thus fulfilling the two vital conditions for the emergence of a genius.

In his study of Leonardo da Vinci (1910*c*), Freud stresses the importance of sexual seduction carried out by the mother on the mouth of her infant. In a footnote added to the 1911 edition of *The Interpretation of Dreams* (*ID* 398 n.), he postulates that people favoured by their mothers show optimism in life and in their own success. He later repeats the same idea at the end of 'A Childhood Recollection from *Dichtung und Wahrheit*': 'If a man has been his mother's undisputed darling he retains throughout life the triumphant feeling, the confidence in success, which not seldom brings actual success along with it. And Goethe might well have given some such heading to his autobiography as: "My strength has its roots in my relation to my mother"' (1917*b*, *SE* 17, 156).

According to Besdine, the libidinal hypercathexis of the boy by his mother, and the fact that she not only looks after him but is responsible for introducing him to many new and important experiences, together give him a specific character structure typified by fear of love, guilt feelings, masochism and narcissism all to a considerable degree. This pattern fits Freud in general fairly well, but is particularly relevant to the four 'Rome' dreams. As I have already suggested, they contain the following features:

– the twofold fear of his own incestuous desire for his mother and of her positive response to that desire (cf. the distant 'views' of Roma-Amor, and memories of his unspoken adolescent love for Gisela Fluss);
– fear of punishment (the departing train, Sant'Angelo prison, the fatal disease of diabetes, shame at 'loss of control', the torments of hell);
– identification with the victim (his father being subjected to antisemitic harassment) and heroic identification with those who fail when on the brink of success (Winckelmann, Hannibal, Masséna).

But the particular form of narcissism at work here still needs to be identified. While in the first two dreams Freud remains outside the city and is happy merely to enjoy the view, in the last two he fulfils his wish: he is in Rome itself. The third dream describes a mythical journey into his mother's pregenital belly; and the Mr Sugar whom he meets there and asks the way (in both senses of the word – route and method) could well be the introjected penis of the father, whose sweet delights make the mother swoon, and with whom Freud, as a child, identified rather easily. No sooner was his father dead than he dreamed overtly of kissing Mother Earth, of possessing Rome. Thus, he dreamed of possessing a maternal image both at the phallic-genital level and at the level of a very early narcissistic sharing in maternal omnipotence. There is more than mere symbiosis in this case. Symbiosis is a passive state, whereas in the third dream Freud examines every detail of the landscape and questions a passer-by – in short, he behaves actively. The symbiosis which the genius inhabits is precisely a symbiosis which Freud inhabits: against an important symbiotic background that gives him great abilities for insight (or empathy), an Oedipal form of self-assertion – he is father of his works – enables him to elaborate cultural products from those insights.

The fourth dream also takes place in Rome. This time the setting is urban: the dreamer is at a street corner, which means that he has changed direction and come to a turning point, as well as that he is in an Euclidean geometrical framework, an architectural layout. The central idea of the dream is that in Rome German is not spoken, but written. In other words, Freud moves without transition – the fourth dream occurred 'soon after' the third – from a dream of syncretic amalgamation with his mother's breast to a much later relationship with his mother, one that began when she taught him to read and write German. It can be seen that the intermediate phase, which is gone through by most people, i.e. by those who will never be anything more than ordinary people, has been skipped by Freud. When he learned to talk, he learned not one mother language but three: his mother, who was kept very busy in the family workshop, was not the only person to teach him how to talk. When he learned to write, on the other hand, he was taught only one language. Thus, after the move to Vienna, the disorder of phonetic codes, lexical systems and pregenital pleasures was succeeded by a period where those pregenital pleasures were placed under the guardianship of genitality and those codes and systems were ordered according to the alphabetical code and the grammatical and syntactical system of written German. This retroactive reorganisation of the old by the recently acquired was probably what predisposed Freud to absorb Hughlings Jackson's pioneering theories ten years earlier than other neurologists in Germany. Freud learned to speak several languages because he had several 'mothers' and because his parents, in their conversation, switched constantly from a language of reference to a language of belonging. His real mother language – real because it was a unique language, because it was that of his actual mother, and because it was taught to him by her – did not really crystallise in his mind until he started learning to read and write. Why did Freud become a genius instead of a dyslectic? It frequently happens, in a multilingual context or in situations where moving house disrupts the child's emotional, sociocultural and linguistic environment, that superimposed codes get scrambled, resulting in writing and learning difficulties. This is another variable that turns up in the childhood of creative geniuses: precocity in the exercise of learning powers. Children who have to face difficulties from life or from their parents that are greater than normal for their age, tend, if they are at the same time loved in a way that encourages their narcissicism and valorises their imaginary omnipotence, to develop a keener intelligence sooner than other children: understanding is a skill they are forced to acquire prematurely, first because it enables them to cope with external conflicts, which adversely affect them and jeopardise their psychical integrity, and then because by being brilliant they are loved even more.

Freud's problems in Freiberg, however, were more than purely linguistic. His parents were involved in a sociocultural conflict of which Sigismund's language problems were only a reflection: as Jews, they wanted to speak German because it was the vehicle for all important exchanges of goods or ideas, and they were living in the midst of Czechs whose nationalist feelings were becoming stronger and stronger.

On top of that, the family structure posed a problem for the very young Freud: his middle-aged father had taken a young second wife; his half-brothers were the same age as his mother; his nephew was older than him and his niece the same age. Here again, the scrambled codes were followed by a simplification and clarification of the situation, when one part of the family emigrated to Manchester and the other moved to Vienna, i.e. after everyone, on reaching a 'street corner', had gone in a different direction. A simple ternary family structure – father, mother and children – corresponded to written German. But neither the old codes, nor the other systems of oral expression, nor the primal horde had been renounced. They lingered on in the background like some kind of reserve force, like potential schemas for possible developments, like instruments of thought that would become available, subsequently, for the task of sublimating the component instincts – instincts whose awakening was contemporaneous with the acquisition of those schemas and instruments. It is easy to see why, at the end of 1896 and the beginning of 1897, Freud conceived the unconscious, the preconscious and consciousness as being not only three different systems of transliteration, but three chronologically successive systems. Written German, which itself has a double system of transliteration (Gothic and Latin/roman) – in the fourth 'Rome' dream, he sees posters in German script, not in Latin as he had expected – functioned as the code of all codes for the young Sigismund.

THE MESSAGE OF THE 'ROME' DREAMS

The 'Rome' dreams suggest a number of conclusions. The first of these throws light on an aspect of the scientific genius that has not, as far as I know, been the subject of much attention.[1] It emerged from a series of discussions I had with my wife, Annie Anzieu, about the four dreams. The structure that is common to them all – a landscape in the first part of the dream, followed by proper names or writing in the second part – involves something seen being immediately followed by something written. Why is it that, in the Irma dream, the dream about the death of his father, and the four 'Rome' dreams, the one sense that is given greater importance than any other is sight? Hearing is essential when a child learns to talk. But sight is the only sense involved in the act of reading; then, when the child moves on from reading to writing, it plays a lesser role. At a pinch, it is possible to write with one's eyes closed. Sight governs not the movements of the hand, but the writing that results from it. When a child uses hand movements to arrange words on paper, he no longer follows a visual external model but an abstract internal one. Writing and counting presuppose the constitution of a mental space, which derives from the body schema and replaces the imaginary space that is a projection of the phantasied body. Thus, the type of intelligence that makes Freud a creator consists of the direct transliteration of what is 'seen', i.e. what is intuitively grasped; that is what gives the 'views' in the 'Rome' dreams, despite the 'mist' shrouding their

1. Though Nicolas Abraham (1972) does describe the characteristic peculiar to creative geniuses as being the ability to 'symbolise symbolisation'.

content, a clarity and definition that surprise the dreamer himself. In so doing, he bypasses a stage that keeps most people captive – that of spoken language. Neither before nor afterwards does oral expression or the spoken word play anything but a minor role in his dreams. Although what he demands of his patients during psychoanalytic sessions is the verbalisation of their actual experience, he himself functions differently. The dreams he has as a patient undergoing self-analysis are written down by him; and it is in writing that he records the immediate associations and broad axes of his interpretation. It is even possible that the subject chosen by Freud for his first book, *On Aphasia* (1891*b*), is of some significance: the inability to speak may have presented itself to him, at the start of his scientific career, which was now at last autonomous, as the admission of a negativity that had to be accepted if he was to progress further – devoting himself to writing meant giving up the spoken word. This makes Freud's interest in the case of Anna O. all the more explicable: one of her main symptoms was a progressive disruption of speech to the point even of speechlessness, for she spoke only in very correct English, and just occasionally in French or Italian, but not in her mother tongue German, which she did however continue to understand. 'She began writing again, but in a peculiar fashion. She wrote with her left hand, the less stiff one, and she used Roman printed letters, copying the alphabet from her edition of Shakespeare' (1895*d*, *SE* 2, 26). It was she, too, who gave an English name – the 'talking cure' – to the cathartic method used on her by Breuer.

It is also easy to see why Freud did not need to undergo psychoanalysis – that is to say, to submit to the imperative of verbalisation – as all modern psychoanalysts must in their turn in order to become analysts. We are able to to find our bearings in the unconscious because we have been taught the code by someone else, who himself has been initiated by yet another person. Because of Freud's hypercathexis of sight and of writing, because of his ability to bypass the intermediate stage and to reason according to the second level of language symbolisation – that of the written, not spoken, language – and according to the superior form of that second level – writing, not reading – he was able directly to transliterate the specific code of the unconscious, a code that was implicit in what he saw in himself and in his patients. Finally, it becomes clear why all the metaphors Freud used to describe the unconscious were borrowed from the medium of writing: in *Studies on Hysteria*, he had likened forgotten memories retrieved in the course of psychical analysis to 'a dossier kept in good order' (cf. p. 148); later, he compared dreams to a rebus, or picture puzzle (cf. p. 330); at this point in his life, psychoanalytic work seemed to him to resemble archaeological excavations that revealed ground plans and inscriptions.

That ability to leap without transition from the body to the code is also, in my view, one of the creative traits of the Argentinian writer, Jorge Luis Borges (Anzieu 1971*a*).

The ordinary person feels things more than he sees them: what he feels is a combination of the olfactory, the gustatory, the tactile and the interoceptive and proprioceptive sensibility, where hearing and sight merge in an indistinct chiaroscuro. For Freud, sight is at once differentiated and differentiating. What he sees in January 1897 is still shrouded to some degree in mist – the mist of uncertainty and inhibition. He has a long way to go before understanding everything about the unconscious, and is afraid of seeing what meets his eyes. But he sees what he sees with such 'clearsightedness' that in the second Rome dream he is 'surprised'. That also means that he has seen something surprising. The ordinary person, when given a code, is normally capable of, and interested in, applying it. The only people who discover and transliterate new codes are those who are able, first, to regress to a stage far back enough for them to retrieve early mental representations, secondly to see those representations clearly, and thirdly to formulate them in writing in a straightforward and relevant manner. The first process, felicitously termed 'controlled regression' in the service of the ego by Hartmann, Kris and Lowenstein, exists, potentially at least, in many human beings. Roughly speaking, it coincides with the indication that analysis is called for; it is held in check by defensive, characterological or neurotic rigidity and by fear of having to face, on the way, anxieties of a psychotic nature (fragmentation, self-destruction, destruction of a loved one). The second process is less widespread, not only because it is inhibited by guilt feelings (it is forbidden to see certain things), but also because the weight of acquired knowledge tends to blur the perception of new things (a form of epistemological resistance) and because we do not dare to believe, alone, that what we see is true (another form of the same resistance). The third process is exceptional: it indicates the presence of a superior intelligence capable, in the form of written language, of structuring data that is not originally symbolised.

My second conclusion has to do with the dynamics of transference. When, early in January 1897, Freud internalised both his dead father and his law, saw Rome and entered it – in other words, possessed symbolically, but not in reality, his mother's love and also entered into possession of his early memories again – he accomplished a further step towards his discovery of the symbolic nucleus around which neuroses and the unconscious are organised. Ambivalence towards his father, which the work of mourning had helped him to recognise, eventually led to ambivalence towards John, whose memory Freud was beginning to retrieve, and whose importance he was on the verge of understanding. But what he had in no way realised was that the memory was coming back to him only because he was going through the same experience in his relationship with Fliess. That is why the symbolism of Rome long continued to work within him. His unappeased desire for Rome persisted even when his self-analysis had almost been completed, after *The Interpretation of Dreams* had been published, and at a time when his friendship with Fliess was on its last legs: 'Otherwise Vienna is Vienna, that is, extremely disgusting. If I closed with "Next Easter in Rome", I would feel like a pious Jew. So I say rather "Until we meet in the summer or autumn in Berlin or where you will"' (*F*, April 16, 1900, 409). The remark was a nice case of compromise-formation between the desire, peculiar to practising Catholics, to spend Holy Week in Rome and the wish that orthodox Jews express to each other at the end of the Passover service: 'Next year in Jerusalem!' In any case, it proved that Freud had ceased to fear the Catholic and papal city of Rome, while at the same time persisting in his belief that a fruitful friendship with Fliess was still possible. Freud eventually went to Rome with his brother in the late summer of 1901. But before he could do so he had first to complete *The Psychopathology of Everyday Life*, realise that his relationship with Fliess was nothing more than a relic of the past, and plan a book on bisexuality that precipitated the break with his friend. By finally travelling to Rome, Freud was putting an end to his 'transference' on to Fliess.

This brings me to my third conclusion. The 'Rome' dreams form part of the work of mourning caused by the death of Jacob Freud at the end of October 1896. Stein (1967), arguing along the same lines, concludes 'that [Freud's] longing to go to Rome lasted as long as his self-analysis, that his self-analysis lasted as long as the mourning for his father, and that the journey (to Rome) marked the completion of mourning' (p. 15). It was not for almost another twenty years, in 1915, that Freud wrote a clinical and theoretical study of mental activity during mourning ('Mourning and Melancholia', 1917*e*), whereas his study of mental activity during dreaming appeared in 1900 (*The Interpretation of Dreams*, 1900*a*). Two factors should be taken into consideration here. In the course of his self-analysis, between 1895 and 1901, Freud accumulated material which he only partially exploited straight away, but on which he subsequently drew in formulating his theory of psychoanalysis. Moreover, Freud continued the process of self-analysis throughout his life; it did not always prove as fruitful as before, but, as various conflicts were revived within him over the years, it did retain contact with processes he had previously glimpsed but not yet included in his theoretical work. It was probably the break with Jung in 1913 and the death of his half-brother Emanuel in 1914, both of them followed by the work of mourning, which, along with Abraham's new theoretical contribution, prompted Freud to write 'Mourning and Melancholia'. In the essay, it is fairly easy to spot the passages where Freud draws on observation of his patients and those where he relies on his own experience. His description, at the beginning of the essay, of similarities between melancholia and profound mourning falls into the first category: 'the same loss of interest in the outside world [. . .] the same loss of capacity to adopt any new object of love that is not connected with thoughts of him' (*SE* 14, 244), that is to say all the mechanisms that are characteristic of narcissistic regression of the libido. On the other hand, it seems to me that Freud is drawing on personal experience when he speaks of 'profoundly painful dejection' (*ibid.* 244); when he remarks that 'when the work of mourning is completed the ego becomes free and uninhibited again' (*ibid.* 245); when he establishes the '*identification* of the ego with the abandoned object', adding: 'thus the shadow of the object fell upon the ego, and the latter could henceforth be judged by a special agency, as though it were an object, the forsaken object' (*ibid.* 249); above all when he takes note of the fact that 'the loss of a love-object is an excellent opportunity for the ambivalence in love-relationships to make itself effective and come into the open' (*ibid.* 250–1); and lastly when he points to what was later called manic defence against depression, the intoxication of a long-awaited triumph, and the gain of energy obtained by 'a suspension [. . .] of expenditures of energy in repression' (*ibid.* 254). 'Mourning and Melancholia' was Melanie Klein's point of departure when she elaborated the notion of the depressive position.

Here we can begin to tie things up. In the middle of 1895, Freud began to enter his mid-life crisis. That crisis was superactivated, from the autumn of 1896 on, by the work of mourning. That crisis and that work were both connected with the depressive position. His father's death reminded Freud of his first separation – the move from Freiberg. That painful separation was succeeded, when the family settled in Vienna, by the difficult Oedipal renunciation, as well as by access to the highest forms of symbolisation – the source of a new freedom and of new triumphs, the freedom and triumphs of the mind. The essence of the depressive position, i.e. the intrication of love and hate for any person on whose love one depends, was grasped by Freud, who then adopted what Elliott Jaques has called a tragic vision of the world, though in Freud's case it was rather a tragic vision of man and, more accurately speaking, of psychical reality.

Here is Freud, then, ready to make use of a legendary Greek hero in order to conceptualise the conflict of instincts and their objects in a more structured and concrete way. But whereas all this is taking place chiefly in

Freud's preconscious, his conscious system is dominated by a feeling of exhilaration resulting from lessened inhibitions (cf. 'God is dead, all is permitted'), from the withdrawal of cathexes invested in infantile objects, from the liberation of intellectual and emotional possibilities, in short from a greater internal freedom of movement – a feeling he tries to get Fliess to share. At the same time, apart from his relationship with Fliess, he feels scientifically and professionally isolated in Vienna, left to his own devices in a city characterised by hypocritical puritanism and, what is more, by hostility to Jews, national minorities, and new ideas. Rome, then, is the shadow of the object which falls upon the ego and makes it recognise itself as an abandoned ego, a third party excluded from the primal scene. Freud was quick to feel the therapeutic benefit of this psychoanalytic work on himself, as can be seen from the way he signed off a letter to Fliess on January 24, 1897: 'I think I have now passed the critical age. My condition is so much more stable' (*F* 228).

Freud's discovery of psychoanalysis, or rather of the first psychoanalytic theory, was part of a process of working over the depressive position during his mid-life crisis. His development of the second topography coincided with a re-working over of that position during his next crisis, the entry into old age. This primal metapsychological situation can explain a number of other points, such as why complementary discoveries made in Freud's wake seem to have coincided with their authors' withdrawal from depressive anxiety after reaching the age of 40, why the few attempts by psychoanalysts, such as Victor Tausk and Wilhelm Reich, to work over the paranoid-schizoid position in their lives and thoughts have failed dramatically, and why the cry of protest raised by Gilles Deleuze and Felix Guattari in their *L'anti-Oedipe, capitalisme et schizophrénie* (1972) met such a response when it came out.

Now for my fourth and final conclusion. In the dream of 'Irma's injection', Freud affirmed his determination, from then on, to fulfil his wishes, at least in his dreams. The 'Rome' dreams go one stage further: to go to Rome would be to fulfil his wishes in their entirety. As Stein (1967) has pointed out, if in the manifest content all roads lead to Rome, that means that in the latent content Rome opens up all roads: 'His longing for Rome maintained his illusion that infantile omnipotence had been achieved and his anguish that that achievement might remain virtual' (p. 29). His actual trip to Rome in 1901 marked the end of his systematic self-analysis, when he recognised that the desire for infantile omnipotence is in fact an illusion.

Prelude to systematic self-analysis (February–May 1897)

Four dreams during this period marked an important new development in Freud's self-analysis – 'Uncle with the yellow beard', 'Villa Secerno', 'Hella', and 'Running up stairs undressed'.

THE DREAM OF 'UNCLE WITH THE YELLOW BEARD' (FEBRUARY 1897)

The unrealisable wish contained in the 'Rome' dreams gives way here to another wish, which for the time being is just as unrealisable – Freud's ambition to become a professor. He first alluded to it in a letter to Fliess on January 24, 1897. Immediately afterwards, Nothnagel informed Freud that he and Krafft-Ebing had just put his name forward (along with that of Frankl-Hochwart) to the university board for an appointment as *professor extraordinarius* (roughly equivalent to an associate professor without salary); but Freud had no illusions and expected to be turned down by the notoriously anti-Semitic Minister (*F* 230). He hastened to compile a bibliographical abstract of his publications (1897*b*). During the days that followed, he discussed the matter with two Jewish colleagues who were also candidates for a professorship. One of them, N., said that he had even less of a chance because he had once been the object of legal proceedings: although the case had been dismissed, it was doubtless going to be used as an excuse for not appointing him. The other colleague, R. (probably his friend Königstein), an ophthalmologist, was a long-standing candidate for the professorship and less willing to take his failure lying down; so he went to the Ministry to find out if it were true that denominational considerations were causing his appointment to be delayed. He told Freud the same evening that he had been led to understand that such was indeed the case.

'On the morning after this visit I had the following dream, which was remarkable among other things for its form. It consisted of two thoughts and two pictures – each thought being succeeded by a picture. I shall, however, report only the first half of the dream here, since the other half has no connection with the purpose for which I am describing the dream.

'I. . . . *My friend R. was my uncle. – I had a great feeling of affection for him.*

'II. *I saw before me his face, somewhat changed. It was as though it had been drawn out lengthways. A yellow beard that surrounded it stood out especially clearly.*

'Then followed the two other pieces which I shall pass over – once more a thought followed by a picture' (*ID* 137–8).

The dream of the 'Uncle with the yellow beard', which is described at the beginning of Chapter 4, 'Distortion in Dreams', occurred, then, around the middle of February 1897. It is the first personal dream mentioned by Freud after the Irma dream and the dreams of convenience. It is intended to illustrate first a general process, whereby distortion in dreams is 'deliberate' and 'a means of *dissimulation*', and secondly a particular example of that process, whereby the affect is reversed into its opposite (*ID* 138–45). Later on in *The Interpretation of Dreams*, Freud comes back more than once to this dream, which, like the Irma dream, though to a lesser extent, acts as a kind of pilot-dream. He mentions them together as examples of:

a) the connection between dreams and events of the previous day (*ID* 165 and 180 n.1);

b) the work of condensation resulting in a composite figure or collective image (*ID* 293);

c) the work of displacement (*ID* 305);

d) representation (*ID* 322).

Further on in the book, Freud interprets the dream of the 'Uncle with the yellow beard' as the fulfilment of a childhood wish (ambition kindled by two prophecies that he would become a great man) (*ID* 191–3). He returns twice to the reversal of affect in this dream, once connecting it with the uncle–nephew relationship in his early childhood, a relationship that was 'the source of all my friendships and all my hatreds' (*ID* 472), and in another passage seeing it as an example of distortion caused by the preconscious (*ID* 570). Finally, in connection with the '*Non vixit*' dream, he remarks: 'It will be noticed that the name Josef plays a great part in my dreams [. . .]. My own ego finds it very easy to hide itself behind people of that name, since Joseph was the name of a man famous in the Bible as an interpreter of dreams' (*ID* 484, n.2).

Freud felt a strong resistance against interpreting this dream. He described it as nonsense and decided to analyse it only because he felt he would never allow a patient to get off the hook by dismissing a dream as nonsense. The underlying wish, whose hold over him had so far escaped him, was to become a university professor. The argument is similar to that of the Irma dream: it is other people who are guilty, I myself am 'beyond reproach'. R. (Königstein) 'had originally been extremely dark; but when black-haired people begin to turn grey they pay for the splendour of their youth. Hair by hair, their black beards go through an unpleasing change of colour: first they turn to a reddish brown, then to a yellowish brown, and only then to a definite grey.' The elongated face and yellow beard belong to Uncle Josef, Jacob's brother, who was much admired by the young Freud, but who was a simpleton and got into trouble with the law. The condensation of the two faces, like one of Galton's composite photographs, is designed to attribute similarities of character to two people who resemble each other physically: in the dreamer's eyes, R., whose beard is also going yellow, becomes a simpleton like Josef, which explains why he has not been appointed professor. As for N., he has himself admitted to having been in trouble with the law. It matters little that he was subsequently cleared. The dream makes him a criminal, so it is not surprising that he, too, has been turned down. Freud, on the other hand, who has nothing in common with the two men and is beyond reproach, has every hope of getting appointed: that is the wish fulfilled by the dream.

The 'great feeling of affection' the dreamer has for R. is simply a way of 'dissimulating' the derisive contempt with which he is regarded by Freud in his latent thoughts. The distortion in this dream consists of a hostile affect being replaced by its opposite. Freud had his first inkling at about this time that a censorship mechanism was responsible for disguising dream-wishes. He gradually became more and more certain of it, and used the word 'censorship' for the first time ten months later, at the end of a letter to Fliess on December 22, 1897.

Is that all there is to the dream? Obviously not, for Freud was dissatisfied with his analysis of it. He subjected it to further interpretation, probably when he was writing up the dream for the first version of *The Interpretation of Dreams* one year later, and after he had mentioned it to Fliess in a letter on March 15, 1898 (*F* 303). His second interpretation conformed strictly to the procedure that Freud demanded of his patients and to his theory of childhood memories. He inserted it in Section B, 'Infantile Material', of Chapter 5, 'The Material and Sources of Dreams', between the 'Yellow lion' dream and the 'Rome' dreams, a position that is certainly significant (*ID* 191–3). Freud had often been told in his childhood that just after he was born an old peasant-woman had prophesied that he would be a great man. He also recalled that when he was about 11 or 12 a café poet predicted he would grow up to be a Cabinet Minister. Those were the happy days of the liberal 'Bürger' (middle-class) government, which was elected after the introduction of the new Austrian constitution in 1867 and even included a number of Jews. The young Sigismund took the prediction seriously and decided he would later study law. It was only at the last moment that he opted for medicine instead. Thus the dream takes him back to a *childhood* wish: he is the Minister who mishandles two 'learned and eminent' candidates 'because they [are] Jews'. But that explanation is too good to be entirely true. Indeed, he presents it to Fliess in such a way as to escape his criticism. He precedes his interpretation with a curious self-justifying statement: 'If it was indeed true that my craving to be addressed with a different title was as strong as all that, it showed a pathological ambition which I did not recognise in myself and which I believed was alien to me. I could not tell how other people who believed they knew me would judge me in this respect. It might be that I was really ambitious; but, if so, my ambition had long ago been transferred to objects quite other than the title and rank of *professor extraordinarius*' (*ID* 192). If we are to believe Freud, then, the ambition manifested by the dream does not belong to the present, but to his childhood. No commentator on the dream has been taken in by Freud's claim. Fromm (1953) regards it as a fine example of rationalisation. Buxbaum (1951), when discussing the dream, quotes Bernfeld's highly pertinent remark: 'Do you know what's wrong with self-analysis? It's the countertransference.' Freud is not yet ready to admit that he is currently ambitious. But his denial is in fact an admission – a phenomenon familiar to psychoanalysts.

Freud goes into the theme of ambition at much greater length later on in his self-analysis: the 'Otto was looking ill' dream, for example, draws a rigorous parallel between Freud's 'megalomaniac'[1] wish to become a professor and his secret hostility towards Fliess. At this point Freud reveals to us only half his dream, but he had probably already gone deeper into its interpretation. In his chapter on the dream-work, he incidentally refers to the person with a yellow beard as an example of a composite figure, and enumerates the people with greying beards that form part of the composition – his friend R., Uncle Josef, 'my father and myself' (*ID* 293). The reproach that the dream directs at R. is in fact aimed at Freud's father, who is understandably replaced by one of his brothers. What did Freud hold against the generation that brought him into the world? Was it the fact that it had made him a Jew, thus preventing him from being appointed professor and standing in the way of his ambition? This would explain why, in the dream, he no longer has anything in common with his fellow Jews and takes revenge on them. Freud admitted to mocking his father about such matters in his observations on the much later '1851 and 1856' dream, which probably dates from mid-1899. The very special affection Freud had for his father masked other feelings. That had already been shown by the reproaches he directed at himself the evening following the funeral. He was getting closer and closer to recognising his ambivalence towards his father.

I have a number of remarks to add to Freud's own comments on the dream. The first is a conjecture: if R. is in fact Königstein – and since the

1. Freud eventually recognised his own megalomaniac wish, but did not, I would contend, succeed in seeing it as a megalomaniac defence against persecutory anxiety. The elucidation of the latter still remains today one of the great problems of psychoanalytic treatment.

first part of his name, *König*, means 'king', and a king with a yellow beard could only be Frederick Barbarossa – then surely Freud is once again identifying with a hero? My second remark concerns the colour yellow, which appears here for the first time in Freud's dreams, and which will turn up again later in two disguised autobiographical fragments, the screen memory of the 'Green meadow with yellow flowers' and the repetitive 'Yellow lion' dream. The sudden appearance of this yellow colour, which is there to be deciphered, explains why the dream's formal structure, a thought followed by an image, is different from that of the preceding dreams, in which a visual scene leads to a formula or to written words. But in fact – and this is my third remark – the dream is constructed around a signifier, the name Josef, which springs immediately to Freud's mind when he comes to analyse the dream, as though he had only one uncle, whereas his father actually had five brothers. The later '*Non vixit*' dream is also constructed around the same name, whose various other associations are then exploited by Freud. Here, it seems to me that Josef must also refer to Josef Breuer, the figure of authority in whose eyes Freud, in the Irma dream, attempted to exonerate himself. He had by then completely broken with Breuer; the latter's panicky reaction to Anna O. and to Freud's progress in his theory of the early sexual aetiology of neuroses brought home to his former disciple that, like Uncle Josef, he was a simpleton – and that maybe that was why he had turned down a professorial career. But, as Freud later came to see, Joseph was the interpreter of dreams in the Bible. In his dream about Uncle Josef, Freud is in a sense dreaming that he is interpreting dreams. Grinstein (G 289) points to two important similarities between the biblical Joseph and Sigmund Freud: they are both the first-born sons of a Jacob by his second wife; they are both ambitious (cf. the dream in the Bible where the stars bow down to him). The final association connected with the name Joseph, which is also one that goes back further in Freud's life, is not specifically mentioned by him; but there is every reason to suppose that he was aware of it either consciously or unconsciously. The doctor who treated him in Freiberg, and who had occasion to intervene in a relatively 'tragic' event (both the doctor and the event were soon to resurface in Freud's self-analysis), was called, as Sajner (1968) has established, Dr Josef Pur. As the dream of the 'One-eyed doctor and schoolmaster' reveals, not much later on in Freud's self-analysis, Pur had lost an eye.

One last point. It is not just the affect that undergoes a reversal into the opposite. The manifest content (by dreaming of his weak uncle, Freud passes himself off as a nephew beyond reproach) is the reversal into the opposite of a latent content which, once again, he elucidated only later and which refers to the rivalry between Sigismund – a weak uncle – and his older and stronger nephew. Like the Irma dream, the dream of 'Uncle with the yellow beard' is a programme-dream – a programme for the exploration not of the body and its erotogenic zones, but of childhood memories of Freiberg.

Freud discovered ambivalence, which in his eyes was probably the essential contribution of this dream, because he was currently experiencing it in his relationship with Fliess, the symbol of all his rival friends from Otto to Dr R. Some ten years later, Freud dreamed of a reconciliation with Fliess, with whom he had broken long before. 'On the fourth or fifth occasion I at last succeeded in understanding the meaning of the dream. It was an incitement to abandon my last remnants of consideration for the person in question and to free myself from him completely, and it had been hypocritically disguised as its opposite' (*ID* 145 n.1). He called it a 'hypocritical Oedipus dream'. He added that footnote, in the third edition of *The Interpretation of Dreams*, at the end of his interpretation of the 'Uncle with the yellow beard' dream. Two months after that dream, another one, the 'Villa Secerno' dream, overtly informed him of the ambivalent nature of his feelings both towards Fliess and towards his father.

THE 'VILLA SECERNO' DREAM (APRIL 27–28, 1897)

Freud and Fliess held their Easter 'congress' on April 18, 1897, in Nuremberg, which they finally chose instead of Prague, and whose mediaeval architecture was not at all to Fliess's taste. Then Fliess went on holiday to Venice, where he stayed at the Casa Kirsch, a *pension* that Freud had recommended to him. Freud returned to Vienna. As always after their meetings, he quickly sent Fliess a new batch of notes (Draft L). This time the topics he touched upon included the following: the case of a woman he had just begun to treat for hysteria, who finally admitted – thus dramatically confirming his theory of daughters being seduced by their fathers – that her father 'regularly took her to bed when she was from 8 to 12 years old and misused her without penetrating ("made her wet", nocturnal visits)' (letter to Fliess, April 28, 1897, *F* 238); the notion that primal scenes are subsequently built up into phantasies if they have been heard and into dreams if they have been seen; the emotional self-abasement caused in girls by their fathers' sexual relations with servant-girls; a girl's phantasies of condoms; a wishful dream of abortion by E. (Draft L, *F* 240–2). I shall return to most of these points later. The letter accompanying Draft L clarifies what these phantasies are: what are conscious in hysteria are the memories of 'primal scenes' (*Urszenen*); in obsessional neurosis it is 'perverse impulses' (*perverse Impulse*) deriving from those scenes; and in paranoia it is 'protective fictions' (*Schutzdichtungen*), or a compromise formation that serves both as a 'sublimation' and a 'self-exoneration' of those scenes or, contingently, scenes imagined in 'masturbation phantasies'. But all three neuroses in fact share the same elements; and access to the memory of the actual scene often requires the work of analysis to proceed by way of phantasies 'set up in front of them' (*F* 239).

Freud had not heard from Fliess, and could not write to him in Venice as he did not know where he was staying. He got hold of his address, probably on April 27. The same day, he talked about Nuremberg with a friend who knew the city well. During the night of April 27–28, 1897, Freud dreamed he received a telegram giving Fliess's address:

Via
'(Venice) Casa SECERNO'
Villa

(*F* 236)

The Interpretation of Dreams says very little about this dream (*ID* 317). It gives it as an example of an alternative in dreams: there was a choice between via, villa and Casa. The name Secerno was an echo of discussions he had had with Fliess in Nuremberg on the subject of etymology. He had probably talked about dreams where ambiguities in the meaning of a word or common expression expressed the dreamer's secret wishes. In return, Fliess gave him 'etymological enjoyment'. The verb *secerno*, which means 'I hide' or 'secrete' in Italian, expressed Freud's annoyance that Fliess had kept his address from him. But the most important aspect of this dream is doubtless the fact that in *The Interpretation of Dreams* Freud mentions it just before discussing the dream he had on the night after his father's funeral, in Section C, 'The Means of Representation in Dreams', of Chapter 6, 'The Dream-Work'.

Freud is much more explicit in his letter to Fliess of April 28. He is annoyed with his friend for a number of reasons, which he decides to spell out in full under the guise of interpreting the dream. Surely what Freud is seeking here is, if not mutual psychoanalysis, at the very least simultaneous self-analysis by Fliess and himself. He wanted Fliess to analyse his own dreams, and they almost fell out because Fliess, for no good reason, wanted 'to substitute the grandfather for the [. . .] father'. Ida Fliess was dragged in as well: she called her husband 'kitten', and Freud wanted to know who had called her that when she was a child. But Fliess could not make up his mind to ask her that question – another cause of annoyance to Freud. What is more, Fliess was not staying at the address he had recommended to him; Fliess had not written, as though he were trying to keep his trip a secret; Fliess had gone on holiday to Italy without Freud instead of keeping his promise that they would hold a 'congress' there, while all Freud could do was study Pompeii and its streets (street = *via*) in books or daydream in front of a Böcklin painting depicting a Roman villa; Fliess did not like Nuremberg's mediaeval architecture; Fliess, by failing to leave an address where Freud could send his latest draft, had placed him in a quandary: should he keep to himself notes that he had intended for another, or despatch them without knowing whether they would reach their destination. 'I wanted to have you as my public, tell you some of what I have been experiencing and finding out in my work. [. . .] I would have had to ask you to keep [my notes] for me as material of value' (*F* 237). This passage proves that the mainspring of Freud's work at the time was based on a 'transferential' type of relationship with Fliess.

But the dream is not just about Fliess. The complete interpretation occurred to Freud only after he had begun treatment of the hysteric mentioned above, who finally admitted that, when between 8 and 12 years old, she had been subjected to repeated sexual approaches by her father, a fresh confirmation, in Freud's view, of his paternal seduction theory. The fact that Fliess misinterpreted one of his own dreams involving a father was a source of resentment to Freud. 'Since I myself am still in doubt about matters concerning fathers, my sensitiveness becomes understandable' (*ibid.*). The secret dream-thought must therefore be: it is revolting that supposedly respectable fathers should behave in such a way towards their children. Freud has found the pretext which reveals, behind his guilt feelings, his hostility towards his father.

May 1897 was a fruitful month for Freud. To his great delight, Fliess began writing to him again: 'I hope that now you will remain your old self again for a long time and will let me go on taking advantage of you as a kindly disposed audience' (*F* 243). All of a sudden, he felt an intense intellectual stimulation once again: 'Things are fermenting and bubbling in me; I am only waiting for a new thrust. I cannot make up my mind about writing the preliminary outline of the total work you desire; I believe what prevents me is an obscure expectation that shortly something essential will turn up' (*ibid.*). He is referring to the theory of the psychical apparatus, which is now having to compete, in Freud's mind and with Fliess's encouragement, with a new subject of scientific investigation: 'I have felt impelled to start working on the dream, where I feel so very certain – and in your judgement am entitled to. [. . .] I have been looking into the literature and feel like the Celtic imp: "Oh, how glad I am that no one, no one knows . . ." No one even suspects that the dream is not nonsense but wish-fulfilment' (*ibid.*). This is the first mention by Freud of his plan to write a book about dreams.

There immediately occurred a process which we noted at the very beginning of Freud's self-analysis: at a time when he was asking himself scientific questions and simultaneously taking an interest in dreams, he had two successive dreams which echoed that interest and that interrogation.

Before looking at those two dreams, let me say a word or two about the intellectual activities in which Freud had been engaged in the meantime. On May 25, 1897, he sent Fliess Draft M, where, describing the 'architecture' of hysteria, he says: 'Some of the scenes are accessible directly, but others only by way of phantasies set up in front of them. The scenes are arranged in the order of increasing resistance. [. . .] Phantasies are formed by amalgamation and distortion analogous to the decomposition of a chemical body which is compounded with another one. For the first sort of distortion consists in a falsification of memory by fragmentation in which it is precisely the chronological relations that are neglected. [. . .] A fragment of the visual scene then combines with a fragment of the auditory one into the phantasy, while the fragment set free links up with something else. Thereby an original connection has become untraceable' (*F*, Draft M, 246–7). As in the Irma dream, chemical symbolism provides a model for the explanation. In the same draft, Freud also puts forward a number of ideas about the way repression is connected with bisexuality (the repressed element is 'what is feminine', a remark that should be understood as a personal admission) and with the unconscious (a 'normal' repression exists within the unconscious itself, and not just between the preconscious and the unconscious). He proposes to 'determine the number and kind of phantasies': their kind includes the (family) 'romance', which he describes for the first time but connects with paranoia (fulfilment of the wish to illegitimise the relatives in question); it was only later that Freud grasped its universality.

Freud describes the 'Hella' and 'Running up stairs undressed' dreams in his next letter of May 31, 1897, and again complains that Fliess has stopped writing to him. With the letter, Freud sends Draft N, an exceptionally rich text (I shall later discuss some of the points contained in it). It is here that the existence of 'hostile impulses', i.e. 'death wishes', against parents – and more particularly against parents of the opposite sex – is recognised for the first time. Freud notes that during mourning there is either a melancholy reaction of remorse (we reproach ourselves for their death), or a hysterical reaction of identification (we are ill like them): these observations were patently prompted by Freud's own experience of the work of mourning since his father's death in October 1896; it was not until much later that Freud enlarged upon and published, in 'Mourning and Melancholia' (1917*e*), the notion of identification with a lost object: at this point he did no more than grasp it intuitively. Belief, which is a phenomenon of the 'system of the ego (the *Cs.*)', is in neuroses refused to the repressed material and granted only to the defending material. For the first time, Freud mentions the application of psychoanalysis to literary works (Goethe's *Werther*) and to morality (holiness is connected with the horror of incest). I shall discuss both these types of application at greater length later on. The formation of symptoms is analogous to that of phantasies: like dreams, their aim is wish-fulfilment. The outbreak of anxiety is linked to repressed phantasies, and the transformation of libido into anxiety, first mentioned by Freud in 1894*a*, takes place in the unconscious. The repression of impulses (*Impulsen*) produces not anxiety but depression. These, then, are just some of the stimulating ideas contained in Draft N.

THE 'HELLA' DREAM (MAY 1897)

The 'Hella' dream, then, dates from the end of May 1897. It does not feature in *The Interpretation of Dreams*.

'Recently I dreamed of [having] over-affectionate feelings for Mathilde [Freud's eldest daughter], only she was called Hella; and afterward I again saw "Hella" before me, printed in heavy type. Solution: Hella is the name of an American niece whose picture we have been sent. Mathilde could be called Hella because she recently shed bitter tears over the defeats of the Greeks. She is enthralled by the mythology of ancient Hellas and naturally regards all Hellenes as heroes. The dream of course shows the fulfilment of my wish to catch a *Pater* as the originator of neurosis and thus [the dream] puts an end to my ever-recurring doubts' (*F*, May 31, 1897, 249).

This is a clear case of wishful thinking on Freud's part. There can be no doubt that he wanted to verify his theory: the dream provided him with confirmation of the wish, but not of the theory. This is one of those dreams of compliance that are so frequent in psychoanalysis. Why this compliance? If fathers, almost without exception, sexually assaulted their children, then Freud's father must also have done so. In order to eliminate that unbearable thought, Freud's unconscious cleverly transposes it: he, Sigmund Freud, who could not be suspected of the slightest sexual impropriety, in fact harbours the same inclinations towards his eldest daughter! But if it is the wish, not the act, that is the source of evil, then his whole theory needs to be changed.

I would like to make some further remarks on the dream. Identification with the victim (in this case, the Greek minority whose rebellion had been crushed by the Turks) is already familiar to us. As for Greek mythology, Freud is just as enthusiastic about it as his eldest daughter; this shift of interest, in relation to the preceding dreams, from Rome to Greece shows that Freud is looking in that direction in the hope of finding some answer to the problem of the psychical apparatus. Confirmation for this can be found in the dream's structure: an incestuous scene concludes with an inscription that refers to Greece. All we need to do is change the woman's name from Hella to Jocasta . . .

The 'Hella' dream should also be looked at in the light of material which Freud had recently been furnished by two of his patients, and which, in a sense, he indirectly refers to here. As we saw in the Irma dream, identification with patients and counter-transference with respect to them are together one of the driving forces of self-analysis, for Freud can remark in himself only what his patients have already allowed him to guess about them. But that means that other people's truth cannot become an objective and universal truth unless it goes through an intermediate stage, that of its appropriation as specifically subjective truth: much of the epistemological as well as the therapeutic importance of psychoanalysis resides in that fact. The first piece of clinical material was provided by the woman patient who, during her prepuberty, was taken to bed by her father and 'made wet' with sperm (cf. p. 218): it is easy to imagine the real nature of what Freud demurely describes as his 'over-affectionate feelings' for his daughter in the dream.

A little later, the 'Being arrested for child-murder' dream, recounted by E. (who had resumed his analysis), pointed up this problem: fathers are guilty not only of seduction wishes but of destructive wishes as well. This is a wishful dream, following *coitus interruptus*. The latent thought is E.'s wish not to make his mistress pregnant. It is that wish – a conscious wish – which is fulfilled in the dream: for if she becomes pregnant despite his precautions, he will get her to have an abortion. According to Freud, the dream's manifest content is provided by the anxiety that arises from that kind of *coitus*: just as E. arrives at his house with a lady, he is arrested by a policeman. E. asks for time to put his affairs in order; he realises he is being charged with having killed a child (*F* 242). I myself see the explanation for that last aspect of the dream as being anxiety about the wish to cause the child's death.

In short, Freud identifies with the despicable head of a family who defiles his daughter, gets women to have abortions (as we have already seen, in the dream of 'Irma's injection', this was one of Freud's underlying wishes vis-à-vis his wife Martha), and takes advantage of female servants (Draft L sees such behaviour as the cause of 'self-abasement' in daughters). This is an attenuated form of epistemological resistance: *I* would never think of things like that, but other people, by doing them, make me think of them. It is an attenuated form because, by using exculpation as a shield (it is not me, but others – a formula central to the later '*Non vixit*' dream), it permits a certain recognition of such thoughts. Thus a formula is hidden behind the name Hella that Freud sees in heavy type in his dream; in 1905, he proposed the following scientific transliteration of it in *Three Essays on the Theory of Sexuality*: beneath the genital primacy that is specific to adults there continues to lurk the 'polymorphously perverse disposition' that we all had as children.

THE 'RUNNING UP STAIRS UNDRESSED' DREAM (MAY 1897)

The 'Running up stairs undressed' dream occurred at about the same time as the 'Hella' dream, and is described in the same letter of May 31, 1897:

'Another time I dreamed that I was going up a staircase with very few clothes on. I was moving, as the dream explicitly emphasised, with great agility. (My heart – reassurance!) Suddenly I noticed, however, that a woman was coming after me, and thereupon set in the sensation so common in dreams, of being glued to the spot, of being paralysed. The accompanying feeling was not anxiety but erotic excitement. So you see how the sensation of paralysis characteristic of sleep was used for the fulfilment of an exhibitionistic wish. Earlier that night I had in fact gone up the stairs from our ground-floor apartment – without a collar, at any rate – and had thought one of our neighbours might be on the stairs' (*F* 249).

Freud's version of the dream is somewhat different in *The Interpretation of Dreams*, where it is discussed in Section C, 'The Somatic Sources of Dreams', of Chapter 5, 'The Material and Sources of Dreams':

'One day I had been trying to discover what might be the meaning of the feelings of being inhibited, of being glued to the spot, of not being able to get something done, and so on, which occur so often in dreams and are so closely akin to feelings of anxiety. That night I had the following dream:

'*I was very incompletely dressed and was going upstairs from a flat on the ground floor to a higher storey. I was going up three steps at a time and was delighted at my agility. Suddenly I saw a maid-servant coming down the stairs – coming towards me, that is. I felt ashamed and tried to hurry, and at this point the feeling of being inhibited set in: I was glued to the steps and unable to budge from the spot*' (*ID* 238). This is one of the dreams examined by Grinstein (G, Chapter 7).

There are two differences between one version of the dream and the other. In the letter to Fliess, the woman suddenly comes up behind him and erotic excitation is admitted; in the published work, the maid-servant suddenly comes down the stairs towards him and there is no mention of erotic excitation.

Let me first state my own conclusions about the dream. From the viewpoint of the body image, the dream is accompanied by an erection and represents the two corresponding sensations of flying (going up nimbly) and rigidity (glued to the spot). From the viewpoint of the infantile wish, the dream expresses inhibition towards incest, as Grinstein rightly notes: it can hardly be a coincidence – though it escapes Grinstein's notice – that Freud, in Draft N, which is enclosed with the letter of May 31 describing the dream, draws a parallel between 'holiness' and 'the horror of incest'.

Freud's comments on the dream are contained in two passages of *The Interpretation of Dreams*, separated – or rather linked – by a brief discussion of 'Embarrassing dreams of being naked' (*ID* 238–40 and 247–8). As usual, his free associations centre on the day's residues (all dreams are a response to a question of the previous day; in Freud's case, the question almost always has a scientific aspect). The previous day he had tried 'to discover what might be the meaning of the feelings of being inhibited, of being glued to the spot, of not being able to get something done.' During the night, the dream gave him the *experience* of those feelings, and confirmed something he already knew from his patients – that 'dreams find no difficulty in representing motor acts carried out to perfection,' and also that dreams of incomplete dress or nakedness are dreams of exhibiting.

At a personal level, the dream alludes to two actual circumstances in Freud's life: 1) His residence at No. 19 Berggasse occupied two floors, with his consulting-room and study on the mezzanine and his living rooms on the floor above; to get from one to the other he had to take the main stairs of the building. On the evening before the dream, Freud went up to his flat late, having taken off his collar, tie and cuffs as he usually did when working long hours. It had occurred to him that while in that state he might meet a neighbour on the stairs; 2) The staircase was also like the one in the house of the old woman to whom he gave injections twice a day. When paying morning visits to the house Freud usually felt the need to clear his throat as he climbed the staircase; and as there was no spittoon he acquired the bad habit of spitting on the stairs, with the result that the concierge grumbled audibly and stopped saying good morning. The day before the dream, the old woman's maid-servant had even scolded him for not wiping his boots before coming in.

What do these two circumstances symbolise? If he can fly up the stairs, it proves that his heart is in good shape. If he coughs when going up those same stairs, it is because he smokes too much: 'Pharyngitis as well as heart trouble are both regarded as punishments for the vice of smoking.' The dreamer's neurotic symptoms, then, appear openly in his dreams; he had himself pointed out earlier on (1895*d*, *SE* 2, 296) that in the psychotherapy of hysteria symptoms 'join in the conversation'. In the first part of his interpretation, carried out immediately after the dream, Freud goes no further than that. But we know that symptoms are meaningful only in the intersubjective relationship they convey. Now it was Fliess who had issued the 'no smoking' order already alluded to by Freud's dream the night after his father's funeral. So it must be Fliess, too, who is paralysing him, Fliess to whom Freud wishes to reveal the nakedness of his being through self-analysis.

Two months later, at the beginning of July, Freud took his interpretation of the dream further, for, as he told Fliess in his letter of July 7, he had just discovered the meaning of dreams of nakedness: 'There is an interesting dream of wandering about among strangers, totally or half undressed and with feelings of shame and anxiety. Oddly enough, it is the rule that people do not notice it – for which we must thank wish-fulfilment. This dream material, which goes back to exhibiting in childhood, has been misunderstood and worked over didactically in a well-known fairy tale. (The king's imaginary clothes – "Talisman".) The ego habitually misinterprets other dreams in the same way' (*F* 255) – a warning he would have been well advised to heed when interpreting the 'Hella' dream!

Dreams of being undressed or of jumping into water are common in the early stages of psychoanalysis. Fromm (1953) was surely wrong when he criticised Freud's remarks on the sexual and exhibitionistic meaning of dreams of nakedness in the following terms: 'Nakedness can, for instance, be a symbol of truthfulness. To be naked can stand for being oneself without pretence.' But what does Freud actually say in *The Interpretation of Dreams*? That children, far from feeling ashamed at being naked, enjoy it immensely (his first intuition of infantile sexuality). But he does not lose sight of the non-sexual aspect of the symbol: those observing our nakedness in such dreams represent 'the wishful contrary', in other words the wish to keep something secret from them. This throws light on Hans Christian Andersen's well-known fairy tale, in which the emperor makes his subjects believe that he is wearing a costly garment whereas he is in fact stark naked; on the myth of a long-lost Paradise where mankind was naked; and on the legend of Odysseus who was caught unawares by Nausicaa – and who symbolises the tormented and unwanted wanderer, according to a passage in Gottfried Keller's autobiographical novel, *Der grüne Heinrich* (*The Green Henry*), drawn to Freud's attention by Fliess.

Grinstein (G 201–7), after analysing the novel in detail, makes an interesting comparison between Freud and Henry Lee, the hero of the book (alias Keller himself), who is clearly inhibited towards women, and more particularly towards Judith, a widow (the mother figure): both men were writers, influenced by the essay on Nature attributed to Goethe, and engaged in writing largely autobiographical works; both had to struggle to make ends meet and were afraid they might not be doing the right work; both conflicted with elders and teachers; and both their lives were deeply influenced by the deaths of their fathers.

Freud passed on his thoughts about nakedness to Fliess, in the same letter where he admits to feeling paralysed by him (*F* 255). The childhood memory underlying the dream was not retrieved by Freud until early October (see his two letters to Fliess of October 3–4 and October 15, 1897), by which time a whole series of subsequent dreams had focussed his attention on the central figure of that memory – Monika Zajíc, the nurse who looked after Freud in Freiberg. This enabled Freud to add a third interpretation of the dream to the two he had already suggested: 'The staircase dream to which I have referred was one of a series of dreams; and I understood the interpretation of the other members of the series. Since this particular dream was surrounded by the others it must have dealt with the same subject. Now these other dreams were based on a recollection of a nurse in whose charge I had been from some date during my earliest infancy till I was two and a half. I even retain an obscure conscious memory of her. According to what I was told not long ago by my mother, she was old and ugly, but very sharp and efficient. From what I can infer from my own dreams her treatment of me was not always excessive in amiability and her words could be harsh if I failed to reach the required standard of cleanliness. And thus the maid-servant, since she had undertaken the job of carrying on this educational work, acquired the right to be treated in my dream as a reincarnation of the prehistoric old nurse. It is reasonable to suppose that the child loved the old woman who taught him these lessons, in spite of her rough treatment of him' (*ID* 247–8).

Thus, after positing the notion of ambivalence towards the image of the father, Freud now senses a similar ambivalence towards the image of the mother. After having an erotic dream about his own daughter, he has one about his nurse. It is worth noting, incidentally, that the words describing two of the activities in the dream, 'going up' and 'spitting', have a crude sexual secondary meaning in German, and that such other expressions as 'undress', 'delight' and 'glued' can all easily take on sexual overtones. Odysseus' wish to return to his fatherland (or motherland!) makes specific something that was hinted at in the 'Rome' dreams – the yearning for the mother's body and for the nurse's uncovered body against his own. Self-analysis has left the door wide open to spirits, ghosts and *revenants* – in other words to figures from the past who have left their stamp on the child's desires, anxieties and feelings of guilt, and whom he can faintly remember. The quotation from Goethe that heads *The Psychopathology of Everyday Life* (*SE* 6, vii) states this quite clearly:

> *Nun ist die Luft von solchem Spuk so voll,*
> *Dass niemand weiss, wie er ihn meiden soll.*
> *Faust*, Part II, Act V, Scene 5
>
> [Now fills the air so many a haunting shape,
> That no one knows how best he may
> escape.]
> (Bayard Taylor's translation)

It gradually dawns on Freud that the feeling of shame which is paralysing him, thus preventing him from progressing further in his discoveries, dates from very early in his childhood – from the time when his nurse made him ashamed about things 'behind him' (in other words, about his behind), as well as about things in front, and whose circumstances and meaning remain to be elucidated. The old woman who appears just as Freud is exultantly taking flight and glues him to the spot is strongly reminiscent of the Sphinx of Greek legend (ethnologists have discovered a variant of it in presentday American Indian cultures): the Sphinx, a ghost without a tomb who cannot survive unless able to feast on the blood or sperm of her victims, surprises young men by suddenly appearing before them; fear, combined no doubt with desire, causes them to have an erection – as hard as stone – which she then turns to her own advantage.

Later, in his brief essay – 'Medusa's Head' (1940*c*, written in 1922), Freud follows the same line of thought: the terrible sight of the Medusa's head turns the spectator to stone, in other words gives him an erection. If Freud, despite his shame and his paralysis, is able to forge ahead in his investigations it is because he has a correspondent to whom he can relate much, if not all, of what 'haunts' him; it is also because he tries as hard as he can to understand what he feels; lastly, it is because he possesses a reliable deciphering method: 'Two thoughts which occur in immediate sequence without any apparent connection are in fact part of a single unity which has to be discovered; in just the same way, if I write an '*a*' and a '*b*' in succession, they have to be pronounced as a single syllable '*ab*'. The same is true of dreams' (*ID* 247).

FURTHER THEORETICAL AND CLINICAL PROGRESS

The short space of time during which these four dreams occurred was a period of intense scientific activity for Freud. Within less than a month, on May 2, 25 and 31, he sent Fliess Drafts L, M and N, which I have already mentioned in passing (they were the last three papers he was to send his friend before *The Interpretation of Dreams*). Never before had Freud been so prolific. The drafts teem with ideas that he later developed. We find the notions of fixation (Draft L, *F* 242) and of the family romance (Draft M, *F* 248). Freud rounds out his theory of the libido, which he had left untouched since 1894, and of its transformation into anxiety (*F* 251–2). Explanation through the wish is extended to cover two new fields: dreaming serves as a model for the construction of phantasies and of symptoms. Of symptoms Freud simply remarks: 'Thus symptoms, like dreams, are *the fulfilment of a wish*' (*F* 251).

But the discovery of the existence and origins of phantasies was more than 'a great advance' (*F* 239); it was to affect his psychoanalytic theories considerably. The memory of actual traumatic scenes would come to be seen by Freud as less important than images, daydreams and phantasies caused by wishes. This was a normal consequence of his initial discovery about dreams: if the purpose of all psychical processes is, as in the case of dreams, wish-fulfilment, then the wish is a fundamental principle of behaviour and conflict. But it would be some time before Freud became aware of that. He realised, though, that neuroses exhibit not only memories but 'impulses' and 'protective fictions' (*ibid.*). The work of psychoanalysis necessarily involves an investigation of phantasies, as they are superposed on the true cause of symptoms.

It is understandable that Freud was unable to shake off his doubts – a subject he frequently referred to – about his theory of neuroses being caused by parental seduction at an early age. He did, on the other hand, produce a series of insights that he developed in many of his later works:

1. He collected significant Jewish jokes, which he later included in *Jokes and their Relation to the Unconscious* (1905*c*). He had a hunch that jokes have the same symbolic structure as dreams, where indeed they frequently occur. The 'Running up stairs undressed' dream clinched it for him: 'Since "*spuken* [haunting]" is an activity of *spirits*, "*spucken* [spitting] on the stairs" might be loosely rendered as "*esprit d'escalier*".' And Freud then pleaded guilty of lacking, unlike his nurse, 'ready repartee ["*Schlagfertigkeit*", literally "readiness to strike"]' (*ID* 248 n. 1).

2. Freud used the idea of bisexuality, which Fliess first mentioned to him at their Easter 'congress' in Nuremberg, to arrive at an explanation of

repression that was probably a personal projection (it is the feminine element which is repressed), and to draw a conclusion that was to preoccupy him throughout his life: 'What men essentially repress is the pederastic element' (Draft M, *F* 246). A note by Kris rightly points out that the idea alluded to here led to Freud's later insight into the general significance of 'the tendency to inversion in psychoneurotics', of latent homosexuality, and of passivity in infantile life.

3. A psychoanalytic explanation of literary works was also beginning to take shape: 'The mechanism of fiction is the same as that of hysterical phantasies. For his *Werther* Goethe combined something he had experienced, his love for Lotte Kästner, and something he had heard, the fate of young Jerusalem, who died by committing suicide [and] to whom he lent a motive from his own love story. By means of this phantasy he protected himself from the consequences of his experience' (Draft N, *F* 251).

4. Freud would 'very soon uncover the source of morality' (*F* 249). ' "Holy" is something based on the fact that human beings, for the benefit of the larger community, have sacrificed a portion of their sexual liberty and their liberty to indulge in perversions. The horror of incest (something impious) is based on the fact that, as a result of communal sexual life (even in childhood), the members of a family remain together permanently and become incapable of joining with strangers. Thus incest is antisocial – civilisation consists in this progressive renunciation' (Draft N, *F* 252). This anticipates Freud's later views on civilisation as a repression of the sexual instinct: 'Character and Anal Erotism' (1908*b*), *Totem and Taboo* (1912–13), *Civilization and its Discontents* (1930*a*), and *Why War?* (1933*b*).

5. The works on neuroses and on psychology, which Freud had been working on for more than a year, now took second place. For the first time he had the idea of writing the book that would be called *The Interpretation of Dreams* (1900*a*).

After the 'Villa Secerno' dream, the interpretation of which Fliess largely accepted, Freud became increasingly dependent on his friend both on a personal level and in his work: 'I am noting [a few scraps] down for you alone and hope you will keep them for me. [. . .] If only you were nearer, so that I could tell you about it more easily' (*F*, May 31, 1897, 249). Each discovery made by Freud led to many others. He had a 'vague' presentiment, mentioned in every letter, of what was in store. For example: 'I believe I am in a cocoon, and God knows what sort of beast will crawl out' (*F*, June 22, 1897, 254).

An idea of what that 'beast' was, suggested by his last four dreams, was to prove decisive. It is contained in Draft N (*F* 250–2): 'Hostile impulses against parents (a wish that they should die) are also an integrating constituent of neuroses. They come to light consciously as obsessional ideas. [. . .] [They] are repressed at periods when compassion for the parents is aroused – at times of their illness or death. [. . .] It seems as though this death wish is directed in sons against their fathers and in daughters against their mothers.' Freud saw evidence for this in a dream by his children's governess, Lisl, in which she wished her mistress would die so her master could marry her. He was certainly also thinking of the case of an obsessional young man who had suffered from homicidal tendencies since his father's death and dared not go out into the street in case they got the better of him; Freud alluded to him, as well as to Mr. E., in a letter to Fliess of October 31, 1895; and he again mentioned the man (adding that his impulse to kill his father had been expressed when he was seven years old) in *The Interpretation of Dreams*, just before he set forth his theory of the Oedipus complex (cf. p. 247) (*ID* 260), and also in connection with the 'Hollthurn' dream (cf. p. 331) (*ID* 457–8).

Systematic self-analysis (June–November 1897)

FREUD'S 'TRANSFERENCE NEUROSIS'

Up to that point, Freud's self-analysis had been occasional and fragmentary. Between June and August 1897, he embarked on the process of making it systematic. Although that process diverted him from his newly-fledged plan to write a book about dreams, it was nonetheless closely connected with it: it was 'a necessary intermediate stage in my work' (letter of August 14, 1897, *F* 261), which would itself be an introduction to 'the psychology of the neuroses in general', which dreams 'contain *in nuce* [in a nutshell]' (letter of July 7, 1897, *F* 255). But that did not mean that Freud's self-analysis had been set in motion by purely intellectual and scientific motives. There needed to be another reason, one which Edith Buxbaum (1951) has called Freud's 'transference neurosis'. It requires some explanation.

The three summer months of 1897 were marked by an aggravation of Freud's personal problems. His basic psychological make-up (obsessive ideas, depressive tendencies, and feelings of impotence, failure and guilt) became more transparent. Such problems, which were apparently never worse than those a normal person would expect to face, may be described as neurotic to the extent that any so-called normal person always has to face neurotic problems; but in no way do they reveal a truly psychopathological mental structure. On this point, I cannot but agree with Suzanne Cassirer-Bernfeld's objections (1952) to Buxbaum's argument.

But if some commentators have gone so far as to talk of Freud's *neurosis*, it is because he himself did so. On June 22 he wrote: 'I have been through some kind of neurotic experience' (*F* 254). On July 7: 'I still do not know what has been happening in me. Something from the deepest depths of my own neurosis set itself against any advance in the understanding of the neuroses, and you have somehow been involved in it' (*F* 255). On August 14: 'After having become very cheerful here, I am now enjoying a period of bad humour. The chief patient I am preoccupied with is myself. My little hysteria, though greatly accentuated by my work, has resolved itself a bit further. The rest is still at a standstill' (*F* 261). Intense and relatively brief psychopathological episodes such as these, concealing a massive regression and considerable restructurings of the instinctual economy occur fairly often during the incubation period of a discovery or a work: Ellenberger (1964) uses the term 'creative illness' to describe them. On a more general plane, R. D. Laing and the anti-psychiatry school have drawn attention to the self-curing nature of psychotic episodes in some patients.

Apart from the summer of 1897, it would seem that Freud never used the word neurosis with reference to himself. The fact that he did so at this point was closely conditioned by circumstances. Like any normal person, Freud had hitherto attached only moderate importance to his personal problems. Those problems were activated by his analysis, chiefly for an experimental purpose, of some of his own dreams: a similar aggravation of symptoms often occurs in the course of psychoanalysis. The work of mourning mobilised his depressive tendencies. But that was not all. Freud had failed to complete a psychoanalytic treatment. He had not succeeded in elaborating a sound theory. He was forced to accept the fact that the obstacle was not purely epistemological (as Bachelard acutely put it), but within himself. By focussing his attention on it, Freud allowed it to invade his person. His 'neurosis' manifested itself in a fresh wave of suffering and a total inhibition in his work. 'I have never before even imagined anything like this period of intellectual paralysis. Every line is torture' (*F*, June 22, 1897, 253).

All the major discoveries which Freud made in the course of his self-analysis, and which were to constitute the basic corpus of psychoanalytic notions, were similarly preceded by a period of paralysis. The final discovery in the series was no more than intuited by him as he finished writing *The Interpretation of Dreams*: it was that of the phantasy underlying such paralysis – castration phantasy (cf. my paper 'Paralysie et création: naissance d'un concept freudien'; D. Anzieu, 1971*b*).

His current block was closely connected with Fliess: 'My writing paralysis seems to me designed to inhibit our communication. I have no guarantees of this, just feelings of a highly obscure nature' (*F*, July 7, 1897, 255). In mid-July Freud went to see his sister-in-law Minna in Salzburg, and then visited her mother in Reichenhall. He then returned to Vienna to make arrangements for his father's gravestone. At the end of July, he was at last able to join his family, who were on holiday at Aussee. It was there, apparently (J I, 357–8), that he began his systematic self-analysis.

He wrote fewer letters to Fliess and had less to say in them. Freud had looked forward to his August meeting with his friend, yet put it off: 'I must keep reminding myself that I did do a good deed yesterday by cancelling; otherwise I would regret it too much. [. . .] [I am] too lazy to think, and have not succeeded here in diminishing the agitation in my head and feelings. [. . .] The analysis is more difficult than any other. It is, in fact, what paralyses my psychic strength for describing and communicating what I have won so far. Still, I believe it must be done and is a necessary intermediate stage in my work' (*F*, August 14, 1897, 259–61). Freud even brought his phobia of train journeys into his dialogue with Fliess: 'Martha is very much looking forward to the trip though the daily reports of train accidents are not exactly apt to put the father and mother of a family in the mood for it. You will laugh – and rightly so – but I must confess to new anxieties which come and go, but in between last for half a day. Half an hour ago I was pulled out of my fear of the next train accident when the thought occurred to me: W. and I. also are travelling, after all. [. . .] But this must remain strictly between us' (*F*, August 18, 1897, 262). The journey referred to was the magnificent tour of northern Italy that Freud went on with Martha from the end of August to the middle of September. It included Venice, Pisa, Leghorn, Siena, San Gimignano, near Lake Trasimeno (like Hannibal, he failed to get any further south – and nearer Rome – than that), Poggibonsi, Chiusi, Orvieto (where he was impressed by Signorelli's frescoes), Bolsena, Spoleto, Assisi, Perugia, Arezzo and finally Florence. The trip enabled Freud to relax; but it was Fliess, again, who had suggested it to Freud so he could familiarise himself with the masterpieces of Italian art.

These facts, when seen in combination, add weight to Edith Buxbaum's hypothesis of a 'transference neurosis'. Freud had engaged in a dialogue with Fliess, whom he expected to give him and his work full recognition. The dialogue led him to ask questions about the meaning of life and of his work, while at the same time, to his considerable alarm, casting doubt not only on his own worth but on that of his interlocutor. Behind all that, a specific anxiety was at work: the 'Hella' and 'Running up stairs undressed' dreams caused a resistance in him to any further exploration of incestuous wishes. Buxbaum's hypothesis has, however, to be qualified slightly: Freud's 'transference neurosis' vis-à-vis Fliess occurred at a very specific moment, and was related to the intense work of mourning caused in Freud by his father's death. The crucial discoveries he was about to make in October 1897 also occurred at a very specific moment – the month that included the first anniversary of that death.

THE COLLAPSE OF THE SEXUAL SEDUCTION THEORY

On September 21, the very day after he got back to Vienna, Freud lost no time in telling Fliess about the first result of his investigations (*F*, September 21, 1897, 264–6). It was a theoretical result only, but one that destroyed the idea to which he was most attached, and the keystone of his system – the sexual seduction theory, which he had first told Fliess about in May 1893. There were four reasons for his change of mind: he found it impossible to bring his analysis to a real conclusion; he could not believe that all fathers of hysterical women were perverts; there were no criteria, in the unconscious, that made it possible to distinguish between an actual event and a phantasy; lastly, he realised that in the most deep-reaching psychosis and delirium, where the unconscious takes over the whole personality, no memory of childhood seduction is revealed. Freud was on the verge of a breakdown. He would have to give up 'the complete resolution of a neurosis and the certain knowledge of its aetiology in childhood', and maybe return to the theory of hereditary disposition. He would have to abandon his 'expectation of eternal fame', as well as that of 'certain wealth, complete independence, travels, and lifting the children above the severe worries that robbed me of my youth'.

It looked as though Freud was doomed once again to fall at the last fence. But on this occasion he did not. His self-analysis had begun to change the balance of his psychical economy. He sensed what would save him. 'In this collapse of everything valuable, the psychological alone has remained untouched. The dreams [book] stands entirely secure.' 'I have more the feeling of a victory than a defeat.' He thought of Hamlet again: ' "To be in readiness": to be cheerful is everything'.[1] He could hardly wait to 'slip' off to Berlin the next Saturday evening and see Fliess on Sunday the 28th,

1. 'Freud was quoting from memory. The exact text is: "The readiness is all." A parapraxis? Possibly, but it proves little except that Freud was familiar enough with the English original to risk quoting it from memory. Perhaps the only point to be made is that, before his eagerly-awaited meeting with Fliess, Freud remembered the words uttered by Hamlet before his fatal duel with his arch-enemy Laertes' (J. Starobinski, 1967, p. viii).

between two night trains, in the hope that his friend would be able to clear matters up in his mind. After promising, though very reluctantly, to take advantage of his trip to visit someone who had moved to Berlin from Vienna and to pass on greetings and messages from his family, Freud forgot the name of the street where the man lived. His forgetfulness in this case, as well as his inability, on another occasion, to remember the name of the painter Signorelli, formed the basis of two analyses which he published together under the title 'The Mechanism of Forgetfulness' (1898*b*), and again, in a slightly different form, as part of *The Psychopathology of Everyday Life* (1901*b*; see also p. 359).

THE RECOLLECTION OF MEMORIES FROM HIS SECOND YEAR (SEPTEMBER 29 – OCTOBER 3, 1897)

Freud returned to Vienna on September 29. Once again, the magic had worked: he was powerfully stimulated by his 'congress' with Fliess. His self-analysis gathered pace and began to produce results on a personal level. On October 3 he wrote: 'For the last four days my self-analysis, which I consider indispensable for the clarification of the whole problem, has continued in dreams and has presented me with the most valuable elucidations and clues. At certain points I have the feeling of being at the end, and so far I have always known where the next dream-night would continue' (*F* 268). This last remark is important from the point of view of psychoanalytic technique: Freud had discovered that a dream should not be interpreted in isolation and that the dynamic concatenation of several dreams had a meaning. Next day, he added to his already complete letter a description of the dream he had had during the night about a sheep's head. Freud continued to send off other letters, on October 15, 27 and 31, without always waiting for Fliess's reply.

Freud was rediscovering almost all the childhood memories that had a bearing on his later life. His previously analysed dreams could now be seen to have fulfilled the function of introducing characters whose true role was at last being revealed: his half-brother Emanuel, his parents Jacob and Amalie, his nurse Monika Zajíc, his nephew and niece John and Pauline, and his earliest playmates. His previously recalled memories were of prepuberty and adolescence. His new memories focussed on the first three years of life, which Freud suspected of being crucial to the formation of the personality, and which in his case coincided with his Freiberg period.

So what does the letter of October 3 say? Freud finds no attempt at sexual seduction on the part of his father; on the other hand, he has to admit to jealousy of him, something he had already suspected. He discovers an erotic attachment to his mother, which was aroused during a journey with her to Vienna when he was between the ages of 'two and two-and-a-half years'[1] during which they spent the night together and he saw her naked.[2] Freud remembers that, when he was about one, he reacted to the birth of his first brother, Julius, with jealousy and ill-wishes towards him as though he were a rival. A few months later, his wishes were fulfilled and the baby died, leaving Freud with lasting feelings of guilt. Freud also had two half-brothers from his father's previous marriage. One of them, Emanuel, had two children, who, although more or less the same age as Sigismund, were his nephew and niece. Sigismund tried to emulate John, who was a few months older than him. John and Julius 'have determined, then, what is neurotic, but also what is intense, in all my friendships' (*F* 268). What is more, John and Sigismund were cruel to Pauline, the former's younger sister and the latter's niece.

The recollection of these memories was closely connected with Fliess. Fliess had noted the same erotic arousal, in similar circumstances, of his son Robert towards his mother. Pauline was the name of the dead sister Fliess so adored, the name he would have given his first child if it had been a girl, and the name he later gave his daughter, who was born at the end of 1898. The figure to whom Freud attached the greatest importance was his nurse, an 'ugly, elderly, but clever' woman. She was the 'prime originator' of his neurosis. She spoke Czech; she was Catholic and told him all about God and Hell; she gave him a high opinion of his own capacities, and for that reason the adult Freud felt deeply grateful towards her. He omits to mention, however, that the nurse in question, a 40-year-old spinster, was a daughter of the Zajícs, who owned, and shared, the Freuds' house in Freiberg.

THE 'SHEEP'S-HEAD' DREAM (OCTOBER 3–4, 1897)

The night after writing the letter Freud had a dream, which he described in a postscript (*F* 269). Two occurrences during the day served as a point of departure for the dream. Martha asked him for her 20 florins for the weekly household expenses – which was a nuisance as his practice had not yet got back to normal after the holidays. Freud saw an elderly woman patient, Mrs Q., who had been set to him by Fliess, and whose husband was a doctor. The doctor stipulated that a fee should be paid for the consultation, though Freud had been unwilling to take money from the wife of a

1. Freud was in all likelihood wrong about the date of their journey: he did not set foot outside Freiberg until his family moved to Vienna, when he was three-and-a-half. His memory is more likely to date from a journey he took from Leipzig to Vienna when he was almost four.

2. Freud uses the Latin words *matrem* and *nudam* in his letter.

colleague. Freud describes two fragments of the dream, one in his letter to Fliess, the other in *The Interpretation of Dreams*; the context, at least, would seem to justify the two passages being bracketed together:

1. '*I took out a subscription in S. and R.'s bookshop for a periodical costing* TWENTY FLORINS *a year*' (*ID* 166).

2. 'Today's dream has, under the strangest disguises, produced the following: she was my teacher in sexual matters and complained because I was clumsy and unable to do anything.

'(Neurotic impotence always comes about in this way. The fear of not being able to do anything at all in school thus obtains its sexual substratum.) At the same time I saw the skull of a small animal and in the dream I thought "pig", but in the analysis I associated it with your wish two years ago that I might find, as Goethe once did, a skull on the Lido to enlighten me. But I did not find it. So [I was] a "little blockhead" ["*Ein Kleiner Schafskopf*", literally "a little sheep's-head"]. The whole dream was full of the most mortifying allusions to my present impotence as a therapist. Perhaps this is where the inclination to believe in the incurability of hysteria begins. Moreover, she washed me in reddish water in which she had previously washed herself. (The interpretation is not difficult; I find nothing like this in the chain of my memories; so I regard it as a genuine ancient discovery.) And she made me steal zehners (ten-kreuzer coins) to give them to her. There is a long chain from these first silver zehners to the heap of paper ten-florin notes which I saw in the dream as Martha's weekly housekeeping money. The dream could be summed up as "bad treatment". Just as the old woman got money from me for her bad treatment, so today I get money for the bad treatment of my patients. A special part was played by Mrs Q., whose remark you reported to me: that I should not take anything from her, as she was the wife of a colleague (he of course made it a condition that I should)' (*F* 269–70).

Thus, the two key elements of the dream are: bad treatment and a sheep's-head. The bad treatment is what the nurse metes out on Freud: she would wash him in the reddish water she had already washed her private parts in when she was menstruating; she encouraged him to steal ten-kreuzer coins for her. But the bad treatment is also what Freud administers to his patients: he is a doctor who is incapable of curing hysteria completely, and in return for his services he accepts money, like the nurse; at the same time, he is incapable of earning enough to provide for his family. The word *Schafskopf*, which is an insult in German, reduplicates another insult, 'pig', which the nurse must have used to scold the young Sigismund when he dirtied himself (cf. the 'Running up stairs undressed' dream). Freud is a little *Schafskopf*, in other words a 'muttonhead' who has failed to discover his 'sheep's skull'. This is the kernel of his neurotic feeling of incompetence, which has recently reached its peak.

As in the Irma dream, the symbol also represents the process of self-analysis. Two years previously, in August 1895, when Freud visited Venice for the first time, Fliess had expressed the hope that he would find a skull on the Lido which would enlighten him, as it did Goethe. For Goethe came up with his so-called 'vertebral' theory of the skull after finding the remains of a sheep's-head on that beach. Freud returned to the subject in his second discussion of a later dream, 'Goethe's attack on Herr M.' (*OD* 664).

Introduced by Fliess, Goethe now begins to feature in Freud's self-analysis, playing an ever more important role as it goes on. Quotations from Goethe have already appeared several times in Freud's letters to Fliess, and on each occasion they have played a symbolic role. Just as Freud is embarking upon a systematic investigation of his childhood memories, what could be more normal than for him to allude to Eckermann's *Conversations with Goethe*, which describe Goethe's quest for his family? What could be more normal than for him to make Fliess his Eckermann? Besides, do not most of Freud's secret hopes – that he will never die, but remain eternally youthful, that he will desire attractive women patients and give them the pleasure they are deprived of, that he will become rich, famous and powerful, and conquer the secrets of human knowledge – strongly echo the theme of *Faust*?

Freud at last had within his grasp memories which could be verified, and would therefore enable him to settle an important theoretical issue, depending on whether they proved to be phantasies or to be based on actual events. He checked with his mother. She confirmed everything about the nurse, except on one vital point: *she*, not Sigismund, was the thief. This emerged at the time of Anna's birth, when the money and toys that had been given to Sigismund were found among her things: 'Your brother Philipp himself fetched the policeman; she then was given ten months in prison' (*F*, October 15, 1897, 271). Incidentally, now that it has been established that the nurse belonged to the Zajíc family, we may surmise that the incident had serious repercussions on relations between the two families and probably hastened the Freuds' departure from Freiberg.

Freud's interpretation of the 'Sheep's-head' dream was therefore incorrect in one respect. 'The correct interpretation is: I = she, and the mother of the doctor equals my mother.' Why did he make that mistake? 'So far was I from knowing that she was a thief that I made a wrong interpretation.' That was not the right reason. Freud's other associations are clear: he steals from the mother of a colleague; he steals from the mother of his own children. What Freud only partially spotted here – an inevitable resistance at that stage of his analysis – was his feminine identification, which was already latent in the Irma dream. He did not overcome that identification until he was on the point of shaking off his 'transference' on to Fliess. He then discovered, in the mother-identifying fixation, the genesis of homosexuality.

THE SCREEN MEMORY OF THE 'WARDROBE' SCENE

Freud's talk with his mother enabled him to progress further. 'I said to myself that if the old woman disappeared from my life so suddenly, it must be possible to demonstrate the impression this made on me. Where is it then? Thereupon a scene occurred to me which in the course of twenty-five years has occasionally emerged in my conscious memory without my understanding it. My mother was nowhere to be found: I was crying in despair. My brother Philipp (twenty years older than I) unlocked a wardrobe [*Kasten*] for me, and when I did not find my mother inside it either, I cried even more until, slender and beautiful, she came in through the door' (*F* 271). The purely rational explanation he had hitherto given himself was that he had been teased by his brother, who stopped misbehaving as soon as his mother arrived (*SE* 6, 50). 'Now I suddenly understand it. I had asked him to [unlock the wardrobe]. When I missed my mother, I was afraid she had vanished from me, just as the old woman had a short time before. So I must have heard that the old woman had been locked up and therefore must have believed that my mother had been locked up too – or rather, had been "boxed up" [*eingekastelt*] – for my brother Philipp, who is now 63 years old, to this very day is still fond of using such puns. The fact that I turned to him in particular proves that I was well aware of his share in the disappearance of the nurse' (*F* 271–2).

But that deduction does not explain, whatever Freud may say about it in the first edition of *The Psychopathology of Everyday Life* (1901*b*), 'why, in the translation of this visual childhood scene my mother's slimness was emphasised: it must have struck me as having just been restored to her' (*SE* 6, 51). True, as in dreams, semantic ambiguity provides the key to the puzzle of this memory. But it was only much later (in the 10th edition of *The Psychopathology of Everyday Life* in 1924) that Freud mentioned the sexual symbolism of the wardrobe or cupboard, which represented his 'mother's inside'. Worried by the birth of his sister Anna after that of his brother Julius, Sigismund must have wondered if his mother was pregnant again. The memory therefore accentuated the reassuring slimness of his mother and preserved the affect of 'restoration' he experienced at the time. The footnote Freud added in 1924 is as follows: 'Anyone who is interested in the mental life of these years of childhood will find it easy to guess the deeper determinant of the demand made on the big brother. The child of not yet three had understood that the little sister who had recently arrived had grown inside his mother. He was very far from approving of this addition to the family, and was full of mistrust and anxiety that his mother's inside might conceal still more children. The wardrobe or cupboard was a symbol for him of his mother's inside. So he insisted on looking into this cupboard, and turned for this to his big brother, who (as is clear from other material) had taken his father's place as the child's rival. Besides the well-founded suspicion that his brother had had the lost nurse "boxed up", there was a further suspicion against him – namely that he had in some way introduced the recently born baby into his mother's inside. The affect of disappointment when the cupboard was found to be empty derived, therefore, from the superficial motivation for the child's demand. As regards the *deeper* trend of thought, the affect was in the wrong place. On the other hand, his great satisfaction over his mother's slimness on her return can only be fully understood in the light of this deeper layer' (*SE* 6, 51 n.2).

The triangular structure on which the memory is based is therefore as follows: the young Sigismund is angry with Philipp, who has already had his dear nurse dismissed, for having done the same thing to his mother by making her pregnant. Behind the memory of the cupboard episode, then, there is a belief; that belief itself arises from a phantasy, whose content is gradually, during the first fortnight of October 1897, recognised by Freud as being 'Oedipal'.

The terms whose equation was produced by the Irma dream, and which underwent appropriate processes of substitution in subsequent dreams, are here resolved. The birth of Freud's daughter Anna echoes the problems once posed by the birth of his sister Anna – an event which Freud cannot remember (cf. 1899*a*), and whose screen memory (a term he was later to use) was probably the cupboard scene. The key triangles:

Otto –	Irma (a patient)	– Sigmund
Otto –	Martha	– Sigmund

end up as follows:

Fliess –	Mrs Q. (a patient)	– Sigmund
Philipp –	Amalie	– Sigismund
Jacob –	the nurse	– Sigismund

Freud is able to answer the theoretical question still in suspense. His 'neurosis' was caused not by an actual sexual trauma, but by incestuous phantasies. Moreover, hardly had he embarked on his book on dreams before he was thinking of another book to follow it up – *The Psychopathology of Everyday Life* (1901*b*). Freud's self-analysis had begun by focussing on dreams and the way they are distorted. It was now going to change course and focus on memories and the way they are distorted.

THE DREAM OF THE 'ONE-EYED DOCTOR AND SCHOOLMASTER' (MID-OCTOBER 1897)

Whereas Freud's analysis, activated by a dream, of his memories of the nurse led him to perceive the female protagonist in the Oedipal relationship, it was his childhood doctor, appearing in another dream, who played the role of the male figure. The dream was of the 'One-eyed doctor and schoolmaster', which Freud had at about the same time as the 'Sheep's-head' dream or slightly afterwards (he alludes to it in his letter of October 15, 1897). Freud, who describes it in Chapter I of *The Interpretation of Dreams*, on 'The Scientific Literature Dealing with the Problems of Dreams', sees it as confirmation of the assertion by several earlier authors that distant memories – for example memories from our earliest childhood – which we believe we have forgotten make their way back in dreams:

'I had a dream of someone who I knew in my dream was the doctor in my native town. His face was indistinct, but was confused with a picture of one of the masters at my secondary school, whom I still meet occasionally' (*ID* 17).

The dream shows a great deal of resentment against the doctor (*F*, October 15, 1897, 271). Yet Freud's history master, Professor K., was a harmless enough man. He could not understand why he had associated the two figures. Once again his mother explained everything: both men were one-eyed! Of all his schoolmasters, Professor K. was the only one with such a disability. But the mystery was not solved by that completely external parallel between the two men. The full explanation came only in the later editions of *The Interpretation of Dreams*. In the editions that came out between 1909 and 1922, Freud added to the sentence 'It was 38 years since I had seen the doctor, and so far as I know I had never thought of him in my waking life' the following clause: 'though a scar on my chin might have reminded me of his attentions'.

Also in 1909, Freud inserted a long addition on examination dreams which included the following passage: 'In my dreams of school examinations, I am invariably examined in History, in which I did brilliantly – though only, it is true, because [in the oral examination] my kindly master (the one-eyed benefactor of another dream, see p. 17) did not fail to notice that on the paper of questions which I handed him back I had run my finger-nail through the middle one of the three questions included, to warn him not to insist upon that particular one' (*ID* 275).

Lastly, a footnote added in 1919, in connection with a dream he had had when anxiously awaiting news of one of his sons who was on the front, states that he found in the dream 'allusions [which] reminded me unmistakably of an accident of my own which I had brought on myself when I was between two and three years old. I had climbed up on to a stool in the store-closet to get something nice that was lying on a cupboard or table. The stool had tipped over and its corner had struck me behind my lower jaw; I might easily, I reflected, have knocked out all my teeth' (*ID* 560). In the disguised autobiographical fragment of 'Screen Memories' (1899*a*) which describes the 'Green meadow with yellow flowers', Freud says he has no recollection of the incident, even though he lost a lot of blood, had several stitches, and could still feel the scar. In *Introductory Lectures on Psycho-Analysis* (1916–17, *SE* 15, 201), he added a further detail: 'I also learnt [from my mother] what the accident was for which [the one-eyed doctor] had come to my help.'

Why, then, did Freud not tell this to Fliess or publish it in the first edition of *The Interpretation of Dreams*? Why did he spread his interpretation of the dream over so many years and so many publications? It becomes easier to understand Freud's inhibition if it is seen in context, in other words as part of his self-analysis coming between the 'Uncle with the yellow beard' dream and the discovery of the Oedipus complex. He displays offensive contempt for his colleagues R. and N. and for his Uncle Josef, for whom he has a great feeling of affection. The kindly history master is paralleled by an obnoxious doctor. Freud is struggling with the ambivalence of his feelings – an ambivalence which, in the case of a son, is electively directed at his father. We can now see which phantasy complements the Oedipus phantasy: the scar has marked on his flesh the punishment for his incestuous wishes.

The dream obviously has the same meaning in the transference: Fliess is the one-eyed man *par excellence* (cf. the later dream 'My son, the Myops', where he is identified with the Cyclops). He personifies for Freud the two faces of the kindly schoolmaster and the obnoxious doctor. This is why Freud is sometimes almost too paralysed to write to him, and sometimes keen to see him, listen to him and tell him all. On October 15, the day Freud informed Fliess that he had discovered the Oedipus myth, he made a big promise: 'If the analysis fulfils what I expect of it, I shall work on it systematically and then put it before you.' But on October 27 he was forced to apologise to Fliess for the inhibition that had prevented him from wishing his friend a happy birthday (Fliess had just turned 39). The ambiguity of Freud's 'transference' manifested itself even in his scientific work: 'I have kept my interest focussed so exclusively on the analysis that I have not yet even attempted to try out, instead of my hypothesis that in every instance repression starts from the feminine aspect and is directed against the male one, the opposite hypothesis proposed by you' (*F* 273). His inhibition, then, was well and truly due to the mobilisation of an unavowed homosexual wish.

THE DISCOVERY OF THE OEDIPUS MYTH AND THE BLUNDER IN THE OLD WOMAN'S INJECTION

How did Freud marshal and understand the discoveries he had just made about his own past? By making them universal and pointing up their symbolic structure. That structure was not provided this time by chemistry, archaeology or linguistics, but by legend as embodied in tragedy. After taking as examples the rules that govern combinations of substances or words, Freud saw the symbolic function he attributed to dreams as residing in myth – a set of rules which, according to the ancients, governed human destiny. Myth provided the very substance that makes up the process of psychoanalysis. 'I have found, in my own case too, [the phenomenon of] being in love with my mother and jealous of my father, and I now consider it a universal event in early childhood. [. . .] If this is so, we can understand the gripping power of *Oedipus Rex*' (*F*, October 15, 1897, 272). In *The Interpretation of Dreams*, discreetly included under the heading 'Dreams of the Death of Persons of whom the Dreamer is Fond' (Chapter 5, Section IV, β), Freud returned to the ideas contained in his letter of October 15 and further developed them: 'King Oedipus, who slew his father Laïus and married his mother Jocasta, merely shows us the fulfilment of our own childhood wishes. [. . .] We shrink back from him with the whole force of the repression by which those wishes have since that time been held down within us. While the poet, as he unravels the past, brings to light the guilt of Oedipus, he is at the same time compelling us to recognise our own inner minds, in which those same impulses, though suppressed, are still to be found. [. . .] Like Oedipus, we live in ignorance of these wishes, repugnant to morality, which have been forced upon us by Nature, and after their revelation we may all of us well seek to close our eyes to the scenes of our childhood' (*ID* 262–3).

Thus myths, like dreams and phantasies, are wish-fulfilments. The term 'complex' was invented by a group of Swiss psychoanalysts led by Jung shortly before they broke with Freud, and only in 1910 did Freud himself use the expression 'Oedipus complex' in the first of his 'Contributions to the Psychology of Love' (1910*h*). Similarly, it was Stekel and Rank, themselves future dissidents, who prompted Freud to add a section on symbolic dreams to *The Interpretation of Dreams* in 1909 and 1914 (Chapter 6, Section V, 'Representation by symbols in dreams – some further typical dreams'), which was principally inspired by Stekel, and to insert between the end of Chapter 6 and the beginning of Chapter 7 two essays by Rank entitled 'Dreams and Creative Writing' and 'Dreams and Myths' (they were omitted from the 1930 edition).

As a result, the public has gained a distorted idea of Freud's discoveries: the simplistic symbolic system whereby anything long is a penis and anything hollow a vagina is in fact more allegorical than symbolic, and however indisputable the role played by allegory in psychoanalysis it is dwarfed by that of symbolic thought, which is the very foundation of language, mathematics, culture and the family. Freud was little interested in the symbolism of dreams before 1900. He did, however, grasp the importance of what Jacques Lacan was to call 'the Symbolic' in many psychical products, both individual (dreams, symptoms) and cultural (myths). What enlightened Freud was the *myth* of Oedipus. What he introduced into the human sciences, as Thomas Mann rightly pointed out (1936), was the myth as a general category that enables the facts to be specifically understood.

In the course of his discovery of the Oedipus myth, Freud completes the threefold process – at once subjective, objective, and self-representing – which began to get under way at the start of his self-analysis. It is the discovery of a universal truth; the discovery of himself; and the discovery of itself, by which I mean the correlative discovery of the very process through which the main discovery is made. By inventing the Oedipus complex, Freud symbolically realises his own Oedipus complex. As I have already said, for him, for any psychoanalyst, perhaps for anyone, dreams represent the body of the mother, the primal place where infantile wishes are fulfilled. To understand dreams, to understand one's own dreams, is to repossess that lost body. In Freud's case, that repossession became both more specific and more general in October 1897. He was a new Oedipus, conquering the unconscious, and grasping one of its essential structures. No doubt any great discovery represents one of the infinitely varied forms of Oedipal reconquest.

Reams have been written, and could still be written, about Freud's discovery. I shall restrict myself to quoting some remarks, not by a professional psychoanalyst, but by an essayist and literary critic with a thorough knowledge of psychoanalysis, Jean Starobinski (1967, p. xix and 1970, p. 298): 'The unconscious is not just language: it is dramaturgy, that is to say the staging of speech, spoken action (between the extremes of clamour and silence). *Oedipus Rex*, quintessential mythical drama, is instinct made visible in as pure a form as possible. Oedipus has no unconscious because he *is* our unconscious, by which I mean one of the essential roles that our wish has assumed. [. . .] It would be preposterous to attribute a psychology to him: he is already a psychical agency. [. . .] There is nothing behind Oedipus, because Oedipus is depth itself.'

Freud himself was an Oedipus in his feelings towards his parents. He was an Oedipus, too, because he solved the riddle of neurosis, which is fundamentally the riddle of every man. Already his fertile mind sensed that the same unconscious forces were at work in the tragedy *Hamlet*, with its incestuous wish for the mother, and homicidal wish for the father substitute. But there was an essential difference: whereas the Oedipus of legend had no complex (he fulfilled his wishes in an innocent, almost natural way, and encountered problems only afterwards), Hamlet is typical of someone grappling with that complex, haunted by unconscious guilt feelings because of that twofold wish, and paralysed by them in his actions, emotions, and life in general. 'Thus conscience doth make cowards of us all,' says Hamlet. He can neither respond to Ophelia's love nor wreak vengeance, as ordered by his father's ghost, on his uncle, who is his mother's lover. In other respects, when faced with matters that do not activate that complex in him, Hamlet, far from being timorous and irresolute, acts in a determined and impulsive manner – he, 'the same man who sends his courtiers to their death without a scruple and who is positively precipitate in murdering Laertes,' as Freud points out in the same letter to Fliess (*F* 273).

But Freud, curiously, has once again made a mistake, and once again it is connected with his 'transference' on to Fliess. Starobinski (1967, p. x, n.1, and 1970, p. 289) spotted it: 'Hamlet is unaware that the button has been taken off the foil or that its tip has been poisoned. So Hamlet kills Laertes unwittingly and unintentionally. Why, in his letter to Fliess, did Freud claim that Hamlet deliberately intended to commit a form of fratricide? Or could it be that a remarkable slip of the pen led him to write Laertes when he really meant Polonius?'

Let us return to Freud's letter to Fliess. In the end, Hamlet displays the behaviour of a 'hysteric' in his sexual alienation, in his transferring of the deed from his own father to someone else's (Ophelia's), and in the way he brings down punishment on himself (*F* 273). Freud repeats the same argument in *The Interpretation of Dreams* (*ID* 264–6), but makes two additional points. The first concerns a 'secular advance of repression', which was to form one of the main themes of *Totem and Taboo* (1912–13). The second relates *Hamlet* to Shakespeare's supposed personality: 'I observe in a book on Shakespeare by Georg Brandes (1896) a statement that *Hamlet* was written immediately after the death of Shakespeare's father (in 1601), that is, under the immediate impact of his bereavement and, as we may well assume, while his childhood feelings about his father had been freshly revived. It is known, too, that Shakespeare's own son who died at an early age bore the name of "Hamnet", which is identical with "Hamlet".'

Starobinski (1967, p. xvi) draws attention to Freud's identification with Shakespeare in that passage: 'By stressing the close chronological connection between the death of Shakespeare's father and the writing of *Hamlet*, Freud implies, without actually saying so, that poetic creation occurred in this case under the same circumstances as the discovery of the Oedipus theory, which resulted from Freud's analysis of his dreams during the months following the death of his father. *The Interpretation of Dreams* is intended to play the same role in the sphere of scientific knowledge as that played by *Hamlet* in the development of Shakespeare's dramatic *oeuvre*. Freud is a Shakespeare who has analysed himself.'

The application of the Oedipus myth to the psychology of the unconscious did, however, run into one problem which Freud experienced for himself: *Oedipus Rex* is a tragedy of fate, yet modern man cannot be expected to believe that events are dictated by fate. A symptomatic act provided an answer to the problem. Every morning Freud would visit the old woman (who has already been mentioned) in order to put a few drops of eye-lotion (collyrium) into her eye and give her a morphine injection. He was used to performing the two operations automatically. One morning, between October 4 and 15, he made a blunder – fortunately the one of the two possible errors that was harmless: he put morphine into the eye instead of collyrium. He immediately saw what he had done and corrected his mistake. But he soon realised, when he thought of the phrase 'to do violence to the old woman' or 'to commit a blunder on the old woman' (the German verb *vergreifen* had both meanings), that he had been about to give fate a helping hand.

Freud explained the feeling of fate in the same letter to Fliess: 'Everyone in the audience was once a budding Oedipus in fantasy and each recoils in horror from the dream fulfilment here transplanted into reality' (*F* 272). But the explanation of his act came only later, in *The Psychopathology of Everyday Life*: 'I was under the influence of a dream which had been told me by a young man the previous evening and the content of which could only point to sexual intercourse with his own mother. [. . .] While absorbed in thoughts of this kind I came to my patient, who is over 90, and I must have been on the way to grasping the universal human application of the Oedipus myth as correlated with the Fate which is revealed in the oracles; for at that point I did violence to or committed a blunder on "the old woman"' (*SE* 6, 178).

This passage tells us much about the way Freud came to make his discovery. In his self-analysis, he found residues of his childhood Oedipal feelings. But the truth of the Oedipus theory was fully brought home to him by his patients' analyses. There was a close interdependence between the two forms of analysis: his self-analysis, in relation to his psychotherapeutic work, served as an exercise in producing proof; conversely, the knowledge he acquired from treating his patients helped him in his self-analysis. The patient referred to here is certainly the young man with an obsessional neurosis (already mentioned on p. 231), who had suffered from homicidal tendencies since his father's death, and who, in my view, put Freud on the right track for his discovery, at the end of May 1897, of the death-wish against the parent of the same sex. It is easy to imagine what a revelation it must have been for Freud to hear his patient describe how he had committed incest with his mother in a dream (he refers to the young man in *The Interpretation of Dreams* just before setting forth his discovery of the Oedipus myth: *ID* 260).

From an epistemological point of view, this is crucial to Freud's discovery: it was hysterical girls or young women who enabled Freud to discover the meaning of dreams; but it was an obsessional young man who led him to the discovery of the Oedipus complex. Psychoanalysis, whose ground-plan was laid by Freud's totally new approach to hysteria, was properly founded only when it enabled him to understand obsessional neurosis.

Oedipus' problem is one of filiation. He wonders who his parents are. The oracle – a materialisation of his internal voice – prompts him to ask himself that question. This is one aspect of a problem that bothers all children: where do children come from? It is echoed in such philosophical preoccupations as: Who am I? Where does man come from? Who is man the son of? The answers to those questions presuppose that two differences are recognised – the difference between the sexes and the difference between one generation and the next. Every society has a system that lays down rules of kinship. Man is a civilised being largely because when he is born he escapes from the natural order of things, and because through that system of kinship he forms part of the human order – an order so patently symbolic that Claude Lévi-Strauss (1949) needed the help of an algebraist in order to represent it. It was a question that taxed Freud's mind while he was still very young, and was the prime motivation for his scientific curiosity. It is true that in his case, the riddle of kinship was particularly complicated. On top of the familial criss-crossings common in Jewish communities, there were his father's two (or three) marriages. The very young Sigismund, in Freiberg, must have spontaneously classified those around him into couples, according to age, as follows:

– Jacob and the nurse, the 'old' people (both about 40);
– Emanuel and his wife, the uncle and aunt (between 25 and 30);

– Philipp and Amalie, the young adults (both just over 20);
– John and Pauline, his nephew and niece, who were in fact much more like cousins of his own age (cf. 1899*a*).

But that classification was invalidated by the facts of family life. Why did Jacob share Amalie's bed? How was it possible that the nurse could be dismissed? How could Emanuel be his brother when he had children the same age as Sigismund? How can a nephew be older than his uncle? Freud's family tree (see Table 3) was a jigsaw puzzle that fell into place only after he had had an important conversation, at the age of 19, with Emanuel.

TABLE 3. *Sigmund Freud's family tree*

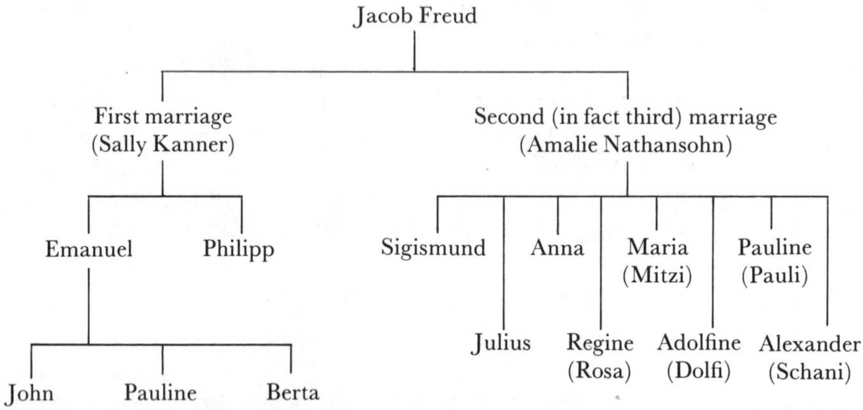

Doubtless only someone faced with such a problematic family configuration could have discovered the Oedipus complex. Those who criticise Freud for having put sex at the heart of all human problems, and who suspect him, for that reason, of taking an unhealthy interest in people's private lives and sexual pleasures, are quite mistaken about both the man and his discovery. Freud succeeded where others had until then failed, the latest in the series being Breuer. He studied the psychological repercussions of sexual problems with the cold, clinical eye of an anatomist. He was interested in neither the physiology of pleasure nor the stratagems of courtship. For him sex meant a kind of human relationship which brings into play two structures – that of the sexes and that of the generations – and which develops along certain specific lines. Everyone is the offspring of his or her father and mother: it is a fate which no one can escape, a fate to which we are all inevitably doomed by the oracle. Jacob Freud's death triggered off in his son the return of the riddles as well as opening the way to their solution. We escape our fate by fulfilling it. We escape childhood by becoming a grown-up. When we have symbolically killed our father, we can in turn become a father. Then, too, it is our turn to complete the cycle and wish the death of our children, just as Laïus wished the death of the new-born Oedipus. During the 1914–18 war, Freud had the same hostile dream about his son, who was on the front, as he had had about his father: he dreamt that he had received news of his death; but his son's imaginary 'accident' reminded him of his own accident as a child, when he tipped over a stool and knocked his jaw, with the result that he was left with a scar on his chin – an accident which he at last decided to mention openly in *The Interpretation of Dreams* (*ID* 558–60).

Freud was thrilled with his self-analysis. 'I cannot convey to you any idea of the intellectual beauty of this work' (*F*, October 3, 1897, 269). It made up for his lack of patients. 'I live only for the "inner" work' (*F*, October 27, 1897, 274). 'Since I have free time, I let myself be persuaded to take on two cases for treatment without a fee. Including myself, that makes three analyses that bring in nothing' (*F*, October 31, 1897, 276). His practice then picked up and put an end to that intense phase of self-analysis. On November 5 (*F* 277), it was once more 'at a standstill'. On the 14th he found out why. 'I can analyse myself only with the help of knowledge obtained objectively (like an outsider). True self-analysis is impossible; otherwise there would be no [neurotic] illness. Since I am still contending with some kind of puzzle in my patients, this is bound to hold me up in my self-analysis as well' (*F*, November 14, 1897, 281).

There was another reason. Freud was unhappy at the indifference shown by Fliess towards the discoveries that had emerged from his self-analysis. 'You said nothing about my interpretation of *Oedipus Rex* and *Hamlet*. [. . .] I have not told it to anyone else, because I can well imagine in advance the bewildered rejection' it would get (*F*, November 5, 1897, 277). Freud consoled himself by reading James Mark Baldwin's latest book, *Mental Development in the Child and the Race* (1895), in which he found several views similar to his own, and by spending a 'stimulating' evening with his friend Emanuel Löwy, who was professor of archaeology in Rome, and who revived Freud's longing to visit the Eternal City.

THE CHARACTERISTICS AND FIRST EFFECTS OF FREUD'S SELF-ANALYSIS IN SEPTEMBER AND OCTOBER 1897

Freud's systematic self-analysis in September and October 1897 has four major characteristics:

1. It forms part of a general cultural trend, which had remained purely

philosophical up to then, aimed at seeking after the truth and at self-knowledge. 'Being totally honest with oneself is a good exercise' (*F*, October 15, 1897, 272). There, Freud divines the essence of neurosis – unrecognised truth – and the essence of psychoanalysis – reestablished truth.

2. That establishment of the truth does not merely commit the soul in its entirety, in Plato's phrase; it brings into play the body, whose powers of symbolic expression, first sensed by Freud when he was investigating hysterical conversion, had now fully come home to him. 'Under the influence of analysis my cardiac symptoms are now very frequently replaced by gastrointestinal symptoms' (*F*, October 31, 1897, 276). Freud did not subsequently mention his heart-trouble again, so it would seem that it had cleared up. His digestive problems, which are alluded to in the dream where he is chided for uncleanliness, heralded the phase that was to follow – regression to the anal stage.

3. Self-analysis establishes the truth by reestablishing the personal past. It is here that psychoanalysis shows an affinity with poetry. Freud quotes the 'Dedication' of Goethe's *Faust*: 'And the shades of loved ones appear; with them, like an old, half-forgotten myth, first love and friendship.' He then adds: 'And also first fright and discord. Many a sad secret of life is here followed back to its first roots; many a pride and privilege are made aware of their humble origins' (*F*, October 27, 1897, 274). Freud (1930*e*) again used the quotation in his address delivered in the Goethe House in Frankfurt, adding that they were 'words which we could repeat for each of our analyses'. In the same letter to Fliess of October 27, he explains that the poet, 'using his privilege to ennoble', differs from the psychoanalyst in his ability to 'sublimate' – a notion which he was later to develop considerably. In his writings, Freud often expressed regret at not being a poet: the poet has an immediate understanding of the human heart that the psychoanalyst can achieve only after a long and laborious process.

4. Although Freud's self-analysis required, in order to progress, the objective knowledge he was deriving concurrently from his psychoanalyses of others, conversely self-analysis constituted a fruitful reversal of roles. 'All of what I experienced with my patients, as a third [person] I find again here' (*F*, October 27, 1897, 274). The first process was responsible for Freud's discovery of the Oedipus complex. Three other discoveries, on the other hand, were the direct result of his intensive self-analysis during October: a) the secondary gain from illness; b) the analysis of resistances; and c) the various stages of psychosexual development:

a) 'My insight that the difficulties in treatment are due to the fact that in the end one is laying bare the patient's evil inclinations, his will to remain ill, is becoming stronger and clearer' (*F*, October 3, 1879, 269). 'This morning I had a pleasant feeling. [. . .] It was in some way connected with the idea that one would have to begin the analysis of hysteria by uncovering the actual, operative motives for accepting the illness' (*F*, November 18, 1897, 283).

b) Freud no longer regarded resistance as an obstacle to treatment, but made it part of that treatment. He saw it as a positive manifestation of the patient's 'infantile character'. 'I dig it out by my work; it struggles; and the person who initially was such a good, noble human being becomes mean, untruthful, or obstinate, a malingerer – until I tell him so and thus make it possible for him to overcome this character. In this way resistance has become something actual and tangible to me' (*F*, October 27, 1897, 274). This passage also shows Freud's activistic and dominating countertransference, which was only reinforced by his practice of hypnotic counter-suggestion, and which was to manifest itself, though to a lesser and lesser degree, throughout his career as a psychoanalyst.

c) On November 14, 1897 (*F* 278–81), Freud wrote a long letter entirely devoted to the development of the libido, and to the notion – which, as we have seen, made its first appearance in his correspondence with Fliess at the time of his 'Rome' dreams at the beginning of 1897 – of pregenital sexual zones, the 'regions of the anus and of the mouth and throat', which become desexualised in the course of normal development, but to which the neurotic regresses. Freud distinguishes between normal repression and neurotic repression, refers to a 'male genital zone' in girls (that is, the clitoral zone), and contends that the choice of neurosis depends on the stage of development at which repression occurs.

Freud's paper, 'Sexuality in the Aetiology of the Neuroses' (1898*a*), whose importance seems to have escaped Fliess as well as most other readers, contains the immediate conclusion that Freud drew from this spate of new ideas: he gave up for good, in his treatment, any last remnants of hypnotic suggestion and any technique of concentration. Psychoanalytic technique as we know it today had been born.

CHAPTER 4

The discovery of the primal scene and the first version of *The Interpretation of Dreams*

'The psychology is proceeding in a strange manner; it is nearly finished, as if in a dream . . .'

(*F*, June 20, 1898, 318)

Freud's first attempt to break away from Fliess (December 1897–February 1898)

THE 'CONGRESS' WITH FLIESS AT CHRISTMAS 1897 AND THE MEMORY OF HIS CHILDHOOD PHOBIA IN BRESLAU STATION

From December 1897 to February 1898, Freud gradually resumed his work on dreams. He came up with some new ideas on psychoanalysis and psychology. His relationship with Fliess began to be of paramount importance.

Freud's new ideas were as follows: myths, legends and religious beliefs are all projections into the outside world of our 'dim inner perception' of the psychical apparatus (*F* 286); this was to be one of the main ideas of *The Psychopathology of Everyday Life* and of *Totem and Taboo*. Masturbation is 'the primary addiction' for which the other addictions (alcohol, morphine, tobacco) are merely substitutes (*F* 287); I quoted this passage in its entirety in connection with the cocaine episode (p. 44, n.1). Happiness is given a psychoanalytic definition: it is 'the belated fulfilment of a prehistoric wish,' in other words an infantile wish; wealth does not bring happiness, because money is not the object of such a wish (*F* 294).

Freud's most important new idea concerned the anal stage: 'the most disparate things are readily united as an obsessional idea under a single word with multiple meanings. The tendency toward breaking through makes use of these ambiguous words as though it were killing several flies at one blow' (*F* 287). Freud provides two examples of this from his own cases: a girl apprentice's obsessional idea of having to *do/make* [*machen*] more; and the way the word *Abort* ('toilet'), which is similar to the word *Abortus* ('abortion'), can mask things to do with birth, miscarriage and menstruation. Freud also equates money with excrement, and points out the significance of such expressions as 'filthy lucre' (cf. the ironical phrase *pecunia non olet*).

The fragments of letters to Fliess quoted by Schur give us a more precise and complete idea of the sudden importance assumed by anal material in Freud's thinking at that time. Freud was certainly encouraged by Fliess's no doubt favourable reaction to his ideas when they met in Breslau at Christmas 1897. With his letter of January 4, 1898 he enclosed No. 2 of his 'Scatological reports' (Freud actually used a witty neologism, written partly in Greek and partly in German: *Δρεκκologischen Berichte* – the German word *Dreck* means mud, dirt, filth or faeces). On January 16 he told Fliess that he had enclosed 'No. 3 of the *Δρ* . . .' (from then on, his abbreviation for the *Δρεκκologischen Berichte*), and added that he was 'well and in good spirits'.

Since writing 'Project for a Scientific Psychology' in October 1895, Freud had shown little interest, in his theoretical work, in the importance of verbal association, though in December 1896 he did make it one of the characteristics of the preconscious. He now approached the question from a new angle, that of the double meaning of certain expressions. Up to then, he had encountered them in his own dreams or memories, such as the 'Close the eyes' and 'Sheep's-head' dreams, or his memory of being afraid that his mother had been 'boxed' up. He now began to take an interest in double meanings that he came across in books or in his patients' case histories. For the first time, he mentioned to Fliess – and explained as being the result of such a mental process – a notion he had already used in previous publications[1] to illustrate one of the effects of repression, namely censorship: 'Have you ever seen a foreign newspaper which passed Russian censorship at the frontier? Words, whole clauses and sentences are blacked out so that the rest becomes unintelligible. A *Russian censorship* of this kind comes about in psychoses and produces the apparently meaningless *deliria*' (*F*, December 22, 1897, 289).

Herr E. immediately provided Freud – which is hardly surprising in view of the close links between the former's psychical activity and the latter's psychoanalytic activity – an example of a very unusual double meaning at both a phonemic and semantic level. When he was aged ten

1. *Studies on Hysteria* (1895*d*, *SE* 2, 269, 282), and 'Further Remarks on the Neuro-Psychoses of Defence' (1896*b*, *SE* 3, 182–5).

Herr E. had an anxiety-attack when he tried but failed to catch a black beetle [*Käfer*]. One day, he mentioned to Freud that his mother had been unable to make up her mind about getting married, and that he had gathered this information, after his mother's death, from a conversation between his grandmother and his aunt. Suddenly, Herr E. talked about the *Käfer* again, and then about a *Marienkäfer* (ladybird), which reminded him of his mother, Marie. Then he laughed, but did not know why. 'Then we broke off and next time he told me that before the session the meaning of *Käfer* had occurred to him; namely: *que faire?* = being unable to make up one's mind . . .' (*F*, December 29, 1897, 290).

The planned 'congress' with Fliess in Breslau at Christmas now occupied Freud's mind. He hoped that their meeting would give impetus to his book on dreams. He asked Fliess to take with him to Breslau the examples of dreams he had sent him. He gave two lectures on dreams to the B'nai B'rith society.

Freud was reminded of their earlier plan to meet in Prague, which gave rise to the fourth Rome dream. His interest in the dream must also have been revived by his conversation with Löwy.

Freud resumed his analysis of the fourth Rome dream and probably completed it at this point, as I have already suggested (cf. p. 198). In any case, he first mentioned the dream in his letter to Fliess of December 3, 1897. During his last journey to Italy, he had been unable, on his way to Rome, to get any farther than Lake Trasimeno, just like the celebrated Carthaginian, Hannibal, when fighting the Romans. Moreover, he remembered a sentence from a classical German author: 'Which of the two, it may be debated, walked up and down his study with the greater impatience after he had formed his plan of going to Rome – Winckelmann, the Vice-Principal, or Hannibal, the Commander-in-Chief?'

The decision taken by Winckelmann, the founder of classical archaeology in the eighteenth century, to visit Rome was the turning-point of his career. The Semitic warrior, Hannibal, had been one of Freud's heroes at school, at the point in his life when he first encountered anti-Semitism. Freud then moves on to the memory which triggered off the dream (and which I have already described): when Freud was between 10 and 12 years old, his father told him how he had offered no resistance to an anti-Semitic bully. 'Thus the wish to go to Rome had become in my dream-life a cloak and symbol for a number of other passionate wishes. Their realisation was to be pursued with all the perseverance and single-mindedness of the Carthaginian, though their fulfilment seemed at the moment just as little favoured by destiny as was Hannibal's lifelong wish to enter Rome' (*ID* 196–7). It is likely, as Jones surmised (J II, 21), that the taboo of incest was the ultimate hurdle which prevented Freud from reaching Rome. The fact that he finally got there, in 1901, was the result of a more complete resolution of his Oedipus complex.

Why, in his letter to Fliess, does Freud interpret the dream from one angle only, that of his 'neurotic' longing for Rome, and omit to mention his dissatisfaction with his father? Surely because he is reliving the same complex of emotions in his relationship with Fliess. He is disappointed in Fliess, but does not yet dare to admit this openly to himself. Buxbaum (1951) goes even further: Hannibal meant to defeat the Romans; Freud intended to defeat Fliess, the reincarnation of John. That would explain the paragraph in the letter that comes immediately after his analysis of the dream: 'Since I have been studying the unconscious, I have become so interesting to myself. A pity that one always keeps one's mouth shut about the most intimate things.' He then goes on to quote *Faust* yet again: 'The best you know, you may not tell to *boys*.' This was one of Freud's favourite quotations. In his address delivered in the Goethe House at Frankfurt (1930*e*), he commented on it in the following terms: 'Goethe was not only, as a poet, a great self-revealer, but also, in spite of the abundance of autobiographical records, a careful concealer.' In the present case, the quotation must surely be interpreted as an oblique reference to Freud's reticence vis-à-vis Fliess.

From February 1898 onwards, Freud's correspondence to Fliess changed in character. It no longer contained descriptions of dreams. True, Fliess still learnt of them through the successive chapters of *The Interpretation of Dreams* which Freud sent him in manuscript. But such a roundabout channel was in itself significant: under the cover of a scientific work – and not, as before, through direct communication – Fliess was given to understand Freud's feelings for him.

The reason that Freud agreed to go to Breslau for their 'congress', after earlier displaying resistances about a similar meeting in Prague, is that he has just exorcised all that Breslau symbolised. He says as much in the same letter of December 3, in which he talks of completing his interpretation of the fourth Rome dream; 'Breslau also plays a role in my childhood memories. At the age of three years I passed through the station when we moved from Freiberg to Leipzig, and the gas flames which I saw for the first time reminded me of spirits burning in hell. [. . .] My travel anxiety, now overcome, also is bound up with this' (*F*, December 3, 1897, 285). Here we see one of the curative effects of self-analysis: his fear of travelling by rail disappears – partly at least: Freud returns to the subject in 1900 (see p. 522) – when he becomes aware of the original memory. As Buxbaum (1951) has pointed out, the gaslight at Breslau station meant that hell and damnation awaits the son who covets his father's wife and who wants to kill the father for that reason.

In Freud's later life, all that remained of his phobia of railways was a tendency to get to the station very early when intending to catch a train. Evidence provided by Sachs (1945), Ernst Simmel, as told to Bernfeld (1946), and Reik (1949*a*) suggest that Freud may even have suffered from agoraphobia. The triumphant invocation of the gods of hell at the beginning of *The Interpretation of Dreams* (a quotation from the *Aeneid*) represented his revenge over them. Jones (J I, 14) ascribes Freud's fear of travelling by train to separation anxiety and to a fear of losing his home, that is to say his mother's breast. This is surely the right explanation: Sigismund's first rail journey was bound up with his family's emigration, in other words with a real separation from the town and the house where he was born, and any such journey would tend to be experienced as a traumatic repetition. Freud's dreams at the beginning of 1898 helped him to work through that memory of emigration and that separation anxiety.

The Breslau 'congress' (December 22–28, 1897) did not go off as well as their previous such meetings. Fliess was more concerned to get Freud interested in his own ideas than he was interested in Freud's discoveries, and expatiated on his new theory: biological bisexuality extended, in man, to a psychical bisexuality, he claimed; and that bisexuality was paralleled by the peculiar bilaterality of the human organism, since left and right were as different and as complementary as the two sexes. Normally, Freud was only too willing to take at face value Fliess's major scientific 'phantasies', such as the connection between sex and the nose, and the difference in the periodicity of men (23 days) and women (28). But this time he did not go along with Fliess. Indeed, anyone with only a slightly scientific turn of mind would have baulked at such a gratuitous link between bisexuality and bilaterity.

As soon as he got back to Vienna, Freud confirmed his disagreement in writing (letter of December 29, 1897), which was something he had never done before: 'Incidentally the question that follows from [the left-handedness theory] is the first in a long time on which our hunches and inclinations have not taken the same path' (*F* 291). But he went further than that, and earlier in the same letter poked fun at his friend's theory: 'Bi-bi is ringing in my ears, but I am still feeling too well for serious work.' It is not difficult to guess that 'bi-bi' means 'bisexuality-bilaterality'. Fliess answered immediately, taking exception to his friend's remarks. On January 4, 1898, Freud hastened to write back in conciliatory terms, accepting that he might be wrong but not shifting his position at all: 'I literally embraced your stress on bisexuality and consider this idea of yours to be the most significant one for my subject since that of "defence". If I had a disinclination on personal grounds, because I am in part neurotic myself, this disinclination would certainly have been directed toward bisexuality, which, after all, we hold responsible for the inclination to repression. It seems to me that I object only to the permeation of bisexuality and bilaterality that you demand. [. . .] I had the impression, furthermore, that you considered me to be partially left-handed; if so, you would tell me, since there is nothing in this bit of self-knowledge that might hurt me. [. . .] The aversion to your conception of left-handedness I have so far felt may rest on unconscious motives. If they are hysterical, they certainly have nothing to do with the subject matter, but merely latch onto a catchword' (*F* 292–3).

Freud very probably had the dream 'My son, the Myops' some time between December 29 and January 4, or else just before or afterwards. It was his first dream – or rather, published dream – after his discovery of the Oedipus complex. Freud later adopted the theory of psychical bisexuality after recasting it and forgetting that he owed the germ of the idea to Fliess. That was the cause of their quarrel in 1900 and their final break in 1904. I would tend to agree with Edith Buxbaum (1951), despite Jones's reservations (J I, 345 n.2), when she interprets one passage of the letter just quoted – 'I literally embraced your stress on bisexuality and consider this idea of yours to be the most significant one *for my subject*' [my italics] – as a *lapsus calami* of Freud's wish to appropriate Fliess's theory of bisexuality.

THE 'MY SON, THE MYOPS' DREAM (JANUARY 1898)

'Another time I had a dream that a man I knew on the staff of the University said to me: "*My son, the Myops* [*der Myop*]." Then followed a dialogue made up of short remarks and rejoinders. After this, however, there was yet a third piece of dream in which I myself and my sons figured. So far as the dream's latent content was concerned, Professor M. and his son were men of straw – a mere screen for me and my eldest son' (*ID* 269). 'Here is the missing main dream, which introduces an absurd and unintelligible verbal form which requires an explanation.

'On account of certain events which had occurred in the city of Rome, it had become necessary to remove the children to safety, and this was done. The scene was then in front of a gateway, double doors in the ancient style (the "Porta Romana" at Siena, as I was aware during the dream itself). I was sitting on the edge of a fountain and was greatly depressed and almost in tears. A female figure – an attendant or nun – brought two boys out and handed them over to their father, who was not myself. The elder of the two was clearly my eldest son; I did not see the other one's face. The woman who brought out the boy asked him to kiss her good-bye. She was noticeable for having a red nose. The boy refused to kiss her, but, holding out his hand in farewell, said "AUF GESERES" to her, and then "AUF UNGESERES" to the two of us (or to one of us). I had a notion that this last phrase denoted a preference' (*ID* 441–2).

Freud includes the dream in Section G, 'Absurd dreams', of Chapter 6, 'The Dream-Work'. Grinstein devotes a chapter to it (G, Chapter 13). I propose to analyse the dream more particularly from three of the five angles mentioned above, namely Freud's relationship with Fliess, the fulfilment of a wish of the previous day, and the fulfilment of an infantile wish. The quotations that follow are taken from the free associations which Freud analyses after his account of the dream in *The Interpretation of Dreams*.

The dream marked a turning-point in Freud's relationship with Fliess: his attitude towards his 'mentor' was beginning to become less admirative and more critical. His criticism expressed itself in the neologisms coined by the dream – *der Myop, Auf Geseres*, and *Auf Ungeseres*.

German does not have a word similar to 'myopic', which derives from the Greek μύειν (to blink) and ὤψ (eye); the normal word used is *kurzsichtig*, which is the exact equivalent of 'short-sighted'. *Myop* is therefore an *ad hoc* form constructed by the dreamer on the pattern of *Zyklop* ('Cyclops'). There is a clear reference to the Breslau 'congress': 'My friend had been telling me his views on the biological significance of *bilateral symmetry* and had begun a sentence with the words "If we had an eye in the middle of our foreheads like a Cyclops . . ."' Now the Cyclops existed only in classical Greek mythology. The latent thought of the dreamer is probably as follows: the use of an analogy with the Cyclops in a supposedly scientific argument is 'short-sighted' – or one-eyed. An earlier portion of Freud's analysis of the dream suggests the same thing: 'I remembered how, the previous Easter, my Berlin friend and I had been walking through the streets of Breslau, a town in which we were strangers. A little girl asked me the way to a particular street, and I was obliged to confess that I did not know; and I remarked to my friend: "It is to be hoped that when she grows up that little girl will show more discrimination in her choice of the people she gets to direct her."' Freud is here voicing doubts about his own discrimination in having chosen Fliess to direct him since 1893 or 1894.

There are two other significant details here. First, Freud gets the date wrong: their Easter 'congress' had been in Nuremberg, and it was at Christmas, just before the dream, that they met in Breslau. This parapraxis may in fact have been an attempt by Freud to cover his tracks at the time of the publication of *The Interpretation of Dreams* – he was paying dearly for his revelation of personal details. But the fusion in Freud's mind of the two occasions when Fliess discussed bisexuality would seem to herald his subsequent cryptomnesia and the priority dispute that occurred between the two men. The second detail concerns Freud's female/passive identification (he is the little girl who chooses the wrong person to direct her) vis-à-vis the male/active Fliess. Thus Freud's interest, now enthusiastic, now hesitant, in the notion of bisexuality is directly connected with a 'transference effect' of a homosexual nature. Freud still had a long way to go before he was able to realise the latent submission and homosexuality that bound him to Fliess. It was only after Freud had shaken off that bond that psychoanalysis became an independent science.

Auf Geseres is a composite expression constructed on the pattern of *Auf Wiedersehen* ('goodbye', or, more literally, 'till we see each other again'), which the boy could normally be expected, in the context of the dream, to utter when taking his leave. 'According to information I have received from philologists, "*Geseres*" is a genuine Hebrew word derived from a verb "*goiser*", and is best translated by "imposed sufferings" or "doom". The use of the word in slang would incline one to suppose that it meant "weeping and wailing".' *Auf Geseres*, then, could be translated as 'till wailing'. Its opposite, *Auf Ungeseres* (literally, 'till non-wailing'), is 'quite meaningless', says Freud. *Ungeseres* is a hybrid word (*un* is a German negative prefix and *Geseres* a Hebrew noun) which is coined by the dreamer out of pure 'bilateral symmetry' and which has no meaning. It makes a mockery of Fliess's purely gratuitous theory about bilateral symmetry. Thus, the absurdity of the signifier is to be taken literally. Form here expresses the content of Freud's assessment of Fliess's theory: it is absurd, it is nonsense. Freud is, however, careful not to say as much in his analysis.

He then focusses on the short remark at the end of the dream, namely that the word '*Ungeseres*' denotes a preference over '*Geseres*'. He sees an analogy with caviare: *unsalted* [*ungesalzen*] caviare is more highly esteemed than *salted* [*gesalzen*]. Similarly, *unleavened* [*ungesauert*] bread is eaten at the Jewish Easter in memory of the fact that 'in their flight out of Egypt the Children of Israel had not time to allow their dough to rise'. The full significance of that 'preference' dawns on Freud a little further on in his analysis when he recalls an anecdote that establishes a connection between the first portion of the dream ('My son, the Myops') and the last (*Auf Geseres/Auf Ungeseres*). Professor M.'s son had a disease of the eyes which gave cause for anxiety. The doctor explained that 'so long as it remained *on one side* it was of no importance.' The affection cleared up in the one eye but soon appeared in the other. The boy's mother was terrified. The doctor 'now went over *to the other side*,' in other words completely changed his opinion: '"Why are you making such a '*Geseres*'?" he shouted at the mother, "if *one* side has got well, so will the *other*." And he was right.'

Freud changes his opinion in a similar way between his letter of December 29, 1897, and that of January 4, 1898. In the first, he simply plays down his reservations about Fliess's theory of bilaterality, whereas in the second he enthusiastically supports his notion of bisexuality. In this way he shows his 'preference', which is to preserve Fliess's friendship by ignoring the deepening disagreement he can feel opening up between them. Freud must have been aware that he was acting in a contradictory, 'crazy way', for he remarks at the end of his analysis: 'After the child had turned to *one side* to say farewell words, he turned to the *other side* to say the contrary, as though to restore the balance. *It was as though he was acting with due attention to bilateral symmetry!*'

Let me now turn to the wishes that seek fulfilment in the dream. The previous day's wish is related to Freud's six children as a whole, and more especially to his sons and to his eldest son. It is the wish that they should avoid two dangers which threaten them – a social danger, anti-Semitism, and a sexual danger, that of contracting syphilis as a result of relations with prostitutes or women of easy virtue. Freud's series of free associations starts by highlighting the first danger: the dream is a visualisation of a scene in Swinburne's poem *Super Flumina Babylonis*, whose first line, '*By the waters*[1] *of Babylon we sat down and wept*,' is quoted by Freud. The poem is partly based on Psalm 137, which is the song of lamentations (*Geseres*) of exiled Jews. The same danger is hinted at by other features of the dream: the need to flee Rome (the Roman emperor Titus destroyed the Temple at Jerusalem and caused the Diaspora of the Jews; anti-Semitic persecution was continued by the Rome-based Catholic Church); the allusion to the massacre of the Holy Innocents (on noticing a door-plate in Breslau bearing the name of a certain Dr Herodes, Freud had remarked to Fliess: 'Let us hope that our colleague does not happen to be a children's doctor'); the play *Das neue Ghetto* (*The New Ghetto*) by the founder of Zionism, Theodor Herzl, which had a great effect on Freud (probably because of its message (G 318–21): the physical walls of the ghetto have been pulled down, but anti-Semitism imprisons the Jews in a new moral ghetto from which it is risky for them to try to break out); the news that a Jewish doctor had been obliged to resign the position he had secured with great difficulty in a state asylum; and lastly the Dreyfus affair in France (though Freud does not refer to it in his analysis of the dream, but mentions it in a letter to

1. The word used in the Psalm is 'rivers', not 'waters'.

Fliess a month later).[1] The deeper idea is reminiscent of the ancient Roman proverb: the Capitol (where triumphers were welcomed) was near the Tarpeian Rock (from which traitors were hurled to their death); Devil's Island (the penal colony to which Dreyfus was sent) lay in store for any ambitious Jew who, like himself, had hopes of making a career in the army, and, as Freud discovered to his surprise during his tour of northern Italy, the insane asylum in Siena was near the Porta Romana.

The second danger emerges only at the end of his analysis of the dream: the desk used by Professor M.'s son at the time of his eye disease was handed over as a gift to Freud's eldest son, Martin. The special construction of the desk was intended 'to save the child from being *short-sighted* [*kurzsichtig*] and *one-sided* [*einseitig*]. [. . .] My concern about one-sidedness had more than one meaning: it could refer not only to physical one-sidedness but also to one-sidedness of intellectual development'. The allusion was clarified in later dreams ('Frau Doni and the three children', and '*Autodidasker*'), when Freud's concern resurfaced: Martin had a gift for poetry, which caused his mother to worry about his future. Although nowhere in his analysis does Freud mention the father's wish to prevent his son from having sexual relations believed to be dangerous for his health, that wish is clearly present in the actual text of the dream: the father gets the women to hand over the boys, and the one she asks to kiss her goodbye refuses to do so; moreover, the woman is an 'attendant' or a 'nun', in other words a forbidden woman.

But 'bilateral symmetry' suggests that this manifest passage may also contain a reversal into its opposite of the following latent content: in his thoughts, Freud entrusts his children to their 'governess', should he die, but also, no doubt, to Minna – his sister-in-law and therefore a forbidden woman – who had been living with the Freuds for the last eighteen months to help Martha bring up the children.

What was the infantile wish that over-determined those waking wishes? According to the dream, 'a female figure [. . .] brought two boys out and handed them over to their father, who was not myself.' If Freud is not the father, then he must appear in the dream as a son. 'The elder of the two was clearly my eldest son; I did not see the other one's face' – probably an allusion to his younger brother Julius, who was born in Freiberg and died at the age of six months. 'She was noticeable for having a red nose' – a reference to the nurse, who, as Freud had recently learnt from a conversation with his mother, drank, was dirty, and used to steal, for which reason

1. Nothing in this dream justifies the interpretation formulated by Maylan (1930), who, writing from an anti-Semitic point of view, claims that Freud's neurosis was the result of a repressed wish to be converted to Christianity!

she was dismissed. Thus, both the separation from the nurse and the departure 'into exile' from Freiberg are represented in the dream. The departure, which had become necessary 'on account of certain events' (obviously an understatement), resulted in the two branches of the family being separated. It is the wish to nullify that separation that the dream fulfils: on one side Freud says 'goodbye' to those from whom he is separated; and on the other side he says 'un-goodbye'. Jacob, his young wife and the two children from his second marriage (Sigismund and Anna) went 'to one side', to Vienna – the unhappy (*Geseres*) side. The two sons from Jacob's first marriage (Emanuel, with his wife and children, and Philipp) went 'to another side', to Manchester – the happy (*Ungeseres*) side.

The wish underlying the 'preference' at the end of the dream is as follows: if I had left with the other branch of the family and gone to England, if I had been Emanuel's son, I would have escaped anti-Semitism. The screen memory of the meadow with yellow flowers (published in 1899) completes the wish: and I would have continued my warlike games with my nephew John and my sexual games with my niece Pauline. The second sentence of the dream now becomes comprehensible: 'The scene was then in front of a gateway, double doors in the ancient style.' 'In front of a gateway' suggests the sexual term *ante portas*; 'the ancient style' denotes an old memory. It was because the boy had tried to see Pauline's double doors – the anal and vaginal orifices – that he was punished by an affliction of his sight (he became 'short-sighted' or 'one-eyed'), and exiled far from the object of his curiosity. Short-sightedness here fulfils both the forbiddance (you will lose your sight if you look at what is forbidden, namely the female sexual organs) and the wish (short-sighted people see better from close to; let me come closer so I can see better).

In this respect, the verbal opposites that conclude the dream, *Auf Geseres/Auf Ungeseres*, are determined specifically by the persons to whom each of them is addressed – a woman in the first case, a man in the second. They therefore represent the difference between the sexes: the male sex is *Geseres*, in other words the cause of something imposed, or doomed to occur (the first meaning of *Geseres*), as well as the cause of weeping and wailing (the second meaning of *Geseres*); the other sex is defined negatively, by the lack or absence (*Un-*) of the first. Freud, in his analysis, describes *Auf Ungeseres* as being 'quite meaningless'. Both the thing and the word were indeed meaningless for a three-and-a-half-year-old child (Sigismund's age when he left Freiberg). What is quite certain, however, is that each sex has a 'preference' for the other.

One or two further remarks may be made on the dream in addition to the three approaches I have just proposed. It followed the usual pattern of the dreams that Freud had had since beginning self-analysis, the first part consisting of a visual scene, and the second of a word or sentence that is read or heard. It confirmed to Freud that the latent content (the dream-thoughts) can be expressed as much in the form and style of the dream, in the impression it leaves, as in its manifest content. The predominant impression given by the dream is one of absurdity, and it closes on an absurd note, just as the Irma dream ends with the formula for trimethylamin. Morever, it is included in the chapter on absurd dreams, and helps to prove that any feeling of immediate absurdity in a dream is an integral part of its thoughts. 'The dream-work produces absurd dreams and dreams containing individual absurd elements if it is faced with the necessity of representing any criticism, ridicule or derision which may be present in the dream-thoughts.'

As Buxbaum (1951) has rightly suggested, this dream answers the question: do there exist dreams without sense, that is to say, dreams whose meaning is nonsense? As I have already said, the meaning of the dream, which Freud does not make entirely explicit, is that the idea of bilaterality is nonsense. He is as disappointed and scornful as he was when his father told him how he stepped out of the path of an anti-Semitic Gentile in the streets of Freiberg. He ends his analysis along the lines of 'a word to the wise is enough': 'Dreams, then, are often most profound when they seem most crazy. In every epoch of history those who have had something to say but could not say it without peril have eagerly assumed a fool's cap. [. . .] Hamlet, who had to disguise himself as a madman, was behaving just as dreams do in reality [. . .] concealing the true circumstances under a cloak of wit and unintelligibility.'

Once again, sight plays a central role in the dream and is implied in its key phrase 'My son, the Myops'. To see is to be able to keep an object at the right distance between danger and the wish – far enough away for it not to be a threat, but within view so it can be kept under control. It is a typically hysterophobic compromise between sexual curiosity and castration anxiety. When looked at from this angle, the position that Freud asks Fliess to occupy becomes clearer: Fliess is the contraphobic object on which Freud fixes his ambivalence, and which protects him from his phobias (for example, of travelling by train or of dying prematurely as a result of smoking too heavily). Whereas conversion hysteria is the subject focussed upon in *Studies on Hysteria*, one of Freud's major advances in psychopathology, which can be seen from his correspondence with Fliess since the death of his father, and which is clearly due to his self-analysis, is an understanding of anxiety hysteria.

Hannibal was one-eyed; he had lost an eye while advancing through the marshes of Etruria. Charcot squinted, in other words he was visually gauche. In his letter of January 4, 1898, Freud was prepared to admit to being 'partially left-handed' so that Fliess would be encouraged to believe, against all the evidence, that he had a better perception of things than Freud. The construction of the dream is based on the contrast between *kurzsichtig* ('short-sighted') and *Scharfblick* ('discrimination' – or, literally, 'sharp-sightedness' – which is lacking in the little girl who asks Freud the way in Breslau). But the most surprising thing of all is surely that in all Freud's associations to the dream there is no mention of Oedipus, who blinded himself after realising he had committed incest and parricide. Freud had discovered the Oedipus complex in October 1897. Since then, he had been reluctant to 'see' the consequence of the twofold incestuous and parricidal wish, namely a certain threat whose substitute in the dream took the form of an eye disease, and whose bodily trace and actual existence in real life took the form of a scar on the chin, which had resulted from a long-forgotten misdeed or accident and been treated by the one-eyed doctor.

The belief that the difference between the sexes is the result of women having been castrated is an infantile sexual theory and a 'primal' phantasy. Freud needed to complete the rest of his self-analysis, with its large number of dreams, before he could work through to an awareness of that belief, that phantasy, and their related anxiety. He would need to find, or rather become receptive to, the signifier capable of acting as an intermediary that would show him the way. Meanwhile, Fliess's assertion that human beings are fundamentally bisexual was used by Freud as an ideological defence against the recognition of castration anxiety and against the recall of that infantile sexual theory.

At the same time, Freud was aware, as yet only partially, but clearly, of the phantasied and ideological nature of Fliess's theory, which for that very reason dissatisfied him, and which he resolved to criticise. Freud already had strong doubts about the hypothesis that psychical bisexuality derived from biological bisexuality – a hypothesis no more sophisticated than infantile sexual theories. Bisexuality is the result of both masculine and feminine identifications, in other words, of a purely psychical process: that was to be the specifically psychoanalytic explanation of the phenomenon. Freud was beginning to realise that what he experienced so intensely in his 'transferential' relationship with Fliess was precisely such a bisexual identification – a double identification in all likelihood represented by the 'double doors' of the dream.

Bisexuality, Fliess's cherished theory, was a premature idea for Freud, and accordingly did not hold his attention for long. By January 16, 1898, he had already moved on to other concerns: 'All sorts of little things are teeming; dream and hysteria fit together ever more neatly. The details are now standing in the way of the large problems touched upon in Breslau' (*F* 294). This shows that Freud was now capable of shaking off Fliess's influence when it seemed likely to cause him to swerve from his own course, and of returning to his own scientific work, which he believed to be more important. He said the same thing once again on March 15: 'I do not in the least underestimate bisexuality either; I expect it to provide all further enlightenment [. . .]. It is only that at the moment I feel remote from it because, buried in a dark shaft, I see nothing else' (*F* 303).

Work on *The Interpretation of Dreams* gets under way (February–July 1898)

THE 'OTTO WAS LOOKING ILL' DREAM (FEBRUARY 1898)

That Freud's self-analysis had recovered its internal dynamic can be seen from the 'Otto was looking ill' dream, which in my view probably dates from February 1898. Certain features of it seem to be contained in Freud's letter to Fliess of February 9: a) Freud had just been on quite a long journey to Hungary for a consultation; b) he was reading the literature on dreams, which, apart from Fechner's thoughts on the subject, disappointed him; and he had taken a major decision: 'My self-analysis is at rest in favour of the dream book [*The Interpretation of Dreams*]'; c) he was following Emile Zola's trial ('A fine fellow'), which had just opened in Paris (Zola was being prosecuted for his celebrated open letter 'J'accuse . . . !', in which he denounced the machinations of Dreyfus's accusers); d) 'A rumour has it that we are to be invested with the title of professor at the emperor's jubilee on December 2. I do not believe it, but had a delightful dream about it, which unfortunately cannot be published because its background, its second meaning, shifts back and forth between my nurse (my mother) and my wife' (*F* 299). This description of the dream does not tally with any of those related in *The Interpretation of Dreams*, though its theme is to be found in the 'Three Fates' dream. I am tempted to see a connection between it and another day's residue which Freud does not mention, and which has so far escaped the notice of other commentators: on January 30, 1898 Freud greeted with jubilation the news that Ida Fliess was pregnant for a second time, and promised to 'listen most devoutly' at their next 'congress'. It is likely that Freud felt some sexual curiosity about his friend's wife, as well as guilt feelings towards Fliess himself. So Freud had another dream, publishable this time, in which those guilt feelings are displaced from Fliess on to

Otto. The previous day, just as on the day before the Irma dream, he had been visited by his family doctor, Oscar Rie (alias 'my friend Otto'), who had married one of Ida Fliess's sisters in 1896 and thus become Fliess's brother-in-law. Martha thought Otto looked tired. The dream is as follows: '*My friend Otto was looking ill. His face was brown and he had protruding eyes.*'

The dream is described and analysed by Freud in subsection (β), 'Dreams of the death of persons of whom the dreamer is fond' (Chapter 5, 'The Material and Sources of Dreams', Section D, 'Typical Dreams') as an example of the dreamer's egoism (*ID* 269–71). He returns to the dream in Section C, 'Wish-Fulfilment', of Chapter 7, 'The Psychology of the Dream-Processes', to show how the day's residues can be received into a dream only if they 'submit' to a wish (*ID* 555–6).

The key to the dream is the memory of an excursion to the Raxalpe mountain plateau six years earlier, probably in August 1891, with Professor Kassowitz, who headed the Institute for Children's Diseases where Freud was director of the neurological department. The carriage taking them there had tipped over an embankment, and they were forced to spend the night in a neighbouring inn. A distinguished gentleman, a baron, with unmistakable signs of Basedow's disease, volunteered to help them. But when taken up on his offer and asked if he could provide a night-shirt, he declined.

Similarly, Freud had asked Otto, some years before, to take charge of his children's sexual education, especially at the age of puberty, if ever anything should happen to him. Now Freud knew of two people called Basedow – one was a physician who gave his name to the disease attributed to Otto in the dream, and the other a well-known educationalist, philanthropist, and follower of Rousseau. One of the meanings of the dream is: if something were to happen to me, Otto would do no more for my children than the noble helper did for us after our road accident. In identifying Otto with the baron, Freud identifies himself with Professor Kassowitz, much of whose career was spent outside the academic world, and who had achieved his well-merited professorship only late in life. Another meaning of the dream is, once again, that Freud wants to be appointed professor. As on the first occasion when that ambition made itself felt (in the 'Uncle with the yellow beard' dream), Jewish colleagues are snubbed (Fliess is fast becoming the symbol of such treatment). The third meaning is as follows: Freud is afraid of having Basedow's disease (exophthalmic goitre). We subsequently learn that it acts as a substitute for a venereal disease.

These are the meanings Freud recognises in the dream, at least in his published analysis. But the day's residues, to which Freud does not refer, throw light on the Oedipal 'transference' on to Fliess that is taking place. In the Irma dream, Freud expressed jealousy of his colleague and friend, Otto, whom Freud's wife, Martha, allowed to examine her. Here, in my view, he fears Fliess may be jealous because his wife, Ida, is subjected to Freud's sexual curiosity. The dream is careful to replace Fliess by another of Freud's friends, Otto (Oscar Rie), who in the meantime has become Fliess's brother-in-law, and to specify, somewhat ambiguously, that he was 'looking ill' ('*schaut schlecht aus*' in both its meanings: 'looking evil' and 'looking sick').

THE WRITING OF THE FIRST VERSION OF *THE INTERPRETATION OF DREAMS*

From February 1898 on, Freud was driven by two psychical forces – the continuation of his self-analysis, involving new dreams, and the writing of the first version of *The Interpretation of Dreams*, which looked back over earlier dreams. The two forces acted in tandem until the summer of 1898, when Freud finally abandoned his first version of the 'dream book' and his self-analysis began to focus on products of the unconscious other than dreams, such as the forgetting of names and screen memories.

For the sake of clarity, I shall examine the two forces separately; but first their juxtaposition needs to be emphasised. While continuing to accumulate personal dream material, which he was to include, a year later, in the second and, apart from additions, final version of the book, Freud wrote up the discoveries he had already made as a result of earlier dreams. A point that has escaped the notice of other commentators is that when doing so he described, one by one, the main stages of his personal and intellectual achievements up to then: in other words, the first version was a diachronic one. Freud got 'stuck', to use his own words, when he began to tackle the psychology of dreams during the summer of 1898 – that is to say, when he adopted a synchronic approach. It took him the whole first half of 1899 to develop that second approach and to differentiate it in a chapter on the dream-work – about half of which consisted of passages or sections written in the spring of 1898, and half of additions dating from the spring of 1899 – and in a final, specifically metapsychological chapter which he wrote on holiday in September 1899, while also correcting the proofs of previous chapters. The beginning of the sixth and final chapter of this book (pp. 458–511) consists of a detailed analysis of *The Interpretation of Dreams* from both a diachronic and a synchronic angle.

The letters to Fliess give some idea of what the first version of the dream book must have been like. After writing *Studies on Hysteria* with Breuer and then breaking with him in order to forge ahead alone, Freud toyed alternately with the idea of writing a book on normal and general psychology (of which 'Project for a Scientific Psychology', written in the autumn of 1895, was an initial abandoned version) and a book which would propose an overall theory of neuroses (until 1900, the latter work got no further than a handful of drafts sent to Fliess and some published articles). The idea that 'dreams [. . .] contain *in nuce* [in a nutshell] the psychology of the neuroses in general' appeared for the first time in a letter to Fliess of July 7, 1897 (*F* 255). The idea grew out of a passage in Draft N, of May 31, 1897, which stated that 'symptoms, like dreams, are *the fulfilment of a wish*' (*F* 251).

Freud's plan to write something on dreams germinated in December 1897: it is implicit in his request to Fliess, before their next 'congress' at Christmas, 'to bring for me to Breslau the dream examples I sent you (insofar as they are on separate sheets)' (*F*, December 12, 1897, 286). Meanwhile, Freud had discovered the Oedipus complex. The Breslau 'congress' at Christmas 1897 gave Freud's plan fresh impetus. After politely but firmly voicing his disagreement with Fliess's competing theories on bilaterality and bisexuality, as I have already described, Freud wrote, on January 16, 1898: 'All sorts of little things are teeming: dream and hysteria fit together ever more neatly' (*F* 294).

By February 9, 1898, his plan was beginning to take concrete shape ('My self-analysis is at rest in favour of the dream book') and to excite him considerably. It is even possible to guess what the two first chapters he was writing were about: one was a historical and bibliographical introduction to the subject, and the other gave examples of his own dreams. 'I am, by the way, for no accountable reason in a splendid mood and have found my daytime interest.[1] I am deep in the dream book, am writing it fluently, and enjoy the thought of all the "head shaking" over the indiscretions and audacities it contains. If only it weren't necessary to do a lot of reading! I am already fed up with what little literature there is. The only sensible thought occurred to old Fechner in his sublime simplicity: the dream process is played out in a different psychic territory. I shall report on the first crude map of this territory' (*F*, February 9, 1898, 298–9).

Fliess reacted by expressing admiration and just a touch of jealousy. We know of his reaction from Freud's letter of March 10, 1898 ('It was no small feat on your part to see the dream book lying finished before you'), and from his analysis, in *The Interpretation of Dreams*, of the 'Botanical monograph' dream, which was triggered off by Fliess's reaction, and which I shall discuss later. The rest of Freud's letter contains an outline of his

1. Schur (S 142, n.44) notes the play on words that Freud makes here when he calls the dream-book his interest of the *day*.

metapsychological theory of dreams and a discovery of considerable importance: there needs to be a combination of two wishes – a wish of the previous day and a prehistoric wish – before a dream can occur: 'It has come to a halt again, and meanwhile the problem has deepened and widened. It seems to me that the theory of wish-fulfilment has brought only the psychological solution and not the biological – or, rather, metapsychical – one. (I am going to ask you seriously, by the way, whether I may use the name metapsychology for my psychology that leads behind consciousness.) Biologically, dream life seems to me to derive entirely from the residues of the prehistoric period of life (between the ages of one and three) – the same period which is the source of the unconscious and alone contains the aetiology of all the psychoneuroses, the period normally characterised by an amnesia analogous to hysterical amnesia. This formula suggests itself to me: What is *seen* in the prehistoric period produces dreams; what is *heard* in it produces phantasies; what is *experienced sexually* in it produces the psychoneuroses. The repetition of what was experienced in that period is in itself the fulfilment of a wish; a recent wish only leads to a dream if it can put itself in connection with material from this prehistoric period, if the recent wish is a derivative of a prehistoric one or can get itself adopted by one. It is still an open question how far I shall be able to adhere to this extreme theory and how far I can expose it to view in the dream book' (*F* 301–2).

Five days later, Freud had progressed to the extent that he was able to send Fliess his plan of the book and a draft of the second chapter:

'The idea occurred to me that you might like to read my dream study but are too discreet to ask for it. It goes without saying that I would have sent it to you before it goes to press. But since it now has again come to a halt, I can just as well send it to you in fragments. A few explanations about them. This is the second chapter. The first, on the literature, has not yet been written. It is succeeded by:

3. Dream Material
4. Typical Dreams
5. The Psychical Process in Dreaming
6. Dreams and Neuroses

'I shall return to two dreams described here in subsequent chapters, where their still incomplete interpretation will be finished. I hope you will not object to the candid remarks in the dream about the professorship. The philistines here will rejoice at being able to say that with this I have put myself beyond the pale. The thing in the dream which may strike you as odd will find its explanation later on (my ambition). Comments on *Oedipus Rex*, the talisman fairy tale, and possibly *Hamlet*, will find their place. I first must read up on the Oedipus legend – do not yet know where.

'While I hesitate to burden you at a time when you feel disinclined to work, I set against this the thought that this thing, with its minimal speculative content, will probably only amuse you in a harmless sort of way.

'As far as hysteria is concerned, I am at present completely disoriented' (*F*, March 15, 1898, 303–4).

The two dreams that feature in the second chapter sent to Fliess are certainly the Irma dream and the 'Uncle with the yellow beard' dream (which Freud calls the 'dream about the professorship'). This second chapter of the first version is therefore the beginning of two chapters in the final version, Chapter 2, 'The Method of Interpreting Dreams: an Analysis of a Specimen Dream' (the Irma dream), and Chapter 4, 'Distortion in Dreams', which centres on the 'Uncle with the yellow beard' dream. This letter makes it possible to draw up a comparative table of the plans of the book's first and second versions (see Table 4; except when in square brackets, the chapter headings are Freud's).

TABLE 1. *The first and second versions of* The Interpretation of Dreams*: a comparison*

First version (1898)	*Second version (edition published at the end of 1899)*
1. Literature on the Subject.	Chap. 1: The Scientific Literature Dealing with the Problems of Dreams.
2. [The Method and Two Examples.]	Chap. 2: The Method of Interpreting Dreams: an Analysis of a Specimen Dream. Chap. 4: Distortion in Dreams.
3. Dream Material.	Chap. 5: The Material and Sources of Dreams; (A) Recent and Indifferent Material in Dreams; (B) Infantile Material as a Source of Dreams; (C) The Somatic Sources of Dreams. Chap. 3: A Dream is the Fulfilment of a Wish.
4. Typical Dreams.	Chap. 5, (D): Typical Dreams; (α) Embarrassing Dreams of Being Naked; (β) Dreams of the Death of Persons of whom the Dreamer is Fond; (γ) Other Typical Dreams.
5. Psychical Processes in Dreams.	Chap. 6: The Dream-Work. Chap. 7: The Psychology of the Dream-Processes.
6. Dreams and Neuroses.	[Abandoned in the final version; partly dealt with in Chap. 7.]

It is also worth noting that the same letter of March 15, 1898, mentions for the first time, and in enthusiastic terms, the German-speaking Swiss writer, Conrad Ferdinand Meyer: the writing of the first version was so to speak accompanied (in a musical sense) by Freud's reading of Meyer's novels, short stories and poems.

Fliess immediately read the manuscript sent to him by Freud, and apart from one or two reservations reacted very encouragingly. Freud replied on March 24 to express his satisfaction, answer his friend's objections, and tell him about the next chapter, which he had begun to write (Chapter 3 of the first version), and which dealt with the somatic sources of dreams (Section C of Chapter 5 of the final version) and with anxiety dreams (Chapter 3 of the final version: anxiety dreams are only apparently a contradiction of the theory of dreams as wish-fulfilments). Freud announced that he would return to the problem of anxiety in the sixth and last chapter of the first version; he in fact did so, in the final version, in Section D, 'Arousal by Dreams – The Function of Dreams – Anxiety-Dreams', of Chapter 7, the last in the book.

Freud never tackled a problem without basing his argument on actual, concrete facts. Which, then, of his own dreams did he draw on in this case? In the final version, it was 'My mother and the bird-beaked figures', an anxiety dream he had at the age of about seven or eight. As there is no other firm evidence that makes it possible to date Freud's retrospective analysis of this childhood dream, I would postulate that he did so during the last half of March 1898. For he says that it is dozens of years since he had a true anxiety dream, and that he realises it is possible to interpret dream material very long after the event if it remains vivid enough (he says so in Chapter 1, 'The Scientific Literature Dealing with the Problems of Dreams'). The essential passage of his letter to Fliess of March 24, 1898, runs as follows:

'You will not be surprised if I write to you today about your evaluation of my dream manuscript, which made my day. [. . .]

'Fortunately I can answer your objections by referring to later chapters. I have just stopped before one such chapter, which will deal with the somatic stimuli of dreams. It will also touch upon anxiety dreams, on which light will be shed once again in the last chapter on "Dreams and Neurosis". But in the account you have read I shall include cross-references, to avoid the impression it gave you that the author is making things too easy for himself here.

'I do not at all think of this version as final. First I want to put my own ideas into shape, then study the literature in detail, and thereafter insert or revise where this is indicated by my reading. I cannot do the reading until I have finished what I myself have to say, and I can compose the details only in the process of writing. So far another twenty-four pages are finished; but I suspect no other section will turn out to be as amusing and as rounded out as what you have read.

'I hope you will tell me more about many particular points when we meet. You shall not refuse me the duties of the first audience and supreme judge' (*F* 304–5).

In the course of the next few days, Freud continued to write equally fast and in the same state of great mental concentration. He refers to his book, more succinctly this time, on April 3: 'At odd hours [these three words are in English in the original] I go on writing the dream book; another section dealing with the sources of dreams and typical dreams is nearly finished, but it is far less satisfactory than the first one and probably needs revision. Otherwise science says nothing whatsoever to me; nor is there any interest alive in me in anything but the dream' (*F* 306–7). The new, 'nearly finished' section in fact consisted of Chapters 3 and 4, respectively 'Dream Material' and 'Typical Dreams' (dreams of nakedness, Oedipal dreams), of the first version.

Their planned 'congress' in Vienna at Easter could not take place because Fliess was ill and his wife indisposed because of her pregnancy. Freud made up for his disappointment by going on a quick trip to Istria (Gorizia, Aquileia, Grado and Divaça) with his younger brother, Alexander. As soon as he returned, he sent Fliess an enthusiastic account of the trip (*F*, April 14, 1898, 307–10). He expresses his indignation at a scathing review, in the latest issue of the *Wiener klinische Rundschau*, of Fliess's recently published book, *Die Beziehungen zwischen Nase und weiblichen Geschlechtsorganen* (The relationship between the nose and the female sexual organs). He then had the dream of 'Goethe's attack on Herr M.', and on April 27 informed Fliess that as the periodical had not bothered to answer his protest about the review he had decided to resign from its editorial board.

Meanwhile, Freud completed the chapter he was working on (comprising Chapters 3 and 4 of the plan of his first version). He sent it to Fliess on May 1, 1898, mentioning at the same time that he was having difficulty in writing Chapter 5 of the first version, 'Psychical Processes in Dreams': 'Enclosed "Caput 3" of the dream. You will find me somewhat unpalatable; I am completely involved in the dream book and completely stupid about it. I have now written the section on psychology in which I had got stuck, but I do not like it, nor will it remain. The chapter you have now is stylistically still quite crude and bad in some parts, that is, written without much liveliness. I have left some gaps in regard to the somatic stimuli, which still need to be brought out more strongly. Naturally I expect you to make various vigorous pronouncements about it when we see each other again. The conclusions, I believe, are correct' (*F* 312). A few days later, during the night of May 10–11, Freud had the 'Castle by the sea' dream. Another dream, that of the 'Hall with machines', also dates from May; it is not referred to in the correspondence with Fliess.

The letter of May 1 contains the following passage: 'What you said about the two hands of the clock of life again sounds so familiar and self-evident that it must be a fabulous novelty and a marvellous truth. May has come, and so at the end of May I shall hear about it. I feel parched; some spring within me has gone dry and all sensibilities are withering. I do not want to give you too detailed a description lest it sound too much like complaining. You will tell me whether it is old age or just one of the many periodic fluctuations.

'I have the impression that you might have determined the sex of your next child, so that this time Paulinchen [little Pauline] may well become a reality.'

For a proper understanding of this passage, it must be remembered that Freud was born on May 6, 1856, and that according to Fliess's theory the dates of a person's birth, illness, and death are determined by cyclical periods. Fliess's calculations showed that in his own case the age of 40 was to be feared (he would be 40 in October 1898). Freud, on the other hand, had long regarded his own 41st year as critical, though he subsequently shifted his fear of death on to his 51st year (23 and 28 – the number of days, according to Fliess, in the male and female cycles respectively – add up to 51), and then on to the 61st. So if Freud were to survive his 41st year – which seemed likely, as he would be 42 in five days' time – he could stop worrying for another nine years. As I have already mentioned (p. 96), Schur argues that Freud's superstitious fears were influenced by certain Jewish beliefs about 'bad' numbers.

Fliess was full of praise for Freud's manuscript and plan. Writing on May 18, Freud was all the more grateful towards his preferred and kindly reader because that fateful date had passed: 'I am so immensely glad that you are giving me the gift of the Other. [. . .] I cannot write entirely without an audience, but do not at all mind writing only for you.'

It was some time before he wrote again. He announced, in a letter of June 9, that he was having difficulty with the first version of the dream book: 'With the continuation of the dream [book] something is amiss [*es hapert*, a Viennese colloquialism]. (Ida will explain the word to you.) True, I have already got to page 14, but it is impossible to publish it, perhaps even to show it to someone else. A mere trial run. For it is wretchedly difficult to set out the new psychology insofar as it pertains to the dream; it is of necessity fragmentary, and all the obscure parts which I, in a state of inertia, have so far put off, demand elucidation. I need a lot of patience, a cheerful frame of mind, and a few good ideas. So I am stuck at the relationship of the two systems of thinking; I must deal with them in earnest. For a while I again shall be of no use to anyone. The tension of uncertainty makes for an infamously unpleasant state, which one feels almost physically' (*F* 315–6).

On the other hand, Freud was still devouring the works of Conrad Ferdinand Meyer, in which he found examples of 'the idea of deferred action'; and he began writing a short essay on one of his short stories, *Die Richterin* (The female judge). The essay, which he enclosed with his next letter, on June 20, develops the idea that the family romance is a defence against brother-and-sister incest. While adding, at the end of the letter, that he had almost finished writing Chapter 5, 'Psychical Processes in Dreams', Freud uses a curiously significant phrase to describe his creative state of mind: the chapter, he says, was 'composed as if in a dream'. Many literary and scientific creators have made the same admission, which should, I contend, be taken literally and not merely as a figure of speech: the psychical work of creation is similar in nature to the psychical work of the dream. There are differences, though: creation is a more or less intentional, self-provoked dream, a dream experienced in both a waking and, above all, a rapt state, a dream that the creator transcribes almost immediately while it occupies his consciousness.

Here is the passage in question: 'The psychology is proceeding in a strange manner; it is nearly finished, composed as if in a dream and certainly, in this form, not fit for publication, nor intended for it, as the style shows. I feel very timid about it. All its themes come from the work on neurosis, not from that on dreams. I shall do nothing that is definitive any more before the holidays' (*F* 318). In the same letter, as Schur notes, Freud reported to Fliess some observations on his own family pertaining to Fliess's 'period' of 28. Schur remarks: 'And [he] added teasingly that his head and Fliess's head were after all two very different heads, even if both were labile – because his head now felt very good. He could, however, replace headache or cardiac symptoms with backache, which had the tendency of irradiation into various zones of the skin in common with his previous cardiac pain. Here Freud obviously recognised that such symptoms were what we would now call "psychosomatic", and did not take them seriously' (S 149–50).

Freud's creative state continued (everything 'follows the dictates of the unconscious', as he put it). He swiftly completed his chapter on 'the psychology' and sent it to Fliess on July 7: 'Here it is. It was difficult for me to make up my mind to let it out of my hands. Personal intimacy would not have been a sufficient reason; it also took our intellectual honesty to each other. It completely follows the dictates of the unconscious, on the well-known principle of Itzig, the Sunday rider. "Itzig, where are you going?" "Do I know? Ask the horse!" I did not start a single paragraph knowing where I would end up. It is of course not written for the reader; after the first two pages I gave up any attempt at stylisation. On the other hand, I do of course believe in the conclusions. I do not yet have the slightest idea what form the content will finally take' (*F* 319).

I disagree with the editors of *The Origins of Psycho-Analysis* (Freud 1950*a*) when they say, in a footnote, that what Freud enclosed with the letter was apparently 'another chapter of *The Interpretation of Dreams*, probably [. . .] the analysis of a specific dream'. It is surely logical to assume that it was in fact the chapter on 'the psychology' which the previous letter had described as 'nearly finished', and which obviously contained examples of his own dreams. If one looks at the series of personal dreams that Freud included in Chapter 6, 'The Dream-Work', of the final version, it would seem plausible that the dreams dealt with in the chapter enclosed on July 7 all concerned Fliess (hence Freud's invocation of their 'personal intimacy' and 'intellectual honesty'). Two of the dreams in Chapter 6 of the final version date from the time when Freud was writing the first version: the 'Botanical monograph' (March 1898), which he uses as his main example of condensation and displacement; and 'Goethe's attack on Herr M.' (April 1898), his main example of the means of representation. Dreams dating from before the discovery of the Oedipus complex and already described in letters to Fliess also serve as examples of the means of representation: the 'Close the eyes' dream after his father's death (October 1896), the 'Rome' dreams (January 1897), and the 'Villa Secerno' dream (April 1897), which, it should be remembered, came as a reaction to Freud's disappointment in Fliess. The 'My son, the Myops' dream (January 1898), which enabled Freud to shake off Fliess's beloved notions of bisexuality and bilaterality and to start his own book on dreams, is used to illustrate the 'apparent absurdity' of dreams. Two last dreams dating from the time when Freud was writing the first version are quoted in Chapter 6 of the final version: the 'Hall with machines' (May 1898), as another example of the means of representation, and the 'Castle by the sea' (May 1898), as an example of the preservation of affects in dreams. But I think it unlikely that Freud had already included them in the chapter he sent Fliess on July 7. The 'Castle by the sea' dream is, though Freud does not say so explicitly, a dream of triumphing over Fliess. The dream-content consists of a superb landscape and of victory. Freud had the dream at a time when Fliess was ill and could not come to see him in Vienna; so instead Freud went on a wonderful trip to Istria, and, on his return, learnt of the devastating review of Fliess's book.

The most likely hypothesis is that the chapter sent to Fliess on July 7 contained a description and analysis of most of the dreams I have just cited; the three earlier dreams were already familiar to Fliess; and the new dreams, which had probably not yet been sent to him, all involved him more or less overtly.

Freud's wife and children spent July at Aussee. Freud and Fliess held a 'congress' there or in Munich towards the end of the month. Freud, who had made good progress with his dream book and been praised by Fliess, was now more willing to accept the latter's biological theories (which, it will be remembered, he had discounted after their previous 'congress' in Breslau at Christmas). In a letter of July 30, 1898 (*F* 320–1), he recalled their meeting with enthusiasm, and accorded Fliess the title of 'the Kepler of biology'. But he also wrote:

'Do not let yourself be deterred from writing to me about the ellipses,[1] although at present I am passing through such an unreasonable segment [of ellipses] of my own. For each should give what he has, without consideration for the other. I am doing the same thing; the lack of constraint is the main attraction of our correspondence.

'I would so much like to give you what *you do not* have: a free head [free of headaches]; but you know that this is not possible. The incompleteness of your findings does not trouble me at all; you know that I do not reflect; I receive, enjoy, marvel, and have great expectations.'

Schur comments on this passage as follows: 'This letter indicates another progress in Freud's self-analysis. He treated himself with the same objectivity that an analyst shows toward a patient who seemingly does not produce new, very important material. He did not lose his self-confidence, and spoke proudly of his inner resilience. Freud's emphasis on the unconstrained freedom of expression in his correspondence with Fliess explains his past and future frankness toward the latter. [. . .] He also expressed compassion and sadness, that he could not give Fliess something which the latter lacked: a "free head". While Freud was referring to Fliess's recurrent headaches which soon required further surgery, this phrase also had another meaning, that of keeping one's thinking clear' (S 151).

I would make two further points. First, July and the beginning of August

1. Freud and Fliess obviously used the term 'ellipse' to mean a period of feeling below par.

were marked, in Freud's case, not only by more frequent dreams, but by the reappearance in them ('Hollthurn', the 'Open-air closet', and 'Count Thun') of the theme of 'faeces', to use Freud's own word. Secondly, he could make no further progress with his dream book, perhaps because of the emergence of this new theme, but more certainly as a result of his inability to relate dream psychology to general psychology, or to articulate the unconscious, the preconscious and consciousness – in other words he was unable to make head or tail of metapsychology, despite the benefit of reading, in August, Theodor Lipps' *Grundtatsachen des Seelenlebens* (1883), which provides solid evidence for the existence of unconscious mental processes.

Pauline Fliess was born in the last week of August. Freud and Martha spent the first two weeks of September travelling in Dalmatia. It was during that trip that Freud had the 'Three Fates' dream. On his return to Vienna, Freud had lost his enthusiasm and was happy merely to reaffirm his convictions: 'I wish you thought less of my masterly skills and I had you close by so that I could hear your criticisms more often. I am not at all in disagreement with you, not at all inclined to leave the psychology hanging in the air without an organic basis. But apart from this conviction [that there must be such a basis], I do not know how to go on, neither theoretically nor therapeutically, and therefore must behave as if only the psychological were under consideration. Why I cannot yet fit it together [the psychological and the organic] I have not even begun to fathom' (*F*, September 22, 1898, 326).

Freud's intellectual stagnation was confirmed by his letters of September 27 and October 9. The one he wrote on October 23 finally announced his decision to accept the consequences of his state and abandon the first version of the dream book, while not, however, giving up all hope of achieving something one day:

'Once again there is a glimmer of light on the horizon, as though this year I shall be in a position to find my way back to the truth from grave errors. But as yet there is no light – and I do not want to talk about it, so as not to spend myself before our meeting, on which I have been counting for some time.

'I am not sufficiently collected, to be sure, to do anything in addition, other than possibly studying the topography of Rome, the longing for which becomes ever more tormenting. The dream [book] is lying still, immutably; I lack the incentive to finish it for publication, and the gap in the psychology as well as the gap left by the [removal of the] thoroughly analysed sample [dream] are obstacles to bringing it to a conclusion which so far I have not been able to overcome. In other respects I am completely lonely; this year I even gave up lecturing so as not to have to talk about anything that I still hope to learn myself. [. . .]

'I have learned one lesson, however, which makes an old man of me. If ascertaining the few points required for explanation of the neuroses entails so much work, time, and error, how can I ever hope to gain an insight into the whole of mental activity, which was once my proud expectation?' (*F* 332).

Much had happened between October 9 and October 23. Fliess had had an operation. The 'unfavourable reports' that came through during the first few days after surgery stimulated the '*Non vixit*' dream. At the same time, a boil on the scrotum caused Freud enormous pain and gave rise to the 'Riding on a horse' dream. On October 18, Freud's sister Rosa, who had recently married, had a baby girl, like Ida Fliess. Finally, October 24 was Fliess's 40th birthday, a day much dreaded by him because he believed that his 40th year constituted a critical phase of his life. Freud wrote to him on the 23rd to wish him a happy birthday. In place of the now temporarily abandoned dream book, death was now to be the dominant theme of Freud's internal life for several months to come.

Dreams dreamt by Freud while writing the first version of *The Interpretation of Dreams*

THE DREAM OF THE 'BOTANICAL MONOGRAPH' (MARCH 8, 9 OR 10, 1898)

Thus, from very early February 1898 on, Freud had embarked on an enterprise that was to mobilise his energies for more than a year and a half – the writing of the 'dream book'. He worked on it fruitfully right up until the summer holidays of 1898. Then came a period when he could advance no further. He overcame that stumbling block by inventing new forms of self-analysis centred on the forgetting of names and on screen memories. He gradually got going again on *The Interpretation of Dreams* in mid-January 1899, and had finished writing it by the beginning of September of the same year.

When Freud said he was giving up his self-analysis in order to devote himself to his book, he was telling only part of the truth. It is true that he stopped the intensive and systematic self-analysis that had reached its peak in October 1897 and resulted in the discovery of the Oedipus complex and the recollection of his earliest childhood memories. But he had not given up occasionally analysing his own dreams. Those dreamt in 1898 made up a large proportion of the examples cited in the final version. They continued to answer the problems that Freud was posing himself, such as how to illustrate his book with examples, and how better to understand the mechanisms of dreams. But no one can undertake a task of that kind without stumbling on the very deepest motivating forces of the personality. As in the spring of 1897 and in November 1898, Freud ran into another period of paralysis, which caused further bouts of intensive self-analysis.

On March 8 or 9, 1898,[1] Freud received a letter from Berlin: 'I am very much occupied with your dream-book. *I see it lying finished before me and I see myself turning over its pages*' (*ID* 172). That morning, Freud had seen a new book on the genus Cyclamen in the window of a bookshop.[2] The same evening, he had a long conversation with his friend Königstein. They talked about the *Festschrift – 30 Jahre experimentelle Pathologie* (Thirty years of experimental pathology), published by Deuticke, Leipzig–Vienna – in honour of Professor Salomon Stricker, director of the Institute of Pathological Anatomy. It was there, in September 1884, while Freud was on holiday, that Koller had asked Dr Gärtner, an assistant, to experiment with cocaine as a local anaesthetic in the eye; they tried it on a frog, a rabbit, a dog, and finally on themselves, thus succeeding in making the great discovery that Freud had just overlooked. The *Festschrift* mentioned their find as one of the laboratory's achievements, yet made no mention of Freud's role in paving the way for his colleagues' discovery. Although Freud was used to not being given proper credit for his work, he always felt mortified. He also talked to Königstein about the problems of remunerations for medical treatment between professional colleagues, about a patient of Freud's called Flora, and about a friend of his wife, Frau L., who had met Martha two days before the dream, and whom he had treated some years earlier. It was Frau L. who had been accustomed to receiving a bouquet of flowers from her husband on her birthday; one year, he forgot, causing her to burst into tears. His excuses only made matters worse, 'for she recognised that her husband's forgetfulness was a proof that she no longer had the same place in his thoughts as she had formerly'. Freud had recently used this example as evidence that forgetfulness expresses the secret intentions of the person who forgets – an extension of the mechanism Freud had discovered in dreams to include memory. His conversation with

1. What is certain is the chronological order of the three events – the arrival of Fliess's letter, the 'Botanical monograph' dream the following night, and Freud's answer to Fliess on March 10. As Freud tended to answer letters promptly, and as this particular letter seems to have been written with the dream still clear in his mind, we may reasonably suppose that Fliess's letter arrived on March 8 or 9, and that the dream occurred during the night of the 8/9 or 9/10.

2. Vandendriessche (1972) tracked down the book in question: *Die Gattung Cyclamen L. Eine systematische und biologische Monographie.* Mit 6 lithogr. Tafeln (The genus Cyclamen L. A systematic and biological monograph. With 6 coloured plates), by Dr Friedrich Hildebrand. Published by G. Fischer, Jena, 1898, 190pp.

Königstein was interrupted when they were joined by Professor Gärtner ('Gärtner' is the German for gardener) and his young wife. Freud congratulated them both on their 'blooming' looks.

Vandendriessche (1972) stresses the extent to which the relationship between sight and writing (whose importance in the dreams preceding the discovery of the Oedipus complex I have already emphasised) again became an essential feature of the day's residues leading up to the 'Botanical monograph' dream, which coincided with the beginning of the first version of the dream book and Freud's hopes of making fresh discoveries. The monograph of the genus Cyclamen, like the Philippson Bible, combined text and illustrations. Moreover, Gärtner's contribution to the *Festschrift* in honour of Professor Stricker described a new method of teaching medicine he had devised: he illustrated his lectures with projected diagrams.

That night, Freud had the following dream, of which he gives three versions in *The Interpretation of Dreams* – variations which Grinstein (G 65) interprets as an indication that heavily affect-laden material is being suppressed:

1) *'I had written a* MONOGRAPH *on a certain (indistinct) species of plant'* (*ID* 165);

2) *'I had written a monograph on a certain plant. The book lay before me and I was at the moment turning over a folded coloured plate. Bound up in each copy there was a dried specimen of the plant, as though it had been taken from a herbarium'* (*ID* 169);

3) *'I had written a monograph on an (unspecified) genus of plants. The book lay before me and I was at the moment turning over a folded coloured plate. Bound up in the copy there was a dried specimen of the plant'* (*ID* 282).

The first two versions are described and analysed at some length at the beginning of Section A, 'Recent and Indifferent Material in Dreams', of Chapter 5, 'The Material and Sources of Dreams' (*ID* 169–76). The dream is cited as illustration of the fact that 'in every dream it is possible to find a point of contact with the experiences of the previous day' (*ID* 165). Freud cites it briefly in Section B of the same chapter, 'Infantile Material as a Source of Dreams', as an example of a childhood memory re-emerging in a dream (*ID* 191). The third version of the dream is related and analysed in Section A of Chapter 6 as an example of condensation (*ID* 282–4). The dream is briefly referred to twice again in the same chapter, in Section B as an example of displacement (*ID* 305), and in Section H as an example of the suppression of affects in dreams (*ID* 467). Grinstein devotes Chapter 2 of his book to the dream.

The following morning, Freud interpreted his dream and, probably the same day, sent Fliess the theoretical findings he believed to have been confirmed by his interpretation. Dream-life derives from the residues of the 'prehistoric period' of life, i.e. the first three years, a period which is the source of the unconscious and which is subsequently blotted out by amnesia. 'A recent wish only leads to a dream if it can put itself in connection with material from this prehistoric period, if the recent wish is a derivative of a prehistoric one or can get itself adopted by one' (*F* 302). Freud does no more than allude to the image that instigated the dream: 'It was no small feat on your part to see the dream-book lying finished before you' (*F* 301). The Irma dream enabled Freud to discover that dreams are the fulfilment of the previous day's wishes. The 'Botanical monograph' dream produced the fresh discovery Freud had been hoping for: a suppressed wish of the previous day results in a dream only if it can put itself in connection with a suppressed childhood wish.

Freud makes three interpretations of the dream. One of them is a mere outline. Another is fully elaborated. The third is deliberately concealed by him from the reader, but can easily be pieced together.

1) The first interpretation is offered by Freud at the beginning of his analysis of the dream. Cyclamens were Martha's favourite flowers, whereas Sigmund adored artichokes, which she often cooked for him. 'I reproached myself for so rarely remembering to *bring* her *flowers*, which was what she liked.' Freud, then, identified with his former patient's husband. One thinks immediately of the symbolic meaning of the expression 'to offer one's wife flowers': this would suggest that Freud was failing to give Martha tokens of his virility. True, Freud felt he was growing old – and later said so in a letter to Fliess – but at the same time he had a feeling of 'satisfaction'. Once again, a dream was enabling him to justify himself in Martha's eyes, by placing her on the same level as young women friends or patients in 'the bloom of life', the prototype of such women being of course Irma. We may therefore attribute the following meaning to the dream: I certainly feel less sexual desire for Martha; but I have proved myself capable of writing important monographs (on cocaine, on hysteria, and, in the near future, on dreams, in other words on sexuality); in any case, with six children, I have proved myself.

Eric Fromm (1953) reinterpreted this dream according to another set of symbols – dried flowers, the negation of aliveness and beauty. According to Fromm, the dream expresses Freud's feeling of having failed in that aspect of his life which is symbolised by love and tenderness, and of having sacrificed those emotions to the only thing he held dear, ambition: 'In fact, the dream is expressive of a deep contradiction in Freud's total personality and his lifework. The main subject matter of his interest and his studies is love and sex. But he is a puritan. [. . .] He has dried the flower, made sex and love the object of scientific inspection and speculation, rather than leave it alive' (p. 93). Freud undoubtedly conformed to the model of the austere Germanic scientist exemplified by his teachers. But his seriousness derived not only from the puritanism of the age in which he lived, but from Jewish moral standards, to which he firmly adhered. In this particular context, I would contend that the dried flower symbolises rather the art of growing old. Lastly, Fromm is surely wrong when he accuses Freud of restricting dreams to the satisfaction of wishes and not realising that they reflect the whole of mental activity. Such an interpretation fails to understand the mechanisms of the dream-work, some of which Freud had just discovered in December and January.

Roazen (1969), in the book in which retrospectively he takes up the cudgels on behalf of Victor Tausk against Freud, paints a curious picture of Freud as someone who fairly early on decathected from sexual relations, was subsequently attracted by intelligent, narcissistic women with whom he did not consummate his desires, and displayed jealousy of his children's and disciples' sexual activities. Is this not a roundabout way of criticising psychoanalysis itself – by making its discoverer impotent? There can be no doubt that Freud, in the most objective and dispassionate manner, added to existing knowledge of both adult and infantile sexuality, and, in the course of doing so, greatly embarrassed his contemporaries. Equally, there can be no doubt that Freud was passionately in love with his fiancée, then settled down to the kind of emotionally and sexually stable relationship that irritates many people today, whose mores have little to do with those of Freud's time. But then Freud has always had a knack for getting under people's skins . . .

The most striking thing about Roazen's thesis is the flimsiness, and often absence, of evidence in support of it. Thus he writes: 'Evidently sexual relations between Freud and his wife came to an early end. By the age of 41 he was writing to his most intimate friend that "sexual excitation is of no more use to a person like me"'.[1] 'Freud's potency may have been influenced by his dislike of contraceptives. And since Martha was very easily impregnated, failing to withdraw was apt to mean children, which was bound to make the couple more anxious about intercourse. Just a year before Freud wrote that letter about sexuality being of no more use to him, Martha had been expecting (or hoping) to enter menopause, even though

1. Letter to Fliess of October 31, 1897, as translated in *SE* 1, 267. Compare the translation in *F* 276 quoted on the opposite page.

she was only thirty-five years old.[1] Instead, her suspected menopause turned out to be her last child, Anna. Nevertheless, apparently Martha did have a very premature menopause soon thereafter' (pp. 39–40). There are several weaknesses in Roazen's argument. First of all, if Martha had an early menopause, which is perfectly possible, that would not have stopped her having sex with her husband. On the contrary, once freed from the need to withdraw or use contraceptive sheaths, he must surely have enjoyed happier and more relaxed, if less frequent, sexual relations with Martha. When seen from this angle, the 'Botanical monograph' dream takes on a new significance: it was Martha who, having just entered the period in her life when she could no longer have children, had become a 'dried flower'; Sigmund could now follow his natural bent and satisfy with her all his whims; when he was an adolescent, the only whims he could satisfy were those of a reader of books; but now he could give free rein to his sexual desire without fearing the consequences.

Moreover, Roazen is wrong when he says there was an interval of 'exactly a year' between the beginning of Martha's sixth pregnancy (which she became aware of in April or May of 1895 – Anna was born on December 3, 1895), and the letter in question (which, as Roazen fails to mention, Freud sent to Fliess on October 31, 1897): the interval was in fact two and a half years. Thirdly, the sentence quoted from the letter to Fliess is taken quite arbitrarily out of context. Freud had just discovered the Oedipus complex, but after three weeks of creative drive and exhilaration his enthusiasm began to wane: his self-analysis became 'obscure' again and was no longer producing 'results'. Here is the whole passage: 'The most disagreeable part of it is the moods, which often completely hide reality. Sexual excitement, too, is no longer of use for someone like me. But I am still pursuing it happily'.[2]

What exactly were the theoretical problems then exercising Freud's mind? At the end of his previous letter, dated October 27 and therefore written four days before the letter in question, Freud deals with such questions as 'sexual excitement', the absence of its discharge in cases of hysteria, masturbation and its accompanying phantasies, which replace childhood sexual games after the latter have been forbidden. The sentence picked on by Roazen should therefore be understood in two senses – one carnal: after the euphoria of his discovery, Freud was going through a

1. Roazen's source for this statement is 'conversations with Dr. Esti Freud on April 30, 1966, and August 27, 1966'.

2. The passage is here quoted in the translation by Jeffrey Moussaieff Masson (*F* 276). Masson points out in note 2 on that page that the last sentence is ambiguous and could refer either to sexuality or, 'more likely', to Freud's self-analysis.

phase of general inhibition and, more particularly, sexual inhibition; and the other intellectual: Freud was making no more headway in his theories about the problem of 'sexual excitement'; 'someone like me' meant 'a person in an uncomfortable frame of mind, like myself at the moment'. In his letter of October 27, Freud had after all said: 'All of what I experienced with my patients, as a third [person] I find again here' and 'Resistance has become something actual and tangible to me' (*F* 274). Roazen tries to make out that a passing inhibition was a permanent condition, and to bolster an ill-founded assertion by using the expression 'evidently' – which is intellectually dishonest to say the least.

The facts are these. That Freud, like any other man in his forties who has entered his mid-life crisis and climacteric, should have experienced a diminished sexual appetite and activity is not only likely, but can be deduced from other passages in his correspondence. In March 1896, he said he was 'delighted with the [idea of the] male menopause' that Fliess had derived from his theory of periodicity (*F*, March 1, 1896, 174). In January 1897, he admitted: 'I think I have now passed the critical age. My condition is so much more stable' (*F*, January 24, 1897, 228). And in November 1900, after the relative failure of *The Interpretation of Dreams*, he sent Fliess a self-portrait which in retrospect illustrates the 'Botanical monograph' dream rather well:

'In my spare time I take care not to reflect on it. I give myself over to my fantasies, play chess, read English novels; everything serious is banished. For two months I have not written a single line of what I have learned or surmised. As soon as I am free of my trade, I live like a pleasure-seeking philistine. You know how limited my pleasures are. I am not allowed to smoke anything decent; alcohol does nothing for me; I am done begetting children; and I am cut off from contact with people. So I vegetate harmlessly, carefully keeping my attention diverted from the subject on which I work during the day. Under this regimen I am cheerful and equal to my eight victims and tormentors.

'On Saturday evenings I look forward to an orgy of taroc, and every second Tuesday I spend among my Jewish brethren, to whom I recently gave another lecture' (*F*, March 11, 1900, 404).

A diminished sex life is not the same thing as no sex life at all. Freud was in the grips of his mid-life crisis; his carnal appetites had waned, he was worried about death, and he was sorry he could no longer procreate; but create he could – and did.

2) The interpretation of the dream proposed by Freud relates his current situation to a series of memories. His work was being criticised by

his colleagues, just like his hobbies. His monograph on cocaine, which enabled Koller to make his discovery, was long forgotten – cocaine, which is obtained from the dried leaves of the coca plant. At his secondary school, the boys were asked to clean a herbarium that had been eaten by bookworms; but the young Freud was given only a few sheets. Botany had never particularly interested him: during his medical studies, he almost failed an examination in which he was asked to identify a crucifer. He had otherwise been a conscientious medical student and always wanted to learn things only out of monographs. Despite his limited means he succeeded in getting hold of a number of volumes of the proceedings of medical societies, whose coloured plates enthralled him. Later, he made his own drawings to illustrate his articles, but so badly that he was made fun of by his colleagues. Again during his student days, Freud developed a passion for books, like a bookworm. It was an expensive passion, and earned a rebuke from his father.

Then Freud recounts the childhood memory that contains the primal scene: 'It had once amused my father to hand over a book with *coloured plates* (an account of a journey through Persia) for me and my eldest sister to destroy. Not easy to justify from the educational point of view! I had been five years old at the time and my sister not yet three; and the picture of the two of us blissfully pulling the book to pieces (leaf by leaf, like an *artichoke*, I found myself saying) was almost the only plastic memory that I retained from that period of my life. Then, when I became a student, I had developed a passion for collecting and owning books, which was analogous to my liking for learning out of monographs: a *favourite hobby*. (The idea of "*favourite*" had already appeared in connection with cyclamens and artichokes.) I had become a *book-worm*. I had always, from the time I first began to think about myself, referred this first passion of mine back to the childhood memory I have mentioned. Or rather, I had recognised that the childhood scene was a "screen memory" for my later bibliophile propensities. And I had early discovered, of course, that passions often lead to sorrow' (*ID* 172–3).

The reference to the screen memory (cf. Freud's paper 1899*a*) can only have been added when Freud wrote the second version of *The Interpretation of Dreams*. But it does suggest a parallel between the contents of the two screen memories – the Freiberg memory, which Freud analysed at the very beginning of 1899, where Sigismund and John 'snatched the flowers' from the young Pauline, and the Vienna memory, where Sigismund took immense pleasure in 'pulling to pieces' an illustrated book with his younger sister, Anna: the two memories retrieve scenes of sexual play with little girls slightly younger than him who are also close relations (a niece or a sister). It is all the more surprising that Jacob Freud allowed his children to tear up an illustrated book because there is great respect for books in Jewish households (they must not be put on the floor or torn), and because he was a self-taught man with a passion for reading. Jacob's tolerance in this respect undoubtedly facilitated the erotisation of knowledge in the young Sigismund. Thus, the subsequent elucidation of the screen memory of flowers snatched from Pauline threw light on the later memory of the book pulled to pieces with Anna. Conversely, however, the recollection of the second memory in March 1898 paved the way for the recollection of the first in January 1899.

This context illuminates Freud's memory, prompted by the dream, of his father rebuking him when he was 17 for buying too many books. The latent thought, then, is a criticism by Freud of his father's contradictory attitude in allowing a book to be wasted and then frowning on money being wasted on books. But that is not all. His father's rebuke about books is mentioned here instead of other rebukes about women: Jacob must have warned his son against associating with women of easy virtue (the kind one visits incognito) and against the diseases which can be caught from them, and which turn a man's virility and even his intelligence into a dried flower.

The 'Botanical monograph' dream picks up the momentum that had fallen off since the discovery of the Oedipus complex – the momentum of Freud's recollection of his own infantile sexuality. An incidental remark he makes, a trifle incongruously, later on in his analysis of the dream, confirms that what is involved here is sexual curiosity about his closest sister, Anna (who, by the way, was born in Freiberg): 'What, it may be asked, would have happened if Professor Gärtner and his wife with her blooming looks had not come up to us or if the patient we were talking about had been called Anna instead of Flora?' (*ID* 176).

The flowers in the dream thus formed a transition that led to Freud's subsequent recollection of the Freiberg screen memory 'Green meadow with yellow flowers'. Grinstein (G 60–61 and 64) points out how the plants that appear in the two screen memories correspond botanically. In the first we find the artichoke (the Compositae family), a member of the Cruciferae family (in the botany examination), and the genus Cyclamen (the Primulacea family); in the second, the coltsfoot or the dandelion (Compositae), the wallflower (Cruciferae), and the yellow alpine flowers (Primulacea).[1]

1. Taxonomy, or the scientific classification of living organisms, is arranged in increasingly specific groups, such as the class (in this case, the Dicotyledonae), the family (Primulacea or Compositae) and the genus (Cyclamen in the Primulacea family, and coltsfoot in the Compositae family).

A point also worth noting – and one overlooked by Grinstein – is the range of colours covered by the flowers in question: the cyclamen has pinkish-mauvish-brown flowers (reminiscent of the colours that feature in the laryngeal-cum-gynaecological examination in the Irma dream); the flower of the dandelion is yellow (like Pauline's dress); the yellow alpine flowers take on a darker yellow-brown shade (like the wallflower) at high altitudes. In my view, the transition between the two screen memories was effected by Freud's elucidation of the 'Yellow lion' memory (cf. pp. 354–8). It should also be noted that at that period artichokes were regarded in the Germanic countries as rather distinguished decorative plants.

The presence of an incestuous wish seeking fulfilment through sexual games with his sister and niece is disguised in these two screen memories. But the other dimension of the Oedipal wish is also present in the latent dream-thoughts. This is suggested by a quotation from *Hamlet*:

> There needs no ghost, my lord, come from the grave
> To tell us this.
>
> (*ID* 175)

The parricidal wish is particularly evident in the daydream Freud had on the morning after the dream, in which he imagined himself being operated on for glaucoma, like his father (cf. *lex talionis*, or an eye for an eye). This is shrewdly remarked on by Grinstein: 'What strikes us immediately are the parallels to *Oedipus Rex*. In Freud's phantasy he is incognito and hence his identity is unknown; in the Sophocles drama, the identity of Oedipus – who he really is – is unknown. Freud does not know the surgeon who will operate on him, only that he is to be recommended by Fliess; Oedipus did not know who Laius was when he met him, fought with him, and killed him in the defile. In his phantasy Freud has glaucoma and submits to surgery; Oedipus, made aware of his crime by the blind prophet Tiresias, enucleates his own eyes. The castration significance of Freud's phantasy and the deed of Oedipus is very clear' (G 52–3). Clear, maybe, for the reader with some knowledge of psychoanalysis, but obscure and harrowing for Freud, who was tackling the problem in the course of solitary self-analysis. That solitary self-analysis fulfilled a function similar to the one he had ascribed to masturbation in a letter to Fliess two and a half months before: 'The insight has dawned on me that masturbation is the one major habit, the "primary addiction", and it is only as a substitute and replacement for it that the other addictions – to alcohol, morphine, tobacco, and the like – come into existence' (*F*, December 22, 1897, 287).

I would contend that the present action in the dream – opening a folded plate on which a flower is 'reproduced' – represents an intellectualisation of a past, carnal action – opening the folded 'flower' of a little girl, in other words her sexual organs, whose purpose is, precisely, to 'reproduce', and where the little boy imagines he can see the results of castration. The reproductive functions of the human body are often explained to small children through the analogy of botanical examples. Before seeing his mother in the nude and feeling erotically stimulated by her during a train journey to Leipzig at the age of about three-and-a-half, Sigismund saw Pauline's 'cyclamen' in Freiberg. The following description of the cyclamen, taken from a book on botany, is so eloquent as to need no comment: the cyclamen has green leaves with broad reddish leaf-stalks and a carmine-pink flower.

The quotation from Goethe shortly to be discussed (p. 290) is also relevant: the to-ing and fro-ing of the shuttles and the knitting together of the threads represent both the movements of masturbation and the phantasy of coitus that accompanies it. In the nineteenth century, parents and educators on the whole forbade masturbation more explicitly and strictly than they did incest.

But let us return to Freud's interpretation of his dream. One reproach is common to all these memories, that of being too absorbed in doing what he wanted to do – a topic brought up in his conversation with Königstein: Freud would have discovered the anaesthetising properties of cocaine had he not broken off his research in order to join his fiancée on holiday; he would have become well-known instead of remaining unknown. Louis S. Lipschutz, quoted by Grinstein (G 53, n.1), has suggested that the incognito phantasy (Freud, in his daydream, imagines himself being operated on, incognito, in Fliess's house) may have represented a reversal of Freud's wish to be cognito, i.e. to be recognised and famous. The meaning of the dream is the wish to escape all these reproaches. He blamed Martha (without justification, as we saw on p. 41) for the fact that he had failed to make the discovery. In any case, his monograph on cocaine had been a useful piece of work. He had always shown himself to be a hard-working student: he could surely afford to have a few pastimes; it was better to have a passion for books than for other things. Similarly, the valuable monograph he was writing on dreams surely excused his current extravagances, such as smoking and collecting antiques. 'Once again the dream, like the one we first analysed – the dream of Irma's injection – turns out to have been in the nature of a self-justification, a plea on behalf of my own rights. Indeed, it carried the subject that was raised in the earlier dream a stage further and discussed it with reference to fresh material that had arisen in the interval between the two dreams' (*ID* 173).

Thus, two key moments in the genesis of *The Interpretation of Dreams* – the one when Freud became certain of understanding the meaning of dreams, and the one when he felt self-confident enough to decide to write a book about them – were accompanied by two parallel dreams, which helped him to overcome an inner conspiracy of doubts and reproaches. Never before, no doubt, had a reader or even a confidant been able to monitor so closely the inhibition of a creator toiling over the gestation of his work and battling against resistance to discovery. At first Freud did not feel himself up to his task or his ambitions. Like Joseph and the ancient interpreters of dreams, it was in his own dreams that he derived confidence in himself, his work, and his ideas. That confidence welled up from his very first years: the memory of the book he pulled to pieces symbolised the happy period of his childhood, just as his father later made the Philippson Bible a symbol of his thirst for knowledge (see pp. 300–4). It was no coincidence that Freud concluded *The Interpretation of Dreams* with a kind of apologia of the unconscious. Dreams, he said, pursue and complete the work of our waking lives. There is nothing surprising in that, because they are driven by the same psychical forces that enable the waking intellect to work. But, as Freud went on to assert clearly, dreams can do more than that. Drawing strength from deep-lying impulses, dreams are capable of fashioning future actions. 'The respect paid to dreams in antiquity is, however, based upon correct psychological insight and is the homage paid to the uncontrolled and indestructible forces in the human mind, to the "daemonic" power which produces the dream-wish and which we find at work in our unconscious' (*ID* 614). The 'Botanical monograph' dream was in all likelihood the first occasion when Freud felt such a strong insight on this point. Like Fliess, he saw the dream book finished and could leaf through it like the first book which fascinated him as a child. The confidence required to write it was thus put within his grasp. *Traumbuch* means 'book on dreams' (and even 'key to dreams'), but also 'dreamt-of book' and 'dream book'.

The symbolic organisation of the Irma dream hinged on an injection of trimethylamin, i.e. on a chemical series; here, it hinges on botanical classification. The dream's structure is no longer based on ternary subdivision, nor does it pose the problem of how to combine elements. It now deals with the specific characteristics that make it possible to differentiate between plant genera – characteristics which, according to botanical science, mainly reside first in the shape of the stem, leaf and flower of plants, and secondly in their reproductive systems. The underlying structure is here one of binary opposition: why are there two sexes, and what distinguishes between them?

The visual representation in which that question and that structure are condensed is one of pulling to pieces *leaf by leaf* (which combines the two series of associations symbolised by the words monograph and botany) rather than of a *dried flower*. 'In the course of the work of analysis I was reminded of my conversation with Dr Königstein. [. . .] All the trains of thought starting from the dream – the thoughts about my wife's and my own favourite flowers, about cocaine, about the awkwardness of medical treatment among colleagues, about my preference for studying monographs and about my neglect of certain branches of science such as botany – all of these trains of thought, when they were further pursued, led ultimately to one or other of the many ramifications of my conversation with Dr Königstein' (*ID* 173). Freud devotes two pages to analysing the flurry of different events, memories, images and words prompted by the theme of the botanical monograph (*ID* 282–4). The metaphors that occur to him to describe the dream-work involve 'connecting paths' and 'a weaver'. The latter metaphor is once again inspired by Goethe's *Faust*, and comes from the scene where Mephistopheles describes the 'factory of thoughts' to the student (Part I, Scene 4):

> Ein Tritt tausend Fäden regt,
> Die Schifflein herüber hinüber schiessen,
> Die Fäden ungesehen fliessen,
> Ein Schlag tausend Verbindungen schlägt.
>
> [. . . a thousand threads one treadle throws,
> Where fly the shuttles hither and thither,
> Unseen the threads are knit together,
> And an infinite combination grows.]
> (*ID* 283)

Thus, Fliess's name (*fliessen* means 'to flow') appears in this passage; thus, too, Freud sees himself confronting Mephistopheles. His immediate theoretical findings, most of which he tells Fliess about in his letter of March 10, are as follows: the overdetermination of each element of the dream content is confirmed; the close connection between dreams and events of the previous day disguises the fact that dreams also contain childhood wishes and could not exist without the material supplied by them; events of apparently little importance which are given prominence by the dream constitute a distortion of the dreamer's fundamental concerns; the distortion is a result of censorship.

3) Freud repeats that his interpretation is incomplete while at the same time leaving clues that enable the reader to complete it himself. 'I can assure my readers that the ultimate meaning of the dream, which I have not disclosed, is intimately related to the subject of the childhood scene'

(*ID* 191). In the same paragraph, tucked away among other considerations, are some interesting clues. The expression 'pulled to pieces leaf by leaf like an artichoke' was commonly used at the time in connection with the dismemberment of the Chinese empire. Later in the book, Freud introduces the notion of displacement: the dream is 'differently centred' from the thoughts that make it up; the central point is botany, while 'the dream-thoughts [are] concerned with the complications and conflicts arising between colleagues from their professional obligations, and further with the charge that I was in the habit of sacrificing too much for the sake of my hobbies' (*ID* 305). He returns to the dream later in the book: 'The thoughts corresponding to it consisted of a passionately agitated plea on behalf of my liberty to act as I chose to act and to govern my life as seemed right to me and me alone. The dream that arose from them has an indifferent ring about it: "I had written a monograph; it lay before me; it contained coloured plates; dried plants accompanied each copy." This reminds one of the peace that has descended upon a battlefield strewn with corpses; no trace is left of the struggle which raged over it' (*ID* 467).

It is difficult not to interpret these remarks as allusions to Freud's recent disagreement with Fliess over bilaterality and bisexuality. Freud's account of the daydream he had the day after the dream, which he includes in his analysis, points in the same direction: 'If ever I got glaucoma, I had thought, I should travel to Berlin and get myself operated on, incognito, in my friend's [Fliess's] house, by a surgeon recommended by him' (*ID* 170). It is this daydream which introduces into the dream analysis the theme of cocaine, necessary for the operation, and the awkwardness of paying for medical treatment by professional colleagues. Freud realises that this conscious daytime phantasy masks a memory. Jacob Freud, who suffered from glaucoma, had in fact been operated on by Königstein in Freud's presence; Dr Koller had been in charge of the cocaine anaesthesia. Koller had commented on the fact that this case had brought together all three men who had had a share in the introduction of cocaine. Freud, then, identifies with his father, and sees Fliess as the ungrateful Koller, who later took all the credit for the discovery.

A third meaning of the dream – its 'transferential' meaning – then becomes obvious. Fliess had written saying that he saw Freud's book lying finished before him and saw himself turning over its pages. The image immediately reminded Freud of the childhood scene where he and his sister pulled a book to pieces page by page. The reason Fliess was so impatient to receive a copy of the dream book must therefore be that he wanted to pull it to pieces. This third meaning ties up with the second, once the roles are reversed. Freud tore Fliess's bilaterality theories to pieces. But

Fliess did not give as good as he got. He showed interest in the dream book – this was 'the peace upon a battlefield'. But deep down Freud felt he was right to affirm the 'unilaterality' of his own work, to defend his liberty to act as he pleased, and to go his own way. He used the same term he had used in discussing a recent dream, 'My son, the Myops': 'So, too, "monograph" in the dream touches upon two subjects: the one-sidedness [*Einseitigkeit*, which can also be translated as 'unilaterality'] of my studies and the costliness of my favourite hobbies' (*ID* 283).

The presence of the 'cyclamen' in the dream would seem therefore to be overdetermined. As a thing presentation, it refers, as we have already seen, to infantile and incestuous sexual curiosity about the female sexual organs. As a word presentation, it has connotations of the 'cycle' (a reference to Fliess's periodicity theory) and recalls the Cyclops of the 'My son, the Myops' dream. Eva Rosenblum has even gone so far as to put forward the hypothesis that Freud, stretching the rules of etymology, applied the word Cyclops to anyone who saw cycles everywhere. Consciously, Freud's attitude to Fliess's work was one of keen interest and approval. In his preconscious, he was becoming increasingly aware of its whimsicality. And he demanded the right to follow his own whims by devoting himself to the dream book without having to respond any more to Fliess's bothersome talk of bisexuality and bilaterality. Like the wife whose husband forgot to bring her flowers, Fliess, cast for the first time by Freud as the female half of the couple, 'no longer had the same place in his thoughts as [he] had formerly'. Freud was in the process of 'turning the page' in his relationship with Fliess; but he maintained a 'passion' for him against which he fought, and took from him an idea – that of bisexuality – which he found increasingly persuasive, and which he secretly wanted to appropriate, just as Koller had appropriated his theory about cocaine. For Fliess, bisexuality was a biological phenomenon to do with periods and 'cycles'. Freud would turn it into a psychological phenomenon involving phantasies connected with the difference between the sexes.

We are now in a position to assess the role of this dream in Freud's self-analysis and in the discovery of psychoanalysis: just as he was getting down to the task of writing the first version of his book, the dream gave him the same intellectual and emotional impetus he had derived from the dream of 'Irma's injection', two and a half years earlier, when he undertook his dual investigation of dreams and of himself. The 'botanical' examination of the female sexual organs corresponds with the laryngeal-cum-gynaecological examination of Irma. The difference here is that the genitals/nose parallel, which was a tribute to Fliess, has been replaced by a female genitals/flower parallel, in which scientific dependence on Fliess remains both present and contested (the word 'cyclamen' contains elements of both 'cycle' and 'Cyclops'), and which contains three other references that were to prove more fruitful – the reference to Goethe, whose scientific 'monographs' brought him fame earlier than his literary works did; the reference to a symbol commonly found in vernacular language (flower = female genitals); and the still preconscious reference to phantasied scenarios of his own childhood.

A person who senses that he is becoming a creator inevitably imagines, deep down, a scene of procreation. But, as I have already suggested, such a scene was for Freud an aim in itself as well as a driving force of discovery. The dried flowers kept in the herbarium of his memory were being given both life and the indestructible colours of desire by his self-analysis. The material which Freud here divined (up to then he had merely glimpsed it in his patients or through his mother's accounts of his childhood), and which he was to continue to recollect ever more extensively, eventually formed the substance of another book, *Three Essays on the Theory of Sexuality* (1905*d*).

Freud looked forward to his dreams all the more expectantly because he needed them for his book. There was nothing odd in the fact that he should dream a dream that could be dissected and inserted into the monograph he was dreaming of devoting to dreams. This work in progress, unlike the monograph on children's cerebral paralysis (1897*a*), which he had written only because he had to, was his favourite book, the one in which he indulged his whims, the book of his wishes in both senses – the book he wished to write and the book in which he was exhibiting his wishes.

In this sense, the dream of the 'Botanical monograph' is a narcissistic dream (are not the acts of creating and dreaming always a regression to narcissim?): his dream book would be better than the recently published works by Fliess and by Janet, one of which, on the connection between the nose and the female sexual organs (1897), was extremely far-fetched and had been very badly reviewed, and the other of which, on *Névroses et idées fixes* (1898), was too superficial. Freud referred to Janet's book in the same letter of March 10, written the day after the dream.

Lastly, let us consider the affect of the 'Botanical monograph' dream. It is quite the opposite of an anxiety dream. As Eva Rosenblum has suggested to me, it is a dream of wonderment – the wonderment of a child at the colour illustrations of a traveller's tale, the wonderment of a boy at the body of his young mother, who is as attractive as a multi-coloured picture-book, the wonderment of the male at the mystery of femaleness, and the wonderment of the connoisseur at the weaver's masterpiece: Freud used Goethe's metaphor in his speech of thanks when he was awarded the Goethe Prize in 1930: 'Psychoanalysis can supply some information which cannot be arrived at by other means, and can thus demonstrate new connecting threads in the "weaver's masterpiece" spread between the instinctual endowments, the experiences and the works of an artist. [. . .] In the case of Goethe we have not yet succeeded very far. This is because Goethe was not only, as a poet, a great self-revealer, but also, in spite of the abundance of autobiographical records, a careful concealer' (1930*e*, *SE* 21, 212). In a word, then, wonderment at the creative process.

Do not the two actions of the weaver – raising the warp yarns to receive the weft, and uniting the two surfaces by tucking them into each other – provide a connection between the sexual act (opening the female genitals, then covering them), the act of reading (leafing through and opening up a book, but also comparing the text with the illustrations), and the creative process (transforming internal images into a text)?[1] But at the same time, to possess is to deflower, to read is to tear up, and to create is to destroy. A certain wish to destroy is also part of the passions that cause suffering. Whereas at the time of the Irma dream Freud was engrossed with the essay 'On Nature' attributed to Goethe, he was now deeply concerned with Faust's problems in facing the negating power embodied by Mephistopheles: he was about to discover the origins of that negating power in the unconscious.

THE DREAM OF 'MY MOTHER AND THE BIRD-BEAKED FIGURES'

In the seventh and last chapter of *The Interpretation of Dreams*, which is devoted to 'The Psychology of the Dream-Processes', Freud goes back to several of his own dreams (already described and analysed in earlier chapters) in order to illustrate those processes. He mentions only two new dreams – a punishment dream and an anxiety dream. He had the first (about his son on the front line and a sum of money) during the First World War, and added it in 1919 to the fifth edition of the book as an example of the way a dream can satisfy both a wish of the previous day and a childhood wish. The second dream ('My mother and the bird-beaked figures') appears in Section D, 'Arousal by Dreams – The Function of Dreams – Anxiety Dreams' in all editions). It happens to be the last of Freud's own dreams described in the book. It is immediately followed by a patient's dream (a dream of being paralysed when pursued by a man with

1. Vandendriessche (1972) argues that this dream contains the first glimmerings of the concept of sublimation which Freud later outlined in his paper on screen memories (1899*a*) and named in his study of Leonardo da Vinci (1910*c*): the instinct to see, having succeeded in freeing itself from repression, is sublimated into a wish to know, which is then reinforced by another pre-existent and important instinct, the investigative instinct.

a hatchet) and a description of a case of *pavor nocturnus* in a child quoted by Debacker. Grinstein rightly points out that the other dream and Debacker's case form part of Freud's associations to the dream of 'My mother and the bird-beaked figures' and enable it to be interpreted fully. There are two other references to patients in Section F (the last section of the chapter), but they concern symptoms, not dreams.

Thus Freud's dream followed by the patient's dream about being pursued by a man with a hatchet constitutes a kind of personal 'last word' by the author. Whereas all the other dreams dreamt by Freud and described in *The Interpretation of Dreams* occurred during his self-analysis, between 1895 and 1899, 'My mother and the bird-beaked figures' was an early dream. Indeed, it is the only dream from Freud's childhood that features in his complete works and in all his letters so far published. It has been analysed by Eva Rosenfeld (1956) and by Grinstein (G, Chapter 19), both of whom focus chiefly on its cultural source, the Philippson Bible, with its illustrations of bird-headed Egyptian gods.

It is difficult to say exactly when Freud analysed the dream retrospectively. I suggest later on that there is good reason to suppose he did so some time between the summers of 1897 and 1898. The letter to Fliess of March 24, 1898 (already referred to on p. 271), in which Freud announces that he has begun writing about 'anxiety dreams', would suggest that he interpreted the dream towards the end of March 1898. After meticulous study of the dream, I am convinced that logically his interpretation must have taken place between the dream of the 'Botanical monograph' just discussed and the 'Count Thun' dream (the summer of 1898).

Here is Freud's account of the dream:

'It is dozens of years since I myself had a true anxiety-dream. But I remember one from my seventh or eighth year, which I submitted to interpretation some thirty years later. It was a very vivid one, and in it I saw *my beloved mother, with a peculiarly peaceful, sleeping expression on her features, being carried into the room by two (or three) people with birds' beaks and laid upon the bed.* I awoke in tears and screaming, and interrupted my parents' sleep. The strangely draped and unnaturally tall figures with birds' beaks were derived from the illustrations to Philippson's Bible. I fancy they must have been gods with falcons' heads from an ancient Egyptian funerary relief. Besides this, the analysis brought to mind an ill-mannered boy, a son of a *concierge*, who used to play with us on the grass in front of the house when we were children, and who I am inclined to think was called Philipp. It seems to me that it was from this boy that I first heard the vulgar term for sexual intercourse, instead of which educated people always use a latin word, "to copulate" [*coitieren*], and which was clearly enough indicated by the choice of the falcons' heads.[1] I must have guessed the sexual significance of the word from my young instructor, who was well acquainted with the facts of life. The expression on my mother's features in the dream was copied from the view I had had of my grandfather a few days before his death as he lay snoring in a coma. The interpretation carried out in the dream by the "secondary revision" must therefore have been that my mother was dying; the funerary relief fitted in with this. I awoke in anxiety, which did not cease till I had woken my parents up. I remember that I suddenly grew calm when I saw my mother's face, as though I had needed to be reassured that she was not dead. But this "secondary" interpretation of the dream had already been made under the influence of the anxiety which had developed. I was not anxious because I had dreamt that my mother was dying; but I interpreted the dream in that sense in my preconscious revision of it because I was already under the influence of the anxiety. The anxiety can be traced back, when repression is taken into account, to an obscure and evidently sexual craving that had found appropriate expression in the visual content of the dream' (*ID* 583–4).

In view of the brevity of the dream and its exceptionally important position in *The Interpretation of Dreams*, it may be of interest to analyse it literally.

'It is dozens of years since I myself had a true anxiety-dream [in other words, one causing the dreamer to awake immediately].'

The somewhat extreme nature of this statement may conceal a negation. The later dream about his son at the front and a sum of money received was also an anxiety dream which caused him to wake up in the middle of the night. It is possible that Freud had had no anxiety dreams since adolescence, following the establishment in his psyche of a hysterophobic system of anxiety displacement, then as a result of his elucidation of the contents and mechanisms of his anxiety in the course of self-analysis. Nonetheless, I understand this first sentence to have the same latent content as the dream of 'Irma's injection' and others: 'No, I am not guilty, I have not been guilty for a long time.'

'But I remember one from my seventh or eighth year . . .'

The date of the dream is incorrect. There are many other mistakes about figures and proper names in *The Interpretation of Dreams*; but whereas Freud

1. In German slang, one of the words meaning 'to have sexual intercourse' is *vögeln*, which is the same as the dative plural of *Vogel* (a bird). This homonymity has given rise to a well-known punning couplet:

Vögeln muss man jeden Tag
Frisches Wasser geben.
(Screw you must every day *or* To birds you must every day
Give fresh water.)

subsequently corrected and explained the others in later editions or in *The Psychopathology of Everyday Life*, this one slipped through the net. It was Jones who pointed it out to Eva Rosenfeld (1956). Freud's paternal grandfather, Schlomo, died on February 21, 1856. Shortly afterwards, Sigismund was born, and given Schlomo as his Jewish first name in memory of his grandfather. His mother's father, a Nathansohn, who must be the grandfather in question, and whose first name was Jacob, died on October 3, 1865. Freud, who was born on May 6, 1856, was therefore nine and a half at the time. Why does he say the dream dates from his seventh or eighth year? Neither Jones, nor Rosenfeld, nor Grinstein answers that question. So what did happen when he was seven or eight? Surely the incident referred to – which Freud recalled a little later on when analysing the 'Count Thun' dream in the summer of 1898 – is the one where he deliberately urinated in his parents' bedroom, and his father, usually of such a kindly disposition, rebuked him with a curse that Freud strove throughout his life to prove wrong: 'The boy will come to nothing.' The memory of that trauma, then, underwent a defensive working out through the dream Freud had about two years later, when his maternal grandfather died.

'. . . which I submitted to interpretation some thirty years later.'

If the dream does in fact date from the autumn of 1865, it must have been interpreted by Freud at some point during or after the autumn of 1895, in other words later, which is logical enough, than his first analysis of one of his own dreams, the Irma dream (July 23–24, 1895). But his systematic self-analysis began only in the spring of 1897, and resulted in October of that year in the recollection of many childhood memories and the discovery of the Oedipus complex. This would suggest that Freud interpreted the dream of 'My mother and the bird-beaked figures' some time between the summer of 1897 and the summer of 1898, the date at which he elucidated the memory of urinating in his parents' bedroom.

'It was a very vivid one . . .'

The 'wish' was very vivid.

'. . . and in it I saw *my beloved mother* . . .'

The German, literally translated, says 'the mother'. It is true that German is not as systematically fond of the possessive form as English or French. Even so, an impersonal tone is set from the very first word of the dream itself, and continues not only throughout the rest of it, but in the analysis as well. A mother is carried away (cf. 'a child is beaten'), in other words taken away from her child, who loves her. This is represented by the fact that the child who has the dream is absent from the manifest content; there is only the mother with two (or three) other people. The latent wish is clearly the reverse: the child would like to have his mother all to himself. The absence of the child from the dream therefore indicates the presence of the incest taboo.

'. . . *with a peculiarly peaceful, sleeping expression on her features* . . .'

Sigismund's mother must have been particularly distressed by the death of her father in 1865. The latent thought could well be: I am consoling my mother with my love, and she is falling peacefully asleep, just as she herself used to calm me and send me to sleep when I was little. But when we refer to the original scene, which happens to be the same thing as the primal scene, the meaning changes. In actual fact, the child spies on the parental couple in their bedroom. The mother is lying on the bed after sexual intercourse, her face shows contentment and gratification, and her eyes are closed on her own well-being. In his phantasy, the child imagines that she has died (of pleasure). In several languages, orgasm is popularly referred to as 'dying a little': such everyday metaphors often find their way into dreams.

'. . . *being carried into the room* . . .'

It is the child that is 'carried into' his parents' bedroom out of curiosity and jealousy. One of the characteristics of dream syntax is that a sentence made up of several propositions with a single subject in the manifest content conceals in the latent content several actions with different subjects (condensation).

'. . . *by two (or three) people* . . .'

As I have already pointed out, Freud succeeded during his self-analysis in elucidating the confusion he felt as a child about his family situation. Emanuel and Philipp, Jacob Freud's sons by his first marriage, were respectively 23 and 22 years older than Sigismund, the first-born child of Jacob's third marriage. Freud's mother, Amalie, was twenty years younger than her husband and one year younger than her stepson Philipp. In his phantasy, Sigismund paired off the people of the same age – his father Jacob with the nurse Monika Zajíc, and his mother Amalie with Philipp. But Sigismund realised that Jacob in fact shared his bed with Amalie. Thus, the 'two people' in the dream who lay the mother on the bed are in all likelihood Jacob, the grandfather figure, and Philipp, the father figure.

But why '*two (or three)*'? The third person, who is parenthetically present, is obviously the young Sigismund, dreamer of the dream, intruder into the parents' bedroom, and outsider excluded from the primal scene. Here again, the letter of the text – not just its syntax and logic, but its typography – acts as a symbolic representation of a phantasied position or of an unconscious topographical state: the child is 'parenthetically' present at the primal scene.

However, there is a chronological discrepancy between the likely explanation for this part of the sentence and the explanations that we have already found for earlier phrases, which refer to events that took place in the Freuds' Vienna apartment when Sigmund was between seven and ten years old: here we are taken back to an earlier time and place, to the house in Freiberg where Freud was born and which he left at the age of three and a half. In his analysis of the 'Count Thun' dream, Freud mentions another, earlier case of urinary incontinence (unintentional this time) dating from the Freiberg period. The scene had often been described to him, though he could not himself recall the actual train of events. He did know, however, that he had been able to disarm his parents' anger with a childish witticism (cf. pp. 344–5).

There would seem, then, to be three different and interwoven layers here: 1) A scene of incontinence, which was forgotten because Freud's own shame and his father's rebuke about him being unable to control himself were dispelled by a childish witticism that was remembered by the family and later often referred to admiringly by them; 2) A voluntary act, which was at once the *mise-en-scène* of a phantasied wish to see the primal scene, and the reproduction, in order to deflect possible parental criticism, of the previous scene, which had had a happy end; but the second scene went wrong, because this time the father had the last word; 3) As his maternal grandfather lay dying, an attempt to take control of the previous scene by repeating it vindictively in a dream: if Jacob, a grandfather figure though actually my father, died, it would be me, now that Philipp is no longer with us, who would carry him into my mother's bedroom, lay him on the bed, and peacefully put him to sleep; but that attempt, too, fails in the dream itself, which becomes an anxiety dream where the child has a hallucination that his mother is dead, i.e. that he has lost her.

'. . . *with birds' beaks* . . .'

Why beaks? The Egyptian gods to which the dream refers have a human body with a complete bird's head, not just a beak. The part (the beak) is given for the whole (the head), which is itself part of a composite being. This is an example of metonymic relationship. But the presence of the beak in the dream is overdetermined by a metaphorical relationship. A beak is elongated and hard, like an erect penis, which the child no doubt glimpsed in his parents' bedroom (the second layer of the memory). In the first relationship, the beak represents the hostile god to whom the Jews would be well advised to submit. In the second relationship, the beak represents the father's genitals, which the Bible forbids the son to look at: the child, under pain of death, must submit to this father – just as the Jews must submit to the hostile god – by abandoning hope of possessing his beloved mother.

Sigismund may have been unaware of the fact that Isis was supposed to have revived by fellatio the sleeping penis of her dismembered husband, Osiris. But he would certainly have remarked that the bird-headed Egyptian god, Thoth, is pronounced in German the same way as *Tot* (the German word for 'a dead person').

'I awoke in tears and screaming, and interrupted my parents' sleep.'

This is a wish-fulfilment which comes about not *in* the dream, but as an immediate result of it: the parents are dragged from their bed, and their supposed sexual intercourse is interrupted.

'The strangely draped and unnaturally tall figures with birds' beaks . . .'

The child who unexpectedly enters his parents' bedroom notices that strange things go on under the rumpled sheets, and, in particular, unnaturally elongated things (the second layer of the memory).

'. . . were derived from the illustrations to Philippson's Bible.'

This edition of the Bible by the Philippson brothers (*Die Israelitische Bibel*, Leipzig 1858) was something of an exploit for the period – and is still called into question today by traditionalist Jews. The edition was bilingual, with the Hebrew text and a German translation, in other words it aimed to get the Jewish heritage adopted by Germanic culture; it was illustrated with 500 woodcuts, despite the fact that the second commandment forbids 'graven images' of God; and it contained a commentary which did not restrict itself to strictly theological considerations, but discussed archaeology and the comparative history of religions from an 'objective' point of view, very much in the spirit of Moses Mendelssohn's new Jewish philosophy.

It was this edition which Jacob Freud, a liberal-minded man who kept up with the developments of his time, showed his son when he was about seven, with the result that Sigismund was attracted by Egypt, identified with Joseph, the interpreter of dreams, and became interested in Moses the lawgiver (about whom he wrote a book right at the end of his life, in which he tried very hard to prove that Moses was of Egyptian origin). Jacob had already given an illustrated book on Persia to the five-year-old Sigismund and his three-year-old sister, who together 'pulled it to pieces' with incestuous delight under the benevolent eye of their father (the memory referred to by the dream of the 'Botanical monograph'). The combination of written text and illustrations was, then, not only familiar to the young Freud, but eroticised – a precondition for his being able to discover that dreams are picture puzzles, and for his successful attempt at deciphering them.

Jones tells us that Jacob Freud presented a copy of the Philippson Bible (which he had preserved) to Sigmund on the occasion of the latter's 35th birthday. His inscription in Hebrew has already been quoted (p. 96). Freud's symbolic identification with his father not only fostered his thirst for knowledge, but also encouraged him to transgress in an area that was no longer Oedipal except in a symbolic sense. Gods may be represented in a figurative form; the customs, habits and beliefs of enemies may be studied; it is preferable, even, to know them well in order better to combat them. To know is to transgress fears and prejudices, as Philippson had done, then to demystify them and establish new laws. The Bible, and then more generally culture, acted for Freud as a symbolic guarantee of the truth. The Freudian registration of proof is twofold: it is as much cultural as it is clinical.

'I fancy they must have been gods with falcons' heads from an ancient Egyptian funerary relief.'

Do the illustrations in the Philippson Bible have as much to tell us as Rosenfeld and Grinstein claim? Rather than commit myself one way or the other, I shall simply outline their theories.

Eva Rosenfeld stresses the symbolic value of birds for Freud: they foreshadow his notion of infantile totemism and the vulture he discovered (wrongly in fact, for it was a kite) in a childhood memory and a painting by Leonardo da Vinci. She discovered among the collection of antiques left by Freud after his death a falcon-headed god and a funerary barge – a materialisation of the images in his dream. Basing her argument on a representation of a falcon-headed sphinx and on the onomastic similarity of the two Thebes, the capital of Egypt and the Greek kingdom ruled over by Laïus and Jocasta, she contends that the dream contains in embryo the discovery of the Oedipus complex. As Grinstein rightly points out, Freud's keen interest in the gargoyles of Notre-Dame-de-Paris should be seen in the same light.

Grinstein reproduces four woodcuts from the Philippson Bible that echo the dream in several respects, and tries to find, in corresponding passages of the Bible, elements that might have made an impression on the young Sigismund.

One woodcut reproduced in Grinstein's book shows a succession of Egyptian gods, several with birds' heads. In the Philippson Bible, the woodcut illustrates the passage in Deuteronomy (4: 28) where Moses gives his law to the Israelites and condemns the 'graven images' of gods that are common in other religions.

Another woodcut (Figure 1 overleaf), which illustrates the passage in the Bible where Samuel anoints Saul, contains Egyptian figures with

Figure 1 Woodcut from the Philippson Bible

falcon-like heads. But Grinstein finds little indication, either in the text (I Samuel, 10: 2) or in Philippson's commentary, that this illustration had any special significance for Freud. But what about the illustration itself? If we give free rein to our imagination while looking at it, surely it evokes a scene of masturbation? The case of the boy suffering from *pavor nocturnus* mentioned by Freud just after his analysis of the dream of 'My mother and the bird-beaked figures' (when 13, Albert G. had nightmares in which the Devil undressed and burned him, and he screamed: 'No, no, not me; I've not done anything!' or 'Please not! I won't do it again!') seemed to him to have been caused by intense anxiety at having masturbated, and not by cerebral anaemia as Debacker claimed.

Figure 2 no doubt tallies most closely with the dream's manifest scene: it shows a bier ('bed') on the back of an elongated sphinx-like figure. Lying on this bier is the body of a man or woman with 'a peaceful, sleeping

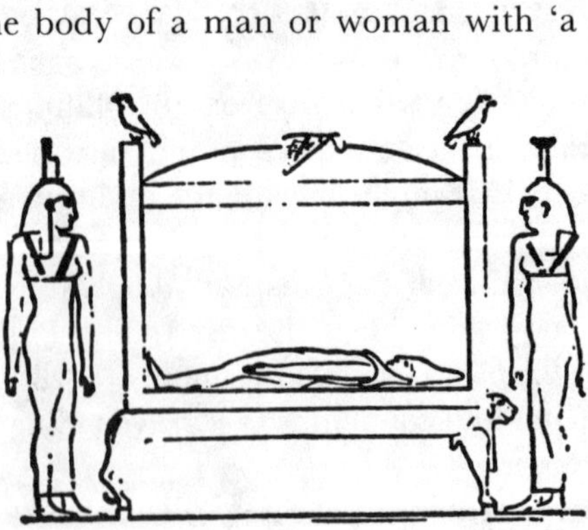

Figure 2 Woodcut from the Philippson Bible

expression' on its face. On either side there are 'strangely draped' figures which seem to be guarding the bier ('two (or three) people'). They have human heads, but there is a bird on top of each of the two columns of the bier. The picture illustrates the line from II Samuel (3: 31) which says: 'And King David followed the bier' (of Abner). The story of King Saul, of his loyal commander-in-chief Abner, and of his saviour, son-in-law and finally enemy, David, teems with incestuous themes (Saul took his daughter back from David and gave her to another man to marry; after Saul's death, Abner slept with the latter's concubine) and parricides or fratricides (Saul's attitude to David was constantly ambivalent; Abner killed one of David's commanders, then the dead man's brother took revenge by killing Abner just as he was reconciled with David). The parallel drawn by Grinstein deserves to be taken further. It is possible to identify in the picture the wings of Horus, who represents the Sun (and therefore the penis) as it rises again, and Osiris, whose genitals are asleep, lying dead in his mummy wrappings and being mourned by his wife Isis: a reversal into the opposite of the dream image where the child watches over his dead mother.

Figure 3, which shows a funerary barge with bird-headed gods (unless of course it is the Sun's boat crossing the Nile), illustrates the return of David (II Samuel, 19: 18), whom the boat has fetched from the other side of the Jordan, and evokes the same kind of themes (Absalom killed his half-brother Amnon, guilty of having raped their sister Tamar, and then prepared to depose their father, King David; David fled across the Jordan, purposely leaving behind his concubines, whom Absalom rapidly and flauntingly possessed; David had decided to be lenient, but his men disregarded his orders and killed Absalom; then they went to fetch David, who wept long over his beloved son before agreeing to return). This legend of a powerful, warm-hearted father who forgives his son for his incestuous and parricidal desires may well, as Grinstein suggests, have reinforced in

Figure 3 Woodcut from the Philippson Bible

Sigismund a certain paternal image that was already tending in that direction: in that case, the ego-ideal would have been strengthened at the expense of the super-ego.

But Grinstein fails to mention the passage in Deuteronomy (22: 30 and 23: 1), which forms part of Moses' Tables of the Law, and which seems to have stronger connections with Sigismund's anxiety dream: 'A man shall not take his father's wife, nor discover his father's skirt. He that is wounded in the stones, or hath his privy member cut off, shall not enter into the congregation of the Lord.' These two verses, coming one after the other, must have had a powerful impact on the young Freud.

'Besides this, the analysis brought to mind an ill-mannered boy, a son of a *concierge*, who used to play with us on the grass in front of the house when we were children . . .'

We are now explicitly in Freiberg (the first layer of the memory), on the meadow that was the setting for the screen memory which Freud was to interpret at the very beginning of 1899. Sigismund is playing with John, who is his nephew, but older than him, and with his niece Pauline, who is a little younger: the two boys snatch a bunch of flowers from the girl (an easy picture puzzle to solve: they 'deflower' her).

This meadow has a dual derivation in relation to sexual curiosity, just as the bird's beak had in relation to defence. There is a metonymic derivation: the apparently neutral memory of the meadow subsists, out of contiguity, in place of the pleasure- and anxiety-laden games that occurred there – the game of Pauline's 'deflowering' and the game of obscene puns produced by the *concierge's* son. And there is a metaphorical derivation: like all undulating countryside, the meadow is a metaphor for the mother's body. Freud refers explicitly to this metaphor in the 1909 edition of *The Interpretation of Dreams*: he points out that places the dreamer has a feeling of having been to before ('*déjà vu*') are invariably the genitals of the dreamer's mother (*ID* 399).

In the mid-nineteenth century, *concierge's* children were usually ill-mannered and crude, and bourgeois families never allowed their own children to play with them: here again, Sigismund's transgression must have been facilitated by a certain degree of tolerance in his milieu. Moreover, Monika Zajíc, the nurse who looked after Sigismund, and who came from the family living in the same house as the Freuds, was, as we have seen, crotchety, rude, dirty and dishonest.

'. . . and who I am inclined to think was called Philipp.'

There is little chance of ever finding out his real name. But two remarks are, I think, called for. First, if you put the words Philipp and son (of the *concierge*) together, you get the name Philippson. This play on words, which combines the quick-witted, ill-mannered Philipp and the serious, earnest editor of the Bible, can be interpreted in the same way as earlier remarks: one must identify with the enemy in order better to know and control him; and although it may legitimately be forbidden to do certain things, there is nothing that one can be forbidden to know.

Secondly, there is Sigismund's half-brother, who is also called Philipp. Freud's interpretation of the screen memory of 'the wardrobe', in which Philipp played such an important part, dates from mid-October 1897. As Jones has remarked, it was no doubt easier for Sigismund to live out his Oedipus complex by shifting it from his father on to Philipp. This fragment of the dream can therefore be translated as: 'I am inclined to think that the "guilty person" (guilty of intercourse – of "*vögeln*" – with the mother) was called Philipp.'

'It seems to me that it was from this boy that I first heard the vulgar term for sexual intercourse, instead of which educated people always use a latin word, "to copulate", and which was clearly enough indicated by the choice of the falcons' heads.'

Vögeln is both the dative plural form of *Vogel* (a bird) and an indecent term, not normally found in German dictionaries, meaning 'to have sexual intercourse'. The dream turns the play on words into a picture puzzle: by representing a woman being carried to bed by several men (the pun does not work with the singular form) whose heads are like those of birds (*Vögeln*), it means that the man is, so to speak, 'birding' the woman.

But why does Freud talk of 'falcons' heads' when the pun requires 'birds' heads'? His choice of the falcon, which is a bird of prey, is a metaphorical allusion to a sadistic representation of intercourse.

The distressing thought, which wakes Sigismund up, that his mother is dead is the logical consequence of that. The need to write a verb derived from the Latin word *coïtus* (= *coït tue*; a new play on words, this time in French, we can assume Freud knew of) is an allusion of the same sort, but Freud isn't satisfied just with allusions. The nightmare which one of Freud's patients had had repeatedly when he was between 11 and 13 ('*A man with a hatchet was pursuing him; he tried to run away, but seemed to be paralysed and could not move from the spot*'), and which Freud recounts immediately after discussing the dream of 'My mother and the bird-beaked figures', prompts him to make the following explicit comments: the nightmare had resulted from the patient witnessing with horror, when he was nine, his parents making love – a scene which he interpreted as having involved 'violence and struggling', and which left traces of blood on the bed. The fact that the patient is stated to have been nine at the time would tend to confirm not only the dating of the dream of 'My mother and the bird-beaked figures'

(Freud was nine and a half when he had the dream, not seven or eight), but also Freud's need to identify with the patient in order both to understand him and to understand himself.

'I must have guessed the sexual significance of the word from the face of my young instructor, who was well acquainted with the facts of life.'

The end of the sentence is ironical: people who use excessively crude language when talking about certain things are often trying to distract attention from the fact that they are unable to do those things. The beginning of the sentence alludes to mime as a visual and gestural expression of meaning – which is also the technique of the picture puzzle. It is worth noting that the dream contains three facial expressions: that of the sleeping mother (sensual pleasure), that of the dying grandfather (death), and that of the *concierge's* son (meaning). The presence of the notion of meaning *qua* meaning at this point in *The Interpretation of Dreams* seems to me to be highly significant: death is inevitable sooner or later; physical pleasure, even when freed from inhibition, remains a limited experience; the possibility of understanding and the pleasure afforded by success in doing so are, on the other hand, unlimited.

'The expression on my mother's features in the dream was copied from the view I had had of my grandfather a few days before his death as he lay snoring in a coma.'

This is an example of condensation.

'The interpretation carried out in the dream by the "secondary revision" must therefore have been that my mother was dying; the funerary relief fitted in with this.'

Freud, then, was paying increasing attention to the process of secondary revision, on which he was probably writing a few pages at about the same time for the first version of his book. After being revised and added to, they made up Section I (the last) of Chapter 6 in the final version. As regards the need felt by Freud to provide proof for his theories, he was clearly very pleased to be able, in a short and straightforward child's dream, to differentiate between a latent content, an intermediate manifest content, and a final manifest content resulting from secondary revision, whereas other examples in the book could be rejected either because they were the dreams of patients (and therefore involved abnormal psychological processes), or because they were dreams of his own dreamt *after* he had taken the decision to analyse them (thus making him both judge and judged).

'I awoke in anxiety, which did not cease till I had woken my parents up. I remember that I suddenly grew calm when I saw my mother's face, as though I had needed to be reassured that she was not dead.'

Here we have the same process as in the scene with the wardrobe, where

Sigismund suddenly grew calm when he saw his 'beautiful and slim' mother, i.e. when he thought: 'So she is not pregnant.'

'But this "secondary" interpretation of the dream had already been made under the influence of the anxiety which had developed. I was not anxious because I had dreamt that my mother was dying; but I interpreted the dream in that sense in my preconscious revision of it because I was already under the influence of that anxiety.'

This is a perfect example of what Bion has since called the need to understand. Understanding what goes on between parents derives from what, according to myths and sacred legends, goes on between gods or heroes. But to understand is also to want to see, and also to want to do oneself: hence the arousal of anxiety. Anxiety, in turn, needs to be understood in order to be dominated, and death (or separation) supplies one of the figures that make that possible. In other words, interpretation is a spontaneous and primal psychical activity. A dream contains not only a representation of latent thoughts (the picture puzzle), but also a representation of its own processes (a topography) and, lastly, a preconscious and defensive interpretation of itself. These are the characteristics that make the meaning of dreams decipherable. The psychoanalyst merely takes charge of the psychical apparatus' natural and vital urge to interpret, and steers it towards the truth.

'The anxiety can be traced back, when repression is taken into account, to an obscure and evidently sexual craving that had found appropriate expression in the visual content of the dream.'

The subject of the sentence is ambiguous: is it anxiety in general, or his particular anxiety on awaking after the dream? I have already remarked on the impersonal tone of the whole passage. Freud refrains from mentioning too many personal details, partly because he regards his case not as intrinsically interesting but as typical of universal mental processes. Hence the lack of a possessive pronoun. The craving is obscure only to the reader, because Freud does not want to be more specific about it; but it is doubtless quite clear to him.

If taken as an assertion, the sentence means that repressed libido is transformed into anxiety – an idea that Freud had already arrived at in 1895 in the course of his work on actual neuroses. If taken as a personal explanation (and enlarged upon by my own comments), it means that when Sigismund was about nine and a half masturbation was accompanied by phantasies of exclusive possession of the mother and by death-wishes against the father and against other rival children, and that it caused him to feel anxiety at three levels – unconscious anxiety at having transgressed the incest taboo, unconscious fear of retaliation by the father, and preconscious anxiety at having failed to observe the prohibition of masturbation. This last prohibition, because it is a preconscious one, and because it was common and particularly strict in the puritanical atmosphere of mid- to late-nineteenth-century Europe, may, as I have already pointed out, have carried more weight with the young Freud than the Oedipal prohibition; but the adult Freud's stroke of genius was to have shown that the psychical force of the first (preconscious) prohibition derived entirely from the second (unconscious) prohibition. However, the gulf between the two types of prohibition meant that Freud's guilt feelings attached themselves to masturbation, a fact that doubtless made it easier for him to discover the Oedipus complex.

Yet Freud's suggested interpretation of the 'obscure craving' in his dream is unsatisfactory; and the insistence with which he plays down the specific anxiety most prominent in the dream (about the death of his mother) by tracing it back to something else strikes me as suspect. I see a different meaning here. The internal process of the Oedipal phase was drawing to a close, and Sigismund was bidding farewell to his beloved mother, the mother of his infancy, his Oedipal mother. Henceforth, she would be dead for him, in other words he was abandoning incestuous possession of her. The post-Oedipal super-ego was thus at work, tempered, however, by the ego-ideal, as we have seen. Freud was thus able both to abandon his mother as a libidinal object and to seek substitutes for her in the sphere of thought, in other words to retrieve her image by taking possession of an unknown area of knowledge and by delighting in that possession.

The question I asked at the beginning of my discussion of this dream – why is it so placed as to be Freud's personal *last word* in *The Interpretation of Dreams*? – can now be answered. We have examined the three layers of memory which undergo condensation in the dream: at the age of two, when rebuked by his father, Sigismund had the last word, which was a witticism; when he was about seven or eight, it was his father who had the last word by predicting that he would be a good-for-nothing; and when he was nine and a half, it was death that had the last word. We now come to his manhood and to the fourth layer – that of the self-analysis set in motion by the work of mourning following his father's death in October 1896. Freud was in the process of completing the discovery which would refute his father's curse once and for all and bring him the symbolic possession of his beloved mother. At the same time as he was doing that, he was aware of exactly what he was doing: for the first time, he fully grasped the significance that a major discovery has for the person making it. He was able to interpret his anxiety dream, a relic of prepuberty and of some traumatic childhood scenes. He was able to forge ahead with the writing of his book, which was at once a last word to his father and the last word on him. By placing the interpretation of the dream at the end of his book, he was confirming that he had taken back his beloved mother from his father and regained possession of her; but, more than that, he was indicating that he now had the last word on death, the last word on anxiety, the last word on separation from the primally loved object. For death, anxiety and separation are inevitable facts of life which we can counter (indeed, only counter) with words and sentences which run through our heads, or which we expect to hear from those to whom we are important – words and sentences which speak from the point of view not of the super-ego or ideal ego, but of the ego-ideal, and which restore us by talking of good internal objects which have been destroyed and reintrojected by us.

One last point: Freud was not only a psychoanalyst but a collector, and was surrounded, while he worked, by an array of antique objects and Egyptian figurines bearing the heads of domesticated falcons or wild hawks. It was vital for him that the hostile god whose ally he had become – the unconscious – should remain constantly in view while he treated his patients so that he could better control it, just as Philippson felt that Jews should acquaint themselves with other religions and cultures in order better to preserve their own. Freud says clearly in his analysis of the dream that if we face up to bad objects, call them by their names, and work out their mechanisms, we can hold them at our mercy.

THE DREAM OF 'GOETHE'S ATTACK ON HERR M.' (BETWEEN APRIL 14 AND 27, 1898)

As has already been noted (p. 269), on March 15, 1898, Freud sent Fliess the manuscript of his second chapter, which contained his analysis of two pilot dreams (probably the Irma and the 'Uncle with the yellow beard' dreams) and some remarks on the Oedipus myth. On March 24, he answered Fliess's objections and began writing the chapter on the somatic stimuli of dreams and on anxiety-dreams. By April 3, the chapter was almost finished. Their scheduled Easter 'congress' had to be cancelled because Fliess was ill and his wife well into her pregnancy. Freud seized this opportunity of going on a trip with Alexander to Istria, which was then Austrian, and as soon as he got back on April 14 sent Fliess a vivid account of their experiences. He had been struck by the number of ancient priapic statues he had seen, and suggested a possible symbolic interpretation of them in his letter: 'Priapus stood for permanent erection, a wish-fulfilment representing the opposite of psychological impotence' (*F* 308).

But immediately upon his return Freud had to deal with an unpleasant incident. Fliess's first book, on the relationship between the nose and the female sexual organs, had been brought out by Deuticke in Vienna the previous year. *Wiener klinische Rundschau*, the journal to which Freud regularly contributed important articles, had just published a devastating review of the book. Grinstein reproduces the text in full (G 248–9). Here are some typical extracts: 'The book [. . .] is quite voluminous despite its meagre content. [. . .] It is not the task of science to criticise the phantasy-products of this author. [. . .] The reader obtains the impression in many places of the book that the author is making fun of him.' In the same letter of April 14, an indignant Freud told Fliess that he had just written a letter of protest to the editor. As he received no satisfactory reply from him, he told Fliess on April 27 that he had withdrawn his name from the list of contributors printed on the cover. At about this time (probably between April 14 and 27, 1898), Freud had the following dream:

'Here is yet another absurd dream which plays about with numbers. *One of my acquaintances, Herr M., had been attacked in an essay with an unjustifiable degree of violence, as we all thought – by no less a person than Goethe. Herr M. was naturally crushed by the attack. He complained of it bitterly to some company at table; his veneration for Goethe had not been affected, however, by this personal experience. I tried to throw a little light on the chronological data, which seemed to me improbable. Goethe died in 1832. Since his attack on Herr M. must naturally have been made earlier than that, Herr M. must have been quite a young man at the time. It seemed to be a plausible notion that he was eighteen. I was not quite sure, however, what year we were actually in, so that my whole calculation melted into obscurity. Incidentally, the attack was contained in Goethe's well-known essay on "Nature".*' (*ID* 439).

This dream and Freud's analysis of it are included in Chapter 6, Section G, of *The Interpretation of Dreams* as an example of an absurd dream (*ID* 439–41 and 448–9). It is to be found in the middle of a highly significant series of Freud's dreams – 'Father on his death-bed like Garibaldi', 'Count Thun', '1851 and 1856', and 'My son, the Myops'. The last of these dreams coincided with Freud's first serious disagreement with Fliess; as for the others, all of which were dreamt at a later date, their absurdity was explained by Freud as an expression of hostility towards his dead father; so it is easy to guess how Fliess was perceived by Freud. The dream of 'Goethe's attack on Herr M.' had already been referred to, without being described in detail, in Section C of the same chapter, 'The Means of Representation in Dreams', as an example of a reversal into the opposite, along with the '*Sappho*' dream (by one of Freud's male patients), which was based on Alphonse Daudet's novel of the same name (*ID* 326–7 and 337 n.1). An almost identical description of the dream, with a shorter analysis, is to be found in *On Dreams* (1901*a*, *OD* 662–5). Grinstein devotes Chapter 10 of his book to the dream.

By subjecting each fragment of the dream to his associations of ideas, Freud elucidates the polysemy of the 'attack'. One of the meanings of the word alludes to the 'crushing' review of Fliess's book and of the purely gratuitous juggling with ideas and figures it contained. Fliess, for example, explained Goethe's lifespan (1749–1832, or nearly 84 years) as being a multiple of 28, the number of days in the 'female' cycle. Consciously, Freud was shocked by the criticism of Fliess. In the dream, he unconsciously agrees with it (the dream anticipated his break with Fliess by several years). But in his analysis of the dream, as in the case of the Irma dream, Freud takes the blame for Fliess's error: he explains that it is he, Freud, who is in fact being attacked because of his theory of the sexual aetiology of neuroses. However, in his introductory sentence to the dream, Freud says that it is an 'absurd dream which plays about with numbers': the subtext here is surely that Fliess's theory is absurd and plays about with numbers.

A second meaning of the word 'attack' refers to the deterioration of the mental faculties caused by general paralysis, the last stage of syphilis contracted in one's youth. This happened to be the case with Herr M.'s brother, whom Freud had recently examined and asked to do several tests involving memory, sums, and awareness of time. In the dream, Freud is unsure what year he is in, and thus identifies with the paralytic.

In a third meaning, the attack refers to the sudden mental illness suffered by the brother of one of Freud's women patients. His frenzy began with him screaming 'Nature! Nature!' (the doctors erroneously took his exclamation to be a reference to the celebrated essay attributed to Goethe – the very same one which had determined the adolescent Freud's vocation – and as evidence of overwork at his studies in natural philosophy), and ended with him mutilating his own genitals: so 'Nature' referred to the sexual organs. Freud recognises his own identification with the paralytic, but draw no parallel of a similar kind with the second patient. Thus he under-interprets this third set of associations by seeing it merely as an expression of intellectual unpleasantness – that of seeing his theories about the sexual 'nature' of the neuroses being strongly criticised. Of the far greater unpleasantness of being attacked in the genitals by an ideal, yet strict and omnipotent father like Goethe, nothing at all is said; for the 'nothing' to which the organ of Oedipal desire is in danger of being reduced is so horrible as to preclude expression. Quite logically, a phantasied emasculation of the body corresponds with a radical scotomisation of speech and thought.

At this point, thematic analysis can get us no further. Primary thought has its own logic, and it is through that logic that it succeeds in giving meaning to things – affects and instincts, for example – which originally have none. The formal process revealed by this dream is that of the reversal into the opposite. Freud's insight into that process came when he was analysing one of his patients' dreams, which he called 'a lovely dream', and which is based, in reverse, on the introduction to *Sappho*, the novel by Alphonse Daudet (who was himself syphilitic – did Freud know, one wonders? – and who wrote a book about his experience of tabes). In the novel, the hero carries upstairs the woman whom he has just met, and who is about to yield to his desires. At the foot of the stairs, she seems light – a premonition of what he is about to discover: that she is a *femme légère*, or woman of easy virtue. But as he goes up each flight of stairs, the woman seems increasingly heavy, which anticipates a second discovery: that she is a mature woman, a symbolic representation of the paralysing despair their liaison will result in. Grinstein (G 257–61) establishes a detailed parallel between the framework of the novel and the phantasy scenario of the dream.

Freud's patient, a man suffering from claustrophobia, who had recently ended his love affair with an actress of humble origin, and had just seen a play with the same theme as *Sappho*, dreamt of walking uphill, first with difficulty, then much more easily. Analysis of the dream reveals some of the implications of this reversal: the man's liaison with a woman of easy virtue was sexually satisfying for him, but brought him right down the social scale; conversely, for the actress, their relationship represented an important stage in her social rise. Which of them, then, can be said to have gained the upper hand? In the childhood memory recalled by the patient during analysis, he was being suckled by his wet-nurse (who had in fact been his mother) in the place of his brother. Carrying a desired woman in his arms was therefore a reversed repetition of the primal situation of infantile pleasure where, having eliminated all his rivals, he was carried by his mother and was in close physical contact with her.

In the dream of 'Goethe's attack on Herr M.', Freud, as often, tested on himself the veracity of a process he had first observed in his patients. He was turning his back on Fliess, just as Sappho in the novel eventually turns her back on the young man she originally seduced. But when men alone are involved, turning one's back on someone has a homosexual connotation, and one which is reinforced by the Lesbian overtones of the name Sappho. So Freud was beginning to have an inkling of the latent homosexual nature of his submission to Fliess. Eighteen-thirty-two was indeed the year of Goethe's death; but it was also the date when Sigmund's elder half-brother, Emanuel, was born to Jacob Freud's first wife. The confusion over dates, which is attributed to the paralytic patient, is the channel through which a wish typical of sibling rivalry is expressed: if only the date of Emanuel's birth had also been that of his death . . . As for the cries of 'Nature! Nature!', they reminded Freud of a personal experience. Shortly before he was 18, he had attended a series of lectures on comparative anatomy at which he had heard a quotation from Goethe's famous essay for the first time; his enthusiasm was such that he decided on a medical career. The conjunction of the theme of 'comparative anatomy' and the formal process of reversal into the opposite marks the emergence of the infantile belief that the conformation of the female genitals is the opposite, as a result of removal, of the conformation of the male genitals.

The formal process governing the dream-work is that of reversal. As Freud remarks, calculations based on the date of birth become calculations based on the date of death. The critical reviewer of Fliess's book was quite young: in the dream, it is the criticised person who is quite young. The thought 'quite a young man could today criticise Goethe' becomes 'Goethe criticises quite a young man'. Freud then hints at another meaning of the dream: the crazy fool is not the person one thinks, not the person who is attacked, but the reverse. This reversal into the opposite is contained in embryo in another, equally critical review of Fliess's book, which Freud quotes in his discussion of the dream: 'One wonders whether it is the author or oneself who is crazy' (*ID* 440).

Reversal is a dangerous operation, as it can backfire on the person who propounds it. If Freud thinks, or at least writes, that the meaning of the dream is that he wanted to avenge Fliess for the criticism he had suffered, first by reversing it, and secondly by taking his place, it could be that the dream has precisely the *reverse* meaning. Freud tries to make calculations, like Fliess, but his 'whole calculation melted into obscurity'. 'I behaved like a paralytic, and the dream was a mass of absurdities' (*ID* 440): so the meaning is that he finds Fliess's calculations absurd. Freud repeats his belief that feelings and reactions experienced after a dream form part of its content. As in the 'My son, the Myops' dream, the feeling of absurdity in this dream was in fact directed at Fliess's theory. Confirmation of that came when Freud, on the brink of breaking with his friend in the autumn of 1900, chose to include the dream in *On Dreams*, and to make a number of additional points about it. When a student, Fliess complained so noisily about a senile professor that he obtained his resignation; the implication is that it is now Fliess's turn to suffer the same fate. Freud himself had served in hospital under a 'fossil' chief (he draws a parallel with the sheep's head discovered by Goethe on the Lido beach); some of his young contemporaries concocted a parody of what was then a popular song: 'This was written by no Goethe . . .'

Eva Rosenblum points out that one phrase in the dream – '*welches Jahr wir gegenwärtig schreiben*' (literally, 'what year we are now writing') – is an archaic German form that might have been used by Goethe. So it is Freud who, in this dream, writes like Goethe and who, like him, has discovered his sheep's head, i.e. the meaning of dreams and the Oedipus complex. Now if Freud, as it now appears, identifies with Goethe and his discovery, it is he who, in the dream, attacks Herr M. (Fliess). Freud hints at this in the first edition of *The Interpretation of Dreams*: 'I think, moreover, that all these dreams of turning things round the other way include a reference to the contemptuous implications of the idea of "turning one's back on something"' (*ID* 327).[1] In 1911, he added: 'It is remarkable to observe, moreover, how frequently reversal is employed precisely in dreams arising from repressed homosexual impulses.' Reversal in the dream-processes is therefore the transposition, on a formal plane, of a latent content of inversion.

By the time Freud had finished analysing this dream, the equation of the problem was clear in his mind: there exists a middle term between the general feeling of paralysis, the Oedipal prohibition, and the difference between the sexes. That middle term is in all likelihood an infantile phantasy. But of what kind? Explicit recognition of it cannot be obtained through purely intellectual processes. If an individual is to shake off an infantile belief, he has to rebel overtly against the threat, contained in that belief, of general paralysis (a rebellion already perceptible in the affect of the dream: the 'unjustifiable degree of violence' of the attack), and needs the courage to imagine that transgression of the prohibition is possible. Surely that act of shaking off, that rebellion, that transgression, and the symbolic realisation of a very early phantasy are implicit in all creation?

THE DREAM OF THE 'CASTLE BY THE SEA' (ALSO KNOWN AS THE 'BREAKFAST-SHIP DREAM') (MAY 10–11, 1898)

On May 1, 1898 (*F* 312), Freud sent Fliess the manuscript of Chapter 3 of the first version of his dream book, which was on dream material. He was worried because the Spanish-American war had just broken out, and the Spanish fleet was reported to have left the Azores. New York was in a state of nervous anxiety, as there were fears it might be attacked or bombarded from the sea. Martha's brother, Eli Bernays, his wife Anna,

1. The German *Kehrseite* can mean both 'reverse' and 'backside'.

who was Sigmund's sister, and their children lived in New York. On May 7, news came through of the battle of Manila, which had taken place on May 1 and resulted in victory for the Americans.

On May 10, the Viennese newspaper, *Neue freie Presse*, published a detailed account of the battle, which Adams (1953) consulted and compared with Freud's subsequent dream. It may be summarised as follows: Admiral George Dewey's ships, in single file as though on parade, sailed past the Spanish fleet, which was sheltering in the Bay of Manila. Their action seemed all the more reckless because they did not answer the Spanish fire. Dewey talked imperturbably of the weather and the view, while the ellipse of his ships gradually closed in. After thirteen minutes he gave the order to start a terrible and unceasing barrage on the Spanish positions. Two hours later, at exactly breakfast-time, he stopped the bombardment so his men could eat. The Spanish were by then putting up almost no resistance. After breakfast, when the smoke had cleared, the American barrage resumed, destroying all the enemy ships. The Spanish flagship lost its successive captains, and was then cut in half. At 12.30 p.m., the white flag was hoisted. News of the battle reached the rest of the world only some days later, as cable lines to Manila had been cut.

On the same day that he read about the battle in the paper, Freud was struck by the bright colours of the toy bricks his children were playing with. That night, he had the following dream:

'*A castle by the sea; later it was no longer immediately on the sea, but on a narrow canal leading to the sea. The Governor was a Herr P. I was standing with him in a big reception room – with three windows in front of which there rose buttresses with what looked like crenellations. I had been attached to the garrison as something in the nature of a volunteer naval officer. We feared the arrival of enemy warships, since we were in a state of war. Herr P. intended to leave, and gave me instructions as to what was to be done if the event that we feared took place. His invalid wife was with their children in the threatened castle. If the bombardment began, the great hall was to be evacuated. He breathed heavily and turned to go; I held him back and asked him how I was to communicate with him in case of necessity. He added something in reply, but immediately fell down dead. No doubt I had put an unnecessary strain upon him with my questions. After his death, which made no further impression on me, I wondered whether his widow would remain in the castle, whether I should report his death to the Higher Command and whether I should take over command of the castle as being next in the order of rank. I was standing at the window, and observing the ships as they went past. They were merchant vessels rushing past rapidly through the dark water, some of them with several funnels and others with bulging decks* (just like the station buildings in the introductory dream – not reported here). *Then my brother was standing beside me and we were both looking out of the window at the canal. At the sight of one ship we were frightened and cried out: "Here comes the warship!" But it turned out that it was only the same ships that I already knew returning. There now came a small ship, cut off short, in a comic fashion, in the middle. On its deck some curious cup-shaped or box-shaped objects were visible. We called out with one voice: "That's the breakfast-ship"'* [*Frühstückschiff*] (*ID* 463–4).

The description of this dream and Freud's analysis of it are included in Section H, 'Affects in Dreams', of Chapter 6, 'The Dream-Work', where Freud discusses the way 'the dream-work brings about a suppression of affects' (*ID* 463–8). He returns to the dream in Section B, 'Regression', of Chapter 7, 'The Psychology of the Dream-Processes', in order to illustrate the fact that the specifically visual state of excitation in dreams 'has been set up by a *memory*, [. . .] it is a *revival* of a visual excitation which was originally an immediate one' (*ID* 546–7).

Freud describes the dream as his 'most vivid and beautiful dream of the last few years'. But at the same time his argument lacks conviction: on the one hand he disagrees with Scherner, asserting that the dream-content is due much more to an infantile scene, for which the dream is '*a substitute* [. . .] *modified by being transferred on to a recent experience*', than to internal sources of stimulation during sleep; yet all he proves with the example of the 'Castle by the sea' dream is that the visual hallucination peculiar to this dream derived from two recent memories (his trip to Istria, and the Ankerstein toy bricks played with by his children), i.e. from some day's residues, and not from an infantile memory. Freud's hunch that an infantile memory was somehow involved and his failure to bring it to light are characteristic of this phase in his self-analysis, when he was beginning to recall memories from the second part of his childhood (between the ages of five and ten in Vienna), but had not yet recognised the screen memory of a country scene with intense colours that occurred in Freiberg when he was about three – intense colours which later turned out to have represented the very intense sexual emotions he experienced at that time.

In the dream's intensely coloured images we find combined the toy bricks, the account of the naval battle, and Freud's two trips to the Adriatic with Alexander (to Venice in the summer of 1897, and to Istria at Easter a year later). During the second trip, they visited the museum in Aquileia and saw its collection of Etruscan funerary relics; then they had a picnic on the boat that took them on an excursion to Grado. A detailed and exuberant description of this trip can be found in Freud's letter to Fliess of April 14, 1898 (*F* 307–10). The River Isonzo and the lagoons were blue, and the Karst (the limestone plateau behind Trieste) brown. His whole description of the journey bubbles with enthusiasm, in strong contrast with the dramatic, gloomy atmosphere of the dream. The meaning of the latter was connected with Freud's worries about his family's future were he to die prematurely. He identified with his endangered brother-in-law in New York and with the admiral killed during the battle.

This fear of an imminent death had gradually become more insistent in Freud's dreams and now occupied a central position. The key to it can be found in a verbal expression at the end of the dream – yet another case of a visual scene being succeeded by symbolisation. The 'breakfast-ship' is an allusion to the two flagships involved in the battle, one which holds its fire in order to have breakfast, and the other which is defeated, smashed, and broken in two. Freud was also reminded of some Etruscan objects which had attracted his interest (probably in Aquileia) – a parallel with the Egyptian funerary barge in the dream of 'My mother and the bird-beaked figures'. The objects in question, which were not unlike breakfast-sets, were in fact lady's *toilettes* (toilet-sets) – Sigmund and Alexander jokingly wondered whether to take one home with them for Martha – made of terracotta and covered with black glaze (like all Etruscan domestic pottery). The dream-object, then, meant a black '*toilette*', i.e. mourning dress. There was also an allusion to the funeral boats in which in early times dead bodies were placed and committed to the sea for burial. Moreover, as Freud himself points out in his analysis, the English word 'breakfast' literally means 'breaking fast': 'The "breaking" related once more to the shipwreck [ship-break] and the fasting was connected with the black dress or *toilette*.'

Buxbaum (1951) regards this dream as marking a further step forward by Freud in the analysis of his relationship with Fliess and with his father. Instead of meeting Fliess, who was ill, Freud went to Istria with Alexander. The fear that he might die without providing for his children was punishment for his death-wishes against his father and his friend: he who wants to commit murder because of incestuous wishes is afraid of being subjected to *lex talionis* and of dying himself. Thus, it is increasingly clear that Freud is in the process of extricating himself from Fliess's influence: Fliess is no longer the 'governor' of Freud's scientific work; Freud has the impression that he is 'putting a strain' on Fliess 'with his questions'; he decides to take his place and go ahead with his own research without paying any attention to his friend's theories. The work of mourning that followed his father's death (the 'merchant vessels' in the dream allude to Jacob's profession) continues as a work of mourning connected with his contingent separation from Fliess.

Let us examine this dream, as we have earlier ones, from some other angles. The latent infantile wish is an Oedipal one: the Governor, Herr P. (the father) falls down dead; his widow remains in the castle, where she is 'threatened' (by incest); Freud takes the place of the Governor, and is suddenly afraid for his own life. But the dream in fact ends with a scene where he sees 'a small ship, cut off short, in a comic fashion, in the middle': thus the Oedipal punishment is not death but castration; however, Freud – quite understandably – is still not able to grasp, clearly and intellectually, this fact, which is presented by the dream in the form of thinking in images.

I say understandably, because the infantile wish is interlocked with memories of infantile scenes which have not yet been fully enough recalled or elucidated by Freud. The 'bulging decks', heavy breathing, and rushing ships suggest the bed, sheets and parental intercourse of the dream of 'My mother and the bird-beaked figures'. Intense colours already featured in the memory of the picture book on Persia that was pulled to pieces. But the wish to deflower Pauline, which was revealed at the beginning of 1899 by Freud's analysis of the screen memory, remained repressed, though it was by then nudging its way closer and closer to consciousness: when asked 'how far one could penetrate into the cave', the salacious guide of the Divaça cave (recently visited by Freud and his brother) gave the following answer – which Freud felt the need to report to Fliess in his letter of April 14, 1898: 'It's like with a virgin; the farther you get, the more beautiful it is' (*F* 309). The power of the 'bombardment' was such that it cut off the small ship in the middle: the defloration is phantasied as sadistic and destructive. Here we have a phantasy underlying a masturbatory daydream – masturbation, the breakfast of one's sex life . . .

When looked at from the angle of the body image, the dream effects a symbolic exploration of the female body (the castle, the sea, the canal). As I already remarked in connection with the 'Rome' dreams, the landscape is seen from afar (from behind a fortified wall), and it is seen thanks to the reassuring presence of a companion, who is first a father figure (the 'governor'), then Freud's younger brother Alexander. The exploration culminates with the act of taking possession (the 'bombardment', the ships which 'rush rapidly through the water'), a source of both anxiety and intense pleasure.

THE DREAM OF THE 'HALL WITH MACHINES' (ALSO KNOWN AS THE 'SANATORIUM' OR 'DISHONESTY' DREAM) (MAY 1898)

During the next few days, towards mid-May 1898, Freud's mind continued to be exercised by the theme of death, as he revealed in a footnote to a new dream (a footnote that enables it to be dated): 'My not being able to find my hat was an occurrence from waking life which was used in more than one sense. Our housemaid, who was a genius at putting things away, had hidden it. – The end of this dream also concealed a rejection of some melancholy thoughts about death: "I am far from having done my duty, so I must not go yet." – Birth and death were dealt with in it, just as they had been in the dream of Goethe and the paralytic patient, which I had dreamt a short time before' (*ID* 337, n.1).

The dream and Freud's comments on it run as follows:

'This "not being able to do anything" does not always appear in dreams as a sensation but is sometimes simply a part of the content of the dream. A case of this sort seems to me particularly well qualified to throw light on the meaning of this feature of dreaming. Here is an abridged version of a dream in which I was apparently charged with dishonesty. *The place was a mixture of a private sanatorium and several other institutions. A manservant appeared to summon me to an examination* ['*Untersuchung*', which also means an enquiry]. *I knew in the dream that something had been missed and that the examination was due to a suspicion that I had appropriated the missing article.* (The analysis showed that the examination was to be taken in two senses and included a medical examination.) *Conscious of my innocence and of the fact that I held the position of a consultant in the establishment, I accompanied* ['*gehen*', which also means to walk or to leave] *the servant quietly. At the door we were met by another servant, who said, pointing at me: "Why have you brought him? He's a respectable person." I then went, unattended, into a large hall, with machines standing in it, which reminded me of an Inferno with its hellish instruments of punishment* ['*Strafaufgabe*']. *Stretched out on one apparatus I saw one of my colleagues, who had every reason to take some notice of me; but he paid no attention. I was then told I could go* ['*gehen*']. *But I could not find my hat and could not go* ['*gehen*'] *after all.*

'The wish-fulfilment of the dream evidently lay in my being recognized as an honest man and told I could go. There must therefore have been all kinds of material in the dream-thoughts containing a contradiction of this. That I could go was a sign of my absolution. If therefore something happened at the end of the dream which prevented my going, it seems plausible to suppose that the suppressed material containing the contradiction was making itself felt at that point. My not being able to find my hat meant accordingly: "After all you're *not* an honest man." Thus the "not being able to do something" in this dream was a way of expressing a contradiction – a "no" –; so that my earlier statement that dreams cannot express a "no" requires correction' (*ID* 336–7).

The dream and its brief analysis, which is completed by a short footnote (part of which has already been quoted), are to be found at the end of Section C, 'The Means of Representation in Dreams', of Chapter 6, 'The Dream-Work'. In the edition of 1900, they come quite soon after the passage where Freud compares his preceding dream ('Goethe's attack on

Herr M.') with Daudet's *Sappho*. In between, we find the dream of 'Phantasies during sleep' (which is also critical of Fliess) and some observations (which probably date from the time when he wrote the second version) on the difference between the intensity or vividness of dream-images and the psychical intensity of dream-thoughts; Freud draws a parallel with Nietzsche's notion (though he does not mention him by name) of 'a transvaluation of all psychical values'. Grinstein investigates the dream very thoroughly (G, Chapter 11).

Freud's wish to exonerate himself, which had been operating since the beginning of his self-analysis, takes the specific form, in this dream, of a wish to avoid the accusation of dishonesty and the punishment of hell. The notion of dishonesty relates to Fliess, whose theories Freud appropriates while at the same time criticising them, and to the nurse, Monika Zajíc, who, as we saw, forced the young Sigismund to steal zehners (small coins), and who, in her uncouth fashion, taught him how to wash. The notion of hell is another allusion to the nurse, who threatened the child with the flames of hell, as well as being a continuation of the theme of going down into the underworld and visitng Tartarus (where the greatest criminals were tortured on machines), in other words a continuation of his heroic identification with Aeneas and Dante.

The key to the dream is to be found in the expression 'I could not go', which means two things: 'I am not absolved', and 'I have not completed my task, I must not die'.[1] A quotation from Schiller's play, *Fiesco* (Act III, Scene 4), provides a link: 'The Moor has done his duty, the Moor *can go* ["*gehen*"].' Freud points out in a footnote that there is a further pun on the double meaning of the verb '*gehen*': 'Then came a facetious conundrum: "How old was the Moor when he had done his duty?" – "One year old, because then he could go ['*gehen*' – both 'to go' and 'to walk']." (It appears that I came into the world with such a tangle of black hair that my young mother declared I was a little Moor.)' (*ID* 337, n.1).

As Grinstein demonstrates in detail (G 268–80), *Fiesco*, which Schiller wrote in 1783, is a particularly black play. Freud's reference to it seems to me to follow on from the stories that Sigismund used to read in the Philippson Bible at the time he had the dream of 'My mother and the bird-beaked figures'. A parallel can easily be drawn between several of the play's themes and Freud's own problems:

– *Ambition*: in 1547, Fiesco, the Count of Lavagna, wants by hook or by crook to oust Andreas Doria, the Duke of Genoa, and take his place: there

1. Stein (1968*a*) interprets this as follows: the infantile wish fulfilled in the dream is a wish to remain with his mother; hence the statement 'I cannot go'; hence, too, the difficulty of avoiding the accusation of dishonesty, since the wish in question is obviously felt to be reprehensible.

is a connection here with Freud's semi-unconscious ambition to become a *professor extraordinarius*, even if it meant riding roughshod over his colleagues.

– *Homicidal rivalry* towards father and brother figures: a group of conspirators, which includes Verrina, an elderly, upright republican, and is later joined by Fiesco, wants to kill the duke; the latter's nephew, Gianettino, also plans independently to kill the duke and to eliminate Fiesco as well.

– *Betrayal*: the Moor of Tunis, Muley Hassan, betrays a succession of people – first, his original master, Gianettino, after failing to follow his instructions to kill Fiesco, then his second master Fiesco, by telling the duke that Fiesco is plotting against him; in the meantime, he betrays Julia by telling Fiesco that he has been instructed by her to mix poison in Leonora's chocolate every day (Leonora is Fiesco's wife); lastly, he becomes a thief and an incendiary.

– *Contempt for women*: Fiesco publicly pays court to Julia, the duke's niece and Gianettino's sister, solely to put Doria off his guard; he gets her to confess her passion for him in the presence of his wife, Leonora, who is concealed behind a tapestry, then humiliates Julia, before she is led away to prison, by suddenly drawing back the tapestry and revealing his wife; Gianettino ravishes Verrina's daughter, Bertha, who is engaged to the young Bourgognino; Fiesco mistakenly kills Leonora, who is wearing the dead Gianettino's scarlet cloak and hat.

– *Punishment*: after thwarting the Moor's attempt to kill him, Fiesco has him tortured on the wheel; in the end, he sends him to the gallows for theft and arson; Bourgognino avenges Bertha by killing Gianettino; at the end of the play, Verrina pulls off the purple cloak that Fiesco has just donned on becoming the Duke of Genoa, and pushes him into the sea, where he drowns.

Grinstein spots a connection between another line from the play and Freud's dream: at one point, Fiesco, now ready to lead the conspiracy, declares: 'All the machines are ready for the grand attempt – the instruments are tuned for the terrific concert' (Act II, Scene 16). He also corrects Freud's quotation from the play: when Fiesco has been convinced by the Moor that Julia wants to poison Leonora, he dismisses him, at which point the Moor says: 'The Moor has done his work [Freud mistakenly wrote "his duty" – but the two words are often confused], the Moor can go' (Act III, Scene 4).

Freud's quip about the Moor who could go/walk at the age of one doubtless ties up with an episode from his infancy which has already been mentioned by him, and which recurs in several later dreams without being made explicit: he was nearly one-and-a-half when his brother Julius was born, and nearly two when Julius died of a gastro-intestinal disorder. It is easy to see why Freud remarked, in his footnote, that 'birth and death were dealt with in [this dream]'.

One last point, already made by Grinstein, is also worth mentioning. The *hat* is a symbol of the male sexual organ: Freud was not yet fully aware of this, but later on, in the third edition of *The Interpretation of Dreams* (1911), he added a passage entitled 'A Hat as a Symbol of a Man (or of Male Genitals)' (Section E, Chapter 6, *ID* 360–62). So the lack of the hat in the dream refers – though Freud cannot yet realise this – to the lack of male genitals. The thematic similarity between this dream and an otherwise undatable dream, 'Phantasies during sleep', suggests that the latter, which I shall now examine, occurred some time after the 'Hall with machines' dream, probably in June 1898.

THE DREAM OF 'PHANTASIES DURING SLEEP' (JUNE 1898?)

'In a few cases we find to our surprise that the impression of clarity or indistinctness given by the dream has no connection at all with the make-up of the dream itself but arises from the material of the dream-thoughts and is a constituent of it. Thus I remember a dream of mine which struck me when I woke up as being so particularly well-constructed, flawless and clear that, while I was still half-dazed with sleep, I thought of introducing a new category of dreams which were not subject to the mechanisms of condensation and displacement but were to be described as "phantasies during sleep". Closer examination proved that this rarity among dreams showed the same gaps and flaws in its structure as any other; and for that reason I dropped the category of "dream-phantasies". The content of the dream, when it was arrived at, represented me as laying before my friend [Fliess] a difficult and long-sought theory of bisexuality; and the wish-fulfilling power of the dream was responsible for our regarding this theory (which, incidentally, was not given in the dream) as clear and flawless ["*lückenlos*", literally "without gaps" or "gapless"]. Thus what I had taken to be a judgment on the completed dream was actually a part, and indeed the essential part, of the dream-content. The dream-work had in this case encroached, as it were, upon my first waking thoughts and had conveyed to me as a *judgement* upon the dream the part of the material of the dream-thoughts which it had not succeeded in representing accurately in the dream' (*ID* 331–2).

This dream confirms that Freud did not share Fliess's enthusiasm; he found his theory (that of periodicity and bilaterality) extremely 'indistinct' and 'full of gaps', not subjectable to the 'mechanisms' of scientific proof, and, in a word, pure 'phantasy'. One of the wishes fulfilled in the dream is probably the following: my own theory of the dream-work which I am now elaborating will, unlike his, be 'well-constructed, flawless and clear'. But the wish-fulfilment in the dream – of the wish to acquire knowledge, to have scientific ambitions, to outstrip a rival – is too bluntly expressed. When Freud wakes up, secondary revision swiftly changes its meaning: it is not my friend who had phantasies, it is I who, carried away by my own enthusiasm, made the mistake of adding to my dream theory the purely imaginary category of phantasies during sleep. Once again, then, Freud prefers to take the blame for his friend's mistake and thus get him excused.

But another wish, which is spelt out by the dream, anticipates what actually happened later: Freud adopted the theory of bisexuality, and the priority dispute that ensued finished off his already dying friendship with Fliess. However, if that wish, which is now fully preconscious for Freud, is spelt out by the dream ('the content of the dream, when it was arrived at, represented me as laying before my friend a difficult and long-sought theory of bisexuality'), it is because it masks another, this time unconscious, wish – the wish that there should be no gaps. More precisely, Freud's conscious scientific wish to arrive at a 'gapless' dream theory is hypercathected by the unconscious wish, produced by an infantile sexual theory, that the thing itself, and not just the discussion of it, should be 'gapless'. That thing is 'a phantasy' (Freud's dream, anticipating – as often – his conceptual thought, says so explicitly) concerning 'bisexuality' (i.e. the difference between the sexes).

The meaning of the dream dawned on Freud much later. In the 1911 and 1914 editions of *The Interpretation of Dreams*, after the passage dealing with the dream of 'Phantasies during sleep', Freud characteristically added two dreams by patients which clearly contain further associations to his own dream. In the first, the dreamer makes a mistake over his hotel room number and bursts in unannounced on an elderly lady and her two daughters as they are undressing. 'He proceeded: "Here there are some gaps in the dream; there's something missing. Finally there was a man in the room who tried to throw me out, and I had to have a struggle with him".' Interpretation produced the following conclusion: 'The "gaps" were the genital apertures of the women who were going to bed; and "there's something missing" described the principal feature of the female genitalia' (*ID* 332–3). The second dream, by another patient, consists of a similarly imprecise narrative: 'then came an obscure patch, an interruption', which occurs between a scene in a restaurant and a scene in a brothel. Here again, Freud's interpretation pointed to the recollection of a scene of boyish sexual curiosity, when he had 'inspected [. . .] the genitals of a sister who was a few years his junior' (*ID* 333).

Thus, if my dating of this dream is correct, Freud was asking himself, as he finished writing the first version of his dream book, whether his theory was 'gapless', whether all infantile sexuality could be explained by the Oedipus complex, whether certain dreams did not escape 'the mechanisms of condensation and displacement' – mechanisms which at that time he ascribed solely to thing-presentations. An answer came in the form of a dream which he could not immediately understand, but which showed that a word-presentation ('gaps' in a narrative or a theory) can act as a substitute for an anxiety-laden thing-presentation (the visible 'gaps' in little girls' genitals) – another example of the way Freud's thought leapt from the visual to the textual. The dream also contained a 'bisexual', and no longer a purely Oedipal, infantile sexual phantasy.

Freud did not understand the dream because he was not yet ready to grasp either that thought process or that phantasy. Not unnaturally, then, he 'interrupted' the writing of the first version and left it in the air, as though he had run into an 'obscure patch'. It was now his own theories on the dream-work and on infantile sexuality that no longer seemed to him sufficiently 'well-constructed, flawless and clear.'

The important dreams of the summer of 1898

THE 'HOLLTHURN' DREAM (JULY 18–19, 1898)

June and the beginning of July 1898 were eventful in various ways. At the same time as he was finishing Chapter 5, 'The Psychical Processes in Dreams', of the first version of his book (the chapter sent to Fliess on July 7), Freud continued to read the novels of Conrad Ferdinand Meyer with great enthusiasm. He was visited in Vienna by Emanuel and his son, John. He spent a weekend at Aussee, where his family had already gone for the summer holidays: he found them 'with colds and frozen stiff' (*F*, June 20, 1898, 317). He made two other journeys, one for a consultation near Königgrätz (now Hradec Králové) in Bohemia (*F*, July 7, 1898, 319), the other, at about the middle of June, to meet his sister-in-law Minna in Salzburg and take her to see her and Martha's mother in Reichenhall (J I, 368). Freud had also met Minna the previous year in Salzburg, in mid-July, and gone on a short walking tour with her before visiting her mother in Reichenhall (J I 367).

The summer of 1898 turned out to be very hot. On the evening of July

18,[1] Freud set off for another consultation, this time at Pörtschach in Carinthia. Travelling conditions were uncomfortable. The train was packed. He found a seat in a compartment already occupied by a stand-offish couple who were clearly annoyed by his intrusion and refused to let him open the window despite the heat. They were travelling on a free pass. Although suffocating, Freud managed to get to sleep. When the train arrived at Marburg, he woke up in the middle of the following dream:

'Included in yet another of my dreams there was an expression of surprise at something I had experienced in it; but the surprise was accompanied by such a striking, far-fetched and almost brilliant attempt at an explanation that, if only on *its* account, I cannot resist submitting the whole dream to analysis, quite apart from the dream's possessing two other points to attract our interest. I was travelling along the *Südbahn* railway-line during the night of July 18–19, and in my sleep I heard: *"Hollthurn, ten minutes" being called out. I at once thought of holothurians* [sea-slugs] – *of a natural history museum – that this was the spot at which valiant men had fought in vain against the superior power of the ruler of their country – yes, the Counter-Reformation in Austria – it was as though it were a place in Styria or the Tyrol. I then saw indistinctly a small museum, in which the relics or belongings of these men were preserved. I should have liked to get out, but hesitated to do so. There were women with fruit on the platform. They were crouching on the ground and holding up their baskets invitingly. – I hesitated because I was not sure whether there was time, but we were still not moving. – I was suddenly in another compartment, in which the upholstery and seats were so narrow that one's back pressed directly against the back of the carriage.*[2] *I was surprised by this, but I reflected that* I MIGHT HAVE CHANGED CARRIAGES WHILE I WAS IN A SLEEPING STATE. *There were several people, including an English brother and sister; a row of books were distinctly visible on a shelf on the wall. I saw "The Wealth of Nations" and "Matter and Motion" (by Clerk-Maxwell), a thick volume and bound in brown cloth. The man asked his sister about a book by Schiller, whether she had forgotten it. It seemed as though the books were sometimes mine and sometimes theirs. I felt inclined at that point to intervene in the conversation in a confirmatory or substantiating sense* . . . I woke up perspiring all over, because all the windows were shut. The train was drawing up at Marburg [in Styria].

'While I was writing the dream down a new piece of it occurred to me,

1. Freud himself says the journey and the dream took place during the night of July 18–19, without specifying which year. It could only have been 1898, both because of the socio-professional circumstances, and because of the content of the dream itself, which marks the beginning of a series of 'excrement' dreams.

2. This description was unintelligible even to myself; but I have followed the fundamental rule of reporting a dream in the words which occurred to me as I was writing it down. The wording chosen is itself part of what is represented by the dream.

which my memory had tried to pass over. *I said* [in English] *to the brother and sister, referring to a particular work: "It is from . . .", but corrected myself: "It is by . . ." "Yes," the man commented to his sister, "he said that right"'* (*ID* 455–6).

This dream and Freud's initial analysis of it are to be found at the end of Section G, 'Absurd Dreams – Intellectual Activity in Dreams', of Chapter 6, 'The Dream-Work' (*ID* 455–9). Further remarks, which refer to the 'gross indecency' of the dream and specify the youthful memory that lay behind it (Freud's first visit to England at the age of 19), are included in Section A, 'The Forgetting of Dreams', of Chapter 7, 'The Psychology of the Dream-Processes' (*ID* 519–20). Freud points out in *The Psychopathology of Everyday Life* that, in his discussion of the dream, he had mistakenly referred to Marburg as Schiller's birthplace, whereas he was in fact born in Marbach. He explains the error by indicating that Marburg was the name of 'a business friend of my father's' and suggests that 'anyone who reads through the dream [. . .] will in part find undisguisedly, and will in part be able to guess from hints, that I have broken off at thoughts which would have contained an unfriendly criticism of my father' – doubtless an allusion to Jacob's ill-starred business activities, which were a subject of shame and annoyance to his children (*PEL* 217–19). The dream is analysed by Grinstein (G, Chapter 14).

Freud scarcely discusses his associations in detail, revealing little more than the results of his interpretation.

One line of interpretation, then, is that the dream-thoughts are so grossly rude and indecent that he cannot relate them. He simply indicates the following association in connection with *Ma*tter and *Mo*tion: '*Mo*lière's "Le *ma*lade imaginaire" – "La *ma*tière est-elle laudable?" – A *mo*tion of the bowels.' The aim is to take revenge on his disagreeable fellow-travellers. The rudeness is the product of what Freud was later to call anal erotism.

Let us attempt to delve into some of the details not revealed by Freud. *The Wealth of Nations* (1776), by the English economist Adam Smith, was the first work to try to synthesise data on economics and postulate the principle of *laissez-faire*. It was a pioneering, revolutionary and voluminous work, as Freud imagined his dream book would be. Another parallel between Smith and Freud, as Grinstein remarks, is that they both believed that man is fundamentally egocentric, that he is governed by natural laws, and that *laissez-faire* or, so to speak, *laissez-dire* is the best way of restoring economic or psychical equilibrium. *The Wealth of Nations* is divided into five books, just as the holothurians have five sectors and Freud had at that point written five chapters of the first version of the dream book.

Matter and Motion (1877), by the English physicist James Clerk-Maxwell, who became famous for his discoveries on the nature of electrical phenomena, is a slim volume of some 100 pages; in it he sets forth a purely physical and mathematical theory that tries to synthesise data on matter and motion, using the concept of energy as a basis. In its size, rigour of thought, and scientific principles, the book succeeds in doing what Freud had merely outlined, in manuscript form, with his 'Project for a Scientific Psychology' (1950*a*). The concepts of *inertia* and *facilitation* are explicitly discussed in both texts, and are used in a sexual sense in Freud's analysis of the dream: the disagreeable man in Freud's compartment on the train 'sat there motionless'; Freud's presence had not facilitated 'the affectionate exchanges which they had planned'.

The reference in the dream to these two books is overdetermined. Adam Smith acted as a model for Freud's study of 'psychoeconomics', and Clerk-Maxwell as a model for his study of 'psychodynamics' (G 348). Both men were English, like the older branch of his family, whom he so envied. The titles of the two books have anal symbolic overtones: matter can easily be faecal, and motion, as Freud points out, can refer to the bowels; as for wealth, Freud had already equated faeces with money. Lastly, Clerk-Maxwell's book is 'a thick volume and bound in brown cloth', a further allusion to excrement.

Le malade imaginaire (1673) was the last play written by Molière, who died on stage while acting in its title role – a fact which Grinstein fails to mention but which was probably known to Freud. We find here the same masochistic theme as in the identification with Moses – the notion of completing one's life work and dying immediately afterwards, of meeting with fame at the same time as meeting one's death. Grinstein does, however (G 350–52), suggest four other reasons why the play was significant for Freud: its satire of the medical profession's reactionary attitude and resistance to new ideas; the reference by Louison, the younger daughter of Argan (the *malade imaginaire*), to a primal scene of love-making between her elder sister, Angélique, and the man who loves her, Cléante (Argan refuses to let them be married, and wants Angélique either to marry Thomas Diafoirus, a prospective doctor, or to go into a convent); the play's emphasis on going to the lavatory and taking enemas, i.e. on anality; and lastly, its satire of an enfeebled, sickly, fallen father figure with a preposterously infantile interest in his own stool.

This scatological dimension of the dream, which is relatively new in Freud's self-analysis, is overlaid by more familiar dimensions – infantile sexuality, Oedipal wishes, the incest taboo, and the difference between the sexes. These constitute a second line of interpretation, which I now propose to examine.

The two fellow-travellers in the dream are English, and they are brother and sister. It was too soon for Freud to spot the connection here with a childhood scene involving his nephew and niece, John and Pauline, who were also brother and sister, and who had since become English. But there was another connection, this time with a contemporary, not a distant, situation, of which Freud must have been aware though he does not mention it: he had just spent a weekend with his sister-in-law Minna, during which they made plans for their trip to Italy later that summer. The mutual pleasure that Sigmund and Minna derived from intellectual conversation and travelling together was possible only because the incest taboo was fully and spontaneously in operation between them. Jones (J I, 168), denying certain malicious rumours, states quite categorically that there was never any emotional or sexual relationship between Freud and his sister-in-law. This dream confirms that there could have been nothing between them: the married couple on the train who had planned affectionate exchanges during the night are replaced in the dream by a brother-and-sister couple. But, by becoming actual once again, the incest taboo inexorably, yet still indistinctly, revived Freud's memories of the incestuous games of his childhood.

The problem of the difference between the sexes is called to mind by the holothurians, whose name, condensed with Marburg, the station at which the train stopped, produced the 'Hollthurn' of the dream, which is not the name of any real place. Holothurians are molluscs and belong to one of the five classes of the phylum Echinodermata (literally 'hedgehog-skinned'), which also includes sea-urchins and starfish. Echinodermata are bilaterally symmetrical invertebrates (a discreet allusion to Fliess); their bodies are divided into five sectors or rays. Holothurians, which are also known as sea slugs or sea cucumbers, differ from the other Echinodermata in that they are shaped like a penis or a piece of excrement. The dream manifestly uses them as an anal phallic symbol, though Freud himself does not say so.

The youthful memory that comes back to him is of his first trip to England in 1875 at the age of 19 (the first edition of *The Interpretation of Dreams* gives his age as 17, which is probably a misprint, as all other editions give it as 19). During his stay in Manchester, Freud had a conversation with his half-brother Emanuel which shed valuable light on his genealogy. It was during his visit to England that Freud made the grammatical mistake referred to by the dream: while on the shore of the Irish Sea, he picked up a starfish (a class related to the holothurians) and said: 'He is alive' instead of 'It is alive'. In the manifest content of the dream, this mistake is replaced by another one ('It is from . . .' instead of 'It is by . . .'), whose meaning I shall examine shortly.

Thus the dream, says Freud, wanted to point out that he was 'using a word indicating gender or sex [*Geschlechtswort*] in the wrong place – of my bringing in sex (the word "he") where it did not belong' (*ID* 519–20). But he does not take his analysis any further. Blame for bringing in sex where it did not belong had current relevance for Freud, as it was the charge brought by Breuer and other Viennese doctors against his audacious sexual theories. But nothing from Freud's present occurs in the dream without being overdetermined by a childhood scene. He was now getting closer and closer to the recollection of that scene – a scene where he was interested in sex, where the masculine gender appeared in a place where he did not expect it, and where he found an answer to the question: 'What is the point of the difference between the sexes?'

The insults directed by the dreamer at his travelling-companions conceal a latent critical attitude towards his father. Freud does no more than hint at this third line of interpretation, in connection with the grammatical mistake corrected by the dream: '"*Das Buch ist von Schiller*" should be translated into English not with a "from" but with a "by".' He notes that the English preposition 'from' is pronounced in the same way as the German adjective '*fromm*' ('pious'). But he fails to add that the English 'by' has the same sound as the German '*bei*', which means 'next to' or 'with' and combines with a noun like '*Schlaf*' ('sleep') to form '*Beischlaf*' ('sexual intercourse'). Replacing 'from' with 'by' is the same thing as replacing a pious image of his father with the unseemly image of a sexually active father. What Freud at least hints at by his remark concerning the double meaning of 'from' is that grammatical incorrectness masks a more serious form of incorrectness – impiety towards the sacred person of the father. The price Freud pays for his determination not to be unmasked is his slip over Schiller's birthplace. He says it was Marburg (in Germany, whereas the Marburg Freud arrived at was in the Austrian province of Styria, now part of Yugoslavia), yet 'as every German schoolboy knows', he says in a footnote added in 1909 to *The Interpretation of Dreams*, Schiller was in fact born at Marbach. But Marburg was the name of a business friend of his father's, which Freud wished to suppress because the name would result in his adopting an offensive attitude towards his father (the relevant passage in *The Psychopathology of Everyday Life* has already been quoted on p. 326).

Freud's increasingly overt disrespect for his father was accompanied by increasingly fierce ambition, whose existence, to his great surprise, had already been revealed by earlier dreams. This theme is represented in the 'Hollthurn' dream by the allusion to a play by Schiller on the Counter-Reformation. Schiller wrote three plays – *Wallenstein's Camp*, *Piccolomini* and *The Death of Wallenstein* – on the great general of the Counter-Reformation, Albrecht Eusebius von Wallenstein (1583–1634), who ended up accused of high treason and was murdered because of his personal ambition, thirst for power, and double-dealing. In other words, he was a man who in more than one respect resembled Fiesco, the central character of another Schiller play alluded to by the previous dream. It is worth noting that for the time being Goethe had been eclipsed by the blacker, more violent Schiller as a cultural reference in Freud's dreams.

That impiety should express itself in the form of grammatical incorrectness was a fresh example of the way dreams use a linguistic device to express a wish. This led Freud to expand his theory of the dream-work: latent wishes could be represented by word-presentations just as well as by thing-presentations. Following up that line of investigation, Freud wrote – possibly straight away, possibly only the following spring when he went back to and completed his first version – the introduction to Chapter 6, on 'The Dream-Work'. Part of it runs as follows:

'The dream-thoughts and the dream-content are presented to us like two versions of the same subject-matter in two different languages. Or, more properly, the dream-content seems like a transcript ["*Übertragung*"] of the dream-thoughts into another mode of expression, whose characters and syntactic laws it is our business to discover by comparing the original and the translation. The dream-thoughts are immediately comprehensible, as soon as we have learnt them. The dream-content, on the other hand, is expressed as it were in a pictographic script ["*Bilderschrift*", literally "picture-writing"], the characters of which have to be transposed ["*übertragen*"] individually into the language of the dream-thoughts. If we attempted to read these characters according to their pictorial value [*Bilderwert*] instead of according to their symbolic relation, we should clearly be led into error. Suppose I have a picture-puzzle [*Bilderrätsel*], a rebus, in front of me. It depicts a house with a boat on its roof, a single letter of the alphabet, the figure of a running man whose head has been conjured away, and so on. Now I might be misled into raising objections and declaring that the picture as a whole and its component parts are nonsensical. A boat has no business to be on the roof of a house, and a headless man cannot run. Moreover, the man is bigger than the house; and if the whole picture is intended to represent a landscape, letters of the alphabet are out of place in it since such objects do not occur in nature. But obviously we can only form a proper judgment of the rebus if we put aside criticisms such as these of the whole composition and its parts and if, instead, we try to replace each separate element [*Bild*] by a syllable or word that can be represented by that element in some way or other. The words which are put together in this way are no longer nonsensical but may form a poetical phrase of the greatest beauty and significance. A dream is a picture-puzzle of this sort and our predecessors in the field of dream-interpretation have made the mistake of treating the rebus as a pictorial composition: and as such it has seemed to them nonsensical and worthless' (*ID* 277–8).

As has already been pointed out, it was not until the second edition, in 1909, that Freud first likened dreams to hieroglyphs: 'The productions of the dream-work, which, it must be remembered, *are not made with the intention of being understood*, present no greater difficulties to their translators than do the ancient hieroglyphic scripts to those who seek to read them' (*ID* 341).

Let us return to the 'Hollthurn' dream and investigate one last line of interpretation. Changing compartments is itself explained in the dream as a case of '*automatisme ambulatoire*' (Freud uses the French term). Freud had identified with a former patient of his, who had reproached himself with murderous inclinations after the death of his parents; the man eventually stopped going out at all, remaining cooped up at home for fear of committing a crime in an unconscious state. It was in the company of that very same man, now cured, that Freud had travelled to Königgrätz at the beginning of July for a consultation (he had been sent for by the man's relatives). It was a pleasant journey: they had a compartment to themselves, and left the windows open all night. 'I knew that the root of his illness had been hostile impulses against his father, dating from his childhood and involving a sexual situation. In so far, therefore, as I was identifying myself with him, I was seeking to confess something analogous.'

It was the same patient who had described a dream of incest with his mother, over which Freud was pondering at the time when he gave the old lady the wrong injection (see page 246) and was discovering the Oedipus myth. The patient also features in another passage of *The Interpretation of Dreams*, in Section (β), 'Dreams of the Death of Persons of whom the Dreamer is Fond', precisely just before Freud's explanation of the Oedipus complex: 'On another occasion I had an opportunity of obtaining a deep insight into the unconscious mind of a young man whose life was made almost impossible by an obsessional neurosis. He was unable to go out into the street because he was tortured by the fear that he would kill everyone he met. He spent his days in preparing his alibi in case he might be charged with one of the murders committed in the town. It is unnecessary to add that he was a man of equally high morals and education. The analysis (which, incidentally, led to his recovery) showed that the basis of this distressing obsession was an impulse to murder his somewhat over-severe father. This impulse, to his astonishment, had been consciously expressed when he was seven years old, but it had, of course, originated much earlier in his childhood. After his father's painful illness and death, the patient's obsessional self-reproaches appeared – he was in his 31st year at the time – taking the shape of a phobia transferred on to strangers. A person, he felt, who was capable of wanting to push his own father over a precipice from the top of a mountain was not to be trusted to respect the lives of those less closely related to him; he was quite right to shut himself up in his room' (*ID* 260). The fact that this patient had since recovered not only gave Freud confidence in his medical and therapeutic abilities, but also reassured him the danger that he faced in making himself aware of his own hostile impulses was only relative.

Freud was then able to pin down the phantasy on which the dream hinged. His two recent travelling-companions had probably intended to have sexual intercourse on the train during the night, and had been disturbed by him. 'This phantasy went back [. . .] to a scene of early childhood in which the child, probably driven by sexual curiosity, had forced his way into his parents' bedroom and been turned out of it by his father's orders' (*ID* 458–9). Freud had already postulated several times, in the manuscripts he sent to Fliess, that his patients' phantasies and dreams originated in 'primal scenes'. This is the first time that the primal scene is mentioned by Freud in connection with one of his own dreams. It had already been implicit in the probably recent recollection and analysis of the childhood dream of 'My mother and the bird-beaked figures'. But he did not yet specify its connection with 'scatology', or indicate the exact circumstances of its occurrence in his childhood. He continued to present the primal scene more as a general fact than as a personal experience.

THE 'OPEN-AIR CLOSET' DREAM (JULY–AUGUST 1898)

Some nights later, Freud had a more overtly anal dream. It came after a hot summer's day – which could not have been a Sunday, for we know that Freud delivered a lecture that evening. Grinstein (G 434) has established that apart from July 18 and 19, when Freud went on the journey that instigated the 'Hollthurn' dream, the hottest days in Vienna – excluding Sundays, and before Freud left for his summer holidays – were Saturday, July 23, Thursday, August 4 and Monday, August 8. It was also at the end of July that Freud had a 'congress' with Fliess (whether before or after this dream, and whether in Munich or in Aussee, is unknown; cf. the letter of July 30 already quoted on p. 276).

On that very hot afternoon, then, a tired and depressed Freud, who was unhappy with his lecture on the connection between hysteria and the perversions, longed to join his family at Aussee, with its landscape of hills and bushes. One of the people who had attended his lecture followed him to a café and began to flatter him embarrassingly, explaining, says Freud, 'how I had cleansed the *Augean stables* of errors and prejudices in my theory of the neuroses'. Before going to sleep, Freud leafed through a recently published edition of Rabelais illustrated by Garnier and read one of Conrad Ferdinand Meyer's short stories, *Die Leiden eines Knaben* (A boy's sorrows), which reminded him of the childhood scene that had featured in his preceding dream. (Fliess, it will be remembered, had recommended Meyer to Freud, who subsequently became an avid reader of his works. The same day that Freud had returned from Aussee, on June 20, he sent Fliess a brief essay on a short story by Meyer, *Die Richterin*, which, after *Werther* and *Hamlet*, was the third literary work to be subjected to psychoanalysis (*F* 317–18); in it, Freud pointed to the latent theme of an emotional attachment for one's sister in a manner that foreshadowed his subsequent work on Jensen's *Gradiva* (1907*a*).) Freud then fell asleep and had a dream:

'I will here give as an instance a dream in which the indifferent feeling-tone of the content of the dream can be explained by the antithesis between the dream-thoughts. It is a short dream, which will fill every reader with disgust.

'*A hill, on which there was something like an open-air closet: a very long seat with a large hole at the end of it. Its back edge was thickly covered with small heaps of faeces* [Kot] *of all sizes and degrees of freshness. There were bushes behind the seat. I micturated on the seat; a long stream of urine washed everything clean; the lumps of faeces* [Kotplatzen] *came away easily and fell into the opening. It was as though at the end there was still some left*' (*ID* 468–9).

The dream and its analysis are to be found in Section H, 'Affects in Dreams', of Chapter 6, 'The Dream-Work' (*ID* 468–71), just after the dream of the 'Castle by the sea'. Grinstein devotes a chapter to it (G, Chapter 18).

Freud's remarks show that the dream reacted against his weariness of the previous day and feeling of displeasure at his own worthlessness by supplying him with reasons for megalomania. He is the Hercules who has discovered the infantile aetiology of the neuroses; he has thus saved his own children from falling ill; he is highly esteemed by his patients; he is Gulliver, who, by urinating, extinguished the great fire in Lilliput; he is Gargantua, who revenged himself in the same way on the Parisians by sitting astride the towers of Notre-Dame (which Freud repeatedly visited when he was in Paris). As soon as Freud intervenes, the faeces are washed away. In other words, '*Afflavit et dissipati sunt*' ('He blew and they were scattered') – the inscription on the medal struck to commemorate the destruction by the English of the 'invincible' Spanish Armada. Freud quoted the inscription, this time correctly ('*Flavit*', not '*Afflavit*'), in a letter to Fliess of January 3, 1897, mentioning that he intended one day to put it at the head of one of his future chapters (cf. p. 176).

The dream is an example of what one might call the neutralisation of affects, a notion that appears only in the second version of *The Interpretation of Dreams*:

'The day-time mood of revulsion and disgust persisted into the dream in so far as it was able to provide almost the entire material of its manifest content. But during the night a contrary mood of powerful and even exaggerated self-assertiveness arose and displaced the former one. The content of the dream had to find a form which would enable it to express both the delusions of inferiority and the megalomania in the same material. The compromise between them produced an ambiguous [*zweideutig* – literally, 'with two meanings'] dream-content; but it also resulted in an indifferent feeling-tone owing to the mutual inhibition of these contrary impulses.

'According to the theory of wish-fulfilment, this dream would not have become possible if the antithetical megalomanic train of thought (which, it is true, was suppressed, but had a pleasurable tone) had not emerged in addition to the feeling of disgust. For what is distressing may not be represented in a dream; nothing in our dream-thoughts which is distressing can force an entry into a dream unless it at the same time lends a disguise to the fulfilment of the wish' (*ID* 470–71).

I propose to enlarge upon Freud's comments by stressing first of all, as does Grinstein, his identification with three heroes, Hercules, Gulliver, and Gargantua – one Greek, one English and one French, an allusion to the three cultures, apart from German culture, that were important for Freud.

Hercules cleaned out the stables of King Augeas, which contained 3,000 head of cattle, in a single day. He did so by making a breach in the surrounding wall and diverting the waters of the nearby rivers of Alpheus and Peneus (a name that recalls the word 'penis') through the stables. One of the themes here, though it is latent in the dream, is the transition from the anal to the urethral stage; another is that of instinctual control, which Freud took up again in *Civilization and its Discontents* (1930*a*) and in his paper 'The Acquisition and Control of Fire' (1932*a*). The symbolic equation: faeces = gift is represented by a piece of furniture, similar to the seat of the closet in the dream, which had been given to him by a grateful woman patient.

Like Gulliver, Freud is a kind of traveller who has seen strange things.

To put out the fire that had started in the palace of the Lilliputian Queen, Gulliver urinated on it. As punishment for that crime, he had the choice between being put to death and having his eyes put out (cf. the blinded Oedipus). This is an obvious allusion to the infantile belief that a boy engages in sexual intercourse by urinating in the 'palace' of his mother; urine puts out the 'fire' of sexual desire (cf. 1932*a*).

Lastly, the dream reproduces one of Jules Garnier's 151 coloured illustrations (Plate XVI to be precise) for *Rabelais et l'Oeuvre* (1st edition, 1897), which were unbound and separate from the text in a cover of their own (so that Freud could have turned them over 'leaf by leaf', as in the memory recalled by the 'Botanical monograph' dream). Notre-Dame Cathedral is depicted on a hill, as in the dream; Gargantua is 'astride' it and is urinating into the 'hole' between the two towers; a long stream of urine is washing everything clean; the various browns used for the buildings and the shading correspond to the heaps of faeces in the dream. The transcription could not be clearer: in his dream, Freud substitutes himself for the father astride the mother (= Notre-Dame); intercourse is urethral, and not yet genital. The underlying memory has not yet been clearly recalled.

But as often with Freud a heroic or megalomanic identification is matched by a masochistic identification with the victim. Here, he identifies with Julian Boufflers, the central character in Meyer's short story, *Die Leiden eines Knaben*. Grinstein (G 440–44) draws a detailed parallel between Freud and Julian. Both had been cursed and rejected by their fathers, who believed them incapable of intellectual achievement. Both wished to be recognised by their fathers (Julian was a son by a first marriage, Sigismund by a second), as well as by the King, in Julian's case, and by the Emperor of Austria, in Freud's (he wanted to be appointed professor by him). Both were criticised, one by his schoolmates, the other by his professional colleagues. Julian achieved his ambition in his dreams (during delirium), while Freud did so by discovering the 'secret of dreams'. They were both given a strict education and probably beaten, Julian by the Jesuits, and Sigismund by his Catholic nurse; in either case, the educators obtained money through fraudulent means. Both were innocent victims: Julian was caught up in the machinations of the church against his father, Marshal Boufflers, while Sigmund suffered from anti-Semitism. Both were the object of false accusations: Freud was constantly trying to exonerate himself in his dreams; Julian was persuaded by a schoolfriend to draw a bee and label it '*bête à miel*' ('animal with honey'); when the schoolteacher, Father Amiel, saw it he understood the pun on *bête Amiel* ('stupid Amiel'), with the result that Julian was severely beaten by another Father, fell ill and subsequently died.

It is worth noting in both cases the importance of the 'double meaning' and the danger of releasing aggressive and sexual instincts. Earlier on, Julian had been seen sitting with his girlfriend, Mirabelle, and had made fun of Father Amiel's 'nose' (= penis). The twofold Oedipal wish is punished by the lash and by death: one and the same problem faced Gulliver, Panurge and Freud, who must also have been struck by the similarity of first names. His younger brother *Julius* (which is almost identical with Julian) had died; Freud feared the same fate. The illustrator of Rabelais, *Jules*-Arsène Garnier (1847–89), died in such destitution that his friends organised an exhibition of his Rabelais paintings to raise funds for his widow and children. But we cannot be sure that Freud knew of this.

This dream has a leit-motif – coming to the end of one's life, coming to nothing, coming to the final nothingness – whose origins and precise formulation were to become clear in the dream that followed shortly after it, that of 'Count Thun'. In the meantime, the conclusion that imposed itself on the dreamer was that the transition from the anal to the urethral stage was dangerous. The reason it was dangerous was that it implied recognition of the difference between the sexes and of the dangers that phantasy infers from that difference.

THE 'COUNT THUN' DREAM (AUGUST 1898)

Freud had this dream not long after its two predecessors, and like them its content is 'scatological'. It was also dreamt on a train, during the night he left Vienna for the summer holidays, and after a 'congress' with Fliess. 'Freud worked late that year. The children had been ill and his wife was in need of rest. So instead of joining them and infecting them with a cold he had just contracted he went early in August to Munich. [. . .] Then Minna joined him and they travelled together to Kufstein and Innsbruck' (J I, 368). As Aussee is on the Vienna–Salzburg–Munich railway line, it is likely that Freud stopped there briefly to see his family. That would explain why the preamble to the dream mentions that he took 'the train for my summer holiday at Aussee'.[1] Minna Bernays, it will be remembered, had come to live with the Freuds in October 1896, around the time when Jacob Freud died; in July 1897 and June 1898, Freud spent a weekend with her in Salzburg. But this was the first time they had set off together for a holiday.

1. Another, less likely hypothesis is that Freud was only going for the weekend to Aussee; in that case, the dream would date either from mid-June (when he found his family 'with colds and frozen stiff') or from the end of July (when he met Fliess). Some doubt, then, hangs over the chronological order of the 'Hollthurn', 'Open-air closet', and 'Count Thun' dreams, though this in no way affects their obvious affinity. Uncertainty over the date of the dream concerns only the month, not the year, as Freud's associations refer to the Jubilee for Emperor Franz Josef I, which took place in 1898.

In the same passage, Jones gives a detailed itinerary of their trip; and Freud wrote about it enthusiastically in a letter to Fliess written on August 20 after his return to Aussee.

But Freud, when describing the day's residues, fails to mention his projected trip despite its importance to him. It was at about this time that he was beginning to discover in his sister-in-law an intelligent and open-minded person with whom he could discuss his investigations: Minna replaced not only Martha, who was worn out by the task of bringing up her many children and could no longer follow her husband in his intellectual speculations, but also Fliess, with whom Freud disagreed more and more on points of theory. It is worth noting, too, that the 'specimen dream' of 'Irma's injection' occurred shortly after Freud's arrival in Bellevue for the summer holidays in 1895, and that the discovery of the Oedipus complex took place on his return from the summer holidays of 1897. Holidays were a time when he could rest, be on the move, and think, all at the same time: he cathected them as a period when he could be free, i.e. fulfil his wishes in life and in his dreams more freely, and also as a time when he expected to come up with some new discovery.

The day's residues that Freud does mention are discussed at two different points in his book. In the first passage, which includes a complete description of the dream (quoted below), he refers to his encounter with the Austrian Prime Minister, Count Thun, on a railway platform. In the second passage, where only part of the dream is described, Freud mentions three other events of the previous day: a) he had hired a cab to take him to Dornbach on the outskirts of Vienna; the driver did not know the way, so Freud had to guide him; b) he had called off a trip to Italy he was due to make with his brother, Alexander: 'This cancellation had been a kind of punishment for the complaints he used to make that I was in the habit of overtiring him [. . .] by insisting upon moving too rapidly from place to place' (*ID* 432); but Freud omits to mention another reason for the cancellation: whereas up to then he had always gone to Italy with Alexander (in August 1895, September 1896, September 1897 with Martha as well, and April 1898 – to Istria, which was not Italian at that time), on this occasion it was with Minna that he intended to travel; we find here the same latent thought as in the 'Hollthurn' dream: he prefers the sister to the brother; c) Alexander had accompanied Freud to the station, then gone to the suburban railway station adjoining the main line terminus in order to take a train to the suburb of Purkersdorf, despite the fact that he could equally well have reached his destination by taking the same train as Freud and getting off at Purkersdorf.

Let me fill in some of the social and political background to the dream.

Emperor Franz Josef was due to celebrate his 50th Jubilee on December 2, 1898. In a letter to Fliess of February 9, 1898 (*F* 299), Freud had mentioned his hopes – which were to prove unfounded – of being invested as professor on that day. He also said he had had a 'delightful' dream, which was unfortunately unpublishable (cf. p. 265). The emperor had come to the throne on December 2, 1848, at the age of 18, following the abdication of his uncle, Emperor Ferdinand, and before the Czech, Italian and Hungarian uprisings were crushed. Jones mentions that Freud's mother had moved to Vienna with her parents while still a child: 'She had vivid memories of the 1848 revolution there; she had preserved a picture with shot holes dating from that event (J I, 3). Sigismund must have been struck by his mother's reminiscences.

Indeed, the memory of the various revolutions which broke out in most European countries in 1848, and which were all followed by a period of brutal repression, was still very much alive at the end of the nineteenth century: it fuelled the resentment of the Czech and Hungarian nationalist movements which were beginning once again to perturb the Austro-Hungarian Monarchy (until 1867 known as the Hapsburg Empire). The dream alludes to two liberal-minded prime ministers who tried to satisfy those aspirations, but who at the same time were associated with the rise of anti-Semitism. Count Taaffe (1833–95) was prime minister from 1868 to 1870, and from 1879 to 1893; he made concessions to the Czechs, persuaded them to abandon their policy of abstaining from participation in parliamentary affairs, and authorised the Czech language at Prague University. Count Thun (1847–1916), governor of Bohemia from 1889 to 1896, during which time he attempted in vain to reconcile the Czechs with the Germans, had been prime minister since March 1898. He was unsuccessful in office and resigned in 1899. As though echoing that context, the atmosphere of the dream is undoubtedly a 'revolutionary' one.

In view of the importance and length of the comments that can be made on this dream, I have decided, in the interests of clarity, to cast some of them in the form of footnotes to the dream itself. Freud's own footnotes are indicated as such. In all other cases, the footnotes are by me or by Eva Rosenblum, who was particularly helpful to me in the study of this dream.

On the train taking him to Aussee, probably the first stage of his journey before joining Minna, Freud had the following dream:

'The next dream calls for a rather long preamble:

'I had driven to the Western Station [in Vienna] to take the train for my summer holiday at Aussee, but had arrived on the platform while an earlier train, going to Ischl, was still standing in the station. There I had seen Count Thun who was once again travelling to Ischl for an audience with the Emperor. Though it was raining, he had arrived in an open carriage. He had walked straight in through the entrance for the Local Trains. The ticket inspector at the gate had not recognised him and had tried to take his ticket, but he had waved the man aside with a curt motion of his hand and without giving any explanation. After the train for Ischl had gone out, I ought by rights to have left the platform again and returned to the waiting room; and it had cost me some trouble to arrange matters so that I was allowed to stop on the platform. I had passed the time in keeping a look-out to see if anyone came along and tried to get a reserved compartment by exercising some sort of "pull". I had intended in that case to make a loud protest: that is to say to claim equal rights. Meantime I had been humming a tune to myself which I recognised as Figaro's aria from *Le Nozze di Figaro*):

> Se vuol ballare, signor contino,
> Se vuol ballare, signor contino,
> Il chitarino le suonero
> [If my Lord Count is inclined to go dancing,
> If my Lord Count is inclined to go dancing,
> I'll be quite ready to play him a tune]

(It is a little doubtful whether anyone else would have recognised the tune.)

'The whole evening I had been in high spirits and in a combative mood. I had chaffed my waiter and my cab-driver – without, I hope, hurting their feelings. And now all kinds of insolent and revolutionary ideas were going through my head, in keeping with Figaro's words and with my recollections of Beaumarchais' comedy which I had seen acted by the *Comédie Française*. I thought of the phrase about the great gentlemen who had taken the trouble to be born, and of the *droit du Seigneur* which Count Almaviva tried to exercise over Susanna. I thought, too, of how our malicious opposition journalists made jokes over Count Thun's name, calling him instead "Count Nichtsthun".[1] Not that I envied him. He was on his way to a difficult audience with the Emperor, while *I* was the real Count Do-nothing – just off on my holidays. There followed all sorts of enjoyable plans for the holidays. At this point a gentleman came on to the platform whom I recognised as a Government invigilator at medical examinations, and who by his activities in that capacity had won the flattering nickname of "Government bedfellow" [*Regierungsbeischläfer*][2]. He asked to be given a

1. A pun: *thun* means 'to do' in German, and *nichtsthun* 'to do nothing'. Since the reformed spelling introduced in German-speaking countries in 1901 (cf. E. Ribeiro Hawelka, 1974), this verb has been spelt *tun*; so in modern German the pun is only a phonetic one.

2. *Beischläfer* means 'concubine' (literally, 'he who sleeps (*Schläfer*) with (*bei*)'. *Beischlaf* means 'sexual intercourse' (cf. Freud's mistake over the word 'by' in the 'Hollthurn' dream).

first-class half-compartment to himself in virtue of his official position, and I heard one railwayman saying to another: "Where are we to put the gentleman with the half first-class ticket?" This, I thought to myself, was a fine example of privilege; after all *I* had paid the full first-class fare. And I did in fact get a compartment to myself, but not in a corridor coach, so that there would be no lavatory available during the night. I complained to an official without any success; but I got my own back on him by suggesting that he should at all events have a hole made in the floor of the compartment to meet the possible needs of passengers. And in fact I did wake up at a quarter to three in the morning with a pressing need to micturate, having had the following dream:

'*A crowd of people, a meeting of students.*[1] – *A count (Thun or Taaffe) was speaking. He was challenged to say something about the Germans, and declared with a contemptuous gesture*[2] *that their favourite flower was colt's foot* [Huflattich][3], *and put some sort of dilapidated leaf – or rather the crumpled skeleton of a leaf – into his buttonhole. I fired up – so I fired up* [ich fahre auf],[4] *though I was surprised at my taking such an attitude.*

'(Then, less distinctly:) *It was as though I was in the Aula;*[5] *the entrances were cordoned off and we had to escape.*[6] *I made my way through a series of beautifully furnished rooms, evidently ministerial or public apartments, with furniture upholstered in a colour between brown and violet;*[7] *at last I came to a corridor,*[8] *in which a*

1. The setting and atmosphere are reminiscent of the Irma dream: a) a representation of the unconscious; b) a regression to adolescence ('students'); c) the hubbub of multiple and contradictory identifications that all start talking at the same time in the dream.

2. An allusion to the bed-wetting scene at the age of two, which Freud was shortly to recall: the boy-king Sigismund is speaking. Asked what he has to say about his bed-wetting, an act that has caused him to be mocked, he says something that makes everybody laugh.

3. The colt's foot here replaces the dandelion, whose leaves are indeed dilapidated, as the dream goes on to indicate (whereas the colt's foot has large leaves which cannot become dilapidated). Both are weeds. The colt's foot and the dandelion are discussed at greater length further on.

4. This repetition crept into my record of the dream, apparently through inadvertence. I have let it stand, since the analysis showed that it was significant (Freud's footnote). *Ich fahre auf* has two meanings: 'I fire up', but also 'I travel up' or 'drive up', the sense in which it is used repeatedly later in the dream and in Freud's associations.

5. The Aula is the great ceremonial hall of the University; cf. the 'hall' in which the guests are received at the beginning of the Irma dream. The word also means a royal court: a royal councillor is an 'aulic' councillor. This is an allusion to the professorship that Freud hoped to obtain on the occasion of the Emperor's Jubilee.

6. The same theme as in the dream of 'My son, the Myops': 'It had become necessary to remove the children to safety.'

7. The 'series of beautifully furnished rooms' remind Freud of 'public women'. They contrast with the single room that housed Sigismund and his parents in Freiberg. It was there, in the bed-wetting scene that the dream brings back to him, that Freud promised his father he would buy him 'a nice *new red* bed'. The 'colour between brown and violet', which recurs later in the dream as 'violet-brown', was the colour of the *new* trunk Freud had just bought for the journey.

8. The dream fulfils Freud's wish to have a corridor, so he could get to the lavatory.

housekeeper was sitting, an elderly stout woman.[1] *I avoided speaking to her, but she evidently thought I had a right to pass, for she asked whether she should accompany me with a lamp. I indicated to her, by word or gesture, that she was to stop on the staircase; and I felt I was being very cunning in thus avoiding inspection at the exit. I got downstairs and found a narrow and steep ascending path, along which I went.*[2]

'(Becoming indistinct again) . . . *It was as though the second problem was to get out of the town, just as the first one had been to get out of the house. I was driving in a cab and ordered the driver to drive me to a station. "I can't drive with you along the railway-line itself," I said, after he had raised some objection, as though I had overtired him.*[3] *It was as if I had already driven with him for some of the distance one normally travels by train. The stations were cordoned off. I wondered whether to go to Krems or Znaim, but reflected that the Court would be in residence there, so I decided in favour of Graz,*[4] *or some such place. I was now sitting in the compartment, which was like a carriage on the Stadtbahn* [the suburban railway]*; and in my buttonhole I had a peculiar plaited, long-shaped object, and beside it some violet-brown violets made of a stiff material.*[5] *This greatly struck people.* (At this point the scene broke off.)

'*Once more I was in front of the station, but this time in the company of an elderly gentleman. I thought of a plan for remaining unrecognised; and then saw that this plan had already been put into effect. It was as though thinking and experiencing* [erleben][6] *were one and the same thing. He appeared to be blind, at all events with one eye,*[7] *and I handed him* [vorhalten] *a male glass urinal* [Uringlas][8] *(which we had to buy or had bought in town). So I was a sick-nurse and had to give him the urinal because he*

1. The word used here is not *Frau* ('woman'), but *Frauenzimmer* (literally, 'women's apartment'), a derogatory word for 'woman'. Cf. the female attendant that the boy refuses to kiss in the dream of 'My son, the Myops'. This is both the tolerant nurse, Monika Zajíc, and the witty hostess whose social evenings were greatly enjoyed by Freud: both women caught him *in flagrante delicto* – failing to be clean in the first case, and failing to solve two riddles, which I shall examine later, in the second.

2. The topography of this passage resembles that of the screen memory analysed by Freud at the beginning of 1899, which consists of a sloping meadow and a house at the top. What is more, the house in Freiberg had a staircase leading up to two bedrooms, the Zajícs' and the Freuds'. The nurse (the 'elderly stout woman') lived with the Zajícs and worked for the Freuds.

3. A condensation of two day's residues: the cab-driver who could not find his way, and the friction between Freud and his brother – each had in turn refused to accompany the other; Alexander used to complain that Sigmund overtired him when they went on trips together.

4. Krems in Lower Austria and Znaim in Moravia were neither of them Imperial residences. – Graz is the capital of the province of Styria (footnote in *SE*). Freud associates Graz with the celebrated 'boast' of extremely well-off people: 'What's the price of Graz?'

5. The spikes of colt's foot and dandelion are violet-brown and reddish: a symbolic representation of an erect penis. In his analysis, Freud associates the object on his lapel with a kind of buttonhole known in slang as a *Mädchenfänger*, or 'girl-catcher'.

6. Literally, 'to experience through life'; it gives the noun *Erlebnis*, which means 'lived experience'.

7. Cf. the 'Close the eyes' and 'My son, the Myops' dreams.

8. Literally, 'urine glass'. In his analysis, Freud specifies that it is a *männliches Glas* (a male glass), which cannot fail to suggest the *männliches Glied* (the male organ).

was blind. If the ticket-collector [Kondukteur] *were to see us like that, he would be certain to let us get away without noticing us. Here the man's attitude and his micturating penis appeared in plastic form.*[1] (This was the point at which I awoke, feeling a need to micturate.)' (*ID* 208–211).

The dream and its analysis come in Section B, 'Infantile Material as a Source of Dreams', of Chapter 5, 'The Material and Sources of Dreams'; they illustrate the fact that dreams are related to events not only from the previous day but from childhood (*ID* 208–18). Freud returns to this dream on three other occasions. In Section C of the same chapter, 'The Somatic Sources of Dreams', the dream is mentioned briefly to show 'how an accidental physical need [in this case the need to urinate] can be linked up with the most intense (but at the same time most intensely suppressed) mental impulses' (*ID* 233). Later on, the dream illustrates 'the dream-work in the very act of intentionally fabricating an absurdity for which there was absolutely no occasion in the material' (in Section G, 'Absurd Dreams', of Chapter 6, 'The Dream-Work'). Freud reveals the dream-thought: 'It is absurd to be proud of one's ancestry; it is better to be an ancestor oneself'; this 'absurd' dream is therefore a variant of the 'dreams of a dead father'; we also learn that Freud had called off a trip he was going to make to Italy with Alexander, who accompanied him to the station (*ID* 431–4). Finally, a brief reference in parentheses points out that the same childhood memory, that of the primal scene, lay behind this dream and the 'Open-air closet' dream (*ID* 470). Grinstein devotes two chapters to this dream (G, Chapters 4 and 5).

Freud analyses this dream at greater length than any other in *The Interpretation of Dreams* except the Irma dream. He says that he has held back no part of his interpretation from the reader except for the name of a court councillor and some sexual material. Also pertinent to the interpretation, in my view, are the dream's agoraphobic and claustrophobic elements (he had to escape from the university, and then from the town; the corridor; the steep ascending path); they are obviously a transposition of the feeling of being cooped up in a compartment with no corridor and therefore with no means of going to the lavatory; the intensity of these elements may be ascribed to the railway phobia which Freud had already elucidated, and which, although now residual, was brought to life again by his departure for his holidays.

The dream marks a continuation of Freud's gradual detachment from the omnipotent image of the father. The first section of Freud's analysis

1. Under Jewish law, a son is not allowed to look at his father's sexual organs (cf. pp. 172 and 299).

(*ID* 211–14) refers first to a series of relatively recent memories: the school conspiracy against a bad German-language teacher; the memory of a scene in Shakespeare's *Henry VI Part 3* representing the beginning of the War of the Roses (Richard Plantagenet of the House of York, symbolised by the white rose, is determined to depose King Henry VI of the House of Lancaster, symbolised by the red rose; eventually, Henry's son defeats Richard's son, King Richard III, and becomes King Henry VII); an anti-Semitic provocation during a train journey; the contemporary war of the carnations in Vienna (anti-Semites wore white carnations in their buttonholes, and Social Democrats red ones); a discussion at a German students' club, some years earlier, with the future Social Democrat leader, Viktor Adler, in the course of which Freud boorishly defended materialism.

Then come some deeper symbols. There is the theme of life and death: all flowers wither (cf. the 'Botanical monograph' dream), but that should be no cause for grief. There are scatological themes: a series of insults – 'swine', 'sow', 'dog', 'giraffe' ['*Affe*' is the German for ape], and 'donkey'; the three bodily functions (excreting, urinating and breaking wind), derived from Zola's *Germinal* – *pisser* (Freud thought that the correct translation of *pissenlit* – spelt by him *pisse-en-lit* – in the novel was 'colt's foot', whereas it in fact means 'dandelion'), *chier* (which sounds a little like *chien*), and *péter* (Zola describes children's farting competitions). Freud resolutely explores the phantasies of the anal stage and finds that they are connected with feelings not only of rivalry and rebellion but of megalomania and boastfulness. He thus identifies the origins of the ambition which now expresses itself in his works.

The second set of associations to the dream (*ID* 214–15) contains an allusion to an important personage of the court (*Aula*), who suffered from incontinence of the bowels, and to a female symbol (the series of rooms). These associations are above all a representation in images of the very mechanisms of the dream-work. In 1911, Freud added a footnote referring to an interesting paper by Silberer, who 'tried to show from this part of my dream that the dream-work can succeed in reproducing not only the latent dream-thoughts but also the psychical processes that take place during the formation of dreams'. In 1914, he completed the footnote as follows: 'But he is, I think, overlooking the fact that "the psychical processes that take place during the formation of dreams" were, like the rest, part of the *material* of my thoughts. In this boastful dream I was evidently proud of having discovered those processes.' This sheds light on the meaning of this fragment of the dream. Freud has left the University, where he hopes to return as a professor. He has deviated from official science; he has blazed his own trail, first enlightened by the elderly woman (a condensation of Breuer and the nurse?), then escaping her inspection and embarking alone on a steep path.

The third set of associations, which it is convenient to discuss here even though Freud introduces them at a later point in his book (*ID* 431–4), concerns Freud's recent refusal to accompany his brother Alexander to Italy, the identification of the cab-driver with Count Thun, who was the driver of the State coach of Austria, and the two easy riddles that Freud failed to solve at a soirée. These two riddles confirm my theory about Freud's discovery of the Oedipus myth, i.e. that he was deeply preoccupied by the problem of filiation. Here is the first of them:

Der Herr befiehlt's,	[With the master's request
Der Kutscher tut's,	The driver complies:
Ein jeder hat's,	By all men possessed
Im Grabe ruht's.	In the graveyard it lies.]

The answer, *Vorfahren*, is a pun, similar to the *Vögeln* of the dream of 'My mother and the bird-beaked figures'; *Vorfahren* as a noun means 'ancestors', and as a verb 'to drive up'; it contains the root *fahren* that is found throughout this dream.

Here is the second riddle:

Der Herr befiehlt's	[With the master's request
Der Kutscher tut's	The driver complies:
Nicht jeder hat's,	Not by all men possessed
In der Wiege ruht's.	In the cradle it lies.]

The answer is *Nachkommen*, which as a noun means 'descendants', and as a verb 'to come after' or 'obey'.

The meaning of this part of the dream is therefore: 'It is absurd to be proud of one's ancestry; it is better to be an ancestor oneself.' The context of the dream ('I felt I was being very cunning . . .') ties in with the notion of boastfulness.

The fourth part of Freud's analysis (*ID* 215–17) mentions a series of thoughts about his father and two childhood scenes resulting at last in a personal experience of the primal scene which the previous series of dreams had led us to expect. During the days leading up to his death, Freud's father could no longer control his sphincters. The associations which Freud relegates to footnotes refer to scenes where his father, now in his second childhood, is maltreated. The dream expresses a rebellious and recalcitrant attitude towards authority, whether paternal or political. The first of the two childhood scenes is known to Freud only through descriptions by other people. 'It appears that when I was two years old I still occasionally *wetted the bed*, and when I was reproached for this I *consoled* my father by promising to buy him a nice *new red* bed in N., the nearest town of any size. [. . .] This promise of mine exhibited all the megalomania of childhood.' Jones has established that the town of N. is Neutitschein, but fails to point out its significance when used by Sigismund in his reply (*Neu . . . Schein* = new appearance). That reply, like the two riddles, is based on a pun: the child who was made to feel ashamed of his bed-wetting answered back by being 'cunning' on another level, a verbal level. As for the colour red, which tends to be the favourite colour of children, it can probably be explained by the fact that at that time fine wooden furniture was often painted. In 1914, Freud added: 'We have also learned from the psychoanalysis of neurotic subjects the intimate connection between bed-wetting and the character trait of ambition.'

The second scene took place when Freud was seven or eight years old: 'One evening before going to sleep I disregarded the rules which modesty lays down and obeyed the calls of nature in my parents' bedroom while they were present. In the course of his reprimand, my father let fall the words: "The boy will come to nothing"'.[1] This was a terrible blow and had haunted him ever since – a humiliation which determined the final pattern of his ambition. That ambition was not merely, as he later claimed (1908*b*), the relic of character traits formed at the anal stage. It had an intersubjective meaning: it was the particular channel through which Freud attempted to belie his father's curse and get his true worth recognised by other people. 'References to this scene are still constantly recurring in my dreams and are always linked with an enumeration of my achievements and successes, as though I wanted to say: "You see, I *have* come to something".' The dream, then, contained allusions to Freud's two latest discoveries – an explanation of dreams, and an explanation of hysterical symptoms (cf. 'It was as though thinking and experiencing were one and the same thing'). The expunging of his father's affront then began to look very much like revenge: 'The older man (clearly my father, since his blindness in one eye

1. Freud's account of this memory – no doubt because of his embarrassment – leaves certain questions unanswered. What 'call of nature' did he obey – urination or defecation? Was he still sleeping in his parents' bedroom, as he used to in Freiberg, or had he come in 'unintentionally'? Did he relieve himself on the floor? The link with the preceding scene and with the final image of the dream strongly suggests that it was a case of enuresis. The parallel with the childhood memory, referred to in the third person, that comes at the end of Freud's analysis of the 'Hollthurn' dream ('The child, probably driven by sexual curiosity, had forced his way into his parents' bedroom and been turned out of it by his father's orders'; cf. p. 332) has led all commentators to suppose that Sigismund entered his parents' bedroom out of voyeurism and urinated on the floor (out of pleasure? excitement? fear?). My own analysis of the dreams Freud had had since the dream of 'My mother and the bird-beaked figures' leads me to the same conclusion.

referred to his unilateral glaucoma) was now micturating in front of me, just as I had in front of him in my childhood' (which confirms that the call of nature Sigismund obeyed in his parents' bedroom was urination); the sick father was grateful that thanks to cocaine his son had been able to operate on his glaucoma painlessly; and the son, in his dream, was happy to make fun of him – for two reasons: because he was blind, and because he had to hand him the urinal.

The wealth of detail in the dream and in Freud's analysis of it preclude any exhaustive examination of it here. I shall limit myself to a summary of four of its aspects (as I have with earlier dreams).

As regards 'transference' on to Freud's contemporaries, it should be noted that Fliess, who is completely absent from the dream-thoughts, has been replaced by Freud's younger brother, Alexander, and by his sister-in-law, Minna; the former is the subject of aggressive rejection, the latter the subject of prohibited incestuous desire.

As regards the infantile wish, there is an attempt to take revenge on the prohibiting father figure: to soil him with urine and faeces, to devalue him, to disobey him by chasing girls and going with public women, and to belie the curse once uttered by him by having ambitions and achieving them; Freud identifies both with Count Thun, who is received by the Emperor, and with the literal meaning of his name (*thun* = to do): he has indeed done much.

As regards the body image, the keynote is one of micturition and excretion (the sitting position, occupied seats, the smell of violets, faeces coming out of the anus, crumpled leaves of paper).

As regards the representation of the psychical apparatus and the discovery of psychoanalysis, the need to avoid the control of the super-ego in order to make progress, and the need to 'go it alone' have already been represented on many occasions. The phantasy of the primal scene, which marks the main step forward achieved by analysis of this dream, is present not in the dream-content, but in the phrases that link together the various sections of the description of the dream – 'Becoming indistinct again', 'At this point the scene broke off', 'This was the point at which I awoke, feeling a need to micturate.' Also worth noting is the fact that there are more references to literary works in this dream than in any other of Freud's dreams: he must therefore have felt an increasingly urgent need to produce proof through cultural references.

The key word in the dream is *colt's foot*. Because of its similarity to the *dandelion* (whose diuretic properties are well known, hence the English variant name of 'pissabed', and French name *pissenlit*, or, as Freud refers to it, *pisse-en-lit*), it eventually leads to the glass urinal. The colt's foot and the dandelion both belong to the Compositae family, their main difference being the shape of their leaves, broad and heart-shaped in the first case, and long and notched in the second.

The English word dandelion comes from the French variant name *dent-de-lion* (lion's tooth), which refers to the jagged teeth of the leaves. The German word for dandelion, *Löwenzahn*, means exactly the same thing. In his associations, Freud alludes to other popular names for the dandelion: *Salathund*, or 'dog salad' (paralleled by the English variant name, 'dog-in-the-manger'; the French for 'dog', *chien*, reminded Freud of *chier*), and 'mole salad'; its young leaves are often eaten in salads. Freud points out in his analysis that the word for colt's foot, *Huflattich*, literally means 'hoof lettuce'. This contemptuous term (cf. 'the contemptuous gesture' in the dream) means, in Freud's view, that it is a salad plant which deserves no better fate than to be nibbled by hoofed animals (as can be seen from the English name, colt's foot). *Huflattich* is assonant with *Huffladen* ('cow-pat') and with *flatus* ('wind', 'jet'), which comes from the Latin verb *flare* that is found in the motto *Flavit et dissipati sunt* already quoted by Freud (cf. p. 333–4): these are, therefore, scatological assonances. The scientific name for the colt's foot, *Tussilago farfara*, refers to its cough-curing properties (*tussis* = cough). The colt's foot and the dandelion are widespread in Europe; their yellow flowers blossom in spring or, in the mountains, in early summer. They are popularly regarded as stubborn 'weeds' that are difficult to get rid of. The milky fluid in the dandelion's hollow stem was once – erroneously – believed to be poisonous. In Freud's time at least (I am told by Eva Rosenblum) young children were warned that they might die if they touched its 'milk' and then ate bread. The French expression '*manger les pissenlits par la racine* (cf. the English 'pushing up the daisies') would seem to derive from that belief: the milk of the dandelion poisoned the 'dead' who consumed it. The analogy between the urethra and the dandelion's hollow stem is also found in the German expression *Pfaffenröhrl* (literally, 'priestling's tube'), a derisive term for the penis of curates, men supposed to have no sex life. In his associations, Freud recalls that at a recent *Gschnas* (a bohemian party during which rare objects were constructed out of preferably comic and worthless materials) a poisoned chalice, jokingly said to have belonged to Lucrezia Borgia and made out of a male urinal, was exhibited.

Throughout this series of associations, there is a condensation of three threats directed at children – when they are weaned, when they wet their beds, and when they attempt to masturbate: mothers and wet-nurses smear their nipples with some repulsive substance to stop the baby sucking; if you go on peeing in bed, you will never be married; if you make the milk come out of your penis, you will be poisoned. Thus, the colt's foot in this dream plays a role that is halfway between the *cyclamen* of the 'Botanical monograph' dream, and the *dandelion* of the screen memory that Freud interpreted at the beginning of 1899. The violet-brown colour of the colt's foot's elongated bud is echoed in this dream by the colour of the furniture in the public apartments and by the colour of the violets made of a stiff material which Freud wears in his buttonhole: this is an image of an erect penis, the anal-penis already suggested by the holothurian of the 'Hollthurn' dream. In the dream of the 'Botanical monograph', Freud mentions that he and his wife each had a favourite flower, the artichoke and the cyclamen respectively. This dream follows up the same idea: each sex has a corresponding botanical characteristic and a colour: an elongated violet-brown bud is the penis, while a little yellow flower represents a girl's sexual organs. The desire to 'deflower' the latter makes the former erect; but that is a conclusion which Freud arrived at only in early 1899. For the time being, he merely remarked: 'Notice, too, the juxtaposition in symbolism of the male urinal and the female trunk or box' (*ID* 216).

Let us return to the dreamer's relationship with the father figure and his use of cultural references. This dream spells out the adolescent's protest, already outlined in an earlier dream, 'Goethe's attack on Herr M.', against the father's prohibition as regards the company of loose women (either they give you syphilis or you get deeply involved with them and come down in the world). But it goes further than that. It derides the author of the threat – namely, that if you satisfy your sexual desires illegally, you will become a degenerate person – by turning it back against him. The representation of himself as a paralytic in the dream of 'Goethe's attack on Herr M.' is reversed in the 'Count Thun' dream into a representation of the father as being in a state of senile dementia: he has only one eye, he is doddering, he is losing his memory, and he is incontinent (allusions to the operation on his father for glaucoma some years previously, and to his recent terminal illness, both of which Freud attended).

This dream prompts a host of cultural references in Freud's mind. Sometimes they are works of protest, such as Beaumarchais' *Le mariage de Figaro* (1778), Rabelais' *Gargantua et Pantagruel* (1540–67), and Zola's *Germinal* (1885) and *La terre* (1888), in which sexual conflicts resulting in fatal 'accidents' or rapes in front of witnesses are presented as signs of the physical and social degeneration of syphilitics, defectives, and the old. In other cases, the theme is 'rebellion', as in Felix Dahn's *Odin's Consolation* (1880), which relates the myth of the god Odin, who is indirectly responsible for the death of his favourite son; as in Franz Grillparzer's play, *The Waves of the Sea and of Love* (1831), about the tribulations of Hero, who, just as she is about to break the vows of chastity she took when becoming a priestess, unintentionally causes the death of her beloved Leander; as in Conrad Ferdinand Meyer's short story, *Die Leiden eines Knaben* (cf. the previous dream of the 'Open-air closet'), in which a father gets rid of his son by a first marriage by sending him off to a Jesuit boarding school, where he is called 'an idiot' by his schoolmates and on one occasion is so violently beaten by a Father that he becomes delirious and dies of brain fever. Grinstein gives very detailed summaries of all these works, as well as of Oskar Panizza's play, *Das Liebeskonzil* (*The love council*), which is the last and most essential of all Freud's associations to this dream, and is described by him, in a footnote, as 'a strongly revolutionary literary play'.

Panizza, a writer and psychiatrist from Munich,[1] published his play in 1895. There were no re-editions of it for many years; and its first performance apparently took place in Paris only in 1968. The play is dedicated to the German writer, Ulrich von Hutten, who was connected with the Reformation movement, and who died, presumably of syphilis, at the age of 35 in 1523. The action takes place in 1495, the year that the first cases of syphilis reportedly appeared in Europe. God, the Virgin Mary, and Christ wish to punish the rampant debauchery of the human race and the Church. To do so, they call on the services of the Devil. He conjures up an extraordinarily seductive creature – beautiful, promiscuous and infected with syphilis – who sets about contaminating mankind. As she has been told to proceed in descending order of rank, she begins with the Pope.

The scandalous nature of the plot is reinforced by the way the characters are presented. God has a gammy leg, His sight and memory are failing, and He is too old to continue creating. The only thing that cheers Him up are the lubricious pranks of the 'angels', who, before they died, were perverse young girls. Freud makes a point that was missed not only by his contemporaries but by most theatre critics when the play was put on in Paris: 'God the Father is ignominiously treated as a paralytic old man' (*ID* 217 n.1). Thus, when the Pope catches syphilis as punishment for his lechery, he turns out to be following in God's footsteps. At the end of the 19th century, it was just beginning to be realised that general paralysis was one of the complications of syphilis and that syphilis could be hereditary:

1. Oskar Panizza (1853–1921) was prosecuted in Germany for most of his works, all of which were pamphlets against Catholicism or the Emperor. Although he took the precaution of getting *Das Liebeskonzil* published in Switzerland, it still resulted in his getting a year's prison sentence in Germany. In 1898, he sought refuge in Paris, where he continued to write his pamphlets. Freud was probably aware of this, and remembered his own stay in Paris in 1885–86, when he saw a performance of *Le mariage de Figaro* and read Rabelais and Zola. Panizza subsequently returned to Germany to try to prevent his property from being seized. Possibly syphilitic, and without any doubt paranoiac, he died insane (the first hospital to which he was confined in 1905 was the one where he had himself practised).

Christ is depicted in the play as suffering from motor ataxia and mental deficiency . . .

Panizza no doubt intended to show that degenerate Catholics were incapable of visualising God except in their own debauched and unwholesome image. Freud saw his message in terms of infantile phantasies: parents forbid children to do what they themselves did, while at the same time passing on to them their reprehensible wishes; it is because parents fornicate that children degenerate. Freud then recalled the childhood memory where 'one evening before going to sleep I disregarded the rules which modesty lays down and obeyed the calls of nature in my parents' bedroom while they were present.' His father's resulting curse had constantly *paralysed* Freud from that moment on. His unsuccessful discovery of the properties of cocaine and the discovery of psychoanalysis in which he was currently engaged were arguments he could use in his never-ending appeal against that judgment. When his father later reiterated his curse by forbidding the adolescent Freud to keep female company, he ensured that his son would not be able to get up to any mischief with girls but would nonetheless suffer the ignominy of being suspected of such misbehaviour. Through the medium of the 'Count Thun' dream, Freud was no longer appealing but contesting. He was challenging the validity of the judgment. He was asserting his right to have desires. He was becoming aware that paralysis of thought, like paralysis of action, is the result of an unspoken, yet understood, threat closely bound up with the father's curse – a threat directed at the 'micturating penis'. In the last image of the dream, he feels reassured when he sees that same penis still in working order . . .

Prohibition performs a fundamental function in the human psychical economy – that of preventing certain acts that are harmful to oneself and to other people. But while action naturally has to be governed by prohibition, thought has to overcome all forms of prohibition in order to be able to understand or create: transgression is a precondition of its progress. Freud realised that to see oneself as a defective is to bar oneself from understanding, and that to see oneself as a syphilitic is to bar oneself from procreating or creating. He realised that one and the same anxiety had made him deaf when giving treatment and blind when working out theories – an anxiety caused by the wish to see the difference between the sexes, to catch his parents making love, to imagine what they felt, and to try to feel it for himself. That anxiety was rooted in an unconscious phantasy – that of being deprived of the physical (and psychical) possibility of sexual pleasure because in his body and in his mind he had experienced the twofold wish to commit incest and parricide. It was only later that Freud gave a name to this phantasy. But he could already sense it with sufficient clarity to be able to continue making therapeutic and theoretical progress – as he was to continue to do right up to his death some forty years later. He no longer believed in the theory of nervous degeneracy as the cause of hysteria nor in the more general theory of heredity in mental disorders, which continued to be upheld by Charcot, Breuer and the rest of the nineteenth-century scientific establishment. Freud's repeated identification with a paralytic in his dream ended up by revealing to him the extent to which such theories were simply the rationalisation of a phantasy.

FROM THE PHANTASY OF THE PRIMAL SCENE TO CASTRATION ANXIETY

I now propose to leave aside for the moment the diachronic chain of events which we have been following in detail, and to try to identify the synchrony of the mental processes behind the new discovery that Freud was making. The work, pursuing its own course, that of deriving the concept of the castration complex, was guided by two considerations.

General paralysis marks the final stage in the development of syphilis and gradually affects both body and mind, whereas castration impairs a single biological function. In Freud's phantasy scenario, the representation of castration – which is impossible to represent because it is too horrible – is replaced by general paralysis. It could also be said that, as in Panizza's play, where an already paralytic God gets the Devil to invent syphilis, there is a reversal of the normal sequence of cause and effect. For, in psychical reality, the castration phantasy, as a result of the intense anxiety it arouses, produces sexual and intellectual inhibitions; conversely, in organic reality, it is general paralysis that results in sexual inactivity, just as doctors treating the brother of one of Freud's women patients (quoted in connection with the dream of 'Goethe's attack on Herr M.') believed that intellectual overwork had caused him to go mad and emasculate himself. So a whole is substituted for a part, and an effect for a cause: the derivation of the concept of the castration complex from a general feeling of paralysis and from medical familiarity with paralytics is therefore a metonymical process.

The second, and simultaneous, derivation is metaphorical. Fear of castration does to desire what general paralysis does to the nervous system. Amnesia regarding infantile sexuality occurs during the latency period after the Oedipal renunciation, just as memory lapses are the first clinically detectable symptom of general paralysis. When fear of castration occurs early, before the phallic phase, for instance at the time of weaning, the infant has difficulty in walking (the erection of his whole body is threatened) and in talking (what his beautiful 'organ' emits is choked and disjointed, or at least uglified) – problems that recall the motor disorders and deterioration of conceptual thought found in paralytics. In either case, sexual transgression is represented as being responsible for the physical punishment inflicted by nature on the debauched adolescent or adult (syphilis) or by the rival parent on the incestuous child (castration). There is a double metaphoric process at work here: the feeling of paralysis is at once a psychical metaphor for a physical illness – general paralysis – and a conscious metaphor for an unconscious anxiety, connected with the castration phantasy.

Ennui, in its powerful seventeenth-century sense (cf. Pascal: 'Nothing is so intolerable to man as to be fully at rest, without any passion, business, diversion, or application. He then becomes aware of his nothingness, abandonment, inadequacy, dependence, helplessness, and emptiness. Without being able to control himself, he will draw up from the depths of his soul boredom, evil, sadness, grief, resentment and despair'), was a variant of this metaphorical process in an age when people were not yet fully aware of the dangers of syphilis, which had only recently reached Europe. Another variant is to be found in Sartre's concept of *nausée*, with its disgust for slime. Although syphilis can now be cured, although the collective consciousness can no longer hold it up as a threat, and although society has become much more sexually tolerant, Samuel Beckett still thinks up characters that resemble paralytics when, in his novels and plays, he wishes to describe the universal, timeless human being racked by the horrors of castration anxiety.

Castration anxiety is one of the major psychical obstacles to creation; similarly, successful creation may result in reparation for the mutilation the creator feels deep down. The 'epistemological resistance' described by Bachelard derives from that mutilation. The creation here being carried out by Freud is, then, a very special kind of creation: it is the discovery of the nature of the main resistance that paralyses all creation.

How is creation at one remove, as in this case, possible from a psychical point of view? Panizza's play, while explaining diachronically the appearance of syphilis on earth, synchronically portrays an already syphilitic God. The ambiguity of its content is echoed by its formal composition; the traditional edifying explanation that syphilis is of 'divine' origin has an indecent double meaning. It signifies, in a metonymical sense which is both holy and conformist, that God afflicted man with the disease in order to punish him for his sins. But it implies, in a metaphorical sense which is both ungodly and revolutionary, that God transmitted His own disease to man.

Like Panizza's play, Freud's dream combines form and content, structure and theme (Freud had already noted the frequency with which dreams borrow their scenario from a literary work that has recently struck the dreamer). As I have already pointed out, dreams represent, in addition to the dreamer's latent thoughts and sexual and aggressive wishes, his epistemological wishes. Freud's dreams represent not only, in their diachrony, transpositions of phantasy scenarios inherent in the dreamer's defensive conflicts, but also, in their synchrony – sometimes directly, literally – formal processes specific to the various levels of thought, such as inclusion, negation, antithesis, associativity, commutativity, reversibility, causality or classification. Freud goes along with the old empiricist saying: 'There is nothing in the mind that has not come through the senses.' Or perhaps he might have adapted it as follows: 'There is nothing in the mind which the mind does not represent to itself.' For the psychical apparatus apprehends not only the external world and the internal world, but the processes through which it apprehends them.

But what I have just said needs qualifying, for we are now one step ahead of Freud. In August 1898, he still had some way to go before realising the existence of such a thing as castration anxiety and its essential role in the psychical economy of neurosis. Yet he was moving closer to that realisation all the time. The exceptional feature of his self-analysis was that its processes were of the same kind as the processes of psychoanalysis: it took place on two levels, that of affects, and that of representation, and constantly interrelated them. But quite apart from the fact that castration anxiety does not necessarily go away when one becomes aware of it (it is possible to loosen its hold over one, but it still continues to exist, with the result that analysis becomes interminable, as Freud accepted (1937*c*) at the end of his life), it is not possible to approach an unknown, testing and formidable psychical reality without embarking on a long process of working through involving failure, recurring symptoms and blind alleys. It is hardly surprising that this phantasy and this anxiety were now Freud's stumbling block, nor that the writing of the first version of his book finally ground to a halt and that throughout the summer of 1898 Freud felt his mind to be 'paralysed' by the problem of the metapsychology of dreams. Before he could complete his discovery and finish his book, he first had to pick up and explore more deeply in his dreams most of the themes that had preceded his self-analysis; he had to stop making dreams the sole focal point of his self-analysis and discover the dynamics of the forgetting of names and of screen memories; lastly, he had to detach himself more thoroughly from his 'transference' on to Fliess.

CHAPTER 5

The discovery of castration anxiety and the second version of *The Interpretation of Dreams*

> 'If we turn back to the dream about the strange task set me by old Brücke of making a dissection of my own pelvis, it will be recalled that in the dream itself I missed the gruesome feeling ['*Grauen*'] appropriate to it. [. . .] The dissection meant the self-analysis which I was carrying out, as it were, in the publication of this present book about dreams – a process which had been so distressing to me in reality that I had postponed the printing of the finished manuscript for more than a year.'
>
> (*ID* 477)

Two disguised autobiographical dreams (August 1898?)

THE DREAMS OF THE 'YELLOW LION' AND OF 'NANSEN'S SCIATICA'

On his return to Aussee, Freud gave Fliess, in a letter of August 20, 1898, an enthusiastic description of his trip to the Engadine (Maloja, Tirano) with Minna. The heat eventually became too much for them, and they cut short the excursions they had planned; the dreaded 'paralysis' which had lurked in the background of the 'Count Thun' dream reappeared: 'A few days later, in Innsbruck, both of us were in a state of almost paralysing weakness' (*F*, August 20, 1898, 322). In the same letter, he referred to another writer – also recommended by Fliess – who now replaced Conrad Ferdinand Meyer: 'Yes, I too have skimmed Nansen; my whole household is full of enthusiasm for him – for Martha, the Scandinavians (Grandmother, who is staying with us, still speaks Swedish) obviously revive a youthful ideal which did not materialise in her life; for Mathilde, who until now has been enthralled by the Greek heroes, the transition has been made to the Vikings; and Martin, as usual, reacted to the three volumes of adventure with a not-at-all-bad poem.

'I shall be able to make good use of Nansen's dreams; they are completely transparent. I know from my own experience that his psychic state is typical of someone who dares to do something new and relies on his confidence and who, by taking a wrong route, probably discovers something original, but far less than he had anticipated. Fortunately, the secure harmony of your nature keeps you at a distance from that. . . .' (*ibid.*, 323).

The book in question is *Farthest North*, by the Norwegian explorer Fridtjof Nansen (1861–1930),[1] which came out in Norwegian in 1897 and was immediately translated into German. This was yet another case of heroic identification: Freud identified with the explorer of unknown regions.

This is, unfortunately, the only evidence – and it is flimsy at that – for supposing that it was during the second half of August 1898 that Freud not only recalled the memory connected with a series of childhood dreams about a yellow lion, but also had the dream of 'Nansen's sciatica'. He describes the memory and the dreams one after the other in *The Interpretation of Dreams*, but attributes them to 'a physician in his thirties', who, he claims, told him about them. But they were in fact a fragment of disguised autobiography, like the screen memory that he analysed at the beginning of 1899. Their autobiographical nature was established simultaneously by Serge Leclaire (1966) in France and by H. Lehmann (1966) in the United States. A further point is worth making. This disguised autobiographical fragment, which comes at the beginning of Section B, 'Infantile Material as a Source of Dreams', of Chapter 5, 'The Material and Sources of Dreams', ties in significantly with the passages that precede and follow it. Just before it, Freud relates a dream of a primal scene told to him by someone who had attended his lectures: the person in question had dreamt of seeing '*his former tutor in bed with the nurse*'. He reported the dream to his elder brother, who confirmed the truth of what he had dreamt: 'The lovers had been in the habit of making the elder boy drunk with beer, whenever circumstances were favourable for intercourse during the night. The younger boy – the dreamer –, who was then three years old and slept in the room with the nurse, was not regarded as an impediment' (*ID* 189–90).

1. In 1911, in the later editions of his two books on dreams, Freud referred to dreams described by another polar explorer, Otto Nordenskjöld, in his book *Antarctic* (1904). In *On Dreams*, Freud summarised them as follows: 'The leader of a polar expedition has recorded that the members of his expedition, while they were wintering in the ice-field and living on a monotonous diet and short rations, regularly dreamt like children of large meals, of mountains of tobacco, and of being back at home' (*OD* 646). A more detailed quotation from Nordenskjöld is to be found in *The Interpretation of Dreams* (*ID* 131 n.1).

The continuity of this dream with the dreams of the 'Open-air closet' and 'Count Thun' (the latter comes at the end of the same section of Chapter 5) is obvious: Freud had proof, based on his own evidence and that of others, that young children observe sexual scenes between adults with a mixture of curiosity and anxiety. While he had abandoned the theory of actual seduction of the child by the adult and now believed that hysteria was caused by a phantasy of seduction, he here describes the primal scene as a fact – but does not yet apprehend the primal phantasy produced in the child on that occasion. His retrospective analysis (which in my view he carried out a little earlier) of another of his childhood dreams, 'My mother and the bird-beaked figures', clearly shows that he still had much ground to cover: he did not understand that what was expressed in that anxiety dream was the anxiety of the primal scene. But between the interpretation of that childhood dream, probably in the spring, and his analysis of the 'Count Thun' dream in the summer Freud made a considerable leap forward.

The passage that comes after the disguised autobiographical fragment recalls a childhood memory stumbled upon when he was analysing the dream of the 'Botanical monograph': when he was five, he and his sister tore up a book with coloured plates. The main result of Freud's analysis of his dreams, since his discovery of the Oedipus myth in October 1897, was a continuing recollection of childhood memories and an ever-increasing awareness of the phantasy content inherent in those memories. The fragment is as follows:

'There is another way in which it can be established with certainty without the assistance of interpretation that a dream contains elements from childhood. This is where the dream is of what has been called the "recurrent" type: that is to say, where a dream was first dreamt in childhood and constantly reappears from time to time during adult sleep. I am able to add to the familiar examples of such dreams a few from my own records, though I have never myself experienced one. A physician in his thirties told me that from the earliest days of his childhood to the present time a yellow lion frequently appeared in his dreams; he was able to give a minute description of it. This lion out of his dreams made its appearance one day in bodily form, as a china ornament that had long disappeared. The young man then learnt from his mother that this object had been his favourite toy during his early childhood, though he himself had forgotten the fact.

'If we turn now from the manifest content of dreams to the dream-thoughts which only analysis uncovers, we find to our astonishment that experiences from childhood also play a part in dreams whose content would never have led one to suppose it. I owe a particularly agreeable and instructive example of a dream of this kind to my respected colleague of the yellow lion. After reading Nansen's narrative of his polar expedition, he had a dream of being in a field of ice and of giving the gallant explorer galvanic treatment for an attack of sciatica from which he was suffering. In the course of analysing the dream, he thought of a story dating from his childhood, which alone, incidentally, made the dream intelligible. One day, when he was a child of three or four, he had heard grown-ups talking of voyages of discovery and had asked his father whether that was a serious illness. He had evidently confused *Reisen* ["voyages"] with *Reissen* ["gripes"], and his brother and sisters saw to it that he never forgot this embarrassing mistake' (*ID* 190–91).

The two memories – of a china ornament representing a yellow lion, and of the confusion over *Reisen* and *Reissen* – certainly date from Freiberg: the ornament, after the family's move to Leipzig, then to Vienna, no doubt embodied Sigismund's nostalgia for his home town, for his second mother, the nurse, and for his niece Pauline, from whom he had snatched a bunch of yellow flowers; the verbal confusion was probably connected with the preparations for the long journey (*Reisen*) which his parents discussed in front of him, and with the suffering (*Reissen*) that the prospect of leaving Freiberg must have caused him. The 'brothers' who saw to it that he never forgot his embarrassing mistake were his half-brothers, Emanuel and Philipp. The 'field of ice' in the dream probably represents separation anxiety and object-loss anxiety. As for the 'galvanic treatment', it irresistibly brings to mind Freud's early medical career, when he relied as much on electrotherapy as on hypnosis.

The china ornament was yellow, like colt's foot and dandelion flowers. Puns on journeys were recurring: *fahren* (to drive), *auffahren* (to fire up), and *Vorfahren* (ancestors) in the 'Count Thun' dream were followed by *Reisen* (voyages) and *Reissen* (pains, aches, gripes) in the Nansen dream. Leclaire (1968, pp. 44–49) remarks that the verb *reissen* (as opposed to the noun *Reissen*) means to wrench, tear, pierce, or pull to pieces. *Vögeln*, too, had two different meanings, as a verb and as a noun, in the dream of 'My mother and the bird-beaked figures'. Thus, the persistence of a particular colour and of puns involving homophony and polysemy – the 'Botanical monograph' dream contained both colours and puns – was edging Freud closer and closer to his recollection of the screen memory in which he snatched a bunch of yellow flowers from a little girl.

Now it was between August 26 and 31, at Aussee, that Freud learned of the birth of Pauline, Fliess's much-wanted daughter. Fliess had been unable either to go with Freud to Italy or to meet elsewhere for their planned Easter 'congress' because of his wife's pregnancy. Pauline was the name of Fliess's sister, who had died young and to whom he was very attached. Pauline was also the name of the niece with whom Sigismund used to play in the green meadows with (again) yellow flowers in Freiberg – Freiberg where he later fell in love, as Freud revealed in early January 1899, with a girl in a yellow dress. The birth of Pauline Fliess is further evidence that the dream of 'Nansen's sciatica' dates from the end of August 1898: its key words, *Reisen/Reissen*, call to mind both the *pains* of Ida Fliess's confinement and Wilhelm Fliess's inability to *travel* and come to see Freud. Increasingly, then, word-presentations were dominating thing-presentations in Freud's dreams.

Freud remained in Aussee until the end of August. He continued working on the metapsychology of dreams and plunged into the study of Theodor Lipps' *Grundtatsachen des Seelenlebens* (1883). Freud was both pleased and slightly disappointed to find that Lipps, a theorist of the unconscious, had already stated his (Freud's) own principles – and with greater clarity (cf. letters to Fliess of August 26 and 31, 1898). The same year, Lipps published another work, *Komik und Humor*, which later prompted Freud to write *Jokes and their Relation to the Unconscious* (1905*c*).

First analyses of name-forgetting

THE FORGETTING OF THE NAME 'JULIUS MOSEN' (AUGUST 1898)

On August 26, 1898, in a letter to Fliess, Freud analysed for the first time the forgetting of a word. 'That happened to me recently with the name of the poet who wrote *Andreas Hofer* ("*Zu Mantua in Banden*"). It must be something with an *au* – Lindau, Feldau. Of course, the man's name is Julius *Mosen*; the "Julius" had not slipped my memory. Now, I was able to prove (i) that I had repressed the name Mosen because of certain connections; (ii) that infantile material played a part in this repression; (iii) that the substitute names that were pushed into the foreground were formed, like symptoms, from both groups of material. The analysis of it turned out to be complete, with no gaps left; unfortunately, I cannot expose it to the public any more than my big dream' (*F* 324). Freud never mentioned this example again, and its interpretation remains hazardous. But it is perhaps worth drawing a parallel between Mosen and Moses, about whom Freud wrote a book at the end of his life (1939*a*), and recalling that Julius was the first name of Freud's hated brother, who was born, and died prematurely, in Freiberg, and to whom Freud has so far alluded only once in his self-analysis – and then without mentioning him by name (*F*, October 3, 1897, 268).

THE FORGETTING OF THE NAME 'SIGNORELLI' (EARLY SEPTEMBER 1898)

On August 31, Freud left with Martha for the Adriatic and the Dalmatian coast. It will be remembered that in 1878, the republic of Bosnia and Herzegovina had left the Ottoman Empire and become part of the Austro-Hungarian Empire. It was the first time that Freud had travelled alone with his wife to southern Europe. She suffered a gastric disorder, and remained in Ragusa (now Dubrovnik) while he forged on to Cattaro (now Kotor). During this trip, Freud analysed his forgetting of another name, this time Signorelli. He reported his findings to Fliess shortly after getting back to Vienna, whose atmosphere quickly depressed him again (*F*, September 22, 1898, 326), and, despite Fliess's earlier objections, re-affirmed his belief that the psychological was independent of the organic (a passage already quoted on p. 277). He immediately wrote a paper entitled 'The Psychical Mechanism of Forgetfulness' (1898*b*) and on September 27 sent it off to the publishers Ziehen and Wernicke (*F* 328). The Signorelli episode formed the basis of his paper, which itself provided a starting point for the opening chapter of *The Psychopathology of Everyday Life*.

His short paper also discussed another example of name-forgetting: Freud once forgot the name of the street (and the *pension*) where he had reluctantly promised to visit someone. He had gone on a 24-hour visit to a friend of his, probably Fliess in Berlin, ('[He] unfortunately lives very far away, and I was full of the things I was going to tell him'), and had promised, during his visit, to take greetings and messages from a family of his acquaintance in Vienna to one of their members, who had moved to the town in question. This of course meant that he would have less time for conversation with his friend. 'My memory for names is not particularly good, but it is incomparably better than for figures and numbers' (1898*b*, *SE* 3, 297), yet he remembered the number of the house but forgot the name of the street. The episode is again mentioned, very succinctly, at the end of a footnote in *The Psychopathology of Everyday Life* (*PEL* 12–13 n.1). It probably dates from September 28, 1897, when Freud, who had just begun his systematic self-analysis and was extremely upset about the collapse of his paternal seduction theory, went on a weekend visit to Fliess in Berlin (cf. p. 235).

Let us now look at Freud's analysis of the Signorelli episode (*PEL* 2–7). Freud went on his excursion into Herzegovina in the company of a Berlin lawyer named Freyhau, whom he had just met. They discussed the customs of the Turks living there. Freud mentioned their confidence in doctors and resignation to death. 'If one has to inform them that nothing can be done for a sick person, their reply is: "*Herr* [Sir], what is there to be said? If he could be saved, I know you would have saved him' (*PEL* 3). Freud thought of another anecdote, but refrained from telling it to a stranger because he regarded it as indecent. 'These Turks place a higher value on sexual enjoyment than on anything else [. . .]: '*Herr*, you must know that if *that* comes to an end then life is of no value' (*ibid.*). Their conversation then turned to the subject of painting. Freud mentioned the frescoes of the Last Judgment in Orvieto – 'the greatest I have seen so far,' he wrote to Fliess in the already quoted letter of September 22 – which he had already admired in September 1897 when visiting Italy with Martha and Alexander. All of a sudden, Freud was unable to remember the name of the painter. Botticelli and Boltraffio came to mind, but they were obviously not right. Instead of obstinately striving to find the name, which is what most people do (usually without success), Freud adopted a psychoanalytic method: he allowed his mind to associate freely. The apparently forgotten name, Signorelli, came back to him, as did the Christian name, Luca – 'proof that it had been only a repression and not genuine forgetting' (*F* 327).

Freud's analysis of this act of forgetfulness proceeds exactly like that of a dream – or more precisely like the breakdown of *Hollthurn* into holothurian and Marburg. The second half of the forgotten name, *elli*, remains unaltered since it is also found in one of the substitute names, Botti*celli*. The repressed element was *Signor* (the Italian for 'Sir', which is *Herr* in German), which features at the beginning of the Turkish anecdote – repressed by Freud – about death and sexuality. But that is not the only reason; an act of forgetfulness cannot occur unless it is overdetermined.

The second reason has to do with the string of identical syllables: *bo* is common to *Bo*tticelli, *Bo*ltraffio and *Bo*snia, and calls *Herr* to mind because of *Bo*snia-*Her*zegovina. This explains the first substitute name:

Signorelli → *Herr-elli* → *Bo(ttic)elli*

The breakdown of the name Boltraffio reveals a third reason. *Traffio* is very similar to *Trafoi*, the hamlet in the Engadine where Freud had briefly stayed during his trip with Minna in mid-August, and where he had learned that a patient of his had committed suicide because of an incurable sexual disorder (always unpleasant news for a doctor); this was another example of the repressed link between death and sexuality. The second substitute name, Boltraffio, although apparently less similar than Botticelli to the forgotten name Signorelli, in fact sheds more light on the significance of the act of forgetfulness. We can understand that Freud's latent state of mind caused him to forget a name; but why the name Signorelli?

At this point, a fourth reason becomes evident. The painter Signorelli is connected with that state of mind not only because of the form of his name, but because of the content of his work. Freud does not mention this reason immediately, but suggests it in two footnotes several pages further on (*PEL* 12 n.2, 13 n.1): 'The visual memory that I had of the series of frescoes and of the self-portrait which is introduced into the corner of one of the pictures was *ultra-clear*'; the connection between death and sexuality is the very subject of the Orvieto frescoes, and must have been brought home to Freud all the more vividly because when he visited an Etruscan tomb near Orvieto he saw that it still contained two skeletons.

I have studied these paintings in some detail. Four large semi-circular frescoes occupy the walls of a side-chapel of Orvieto Cathedral. They are: the *Story of the Anti-Christ*, the *End of the World*, the *Resurrection of the Bodies*, the *Inferno*, and *Paradise*. An arc-shaped fresco runs across the top of the entrance to the chapel, with *The Sibyl and the Prophet* on one side, and *The Thunderstruck* on the other. Signorelli (1441?–1523) was one of the first masters of the Umbrian school to draw the human body in an anatomically accurate way. His realism and his powerful muscular nudes influenced Michelangelo. The subject of his series of frescoes, *The Last Judgment*, must have reminded Freud of themes – death as punishment, the torments of hell – which, with the help of his nurse, left a deep impression on the very young Sigismund. But where does sex come in? Surely in Signorelli's treatment of his theme: completely nude men, with fine strong bodies and genitals depicted in every detail; naked women, two of them clasping each other's necks, and one caressing the breast of another; and a hallucinating series of torture scenes that could easily arouse sadistic pleasure in the spectator: people being strangled manually or with ropes and being punched in the back of the neck; feet trampling heads into the ground; naked women being flung flat on their faces by greenish or purplish demons, hugged and squeezed until they can no longer breathe, dragged along the ground, carried with their heads down, or themselves having to carry the horsemen of hell, who jab them and make them bow beneath their weight; above this scene, a flying devil with an obscene leer carries on his back a wild-haired woman who clasps him round the waist with her thighs. Freud must have been struck by the sexual suggestiveness of these scenes, whose central theme is death. In the bottom left-hand corner of the *Anti-Christ* fresco, as though bearing witness to these equivocal horrors,

Signorelli signs his work with a self-portrait. Freud probably identified with him. The names *Sig*mund and *Sig*norelli begin with the same three letters. Freud's self-analysis had portrayed similar scenes: it had taken him down into hell, and he was expecting something like the supreme punishment for his curiosity about the primal scene.

The working over of anxiety about death

THE DREAM OF THE 'THREE FATES' (SEPTEMBER–OCTOBER 1898)

The connection between death and sexuality became more explicit in the dream Freud had after his holiday in Bosnia–Herzegovina and Italy during the first three weeks of September, in other words just after his return to Vienna ahead of his family. After making an excursion to Cattaro without Martha, then rejoining her in Ragusa, they went together to Spalato (now Split) and Trieste. Freud left his wife to recuperate from her gastric disturbance in Merano, and, alone once again, visited Brescia, Milan, Pavia, Monza and Bergamo before returning to Milan to take the train back to Vienna. When in Spalato, Martha had bought a quantity of Turkish stuffs from a shopkeeper called Popovíc (in German, *Popo* is a childish word for 'the backside', and *Witz* – the German transliteration of the Serbo-Croat pronunciation of the syllable *vic* – means a 'joke'; so to a German, as Eva Rosenblum has pointed out to me, the name Popovíc would mean 'a joke about the backside'). On his return to Vienna, Freud had a dream:

'Tired and hungry after a journey, I went to bed, and the major vital needs began to announce their presence in my sleep; I dreamt as follows:

'*I went into a kitchen in search of some pudding. Three women were standing in it; one of them was the hostess of the inn and was twisting something about in her hand, as though she was making Knödel* [dumplings].[1] *She answered that I must wait till she was ready.* (These were not definite spoken words.) *I felt impatient and went off with a sense of injury. I put on an overcoat. But the first I tried on was too long for me. I took it off, rather surprised to find it was trimmed with fur. A second one that I put on had a long strip with a Turkish design let into it. A stranger with a long face and a short pointed beard came up and tried to prevent my putting it on, saying it was his. I showed him that it was embroidered all over with a Turkish pattern. He asked: "What have the*

1. *Knödel* is the diminutive of *Knoten* ('knot'); dumplings, which are difficult to make, are much appreciated in Austria and southern Germany. When they contain meat, they are known as *Fleischknödel*.

Turkish (designs, stripes . . .) to do with you?" But we then became quite friendly with each other' (*ID* 204).

This dream and a first set of associations tying it up with a number of childhood memories are to be found in Section B, 'Infantile Material as a Source of Dreams', of Chapter 5, 'The Material and Sources of Dreams' (*ID* 204–8). A second, much shorter discussion of the dream comes a little further on, in Section C, 'The Somatic Sources of Dreams': 'My dream of the "Three Fates" was clearly a hunger dream. But it succeeded in shifting the craving for nourishment back to a child's longing for his mother's breast, and it made use of an innocent desire as a screen for a more serious one which could not be so openly displayed' (*ID* 233). Grinstein devotes a chapter to this dream (G, Chapter 6). It is also analysed by E. H. Erikson, in *Insight and Responsibility* (1964).

Freud's analysis of the dream throws up three childhood memories, in all of which cultural references predominate: the memory of the first novel he ever read, perhaps when he was 13; the memory of his mother explaining to him, when he was six, that we are all made of earth and must return to earth; and the memory of witticisms about his own name, Freud, to which he was subjected throughout his childhood.

Freud says he never knew 'the name of the novel or of its author'. But he did have a vivid memory of its ending: 'The hero went mad and kept calling out the names of the three women who had brought the greatest happiness and sorrow into his life. One of these names was *Pélagie*.' Grinstein, no doubt correctly, argues that the novel in question was the Reverend Charles Kingsley's *Hypatia*, which was very popular at the time; he analyses it in detail (G 179–90). It is a historical romance which describes the conflict between Christianity, Arianism, Judaism and paganism in Alexandria in the fifth century. A young monk, Philammon, is attracted by a seductive and clever Greek woman slightly older than himself, Hypatia, a pagan who teaches philosophy and mathematics. He tries to convert her to Christianity, but fails. She decides to follow in Iphigenia's footsteps, as she puts it, by giving herself to the prefect of the city, who is a pagan converted to Christianity, in the hope of persuading him to reinstitute the worship of the ancient Greek gods while at the same time proclaiming himself emperor. But their plan falls through. She is caught by a crowd of monks, who rip her clothes off, beat her and tear her to pieces. Earlier, Philammon narrowly escapes his fellow monks, who are angry that he attended Hypatia's lectures. He feels attracted by another Greek beauty, Pelagia, who is the mistress of the chief of a band of Goths – and therefore a prostitute in his eyes. He tries to drag her away from a pagan ceremony in which she plays the role of Aphrodite, and finally discovers what he had always suspected: that she is his sister. He attempts to save her from her life of sin and to make her repent; he struggles with the leader of the Goths and causes him to plunge to his death from a parapet. Pelagia and Philammon both become hermits of exemplary godliness, each in a different part of the desert. Years later, brother and sister meet and die in each other's arms.

As Freud rightly remembered, there is a third important female character in the novel, Miriam, a rich and sinister Jewess who had brought up Pelagia and acted as a go-between for Hypatia and the prefect. Up until his death – but he does not, as Freud implies, die mad – Philammon prays for the two women he has loved, Hypatia, a kind of mother, and Pelagia, his sister. It is during an earlier episode when he is in prison that he goes into a rage and instead of calling on God he cries out three names, those of these two women and of the old monk who is his spiritual mentor. Of the three women who play an important part in Philammon's life, Hypatia represents a good mother figure, Miriam a bad mother figure, and Pelagia the sister. The essential unconscious theme in the novel is the intensity of the young monk's incestuous desire for his sister. This would seem to be confirmed by the quotation from Goethe's *Iphigenie auf Tauris* (1779) which comes towards the end of Freud's analysis:

> *'So seid ihr Götterbilder auch zu Staub.'*
> ['So you too, divine figures, have turned to dust!']

This is the exclamation uttered by Iphigenia, the slave-priestess at Diana's temple in Tauris, when Pylades, who has just been captured together with his friend Orestes, tells her of the many deaths of heroes during the siege of Troy. The dramatic mainspring of the play resides in the fact that Orestes and Iphigenia – who are brother and sister – realise each other's identity, that Iphigenia saves him from being sacrificed, and that Orestes, by rescuing her, fulfils the oracle and is forgiven for his crime (the murder of their mother Clytemnestra).

Early on in his analysis of the dream, Freud mentions the three Fates. In Greek mythology, they were Clotho, who spins the thread of life for each mortal, Lachesis, who determines its length, and Atropos, who cuts it off. Freud viewed them in a rather different way: one of the Fates was the mother who gives life and the breast, an idea he returned to in a subsequent paper, 'The Theme of the Three Caskets' (1913*f*), where he said that one woman bears man, another is his mate, and a third (death) destroys him – 'the three forms taken by the figure of the mother in the course of a man's life.'

The first part of the dream expresses hunger, while the second expresses the desire to be clothed. Hunger brings to mind the woman's breast, which gives life and 'the living creature its first nourishment.' Later in life, the breast arouses sexual desire in men. Dreams are an open invitation to make the most of one's opportunities – to make the most of women, their sweet gentleness, the caresses of their hands, and their *Popo*.

But no sooner is sexual desire aroused than it revives all sorts of prohibitions, and threats of punishment such as death, symbolised by the third Fate. Freud then relates a second childhood memory, of which he had already been reminded by a dream he had had shortly before this one: 'When I was six years old and was given my first lessons by my mother, I was expected to believe that we were all made of earth and must therefore return to earth. This did not suit me and I expressed doubts of the doctrine. My mother thereupon rubbed the palms of her hands together – just as she did in making dumplings, except that there was no dough between them – and showed me the blackish scales of *epidermis* produced by the friction as a proof that we were made of earth. My astonishment at this ocular demonstration knew no bounds and I acquiesced in the belief which I was later to hear expressed in the words: "*Du bist der Natur einen Tod schuldig*" ["Thou owest Nature a death"]' (*ID* 205).

Freud uses the same quotation in a subsequent letter to Fliess (*F*, February 6, 1899, 343). It is in fact a misquotation from Shakespeare's *Henry IV Part I*, Act 5, Scene 1, where Prince Hal says to Falstaff: 'Thou owest God a death.' Freud's replacement of God by Nature is indicative not so much of atheism as of a disturbing mother figure. The woman who gives life is also the third Fate, the giver of death. Women make men happy and send them mad (cf. the memory of the novel he read at the age of 13). Women are extravagant spenders (cf. Martha in Spalato). Women with whom one can seize a good opportunity give one 'special diseases'. His mother's unanswerable demonstration must have symbolised other lessons, which Freud intentionally omits to mention, but which were a common feature of Jewish moral education: relations with prostitutes ruin one's health; masturbation (rubbing *Knödel* in one's hands) is dangerous, one can die of it. This is probably the close connection between death and sexuality which was suggested by the Signorelli frescoes, and which Freud later described in his work on infantile sexuality. Spiritual pleasures should be sufficient to satisfy a young man: with reference to his own student days, Freud quotes from Goethe's *Faust* (Part I, Scene 4):

> '*So wird's Euch an der Weisheit* Brüsten
> *Mit jedem Tage mehr gelüsten.*'
> ['Thus, at the breasts of Wisdom clinging,
> Thou'lt find each day a greater rapture bringing.']

At this point, Freud breaks off the analysis of his dream, as usual, because if he pursued it further he would have to be too explicit about his sex life (Martha, masturbation). As we have already seen, he was prepared to discuss or refer to any other kind of personal question quite openly, even if it was likely to shock – ambition, insults, scatological coarseness, or death-wishes against his father or his friends. But his sex life, as he later told Reik (1948), was *privatissima*. The long process which led Freud, in his theory of the aetiology of psychoneuroses, to substitute phantasies for memories of sexual scenes was bound up with the gradual elucidation of his own phantasies, notably masturbation phantasies.

The first part of the dream also marks the emergence of an initial theory of the instincts, which Freud included in his paper on screen memories (1899*a*) and later replaced with the opposition of the sexual instincts and the ego-instincts: 'Love and hunger, I reflected, meet at a woman's breast.'

The second part of the dream, which centres on the wish to be clothed, soon takes on sexual overtones which bring censorship back into play: 'Turkish things have nothing to do with you.' The Turks' penchant for sexual gratification has already been mentioned in connection with the forgetting of the name Signorelli. Moreover, Freud had known for a year that dreams of being naked were exhibitionist dreams, and that dreams of being clothed were disguised dreams of being naked. The 'overcoats' which Freud in his analysis connects with *Knödel* and a fish's swimming bladder (*Fischblase*) – which, as we shall see later, forms part of the chain of associations beginning with *Pélagie* – 'clearly referred to implements used in sexual technique', in other words the male contraceptive sheath. But in my view there are other sexual meanings in the body image implicit in the 'overcoat [. . .] [which] was too long for me [. . .], rather surprised to find it was trimmed with fur': this 'overcoat' is the mother's 'blackish' epidermis with its abundant pubic hair concealing the mystery of the female genitals; the 'long strip [. . .] let into it' is the part of the boy's body which gets longer when he rubs it between the palms of his hands or when he sees the *matrem nudam* again in his imagination (cf. p. 236). The 'stranger [who] tried to prevent my putting it on, saying it was his' is in fact, through a reversal into the opposite, a very close relative, the father who makes it clear that *he* is the possessor of his mother's body. The dreamer then avoids conflict; he gives up the 'overcoat' he desires; he yields to a threat; the boy submits to his father, adopting a passive position in order to disarm him and win him over: 'But we then became quite friendly with each other.' The dream ends there.

In what way is Freud's relationship with Fliess reflected by the dream? While infantile wishes are evident chiefly in the dream's thing-presentations, it is that relationship which underlies its word-presentations. For the dream makes much of proper names. There is the already mentioned case of Popovíc. *Knödel* recalls a certain Knödl whom Freud's teacher in histology had once accused of plagiarism. His other teacher, Brücke (which means 'bridge' in German), is the link – the 'verbal bridge' – that takes Freud back to the happy times when he was a student whose only desire was for scientific knowledge, for the 'breasts' (*Brüsten*) of wisdom alluded to by Goethe. The name of another teacher on whom Freud modelled himself, Fleischl, brings back the notion of hunger (*Fleisch* means 'meat'; cf. *Fleischknödel*) as well as recalling an unfortunate use of cocaine – a drug that removes not only pain but hunger. Why all this wordplay? As Freud points out in Chapter 1, 'The Scientific Literature Dealing with the Problems of Dreams', the French investigator, Maury, had already cited instances of dreams where the succession of dream-images are linked together merely through a similarity in the sound of the corresponding words (kilometres – kilogramme – Gilolo – Lobelia – Lopez – lotto): 'He specifies two main features of a "*délire*": "(1) A mental act which is spontaneous and as it were automatic; (2) an invalid and irregular association of ideas" (*Le sommeil et les rêves*, Paris, 1878, p. 126)' (*ID* 59). We know that in Freud's dreams a vice of form conceals and, at the same time, expresses a vice in the content, i.e. a vicious wish.

At first sight, Fliess does not appear in this series of puns on proper names. Freud does not mention him by name (plays on his name feature in the 'Hearsing' dream, which I believe to have been dreamt at about the same time). But, as in the dreams cited by Maury, Freud produces a significant chain of verbal associations: (in German) '*Pélagie – Plagiat – Plagiostomen – (Haifische) – Fischblase*' ('*Pélagie – plagiarising – plagiostomes* or sharks – a *fish's swimming-bladder*'), which is completed a little further on by *Plagen* ('the desires which were now plaguing me') (*ID* 206). Freud does not refer either to the bladder (an allusion to urinary incontinence?) or to the plagiostomes, an order of fishes, including rays and sharks, whose main characteristic is their transverse mouth underneath their bodies (an allusion to female genitals glimpsed on little girls' bodies?). But he does say more about the accusation of plagiarism, though without specifying who plagiarised from whom: clearly, Freud is thinking of his own borrowing of Fliess's theory of bisexuality. When reconsidered from that angle, the text of the dream takes on a new meaning: in the first part, the dreamer is involved with a woman who is preparing sweet things for him with caressing hands (heterosexuality); in the second, the dreamer yields to a man, a Turk, who arrogates the equivocal embroidery, designs, and stripes (homosexuality). Moreover, various characteristics of the two overcoats suggest both male and female sexual attributes. I have looked up in the index of the Standard Edition all references to the term bisexuality in *The Interpretation of Dreams*: interestingly, all but one of them are to be found in editions of the book that came out after 1900. The only one in the first edition comes at the end of Section E, 'The Primary and Secondary Processes – Repression', of Chapter 7 (the last), 'The Psychology of the Dream-Processes':

'The theory of the psychoneuroses asserts as an indisputable and invariable fact that only sexual wishful impulses from infancy, which have undergone repression (i.e. a transformation of their affect) during the developmental period of childhood, are capable of being revived during *later* developmental periods (whether as a result of the subject's sexual constitution, which is derived from an initial *bisexuality* [my italics], or as a result of unfavourable influences acting upon the course of his sexual life) and are thus able to furnish the motive force for the formation of psychoneurotic symptoms of every kind. It is only by reference to these sexual forces that we can close the gaps that are still patent in the theory of repression. I will leave it an open question whether these sexual and infantile factors are equally required in the theory of dreams: I will leave that theory incomplete at this point, since I have already gone a step beyond what can be demonstrated in assuming that dream-wishes are invariably derived from the unconscious' (*ID* 605–6).

Freud then adds a long footnote, which includes the following passage: 'There are special reasons, which may not be what my readers expect, why I have not given any exhaustive treatment to the part played in dreams by the world of sexual ideas and why I have avoided analysing dreams of obviously sexual content. Nothing could be further from my own views or from the theoretical opinions which I hold in neuropathology than to regard sexual life as something shameful, with which neither a physician nor a scientific research worker has any concern. Moreover, the moral indignation by which the translator of the *Oneirocritica* of Artemidorus of Daldis allowed himself to be led into withholding the chapter on sexual dreams from the knowledge of his readers strikes me as laughable. What governed my decision was simply my seeing that an explanation of sexual dreams would involve me deeply in the still unresolved problems of perversion and *bisexuality* [my italics]; and I accordingly reserved this material for another occasion' (*ibid.*). This passage cannot have been written until the early summer of 1899, by which time Freud was putting Chapter 7 into shape, not without difficulty, and had already come to a decision to write a subsequent book on infantile and neurotic sexuality (1905*d*). Freud, in a letter to Fliess of August 1, 1899 (*F* 364), refers to bisexuality as a topic he had shelved. The dream of the 'Three Fates', in the autumn of 1898, shows to what extent the question had been nagging Freud – and indeed been giving him a guilty conscience – ever since Fliess had brought it up during their Nuremberg 'congress' at Easter 1897 (which was followed by the dreams of 'Villa Secerno', 'Hella' and 'Running up stairs undressed'), and their Breslau 'congress' at Christmas 1897 (which led to their disagreement over bilaterality and the 'My son, the Myops' dream). It is possible that the idea of bisexuality, which followed on logically from Fliess's pet theory about male and female periods, had already been discussed by the two men, as it appears for the first time in the letter of December 6, 1896, where Freud, deeply involved in the work of mourning after his father's death, outlined the theory of what he was by then calling 'the psychical apparatus': 'In order to account for why the outcome [of premature sexual experience] is sometimes perversion and sometimes neurosis, I avail myself of the bisexuality of all human beings' (*F* 212).

Let us return to the puns on names to be found in Freud's associations to the dream; 'It could scarcely be denied that playing about with names like this was a kind of childish naughtiness. But if I indulged in it, it was as an act of retribution; for my own name had been the victim of feeble witticisms like these on countless occasions' (*ID* 207). *Die Freude* means 'joy' in German, and *Freudenmädchen*, like the French *filles de joie*, means the same thing as the *ärarische Frauenzimmer* ('public women') who were explicitly alluded to by Freud's associations to the 'Count Thun' dream (*ID* 214), and who later reappeared in the '*Non vixit*' dream. When looked at from this angle, the dream of the 'Three Fates' could easily be interpreted as representing a scene in a brothel. When Freud finished writing his dream book in the summer of 1899, he had a day-dream which, before admitting that it was his own, he first attributed to a character in Alphonse Daudet's *Le Nabab* by the name of Monsieur Joyeuse, which translates into German as 'Herr Freudig' (cf. pp. 445–7).

Freud comes to the following conclusion in his analysis of the 'Three Fates' dream; ' "One should never neglect an opportunity, but always take what one can even when it involves doing a small wrong. One should never neglect an opportunity, since life is short and death inevitable." Because this lesson of "*carpe diem*" had among other meanings a sexual one, and because the desire it expressed did not stop short of doing wrong, it had reason to dread the censorship and was obliged to conceal itself behind a dream. All kinds of thoughts having a contrary sense then found voice: memories of a time when the dreamer was content with spiritual food, restraining thoughts of every kind and even threats of the most revolting sexual punishments' (*ID* 206–7). This is another instance of the father's threat about what happens to a son who goes with prostitutes: the pleasure they give him is rewarded with syphilis, and therefore with general paralysis and death. But this time Freud protests against the threat and looks for an answer to it.

Freud does not merely subject the names of his teachers to the phonetic and semantic contortions once suffered by his own name. He well and truly gets his own back on them by showing that he is in good company – for what company could be better than Goethe's? 'Goethe, I recalled, had remarked somewhere upon people's sensitiveness about their names: how we seem to have grown into them like our skin. He had said this *à propos* of a line written on his name by Herder:

> *'Der du von Göttern abstammst, von Gothen oder vom Kote.'* –
> ['Thou who art the offspring of gods or of Goths or of dung –']
> (*ID* 207)

Freud adds another line to that quotation which, although he does not say so, comes (as we have seen: cf. p. 364) from Goethe's *Iphigenie auf Tauris*, and which contains the word *Götterbilder* (divine figures), another echo of his name after *Göttern* (gods), *Gothen* (Goths), and *Kote* (dung or mud).

I should like to make a few other points, some of them based on Grinstein's analysis of the dream (G 170–78). Johann Gottfried von Herder (1744–1803) and Johann Wolfgang von Goethe (1749–1832) shared the same Christian name, Johann, and a similar syllable (*Gott*fried, *Goethe*). Herder, a philosopher and literary historian rose to fame early in life and strongly influenced the young Goethe when he was a student at Strasbourg University. But Herder's contemptuous attitude finally put Goethe off. During the period when they were close friends, Herder, who was suffering from an eye disease, had an operation which involved making an opening into the nose (cf. Jacob Freud's glaucoma and Fliess's operations), and which left him disfigured. Goethe, who enjoyed Herder's culture and caustic wit, visited him twice a day during his convalescence. It was at that time that Herder, writing to Goethe to ask him for some books, penned a short ironic poem ending with the lines quoted above.

Goethe himself relates this incident, as well as reproducing and commenting on Herder's poem, in *Dichtung und Wahrheit* (Truth and fiction relating to my life) (1811–30). Like Goethe, Freud entered into a friendship (with Fliess) which started by being warm and admiring, but which cooled as a result of the other person's character. Just as, in Goethe's case, autobiography and literary creation were closely intertwined, so Freud, in his dream book, combined autobiography and scientific research. *Dichtung und Wahrheit* deals with many matters which are echoed not only in the 'Three Fates' dream (for example, the Gothic architecture of Strasbourg Cathedral, and the Pelagian heresy, which rejected the notion of original sin and was opposed by St Augustine), but in Freud's self-analysis as a whole – such as Goethe's conflicts with his father, his attachment to his sister, the premature death of his brother Hermann Jakob (a topic later discussed in a paper by Freud, 1917*b*), his interest in books from an early age, and his accounts of surgery.

In short, the dream of the 'Three Fates' marks Freud's still not entirely explicit discovery that death and separation from the mother are equivalent in phantasy. It is his mother who explains to him, while they are having an intimate conversation in the kitchen, that he is made of dust and that she is herself mortal. It is his much-mocked family name – *Die Freude*, joy, Freud, *Freudenmädchen* – which marks Sigmund Freud out for the pleasures of the epidermis, whose decomposition into dust is only hastened by those very pleasures. The decomposition of the thing is here duplicated by the decomposition of the word: Freud is affected both in his name and in his infantile wish to possess his mother totally and indefinitely.

In infantile phantasy, dying means losing one's mother, and losing her through one's own fault. This conception of death is characteristic of depressive anxiety, which, as we have already seen on more than one occasion, gave Freud the impetus to carry out his self-analysis. Freud had difficulty in imagining the mother as a destructive force, as something thoroughly malevolent and mortiferous. In phantasy, he could not conceive of a violent death of a child except in terms of being caused by a cruel father. One of Freud's dominant character traits – his need to preserve an idealised image of his mother – was probably encouraged by the presence of two mother figures during his infancy, his mother Amalie, and his nurse Monika Zajíc, whom he split into two part-structures, good and bad respectively. He subsequently succeeded in discovering the image of the phallic mother, which he described in his papers on Leonardo da Vinci (1910*c*) and the Medusa's head (1940*c*). But he failed to formulate fully either the imago of the bad mother or the correlative notion of persecutory anxiety. Retrospectively we are better able to judge Freud's limitations. They make it even more remarkable that he was able, during the second half of his life, to make so many discoveries that in turn enabled his successors to make many others, which he had himself often half-glimpsed in the form of thing-presentations, but which he had failed to turn into word-presentations.

THE DREAM OF 'RIDING ON A HORSE' (LATE OCTOBER 1898)

At the end of September and throughout October 1898, Freud once again felt depressed and intellectually paralysed. He detested Vienna. He felt drained. At first he had very few patients (*F*, September 27, 1898), then was 'buried under an avalanche' of them (*F*, October 9, 1898), with the result that he had to spend ten hours a day on treatment, with no time or energy to spare for his scientific work. He did, however, recover his vigour. He described to Fliess (*F*, September 27, 1898) the case of a young man of 25 whose symptoms had almost entirely prevented him from walking ever since the deaths of his father and brother; Freud realised that the man was identifying with a tabetic uncle (once again the theme of sexual excess eventually leading to general paralysis), and for the first time connected bed-wetting with sexual excitation in infancy. He found it impossible to get back to writing his book, and on October 23 admitted as much to Fliess: 'The dream [book] is lying still, immutably' (already quoted on p. 277). In the same letter, he said he felt 'completely lonely' and 'an old man'. He tried to amuse himself by studying the psychology of Leonardo da Vinci (who was left-handed – a fact he hastened to pass on to Fliess, on October 9, because he knew it would please him), or by longingly poring over the topography of Rome, the inaccessible city.

Freud's physical health was not good. A recent influenza epidemic had left him with an infection; he had difficulty in breathing, his good spirits were undermined, and he feared a recurrence of the cardiac problems he had suffered in the spring of 1894 after an earlier, lingering bout of influenza (*F*, October 23, 1898). As it turned out, the infection in fact took the form of an outbreak of furuncles (or boils). One of these, a particularly large and painful one, was located on the raphe scrotis and caused him considerable fatigue. The ill-placed boil eventually had to be lanced, as he subsequently told Fliess (*F*, November 6, 1898). As we shall see later on, the reason he was slow to relate this event was that at about the same time Fliess had an operation which was the cause of considerable worry to himself and his entourage, and which instigated Freud's '*Non vixit*' dream. It is difficult to establish which came first, the 'Riding on a horse' dream or the '*Non vixit*' dream. The boil plays a role in both dreams, whereas Fliess's operation features only in the second. Freud already had his boil when, right at the end of October, he first heard of Fliess's operation and responded immediately by writing to him (*F*, October 30, 1898, 332–3; quoted by Schur, S 159–60). I agree with Schur that the '*Non vixit*' dream probably dates from a day or two before October 30. This would suggest that the 'Riding on a horse' dream occurred a few days earlier. In any case, the lancing of the boil took place before November 6, the date at which Freud mentioned the operation to Fliess: so this dream could not have occurred later than the very first days of November.

The 'Riding on a horse' – or 'Grey horse' – dream runs as follows:

'*I was riding on a grey horse, timidly and awkwardly to begin with, as though I were only reclining upon it. I met one of my colleagues, P., who was sitting high on a horse, dressed in a tweed suit, and who drew my attention to something (probably to my bad seat). I now began to find myself sitting more and more firmly and comfortably on my highly intelligent horse, and noticed that I was feeling quite at home up there. My saddle was a kind of bolster, which completely filled up the space between its neck and crupper. In this way I rode straight in between two vans. After riding some distance up the street, I turned round and tried to dismount, first in front of a small open chapel that stood in the street frontage. Then I actually did dismount in front of another chapel that stood near it. My hotel was in the same street; I might have let my horse go to it on its own, but I preferred to lead it there. It was as though I should have felt ashamed to arrive at it on horseback. A hotel "boots" was standing in front of the hotel; he showed me a note of mine that had been found, and laughed at me over it. In the note was written, doubly underlined: "No food", and then another remark (indistinct) such as "No work", together with a vague idea that I was in a strange town in which I was doing no work*' (*ID* 229–30).

This dream and its analysis make up the most important example of 'The Somatic Sources of Dreams' in Section C of Chapter 5, 'The Material and Sources of Dreams' (*ID* 229–32). Let us examine and complement the three lines of interpretation suggested by Freud.

a) The boil on Freud's scrotum was hurting him, had taken his appetite away, and was making it hard for him to work (cf. the two exhortations on the note in the dream). He had treated himself with a poultice (cf. the huge saddle). In any case, Freud could not ride and had no inclination to do so. The dream fulfilled Freud's wish not to have any more boils; he imagined himself on horseback, which would be quite impossible with a boil in that particular place; so he could sleep in peace. Freud was beginning to suspect that the prime and universal wish satisfied by all dreams is the wish to sleep; but it was not until a year later that he fully realised that fact. This is yet another case of one of his dreams anticipating a discovery.

b) The horse also symbolised Freud's relationship with his colleagues and patients. P., when Freud last met him, was wearing a *pepper-and-salt* suit (hence the grey horse). One possible cause of his boils had been ascribed to his eating *highly-spiced* food. P. liked to ride *the high horse* over Freud ever since he had taken over one of his women patients on whom he (Freud) had pulled off some remarkable *feats*. Another colleague expressed surprise at this, for he had believed Freud to be 'firmly *in the saddle*' in the patient's house. This intelligent woman (the horse in the dream) had taken Freud wherever she felt inclined, as if he were Itzig, the 'Sunday rider', whose proverbial quip he had quoted in a letter to Fliess of July 7, 1898, accompanying the latest chapter, which 'completely follows the dictates of the unconscious', of the first version of his book: 'Itzig, where are you going?' 'Do I know? Ask the horse!' (*F*, July 7, 1898, 319). Freud does not go on to explain the meaning of this association. In the dream he is the rider who sits more and more firmly in the saddle and does not let his mount take him wherever it wants; so the dream denies his failure just as it denies his boil: I can sleep in peace because I got the upper hand of P. and know how to keep my patient under control. This is another instance of professional rivalry, as is confirmed by the childhood memory underlying the dream-thought: 'Scenes of quarrelling [. . .] between me and a nephew of mine, a year my senior, who was at present living in England' (*ID* 231). After having elucidated his ambivalence towards his father, Freud was now exploring his ambivalence towards John, his twofold rival as regards both seniority and Pauline.

c) Lastly, riding (or mounting) has a crude sexual sense. Freud suggests this in a roundabout way, taking refuge behind the wordplay of a woman patient who had dreamt of Italy, a 'lovely country' she had never visited: the dream had proved easy to interpret when – once again – word-presentations were taken literally: 'to Italy [*gen Italien*] = genitals [*Genitalien*].' This dream, like the previous one of the 'Three Fates', has a setting that recalls Italy, where Freud had spent his last holidays. It can be seen that the inhibition which was preventing Freud from going to Rome, and which once again featured in his recent letter to Fliess of October 23, was of a sexual and Oedipal nature: if there was rivalry with another man, it was over a woman. Here again, Freud's counter-transference on a woman patient had aroused a sexual desire. But this time curiosity about female anatomy and physiology was no longer involved, as it had been with Irma; it was a virile desire to get on top: who would 'mount' the intelligent and semi-docile horse represented by the woman patient in question?

d) Lastly, the dream has a meaning that relates to psychoanalytic technique. More and more, Freud felt the need to adopt – despite his difficulty in doing so – a procedure whereby he allowed himself to be guided by the patient's free associations instead of firing questions at him and steering him in a direction that conformed with the theories of the infant science of psychoanalysis. 'I now let the patient himself choose the subject of the day's work,' he subsequently wrote in his prefatory remarks to the 'Dora' case (*SE* 7, 12). Later again, he said in an address to the Second Psycho-Analytical Congress: 'At its beginning psychoanalytic treatment was inexorable and exhausting. The patient had to say everything himself, and the physician's activity consisted of urging him on incessantly. Today things have a more friendly air' (1910*d*, *SE* 11, 141). Freud's original notes on the beginning of the 'Rat Man' case (October 1, 1907, to January 20, 1908), published by E. Ribeiro Hawelka (1974), illustrate the 'struggle' he entered into with his patient, yet when he presented the case to the Wednesday Society he said (according to Otto Rank's minutes, quoted by E. Ribeiro Hawelka, 1974, p. 10) that 'the technique of analysis has changed insofar as the analyst now no longer seeks what is of interest to him, but lets the patient develop his thoughts naturally'; Rank added in a footnote: 'What we have here for the first time is an account of an analysis carried out successfully according to the free-association method.'

The metaphor of the horse that guides its master, like many key symbols in Freud's dreams, has a double meaning. It was because he gave too much rein to the woman patient in whose house he believed himself to be firmly in the saddle that he was replaced by P. Psychoanalytic treatment has to be carried out rigorously; for patients expect their psychoanalyst to satisfy their every wish, and if he once starts doing so, then stops, they break off their analysis. Freud here anticipated what he later called the 'rule of abstinence', which bars the analyst from having any kind of relationship other than a psychoanalytic one with his patient, and whose symbolic equivalents in this dream are the resolutions 'No food' and 'No work'. But surely the rule of free association and the rule of abstinence are simply two aspects of one fundamental rule? Looking back at Freud's slightly distorted quotation from Goethe's *Faust* in a letter to Fliess of September 27 we can see that it foreshadowed the conclusion of this dream, which he had a month later;

> *Zwar bin ich gescheiter als alle die Laffen* [. . .]
> *Führe meine Leute an der Nase herum*
> *und seh', dass wir nichts wissen können.*
> [It is true I am cleverer than all the coxcombs [. . .]
> I lead my people around by the nose
> and see that we can know nothing.]
> (*F*, September 27, 1898, 329).

THE '*NON VIXIT*' DREAM (END OF OCTOBER 1898)

I have already suggested that this dream dates from October 30, 1898, give or take a day or two. In order for it to be properly understood, further day's residues on top of those already mentioned in connection with the contemporary 'Riding on a horse' dream need to be taken into consideration.

On October 16, 1898, a ceremony took place in the cloisters of Vienna

University in the course of which a memorial to Ernst Fleischl von Marxow, who had died in the cause of science (and whose name has a certain assonance with that of Fliess), was unveiled. Fleischl had been one of Brücke's two assistants in the Physiological Laboratory where Freud began his scientific career in 1876. In the course of an experiment, Fleischl injured his hand; the wound became infected and several fingers had to be amputated. But he then developed amputation neuromata, which caused him unbearable pain despite repeated operations. Fleischl started taking morphine to ease the pain, and became addicted to it. To cure his addiction, Freud advised him to take cocaine orally (he had discovered its anaesthetic properties in 1884). Initially the results seemed miraculous, then Fleischl, who began to take the drug through intradermic injections, developed a cocaine addiction that was worse than his previous morphinism. With a feeling of distress and guilt, Freud then witnessed his friend's gradual physical and mental deterioration (similar to that caused by general paralysis), which eventually led to his death in 1891. Fleischl von Marxow and the local administration of cocaine to treat nasal complaints (a method Fliess believed in) have already been touched upon in my discussion of the Irma and 'Botanical monograph' dreams.

The unveiling ceremony caused Freud to recall another memory. In 1882, before Fleischl's drug addiction, Freud had left Brücke's laboratory in order to earn his living as a doctor and thus be able to get married. His place as demonstrator in the laboratory was taken by his friend Josef Paneth (1857–90), who was one year younger than Freud, and who married Sophie Schwab in 1884 (one of the inconsolable 'widows' in the Irma dream, after whom Freud named one of his own daughters, Sophie). Paneth died of tuberculosis only one year after obtaining the post of assistant he had so coveted. At his funeral, a young man remarked to Freud that that funeral oration rather exaggerated the dead man's qualities, and added: 'No one's irreplaceable.'

So it is that death lies in wait for happiness and genius: these were the latent thoughts which Freud, who was still deep in his mid-life crisis and felt gloomy at the prospect of his own inevitable death, set in motion in his mind when, during the ceremony at the University, he remembered two 'revenants', Fleischl and Paneth. Both were wealthy and had helped him financially. Moreover, certain similarities between first names must have struck Freud, who at that time was particularly interested in plays on words. Ernst was the first name not only of Fleischl but of Brücke, after whom Freud named his eldest son Ernst. Freud was called Sigmund, and so was Exner, Brücke's other assistant, who after the latter's death in 1892 succeeded him as professor of physiology. Josef, as we have already seen, was a name shared by Breuer, the uncle with the yellow beard, and the interpreter of dreams in the Bible.

Another first name full of associations played an important role in the Freud/Fliess relationship: Pauline. The Fliess's long-awaited child, Pauline, was born at the end of August 1898. In late December 1895, when Robert Fliess was born, shortly after Anna Freud, his parents had already pinned their hopes on a daughter. 'Paulinchen' (little Pauline) was mentioned by Freud in letters to Fliess of October 8, October 31 and December 3, 1895, and was again referred to by him on May 1, 1898. Freud had signed off all his recent letters (August 26 and 31, September 22 and 29) with references to the baby's imminent arrival. In his letter of October 9, Freud reminded Fliess that Pauline was the first name of his (Fliess's) much-loved sister, who had died young: 'The well-being that shines forth from your letters does one good and communicates itself. Just watch how soon Paulinchen will turn out to be a reincarnation of your sister' (*F* 330). This name was also a 'revenant' for Freud, who, as soon as he discovered the Oedipus myth in October 1897, described a memory of his nephew John and his niece Pauline in Freiberg (without mentioning them by name): 'The two of us seem occasionally to have behaved cruelly to my niece, who was a year younger' (*F*, October 3, 1897, 268). But that is not all: two days after the unveiling of the Fleischl memorial, a niece was born to Freud: 'My sister Rosa gave birth to a girl on October 18; both are well' (*F*, October 23, 1898, 332).

This letter of October 23 is crucial for a proper understanding of the '*Non vixit*' dream. In it, Freud sent 'good wishes for your happiness from me and my family' for Fliess's birthday (the year before, Freud had forgotten to wish Fliess a happy birthday because he was irritated at his friend's lack of response to the announcement that he had discovered the Oedipus myth; cf. *F*, October 27, 1897). Fliess, who was born on October 24, 1858 (the year when Sigismund's younger brother, Julius, died), had therefore reached his 40th birthday. He was a man obsessed with calculating the periodic cycles that predetermine birth, illness and death, and regarded the age of 40 as the most critical time in his life (we have already seen that the age Freud dreaded was 41, which he had already safely passed). Yet it was precisely at that critical moment that Fliess decided to undergo surgery, no doubt connected with his persistent migraines, which he refused to interpret as being partly psychosomatic, as Freud had suggested; superstition also probably prompted Fliess's choice of date – if it was a critical one, he might as well make it coincide with serious illness rather than death.

Against that context, Fliess's operation prompted considerable concern and was shrouded in mystery: it was his relatives in Vienna who informed Freud of its seriousness and of the family decision that it should not be discussed with anyone. Freud was both worried for his friend's life and offended that he was suspected of being unable to keep a secret. In his letter of October 23, he sent only birthday wishes to Fliess as he did not yet know about the operation. The first reports of it passed on to him by Fliess's parents-in-law were not reassuring, and Freud even toyed with the idea of rushing to his friend's bedside in Berlin. Here is Freud's description of the episode in his analysis of the dream: 'I had heard from my friend in Berlin, whom I have referred to as "Fl." [i.e. Fliess], that he was about to undergo an operation and that I should get further news of his condition from some of his relatives in Vienna. The first reports I received after the operation were not reassuring and made me feel anxious. I should have much preferred to go to him myself, but just at that time I was the victim of a painful complaint which made movement of any kind a torture to me. The dream-thoughts now informed me that I feared for my friend's life. His only sister, whom I had never known, had, as I was aware, died in early youth after a very brief illness. (In the dream *Fl. spoke about his sister and said that in three-quarters of an hour she was dead.*) I must have imagined that his constitution was not much more resistant than his sister's and that, after getting some much worse news of him, I should make the journey after all – and arrive too late, for which I might never cease to reproach myself.' At this point, Freud adds the following footnote: 'It was this phantasy, forming part of the unconscious dream-thoughts, which so insistently demanded "*Non vivit*" instead of "*Non vixit*": "You have come too late, he is no longer alive." I have already explained on pp. 421–3 that "*Non vivit*" was also required by the manifest situation in the dream' (*ID* 480–81). This fear of arriving too late is paralleled by Freud's lateness at the house of mourning which instigated the 'Close the eyes' dream connected with his father's death. There was therefore another anniversary and another revenant: Jacob Freud had died exactly two years before, on October 23, 1896. Fear of having to mourn Fliess and the reactivation of the work of mourning following his father's death reinforced in Freud's mind the anticipated mourning to be carried out over his own future death.

Towards the end of the month, Freud received more encouraging news, possibly from Fliess himself, and hastened to write to him on October 30, 1898: 'After having sent off my last letter with the wishes for your happiness, I reproached myself for having deviated from the traditional formula, which seeks to eradicate every last vestige of suffering or illness. I wanted to sound rational and provide a place and a positive function for that which in any event cannot be avoided. This was nonsense, because wishing does not become reasonable by any correction of this sort. In my inattentive reading I overlooked your first intimation, that you planned to let yourself in for new experimental tortures, and I was therefore greatly surprised to get the news of your operation so soon thereafter' (*F* 332–3).

It was, then, at about this time that Freud had the '*Non vixit*' dream:

'More instruction can be derived from another dream, which I shall report in this connection on account of the very distinct speech which formed its centre-point, although I shall have to put off explaining it fully till I come to discuss affect in dreams. I had a very clear dream. *I had gone to Brücke's laboratory at night, and in response to a gentle knock on the door, I opened it to* (the late) *Professor Fleischl, who came in with a number of strangers and, after exchanging a few words, sat down at his table.* This was followed by a second dream. *My friend Fl.* [Fliess] *had come to Vienna unobtrusively in July. I met him in the street in conversation with my* (deceased) *friend P., and went with them to some place where they sat opposite each other as though they were at a table. I sat in front at its narrow end. Fl. spoke about his sister and said that in three-quarters of an hour she was dead, and added some such words as "that was the threshold". As P. failed to understand him, Fl. turned to me and asked me how much I had told P. about his affairs. Whereupon, overcome by strange emotions, I tried to explain to Fl. that P. (could not understand anything at all, of course, because he) was not alive. But what I actually said – and I myself noticed the mistake – was,* "NON VIXIT". *I then gave P. a piercing look. Under my gaze he turned pale; his form grew indistinct and his eyes a sickly blue – and finally he melted away. I was highly delighted at this and I now realised that Ernst Fleischl, too, had been no more than an apparition, a "revenant"* ["ghost" – literally, "one who returns"]; *and it seemed to me quite possible that people of that kind only existed as long as one liked and could be got rid of if someone else wished it*' (*ID* 421).

This dream and Freud's initial remarks about the relationship between speeches in dreams and speeches heard in real life are to be found in Section F, 'Some Examples – Calculations and Speeches in Dreams', of Chapter 6, 'The Dream-Work' (*ID* 421–5). Further remarks on the over-determination of pleasurable and unpleasurable affects in this dream are included in Section H, 'Affects in Dreams', of the same chapter (*ID* 480–87). A third and shorter reference to this dream comes at the beginning of Section A, 'The Forgetting of Dreams', of Chapter 7, 'The Psychology of the Dream-Processes' (*ID* 513): it underlines the importance of an apparently trivial detail of the dream (the passage: '*As P. failed to understand him, Fl.* [. . .] *asked me . . .*') which nonetheless eventually led Freud back to its underlying childhood memory – his affectionate yet stormy relationship with John. Freud then quotes some lines by Heine, from 'Die Heimkehr'

('The Homecoming') in *Buch der Lieder* (*Book of Songs*), LXXVIII:

Selten habt ihr mich verstanden,
Selten auch verstand ich euch,
Nur wenn wir im Kot uns fanden
So verstanden wir uns gleich.
[Rarely have you understood me,
And rarely too have I understood you.
Not until we both found ourselves in the mud
Did we promptly understand each other.]

It is worth noting the recurrence of the word *Kot* (mud), which appeared in Herder's quip about Goethe quoted by Freud in connection with the 'Three Fates' dream. Grinstein devotes a chapter to the '*Non vixit*' dream (G, Chapter 12).

We scarcely need Freud's associations in order to guess the wish expressed by the dream. Fliess is seriously ill: if he dies, like his quasi-homonym Fleischl, like Sophie Schwab's husband Josef Paneth, like Sigismund's younger brother Julius, Freud will be happy to have survived him. Once again, it is a question of 'May the other person die rather than I!' The person who melts away under Freud's gaze in the dream is Fliess. Freud half-realises what Fliess has become for him – an apparition, a revenant, the ghost of John and of Julius. He is considerably embarrassed by the dream, which marks the end of his strong emotional attachment to Fliess. It is too important to be left out of *The Interpretation of Dreams* (yet further proof that Freud held very little back from the reader), but he cannot bring himself to present 'a complete solution of its conundrums', as it would mean 'sacrificing to my ambition people whom I greatly value'. He is indeed careful not to reveal that solution in the analysis which immediately follows the description of the dream. Sixty pages further on, however, in the second section of his analysis, he does in fact reveal it through a process of fragmented or deferred interpretation with which we are by now familiar.

Here are the memories and phantasies alluded to by Freud in connection with each element of the conundrum.

The theme of lateness. – When Freud worked as a demonstrator at Brücke's laboratory, he sometimes arrived late. One day, Brücke turned up punctually, caught Freud out and gave him a piercing look with his terrible blue eyes. When Freud received news of Fliess, he unconsciously imagined that his friend would die very quickly, as his sister Pauline had done, and that he (Freud) would arrive in Berlin too late and be told: he is not alive (*non vivit*). The dream expresses his wish to escape criticism for such lateness: it is he, Freud, who gives other people a piercing look with his blue eyes; it is Fliess who has come unexpectedly to Vienna (which is untrue in fact, since they had probably met in Salzburg at the end of July).

The theme of indiscretion. – The insistence with which Fliess's parents-in-law warned Freud not to discuss Fliess's condition offended him. Through an indiscretion, Freud had already unintentionally caused trouble between Fleischl and another man called Josef (probably Breuer). The theme of indiscretion reflects the process of the dream-work: in order to be expressed, death-wishes must be directed against dead men like Fleischl and Josef Paneth, and not living rivals like Fliess and Josef Breuer.

The theme of immortality. – *Non vixit* is a further example of a grammatical incongruity in one of Freud's dreams. He realised that the words came from a memorial to Emperor Josef II (another Josef), located in the Imperial Palace in Vienna (a photograph of it is reproduced in G, fig. 9). According to Freud, the monument bore the inscription:

> *Saluti patriae vixit*
> *non diu sed totus.*
> [For the well-being of his country he lived
> Not long but wholly.]

During the ceremony at the University, Freud probably had the following day-dream: like Brücke and Fleischl, Josef Paneth also deserves to have a memorial erected here in his honour; Fliess's sister lives on in the young Pauline; similarly, Sophie Freud is keeping the memory of Josef Paneth alive; the names of children are revenants; the only way to achieve immortality is to have children. The dream expressed Freud's wish for immortality: one day a memorial would be erected to him, the interpreter of dreams, the new Joseph.

All Freud's intentional attempts to cover his tracks are marked by slips of various kinds, and this dream is no exception. Wittels (1924) noted a mistake in Freud's wording of the inscription (he wrote *patriae* instead of *publicae*), and suggested the following explanation, with which Freud himself broadly agreed:

a) *Publica puella* means a prostitute (*Freudenmädchen*); Josef (Breuer) broke with Freud in 1896 out of repugnance for his theory of the sexual aetiology of the neuroses: *publicae* (= sexuality) was therefore omitted because of Josef;
b) *Patriae* has the same root as *pater*: Freud's self-analysis had been activated by his father's death;
c) Freud's teaching signified a liberation of love, hence the negative reactions of his contemporaries and the implicit wish: *Saluti publicae vivit!* (He lives for the public well-being!).

Grinstein usefully outlines the career of Emperor Josef II. Born in 1741, he was the son of Francis I and Maria Theresa, becoming co-regent with the latter after his father's death in 1765. Because of frequent disagreements with his mother, he achieved little of note until her death in 1780, when he became head of the Hapsburg Empire. An impatient and ambitious man, he promulgated many reforms in the spirit of 'the greatest good for the greatest number': he emancipated the serfs, and decreed equality of taxation and equal punishment for equal crimes regardless of the class of the offender; he introduced press freedom; he founded secular hospitals, asylums, orphanages and schools; he granted equal civil rights to the Jews, making them subject to military service for the first time in Europe and raising some to the nobility. To force through his reforms, Josef centralised the state, imposed the German language (thus causing national rebellions in Hungary and in Belgium), and set up a police state. Because of his authoritarian methods, he was deserted by his friends and never gained any popular support. On January 30, 1790 (only a few months after the beginning of the French Revolution), he was forced to withdraw all his reforms, and died three weeks later.

In dreaming about him, Freud was thinking of how failure and death lie in wait for the ambitious, particularly if they are ahead of their time and do not enjoy the support of their peers.

The theme of rivalry with one's elders. – Josef Paneth (1857–90) succeeded Freud as demonstrator in Brücke's laboratory, and hoped eventually to secure one of the posts of assistant occupied by Sigmund Exner (1846–1925) and Ernst Fleischl von Marxow (1846–91). He once expressed eagerness to take the place of the gravely ill Fleischl – but paid dearly for his impatience, since he was the first to die.

But there are other elements, which Freud does not mention in his analysis. Fleischl and, more particularly, Breuer had helped Freud during his studies by making him considerable loans (J I, 174–6). As has been revealed by correspondence which has since come to light (unpublished letter from Freud to Josef Breuer of January 7, 1898, quoted in *L* 243–5), it was in 1898 that Freud, who was by then in a financially stable position, took steps to repay his debt to Breuer, with whom he no longer had any professional relationship. Breuer would not hear of such a thing, since he regarded his payment to Freud as a gift. Freud was furious with Breuer, who was thus preventing him from removing the last token of his dependence. So in the dream he gets rid of Josef, i.e. Breuer.

Fliess was the only person Freud had let into the secret of his animosity towards Breuer. A year and a half later, Freud intimated in a letter to his friend that he would like to 'finish with Breuer', but was inhibited from doing so by an old money debt (*F*, May 20, 1900, 415). On January 16, 1898, he had told Fliess that his debt to Breuer amounted to the considerable sum of 2,300 florins (*F* 294). Whom, now, could Freud let into the secret of his animosity towards Fliess? Freud felt the same mixture of hostility and affection towards Fliess as he had towards Breuer. During the ceremonial unveiling of the memorial to Fleischl, he had reflected: 'What a number of valued friends I have lost, some through death, some through a breach of our friendship! How fortunate that I have found a substitute for them and that I have gained one who means more to me than ever the others could, and that, at a time of life when new friendships cannot easily be formed, I shall never lose his!' (*ID* 486). At the same time, the irreverent remark about nobody being irreplaceable struck a chord in Freud: 'How many people I've followed to the grave already! But I'm still alive. I've survived them all; I'm left in possession of the field' (*ID* 485). He then quoted the well-known joke about the married couple, one of whom says to the other: 'If one of us dies, I shall move to Paris.'

Freud was then able to recall the two childhood memories that lay at the origin of this theme of rivalry with one's elders. The more recent of the two dated from when he was 14: probably for the first time since they had left Freiberg (resulting in the two branches of the family becoming separated), Emanuel and his son John visited Vienna. They were the first revenants in Sigismund's life. Before recollecting the scene that then took place between him and John, Freud – as always seeking cultural references, which in this case, because of the nationality of the revenants, are naturally English – alludes to two tragedies by Shakespeare in two different sections of his analysis. Grinstein comments on them as follows.

Remarking on Josef Paneth's impatient ambitiousness, which is a disguise for his own, Freud writes: 'Wherever there is rank and promotion the way lies open for wishes that call for suppression. Shakespeare's Prince Hal could not, even at his father's sick-bed, resist the temptation of trying on the crown' (*ID* 484). This takes place in Scene 5 of Act 4 of *Henry IV Part 2*. King Henry IV, mortally ill, is lying on his bed; he has had his crown placed on his pillow. Prince Hal, who is heir to the throne, enters and proposes to watch over the king; his brothers and various lords in attendance leave the room; King Henry falls asleep. Prince Hal expresses his affection for his dying father, puts on the crown that will be his, and exits. But the king awakes, calls his attendants, asks why they have left him alone and why his crown has gone, denounces Hal's impatience to see him die and to succeed him, and says that his son's callous haste is helping to finish him off. The prince returns, and the others leave again. The king complains of his son's avidity. Prince Hal excuses himself and says he had thought that his father was dead and that the cares of the crown had contributed to his death, adding that he himself had put on the crown 'To try with it, as with an enemy/ That had before my face murder'd my father,/ The quarrel of a true inheritor', without joy or pride. The king forgives him. Freud was no doubt struck here by the conflict between ambition and filial piety, and by the guilt experienced by the son because he had wished his father dead – a conflict and a guilt that he had himself re-experienced in the course of his self-analysis.

The second quotation, from *Julius Caesar*, needs to be seen in context. Brutus and Cassius lead a conspiracy to preserve the republic against the ambitions of Julius Caesar, who is suspected of wanting to become emperor. Shakespeare, basing his play on Plutarch's account, assumes that Brutus was Caesar's illegitimate son: hence Caesar's celebrated death cry '*Et tu, Brute?*', which appears in Plutarch as '*Et tu, mi fili, Brute?*' ('You too, my son, Brutus?'). Freud quotes a passage from Brutus' speech at Caesar's funeral (Act 3, Scene 2) which is eminently applicable to his own rivalry with John: 'As Caesar loved me, I weep for him; as he was fortunate, I rejoice at it; as he was valiant, I honour him; but, as he was ambitious, I slew him' (*ID* 424). The July of the dream, says Freud, can be explained by the fact that it was named after Julius Caesar. He adds that *Cäsar* [Caesar] is connected with *Kaiser* [emperor], a name present both in the statue of Kaiser Josef II and in the street Kaiser Josefstrasse, i.e. both emperor and father. Freud's distancing of himself from a rival friend was the result of a similar distancing process vis-à-vis his father.

But Freud does not mention that Julius was the first name of his younger brother, who was born a year and a half after him – like Paneth – and died at the age of six months. *Non vixit* applies perfectly well, grammatically, to Julius: 'He did not live' (or, better even, as in the inscription on the monument of Emperor Josef II, *Vixit non diu*: 'He did not live long'). Yet when he discovered the Oedipus myth, Freud told Fliess not only about his nurse's lessons, his sexual curiosity about his mother, and his cruelty to Pauline (with the active help of John), but also about Julius' role in his life (he did not mention his first name any more than he did the names of John and Pauline): 'I greeted my one-year-younger brother (who died after a few months) with adverse wishes and genuine childhood jealousy; and [...] his death left the germ of [self]-reproaches in me' (*F*, October 3, 1897, 268). Thus by October 1897 Freud had retrieved many of the essential memories of his infancy, but he had retrieved them solely as representations. In September and October 1898 it was as affects that those same memories fuelled his dreams. It is easy to see why the second version of his book took into consideration the transformation of affects, a notion overlooked by the first version.

Freud had already alluded to his fights with John in connection with earlier dreams, such as the 'Rome' series and the dream of the 'Uncle with the yellow beard'. But since October 1897 he had made no further mention of John, either in his correspondence with Fliess or in the analysis of his dreams. It was as a result of his two most recent dreams, 'Riding on a horse', and '*Non vixit*', that he had begun to relive, in the 'transference' on to Fliess, his ambivalence towards his childhood rival (John was a revenant par excellence), and to grasp the structuring role which that childhood relationship had had on the way his subsequent friendships developed. Julius, on the other hand, whom Freud had not mentioned since October 1897 either, never appeared again in later letters to Fliess or in the published text of *The Interpretation of Dreams*. Freud's anxiety about death had found its primal scene in that premature demise – a trauma that repeated itself every time someone in his close circle of family and friends died, a material reality built up by his psychical apparatus in order to give body to the punishment anxiety hanging over forbidden sexual desires, the key to his strong identification with victims and, at the same time, phantasied proof of his omnipotence over rivals.

The dénouement of Shakespeare's tragedy, which remained close to historical fact, illustrated perfectly, in Freud's eyes, the inevitability of the punishment which eventually strikes down those who kill their fathers or their brothers. Mark Antony arouses the populace against the conspirators. The latter are defeated at the battle of Philippi and seem to be on the point of being captured. Cassius orders one of his men to stab him, and, in his dying moments, says: 'Caesar, thou art avenged.' Brutus then enters, and says: 'O Julius Caesar! thou art mighty yet! /Thy spirit walks abroad, and turns our swords/ In our own proper entrails.' Brutus, who saw Caesar's ghost for the second time the night before the battle, realises that his time has come: he asks one of his men to hold his sword, and runs on to it shouting: 'Caesar now be still; I kill'd not thee with half so good a will' (Act V, Scene 5).

Freud's associations enabled him to retrieve the memory of another theatrical scene – one he himself acted in with John when he came from England to visit Vienna in 1870. It so happened that they played the roles of Brutus (Sigismund) and Caesar (John) in an extract from a play written by Schiller at the age of 18, *Die Räuber* (*The Robbers*). Here is the plot, based on Grinstein's summary of it (G 297–305). Count Maximilian von Moor, goaded by his physically deformed son Francis, disowns his elder son Charles, because of his delinquent pranks and his debts (the theme of sibling rivalry for his father's succession). Charles, who had hoped his father would forgive him but learns from Francis that he has been disgraced, is forced to take to the forests at the head of a band of robbers. Maximilian then begins to feel remorse over his treatment of Charles. In order to hasten the count's death, Francis arranges for him to be told that his son has been killed in battle. Delighted to see that his plot has had the desired effect, Francis then tries to woo Amelia, Charles' sweetheart and the count's niece, with whom the two brothers were brought up (the theme of transgression of the incest barrier, and of sibling rivalry for a woman: also to be noted is the similarity between the name Amelia and that of Freud's mother, Amalie). Charles appears at the castle in disguise and learns that he is responsible for his father's dying of grief. Amelia falls in love with him but does not recognise him. Francis, certain that the visitor to the castle is Charles, tries to get this 'revenant' killed. Charles rejoins the robbers, who have been concerned at his long absence. That night, while they sleep, he picks up his lute and recites, alone, a dialogue in verse between Brutus and Caesar (quoted in full by Grinstein, G 300–1; this was the interlude enacted by Sigismund and John), in which the dead Caesar appears to his son Brutus as a revenant. Charles, who believes himself to have been responsible for his father's death, here expresses his identification with Brutus and his own suicidal thoughts.

Charles then discovers that his father did not die, but simply fainted, and that he is being held prisoner by Francis in the dungeon: he, then, is yet another 'revenant'. The robbers attack the castle. Francis kills himself. Charles is about to be recognised and loved by Amelia, but in a fit of rage reveals himself to be the leader of a band of robbers and murderers, and wishes death and destruction on his father and his beloved Amelia. The count dies. Charles embraces Amelia, but is reminded by an aged robber, who places a sword between them, that he has sworn an oath of allegiance to the robbers and is not free to go with her. Charles kills her and gives himself up to justice. (Here again, punishment has the last word; it should be remembered, too, that Freud's nurse encouraged him to steal; lastly, the robbers in this play anticipate what Freud later described, in *Totem and Taboo*, as the brother horde united by the same crime.)

Let us turn now to the second, earlier memory dating from Freiberg that lay behind the words *non vixit* in the dream. John and Sigismund once fought over an object, each of them claiming to have got there before the other (cf. the theme of lateness) and therefore to have a better right to it. Sigismund knew he was in the wrong (cf. the wrong tense in the dream) but used force and got the better of his nephew (which is surprising if, as Freud says, he was not yet two at the time – John was nine months his senior).

John hurried to his grandfather (Sigismund's father), and complained about his young uncle (cf. the theme of indiscretion). Sigismund defended himself in a short speech which so struck his parents that they often repeated it to him in later years, thus fixing the memory in his mind: 'I hit him 'cos he hit me.' He used the colloquial verb *wichsen* (bash). 'It wasn't me who bashed him' would have contained the words *nicht gewichst*, which echo *non vixit* (*ID* 424–5). Hence the underlying phantasy forming the connection between this memory and the dream: '"It serves you right if you had to make way for me. Why did you try to push *me* out of the way? I don't need you, I can easily find someone else to play with," and so on' (*ID* 484).

Freud was breaking with Breuer just as he had broken with his father and was preparing to break with Fliess. Like Otto and the uncle with the yellow beard (who was also called Josef), they were all revenants, reincarnations of that first figure who '*früh sich einst dem trüben Blick gezeigt*' ('. . . long since appeared before my troubled gaze'), as Goethe wrote in the Dedication to *Faust, Part I*. Freud suddenly became aware of one of the recurring features of his life: 'My emotional life has always insisted that I should have an intimate friend and a hated enemy. I have always been able to provide myself afresh with both, and it has not infrequently happened that the ideal situation of childhood has been so completely reproduced that friend and enemy have come together in a single individual' (*ID* 483).

But revenants exist only as long as one likes: none of them is irreplaceable. Freud decided to rid himself of remorse and exist in his own right, to face the inevitability of his own end by living on in his children and in his works, and to become a father in every sense of the term. Likewise, the problem of indiscretion was settled: Freud would appear in his work as he really was. 'One is bound to emerge as the only villain among the crowd of noble characters who share one's life' (*ID* 485). He would publish his analysis of the '*Non vixit*' dream. He would tell Fliess about his dreams: 'It is astonishing how often you appear in them. In the *non vixit* dream I am delighted to have outlived you; isn't it terrible to suggest something like this – that is, to have to make it explicit to everyone who understands?' (*F*, September 21, 1899, 374). He left the dialectics of noble souls to psychoneurotics.

It was Plato who said that the essence of language was to reveal the truth. '*It is from*' instead of '*it is by*', and '*non vixit*' instead of '*non vivit*', were warnings whose significance did not escape the dreamer. 'Perhaps, however, my scarcely being able to tell lies any more is a consequence of my occupation with psychoanalysis. As often as I try to distort something I succumb to an error or some other parapraxis that betrays my insincerity,' he wrote not long afterwards (*PEL* 221).

Anxiety about death loomed large in Freud's self-analysis over a period of several months: he who wishes to kill his rivals will be punished with death; that is the law of an eye for an eye. The dead reappear to the culprit in the form of revenants in order to tell him so. Freud counters this anxiety, whose deeper nature escapes him, with narcissistic confidence in his own lucky star, and savours his delight (*Freude*) at having survived so many dead rivals. A memorial will be unveiled to him one day – to the man who revealed the meaning of dreams and who will reveal himself in his book.

Yet again, as after the dream of 'My son, the Myops' and 'Goethe's attack on Herr M.', Freud's relationship with Fliess survived the storm. On November 30, 1898, Freud reported with typical bluntness the 'phenomenon' of feeling angry about Fliess's ill-health and wanting to find fault with Fliess's surgery. At the same time, showing another facet of his ambivalence, he suggested a 'congress' at about Christmas time; he added that if he had made a great deal of his boils in his correspondence, it was because he wanted to put a damper on his expression of sympathy towards Fliess and on the further comments that he (Fliess) would certainly make about his own illness.

The discovery of the condensation of words (autumn 1898)

THE 'HEARSING' DREAM

This dream, which is impossible to date accurately, seems to me to follow on naturally from the one just discussed: it, too, mentions Fliess as well as the English branch of Freud's family. Here is the relevant passage in full:

'In a confused dream of my own of some length, whose central point seemed to be a sea voyage, it appeared that the next stopping place was called "*Hearsing*" and the next after that "*Fliess*". This last word was the name of my friend in B[erlin], who has often been the goal of my travels. "Hearsing" was a compound. One part of it was derived from the names of places on the suburban railway near Vienna, which so often end in "ing": Hietzing, Liesing, Mödling (Medelitz, "*meae deliciae*", was its old name – that is "*meine Freud*" ["my delight"]). The other part was derived from the English word "hearsay". This suggested slander and established the dream's connection with its indifferent instigator of the previous day: a poem in the periodical *Fliegende Blätter* [literally, "flying leaves"] about a slanderous dwarf called "Sagter Hatergesagt" ["He-says Says-he"[1]]. If the syllable "ing" were to be added to the name "Fliess" we should get "Vlissingen", which was in fact the stopping-place [the verb used is *berühren*, "to touch on"] on the sea voyage made by my brother whenever he visited us from England. But the English name for Vlissingen is "Flushing", which in English means "blushing" and reminded me of the patients I have treated for ereutophobia, and also of a recent paper on that neurosis by Bechterew which had caused me some annoyance' (*ID* 298).

This passage is to be found in Section A, 'The Work of Condensation', of Chapter 5, 'The Dream-Work'. It is one of a series of illustrations of how words can be condensed in dreams. The series also includes two other dreams, which I shall discuss later: '*Norekdal*' and '*Autodidasker*'.

No other dream of Freud's displays such concision in the rebus it poses or such obviousness in its syntax. It is a succession of proper names (place names and personal names), all of which exist in real life except Hearsing, which is coined by the dreamer. Most of the proper names also have meanings as common nouns – a fact not always indicated by Freud. Hearsing can be split up into the English words 'hear' and 'sing'. Fliess in German means 'to flow'. Hietzing is reminiscent of the German word *Hitze*, which means 'heat'. Liesing and Mödling, on the other hand, apparently have no particular double meaning, and seem simply to act as a transition to the name Medelitz, which Freud translates by the Latin '*meae deliciae*' and the German '*meine Freud*' (my delight). It is to be noted that the German word for joy is feminine (as is the French word *joie*), and that the schoolmates who joked about Freud's name no doubt harped on the feminine gender of *Freud*. Previous dreams have already alluded to *filles de joie* and to the jibes about his name he had to put up with as a child.

Freud says that Hearsing derives partly from the English word 'hear-say', but does not go into the literal meaning in English of its two limbs, 'hear' and 'sing'. He also sees a parallel between Vlissingen (the Dutch name of the port on Walcheren Island in the mouth of the West Scheldt river) and its English name, Flushing, which also means 'blushing' or 'going red'. He brings in the name of the Russian physiologist Bechterew, who later worked with Pavlov, in connection with 'ereutophobia', on which Bechterew had recently written a paper. This neurotic symptom is also known as 'erythrophobia'; but Freud probably preferred the other term because of its similarity with 'erotophobia', or fear of love. Lastly, the pseudonym of the 'slanderous dwarf' ('He-says Says-he') is an allusion to aggressive verbal usage.

1. A more accurate rendering would be "He-said Said-he", or possibly "He-says Said-he [Translator's note]

Most of the dream's onomastic permutations centre on the syllable 'sing' (e.g. Hearsing, Vlis-sing-en), which evokes the notion of song in both German and English, or on its variants 'zing' (Hiet-zing), 'sing' (Lie-sing) and 'shing' (Flu-shing). Another series of near homophones is to be found at the beginning of the names Fliess, *Fliegenden Blätter*, Vlissingen and Flushing.

We can now perceive the dream's meaning. As regards Fliess and his scientific work, it expresses Freud's unappreciative feelings which we have already encountered elsewhere: according to 'hearsay', Fliess is the object of much criticism – criticism which I share; I act like a 'slanderous dwarf' towards him; his work makes me 'blush'. The underlying infantile wish is probably connected with games of a more or less homosexual character: Freud the girl, delight, the place his brother 'touches', the flushing of the face, the heat of an erection. It is possible that Freud may already have written the passage in *The Interpretation of Dreams* where he draws a parallel between dreams of flying and children's games involving muscular excitation ('romping'), which often give rise to sexual feelings and end in tears (*ID* 271–3).

Enjoyment of puns is probably a displacement and extension of such sexual games, whether solitary or shared. The last remark in the dream ('which had caused me some annoyance') applies in the manifest content to Bechterew's paper, and in the latent content to sexual excitation. Lastly, the technique of psychoanalysis also features in the dream: is not taking delight (*meine Freud*) in hearsay an exact definition of the pleasure taken by the psychoanalyst?

The 'Hearsing' dream is a dream about a sea voyage. The English branch of the family had been the first stopping-place in Freud's life, and Fliess the second. He was now determined to continue his voyage of discovery, alone if necessary. Before successfully completing his long journey home, did not Odysseus have to wrench himself away from each port of call?

THE '*NOREKDAL*' DREAM

This dream is even harder to date than the 'Hearsing' dream; I have assumed it to be more or less contemporary with it because of their contiguity in *The Interpretation of Dreams* and their similarities (verbal condensation and veiled criticism of Fliess):

'On one occasion a medical colleague had sent me a paper he had written, in which the importance of a recent physiological discovery was, in my opinion, overestimated, and in which, above all, the subject was treated in too emotional a manner. The next night I dreamt a sentence which clearly referred to this paper: "*It's written in a positively norekdal style.*" The analysis of the word caused me some difficulty at first. There could be no doubt that it was a parody of the [German] superlatives "*kolossal*" and "*pyramidal*"; but its origin was not so easy to guess. At last I saw that the monstrosity was composed of [*zerfiel*] the two names "Nora" and "Ekdal" – characters in two well-known plays of Ibsen's [*A Doll's House* and *The Wild Duck*]. Some time before, I had read a newspaper article on Ibsen by the same author whose latest work I was criticising in the dream' (*ID* 296).

Grinstein devotes a chapter to this dream (G, Chapter 8). Its location in *The Interpretation of Dreams* suggests two lines of thought. Just before discussing this example, Freud returns to the Irma dream and mentions the group of condensations attached to 'Wilhelm' (Fliess): Munich, Propylaea, propyls, trimethylamin. And just after the '*Norekdal*' dream, he quotes two dreams by patients – '*Maistollmütz*', where he shows that 'a long chain of thoughts and associations led off from each syllable of this verbal hotchpotch [*Wortklumpen*, a word coined by Freud, meaning a verbal heap, with connotations of crudeness]' (*ID* 297); and '*Tutelrein*', in connection with which he adds the following footnote: 'The first reader and critic of this book – and his successors are likely to follow his example – protested that "the dreamer seems to be too ingenious and amusing". This is quite true so long as it refers only to the dreamer. [. . .] The fact is intimately connected with the theory of jokes and the comic. Dreams become ingenious and amusing because the direct and easiest pathway to the expression of their thoughts is barred: they are forced into being so' (*ID* 297 n.1). The protesting reader was Fliess; Freud answered his criticism in his letter of September 11, 1899.

Thus, the 'recent physiological discovery' which the author of the paper had 'overestimated' was very probably Fliess's theory of periodicity, which the latter, in his book of 1897, had indeed treated 'in too emotional a manner', and which had earned him widespread and scathing criticism (echoed in the dream of 'Goethe's attack on Herr M.').

Freud explains the name Norekdal as being a condensation of Nora and Ekdal. Nora is the Christian name of the central character in *A Doll's House* (1879); and Ekdal is the surname of one of the main characters in *The Wild Duck* (1884). Grinstein gives a detailed and comparative analysis of the two plays (G 211–20) which may be summarised as follows.

In *A Doll's House*, Nora, who is married to a banker, Torvald, and has three children, is a young woman of striking immaturity: both her father and her husband have treated her like a 'doll'. An employee of the bank, who has been dismissed by Torvald, intends to take his revenge by revealing that Nora had once been guilty of forging a signature on the receipt for a loan she had obtained without her husband's knowledge. A woman friend of the employee makes sure that the revelation is made, as she believes that marriage should not be based on a lie and that Nora's husband should know the truth. As a result, their marriage breaks up. Nora discovers that her husband does not love her, and in order to stop being a perpetually dominated 'doll' she leaves him and her children.

In *The Wild Duck*, fifteen years before the play opens, Ekdal married Gina, the former housekeeper of the wealthy Werle, without realising that she had once had an affair with her employer. Werle is now developing progressive blindness. His son, Gregers, an old friend of Ekdal's, suffers from overidealism and hates his father. He discovers not only that his father had an affair with Gina, but that, having contracted syphilis, he infected his wife, causing her final illness, and is now going blind for the same reason. Gregers decides to tell Ekdal the whole truth, expecting him to have 'an ennobling experience'; instead, relations between Ekdal and his wife become strained, gloomy, and disillusioned. Their 14-year-old daughter, who has lovingly brought up a wild duck wounded by Werle, is also going blind. Ekdal is obsessed by the idea that her real father is Werle and that she does not love him (Ekdal). She is desperate to show that she does in fact love her father, and is persuaded by Gregers to sacrifice the wild duck as proof of her love. Instead, she shoots herself. The Ekdals are reunited in their grief. Gregers goes mad. Another character, a doctor, remarks that life would be tolerable 'if only we could be rid of the confounded dunce that keeps on pestering us, in our poverty, with the claim of the ideal'.

Both plays contain themes that are to be found in Freud's latest dreams: the withdrawal or refusal of love, the dangerous nature of women, and syphilis, which physically punishes children for the sexual pleasures enjoyed by their father. The new element is an allusion to the aim of psychoanalysis, which is to reveal to people the truth about themselves, whatever the risks involved. Just as Freud criticised Fliess's discoveries, just as he had himself once got into considerable trouble as a result of the unfortunate side-effects of cocaine, whose pharmacological properties he had discovered, so his forthcoming book on dreams, which was going to reveal the innermost truths of the human soul to a still immature general public, would be received with criticism and lack of comprehension. The road from psychoanalysis to disillusionment would be a short one . . .

Ibsen's plays enjoyed 'colossal' popularity in German theatres at that time, and as Schur points out (S 175, n.11) the role of Oswald in *Ghosts* (1881) was as eagerly sought after by leading actors as that of Hamlet: the young Oswald, a victim of congenital syphilis, is stricken with general paralysis, and the play ends with his repeated cry, 'The sun, the sun', which is reminiscent of the cry 'Nature! Nature!' uttered by the mentally ill brother of one of Freud's women patients – one of the sources of the dream of 'Goethe's attack on Herr M.'.

In another passage of *The Interpretation of Dreams*, Freud refers to Ibsen as bringing 'the immemorial struggle between fathers and sons into prominence in his writings' (*ID* 257).

The manifest content of the dream amounts to nothing more than the word 'style'; what does this conceal? *Kolossal* is an allusion to the Colossus of Rhodes, a gigantic statue with feet of clay; this is a way of criticising Fliess. In its form, *pyramidal* is an obsolete German word; in its content, it alludes to the pyramids, imposing monuments built by the Egyptian pharaohs, who oppressed the Jewish people. The following sentence in Freud's analysis is most curious: 'I saw that the monstrosity was composed of [literally, broke down into] the two names "Nora" and "Ekdal"'; it calls to mind the popular description of the primal scene as consisting of a two-headed and eight-limbed monster. This is an allusion to the memory revived by the 'Count Thun' dream: Sigismund urinated in his parents' bedroom, and the bisexual monster of his united parents split up into two bodies, a man like Ekdal and a woman like Nora. Freud imagined himself playing the part of Ibsen in this scene, that is to say – for does not the dream play on words? – the part of *ipse* ('himself' in Latin), just as Signorelli had painted himself in the corner of one of his frescoes. This splitting up of the monstrous couple is the *coup de théâtre* of a dream which is doubly theatrical, both in its language and in its references to Ibsen.

This termination of an amorous exchange is also significant with regard to Freud's transference on to Fliess. Freud wants to stop being the dominated 'doll', the instrument of a rich blind old man, the Jewish prisoner of the pharaoh. Eva Rosenblum has suggested a literal interpretation of the dream which points strongly to its latent homosexuality: Norekdal can equally well break down into no-*rektal* (an English word and a German word). The misspelling of *rektal* (in fact d and t are often interchangeable in Germanic dialects) is yet another attempt to conceal the impropriety of the thought. In that interpretation, Freud had decided to terminate the kind of 'rectal' (i.e. passive, submissive) relationship which, up to then unconsciously, he had built up with Fliess.

But if the dream criticises Fliess, it is also a portrait of the dreamer, Freud: he, and no other, invented that ingenious word, even if he rejects pompousness of style. That was the style we have already seen in the dream of the 'Open-air closet', where Gargantua straddles Notre-Dame and urinates on Paris – a style characteristic of infantile megalomania.

THE '*AUTODIDASKER*' DREAM

This dream, which consists essentially of a composite word coined by the dreamer, belongs to the same series as the preceding dreams, 'Hearsing' and '*Norekdal*', and comes after them in *The Interpretation of Dreams*. It therefore probably dates from the autumn of 1898.

There were two day's residues lying behind the dream. The first involved the Jewish novelist Jakob Julius David (1859–1906), whose two first names must have reminded Freud of his father and his first brother, both of whom were dead. David was a friend of Freud's youngest brother Alexander, who had introduced the two men. Freud had read some of David's novels and given them to Martha to read. David was, moreover, somewhat unbalanced, and it is possible that Freud treated him. The following year, in a letter to Fliess, he wrote: 'J. J. David visited me several times in Vienna; he is an unhappy man and a not inconsiderable poet' (*F*, August 6, 1899, 366).

A summary of David's life, which I have borrowed from Grinstein (G 222–3), makes the dream more readily understandable. David was born in Mährisch-Weisskirchen (and not in Freiberg, as Freud supposed) of a Jewish family that had gradually lost its money and property. His father's behaviour was tyrannical and paradoxical: he once threw his son on the ground, hit him, and then kissed him. He died of cholera in 1866, and his family became destitute. David was a sickly child, whose elementary education was irregular. He read a great deal on his own. After catching typhoid, he became near-sighted and very hard of hearing. When at university, he studied mainly as an autodidact. He endured great deprivations of food and shelter. He scraped a living from his newspaper articles and his novels, then was helped by a sculptor friend, Heinrich Natter, in Gmunden (a town where Freud was once taken by his protector Breuer). In 1899 David wrote a thesis on Pestalozzi (the inventor of a teaching method that encouraged autodidactic methods). His health remained poor, and despite treatment by Nothnagel (no doubt the Professor N. mentioned in Freud's associations) died a premature death in 1906.

Freud relates that one of David's novels, the story of a man of talent who went to the bad after getting involved with a woman, had left a deep impression on Martha and caused her to worry about the future of their children. She discussed this with Sigmund, who had the '*Autodidasker*' dream immediately afterwards. Grinstein has identified the novel in question, and gives a detailed analysis of it (G 223–7), which I shall now summarise. It is an autobiographical novel called *Ein Dichter?* (*A Poet?*). The central character, Josef Bernhofer (we know of the significance of his first name for Freud), is a talented and needy poet who has to struggle against bouts of depression and concern that he will not be able to give his children a proper upbringing. He writes a report on a big fire he has just witnessed and takes it in to the newspaper that employs him. There, he is humiliated by Dr Wortmann, the editor, who says that although beautifully written the report is not factual enough. Bernhofer, he says, is just a very impractical writer of books; as a journalist, he is 'no good' (Freud was similarly criticised by his father when he urinated in his parents' bedroom, then by Brücke for arriving late at the laboratory, and lastly by Josef Breuer for making a financially unwise marriage). As he leaves the newspaper office, Josef Bernhofer tells a colleague a little about himself: he and his wife had two children, both of whom died; since working as a journalist he has been thinking of suicide. One day, after his wife Leni complains of his inability to find a job, he kills himself. Implicit here is the notion that women cause men's downfall.

We have already observed – and will shortly have occasion to observe again – that Martha's concern about her children was heightened by Martin's poetic talent: for were not poets reputed to live in garrets and consort with loose women? Freud's letters to Fliess mention Martin's gifts more than once, though more with admiration or amusement than with apprehension (May 16 and November 14, 1897, March 24 and August 20, 1898, and July 3, 1899).

The second day's residue was a curious episode in Freud's professional, as opposed to family, life. He was baffled by the case of a patient who seemed hysterical but who vehemently denied the existence of any sexual aetiology; Freud therefore suspected he was suffering from an organic disease. He asked Professor N. (probably Nothnagel) to give his opinion. N. was convinced it must be a neurosis. Highly sceptical of this, Freud told the patient he could do nothing for him and recommended him to seek other advice. Whereupon the patient apologised for having lied and revealed precisely the piece of sexual aetiology Freud had been seeking. 'I was relieved but at the same time humiliated. I had to admit that my consultant, not being led astray by considering the anamnesis, had seen more clearly than I had' (*ID* 301). Yet that consultant did not share Freud's views on the sexual aetiology of the neuroses.

That night Freud had a dream:

'On another occasion I had a dream which consisted of two separate pieces. The first piece was the word "*Autodidasker*", which I recalled vividly. The second piece was an exact reproduction of a short and harmless phantasy which I had produced some days before. This phantasy was to the effect that when I next saw Professor N. I must say to him: "The patient about whose condition I consulted you recently is in fact only suffering from a neurosis, just as you suspected." Thus the neologism "Autodidasker" must satisfy two conditions: firstly, it must bear or represent a composite meaning; and secondly, that meaning must be solidly related to the intention I had reproduced from waking life of making amends to Professor N.

'The word "Autodidasker" could easily be analysed into "Autor" [author], "Autodidakt" [self-taught] and "Lasker", with which I also associated the name of Lassalle' (*ID* 298–9).

The dream and an initial detailed analysis of it are to be found at the end of Section A, 'The Work of Condensation', of Chapter 6, 'The Dream-Work' (*ID* 298–302). Freud refers to the dream, more briefly, on several other occasions: in connection with secondary revision (*ID* 493), regression (*ID* 535 and 542), and the primary and secondary processes (*ID* 597). Grinstein devotes a chapter to the dream (G, Chapter 9).

According to Freud, the dream aimed to prove that the fears expressed by Martha and Nothnagel about the future of his children were wrong. After giving his opinion on the case already described, Nothnagel had asked Freud how many children he had and whether they were girls or boys: 'Well, now, be on your guard! Girls are safe enough, but bringing up boys leads to difficulties later on.' This second diagnosis pleased Freud no more than the earlier one. He was convinced that the great danger encountered during adolescence – that of damage caused by a woman – was 'of the kind that a good upbringing averted'. Freud was perspicacious enough to realise that the patient was offering a significant alternative: he was suffering either from general paralysis (once again the spectre of syphilis) or from a neurosis. This was an alternative that his sons were likely to face when they reached puberty. In any case, whether the disorder was organic or psychogenic, the cause was always the same – sexuality, or desire for women.

The dream's meaning is contained in a symbolic neologism, *Autodidasker* (a worthy successor to Hollthurn, Hearsing and *Norekdal*). Freud unravels the conundrum as follows:

a) *Autor*: this refers to J. J. David's autobiographical novel. The summary given above shows that Freud experienced a heroic-masochistic identification with David, who was an important, misunderstood, and unhappy author.

b) *Autodidakt*: Freud does not explain this; but the self-taught person is obviously himself, since he has made discoveries about the neuroses. In the course of perusing the scientific literature on dreams, he had no doubt noticed that once again no other author had suspected what he had discovered. How humiliating, then, it must have been for the self-taught Freud when a colleague with no knowledge of the role of sexuality diagnosed a neurosis more perspicaciously than he had, and then warned him of the dangers of sexuality! Someone who starts his own education all over again by carrying out self-analysis is also self-taught; the process is similar to that described in Goethe's semi-autobiographical *Wilhelm Meisters Lehrjahre* (*The Apprenticeship of Wilhelm Meister*). It should also be remembered that Freud's father was a self-taught man.

c) *Lasker*: Eduard Lasker (1829–84) was one of the leaders of the National Liberal Party in Germany. His name began with the same syllable as that of Ferdinand Lassalle (1825–64), the founder of the German Social Democratic movement. Both were Jewish; both were born in or near Breslau; and Freud had sympathies with both their political movements. But they both died because of women, Lasker from general paralysis (in a short autobiographical novel he related how he refused to marry despite the fact that all women fell in love with him), and Lassalle in a duel (he fell in love with a diplomat's daughter and they planned to marry; when her parents opposed her marrying a commoner and a Jew, the girl declared herself ready to elope with Lassalle – who thereupon lost his nerve; she then broke with him and was reconciled with her former fiancé; her father, when challenged by Lassalle to a duel, allowed himself to be replaced by her fiancé, who shot and killed Lassalle; just before he died, Lassalle wrote: 'I hereby declare that I myself took my life') (based on G 228–33). The meaning of these dream-thoughts is, as Freud says: '*Cherchez la femme*.'

d) *Alex*, an approximate anagram of Lasker, was the shortened form of the name of Freud's younger brother, Alexander, who was still unmarried. Freud was worried about this, as he wanted him to settle down to a happy married life. He felt responsible for the upbringing of this brother, just as he had been for the choice of his name.

Lastly, Freud remarks that the word *Autodidasker* was formed in the same way as the name Sandoz in *L'Oeuvre* (*The Masterpiece*) by Zola, another novelist Freud admired. In that novel, Zola 'introduced himself and his own domestic happiness as an episode. He appears under the name of "Sandoz". The transformation was probably arrived at as follows. If "Zola" is written backwards (the sort of thing children are so fond of doing), we arrive at "Aloz". No doubt this seemed too undisguised. He therefore replaced "Al", which is the first syllable of "Alexander", by "Sand", which is the third syllable of the same name' (*ID* 300). Thus the word *Autodidasker* symbolically represents not only the dreamer's wish, but also a dream-work process which had previously escaped Freud's notice and to which his attention had been drawn by his latest dreams: the mechanism of condensation affects not only thing-presentations but word-presentations.

Grinstein (G 234–42) draws an interesting parallel between Freud and two characters in *L'Oeuvre*, one of whom is in fact Zola in disguise. The book, published in 1886, deals with a successful and happy Naturalist novelist, Pierre Sandoz (Zola), and his Impressionist painter friend, Claude Lantier (based on Paul Cézanne), who is depressed because his painting *Plein Air* has been rejected by the Academy for the Salon. Lantier sleeps with Christine, the model who posed in the nude for the painting, and they settle down together. Cohabitation, parenthood, and eventually marriage have an unwelcome effect on their relationship, which was originally idyllic and good for Lantier's creativity. He is stricken with impotence: he cannot make love to his wife, he cannot paint, he cannot feed his family (his son dies from lack of treatment). But his rejected picture has greatly influenced a new school of painting, Impressionism. One day, Christine forces him to make love to her and promise never to paint again (for years he has been working on a 'masterpiece' which he cannot bring himself to complete). She then falls asleep. Lantier hangs himself from a ladder in front of the canvas, close up against the nude woman depicted in it, whom he has ended up loving more than his living wife – who served as a model for her.

It is easy to imagine which aspects of the novel must have struck a chord in Freud's mind: the conflict between love and creativity (in *Civilization and its Discontents*, he later wrote that women adopt a 'hostile attitude' to the claims of civilization – *Kultur* – because man withdraws his libido from them in order to achieve his cultural aims); the representation of impotence in all its forms, even down to the manner of his suicide (the body hangs like a limp penis in front of the nude woman in the painting); the destruction of love by marriage and parenthood (both of which activate the incest taboo); and lastly the contrast between two husband-and-wife relationships – that of Sandoz, the happy creator, and that of Lantier, the failed creator (a contrast in which Freud recognised his own internal conflict).

Grinstein draws several parallels between Lantier and Freud: both were talented and had to struggle against the criticism they incurred; despite the general public's unfavourable reception, their work created a new and revolutionary school; the theme of sexuality, openly displayed, led to their severe censure; their 'life stories' appear to a large extent in *L'Oeuvre* and in *The Interpretation of Dreams*; and lastly, Lantier is told by Sandoz that he should console himself with the 'illusion that one day [he will] be accepted and understood' – a remark which must have made a deep impression on Freud.

I should like to make some additional points. Once again, the dream displays a wish which the dreamer wants others to recognise. Freud wants his teacher and his wife to regard him as capable of bringing up his children in such a way that happiness will be within their reach. Once again, Freud identifies with the creator of a work of art. Zola follows in the footsteps of Goethe, Shakespeare, Schiller and Signorelli. All these identifications are constructive, whereas those involving scientists, doctors and professors – Brücke, Meynert, Fleischl, Breuer, Königstein, Rie, Nothnagel and Fliess – are vitiated by ambivalence. Freud's work has as much in common with a work of art as it has with a work of science; or at least it elevates something which was previously dealt with only in works of art – the drama of human life (cf. Politzer, 1928) – to the status of a scientifically investigable subject, and it does so through a technique used by many great writers, that of free association.

Let us now try to answer the question which Freud's analysis leaves unanswered: what is the latent meaning of the neologism *Autodidasker*? What is the infantile wish fulfilled in the dream?

There is one field where boys are self-taught – at least the young Freud was: that of auto-erotism. The first use of the word by Freud, however, comes only later, in a letter to Fliess of December 9, 1899. It was a supposedly male preserve, as in Freud's time girls were thought not to masturbate and to be virgins when they got married. In that context, the dilemma which is condensed in the composite neologism *Autodidasker* becomes clear: one alternative open to a young man is to learn the technique of love-making from a woman (cf. the adolescent boy's phantasy of being initiated by his mother), as did Lasker, Lassalle, Bernhofer and Lantier, with the risk of either suffering syphilis and general paralysis if the woman involved is promiscuous or a prostitute, or else shouldering the emotional, financial and educative burden of marriage, and its resultant intellectual sterility; the other alternative is to masturbate. But the second course carries the same risks as the first: at that time, masturbation was condemned by educators as being dangerous, harmful, degrading, and a source of physical and psychical deterioration.

It is not for nothing that the name Breslau recurs several times in Freud's analysis: Lasker and Lassalle were born in, or not far from, that city; close friends of both Professor N. and Freud lived there. It was while passing through Breslau station, in the course of the Freuds' move from Freiberg to Leipzig, that the young Sigismund thought he saw the fires of hell leap up, which, he had been told by his Catholic Czech nurse, would consume him if he were not clean – and also, probably, if he masturbated. As we have seen, Sigismund subsequently hypercathected reading and writing to compensate for the separation from Freiberg and from his nurse; and the pleasure of playing with words (*Autodidasker* is an example) replaced that of playing with the erotogenic zones of his body. Eva Rosenblum has pointed out to me that the very language used by Freud in describing this dream connotes the twin themes of separation ('I had a dream which consisted of two separate pieces') and restructuring ('The intention I had [. . .] of making amends to Professor N.'). Breaking down *Autodidasker* into its constituent parts was a way of ridding auto-erotism of guilt feelings and asserting its formative aspect, which consists of fulfilling the wish to learn by oneself and about oneself. Was not Freud, through his self-analysis, discovering the domain of the unconscious, just as he had once discovered, under the impetus of his nurse and through auto-erotism, his own sexed body, and then, under his mother's influence and by teaching himself, the combination of syllables and words in reading and writing? Jewish children, particularly those with a Hasidic background, were often adept at word-play.

Lasker and Lassalle were the first two Jews who made a successful career in German politics, but the price they had to pay was failure in their love lives. Why should Freud not be one of the first German-speaking Jews to make a successful career as an investigator into the science of psychology, even if the price he had to pay was a restricted sex life and a heroic-masochistic identification, without which creative genius cannot blossom? The patient whom Freud asked Professor N. to examine eventually revealed the sexual aetiology which he had originally concealed. Man is an animal that lives, develops or falls ill for sexual reasons. At the precise moment when Freud began to doubt his own theories and assumed that his diagnosis of the patient was wrong, the very same patient proved his theories correct. Let me repeat a point I made earlier: identification with the victim or the patient (the failed artist, the unrecognised writer, the depressive, the paralytic, the impotent) was just as important for Freud as identification with the creative genius (in this case Zola).

THE 'FRAU DONI' DREAM (DECEMBER 5–6, 1898)

In a letter to Fliess of December 5, 1898, Freud mentioned that he had started research again for his book on dreams, but only with difficulty: 'The literature (on the dream) which I am now reading makes me completely stupid. A horrible punishment for those who write. In the process everything of one's own diffuses. I often cannot remember what I have found that is new, since everything about it is new. The reading stretches ahead, with no end in sight' (*F* 335). This passage proves that Freud was now working on what was to be the first chapter of the final version of his book, 'The Scientific Literature Dealing with the Problems of Dreams'.

Freud goes on in his letter to mention the recent death (on November 28) of Conrad Ferdinand Meyer, his purchase of three 'volumes I lacked' by that writer, *Hutten*, *Pescara* and *Der Heilige*, his enthusiasm for Meyer's work, his gratitude to Fliess for having introduced him to it, his intention of subjecting it to psychoanalytic interpretation, and lastly his great expectations of the 'congress' he and Fliess planned to hold at Christmas.

The following day, on December 6, Sigmund and Martha celebrated the ninth birthday of their eldest and poetically inclined son, Martin. That same day, Freud read, in his daily newspaper *Neue freie Presse*, the announcement dated December 5 of the death in Berlin, on November 30, of Frau Regina Albahary; the death was announced by her husband and their three sons and three daughters; one of the latter, Dona, still bore her maiden name, and was therefore unmarried. The text and date of this death notice were discovered by Grinstein (G 356–9), thus making it possible at last to date the dream accurately. He also established that the deceased woman was of Romanian Jewish origin and died at the age of 55. In his analysis, Freud says he had the dream the night before Martin's birthday, whereas it in fact occurred the night after: he made a similar mistake, as we have seen, over the exact date of his dream about the death of his father. He also says that the dead woman, whose age he does not specify, died in childbirth – a fact not mentioned by the death notice and in any case unlikely since she was 55. He adds: 'My wife told me that the dead woman had been looked after by the same midwife who had attended her at the birth of our two youngest children' (Sophie in 1893 and Anna in 1895). It is quite possible that the dead woman lived in Vienna for part of her life (the death notice gives three places of issue, 'Berlin, Bucharest and Vienna') and gave birth there, or that the midwife in question worked in Berlin (where she attended the dead woman) before moving to Vienna (where she looked after Martha, who was 37 at the time of the dream, i.e. 18 years younger than the dead woman). During the night of December 6, Freud had the following dream:

'*I was going to the hospital with P. through a district in which there were houses and gardens.*[1] *At the same time I had a notion that I had often seen this district before in dreams. I did not know my way about very well. He showed me a road that led round the*

1. The word translated as 'there were' is *vorkommen*, which is not the correct German term; it gives the impression of a play or novel where 'houses and gardens' are somehow in the wings or behind the scenes (note by Eva Rosenblum).

corner to a restaurant (indoors, not a garden). There I asked for Frau Doni and was told that she lived at the back in a small room with three children. I went towards it, but before I got there I met an indistinct figure with my two little girls; I took them with me after I had stood with them for a little while. Some sort of reproach against my wife, for having left them there.

'When I woke up I had a feeling of great satisfaction, the reason for which I explained to myself as being that I was going to discover from this analysis the meaning of "I've dreamt of that before". In fact, however, the analysis taught me nothing of the kind; what it did show me was that the satisfaction belonged to the latent content of the dream and not to any judgment upon it. My satisfaction was with the fact that my marriage had brought me children. P. was a person whose course in life lay for some time alongside mine, who then outdistanced me both socially and materially, but whose marriage was childless. The two events which occasioned the dream will serve, instead of a complete analysis, to indicate its meaning. The day before, I had read in a newspaper the announcement of the death of Frau Dona A—y (which I turned into "Doni" in the dream), who had died in childbirth. My wife told me that the dead woman had been looked after by the same midwife who had attended her at the birth of our two youngest children. The name "Dona" had struck me because I had met it for the first time a short while before in an English novel. The second occasion for the dream was provided by the date on which it occurred. It was on the night before the birthday of my eldest boy – who seems to have some poetic gifts' (*ID* 446–7).

This dream and Freud's analysis of it, reproduced above in full, are to be found in Section G of Chapter 6, 'The Dream-Work', as an example of 'Intellectual Activity in Dreams': judgments passed on dreams after waking usually turn out to be part of the material of the dream-thoughts. This dream belongs to the same series as the dreams of 'Goethe's attack on Herr M.' and 'Hollthurn'. Grinstein, who devotes a chapter to it (G, Chapter 15), has in all likelihood identified the English novel referred to by Freud – George Eliot's *Adam Bede* (1859). In it, Hetty becomes engaged to Adam Bede, and then discovers she is pregnant by Captain Donnithorne, who had earlier seduced her (thus, if she had married him, she would have been called *Frau Donni*thorne). Hetty kills her baby, is deported, and eventually dies. Adam Bede marries another young woman, with whom his brother, too, is in love. Grinstein also summarises Meyer's novelette, *The Tempting of Pescara*, which Freud had recently mentioned to Fliess. In the novelette, which is based on historical events, del Guasto (who is called Don Juan in the book) seduces, impregnates and abandons Giulia, who commits suicide before the baby is born. Pescara, an upright and courageous general, refuses to join the Pope's conspiracy against the Emperor, despite the pleadings of his childless wife, *Donna* Vittoria Colonna, who has ambitions of becoming Queen of Naples as the Pope promised, and who, incidentally, has a gift for poetry (like Jean Martin Freud). Pescara eventually dies of the wounds he received at the battle of Pavia, earlier the same year, when he captured King Francis I of France. It should be added that *Donna* is a common woman's Christian name in Italian novels.

Grinstein makes the following hypotheses about the dream. In his view, it is hostile to Martha and expresses the reproach that she is neglecting her two youngest children; it may also reflect Freud's wish that she should have died in childbirth, thus relieving him of some of his family burdens and enabling him to make a more brilliant career. But the dream in fact concerns Frau Regina Albahary, an older woman, a mother and a grandmother, whom the dreamer replaces with the Christian name of her unmarried daughter *Dona*. This strongly suggests that the hostile feelings are directed at Freud's own mother: if (after he was born) she had remained 'childless' like Dona and Donna Vittoria, if she had made sure that her (next) child would not live, like Giulia and Hetty, the young Freud would have had her all to himself; but, on the other hand, if she had looked after Julius better, he would not have died. The present latent 'satisfaction', expressed by the dream, at having had children would seem, then, to disguise an infantile latent satisfaction at the death of his younger brother Julius. At a deeper level there is also apparently some curiosity about women's genitals and the process of motherhood. In the second edition of *The Interpretation of Dreams* (1909), Freud indicated that, in dreams about places where emphasis is laid on the feeling of having been there before, the places are the mother's genitals, where the dreamer has inevitably been before (*ID* 399). The feeling 'I've dreamt of that before' was a topic which, by the time Freud had the 'Frau Doni' dream, had already been discussed in the pages of the French periodical, the *Revue philosophique*, over a period of two years (1896–98). Freud had clearly followed the discussion of the topic, to which the dream alludes ('a district in which there were houses and gardens'); it was only later, in 1909, that he gave it a psychoanalytic explanation, i.e. a sexual aetiology.

Let me complement Grinstein's remarks with some hypotheses of my own. The 'guide' – a figure that recurs increasingly often in Freud's dreams – no doubt represents both Breuer and Fliess. Frau Doni, who is confused with her unmarried daughter, and who lives 'at the back' with three of her children, could be Freud's unmarried sister-in-law Minna, who lived with the Freuds and probably concerned herself more particularly with the upbringing of their daughters. Martha/Minna shows the same vowel change ('a' becoming 'i') as Dona/Doni. In that case, the latent thought must be: if Martha had died in childbirth, Minna would have lived with me and brought up my children; I would have married and deflowered her. But the letters that appear in the name Minna all occur in the name Monika, the nurse who played such a key role in Freud's earliest infancy.

The double meaning of the expression 'stood' (with his daughters) confirms the underlying presence of a guilty wish on the part of the young Sigismund to exhibit himself to a little girl. The body image which informs the landscape and setting of the dream points in the same direction. In the course of reading the literature on dreams, Freud was probably struck by K. A. Scherner's *Das Leben des Traumes* (*The Life of Dreams*) (1861) and J. Volkelt's *Die Traum-Phantasie* (*Imagination in Dreams*) (1875), both of which are liberally referred to in *The Interpretation of Dreams*, and which postulate and illustrate the symbolism of the body and genitals in dreams – e.g. 'the maiden's garden in the Song of Solomon' (*ID* 346). Freud then worked out how hysterical symptoms can move from the lower to the upper part of the body, i.e. from the genitals to the head: he informed Fliess of this in a letter of January 16, 1899, adding that in young women 'migraine can be used to represent a forcible defloration'. The same notion can also be found in his remarks, in *The Interpretation of Dreams*, about masturbatory dreams of teeth being pulled out or falling out (*ID* 387).

Confrontation with the difference between the sexes

A SECOND DISGUISED AUTOBIOGRAPHICAL FRAGMENT: THE SCREEN MEMORY OF THE 'GREEN MEADOW WITH YELLOW FLOWERS SNATCHED FROM PAULINE' (LATE DECEMBER 1898–EARLY JANUARY 1899)

After recovering from his operation at the end of October 1898, Fliess visited Freud at Christmas. Their meeting once again had a miraculously stimulating effect on Freud: he made a further breakthrough in his self-analysis, enthusiastically resumed writing his book, and in January and February wrote Fliess frequent letters which teemed with new ideas as they had a year previously. As soon as Fliess returned to Berlin, Freud wrote describing the miraculous change that had come over him: 'I live in ill-humour and in darkness until you come; I get things off my chest; rekindle my flickering flame at your steadfast one and feel well again; and after your departure, I again have been given eyes to see, and what I see is beautiful and good' (*F*, January 3–4, 1899, 339).

In the same letter, Freud announced three important pieces of news. His scientific isolation and the contempt with which he believed he was regarded by his contemporaries were no longer total: Havelock Ellis, who specialised in sexual psychopathology, sent Freud an article of his which contained more praise than criticism of the ideas put forward by Freud in *Studies on Hysteria* and later publications. Secondly, the dream book had been given a new lease of life: 'I want to reveal to you only that the dream schema is capable of the most general application, that the key to hysteria as well really lies in dreams. I now also understand why in spite of all my efforts I have not yet finished the dream [book]. If I wait a little longer, I shall be able to present the psychic process in dreams in such a way that it also includes the process in the formation of hysterical symptoms.' Lastly, Freud had accomplished 'a small bit of my self-analysis', which 'confirmed that phantasies are products of later periods and are projected back from what was then the present into earliest childhood; the manner in which this occurs also emerged – once again by a verbal link.' So self-analysis had finally confirmed, in Freud's mind, the role of deferred action and that of word-presentations. It had also revealed to him, he said, that there exists a 'germ of a sexual impulse' in infancy.

Freud's account of this piece of self-analysis takes up half of his paper on *Screen Memories* (1899*a*, *SE* 3, 303–22). It is presented anonymously, rather as if it were a discussion with a former patient, along the lines of a Socratic dialogue. It was Siegfried Bernfeld (1946) who can take the credit for having established that the screen memory in question is in fact disguised autobiographical material.

The text of the screen memory, which Freud then discusses at length in his paper, runs as follows:

'I see a rectangular, rather steeply sloping piece of meadow-land, green and thickly grown; in the green there are a great number of yellow flowers – evidently common dandelions. At the top end of the meadow there is a cottage and in front of the cottage door two women are standing chatting busily, a peasant-woman with a handkerchief on her head and a children's nurse. Three children are playing in the grass. One of them is myself (between the age of two and three); the two others are my boy cousin, who is a year older than me, and his sister, who is almost exactly the same age as I am. We are picking the yellow flowers and each of us is holding a bunch of flowers we have already picked. The little girl has the best bunch; and, as though by mutual agreement, we – the two boys – fall on her and snatch away [*entreissen*] her flowers. She runs up the meadow in tears and as a consolation the peasant-woman gives her a big piece of black bread. Hardly have we seen this than we throw the flowers away, hurry to the cottage and ask to be given some bread too. And we are in fact given some; the peasant-woman cuts the loaf with a long knife. In my memory the bread tastes quite delicious – and at that point the scene breaks off' (*SE* 3, 311).

The characters in this screen memory are easy to identify. The two 'cousins' are in fact Freud's nephew and niece, John and Pauline. The 'peasant-woman' or the 'children's nurse' is probably Monika Zajíc.

Let me first propose a general interpretation of this screen memory; I shall return later to Freud's use of it in his self-analysis.

This is the screen memory that was latent and operative in many of Freud's earlier dreams – those, for instance, which contained a slope, a meadow, or, as in the recent 'Frau Doni' dream, 'a district in which there were houses and gardens'; those which alluded to games played by children when left to their own devices, and sexual curiosity about little girls; or those where yellow was the predominant colour, as in the other disguised autobiographical memory that lay behind the 'Yellow lion' dream. There is also present, behind the screen memory, an individual phantasy which itself ties in with a primal phantasy, probably in this case the phantasy of the consequences of the difference between the sexes: instead of fighting among themselves as they usually do, the two boys, Sigismund and John, gang up on the girl. If girls are not made the same way as boys, what can boys do to girls? But that difference and its consequences are only imagined; they sustain phantasies accompanying masturbation.

The hypothesis that masturbatory day-dreaming is present in this screen memory is supported by two arguments: the increasingly important theme of masturbation in Freud's preceding dreams, and Freud's 'masturbatory' interpretation of one of the memories reported by the Henris in their study of early childhood memories[1] – a study which Freud discusses at some length in his paper: 'Another man reports that his earliest memory is an episode upon a walk in which he broke off [*abbrach*] a branch from a tree. He thinks he can still identify the spot where this happened. There were several other people present, and one of them helped him' (*SE* 3, 306). If the person concerned were a German, says Freud in his interpretation (which comes immediately after his discussion of his own memory of the 'Green meadow with yellow flowers'), the meaning would be obvious:

1. V. and C. Henri, 'Enquête sur les premiers souvenirs d'enfance', *L'Année psychologique*, 1897, 3.

'In German "to pull one out" [*sich einen ausreissen*] is a very common vulgar term for masturbation. The scene would then be putting back into early childhood a seduction to masturbation – someone was helping him to do it – which in fact occurred at a later period' (*ibid.* 319). Freud refers to a variant of this 'vulgar term' in *The Interpretation of Dreams* in connection with a woman patient's 'Language of flowers' dream: she is in a 'garden' where branches have been cut down and thrown into the road, and asks whether she 'may take one' [*sich einen nehmen*]. Freud adds in a footnote: 'That is whether she might pull one down [*sich einen herunterreissen*], i.e. masturbate' (*ID* 348 n.2).

Later on, when discussing typical dreams and, more particularly, the masturbatory symbolism of having teeth extracted, Freud draws attention to the linguistic parallel between two vulgar expressions describing the act of masturbation: *sich einen ausreissen* (to pull one out) and *sich einen herunterreissen* (to pull one down) (*ID* 388). Thus, the semanteme *reissen*, which had regularly recurred in Freud's dreams and recollections over the previous few months (*reisen*, to travel; *reissen*, to feel pain), now took on the primal meaning it had had for the very young Sigismund – a vulgar term for masturbation. He probably learned the word from the foul-mouthed concierge's son, Philipp, who taught him the term *vögeln* (to copulate) (cf. the dream of 'My mother and the bird-beaked figures'), and possibly learned the act itself from John.

Let us now turn to Freud's work of self-analysis in his paper on screen memories. He establishes the fact that the memory of the 'Green meadow with yellow flowers' had come back to him on two occasions where his feelings for a girl were involved. The first occurred during the holidays he spent in Freiberg with old friends, the Fluss family, at the age of 16 (Freud incorrectly says he was 17) just after completing his secondary education. He delighted in rediscovering the beautiful countryside round his birthplace and, in the Fluss household, the comfortable standard of living the Freuds had once enjoyed.[1] He fell in love with Gisela Fluss, who was 15 and still at school. It was his first 'calf-love', but he kept it secret from her. He spent all his time day-dreaming about what would have happened if he had not left Freiberg, and if he had grown up near his loved one, followed his father's profession, and finally married her. When he first met Gisela, she was wearing a yellow dress – but not as yellow as the dandelions in the screen memory, more yellowish-brown like the colour of wallflowers. Freud gets over this little difficulty by explaining that certain flowers which

1. It was the only time in his life that Freud returned to Freiberg. After that episode, the Fluss family also moved to Vienna; when a student, Freud saw a lot of the Fluss boys, but he lost interest in Gisela, who married in Vienna. Later on, Freud was very startled to hear her name mentioned by the 'Rat Man' (1909*d*).

have a light colouring in the lowlands take on darker shades at high altitudes. But this means that the so-called memory must have been constructed, or reorganised, at a later period when he started going on walks in the Alps.

The second occasion occurred three years later, when the 19-year-old Freud went on holiday to England and met Emanuel and his children, John, Pauline and Berta, again. He was by then a medical student and 'a slave' to his books, so there was little danger of his falling in love once more.[1] However, his father and half-brother had concocted a plan whereby Sigmund would switch to studies of a more practical kind, and then settle down in Manchester and marry Pauline. Freud was strongly against the idea; but later, when hard-pressed by the exigencies of life, he thought that there had been much to be said for his father's plan.

This text provides one of the keys to the resentment against Martha that appears in the background of several of Freud's dreams. He had not 'married well', but for love; his marriage had improved neither his station nor his financial circumstances. Just as other dreams had blamed his father for having brought him into the world both poor and Jewish, this day-dream was prompted by similar feelings towards his wife: he held many things against her – the neediness of their first years together, the cocaine episode, the repeated pregnancies, the uncertainty about their children's future. If only he had been Emanuel's son, lived in England, and married Gisela or Pauline, how much easier things would have been!

Freud approaches the interpretation of this childhood memory in just the same way as he did the dreams of the previous autumn, in other words he takes word-presentations quite literally. The image of throwing away the flowers in exchange for the delicious bread – the bread which Sigmund was finding so hard to earn, the bread which married couples share – was a figurative way of representing a common expression, 'to take on a bread-and-butter occupation', which was what his father wanted him to do. Furthermore, the image of snatching flowers from a little girl suggests a verb rich in associations – 'to deflower', a favourite subject of adolescent day-dreams. These images in the screen memory obey the grammatical rules of style and composition. They are the result of two transformations: 'One of these removed the objectionable element [sexual desire] from the protasis by expressing it figuratively; the second forced the apodosis[2] into a

1. Although Pauline left him cold, he was very attracted to her sister Berta (who was born just before the Freuds left Freiberg), and mentioned her several times in his letters to Martha (J I, 29).

2. In a conditional sentence, a protasis is the clause that states the condition, while an apodosis is the main clause. The grammatical structure of the screen memory is as follows: if I had deflowered Gisela or Pauline (the protasis represented by flowers), I would have been happy (the apodosis represented by bread).

shape capable of visual representation [the delicious bread]' (*SE* 3, 317). Thus, this phantasy-memory illustrates 'the most momentous turning-points in your life, the influence of the two most powerful motive forces – hunger and love' (*ibid.*), an allusion to a favourite line of Freud's from Schiller's *Die Weltweisen*. Thus, this childhood memory, probably genuine yet in itself indifferent in content, twice acts at a later date (*deferred action*) as a vehicle and a disguise for sensual adolescent phantasies: its function is to be a *screen memory*.

Freud affirms the primal genuineness of the childhood scene of the 'Green meadow with yellow flowers': indeed, throughout his life, he continued to assert that individual phantasies and collective imagoes originate partly in external reality. Certain details of this screen memory, such as the presence of a second woman or the throwing away of the flowers after they have been snatched from the little girl, seem to him to have no symbolic meaning and to be part of a genuine, and in itself unremarkable, childhood scene. It is precisely because the scene was unremarkable that it was able to remain or become a conscious one. Our childhood memories, because of their very innocence, can serve retrospectively as disguises for unconscious motives that cannot be admitted by consciousness. But they are memorised and give us the impression that we remember them particularly well only because they are informed by such subsequent unconscious motives. An indifferent memory can thus act as a screen for a sexual phantasy. The formation of screen memories obeys the same principle as that of hysterical symptoms: the conflict between a wish and a defence, repression of the wish, displacement, and substitution together result in compromise-formation.

Freud owed this further theoretical step forward directly to his self-analysis. It gave rise to the analogy, to which he referred in his letter of January 3, 1899, between the psychology of hysteria and the psychology of dreams, their common denominator being phantasies. As I have already pointed out, he had drawn a parallel between hysteria and dreams three years earlier. But the two parallels differ. In 1895–96, Freud discovered that dreams had a meaning, just as he had already suspected that hysterical symptoms had a meaning. But Freud now realised that the role played by memories in the production of dreams or of hysterical symptoms was not a direct one, as he had long believed, but took effect indirectly through the phantasies and unconscious day-dreams prompted by those memories. This marked the culmination of a whole series of theoretical and personal discoveries which had begun with his abandonment of the seduction theory and his emphasis on the Oedipus myth. Freud realised that the two questions to which he had devoted his energies – dreams and neuroses – were one and the same thing: psychoanalysis, as a systematic and specific science, had come into being.

I would like to make two more points about this screen memory. First, it contains evidence not only of the displacement of Sigismund's incestuous desire for his old nurse (a mother figure) on to his young niece Pauline, but also of resistance to that transfer in the object-relationship. The boy who plays at seeing or touching the little girl's 'flower' takes fright. At the end of the scene, he runs to seek reassurance from a peasant-woman who gives him something delicious to eat and who doubles up for the nurse: taking refuge at the mother's breast results from fear of sexuality.

Secondly, in the course of describing an 'anonymous' screen memory in his paper, Freud takes the opportunity of recapitulating and publishing most of his childhood memories, almost all of which he had already described to Fliess in the autumn of 1897: '[We] lived comfortably enough in that little corner of the provinces' where he was born; 'A longing for the beautiful woods near our home, in which (as one of my memories from those days tells me) I used to run off from my father, almost before I had learnt to walk'; 'I have no knowledge of the birth of a sister, who is two and a half years younger than I am; my departure, my first sight of the railway and the long carriage-drive before it – none of these has left a trace in my memory. On the other hand, I can remember two small occurrences during the railway-journey' – occurrences which Freud does not describe here, but which are known to us from letters to Fliess: he saw his mother naked (*matrem nudam*) on a journey with her from Leipzig to Vienna (*F*, October 3, 1897), and he was terrified by the gas flames in Breslau station, which reminded him of spirits burning in hell (*F*, December 3, 1897); 'But what should have made most impression on me was an injury to my face which caused a considerable loss of blood and for which I had to have some stitches put in by a surgeon. I can still feel the scar resulting from this accident, but I know of no recollection which points to it, either directly or indirectly'; 'When I was about three, the branch of industry in which my father was concerned met with a catastrophe. He lost all his means and we were forced to leave the place and move to a large town. Long and difficult years followed, of which, as it seems to me, nothing was worth remembering. I never felt really comfortable in the town'; 'From my third year onwards my recollections grew scantier and less clear; there are gaps in them which must cover more than a year; and it is not, I believe, until my sixth or seventh year that the stream of my memories becomes continuous' (*SE* 3, 309–10 and 312–13). All that is missing is the memory of the birth and premature death of Freud's brother Julius, which is referred to in the letter to Fliess of October 3, 1897, but never recalled again; as we have seen, however, it does underlie the anxiety about death which is so strongly present in the recent dreams of the autumn of 1898.

The therapeutic benefits of Freud's further progress in his self-analysis were just as important as the theoretical ones. In his paper on screen memories, the person who is Freud in disguise is said to have been relieved of a slight phobia by means of psychoanalysis. It is also clear that Freud now had a better understanding of his various emotional involvements, of Pauline's role in his early childhood, of his ambivalence towards Martha. He was emerging from his state of 'paralysis'. At both a scientific and a personal level, he had decisively resumed control of his life. It is easy to see why, on the basis of his own experience, Freud henceforth saw the prime aim of psychoanalytic treatment as being the recollection of childhood memories.

Further theoretical progress (January–May 1899)

THE DREAM OF 'FATHER ON HIS DEATH-BED LIKE GARIBALDI' (FEBRUARY–MARCH 1899)

From January to March 1899, Freud's work on the final version of his dream book slowly but surely progressed. He had not only to clear up some theoretical obscurities, but also to overcome two internal resistances – the feeling he was not getting anywhere, and embarrassment at revealing himself in such intimate detail in a published book. Freud's self-analysis and theoretical work on screen memories, which we have just examined, continued steadily over the whole of this period: it was not until May 28 that Freud announced to his friend that he had sent off the manuscript of his paper to the publishers.

On January 16, 1899, Freud told Fliess of his discovery, in hysterics, of an analogy in phantasy between the top and the bottom part of the body (without realising that in so doing he was pinpointing the only scrap of truth in Fliess's pet theory about the relationship between the nose and the sexual organs); in the same letter, he confirmed 'minor advances of the wish-theory' (*F* 340). On January 30, he wrote again, with mounting enthusiasm: 'You probably do not know how much your last visit raised my spirits. I am still living on it. The light has not gone out since then; bits of insight are dawning now here, now there – a genuine reinvigoration by comparison with the desolation of last year. What is rising out of the chaos this time is the connection to the psychology contained in the *Studies on*

Hysteria – the relation to conflict, to life: clinical psychology, as I should like to call it. Puberty is becoming ever more central; phantasy as the key holds fast. Yet there is still nothing big or complete. I diligently make notes of all that is worthwhile so as to present it to you at our congress. I need you as my audience.

'For relaxation I am reading Burckhardt's *History of Greek Civilization*, which is providing me with unexpected parallels. My predilection for the prehistoric in all its human forms has remained the same' (*F* 342). Freud did not immediately send off the letter, and added to it on February 3: 'I could not resolve to send off this letter as if it were completed, and was waiting for new material. But nothing came. Everything is now going in the pages on which I make notes for our congress, and neither my interest nor my energy is sufficient for anything else. [. . .] I merely anticipate what you will say about my notes, which will give you a better insight than ever before, though there is nothing of *first* rank in them' (*F* 342–3). Freud's letter of February 6 is in much the same tone: 'The work is progressing slowly, never without results, but now for a long time again without taking a surprising turn. The secret dossier is getting thicker and thicker and literally longs for its opening at Easter. I myself am getting curious about when Easter in Rome will be possible' (*F* 344).

On February 19, Freud was at once more precise and more enthusiastic. He clearly set out the notion of compromise-formation – proof that he had just accomplished a decisive step forward in elaborating a theory from his screen memory of the 'Green meadow with yellow flowers snatched from Pauline', which had been proving a stumbling block: 'My last generalisation has held good and seems inclined to grow to an unpredictable extent. Not only dreams are wish-fulfilments, so are hysterical attacks. This is true of hysterical symptoms, but probably applies to every product of neurosis, for I recognised it long ago in acute delusional insanity. Reality – wish-fulfilment – it is from these opposites that our mental life springs. I believe I now know what determines the distinction between symptoms that make their way into waking life and dreams. It is enough for the dream to be the wish-fulfilment of the repressed thought, for dreams are kept at a safe distance from reality. But the symptom, set in the midst of life, must be something else besides: it must also be the wish-fulfilment of the repressing thought. A symptom arises where the repressed and the repressing thought can come together in the fulfilment of a wish. The symptom is the wish-fulfilment of the repressing thought, for example, in the form of punishment; self-punishment is the final substitute for self-gratification, which comes from masturbation' (*F* 345).

This is illustrated by two cases, that of X.Y., who suffers from hysterical vomiting because she imagines she is pregnant, and that of Herr E. (a patient already familiar to us), who blushes and sweats when he meets women at the theatre because he imagines he is deflowering them and is ashamed of his phantasy. The phantasy was built up in several stages: his tendency to sweat was caused by a non-sexual trauma at the age of three, when his brother poured soapsuds over his face in the bath; later, when he was 14, he masturbated in the toilet at Interlaken in a peculiar position that enabled him to get a good view of the mountain called the Jungfrau (literally, the 'Virgin'); lastly, at school, where he always sat in the front row of the class (the theatre reproduced the classroom), he had a dispute with his Latin teacher over the expression *operam dare*, which meant 'making an effort' (or in slang 'sweating'); the *entr'acte* at the theatre during which he meets desirable women corresponds to the school break, when he used to sweat.

On March 2, Freud continued in the same vein: 'Things are going almost uniformly well for me. I can hardly wait for Easter to show you in detail a principal part of the story of wish-fulfilment and of the coupling of opposites. [. . .] Yet every few days things become clearer – now here, now there; I have become modest and count on long years of work and patient collecting, with the help of a few useful ideas after vacation and our meetings. Rome is still distant; you do know my Roman dreams' (*F* 346–7). But the most important passage in the letter refers to the therapeutic – and no longer purely intellectual – benefit he has derived from self-analysis: 'The main result of this year's work appears to me to be the surmounting of phantasies; they have indeed lured me far away from what is real. Yet all this work has been very good for my own emotional life; I am apparently much more normal than I was four or five years ago' (*F* 347). So the screen memory which Freud had begun to analyse at the end of December 1898 had finally been elucidated. The benefit he refers to is probably a decrease in his guilt feelings.

At about that time, events on the political scene preoccupied Freud, who was always ready to take up the cudgels on behalf of minorities in the Austro-Hungarian Empire and their nationalist claims. The Hungarian kingdom had been driven by parliamentary obstruction into a state of lawlessness and, for the last year, acute crisis. Earlier, in 1875, the leader of the radical party in favour of national independence, Koloman Tisza (1830–1902), became prime minister of Hungary; his finance minister, Koloman Széll, helped the country's economy to recover. In 1895, the King (who was also Emperor of Austria) appointed a new government with, as its prime minister, Deszo Bánffy, a member of the government party, who won the 1896 elections. Despite his considerable efforts, he was not totally successful in his legislation. By 1898, the opposition to Bánffy gained the upper hand; he even fought a duel with one of his opponents on January 3, 1899. The crisis had reached such proportions by February 26 that, in order not to make matters worse, Bánffy resigned. He was replaced as prime minister by Széll, who in the meantime had founded the successful Hungarian Mortgage Credit Bank. Széll pulled Hungary out of the crisis, restored effective financial arrangements with Austria, and remained in power until 1903.

One day at about that time, towards the end of February or the beginning of March 1899, Freud's son Oliver soiled his bed-clothes. Probably the following night, Freud had a dream:

'Here is another, almost exactly similar, example from a dream of my own. (I lost my father in 1896.) *After his death my father played a political part among the Magyars and brought them together politically*. Here I saw a small and indistinct picture: *a crowd of men as though they were in the Reichstag; someone standing* [steht] *on one or two chairs* [Stuhl], *with other people round him. I remembered how like Garibaldi he had looked on his death-bed, and felt glad that that promise had come true*' (*ID* 427–8).

This dream, followed by an initial analysis, is given as an example of absurdity in dreams, and comes near the beginning of Section G of Chapter 6, 'The Dream-Work (*ID* 427–31). It is preceded by the dream of a patient who had lost his father six years earlier, and who in the dream saw him alive but injured in an accident; it is followed by the second part of Freud's analysis of the 'Count Thun' dream (in the first part of his analysis he had referred to the fact that his father soiled his bed during his terminal illness); Freud concludes, on the topic of absurdity in dreams related to a dead father: 'The authority wielded by a father provokes criticism from his children at an early age, and the severity of the demands he makes upon them leads them, for their own relief, to keep their eyes open to any weakness of their father's; but the filial piety called up in our minds by the figure of a father, particularly after his death, tightens the censorship which prohibits any such criticism from being consciously expressed' (*ID* 435). There then follow, in the same section and on the same theme, the description and analysis of one subsequent dream, '1851 and 1856', and of two earlier dreams, 'Goethe's attack on Herr M.' and 'My son, the Myops'.

Further remarks on the dream of 'Father on his death-bed like Garibaldi' come a little later on, when Freud discusses the question of intellectual activity in dreams, just after the 'Frau Doni' dream: the feeling of satisfaction felt by the dreamer upon awaking is in fact part of the latent dream-thoughts. It is here that Freud mentions that his second son 'soiled his bed-clothes', that he had intentionally given him 'the first name of a great historical figure' (Oliver Cromwell, 1599–1658), and that he had therefore greeted his birth with great satisfaction (*ID* 447–8).

But that did not mean that Freud had discovered the meaning of 'absurd' dreams about a dead father. He returned to the subject at the end of 1899, just after his dream book had come out, in a letter to Fliess: 'Two of my patients have almost simultaneously come up with [self-]reproaches following the nursing and death of their parents and have shown me that my dreams about this were typical. The reproach is in every instance bound to attach itself to revenge, spiteful glee, taking satisfaction in the ill person's excretory difficulties (urine and stools). Truly a neglected corner of psychic life' (*F*, December 9, 1899, 390). The topic continued to be of such keen interest to Freud that he added further remarks about this dream in almost every new edition of his book. It is the only dream in *The Interpretation of Dreams* whose analysis is completed not only by notes in subsequent editions but by three whole paragraphs added, respectively, in 1909 (the question 'If my father were alive, what would he say to this?' prompts the consoling thought that 'the dead person has not lived to witness the event, or a feeling of satisfaction that he can no longer interfere in it'), in 1911 (a man who had nursed his father during his last illness dreamt, after the latter's death, that he '*was alive once more and was talking to him in his usual way, but* (the remarkable thing was that) *he had really died, only he did not know it*'; the dream is intelligible only if the words 'in consequence of the dreamer's wish' are added after 'but he had really died'), and in 1919 (the indifference on the part of the dreamer – 'It's all the same to me whether he's alive or dead' – becomes a dream-representation of his ambivalence). Grinstein devotes a chapter to the dream (G, Chapter 16).

Freud's analysis of the dream in 1899 reveals that it represents in images, i.e. in a figurative form, a kind of proverbial idea which becomes grotesque if taken literally. In a figurative sense, 'to stand [*dastehen*] before [*vor*] one's children's eyes, after one's death, great and unsullied' is an 'elevated' thought. In a literal sense, since *dastehen* can also mean 'to stand up', and *vor* 'in front of', the sentence takes on the following 'absurd' meaning: 'To stand up in front of one's children, after one's death, great and unsullied.' The dream turns this literal version into a picture puzzle: Freud's father is standing up surrounded by a crowd; he is great and unsullied like Garibaldi. But the reversal of meaning produced by the dream goes further than that: it substitutes 'elevated' thoughts for thoughts that are not only 'absurd' but also, and especially, 'common' [*gemein*, in the sense of 'base' or 'ugly']. One of the 'common' thoughts here is that such a 'great and unsullied' man behaved during his old age and illness like a small and dirty child. Freud alludes to this 'common' thought indirectly: his father had had a *post mortem* rise of temperature, and his cheeks had been flushed more and more deeply red. Freud then returns immediately to more elevated thoughts, quoting two lines from the verse epilogue that Goethe wrote to Schiller's *Lied von der Glocke* (*The Song of the Bell*) a few months after his friend's death (he revised it in 1815):

> *Und hinter ihm in wesenlosem Scheine*
> *Lag, was uns alle bändigt, das Gemeine.*
> [Behind him, a shadowy illusion,
> Lay what holds us all in bondage – the things that are common.]

Freud's thoughts 'involuntarily ran on' to this quotation no doubt because he had in mind Goethe's two next lines:

> *Nun glühte seine Wange rot und röter*
> *Von jener Jugend, die uns nie entfliegt*
> [His cheek flushed red and redder yet
> With that unchanging ever-youthful glow.]

Freud is then able to refer to his father's 'complete paralysis (*obstruction*) of the intestines' during his terminal illness without being more specific. The 'common' thoughts are attributed to someone else, a woman who was distressed about the fact that her father had passed a stool [*Stuhl*] at the moment of death or *post mortem* (after his death).

The dream and its analysis are entirely built around the contrast between the elevated and the common. Jacob Freud's ignoble obstruction of the intestines becomes the noble parliamentary obstruction of the Magyars. The nationalist hero is Koloman Széll, whose surname, as Freud was certainly aware, is pronounced in exactly the same way as *selle*, the French word for 'stool' (*Stuhl* in German) in its medical sense, and whose first name has echoes of the word 'colon'. The horrors of the Thirty Years' War, as depicted by Jacques Callot (1592–1635) in his famous series of etchings, *Les grandes misères de la guerre* (1633), to which Freud refers because of the small size of the figures, become in the dream a woodcut from an illustrated history of Austria showing Maria Theresa (1717–80) before the Reichstag [Diet] of Pressburg (1741) in the celebrated episode where the Hungarian nobility responded to her plea for support in the War of the Austrian Succession by vowing '*Moriamur pro rege nostro, Maria Teresia*' ('We will die for our king, Maria Theresa'). (Like most such famous historical 'events', the episode is regarded by historians as apocryphal.)

I would suggest that Freud had other 'common' or 'ugly' thoughts which he does not mention. His father looked like Garibaldi only when he was dead; during his lifetime, he played no great role (an allusion to his ailing business affairs, to the financial hardship he caused his family once they had moved to Vienna, and to the episode where he had allowed a Christian to knock his fur hat off into the mud). The key word in the dream is *Stuhl* (chair). In his associations, Freud says: '[My father] was standing on one or two chairs [*Stühle*]. He had brought them together, and was thus a presiding judge [*Stuhlrichter*, literally "chair-judge"].' The many meanings of *Stuhl* in German can be divided into two categories, one elevated (a throne, a judge's chair, as in *Stuhlrichter*) and the other 'common' (a lavatory seat, stool, mud). So in the dreamer's mind, *Stuhlrichter* had a double meaning: a sitting judge or a defecating judge.

Freud suggests another interpretation of the dream. His children had provided him with something he had hoped, in vain, his father would provide – satisfaction for his megalomania. The feeling of satisfaction with which the dream ends was what Freud had experienced at the birth of his second son. He had hoped it would be a boy so he could call him Oliver after Oliver Cromwell, who readmitted the Jews to England. Cromwell was yet another hero of Freud's adolescent day-dreams of a public career, and gave him all the more reason to admire England. Freud wanted to give his children the advantages he himself had not enjoyed as a child. He saw himself on his death-bed, and sought consolation for his premature death – something he feared – by anticipating the role he hoped to play in the world after his death and vis-à-vis his children. A mechanism of withdrawal from that fear underlies the dream: it is not I who shall die, it is my father who is well and truly dead.

Stein (1968*a*) offers a deeper interpretation of the dream. In his view, it shows Freud torn between a wish for immortality (a variant of the infantile wish for omnipotence) based on an imaginary identification with a phantasied eternal father, with no beginning or end, and an identification with a mortal father resulting in an acceptance of his own mortality (as we have seen, such an acceptance is central to the mid-life crisis of any man, including Freud). This explains why, in his dream, in his analysis of it, and in his additions to subsequent editions, Freud alternates between an image of the father as a revenant, as a being that lives eternally on this side of death, and acknowledgement of the fact that the dead are well and truly dead. But he was not able to formulate that acknowledgement explicitly until the subsequent dream of 'Dissecting my own pelvis'. 'What is involved here is immortality in the strict sense of the term, and not the kind of immortality that a great man achieves in the minds of his descendants through the life's work which he leaves behind – and which may earn him a monument. By bringing a revenant into the world, by identifying his son Oliver with his father Jacob, the dreamer, who thus forges a unity of time between what lies before death and what lies after it, is able to escape his position in the family tree and occupy, outside time and space, the point itself where the principle of the permanence of lineage exists. [. . .] He means: I don't want to have ancestors, I want to be an ancestor. The ambivalence of feelings towards the mortal father masks, then, the infantile aspiration to be the immortal and unbegotten father' (Stein, 1968*a*, pp. 99–100).

Grinstein (G 381–9) draws a parallel between Oliver Cromwell and Giuseppe[1] Garibaldi (1807–82). Both men were described by contemporaries as having a reddish countenance, a characteristic that tallies with the colour of Schiller's cheeks in Goethe's poem. Photographs of Jacob Freud and Garibaldi (G, fig. 12) confirm Freud's remark that the two men looked alike. Cromwell and Garibaldi were also similar in other respects: both worked their way up through the ranks, both were very popular military leaders although they had no military or diplomatic training, both were considered liberators of the people, both had individualistic temperaments which brought them into conflict with the laws of their countries, both were revolutionaries, rough and ready in their speech and cruel in their actions, both were reformers and anti-Catholics. These are characteristics which, almost down to the last detail, were lacking in Jacob Freud – a fact much resented by Sigmund, who used his son Oliver (of the noble first name and ignoble uncleanliness) as a weapon against his father. The essential identificatory clue no doubt resides in the existence of aggression against a father figure: Cromwell had King Charles I executed; Garibaldi took up arms to free Rome from the control of the Pope.

According to Grinstein (G 391), the dream expresses Freud's guilt feelings about that aggressiveness and his fear of horrible punishment of the kind depicted in Jacques Callot's etchings. It is a perfectly valid interpretation, but in my view limits the dream to being no more than the realisation of a childhood wish. I would suggest another, parallel interpretation that sees the dream in terms of the undertaking in which Freud was currently engaged. The text of the dream would read something like this: 'After my father's death, which set my self-analysis in motion, I began to play a role in Austria and to become a great man; I brought the parts of the psychical apparatus together into a whole, but remained caught between two stools, medicine and psychology; my discovery will cause a great upheaval and I shall not become famous until after my death, but I feel glad that the promise made when I was born – that I would be a great man – is about to come true.' Seen from that angle, the dream would seem

1. Giuseppe is the Italian form of Joseph, which, as we have seen, was a name of great importance for Freud.

to be a recapitulative dream: Freud's work now needed only one last stool, i.e. one last word. The dream also expresses his self-confidence: he was about to lead a movement, to make a revolutionary achievement.

THE DREAM OF 'FAMOUS SPEAKERS' (BEGINNING OF 1899?)

The dream of 'Famous speakers', in which Freud sees the first volume of a new series of monographs, consisting of the speeches of Dr Lecher, in a bookshop window, has much the same meaning as the previous dream and was possibly dreamt at about the same time, though it is difficult to date precisely. Dr Lecher, who sat in the German parliament, was a formidable obstructionist speaker, like the opposition members who had just brought down the Hungarian prime minister – and like Freud's dream book, which would, the dreamer no doubt thought, shatter many prejudices and *idées reçues*. Freud made only one point about the dream: 'The position was that a few days earlier I had taken on some new patients for psychological treatment, and was now obliged to talk for ten or eleven hours every day. So it was I myself who was a non-stop speaker [*Dauerredner*]'[1] (*ID* 268–9). I would conclude, then, that it is also his own book which he dreams of seeing in a bookshop window. The book in the dream, he points out, looked like one of the 'monographs on great artists, on world history, on famous cities etc.' which he was in the habit of buying. So Freud no longer saw his book as a botanical monograph, which was how he had imagined it in a dream when he began writing his first version.

THE DREAM OF 'DISSECTING MY OWN PELVIS' (MAY 1899?)

The dream of 'Dissecting my own pelvis', which is also known as the 'Brücke and silver-paper' dream or the 'Self-dissection' dream, is hard to date with exactitude. But it clearly follows on from the previous dreams and alludes to Freud's self-analysis and to the imminent publication of the dream book. It so to speak inscribes the signature of the craftsman on his work. In my view, Freud had the dream some time between yet another stimulating meeting with Fliess in Innsbruck at Easter and his letter of May 28, 1899, which is like a cry of jubilation: 'the dream [book] is suddenly taking shape, without any special motivation, but this time I am sure of it' (*F* 353). The final obstacle that was preventing him from completing the book – the paralysing need to reveal himself in it – had been swept away: 'I have decided that I cannot use any of the disguises, nor can I afford to give up anything because I am not rich enough to keep my finest

1. Freud certainly talked a lot in the course of treating his patients. On January 30, 1899, he wrote to Fliess: 'Today, after twelve hours of work and earnings of 100 florins, I am again at the end of my strength'; this would seem to corroborate my dating of the dream.

and probably my only lasting discovery to myself' (*ibid.*). Although it was an unpleasant step for him to take, he had decided to make his self-analysis public. The rest of the letter exudes the same self-confidence. He had sent his paper on screen memories to the publishers. He had just found confirmation that his psychoanalytic technique was 'near perfect' (*ibid.*). Lastly, his interest in archaeology was at a new peak; he had recently finished Burckhardt's *History of Greek Civilization*, and was in the middle of reading *Ilios* by Heinrich Schliemann, the celebrated archaeologist who discovered the site of Troy: 'I [. . .] enjoyed the account of his childhood. The man was happy when he found Priam's treasure, because happiness comes only with the fulfilment of a childhood wish' (*ibid.*).

Freud was now working uninterruptedly on the final draft of the second version of *The Interpretation of Dreams*. The first chapter was finally taking shape: 'So the dream [book] will be. [. . .] Unfortunately, to frighten one off, the gods have placed the [dream] literature before the presentation. The first time I got stuck in it. This time I shall fight my way through; there is nothing of consequence in it anyway. No other work of mine has been so completely my own, my own dung-heap, my seedling and a *nova species mihi* on top of it. After the literature, there will be deletions, insertions, and the like, and the whole thing should be ready for the printer by the end of July, when I go to the country. I may possibly try to change publishers if I find that Deuticke does not want to pay much for it or is not very eager to have it' (*ibid.*). The comparison between his self-analysis and the 'dung-heap' that acts as a fertiliser to make plants grow follows on directly from the 'stool' of the dream of 'Father on his death-bed like Garibaldi'.

The new dream which left Freud a happy man like Schliemann and prompted him to write such a jubilant letter to Fliess was, in my submission, the dream of 'Dissecting my own pelvis'. Before quoting it, let me point out that before having the dream Freud had had a tired feeling in his legs, as well as a general mood of weariness and self-doubt:

'At the beginning of a dream, which I have so far hardly touched upon, there was a clear expression of astonishment at the subject which had cropped up. *Old Brücke must have set me some task;* STRANGELY ENOUGH, *it related to a dissection of the lower part* [*Untergestell*: "chassis", or literally "under-frame"] *of my own body, my pelvis and legs, which I saw before me as though in the dissecting-room, but without noticing their absence in myself and also without a trace of any gruesome feeling. Louise N. was standing beside me and doing the work with me. The pelvis had been eviscerated, and it was visible now in its superior, now in its inferior, aspect, the two being mixed together. Thick flesh-coloured protuberances (which, in the dream itself, made me think of haemorrhoids) could be seen. Something which lay over it and was like crumpled silver-paper*[1] *had also to be carefully fished out. I was then once more in possession of my legs and was making my way through the town. But (being tired) I took a cab. To my astonishment the cab drove in through the door of a house, which opened and allowed it to pass along a passage which turned a corner at its end and finally led into the open air again.*[2] *Finally I was making a journey through a changing landscape with an Alpine guide who was carrying my belongings. Part of the way he carried me too, out of consideration for my tired legs. The ground was boggy; we went round the edge; people were sitting on the ground like Red Indians or gipsies – among them a girl. Before this I had been making my own way forward over the slippery ground with a constant feeling of surprise that I was able to do it so well after the dissection. At last we reached a small wooden house at the end of which was an open window. There the guide set me down and laid two wooden boards, which were standing ready, upon the window-sill, so as to bridge [überbrücken] the chasm which had to be crossed over from the window. At that point I really became frightened about my legs, but instead of the expected crossing, I saw two grown-up men lying on wooden benches that were along the walls of the hut, and what seemed to be two children sleeping beside them. It was as though what was going to make the crossing possible was not the boards but the children. I awoke in a mental fright*' (*ID* 452–3).

The dream and Freud's initial analysis of it are to be found in Section G, 'Intellectual Activity in Dreams', of Chapter 6, 'The Dream-Work' (*ID* 452–5); the same section includes the recent 'Frau Doni' and 'Father on his death-bed like Garibaldi' dreams, as well as earlier dreams such as 'Goethe's attack on Herr M.' and 'Hollthurn'; Freud inserted the later '1851 and 1856' dream just before the dream of 'Dissecting my own pelvis'. He also discusses the dream at two other points in Chapter 6. The first passage concerns the representation of the proper name of Stannius (a specialist in the nervous system of fishes) by silver-paper, which is technically known as 'stanniol', a derivative of tin (stannium) (*ID* 413). The second passage explains the suppression, in the dream, of the affect of horror (the 'gruesome feeling'). It needs to be quoted in its entirety in view of its important bearing on the interpretation of the dream: 'If we turn back to the dream about the strange task set me by old Brücke of making a dissection of my own pelvis, it will be recalled that in the dream itself I missed the gruesome feeling ['*Grauen*'] appropriate to it. Now this was a wish-fulfilment in more than one sense. The dissection meant the self-analysis which I was carrying out, as it were, in the publication of this present book about dreams [*Traumbuch*] – a process which had been so

1. Stanniol, which was an allusion to the book by Stannius on the nervous system of fishes. (Freud's footnote.)

2. It was the place on the ground-floor of my block of flats where the tenants keep their perambulators; but it was over-determined in several other ways. (Freud's footnote.)

distressing to me in reality that I had postponed the printing of the finished manuscript for more than a year. A wish then arose that I might get over this feeling of distaste [*abhaltend*]; hence it was that I had no gruesome feeling ['*Grauen*'] in the dream. But I should also have been very glad to miss growing grey – '*Grauen*' in the other sense of the word. I was already growing quite grey, and the grey of my hair was another reminder that I must not delay any longer. And, as we have seen, the thought that I should have to leave it to my children to reach the goal of my difficult journey forced its way through to representation at the end of the dream' (*ID* 477–8). *Grauen* does indeed have two quite separate meanings in German, 'to shudder with horror' and 'to grow grey'.

This passage confirms that Freud had the dream at about the time he was completing the manuscript of *The Interpretation of Dreams*, and that he felt a very urgent need, which is characteristic of the mid-life crisis, to complete his work before entering old age and dying. Another double meaning is worth mentioning here: in dreams, travel can be a symbolic representation of death – as Schur (S 175–7) correctly points out; but that theme is here counterbalanced by that of a crossing, of a bridge that makes the crossing possible, which (Schur failed to note) is a literal representation of transgression. To go forward can mean to go and meet one's death; but it also, and above all, means to anticipate and to outstrip death. To transgress is to progress by overcoming inhibitions, anxieties and resistances. The dream of 'Dissecting my own pelvis' gave Freud the confidence he needed to complete his book and publish his discoveries, despite the price that had to be paid – a willingness on his part to expose himself and his self-analysis to public scrutiny.

Grinstein devotes a chapter to the dream (G, Chapter 17). It centres mainly on two books by the English novelist Rider Haggard (1856–1925) to which Freud's associations refer: *She* (1887) – which inspired Pierre Benoît's *L'Atlantide* (1918) – and *The Heart of the World* (1896). The central character of *She*, Leo Vincey, was born, like Freud, in May 1856. He sets off in search of his past, like Freud, in the company of his mentor, Horace Holly. After being shipwrecked, they penetrate an unexplored region of Africa ruled over by the virginal, immortal, cruel and beautiful queen Ayesha, 'She-Who-Must-Be-Obeyed'. For thousands of years, she has been awaiting the man who will seek her out and love her. Over 2,000 years before, she had fallen in love with Leo's ancestor, the priest Kallikrates, and wanted to make him immortal, but only if he would kill the woman with whom he had fled from Egypt. When he refused, she killed him. She has since kept the corpse and awaited his return in another generation. She discovers that Leo is the reincarnation of the priest from whom he is descended, and decides, after killing the native woman who loves him, to make him immortal and marry him. To bring that about, they descend by a difficult and dangerous path into a cavern in the heart of a volcano. They take off their clothes. When Leo hesitates to step into the fire that will give him eternal life, she kisses him, then pours the fire over herself like water and inhales it into her lungs. She shrivels up and, as she dies, begs Leo – in vain – to leap into the fire and wait for her to be reborn centuries later. Leo and Holly escape; but neither of them can forget the love they felt for her, and they live together as brothers for many years.

The novel is fraught with horror. Grinstein (G 401–2) sees it as foreshadowing such concepts as the death instinct and repetition-compulsion. Ayesha is a primal mother figure – the 'eternal feminine' which Freud, following Goethe, mentions in his associations: she is dominating, possessive, caring and protective to those who satisfy her needs, but destroys those who do not. When she is on the point of committing incest (Leo is a filial figure; and the sexual symbolism of the passage down into the volcano and the scene of ecstasy in the cavern is obvious), she dies: the Oedipal act is unattainable. Castration anxiety is represented in an oral sadistic mode by the scene where the natives try to place a hot pot over the head of one of the party, then kill, butcher (cf. the dissection in the dream) and devour him. In his remarks on the dream, Freud contends that the novel also illustrates 'the immortality of our emotions': for over 2,000 years, Ayesha has felt guilt for killing Kallikrates, a guilt she can expiate only by trying to re-enact the original traumatic event with the help of Leo; but in the end the only way out for her is to die. Leo succeeds in doing what each generation of his ancestors had failed to do – seek out Ayesha – but she slips from his grasp when he is about to possess her: thus do children sometimes achieve feats of which their fathers are incapable. But such a realisation of infantile Oedipal wishes causes punishment anxiety.

The other novel by Rider Haggard, *Heart of the World*, is also an account of a mythical exploration (today it would be called science fiction). Ignatio, a chief of the Mexican Indians under Spanish rule, wishes to restore the former Aztec empire. Betrayed by his wife, he obtains the cooperation of the high priest Zibalbay. They go, together with an Englishman called Strickland, to the once holy City of the Heart, which is built on an island in a lake located in the crater of an extinct volcano, and which has gradually been cut off from the rest of the world. Its pyramid contains the high priest's temple. They hope to put an end to its decadence (the inhabitants have long intermarried; strangers or people who bring strangers into the city are sentenced to death; and few children are born) by bringing in new blood from outside. Paradoxically, however, Zibalbay refuses to let his daughter Maya, to whom he is very attached, marry Strickland, whom she loves. He curses her and her children to come, and dies. The lovers succeed in marrying – despite Strickland's being a stranger – by replacing a secret inscription which they find in the temple, and which predicts the destruction of the city and its people, with a fraudulent prophecy implying that they will marry. But they remain prisoners in the city. Their crime is finally denounced by a woman rival of Maya's. They are arrested along with Ignatio, who has taken sides with them, and sentenced to death; their baby is thrown into the lake. Maya in despair then tears loose the symbol of the Heart from the altar. At this point, water pours into the temple, and in the ensuing confusion they escape to the top of the pyramid, where they see the city flooded and destroyed: when the Heart was removed, the secret sluice gates protecting the city from the waters of the lake were opened. Maya becomes psychotic and soon dies. Strickland, although he has succeeded in escaping with Ignatio, cannot put her out of his thoughts and himself dies some years later.

Once again, a relationship with a woman has proved disastrous; a pure and staunch friendship can exist only between men. The destruction of the city is punishment for the incest practised by its inhabitants. Zibalbay opposes his daughter's belonging to another man with such vehemence and rage that he dies. The lessons of the novel are that 'the heart of the world' is love, the basic crime is a sexual one, and violation of taboos brings down death and destruction.

What Freud remembers about the two novels is the idea of 'perilous journeys; [. . .] an adventurous road that had scarcely ever been trodden before, leading into an undiscovered region' (*ID* 454). But, as often, his memory betrays him. He writes: 'The boggy ground over which people had to be carried, and the chasm which they had to cross by means of boards brought along with them, were taken from *She*'. Yet there was only one board carried by Leo's party. He adds: 'The Red Indians, the girl and the wooden house were taken from *Heart of the World*' (*ibid.*). Yet none of the many houses described in that novel is made of wood (G 414).

Grinstein's final interpretation runs as follows. The manifest dream picture ('the cab drove in through the door of a house, which opened and allowed it to pass along a passage'; 'I had been making my own way forward over the slippery ground'; 'the guide [. . .] laid two wooden boards [. . .] upon the window-sill so as to bridge the chasm') contains obvious sexual symbolism. It is equally clear that the object of the desire is incestuous, and that the dissection of his own pelvis, the presence of 'haemorrhoids', and lastly his fear about the use of his legs all represent anxiety about punishment, in this case castration. Such an interpretation is valid but premature: it was not until some months later that Freud arrived at the notion of a castration phantasy. Grinstein rightly notes Freud's constant need for a guide to overcome that anxiety: the prototype of such a mentor at the beginning of his scientific career was of course Ernst Brücke.

Peto (1969) proposes a different interpretation of this dream. In his view, such 'dismemberment' dreams, occurring in the final stages of psychoanalysis, indicate the appearance of a crucial conflict in the transference and provide the necessary impetus for its resolution. When applied to the relationship between Freud and Fliess, his argument seems pertinent. Another meaning of the dream would then be: no one can stop me continuing in the direction I wanted to go; I shall even part from my mentors – from Fliess, just as I did from Brücke and Breuer – if they cease to agree with me; although tired, my legs will not let me down.

Let us return to Freud's remarks and the beginning of his interpretation of the dream. He sees it as having been occasioned by a conversation he had had with Louise N., whom he had offered to lend a book by Rider Haggard, 'a *strange* book, but full of hidden meaning, [. . .] the eternal feminine, the immortality of our emotions', and who had chided him for being so slow in completing the dream book. Freud's fragmentary interpretation is based on that single remark. The idea of publication, which he had been putting off for more than a year, filled him with horror. 'I reflected on the amount of self-discipline it was costing me to offer the public even my book upon dreams – I should have to give away so much of my own private character in it.

> *Das Beste was du wissen kannst,*
> *Darfst du den Buben doch nicht sagen.*
> [After all, the best of what you know
> May not be told to boys.][1]

The task which was imposed on me in the dream of carrying out a dissection of my own body was thus my self-analysis which was linked up with my giving an account of my dreams' (*ID* 453–4). The presence of Brücke in the dream is of particular significance: when working in his laboratory, Freud was tempted on more than one occasion to allow a discovery of his to lie fallow, until an energetic remonstrance on Brücke's

1. This remark by Mephistopheles to Faust (*Faust, Part I*, Scene 4) was a great favourite of Freud's: cf. *F*, December 3, 1897, and February 9, 1898; it concludes his analysis of the 'Uncle with the yellow beard' dream (*ID* 142); and he applied it to Goethe himself on the occasion of his being awarded the Goethe prize in 1930 (1930*e*).

part forced him to publish it. The silver-paper (stanniol) is an allusion to the then standard work by Stannius on the nervous system of fishes and to Freud's own early research into the same subject.

Freud now realised what wish was being expressed by the dream: he had to publish his book at all costs, even if it meant sacrificing his personality. A scientific discovery could not be consigned to oblivion for personal reasons. From Saint Augustine on, many men had written their confessions with the aim of edifying their fellow human beings or achieving literary fame. Freud was the first person to do so for strictly scientific reasons. As he resigned himself to publication, he could not help thinking of his first paper, 'On the Origin of the Posterior Nerve-Roots in the Spinal Cord of Ammocoetes (Petromyzon planeri)' (1877*a*), written over twenty years before when he was 21. He was now 43. It was as if he were starting out all over again.

Rider Haggard's novels provided Freud with the second symbolic key to the dream. In their description of perilous journeys into unknown territory where no one had ever set foot, they represent rather accurately Freud's own exploration of the unconscious: 'The end of the adventure in *She*,' Freud writes, 'is that the guide, instead of finding immortality for herself and the others, perishes in the mysterious subterranean fire.' This clearly alludes to the fear of dying before having achieved one's task – a fear that Freud experienced with increasing intensity as his self-analysis progressed. The wooden house was the excavated Etruscan grave near Orvieto, which Freud had visited during the summer of 1897, and in which 'the skeletons of two grown-up men were lying' on benches. The dream fulfils the wish to escape imminent death: if I have to go down into a grave, why not go as a tourist or, better even, a scientist? After all, Aeneas had succeeded in returning from his journey into the underworld.

The dissection of the pelvis points in the same direction. Freud had had a tired feeling in his legs before the dream, accompanied by 'a tired mood and a doubting thought: "How much longer will my legs carry me?"' The dream gives him back the use of his legs – his legs are fine, he can forge ahead – in other words, it gives him back his self-confidence. He will die, but his work will survive him. The infantile wish for personal immortality, which is still very strong in the previous dream of 'Father on his death-bed like Garibaldi', is replaced here by the adult wish for survival in his descendants and in the minds of his readers. This explains the two sleeping children (probably his paper on Ammocoetes and his dream book) – his children, who will obtain what was refused their father. 'No, my own immortal works have not yet been written,' he tells Louise N. As poets do, Freud was now banking on his work to ensure the immortality of his name: he was in the process of giving up his infantile wish for personal eternity.

Louise N. was present in the dream and during the dissection, 'assisting me in my job'. This is possibly an allusion to Minna, with whom Freud increasingly discussed himself and his work.

Lilla Veszy-Wagner (1969) has compared this dream with Nebuchadnezzar's dream, in the Bible, about the idol with the feet of clay – a dream so horrible that the king awoke and promptly forgot it. It was left to the perspicacious Daniel to piece together an interpretation: when its feet were struck with a stone, the enormous statue of gold, silver, brass, iron and clay broke in pieces and was dispersed like chaff. Veszy-Wagner sees in this type of dream, with its characteristic feeling of 'general paralysis', the expression not so much of castration anxiety as of depersonalisation and fragmentation anxiety. Such dreams in prepsychotics usually herald an imminent outbreak of delirium, as in Nebuchadnezzar's case, or a hypochondriac or suicidal state. In normal people, they occur after great physical fatigue, such as that resulting from standing up for a long period: Freud, for example, had been feeling weariness in his legs for several days. The feeling of heaviness in the legs is used by the dream to represent an autotomia phantasy, in other words, the application to oneself of *lex talionis* ('If thy right eye offend thee, pluck it out and cast it from thee; [. . .] and if thy right hand offend thee, cut it off, and cast it from thee', Matthew 5: 29–30). This applies to Freud's dream: the connection with his father's death, which triggered off Freud's self-analysis, is obvious. For the son, losing his father was like losing his legs; desiring his death was the same thing as cutting himself off from a source of support. But the dream contains another visual image – evisceration at the beginning, and later on a mire or marsh: here, Veszy-Wagner sees a clear identification with a woman who is having her period.

I would go so far as to describe it as an identification with a 'menstruating' woman, for the state of 'mental fright' in which Freud wakes up from the dream foreshadows what he later described as 'the uncanny' (1919*h*): 'Dismembered limbs [. . .] have something peculiarly uncanny about them, especially when [. . .] they prove capable of independent activity in addition' (*SE* 17, 244). This feminine identification, which is very strong in Freud's case, is a reaction of anxiety about the loss of the mother (the individual identifies with the beloved object in order not to lose it) – an anxiety that precedes, and is more intense than, castration anxiety. The dream therefore wishes to deny that loss; hence the references to the perambulators on the ground-floor of his block of flats, to the Alpine guide who carries him as a mother would her child, and to the Etruscan tomb containing 'the skeletons of two grown-up men'. Now Freud knew very well that married couples were buried in the same vault (at least there can have been no doubt about that in Orvieto): so he dreamt of sleeping with the mother in perpetuity. Or rather, publishing his book, producing a scientific work, and dissecting himself was the equivalent of bringing to light that dream deep down within him and then feeling forced, reluctantly, to abandon it.

Twice in later life, Freud had fainting attacks: as in the dream, his legs gave way and the colossus realised the fragility of his feet of clay. The first occasion occurred in Bremen in 1909, just before he left for the United States with Jung and Ferenczi on a trip which he hoped would bring his work worldwide recognition, and for which he had insured his life for a considerable sum: Jung told Freud about some prehistoric cemeteries and mummified bodies that had been discovered in marshland near Bremen. Freud became restive and accused Jung of harbouring unconscious death wishes; he also succeeded in persuading Jung to give up his principle of abstinence and to drink some wine with him (J II, 61).

The second incident occurred in Munich in 1912, again in the presence of Jung, and shortly before his final break with him. Freud asked five colleagues to meet him for lunch to discuss the setting up of another psychoanalytic periodical after Stekel had seceded with the *Zentralblatt*; he began sharply criticising the two Swiss who were present, Jung and Riklin, for writing articles expounding psychoanalysis in Swiss periodicals without mentioning his name. Then he suddenly blacked out: 'His first words as he was coming to were strange: "How sweet it must be to die"' (J I 348). Freud, who continued to carry out self-analysis throughout his life, saw a connection between this second incident and similar symptoms he suffered in the same room in August 1894 during a 'congress' with Fliess (it was Freud's first trip to Munich, on which occasion Fliess told him about trimethylamin): 'There is some piece of unruly homosexual feeling at the root of the matter' (letter to Jones of December 8, 1912, quoted in J I, 348). When Ferenczi drew a parallel between the two incidents in Bremen and Munich, 'in his reply Freud, who in the meantime had analysed his reaction of fainting, expressed the opinion that all his attacks could be traced to the effect on him of his young brother's death when he was a year and seven months old' (J II, 165). Also comparable is the incident where Freud suffered a loss of memory on the Acropolis in 1904 (cf. p. 556).

Let us return to the dream of 'Dissecting my own pelvis'. As Schur remarks (S 177, n.12), the 'eternal feminine' is an allusion to the death and salvation of Faust. *Faust, Part II* ends with the verses:

Chorus Mysticus

Alles Vergängliche	[All that is transient
Ist nur ein Gleichnis;	Is but a symbol;
Das Unzulängliche,	Here imperfection
Hier wirds Ereignis;	Becomes actuality;
Das Unbeschreibliche,	The indescribable
Hier ists getan;	Here is fulfilled;
Das Ewig-Weibliche	The eternal feminine
Zieht uns hinan.	Draws us on high.]

Freud, then, through his self-analysis, was in the process of completing the full Faustian cycle – the development of knowledge, the realisation of all the possibilities of the human mind, an extension of the boundaries of the human condition, downfall, death, rebirth, cure and ascension. This strikingly summarises the working over of the depressive position. Since the 'Rome' dreams, Freud had evolved internally. The dominant feature of those dreams, it will be remembered, was a series of heroic-masochistic identifications with historical figures like Hannibal, Winckelmann and Masséna, who first achieved glory but eventually failed. His identifications with Leo Vincey, Ignatio and Faust were very different: failure was accepted less reluctantly; guilt feelings and anxiety about death were more easily overcome; the crossing of the internal underworld had been completed; reparation for harm done had been made, and in the process opened up the possibility of creativity. It is never possible completely to shake off the temptations of failure, the burden of unconscious guilt, or anxiety at the primal separation from the mother and the final separation of death: this is amply shown by the subsequent incidents in Freud's life which I have just described. What they also demonstrate is the depressive background against which, right up to his death, Freud was constantly able to summon up fresh spurts of creativity.

If we look at this dream in the context of the dynamics of Freud's self-analysis, we see a phenomenon which, as psychoanalysts have since observed, frequently occurs in the final stages of treatment: the prospect of imminent completion may cause one last internal movement of regression and reveal psychical processes that have not yet been explained. Freud had taken the decision to complete his book by exposing himself in it, i.e. to end the systematic self-analysis that had been prompted by the work of mourning following his father's death; true, he continued to resort to self-analysis throughout the rest of his life, but only at irregular intervals. In the dream of 'Dissecting my own pelvis', not only did he resolve to publish his book and thus terminate the psychical 'dissection' of himself, but he embarked on one last process of regression, more deeply than ever before, which allowed him to glimpse – and then only in pictorial form – two new conclusions. The first of these was the subject of further conceptual elucidation by Freud later on; the second proved less fertile.

Nearly a century after the discovery of psychoanalysis, I would offer the following definition of the first conclusion – a fuller definition, in fact, than that subsequently worked out by Freud: anxiety, which lies at the heart of all psychical disorders, differs in character depending on the level of the disorder: fragmentation anxiety in psychosis, object-loss anxiety in narcissistic neuroses and borderline states, and castration anxiety proper in psychoneuroses. In the dream of 'Dissecting my own pelvis', anxiety was so strong that it caused Freud to wake up – something which had possibly not occurred since a dream dating from prepuberty, 'My mother and the bird-beaked figures'. In my view, this dissection dream is a partly successful and partly unsuccessful effort to break down that massive overall anxiety into its three constituent levels – dismemberment and evisceration of one's own body, separation from the mother, and paralysis in the presence of a woman. The second conclusion concerns the maternal imago. Freud's associations lead him to evoke the image of a dangerous woman – dangerous not only because of the prohibited and reprehensible incestuous desires she arouses in the boy, but because of a destructive omnipotence inherent in her. But this image, which is not to be found in the actual text of the dream, remains ill-defined in Freud's analysis. It can only be fully grasped by reading Rider Haggard's novels, as Grinstein has done. On several subsequent occasions, Freud got a little nearer to apprehending this imago without ever grasping it in all its detail.

THE DREAM OF THE 'ETRUSCAN CINERARY URN' (SPRING 1899?)

The dream of 'Dissecting my own pelvis' could also be interpreted more literally: Freud knew and accepted that he was mortal, and was making his final arrangements: if I have to rest in a grave, then let it be an Etruscan grave. When looking at the illustrations of the Philippson Bible as a child, Freud had been struck by the Egyptian funerary barge (cf. the dream of 'My mother and the bird-beaked figures'). Later, in the course of his travels in northern Italy, he was particularly struck by representations of death, notably at Orvieto (the Signorelli frescoes and the excavated Etruscan grave). At Easter, 1898, he visited Aquileia museum, which contained Etruscan funerary objects. A month later, in connection with the Spanish–American naval war, he dreamt of black Etruscan cups (in the dream of the 'Castle by the sea'). He had brought back an Etruscan cinerary urn from one of his trips to Italy. Although he later gave it away, it appears in one of the dreams of thirst which he describes at the beginning of Chapter 3, 'A Dream is the Fulfilment of a Wish'. I believe this dream of the Etruscan cinerary urn to be contemporaneous with the dream of 'Dissecting my own pelvis', partly because of its theme, but also because Freud refers to it as being recent. But it may date from the spring of 1898 just as well as from the spring of 1899:

'Not long ago this same dream of mine showed some modification. I had felt thirsty even before I fell asleep, and I had emptied a glass of water that stood on the table beside my bed. A few hours later during the night I had a fresh attack of thirst, and this had inconvenient results. In order to provide myself with some water I should have had to get up and fetch the glass standing on the table by my wife's bed. I therefore had an appropriate dream that my wife was giving me a drink out of a vase; this vase was an Etruscan cinerary urn which I had brought back from a journey to Italy and had since given away. But the water in it tasted so salty (evidently because of the ashes in the urn) that I woke up. It will be noticed how conveniently everything was arranged in this dream. Since its only purpose was to fulfil a wish, it could be completely egoistical. A love of comfort and convenience is not really compatible with consideration for other people. The introduction of the cinerary urn was probably yet another wish-fulfilment. I was sorry that the vase was no longer in my possession – just as the glass of water on my wife's table was out of my reach. The urn with its ashes fitted in, too, with the salty taste in my mouth which had now grown stronger and which I knew was bound to wake me' (*ID* 124).

Freud's ultimate wish, present at a deeper level in this dream, came true: he was incinerated in England, and his ashes were placed, not in an Etruscan urn, but in his favourite Greek vase.

The writing of the second version of *The Interpretation of Dreams* (May–September 1899)

THE DREAM OF 'BEING IN THE SIXTH FORM' (JUNE 1899)

During the spring and summer of 1899 Freud worked non-stop writing *The Interpretation of Dreams*, then correcting proofs. He gave up the idea of doing any travelling during the summer holidays. He joined his family at a large farmhouse called Riemerlehen, near Berchtesgaden in Bavaria, first for a few days at the end of June, then without a break from the end of July till September 20. It was there, in an arbour in the garden, that he wrote the difficult final chapter of his book. Letters to Fliess tell us how his work was going. On June 9, he was still struggling dispiritedly with the first chapter about the literature on dreams, and announced one last discovery concerning the function of dreams: 'The whole matter again resolves itself for me into a commonplace. Invariably the dream seeks to fulfil *one* wish that has assumed various forms. It is the wish to sleep! We dream in order not to have to wake up, because we want to sleep. *Tant de bruit* . . .' (*F* 354). In *The Interpretation of Dreams* (*ID* 570), Freud says he borrowed this idea from Liébeault's *Le sommeil provoqué et les états analogues* (1889); but Ellenberger has established that Liébeault's works contain no such notion, which would in any case be in direct opposition to the latter's doctrine (E 493 and 563 n.316).

On June 27, Freud was still in the throes of completing the first chapter and about to send in the first signatures to the publisher. He also mentioned the dream of 'Being in the sixth form', which does not feature in *The Interpretation of Dreams*:

'My own dreams have now become absurdly complicated. Recently I was told that on the occasion of Aunt Minna's birthday Annerl said, "On birthdays I am mostly a little bit good." Thereupon I dreamed the familiar school dream, in which I am in *sexta* [sixth form] and say to myself, "In this sort of dream one is mostly in sixth form." The only possible solution: Annerl is my *sexta* [sixth] child. Brr . . .' (*F* 357).

The writing of the first chapter was so difficult that it reminded Freud of a school imposition. At the same time, the 'delivery' of the dream book gave him the feeling he was bringing a new child into the world. The connection with Fliess is not apparent from this description of the dream. We learn more from an earlier passage in the same letter: 'Many thanks for the long letter, which I hardly deserve. It is my lot to wait, and in resignation I have given up my habit of complaining about the unbridgeable distance [which separates us]. I hope the path you have taken will lead you even farther and even deeper, and that as the new Kepler you will unveil the ironclad rules of the biological mechanism to us' (*F* 356). Schur (S 195) spots an ironical allusion here to Schiller's poem *Die Weltweisen* (*The World's Wise Men*), already referred to by Freud in his paper on screen memories and mentioned in a letter to Fliess of May 25. In the poem, Schiller pokes fun at the speculations of wise men:

Einstweilen, bis den Bau der Welt
Philosophie zusammenhält,
Erhält sie das Getriebe
Durch Hunger und durch Liebe
[Meanwhile, until philosophy maintains the
working of the world, it [nature]
maintains the machinery
through hunger and through love.]

Because he had recognised that hunger and love were the two most powerful motive forces in human beings, because of the discoveries he was making about the mental processes, Freud thought he was the new Kepler of psychology – a genuine Kepler, unlike Fliess who, he sensed, would never be anything more than a poor man's Kepler of biology.

THE DREAM OF '1851 AND 1856' (JULY 1899?)

Ambivalence, then, continued to be an increasing ingredient of Freud's relationship with Fliess. The latter played both a positive and an irritating role vis-à-vis Freud. It was he who decided Freud to publish his book, probably during their Easter 'congress'; he was the guide in the dream of 'Dissecting my own pelvis', the reincarnation of Brücke, the romantic heroine who bestows immortality. But he was a guide in relation to whom Freud had to 'dismember' himself and undergo 'defusion' in order to become autonomous. When Freud was in the final stages of writing the dream book, Fliess represented his moral conscience. Freud sent him his manuscript and his proofs as and when they became ready, and asked for criticism. Fliess told Freud to change the plan of the book, to drop a dream here and an epigraph there, to add further chapters; he corrected quotations, tidied up the style, and disapproved of uncalled-for comparisons. It was thanks to him that Freud was able to complete his task: 'The confidence you express is always extremely beneficial to me and has had a stimulating effect for a long time' (*F*, July 22, 1899, 362); 'I cannot tell you how much good your lively interest in this work does me' (*F*, August 1, 1899, 363); 'I find a kind of substitute for our foiled meeting in the heightened liveliness of our correspondence. [. . .] I cannot do without you as the representative of the Other' (*F*, September 21, 1899, 373–4).

Yet Freud took some of Fliess's criticism rather badly, and occasionally paid him back in his own coin. He had lost interest in the writing of the historical-cum-bibliographical chapter, and could not keep it up for more than a few hours a day: 'So I often ask myself whether you really gave me good advice or whether I should curse you for it' (*F*, June 9, 1899, 354–5). He then added perfidiously: 'There is only one possible compensation: you must give me something refreshing to read in your introduction to biology.' Freud's attitude towards Fliess remained unchanged after an initial enjoyable stay with Martha and the rest of his family in Berchtesgaden from June 29 to July 2. It was in the same railway station at Berchtesgaden that Freud had had an attack of travel anxiety at the end of their very first 'congress' in 1890. In the course of recalling the incident, Freud took malicious pleasure in telling Fliess a few home truths: 'At the time I felt somewhat overwhelmed by your superiority; this I felt distinctly. Furthermore, I vaguely sensed something I can express only today: the faint notion that this man had not yet discovered his calling, which later turned out to be the shackling of life with numbers and formulas' (*F*, July 3, 1899, 358). Freud was hinting that the superiority had changed hands: he had got rid of his railway phobia, he was finishing a major book, and he had progressed, whereas his friend's behaviour had simply become more and more wayward. Two and a half months later, Freud was even more explicit: 'My central accomplishment in interpretation comes in the [enclosed] instalment, the absurd dreams. It is astonishing how often you appear in them. In the *non vixit* dream I am delighted to have outlived you; isn't it terrible to suggest something like this – that is, to have to make it explicit to everyone who understands?' (*F*, September 21, 1899, 374).

Fliess, it is true, also had good reason to feel irritated. He was helping Freud as best he could with encouragement, positive criticism, and ideas; he was spending a good deal of time on his manuscript. Yet he was getting nothing of what he expected in return – for instance, Freud gave him no new thoughts on bisexuality. One gets the increasing impression of two men talking into the wind, each interested only in his own theories. The rift between them was accentuated by differences in their personalities and tastes. Fliess disparaged the ancient statuettes of which Freud had just become the proud owner; he described them as 'old and grubby gods' (*F*, August 1, 1899, 363). More seriously, he was shocked at the extreme candour with which Freud had revealed his innermost feelings in his book. Freud tried to get Fliess to see his point of view: 'I have inserted a large number of new dreams, which I hope you will not delete. *Pour faire une omelette il faut casser des oeufs*. Incidentally, only *humana* and *humaniora*; nothing really intimate, that is, personally sexual' (*F*, August 6, 1899, 365); 'You will have to leave me some scope for my "venom" in the interpretations of dreams. It is good for the constitution to get things off one's chest' (*F*, August 27, 1899, 368). This identity between his life and his work, which Freud had at last achieved and wished his friend to recognise, was repugnant to Fliess – or beyond his comprehension. Freud, now convinced that he was on the right track and that his discovery was correct, decided to include in the book most of his own dreams that he had originally decided to leave out. He felt that total sincerity would pay off. The idea of such sincerity was obviously unbearable to Fliess – as indeed it would have been to most people.

Freud was particularly taken aback by one of Fliess's criticisms shortly before the book came out: he felt that the dreamer came across as 'too witty' (*F*, September 11, 1899, 371). Freud countered by saying that it was not his fault if dreams were witty; he had merely recorded the fact. More importantly, he had drawn a more general conclusion from it: 'The ostensible wit of all unconscious processes is intimately related to the theory of the joke and the comic' (*ibid.*). The incident left its mark on Freud, for it proved that Fliess suspected him of interpreting dreams in a wild and fanciful way and had failed to grasp an essential aspect of his discovery, i.e. that word-presentations, like thing-presentations, can be products of the unconscious.

It was in this context that Freud had the '1851 and 1856' dream; it was probably the last of the recorded dreams he had before completing *The Interpretation of Dreams*, since according to Schur (S 189) he composed his interpretation of it right at the end of July 1899.

Freud first referred to an overt disagreement with Fliess over the dream book in a letter of July 17; he had just received proofs of the first chapter from the printers. The problem was the epigraph: 'A motto for the dream [book] has not turned up since you killed Goethe's sentimental one. A reference to repression is all that will remain. *Flectere si nequeo superos, Acheronta movebo*' (*F* 361). Thus, in a single passage, Freud complained of being sterilised by Fliess and came up with the epigraph with which he eventually headed his book.

On July 22, before leaving for the holidays in Berchtesgaden, Freud told Fliess in great detail how much of the book he had already completed and how much remained to be done:

'In regard to the dream [book] things are as follows: it lacked a first chapter, an introduction to the literature, which – unless I am very much mistaken – you also asked for in order to lighten the rest. This was written, was a bitter task for me, and did not turn out very satisfactorily. Most readers will get stuck in this thorny thicket and never get to see the Sleeping Beauty behind it. The rest, with which you are familiar, will be revised, though not very drastically. Sections dealing with the literature will be taken out; a few specific references to the literature which I have only just come upon will be scattered throughout; new dream examples will be inserted as illustrations – none of which amounts to very much. Then the last psychological chapter must be written anew: the wish theory, which, after all, provides the link with what follows; some hypotheses about sleep; coming to terms with anxiety dreams; the interrelations between the wish to sleep and the suppressed. All of it, perhaps, by way of allusions.

'Now, I do not understand what you want to see, and when. Am I to send you this first chapter? And then the continued revisions, before I send them to the printer? You would be taking on a great burden without any pleasure if you still took pains with it. There has been no change in regard to the conditions of publication. Deuticke did not want to let the book go, so I decided not to betray in any way what a difficult decision this was for me. At any rate, a part of the first third of the large task will have been accomplished, that of placing the neuroses and psychoses in [the sphere of] science by means of the theory of repression and wish-fulfilment. (1) The organic-sexual; (2) the factual-clinical; (3) the metapsychological in it. The work is now in its second third; we still need to discuss the first part thoroughly; when the third (Rome, Karlsbad) has been attained, I shall be glad to take a rest' (*F* 362).

July 24, 1899, was the fourth anniversary of the specimen dream of 'Irma's injection'. July 29 was his parents' 44th wedding anniversary. On August 1, when Freud sent Fliess the corrected proofs of the introductory chapter from Berchtesgaden, asking him for his observations and criticisms, he referred to a further subject of major disagreement between them: 'The loss of the big dream that you eliminated is to be compensated for by the insertion of a small collection of dreams (harmless, absurd dreams; calculations and speeches in dreams; affects in dreams). Only the last, psychological chapter needs to be reworked, and that I shall perhaps tackle in September and send you in manuscript form or – bring with me. It occupies my full interest' (*F* 363).

Their lack of understanding was in fact mutual: Freud was no more capable of espousing Fliess's views than Fliess was Freud's:

'The farther the work of the past year recedes, the more satisfied I become. But bisexuality! You are certainly right about it. I am accustoming myself to regarding every sexual act as a process in which four individuals are involved. We have a lot to discuss on this topic.

'A good deal of what you say in your letter distresses me greatly. I wish I could help' (*F* 364).

The '1851 and 1856' dream probably occurred some time around August 1, 1899:

'Here is another absurd dream about a dead father. *I received a communication from the town council of my birthplace concerning the fees due for someone's maintenance in the hospital in the year* 1851, *which had been necessitated by an attack he had had in my house. I was amused by this since, in the first place, I was not yet alive in* 1851 *and, in the second place, my father, to whom it might have related, was already dead. I went to him in the next room, where he was lying on his bed, and told him about it. To my surprise, he recollected that in* 1851 *he had once got drunk and had had to be locked up or detained. It was at a time at which he had been working for the firm of T—. "So you used to drink as well?" I asked; "did you get married soon after that?" I calculated that, of course, I was born in* 1856, *which seemed to be the year which immediately followed the year in question*' (*ID* 435–6).

This dream and Freud's analysis of it are to be found in Section G of Chapter 6, 'The Dream-Work', as an example both of absurd dreams (*ID* 435–9) and of intellectual activity in dreams (*ID* 449–52). Freud's initial analysis of the dream comes after the dreams of 'Father on his death-bed like Garibaldi' and 'Count Thun', and before 'Goethe's attack on Herr M.' and 'My son, the Myops'. He returns to the dream after the dreams of 'Frau Doni and the three children' and 'Goethe's attack on Herr M.', and before the recent dream of 'Dissecting my own pelvis'. A third, shorter discussion takes the example of the number 51 to show how necessary it is to interpret even the least conspicuous details of dreams; it comes at the beginning of Section A, 'The Forgetting of Dreams', of Chapter 7, 'The Psychology of the Dream Processes' (*ID* 513). Freud alludes to this dream a little later in a letter to Fliess: 'You are familiar with my dream which obstinately promises the end of E.'s treatment (among the absurd dreams), and you can well imagine how important this one persistent patient has become to me' (*F*, December 21, 1899, 391). The dream is discussed by Sc' ·r (S 184–91).

According to Freud, t' dream aimed to demonstrate that a difference of four or five years (1851–56) was of no significance. It was the length of time he had set for the psychoanalytic treatment of patients, now that he felt confident of his technique. The treatment of E., which was particularly important for Freud (the case crops up frequently in his self-analysis and in letters to Fliess), was now entering its fifth year, a fact that had prompted Breuer's surprise and criticism. Four or five years was the length of time that Breuer had given him financial support, at a time when Jacob Freud was unable to do so (it might also be noted that Breuer and Freud had ended their collaboration four or five years before the dream). Four or five years was also the length of time, Freud adds, that he made his fiancée wait for their marriage; he recalls gratefully the kindly reaction of his father when told, in somewhat cavalier fashion, that he and Martha had got engaged (an episode reproduced in the dream by '*I went to him in the next room*'). As a student, Freud had exceeded the five years prescribed for medical studies and gone on working for several more years, with the result that his circle of acquaintances wondered whether he would ever take his finals. Lastly, it should be noted, though Freud himself does not mention it, that he was now in his fifth year of self-analysis, since he had had the dream of 'Irma's injection' more than four years previously, on July 24, 1895; it was therefore high time for him to achieve something, to produce his great work.

The dream gave Freud the confidence he needed to do so. First of all, he said to himself, what were five years in comparison with a whole lifetime? Then he had amply shown in the past that even when he had had to wait five years he always attained his objective, be it a medical degree, marriage, or financial independence. Breuer was wrong to criticise him: Freud was convinced he would cure E.'s neurosis (he told Fliess on April 16, 1900, that his treatment had been successfully completed). The accusation of being late which was central to the '*Non vixit*' dream is here rejected once and for all, and even partly turned into a compliment: people who criticise him always end up, somewhat belatedly, by admitting that he was right all along. Jacob was forced to recognise his son's intellectual and professional qualities, which had resulted in his receiving the best medical treatment available. The very same Meynert who had 'attacked' Freud and dismissed him from his laboratory because he had claimed to have found a case of male hysteria, who used to intoxicate himself with chloroform and once had to go into a home as a result (cf. the 'hospital' in the dream), admitted on his death-bed, to an astonished Freud, that he had himself been one of the clearest cases of male hysteria. Similarly, Freud was becoming increasingly convinced that his theories about the neuro-psychoses (the extremely important bearing of the first five years of life on the formation of the personality, the crucial role played by the father in women's sex lives) would eventually, after being ridiculed, gain acceptance. This further withdrawal from the super-ego's criticism was once again prompted by a stimulating ego-ideal based on the image of an understanding father.

The dream also marked a withdrawal from Fliess's theories. Although Freud does not say so, the presence of numbers is an indirect allusion to them. At that time Fliess, no longer able to explain all the phenomena he encountered as being multiples or fractions of 23 and/or 28, decided to bring in two new key numbers 5 and 51 (28 − 23 = 5; 28 + 23 = 51). Freud refused to go along with such a far-fetched hypothesis. Fliess had worked out that his friend (no doubt because of his fundamental bisexuality) would reach a critical point in his life at the age of 51 (28 + 23, i.e. a male cycle + a female cycle). It was the age at which Freud feared he would die, as well as being the age, he said, at which a colleague had died just after being appointed to a professorship. The dream reiterates Freud's misgivings, which he had voiced for the first time in a letter to Fliess of January 3, 1899: a difference of five does not count; 51 is no more certain than 56.

Freud's superstitious fear of the age of 51 appears for the first time in a letter to Fliess of June 22, 1894, in connection with two problems Freud had been facing for about nine months – his cardiac symptoms and the side-effects of his having stopped smoking (cf. Schur, S 51–3). Freud, then aged 38, cannot make up his mind which diagnosis to believe, Fliess's (which would mean his giving up smoking cigars for good) or Breuer's (which would involve only temporary abstinence). Freud then goes on: 'The example of Kundt did not frighten me very much; he who would guarantee me thirteen years until the age of 51 would not have spoiled my pleasure in cigars. My compromise opinion, for which I have no scientific basis, is that I shall go on suffering from various complaints for another four to five to eight years, with good and bad periods, and then between 40 and 50 perish very abruptly from a rupture of the heart; if it is not too close to 40, it is not so bad at all' (*F* 85). The well-known German physicist Kundt had just died, on May 21, 1894, a few days after succeeding Helmholtz as professor of experimental physics at the University of Berlin. It may be assumed that Fliess had told Freud of Kundt's premature death, probably ascribing it to his heavy smoking. Kundt actually died at the age of 54½; we do not know why Freud gave him the fateful age of 51.

It was in a letter of September 29, 1896, that Freud first alluded to the fact that the age of 51 was the sum of 23 + 28. Jacob Freud had been seriously ill since June, and Sigmund did not expect him to live long. His own health, on the other hand, had improved: he had started smoking again, safely passed the age of 40, climbed the Rax mountain, visited northern Italy, and declared himself cured. Then he caught influenza: 'I hope you and your wife and son are again installed most comfortably in the beautiful rooms of von der Heydtstrasse; that you are busily observing and calculating new periods of 28 and 23. [. . .] I have not written to you until today because an influenza with fever, pus, and cardiac symptoms suddenly shattered my well-being; only today did I begin to have an inkling that health might again be possible. I would like so much to hold out until that famous age limit of approximately 51, but I had one day [among them] that made me feel it was unlikely' (*F*, September 29, 1896, 198).

Despite his self-analysis, Freud was unable to rid himself completely of the notion that certain years were fateful and therefore to be feared. He spent his 51st year (1907–08) in a state of anxiety, and, when he came through unscathed, declared that it was a great mistake to believe in superstition. He then fixed the age of 61 (or 62) as the new fateful year. Schur (S 230–2) quotes a letter to Jung of April 16, 1909, which is quite explicit on this point. In it, Freud ascribes that fear to 'the specifically Jewish nature of my mysticism', which he sees as the real reason behind his disturbance of memory on the Acropolis in 1904 (1936*a*). As I pointed out at the beginning of the present work, this mysticism was the prime cause of Freud's superstitious fears: the number 52, which could be spelled out as the Hebrew word for 'dog', was therefore a bad number; and the 52nd birthday was considered a critical one, especially for men (S 25). Fliess's calculations simply provided a belated and flimsy rationalisation for a long-standing fear. It could only have been that fear which led Freud to give credit to Fliess's fanciful theory of periodicity. The latter, incidentally, was the only one of Fliess's three theories which contributed nothing whatsoever to Freud's theory of the unconscious, whereas, as we have seen, bisexuality and the relationship between the nose and the sexual organs probably helped Freud to conceive of the symbolic equivalence of the face and the sexual organs in hysterics, and to suspect the universal existence of a pregenital homosexual instinct.

Let us return to Freud's analysis of the '1851 and 1856' dream. Once again, the manner in which the dream is formulated enables Freud to pinpoint the dream-thoughts. The dream, he says, is clothed in the form of a calculation that knows no rebuttal, or a demonstration of a mathematical conclusion. In this way it expresses his wish a) that he will succeed in drawing a conclusion with his book and with his patient E. just as he has always drawn conclusions in his life and studies, and b) that the conclusions he draws on psychoneuroses and dreams will be regarded as irrefutable. Thus, the symbolism of the dream is not chemical, botanical or grammatical this time, but algebraic: 'It was just as though there were an algebraic equation containing (in addition to numerals) plus and minus signs, indices and radical signs, and as though someone were to copy out the equation without understanding it, taking over both the operational symbols and the numerals into his copy but mixing them all up together' (*ID* 451).

The other dream-thoughts are informed by another kind of symbolism, that of filiation. If I had been a professor's son, I would easily have become a professor. How did my father behave when he was younger, before I came into the world? How long after my father's marriage was I born? The father's role in psychosexual development was one of Freud's important discoveries: in his view, even children who lose their fathers in infancy retain unconscious recollections of him that continue to influence their lives.

Further light is shed on this dream by Sajner's discovery (1968) that Jacob Freud entered into a second – and hitherto unknown – marriage with someone called Rebekka in about 1852, after the death of his first wife Sally (the mother of Emanuel and Philipp),[1] and before his third marriage to Amalie (Sigismund's mother) on July 29, 1855. In his associations, Freud suggests that his parents married in 1851 – a statement that led his early biographers astray; Jones corrected the mistake (J I, 2 n.5). What happened was that Freud got his dates wrong – as do victims of general paralysis – and confused his father's second marriage (1852) with his third (1855), which resulted in Sigismund's own birth in 1856. The last sentence of the dream – 'I calculated that, of course, I was born in 1856, which seemed to be the year which immediately followed the year in question' – therefore takes on several meanings: a) Freud's birth (May 6, 1856) could hardly have followed his parents' marriage (July 29, 1855) sooner, i.e. nine months and one week later; b) his father's second marriage, after his first wife's death, immediately followed the year 1851, since it is certain he remarried in 1852. Schur (S 190) suggests that the date 1851, which must have been so mysterious to the young Sigismund (it was approximately the year when Jacob's first wife died and when he took a new wife, who must also have died rather soon after),[2] may have contributed to Freud's superstitious preoccupation with the age of 51. Perhaps, too, the notion that sons must expiate their fathers' alleged crimes was a component of Freud's fear of death.

Whatever doubts may surround some details of the '1851 and 1856' dream, two things are certain: Freud was anxious about dying at a fateful date; and, once again, a dream gave him enough self-confidence to dominate partially that anxiety by guessing its meaning, and to carry through with determination the task he had undertaken. Death would seem more acceptable to him as long as he had the time (five years) and the good fortune to make a great discovery and publish it.

1. According to Jones (J I, 2), Sally died in 1852, but we do not know who gave him this information. The register of Jews living in Freiberg in 1852 gives Jacob Freud's wife as Rebekka. Her name is no longer listed in 1854, so apparently she had died (Sajner 1968, quoted by Schur, S 20).

2. Unless, of course, Rebekka was repudiated – if we take literally Freud's allusion in the letter to Fliess of September 21, 1897 (when he was in the depths of depression just before his discovery of the Oedipus complex) to the punch line of a Jewish anecdote: 'Rebecca, take off your gown; you are no longer a bride.'

FREUD'S DEVELOPMENT OF THE THEORY OF THE PSYCHICAL APPARATUS

The letters to Fliess of July 22 and August 1, 1899, already quoted, tell us what form the book was taking. Freud had written a new first chapter outlining the existing literature on dreams. He hoped in September to revise completely the final, 'psychological' chapter (on the wish theory, sleep, anxiety dreams, and the interrelations between the wish to sleep and the suppressed), which he had abandoned a few months earlier along with the first version. The rest, i.e. the bulk of the book, was basically the same as the first version, but with two differences: Freud inserted 'new examples of dreams' and added three further sections to Chapter 6, 'The Dream-Work' (in which he had already dealt with condensation, displacement, and representation), namely Sections F (calculations and speeches in dreams), G (absurd dreams, intellectual activity in dreams) and H (affects in dreams). Any additional information the present reader may need will be found at the beginning of the next chapter in a detailed analytical summary, which is both diachronic and synchronic, of *The Interpretation of Dreams*.

On August 6, 1899, Freud answered Fliess, who had found the first chapter tedious: 'You feel about it [the literature on dreams] as I do; the secret probably is that we do not like it at all. But, if we do not want to hand the "scientists" an axe with which to slaughter the poor book, we must put up with it somewhere' (*F* 365). In the same letter, he told Fliess that he was sending him more proofs, and that he had put in some new dreams of his own, which he hoped Fliess would not 'delete' as they included 'nothing really intimate', as well as two other dreams, one dreamt by Fliess's son, and the other, next to it, by Freud's daughter (thus the intellectual contiguity of the fathers was materialised by the joint presence of their children in the book): 'With your permission I shall put Robert's dream among the hunger dreams of children, after Annerl's menu dream. [. . .] At some point the "bigness" in children's dreams must indeed be considered: it is related to children's yearning to be big; to be able for once to eat a bowlful of salad like Papa: the child never has enough, not even of repetitions. Moderation is the hardest thing for the child, as for the neurotic' (*F*, August 6, 1899, 365). The boy was 'under four years old', says *The Interpretation of Dreams*, which was indeed the case with Robert, who had been born at the end of 1895, and whose dream must have been described by Fliess in his latest letter. In the end Freud moved the dream to a different part of his book: instead of putting it with the dreams of hunger (in Chapter 3, 'A Dream Is the Fulfilment of a Wish'), he gave it as an example of the egoism of children (in Chapter 5, Section D, 'Typical Dreams'). He told Fliess about the change on August 27. Here is the relevant passage:

'A child of under four years old reported having dreamt that he had seen a big dish with a big joint of roast meat and vegetables on it. All at once the joint had been eaten up – whole and without being cut up. He had not seen the person who ate it.[1]

'Who can the unknown person have been whose sumptuous banquet of meat was the subject of the little boy's dream? His experiences during the dream-day must enlighten us on the subject. By doctor's orders he had been put on a milk diet for the past few days. On the evening of the dream-day he had been naughty, and as a punishment he had been sent to bed without his supper. He had been through this hunger-cure once before and had been very brave about it. He knew he would get nothing, but would not allow himself to show by so much as a single word that he was hungry. Education had already begun to have an effect on him: it found expression in this dream, which exhibits the beginning of dream-distortion. There can be no doubt that the person whose wishes were aimed at this lavish meal – a meat meal, too – was himself. But since he knew he was not allowed it, he did not venture to sit down at the meal himself, as hungry children do in dreams. (Cf. my little daughter Anna's dream of strawberries on p. 130.) The person who ate the meal remained anonymous' (*ID* 267–8).

Let us return to Freud's letter of August 6, 1899. It contains a remarkable passage on the composition of *The Interpretation of Dreams*: 'The whole thing is planned on the model of an imaginary walk. At the beginning, the dark forest of authors (who do not see the trees), hopelessly lost on wrong tracks. Then a concealed pass through which I lead the reader – my specimen dream with its peculiarities, details, indiscretions, bad jokes – and then suddenly the high ground and the view and the question: "which way do you wish to go now?"' (*F* 365). It is easy to see why Freud added a little further on in the same letter: 'In the last few days I have been very pleased with the work.'

Freud's letter of August 20 was in much the same vein: the typesetting was going slowly; he was sending more proofs to Fliess and begged his

1. The appearance in dreams of things of great size and in great quantities and amounts, and of exaggeration generally, may be another childish characteristic. Children have no more ardent wish than to be big and grown-up and to get as much of things as grown-up people do. They are hard to satisfy, know no such word as 'enough' and insist insatiably on a repetition of things which they have enjoyed or whose taste they have liked. It is only the civilising influence of education that teaches them moderation and how to be content or resigned. Everyone knows that neurotics are equally inclined to be extravagant and immoderate. (Freud's footnote.)

indulgence; he had replaced the big dream deleted by Fliess with 'a small collection of dream fragments'; he dreaded writing the final chapter during the following months. But three new elements made their appearance: he was 'far along in the chapter on "dream-work"' (*Traumarbeit*), in other words Chapter 6; he was writing so much he had writer's cramp; and his younger brother Alexander was going to be appointed *professor extraordinarius* – 'much earlier, in fact, than I' – at the Export Academy, where he already had a lectureship on tariffs (*F* 367). In his letter of August 27, he thanked Fliess for the further amendments he had made to the galley proofs and promised that they would be carefully copied on to the revised proofs when they came back; he said he had sent off 'a stack of writing paper in manuscript form' (probably the final sections of Chapter 6); he was preparing himself for work on 'the last and most thorny chapter'; he repeated his hope that they could have an Easter 'congress' in Rome; and he demanded that Fliess allow him greater latitude in his dream interpretations. When referring to the difficulties of the final chapter, Freud plucked a figure out of the air – a figure which immediately intrigued him: 'Every attempt to make it better than it turns out by itself gives it a forced quality. So it will contain 2,467 mistakes – which I shall leave in it' (*F* 368).

Freud at once tried to explain in a postscript why he had chosen that particular number. He later asked Fliess to return the postscript, and published it in 1901, near the beginning of Chapter 12 of *The Psychopathology of Everyday Life*, as an example of determinism in an apparently arbitrary choice of a number. He explained that he had not chosen the number 2,467 by chance, as nothing in the mind was arbitrary or undetermined. He had just learnt that General E.M., who had been his colonel during his military service (1880), had retired from the post of Master of Ordnance. The general had therefore taken nineteen years over his career. Freud's wife, when told of this, remarked: 'Oughtn't you to be on the retired list too, then?' While writing to Fliess, the thought kept running around in his head: I was 24 during my military service, and I am now 43. The two added together make 67. So the number 2,467 expressed both his annoyance at having failed to get very far during the nineteen years he had been following the colonel's career, and his satisfaction that he still had another twenty-four years ahead of him (*PEL* 242–3). Freud added: 'Since this first example in which an apparently arbitrarily chosen number was explained I have often repeated the same experiment, and with the same result; but the content of the majority of cases is so intimate that they cannot be reported.'

Freud then reached a peak of creative exaltation, and wrote Chapter 7, 'The Psychology of the Dream-Processes', in just two weeks at the end of

August and beginning of September. In his address to celebrate the centenary of Freud's birth, Ernest Jones recalled 'an account Freud's daughter gave me of the time when he was composing the great final chapter of *The Interpretation of Dreams* in the summer of 1899. She recollected that when he was interrupted by being called to a meal he walked as if in a trance, oblivious of his surroundings' (Jones 1956, 19). I shall not discuss the scientific content of Chapter 7 here, as a detailed summary of it will be found in the next chapter (pp. 487–512).

On September 6, Freud wrote to Fliess: 'I am completely into the dream [book], am writing eight to ten pages a day, and have just got over the worst in the psychology – it was agonising. I do not even want to think about how it has turned out. You will tell me whether it can stand at all, but in the galley proofs; reading the manuscript is too much drudgery, and everything can still be changed. In the end I did put more into it than I intended; one always does as one goes deeper, but I am afraid it is – bunk [. . .]. And then they'll really let me have it! When the storm breaks over me, I shall escape to your guest room. You will find something to praise in it in any event, because you are as much on *my* side as the others are *against* me' (*F* 369). Freud, on holiday in the mountains, had no access to a reference library, so Fliess, who remained in Berlin for most of the period, had the thankless task of checking all the quotations.

The same letter contains two remarks of great interest. One of them concerns the question of style: 'My style has unfortunately been bad because I feel too well physically; I have to feel somewhat miserable to write well.' The other has to do with Freud's candour: 'There is a tremendous amount of new material in it, which I shall mark for you in colour. I have avoided sexuality, but filth is unavoidable and asks to be treated humanely.' This proves that whenever in his book Freud cuts short the interpretation of one of his own dreams it is because that interpretation is about to touch upon his sex life.

On September 11, as we shall see later on, Freud finished Chapter 7 and sent it off to Fliess.

THE DAY-DREAM OF 'STOPPING A RUNAWAY HORSE' (SUMMER 1899)

Freud's name meant 'joy' in German, and was therefore subjected to countless unpleasant witticisms, as we saw in the discussion of the 'Three Fates' dream. It also indicated a propensity to dream – like that of Monsieur Joyeuse, one of the characters in Alphonse Daudet's *Le Nabab* (1878), whose name is a French translation of Monsieur Freud: 'While Daudet's Monsieur Joyeuse was wandering, out of work, through the streets of Paris (though his daughters believed that he had a job and was sitting in an office), he was dreaming of developments that might bring him influential help and lead to his finding employment – and he was dreaming in the present tense. Thus dreams make use of the present tense in the same manner and by the same right as day-dreams. The present tense is the one in which wishes are represented as fulfilled' (*ID* 535). The same dreamer is also referred to more briefly, in the previous chapter, as a typical day-dreamer (*ID* 491).

Confusion over names caused Freud, when completing his book during the summer of 1899, to make two slips which he later explained in *The Psychopathology of Everyday Life*: 'While I was writing the later chapters of my book on dream-interpretation, I happened to be at a summer resort without access to libraries and works of reference, and I was forced to incorporate in my manuscript from memory all sorts of references and quotations, subject to later correction. In writing the passage on day-dreams I thought of the excellent example of the poor book-keeper in Alphonse Daudet's *Le Nabab*, in whose person the writer was probably portraying his own reveries. I imagined I had a distinct memory of one of the phantasies which this man – I called him Monsieur Jocelyn – hatched out on his walks through the streets of Paris; and I began to reproduce it from memory. It was a phantasy of how Monsieur Jocelyn boldly threw himself at the head of a runaway horse in the street, and brought it to a stop; how the carriage door opened and a great personage stepped out, pressed Monsieur Jocelyn's hand and said: "You are my saviour. I owe my life to you. What can I do for you?"

'Any inaccuracies in my own account of this phantasy could, I assured myself, easily be corrected at home when I had the book in front of me. But when I finally looked through *Le Nabab* to check this passage in my manuscript, which was ready to go to press, I found, to my very great shame and consternation, no mention of any such reverie on the part of Monsieur Jocelyn; in fact the poor book-keeper did not have this name at all but was called Monsieur Joyeuse. This second error quickly gave me the key to the solution of the first one – the paramnesia. "Joyeux", of which "Joyeuse" is the feminine form, is the only possible way in which I could translate my own name, Freud, into French. Where then could the phantasy, which I had remembered wrongly and ascribed to Daudet, have come from? It could only be a product of my own, a day-dream which I had formed myself and which had not become conscious or which had once been conscious and had since been totally forgotten. Perhaps I invented it myself in Paris where I frequently walked about the streets, lonely and full of longings, greatly in need of a helper and protector, until the great

Charcot took me into his circle. Later I more than once met the author of *Le Nabab* in Charcot's house. But the irritating part of it is that there is scarcely any group of ideas to which I feel so antagonistic as that of being someone's protégé. What can be seen in our country of this relation is enough to rob one of all desire for it, and the role of the favourite child is one which is very little suited indeed to my character. I have always felt an unusually strong urge "to be the strong man myself". And yet *I* had to be reminded of day-dreams like this – which, incidentally, were never fulfilled. Over and above this, the incident is a good illustration of the way in which the relation to one's own self, which is normally kept back, but which emerges victoriously in paranoia, disturbs and confuses us in our objective view of things' (*PEL* 148–50).

Through this day-dream disguised as a pseudo-memory, which coincided with the completion of *The Interpretation of Dreams*, Freud was finally refuting his father's curse ('The boy will come to nothing'): he had written his book, and it was going to be a great book. At the same time, he could hardly fail to detect, in the puerile nature of the day-dream which led him to attribute it to someone else, and in the exploit of stopping the runaway horse, the survival of the infantile wish for omnipotence – a wish he was now going to renounce. He would no longer try to master the unconscious by force, as he would a runaway horse, but by understanding it: all of a sudden, Freud found the final missing link he had so long been seeking. By completing his self-analysis he would be renouncing the infantile wish for omnipotence so bluntly expressed in that day-dream of prowess.

FIRST INTIMATIONS OF CASTRATION ANXIETY (SEPTEMBER 1899)

Since October 1898, in other words for almost a year, castration anxiety had been Freud's main resistance against the completion of his theory, the publication of his self-analysis, and the composition of the final draft of his book. It was the 'gap' representing the missing link in the theory of bisexuality, which was dreamt of as flawless in the 'Phantasies during sleep' dream. It was also becoming more and more present in the latent content of his dreams, and even clearly represented in the dream of 'Dissecting my own pelvis'. It was when completing the seventh and final chapter of his book, in September 1899, that Freud was at last able to describe it, and to start giving it a name. The example given by him – which is the last clinical example cited in *The Interpretation of Dreams*, coming two pages before the end – is not one of his own dreams, but a waking vision described, at the beginning of treatment, by an adolescent suffering from hysterical symptoms. Freud intended it to illustrate the close interdependence between consciousness and the second censorship:

'Here is another example. A fourteen-year-old boy came to me for psychoanalytic treatment suffering from *tic convulsif*, hysterical vomiting, headaches, etc. I began the treatment by assuring him that if he shut his eyes he would see pictures or have ideas, which he was then to communicate to me. He replied in pictures. His last impression before coming to me was revived visually in his memory. He had been playing at draughts with his uncle and saw the board in front of him. He thought of various positions, favourable or unfavourable, and of moves that one must not make. He then saw a dagger lying on the board – an object that belonged to his father but which his imagination placed on the board. Then there was a sickle lying on the board and next a scythe. And there now appeared a picture of an old peasant mowing the grass in front of the patient's distant home with a scythe. After a few days I discovered the meaning of this series of pictures. The boy had been upset by an unhappy family situation. He had a father who was a hard man, liable to fits of rage, who had been unhappily married to the patient's mother, and whose educational methods had consisted of threats. His father had been divorced from his mother, a tender and affectionate woman, had married again and had one day brought a young woman home with him who was to be the boy's new mother. It was during the first few days after this that the fourteen-year-old boy's illness had come on. His suppressed rage against his father was what had constructed this series of pictures with their understandable allusions. The material for them was provided by a recollection from mythology. The sickle was the one with which Zeus castrated his father; the scythe and the picture of the old peasant represented Kronos, the violent old man who devoured his children and on whom Zeus took such unfilial vengeance. His father's marriage gave the boy an opportunity of repaying the reproaches and threats which he had heard from his father long before because he had played with his genitals. (Cf. the playing at draughts; the forbidden moves; the dagger which could be used to kill.) In this case long-repressed memories and derivatives from them which had remained unconscious slipped into consciousness by a roundabout path in the form of apparently meaningless pictures.

'Thus I would look for the *theoretical* value of the study of dreams in the contributions it makes to psychological knowledge and in the preliminary light it throws on the problems of the psychoneuroses' (*ID* 618–19).

Here again, one of Freud's discoveries derives its validity from a twofold reference to clinical experience and mythology. The threat of castration actually made by the father was the original cause of pathogenic anxiety in the boy. But Freud held that anxiety to be a universal phenomenon because Greek mythology mentions castration – of the father by the son –

as one of the earliest events in the history of the gods. The anxiety inherent in this topic caused Freud to make an error, to which he referred in *The Psychopathology of Everyday Life* (*PEL* 218 and 220): it was not Zeus who emasculated his father Kronos, but Kronos who committed that act on his father Uranus. The same error is to be found in the sub-section 'Dreams of the Death of Persons of whom the Dreamer is Fond' (just before the formulation of the Oedipus complex), where Freud quotes the two legends of the father who devours his children and the son who castrates his father and takes his place as examples of mutual hostility between father and son (*ID* 256). In discussing his error, Freud, faithful to his system of adducing evidence, applied this new discovery to himself: he was thus able to connect his 'paralysis', dread of syphilis, fear of women, and guilt feelings with a real or phantasied threat of castration during his childhood directed at him because he had played sexual games with little friends of both sexes – a threat no doubt reiterated when he masturbated, and in any case implicit in the actual curse uttered later on by his father. As a result, renunciation of the infantile wish for omnipotence must have been all the easier.

This is yet another of the many examples in Freud's discovery of psychoanalysis where self-observation interacts with clinical observation. Freud's problems – the bouts of intellectual, emotional and sexual paralysis that affected him from time to time, the gaps he could see in his theory, and the mounting repugnance his dreams were causing him – all concentrated his mind wonderfully and made him receptive to the existence, behind the symptoms of a patient who no doubt reminded him of his own adolescence, of an anxiety-laden castration phantasy. All that remained for him to do was to turn his attention back on himself (we do not know when or how he did so) and understand that he, too, like any psychoneurotic, was subject to the same phantasy and the same anxiety, which are produced by a preconscious cultural threat (castration as punishment for masturbation) and by an unconscious universal threat (castration as punishment for the twofold Oedipal wish to commit incest and parricide). While completing Chapter 7, Freud used the verb 'to emasculate' or 'to castrate' for the second time. The notion of castration, although still only implicit, continued to develop in his mind. Freud's first published use of the expression 'castration complex' was in 1908 in his paper 'On the Sexual Theories of Children' (1908*c*, *SE* 9, 217).

Also worth noting is the replacement of an insight which existed in embryo in the dream of 'Dissecting my own pelvis'. Devouring anxiety ('Kronos, the violent old man who devoured his children') is implicitly linked with castration anxiety. But the oral sadism remains attributed to a father figure. The only passage in *The Interpretation of Dreams* where this is not so, in connection with condensation, comes in a footnote to the 'May-beetle' dream of a woman patient who fails to obtain sexual satisfaction because her husband is impotent. The footnote alludes discreetly to Kleist's play, *Penthesilea* – a significant train of thought when it is remembered that the queen of the Amazons liked to devour her lovers when she needed them no more.

The anxiety, specific to boys, that the threat of castration will be carried out is paralleled in little girls by penis need. Freud describes this notion, though he does not yet name it or explicitly relate it to castration anxiety, when discussing another case just before that of the 14-year-old boy. It concerns a girl who complained that she had 'a feeling in her body as though there was something "stuck into it" which was "moving backwards and forwards" and was "shaking" her through and through'; the sexual meaning of her symptoms could hardly have been clearer, yet the girl described them so innocently that her mother and the second censorship failed to recognise this phantasy of sexual intercourse.

Now that Freud had discovered the Oedipal phantasies (of incest and parricide) and the primal scene phantasy, and was beginning to suspect the existence of a castration phantasy in boys (and a corresponding penis need in girls), he can be said to have laid the basic foundations of the psychoanalytic theory of neuroses.

SOME OBSERVATIONS ON THE TECHNIQUE OF SELF-ANALYSIS

In addition to those of Freud's dreams I have examined – most of which feature in *The Interpretation of Dreams* – the book contains other passages which have a bearing on his self-analysis. They are of two kinds, containing either observations on the technique of self-analysis or brief analyses of other dreams of Freud's which are impossible to date.

Near the beginning of his last chapter, written in September 1899, Freud makes some important observations on how his technique of dream analysis evolved in the course of self-analysis (*ID* 521–6).

Old dreams can be interpreted. It is perfectly possible to analyse childhood dreams. Freud did so successfully with patients' dreams before trying with his own. It is also possible to complete an earlier interpretation at a later date. 'I had kept records of a large number of my own dreams which for one reason or another I had not been able to interpret completely at the time or had left entirely uninterpreted. And now, between one and two years later, I have attempted to interpret some of them for the purpose of obtaining more material in illustration of my views. These attempts have been successful in every instance; indeed the interpretation may be said to have proceeded more easily after this long interval than it did at the time when the dream was a recent experience. A possible explanation of this is that in the meantime I have overcome some of the internal resistances which previously obstructed me' (*ID* 521). This passage reveals an important fact: Freud's interpretation of his dreams was stimulated by the writing of his book. His self-analysis was systematic, then, on three occasions – during his discovery of the Oedipus complex (September–October 1897), during work on the first version of the book (spring 1898), and during the second version (spring–summer 1899).

Freud gives some advice to readers wishing to analyse their own dreams.

a) 'No one should expect that an interpretation of his dreams will fall into his lap like manna from the skies.' It is something that requires strenuous practice. Anyone who attempts interpretation must 'refrain from any criticism, any *parti pris*, and any emotional or intellectual bias'.

b) 'The interpretation of a dream cannot always be accomplished at a single sitting.' When a series of associations has been exhausted, it is a good idea to break off and wait a day or two before exploring another stratum of dream-thoughts. Freud describes this as 'fractional' dream-interpretation (*ID* 523).

c) A complete and coherent interpretation of a dream is not necessarily the right one or the only one: 'For the same dream may perhaps have another interpretation as well, an "over-interpretation", which has escaped him.' The dream-work shows great skill 'in always hitting upon forms of expression that can bear several meanings' (*ibid.*).

d) The interpretation of dreams runs into internal resistances, and may as a result fail or go only half-way. It is a question of the 'relative strength' of the forces involved. The positive forces are 'our intellectual interest, our capacity for self-discipline, our psychological knowledge and our practice in interpreting dreams' (*ID* 525).

e) One dream on its own does not get us very far. Self-analysis is a dynamic process, and draws sustenance from the concatenation of dreams. 'Quite often an immediately succeeding dream allows us to confirm and carry further the interpretation we have tentatively adopted for its predecessor. A whole series of dreams, continuing over a period of weeks or months, is often based upon common ground and must accordingly be interpreted in connection with one another. In the case of two consecutive dreams it can often be observed that one takes as its central point something that is only on the periphery of the other and *vice versa*, so that their interpretations too are mutually complementary' (*ibid.*). This passage highlights an essential characteristic of self-analysis as Freud conceived of and practised it. For him, it was in no way an abstract jigsaw puzzle or an intellectual pastime, but a vital cross-examination to which the subject's dreams provide answers. Dreams recur until the subject has understood and accepted their answers.

f) 'There is often a passage in even the most thoroughly interpreted dream which has to be left obscure; this is because we become aware during the work of interpretation that at that point there is a tangle of dream-thoughts which cannot be unravelled and which moreover adds nothing to our knowledge of the content of the dream. This is the dream's navel, the spot where it reaches down into the unknown' (*ID* 525).

DREAMS BY FREUD WHICH ARE IMPOSSIBLE TO DATE

The few dreams by Freud for which I have been unable to suggest a date are not discussed at length by him. They are short or fragmentary, and serve essentially to illustrate simple dream mechanisms. Here they are in the order in which they appear in *The Interpretation of Dreams*. The first four are examples of the role that can be played by events of the previous day, and appear in the same passage of the book.

1) 'Keeping a woman waiting' (*ID* 165). This dream – Freud was visiting a house into which he had difficulty in gaining admittance, and was in the meantime keeping a woman waiting – was connected with 'a conversation with a female relative the evening before in which I had told her that she would have to *wait* for a purchase she wanted to make till . . . etc.' The theme here is similar to that of the 'Hall with machines' dream.

2) 'Mother and daughter' (*ID* 165). The daughter was the patient who 'had explained to me the previous evening the difficulties her *mother* was putting in the way of her continuing her treatment'. This was a dream of counter-transference.

3) 'Communication from the Social Democratic Committee' (*ID* 166). Freud was a member not of the committee which in the dream treated him as though he were a member, but of the Council of the Humanitarian League, from which he had received a communication simultaneously with one from the Liberal Election Committee. It does not seem possible to interpret this dream.

4) 'Cliff in Böcklin style'[1] (*ID* 166). Freud had received news from his

1. Böcklin was a Swiss painter in vogue at the time. The 'Villa Secerno' dream contains an allusion to his painting, *The Roman Villa*. A woman patient, after being cured by Freud, gave him Böcklin's *Island of the Dead* in May 1900 as a parting gift. Another woman patient secured Freud's professorship, according to Freud, by offering another painting by the same artist to the Minister of Public Education for his Moderne Galerie (February 1902); but, as we shall see later (p. 554), the picture she actually donated was by another, less highly-rated painter.

relatives in England (Emanuel?), and he thought of Dreyfus on the Ile du Diable. The dream would seem to allude to Freud's scientific isolation and to the danger of racial persecution: far from being depressed, Freud was stirred by the prospect.

5) 'Funeral oration by young doctor' (*ID* 178–9). This dream, like the four preceding ones, belongs to Section A, 'Recent and Indifferent Material in Dreams', of Chapter 5, 'The Material and Sources of Dreams', but is discussed separately as an example of the way two distinct events can be condensed into a single one. The day before the dream, Freud had travelled by train with two acquaintances, an eminent medical colleague and the cousin of one of his woman patients, who did not know each other. Freud found himself conversing alternately with one of them (to whom he had recommended a young colleague of great ability who was just starting a medical practice, but whose homely appearance made it hard for him to make his way in families of the better class) and then with the other (asking after the health of his aunt, who was seriously ill at the time; this woman, who came from a distinguished family, was not on good terms with Freud, who had been treating her daughter). During the night, Freud dreamt that the young doctor he had recommended to his first fellow-traveller was sitting in a fashionable drawing-room, surrounded by distinguished and wealthy people, and delivering, with the easy bearing of a man of the world, a funeral oration on the old lady (the aunt of the other fellow-traveller, whom Freud had killed off in his dream). This dream reveals more clearly than those we have examined up to now the death-wish against the bad mother, as well as the professional ambition to have the members of distinguished families as one's patients.

PROOF-READING AND THE PUBLICATION OF *THE INTERPRETATION OF DREAMS* (SEPTEMBER–NOVEMBER 1899)

On September 11, 1899, Freud was in the middle of proof-reading. He sent his final chapter to Fliess, leaving it to his judgment whether it could stand as it was ('The dream material itself is, I believe, unassailable. What I dislike about it is the style, which was quite incapable of noble, simple expression and lapsed into facetious circumlocutions straining after metaphors'). But, more importantly, he wrote: 'I have finished; that is to say, the entire manuscript has been sent off. You can imagine the state I am in, the increase of my normal depression after the elation' (*F* 370). It was in the same letter of September 11 that Freud reacted to Fliess's already mentioned criticism about the dreamer being 'too witty', and first hinted at his next work, *Jokes and their Relation to the Unconscious* (1905*c*). He asked Fliess's permission to reproduce his remark in *The Interpretation of Dreams*; it was inserted at the last moment as a footnote (*ID* 297, n.1; cf. p. 435).

On September 21, Freud, having returned from his holidays to Vienna, was 'sitting again in the familiar place, with seven signatures of proofs in front of me and no medical news'. He was worried about his financial situation (as he was for almost the whole of 1899): 'My mood also depends very strongly on my earnings. [. . .] I came to know the helplessness of poverty and continually fear it.' He continued to be concerned over questions of style: 'Somewhere inside me there is a feeling for form, an appreciation of beauty as a kind of perfection; and the tortuous sentences of my dream book, with their parading of indirect phrases and squinting at ideas, deeply offended one of my ideals. Nor am I far wrong in regarding this lack of form as an indication of insufficient mastery of the material. You must have felt exactly the same thing, and we have always been too honest with each other for either of us to have to pretend in front of the other. The consolation lies in its inevitability; it simply did not turn out any better' (*F* 373–4).

On October 9, Freud wrote: 'Recently I had the satisfaction of finding part of my hypothetical pleasure-unpleasure theory in an English writer, Marshall.[1] [. . .] All but three sheets of the dream book have been printed. The preface I once showed you stays in'. He was disappointed at being passed over once again for appointment to a professorship, but could see for himself the therapeutic benefits of self-analysis: 'My mood, too, is still holding up. Putting it all in the dream book must have done me good' (*F* 378–9). Freud's fertile mind was already focussing on other books: 'Oddly enough, something is at work on the lowest floor. A theory of sexuality may be the immediate successor to the dream book' (*F*, October 11, 1899, 379). 'Now, as to the other five books I am contemplating – we shall have to take our time with them. A long life, material, ideas, freedom from serious interference – and who knows what else; even an occasional strong push from a "friendly quarter"' (*F*, October 27, 1899, 380). But Fliess did not respond to that appeal: 'One cannot say that you are excessively communicative. I do not want to follow your example, even though a depressing uniformity makes it more difficult to communicate' (*F*, November 5, 1899, 381).

1. This was the first time that Freud had mentioned not only the unpleasure principle, but more broadly the theory of pleasure-unpleasure. The works by H. R. Marshall referred to by Freud were *Pain, Pleasure and Aesthetics* (London 1894) and *Aesthetic Principles* (1895).

Printing of *The Interpretation of Dreams* was completed around October 20. Freud immediately sent one of his two complimentary copies to Fliess as a birthday present. The book went on sale on November 4, 1899, though the publishers, Deuticke, preferred to date it 1900.

CHAPTER 6

Freud's theory of the psychical apparatus in *The Interpretation of Dreams* and his further discoveries

'[My mood] is fluctuating; but, as you see, as it says on the coat of arms of our dear Paris:

Fluctuat nec mergitur
[It floats but it does not sink]'
(*F*, September 21, 1899, 374)

The structure of *The Interpretation of Dreams*

ITS GENRE

The Interpretation of Dreams prompts a question which has not, to the best of my knowledge, been examined: to what genre does the book belong?

It is more than a learned monograph or an essay on metapsychology. It is not merely a collection of (very exhaustively analysed) observations. Although its author is clearly very keen to convince his readers and careful to adduce evidence in support of his arguments, it is neither a systematic treatise for specialists nor a more generally informative work for the educated public. It has something of the novel, or rather what was to become known much later as the *nouveau roman*. It also has something of the autobiography. But the scene it sets is peopled by such a huge cast of characters – the friends and patients whose dreams Freud describes – that the resulting tableau of daily life in Vienna at the turn of the century anticipates, in its intricate, interwoven complexity, the world of Proust's *A la recherche du temps perdu*.

Like all pioneering works, *The Interpretation of Dreams* cannot easily be slotted into any classification of genres. It is literature at least as much as it is science. It is a diary, but it also contains reflections on the human condition, like Montaigne's *Essais* or Pascal's *Pensées*. It is the account of an imaginary or extraordinary journey in the course of which an adventurer of the mind encounters myriad phantasies. One is reminded of *Don Quixote* or *Alice in Wonderland*, of course. But there is an important difference: Freud describes phantasies as they really are, and not under the guise of external reality. Other parallels come to mind as well. Each chapter or section of *The Interpretation of Dreams* is arranged more or less as follows: first there is an abstract and rather austere general argument; this is followed by examples which are apparently intended to illustrate the theoretical conclusion of the argument, but which in fact bring to life a host of sometimes commonplace but more often unexpected, wild and shocking wishes, in a visual context where a completely different scene is played out. This compositional technique was precisely that used by the Marquis de Sade in *Justine ou les infortunes de la vertu* (a work which Freud is unlikely to have read).

Freud's book is both the account and the result of the self-analysis which enabled him to isolate himself from the rest of the world for a little over four years, from July 1895 to September 1899, and to reconstruct his own internal reality, mainly with Fliess's help: in that sense, it recalls the exploits of Robinson Crusoe on his island, who with the help of Man Friday recreated his familiar (though external) reality. But Freud apparently did not have Defoe's novel in mind. If he had a model for his book, it was the *Aeneid*, from which he quotes several times. The parallels are striking: Aeneas, the son of a defeated man, was the prototype of the wandering Jew, suffering years of exile, travelling from place to place, braving the perils of the sea, always outwitting his enemies, daring to go down into the underworld and discover not only his past but his future, landing near the mouth of the Tiber and finally founding the settlement that his descendants, after many wars, built up into Rome, the seat of a great civilisation – in other words, the exact image of the hero with whom Freud needed to identify in order to summon up enough courage and faith in himself to embark on his undertaking. Aeneas was the conqueror of an unknown land and the founder of a new law – the Latin counterpart of Moses. Aeneas and Moses could stand as emblems of what the future held in store for Freud, or indeed for psychoanalysis. But Freud's model in life had little to do with the structure of *The Interpretation of Dreams*. His first major work was a book about wishes and their fulfilment in representations.

Almost twenty years later, in *Introductory Lectures on Psycho-Analysis*, Freud introduced his readers to psychoanalysis in a clear and reasoned manner. *The Interpretation of Dreams* is an introduction not to psychoanalysis but to the unconscious; it proceeds according to a certain order – that of the organisation of the mind – but also according to a certain disorder – that of wishes. The book is 'original' in both senses of the term ('earliest' or 'primal', as in the primal scene, and 'original'). On the one hand, it was the first book in the history of psychoanalysis and set the course for the later writings of Freud and his followers. It contains, potentially, such a vast corpus of ideas and data that they have not yet been fully explored and explained: anyone interested in new psychoanalytic ideas, such as those involving the body image, illusion, or linguistic structure, may be surprised to find that *The Interpretation of Dreams* contains them in embryo. Secondly, the book gives an account, halfway between a confession and a family romance, of its own origin – that is to say, of the analysis of Freud's own dreams. *The Interpretation of Dreams* is a work so teeming with ideas that it can be read again and again, and still stimulate further fruitful reflection. It offers a subjective – and objective – account of internal life and of the mind's relationship with reality.

Lastly, let me say a word about the German title, *Die Traumdeutung*, which was a particularly provocative one: it would have suggested to his readers the popular interpretation of dreams by fortune-tellers (the German for astrology is *Sterndeutung*). Theodor Gomperz, who later wrote *Greek Thinkers*, brought out in 1866 a book called *Traumdeutung und Zauberei*, in which he lumped together dream interpretation and witchcraft; his subtitle, *A Survey of the State of Superstition*, left no doubt as to his opinion of the subject. Freud liked to provoke, so he could then shroud himself in the romantic image of the rejected, misunderstood and solitary genius. By choosing a title like that, was he not bound to succeed yet again?

THE PLAN

The Interpretation of Dreams is arranged according to the following plan (the Parts into which I have divided the work are mine, not Freud's; after each of them, I indicate in brackets the corresponding chapters and page numbers in the published work):

– *Part One* (Chapters 1–5; *ID* 1–276; or a total of about 250 pages when passages added after 1900 are taken into account): The indirect history of the discovery of psychoanalysis during the first part of Freud's self-analysis: from the discovery of the meaning of dreams to that of the Oedipus complex (July 1895–October 1897).

– *Part Two* (Chapter 6, except for Section E, which except for two paragraphs was added in various later editions; *ID* 277–508; or a total of about 137 pages when passages added after 1900 are taken into account): The theory of psychical work in dreams; while propounding his theory, Freud divulges at random the various discoveries he had made during the second part of his self-analysis, from January 1898 to the summer of 1899: the symbolism of the body, masturbatory phantasies, anxiety about the primal scene, an ambivalent transference on to Fliess, and so on.

– *Part Three* (Chapter 7; *ID* 509–621; or a total of about 90 pages when passages added after 1900 are taken into account): The theory of the working of the psychical apparatus in general: this theoretical investigation is brought to an end by Freud's first intimations of the castration complex.

The Interpretation of Dreams is headed by three elements which, when combined, anticipate the overall composition of the book. First, a quotation from Graeco-Roman mythology is used as a symbolic cultural referent: *Flectere si nequeo superos, Acheronta movebo.* Then, in his preface, Freud sets out to establish a body of scientific knowledge likely to lead to therapeutic applications: dreams are a paradigm (*Paradigma*) that enables a large number of psychopathological phenomena to be understood (hysteria, phobias, obsessions and delusions) – though he says this aspect will be dealt with in later works. In other words, dreams are a 'paradigm' lost and regained. Thirdly, in addition to these two objective elements, Freud mentions a subjective element: in his examination of the topic, he has preferred his own dreams to those of his patients because the latter contain neurotic features, and to those described in literature because he could draw on his own associations in order to interpret them. He therefore accepts the inevitable and above all painful risk of being thought indecent by revealing many of the intimacies of his mental life to the public gaze.

Each part of the book is itself headed by an introductory passage that outlines its argument or sets its tone. Part One begins with a lengthy chapter devoted to the published literature on dreams; this chapter both underpins and anticipates what follows. Existing, and allegedly scientific, explanations of dreams not only contradict each other, but are of little worth, because they scotomise the meaning of dreams and, so to speak, fail to see the wood for the trees: they reduce an internal psychical event to nothing more than an echo of events outside the psychical apparatus (such as noises, phosphenes, organic disorders, etc.). On the other hand, the many dreams in literature quoted in this first chapter – which feature oral greed, exposure of the dreamer to the fury of crowds or the natural elements, torture, killings, and so on – throw interesting light on the unconscious. But the veil is only partly lifted, for, as readers will see for themselves without needing to be told by Freud, the moral principles of those writing about dreams precluded their mentioning any material involving anal or sexual indecency.

Part Two begins by distinguishing between the manifest and the latent dream-content and by drawing a parallel between dreams and picture puzzles – a perfectly logical introduction to the reasoned analysis of the dream-work that follows.

Part Three opens with an account of a horrific dream reported by a patient: a father falls asleep while his dead son is being watched over by an old man in the next room; he dreams that his child has caught him by the arm and is whispering: 'Don't you see I'm burning?' What has happened is that the old man has dropped off to sleep, and a falling candle has burnt the wrappings and arm of the tiny corpse. Freud refers to this dream on several other occasions as an example, not of the dream-work as in Part Two, but of the way the psychical processes function. But the most striking characteristic of the dreams chosen by Freud as examples is their polysemy and their force as phantasies: they are not simply used as evidence in a logical chain of arguments or as a concrete illustration of a scientific statement. They teem and overflow with meaning. What better representation of a castration phantasy could there be than a burning arm? In cases where Freud has not yet become sufficiently aware of an unconscious process to explain it to us in words, the dreams he describes explain it in images.

If we disregard the numerous additions (and occasional deletions) made by Freud in subsequent editions of *The Interpretation of Dreams* and examine only the first edition of 1900 (published in November 1899), it can be seen to contain 24 headings, just as the *Odyssey* has 24 books, and to follow a hidden and significant pattern of literary composition. This I shall now endeavour to demonstrate through a detailed analysis of each heading (the breakdown and titles of these headings are my own, not Freud's).

PART ONE: A DIACHRONIC ACCOUNT OF THE DISCOVERY OF THE OEDIPUS COMPLEX

The first nine headings, with only minor variations, follow the diachrony of Freud's discovery. They correspond to the first five chapters in the book. I have indicated in brackets after each heading the chapter, and in some cases the section, with which it corresponds in the published work.

Heading 1: The prehistory of the discovery (Chapter 1; *ID* 1–92). – General prehistory: dreams before Freud, the literature on dreams. Personal prehistory: seemingly forgotten childhood memories can reappear in dreams; for example, the image of the one-eyed doctor who treated the young Freud after he had fallen from a stool and cut his jaw returned forty years later in one of his dreams, even though he had no memory of either the fall or the doctor's attentions; thus, the very first personal incident that Freud confided to his readers alludes to the marks left by castration.

This heading was composed in three stages. In May 1897, Freud was 'looking into the literature' on dreams and discovered, to his satisfaction, that no previous author had suspected that 'the dream is not nonsense but wish-fulfilment' (*F*, May 16, 1897, quoted on p. 221). A first draft, written in January–February 1898, was placed at the beginning of the first version of the book (cf. *F*, February 9, 1898: 'I am already fed up with what little literature there is'); this draft was soon abandoned, as Freud was much more interested in elaborating and setting forth his own ideas. He wrote the final draft of Heading I in May–June 1899 when he began composing the second version.

In it, Freud cites a large number of dreams he had found in the literature on the subject.

Section A, 'The Relation of Dreams to Waking Life', gives an example of a totally unrealistic dream: 'Napoleon and the wine merchant' (the merchant makes a sea-voyage to St Helena in order to offer Napoleon some Moselle wines). Section B, 'The Material of Dreams – Memory in Dreams', cites several hypermnesic dreams which prove that seemingly forgotten memories are in fact retained by the mind: '*Asplenium* and the lizards', 'Mussidan in Dordogne', '*Kontuszówka* Liqueur' (dreamt by a patient of Freud's), 'Childhood at Trilport', 'Childhood at Montbrison', and 'Carriage accident' (which reproduced in all its details an accident which had occurred in real life). Subsection 1, 'External Sensory Stimuli', of Section C, 'The Stimuli and Sources of Dreams', describes:

– a series of short dreams, taken from Jessen (1855), which illustrate how dreams can be caused by sensory excitations: 'Stake between the toes' (a piece of straw), 'Being hanged' (a over-tight shirt), 'Falling from a high wall' (a collapsed bedstead), 'Climbing Mount Etna' (feet on a hot-water bottle), 'Being scalped' (a hot poultice on the head), 'Being dragged through a stream' (a damp night-shirt), and 'Being tortured by the Inquisition' (an attack of gout);

– a series of experimentally produced dreams, the first two by Girou de Buzareingues (quoted by Jessen), the others by Maury (1878): 'Travelling at night with cold knees', 'Attending a religious ceremony with an uncovered head', 'Mask of pitch', 'Revolution of 1848', 'Shop in Cairo', 'Mustard plaster', '*Chauffeurs* of La Vendée', 'Orvieto wine', and 'Storm in the Channel';

– general dreams of noises: 'Fire-alarm', 'Crossing of Tagliamento' (dreamt by Napoleon as he was woken by a bomb-explosion), 'Guillotine' (dreamt by Maury as he was woken by the top of his bed falling on his neck), three alarm-clock dreams – 'Church bells', 'Sleigh-bells', and

'Broken crockery' – taken from Hildebrandt (1875), and 'Giants at table', caused by the sound of horses' hooves (described by Simon, 1888).

Subsection 2, 'Internal (Subjective) Sensory Excitations', borrows from Maury three examples of dreams which were continuations of hypnagogic hallucinations experienced before falling asleep. 'Grotesque figures with strange coiffures', 'Well-spread table', and 'Book with very small type'. Subsection 3, 'Internal Organic Somatic Stimuli', although it does not refer to any specific dream, discusses nightmares that are instigated by as yet undetected internal disorders, dreams of orgasm caused by sexual excitement, and so-called 'typical' dreams – of falling, of teeth falling out, of flying, of being naked. Subsection 4, 'Psychical Sources of Stimulation', notes the weakness of existing theories about dreams which, with the exception of Scherner's (1861), allege that they are due to external or internal sensorial stimulation, and overlook the essential role played by psychical factors. Section D, 'Why Dreams are Forgotten after Waking', alludes, without indicating their content, to dreams which, on the contrary, linger long in the memory – unspecified dreams by Freud's patients, and a dream of his own still as fresh as ever in his mind thirty-seven years later (probably 'My mother and the bird-beaked figures').

Section E, 'The Distinguishing Psychological Characteristics of Dreams', focusses on two fundamental ideas in particular picked out by Freud from all the often nonsensical theories he had read about dreams – Fechner's supposition (1889) that 'the scene of action of dreams is different from that of waking ideational life', and Spitta's notion (1882) that dreams 'dramatise' an idea. Fechner is quoted in a letter to Fliess of February 9, 1898 (beginning of the first version of the book), and Spitta in one of June 9, 1899 (beginning of the second version). In addition to associations of dream-images, which are governed by the familiar law of association, Freud discusses verbal associations at some length (he did not grasp their importance until he began the second version of the book); he quotes two instances given by Maury, his precursor in this respect, of dreams where images are linked together merely by assonance, Pèlerinage/Pelletier/pelle, and Kilometres/kilogramme/Gilolo/Lobelia/Lopez/lotto.

Section F, 'The Moral Sense in Dreams', denounces the wide number of contradictory views on this question: some say that we are no better or worse in our dreams than in real life; others argue that the faults, immoral impulses and evil tendencies we fight against in our waking lives are realised in dreams. Among those taking the latter view are Hildebrandt and Maury, whom Freud regards as precursors of his own theory. But both of them allow morality to take precedence over science: Hildebrandt concludes that dreams act as a 'warning' of our hidden weaknesses; and

Maury that they reveal our instincts only because they are dominated by 'psychological automatism', which is the opposite of true mental activity. The same contradiction surrounds the question: are we responsible for what occurs in our dreams? Spitta excuses adolescents whose dreams fulfil their 'sinful thoughts': we are responsible for our acts, not our thoughts, and it is only normal that whatever we struggle against in our waking lives should take place during sleep. Other authors regard immoral, indecent or violent dreams as boding ill for the dreamer's development: he will become either a criminal or a madman. Thus, the Roman who dreamt he had assassinated the Roman Emperor was executed by the Emperor, who believed that thoughts one has in dreams are the same as those one has when awake. On the penultimate page of *The Interpretation of Dreams*, Freud returns to this dream and interprets it from another point of view: the emperor had nothing to fear from his subject, for, as Plato says, the virtuous man is content to *dream* what a wicked man really *does* (*ID* 620).

Section G, 'Theories of Dreaming and its Function', shows up the shortcomings of the various theories and the contradictions between them. The only theory that Freud regards as worthy of interest is Scherner's, which holds that dreaming reflects the symbolising activity of the imagination; the main examples of this are to be found in the way the human body and its various component parts – its internal and external organs, in particular the male and female sexual organs – are represented by a house, streets, a furnace, a basket, a tobacco-pipe, a piece of fur, a courtyard surrounded by houses and traversed by a soft, narrow footpath, and so on. These, again, are observations that appear only in the second version of the book.

Section H (the last), 'The Relations between Dreams and Mental Diseases', quotes two of Freud's precursors in particular. Radestock (1879) writes: 'The supposed possession of property and the imaginary fulfilment of wishes – the withholding or destruction of which actually affords a psychological basis for insanity – often constitute the chief content of a delirium.' Freud adds: 'This passage from Radestock is actually a summary of an acute observation made by Griesinger (1861, p. 106), who shows quite clearly that ideas in dreams and in psychoses have in common the characteristic of being fulfilments of wishes.'

Heading 2: The technique of self-analysis and the specimen dream of 'Irma's injection' (July 24, 1895) (Chapter 2; *ID* 96–121). – According to most of the 'scientific' theories summarised in Heading 1, dreams are meaningless; they can be explained by external and internal sensations, by the memory and by the imagination, but they cannot be interpreted. Yet man has always striven to interpret dreams. Joseph, in the Bible, propounded a 'symbolic' interpretation of the Pharaoh's dream about the 'Seven kine': such an interpretation was intuitive and prophetic. Works supplying keys to the interpretation of dreams, the most famous of which was by Artemidorus of Daldis, propose an artificial system for 'decoding' each element of the dream separately and overlook the significance of its overall content.

Freud then explains why he thinks his own technique of self-analysis (summarised in detail on pp. 450–1) is the right one, and why it requires him to make public his own dreams, and thus his own weaknesses. Likewise, the Irma dream is at once a plea on his own behalf, an act which enables him to get started and become a creator, and a confirmation that even in normal people dreams are fulfilments of wishes. Freud began to analyse the dream in writing the very morning after having it.

Freud originally wrote this heading, and the two that follow it, before composing the first version of the book. It probably dates from May 1897, when he abandoned the theory of the psychical apparatus and 'felt impelled to start working on the dream' (*F*, May 16, 1897, quoted on p. 220). On December 12, 1897, Freud asked Fliess to bring with him, to their next 'congress' in Breslau at Christmas, 'the dream examples I sent you (insofar as they are on separate sheets)'. These were probably the dreams of 'Irma's injection', 'Uncle with the yellow beard', 'Running up stairs undressed', and, possibly, the four 'Rome' dreams and other dreams which he finally did not include in the book. Freud wrote the final draft of these three headings for the first version of the book in January and February 1898.

Heading 3: Simple wish-fulfilment dreams (Chapter 3; *ID* 122–33). – Freud here marshalls his evidence: adults' dreams of convenience and the dreams of young children are clearly wish-fulfilments. He describes his own dreams of feeling thirsty or waking up; one of the former type probably dates from the autumn of 1895, at a time when he thirsted – in his own words – for 'congresses' with Fliess (I am tempted to add here that dreaming may represent an attempt to find the lost mother's breast again); the dream of the 'Etruscan cinerary urn' dates from the spring of 1898 or 1899. The adults' dreams of convenience he cites include the 'Medical student and hospital' (which appears in a letter to Fliess of March 4, 1895), 'Pains in jaw', 'Menstruation', 'Party with Daudet, Bourget and Prévost', and 'Milk stains on vest'. Of the children's dreams, the first five were dreamt by Freud's own children and their friends during the summer of 1896: 'Dachstein', 'Bars of chocolate', 'Rohrer Hütte and the Hameau', 'Trip across Lake Aussee', 'Achilles and Diomede', 'Strawberries' (mentioned in a letter to Fliess of October 31, 1897, and complemented in a footnote by the description of a dream by Freud's mother in which she dreamt of feeling hungry and being a young girl again), and 'Basket of cherries'.

Heading 4: Distortion (Chapter 4; *ID* 134–62). – Except in the preceding cases of simple dreams, wishes fulfilled in dreams are distorted; for as they are repressed they have to be disguised in order to escape censorship (a notion that makes its first appearance in a letter to Fliess of December 22, 1897). Hence the need, when interpreting dreams, to distinguish between the manifest content and the latent content. The dream of his own which Freud then discusses is 'Uncle with the yellow beard' (mid-February 1897): the wish expressed in it – ambition – is still a relatively avowable one. Freud then describes for the first time some of his patients' dreams: 'Supper of smoked salmon' (a dream which illustrated hysterical identification), 'Summer holidays with mother-in-law', 'Barrister's lost cases', 'Little Karl in his coffin', 'Dead daughter in case', 'Arrest for infanticide', and 'False income-tax return'; these were all dreams which apparently contradicted his theory of wish-fulfilment, but which after analysis turned out to corroborate it. Here again, the wishes brought to light are nothing really to be ashamed of – jealousy in love, the wish to do mischief to a friend, the wish to see a loved one after being separated, the wish to have sexual relations without procreating children, and the love of gain. Freud had finished writing his analysis of the 'Uncle with the yellow beard' dream by March 15, 1898, when he sent it to Fliess along with the first version of Headings 2, 3 and 4.

Heading 5: The day's residues (Chapter 5, Section A; *ID* 165–88). – One of the prime sources of dreams resides in the day's residues: the wish fulfilled in the dream is a repressed wish of the previous day, and the reason for censorship is sexual. Freud quotes five short dreams of his own (they are mostly impossible to date, and their underlying wishes are not revealed): 'Keeping a woman waiting', 'Mother and daughter', 'Periodical for 20 florins' (no doubt the same dream as the 'Sheep's-head' dream of October 3–4, 1897), 'Communication from Social Democrats', and 'Cliff in Böcklin style'. He then analyses another of his own dreams in detail, the 'Botanical monograph' (March 1898), whose main theme centres on criticism for spending too much time on his own hobbies, and which leads on to Freud's first exposition of the notion of 'dream-work'. He then gives a more summary account of his dream of the 'Funeral oration by young doctor' (date unknown). There follow five 'innocent' dreams by patients which in fact conceal less and less avowable sexual situations: an open bodice or gaping fly-buttons; a torn condom; a candle and a box symbolising the male and female sexual organs respectively. Four of them were dreamt by the same woman patient ('Market', 'Piano a disgusting old box', 'Candle and candlestick', and 'Box packed with books'); the fifth, 'Winter overcoat', was dreamt by a male patient. Freud wrote the first version of this heading, as well as parts of the following headings (6, 7, 8, 9 and 10), in March and April 1898, and sent them to Fliess on May 1, 1898.

Heading 6: Childhood memories (Chapter 5, Section B; *ID* 189–219). – This is the second source of dreams: in dreams, the child survives with his or her impulses. After briefly referring again to the dreams of 'Childhood at Montbrison', 'Little Karl in his coffin', and 'Rohrer Hütte and the Hameau', Freud gives as his initial examples first a dream of the primal scene, 'Tutor and nurse in bed', told to him by someone who had attended his lectures, and then a woman patient's recurrent dream of 'Pursuit', which was omitted in all subsequent editions. There follow a number of Freud's own dreams: first, two dreams which he disguised and attributed to a colleague, 'Yellow lion' (a childhood dream probably interpreted in the spring or summer of 1898) and 'Nansen's sciatica' (probably dating from August 1898); these are followed by further analysis of the 'Botanical monograph' and 'Uncle with the yellow beard' dreams, already mentioned in Headings 5 and 4 respectively; then come the four 'Rome' dreams (January 1897), in connection with which Freud highlights the wish to avenge the humiliation suffered by his father; he had returned to these dreams in November or December, 1897, well after they had been dreamt, probably in the course of writing his analysis of them (cf. letter to Fliess of December 3, 1897). This series of dreams is completed by five patients' dreams, 'Schoolboy exposed in bed', 'Orthopaedic institute', 'Boys struggling', 'Violent rush', and 'Falling down in the Graben' (the last two dreamt by the same woman). They all illustrate infantile sexuality: homosexual fondling, bed-soiling and shame, threats of punishment for curiosity about the genitals of urinating little girls, and memories of remarks by adults about 'fallen women'.

It was probably in June 1899, when he was writing the second version of his book, that Freud added to this heading two other dreams of his own which are among the richest in associations of all those he dreamt and analysed, 'Three Fates' (September–October 1898) and 'Count Thun' (August 1898). They illustrate the wishes of the oral and anal stages respectively – or, to use Freud's own expressions, 'love and hunger' (the two aspects of sexuality), and 'faeces': so he was able to check in his own dreams the evidence he had gathered from patients' dreams. He examined first the repressed wishes of the previous day, then the repressed wishes of prepuberty and adolescence. When writing the first version of his book, Freud grasped the importance, in his patients, of the pregenital wishes of infancy, as can be seen from his letter to Fliess of March 10, 1898. Finally, when writing the second version, he implicitly confirmed the universality of such wishes because he had discovered them in himself. The completed book, then, mirrors in its arrangement the progression in time of Freud's discoveries. The conclusion of this heading is that dreams always fulfil several wishes (over-determination).

Heading 7: The somatic sources (Chapter 5, almost all of Section C; *ID* 220–38). – By May 1, 1898, Freud was already complaining to Fliess that he was dissatisfied with what he had written on this topic in the first version. It would indeed seem that almost all the material under this heading belongs to the second version. It picks up again and expands Section C of Chapter 1, in particular Subsection 3 on 'Internal Organic Somatic Stimuli': in it we find an account of body symbolism according to Scherner (1861), which is complemented by two short 'dental' dreams from the literature on dreams, 'Two rows of boys', and 'Two rows of drawers'; another of his own dreams, 'Riding on a horse' (October 1898), followed by a reference to the dream of a woman patient, *Gen-Italien*; the idea that dreaming is the guardian of sleep, and that dreams fulfil above all the wish to sleep (as he told Fliess on June 9, 1899); and brief references to dreams already discussed, 'Three Fates' and 'Count Thun' (both his own), 'Cooling apparatus', 'Medical student and hospital', and 'Crossing of Tagliamento', which he had found in Garnier's *Traité des facultés de l'âme* (1872). Freud explored the literature on dreams on two occasions, in February 1898 and in May–June 1899; there is no way of knowing at which point he read Garnier.

Heading 8: Dreams of nakedness and exhibitionism (Chapter 5, end of Section C and Subsection (α) of Section D; *ID* 238–48). – This heading begins with the dream of 'Running up stairs undressed', the discussion of which runs over from the end of Section C to the beginning of Section D. It continues with an analysis of Hans Andersen's fairy tale, *The Emperor's New Clothes* – the first psychoanalytic allusion to a literary work in *The Interpretation of Dreams*. It marks an important turning point in Freud's use of evidence. In the first seven headings, the validity of Freud's argument was backed up by a comparative analysis of dreams cited in scientific literature, his own dreams, and dreams of his patients, children, friends, colleagues and students. He arrived at the conclusion that, whatever the dreamer's age, degree of normality or pathological type, the psychical function of dreams is always the same – wish-fulfilment; that three psychical phenomena, namely the day's residues, childhood memories, and current somatic stimuli, govern that wish-fulfilment; and that the more the wish is repressed the more the dream's meaning is distorted in order to escape censorship.

Heading 8 contains a new type of evidence that was to become specifically Freudian, a comparison between dreams and fairy tales (or legends), or, more precisely, a comparison between individual clinical data and cultural data. Why did Freud change his method of adducing evidence? No doubt because, as I have already pointed out, the further he got into the book, the more the wishes he detected in the dreams he was analysing were likely to shock his readers, and therefore difficult to set forth. One wish is hinted at very indirectly in Heading 8, in connection with the urge of little boys to exhibit their nakedness in front of a mother figure: it is a wish to commit incest, though Freud does not use the word. He described his dream of 'Running up stairs undressed' to Fliess on May 31, 1897. He gave him an equally veiled interpretation of dreams of nakedness in general on July 7, 1897. The writing of this heading in the first version is mentioned among Freud's plans for the book in a letter of March 15, 1898. He had virtually finished the chapter on 'Typical Dreams', consisting of Headings 8, 9 and 10, by April 3, 1898.

Heading 9: From dreams of killing a parent to the Oedipus complex (Chapter 5, Section D, most of Subsection (β); *ID* 248–71). – Freud calls this heading 'Dreams of the Death of Persons of whom the Dreamer is Fond'. After incest comes parenticide. This leads on to the Oedipus 'myth' (Freud had not yet invented the term 'complex' in 1899), a natural result of the incestuous wish being linked up with the parricidal wish. But Freud does not simply state his theory baldly; very gradually and gingerly, Freud takes his readers by the hand and helps them to recognise the horrible notion that the wish to kill a sexual rival exists. He does so in the following sequence: he returns to patients' dreams which portray the death of children in their family, 'Little Karl in his coffin' and 'Dead daughter in case'; he gives an example of sibling rivalry between his own nephews and nieces, and quotes, as an example of such rivalry, the 'Children grew wings' dream; he talks of the 'hostility' between father and son, mother and daughter (and makes his first mythological references – to Kronos devouring his children and Zeus emasculating his father); he gives examples of the child's wish to marry the parent of the opposite sex; he cites several dreams about the death of the mother, one by a woman patient ('Lynx or fox'), others by a hysterical young woman who dreamt she was attending an old woman's funeral or was dressed in mourning; and he describes an obsessional patient's wish to kill his father.

So far, Freud has been cautious in his choice of argument: such wishes are experienced by children or patients. What about normal, civilised adults? At this point, a new form of evidence, which Freud has just tried out in the previous heading, is adduced. He seeks first in myth (the Oedipus myth as adapted in one of Sophocles' tragedies, *Oedipus Rex*), then in literature (*Hamlet*, which is not based on any myth), proof of the universal existence of the twofold wish to commit incest with the parent of the opposite sex and to kill the parent of the same sex. Oedipus carries out that twofold wish; Hamlet represses it. Literature has been enormously influenced by myths. Myths – at least the Oedipus myth – probably sprang from some 'primaeval dream-material': the notion that the genealogy of cultural products can be traced back to the individual unconscious is here expressed for the first time ever. Freud made his discovery in the second week of October 1897, and wrote it up during the second week of March 1898.

So far, then, Freud''s account has more or less followed the chronological order of his discovery:

Heading 2: the Irma dream, July 1895;

Heading 3: dreams of thirst, autumn 1895, children's dreams, summer 1896;

Heading 4: dream of 'Uncle with the yellow beard', mid-February 1897;

Heading 5: dream of the 'Botanical monograph', March 1898;

Heading 6: the 'Rome' dreams, January 1897;

Heading 8: dream of 'Running up stairs undressed', May 1897;

Heading 9: discovery of the Oedipus complex, October 1897.

Headings 1 and 7 do not appear in this list, as they are essentially additions made at the time of the second version. The insertion in Heading 5 of a dream dating from after the discovery of the Oedipus complex can be explained by the fact that Freud dreamt it in March 1898, when he was in the middle of writing the first version. So he placed the dream, which occurred while he was writing the book, at the very point he dreamt it, and he inserted it in the middle of a retrospective account of the dreams he had had while making his discovery; 'in the middle of' should here be taken literally, since this dream of March 1898 comes in Heading 5, halfway through the first ten headings, whose sequence is more or less diachronic.

Although Freud is careful to proceed gradually and to support his theories on the organisation of human wishes with as much evidence as possible, the conclusion he arrives at, i.e. the universality of the Oedipus complex, is something which he finds impossible to uphold any longer. Heading 9 ends with an explanation which aims, so to speak, to soften the blow: Oedipal wishes seem less horrible if they are regarded as something left over from childhood. Freud then demurely explains that the 'egoism' of children persists in the dreams of adults. This finally enables him to mention some of his own dreams (this is the first time in *The Interpretation of Dreams* that Freud's own dreams get left to the end of a heading in this way): 'Famous speakers' (date unknown), the first brief mention of 'My son, the Myops' (January 1898), and 'Otto was looking ill' (probably February 1898). So Freud continues to respect the chronological order of things, even making the moment when a discovery is completed coincide with the moment when an initial phase of writing begins. When correcting the proofs of the second version, in July and August 1899, and possibly as a friendly gesture towards Fliess, Freud preceded three of his own dreams with a dream by the young Robert Fliess, 'Big dish with big joint': the boy, after being sent to bed without his supper because he had been naughty, dreamt of somebody, who did not feature in the manifest content, eating roast meat (the dream is mentioned in letters to Fliess of August 6 and 27, 1899).

Heading 10: Dreams of flying and examination dreams (Chapter 5, Section D, former Subsection (γ) in the 1900 edition, end of Subsection (β) and the whole of Subsection (γ) in the final edition; *ID* 271–4). – In this passage, the consciousness of the author (and possibly the reader) is swamped by the anxiety that has built up during previous headings and peaked with the admission of the existence of a twofold Oedipal wish. This anxiety cannot be held back any longer. It manifests itself in both form and content.

Form: Subsection (γ), in the first edition of 1900, was called 'Other typical dreams' and comprised the last six paragraphs, in which dreams of flying are discussed, of the present Subsection (β) and, inserted between the fifth and sixth paragraphs, the first paragraph of the present Subsection (γ) devoted to 'examination dreams'. Heading 10 underwent more changes in the book's successive editions than any other. It became so expanded with new examples that in 1914 it was transferred to Section E of Chapter 6 with the slightly changed title of 'Some further typical dreams'. 'Dreams of flying' appear, depending on the edition, in their original place, in their new place, or in both. Paragraphs were added, deleted or transferred elsewhere. Subsection (γ) was later limited to examination dreams and as a result its title was changed. Here again, the content varied: Freud added or removed ideas and examples taken from Stekel depending on the state of relations between the two men.

Content: the content of Heading 10 is explicitly described by Freud as consisting of anxiety dreams – dreams where flying ends in falling (in other words, where pleasure, by its very excess, turns into anxiety), and nightmares where the dreamer dreams of failing an imminent examination, or even of one he has already passed ('The ineradicable memories of the punishments that we suffered for our evil deeds in childhood become active within us once more' (*ID* 274). Freud puts forward the idea of presexual muscular pleasure, and draws a parallel between muscular effort or competition, first erections, and dreams of flying. The idea that 'the clownism' of hysterical boys can be explained by 'the interweaving of childhood games played in the nursery and sexual scenes' appeared in a letter to Fliess of December 17, 1896, and not long afterwards (January 24, 1897) Freud drew a parallel between the 'gymnastic feats' of such boys and 'flying and floating'. But he did not mention masturbation, which represents the infantile culmination of the transition from muscular exercise to genital sexuality. For Freud and his contemporaries, it was at once the most widespread and the least effective taboo.

Part One of *The Interpretation of Dreams* ends, then, with fear of punishment and guilt feelings – not with the *idea* of such punishment and such feelings, but with their *presence*, suddenly so real and so powerful that it prevents Freud from realising that they follow on logically from Oedipal wishes and complement his discovery of those wishes. Part One, which is almost entirely diachronic, ends as it began: the series of personal secrets revealed by Freud in the book started with the unconscious memory of falling off a stool and getting a scar as a result (punishment for a forbidden wish to eat something nice), and continued with an evocation of the criticism he encountered for his clumsy or equivocal, real or imaginary, treatment of Irma. Freud has come full circle. We realise that in the course of making his discovery he was driven all along by one particularly strong motivation – the need to exonerate himself – and that it was that same motivation which long caused him to postpone making his discovery public.

PART TWO: A SUPPOSEDLY SYNCHRONIC ACCOUNT WHICH IS IN FACT AGAIN DIACHRONIC

Part Two (Headings 11–18) and Part Three (Headings 19–24) of *The Interpretation of Dreams* are intended to be synchronic. They differ in their degree and type of abstraction. Part Two (Chapter 6) describes the psychical mechanisms peculiar to the dream-work and proves their existence by induction from numerous and varied dreams. Part Three (Chapter 7) sets forth a general theory of the psychical apparatus and relies on a form of reasoning that might be described as partly hypothetical and partly deductive: what characteristics must the psychical apparatus possess if dreams are produced by it? What bearing do those characteristics have on the working of the psychical apparatus as regards activities other than dreaming? But Freud's determined, intellectual and defensive attempt to give a synchronic account was neutralised by the fact that while carrying out self-analysis he continued on a doubly diachronic course: in the process of trying to build up his theory, he evolved internally, and in the process of evolving internally, as opposed to developing his knowledge, he realised the significance of whole new areas of his childhood. Thus, it was because he felt protected by his theoretical construction that he was able to allow more and more deeply repressed wishes, phantasies and anxieties to surge up through the chinks and cracks in his theories.

It was while working on the first version of his book that Freud would seem to have gradually drawn a distinction between Parts Two and Three. On March 15, 1898, he told Fliess there would be a chapter on 'The psychical process in dreaming' and another on 'Dreams and neuroses'. He got stuck on the 'section on psychology': by May 1, 1898, he had written a first draft of it which did not satisfy him. On June 9, 1898, he mentioned how hard he was finding it 'to set out the new psychology'. On June 20, 1898, he remarked that 'the psychology [. . .] is nearly finished, composed as if in a dream'. On August 26, 1898, he talked of his 'germinating metapsychology' for the first time and related it to the theories of the psychologist Theodor Lipps, one of whose books he was reading at the time. Twice, on June 9 and 20, 1898, Freud mentioned one of the reasons for his difficulties: the psychology based on the study of dreams and the psychology based on the study of neurotic symptoms did not tally sufficiently with each other. It is possible that the key notion of the 'dream-work' occurred to Freud only when he was engaged in the writing of the first version and needed to synthesise the psychical processes of dreams; Freud probably found the term 'dream-work' in W. Robert's work on dreams (1886), from which he quotes frequently.

Part Two ('The Dream-Work') follows the following plan:

I. The transformation of latent content into manifest content:
   a) Transformations of thing- and word-presentations in dreams:
      1) Condensation (Heading 11);
      2) Displacement (Heading 12);
      3) Representation (Heading 13).

b) Examination of specific problems related to the transformation of word-presentations:
   1) Preservation of calculations and speech in dreams (Heading 14);
   2) Impression of absurdity in dreams (Heading 15);
   3) Other remarks connected with dreams (Heading 16).

c) Preservation and modifications of affects in dreams (Heading 17).

II. Secondary revision of the manifest content (Heading 18).

A number of headings in Part Two (the first three and the last) were written at the time of the first version. The second version completed these headings where necessary and added others. Generally speaking, the first version dealt only with thing-presentations, and it was the second version which took word-presentations and affects into account. Freud's first reference to the notion of the word-presentation comes in a letter to Fliess of December 22, 1897, shortly after the discovery of the Oedipus complex, in other words at a time when Freud was extending his curiosity from hysteria to obsessional neurosis: it then occurred to him that, while in hysteria the thing-presentation is vital, in obsessional neuroses 'the locality at which the repressed breaks through is the *word-presentation*' notably through words with more than one meaning. But Freud did not expand this notion beyond the sphere of psychopathology until his analysis of the screen memory of the 'Green meadow with yellow flowers snatched from Pauline' led him to realise that the word-presentation was a fundamental fact of general psychology. When informing Fliess, on January 3, 1899, that phantasies are products of later periods which are projected back from the present into the earliest childhood, he added: 'the manner in which this occurs also emerged – once again by a verbal link' (*F* 338).

Part Two is preceded by a short introduction which sets forth such vital notions as the distinction between the manifest content and the latent content, the manner in which the latter is transliterated into the former, and the dream as a picture-puzzle (*ID* 277–8).

Heading 11: Condensation (Verdichtung) (Chapter 6, Section A; *ID* 279–304). – This heading comprises two distinct passages. First of all, dreams condense thing-presentations and presentations of people: Freud here returns to three of his own dreams already discussed, the 'Botanical monograph' (March 1898), 'Irma's injection' (July 1895) and 'Uncle with the yellow beard' (February 1897). This first passage was therefore probably written during the first version. Freud inserts two important dreams by patients between the first and second of his own dreams. They are 'Lovely dream', or '*Sappho*', or again 'Up and down' (dreamt by a claustrophobic man patient), and the 'May-beetle' dream (dreamt by a woman suffering from severe anxiety-states); the first dream focusses on the desire for the breast and the danger of relations with women of the lower classes; the second displays a wish for an erection on the part of the husband and associates sexuality with cruelty.

The second passage shows that dreams also condense word-presentations. Freud cites three of his own dreams, '*Norekdal*', 'Hearsing' and '*Autodidasker*'. He analyses the first two briefly, and solely from a formal viewpoint, without revealing the latent wish. '*Autodidasker*', which is discussed at greater length, centres on the theme of 'coming to grief over a woman' that was already implicit in 'Lovely dream' discussed a little earlier. Coming to grief can take two forms: general paralysis (the result of catching syphilis from women of easy virtue] or neurosis (the result of the frustration, castigation and repression of infantile sexuality, which is awakened by mothers and wet-nurses). These three dreams by Freud almost certainly date from the autumn of 1898. This second passage must therefore have been added during the writing of the second version. Between his first and second dreams, Freud inserts two brief dreams by patients, once again without interpreting the latent wish, '*Maistollmütz*' and '*Tutelrein*'.

The notion of condensation is one of Freud's own discoveries about dreams. In 1914, he added a footnote pointing out that the notion had already been hinted at before him by Du Prel (1885) (*ID* 280 n.1). In the first edition of 1900, he referred to Delage (1891), who noted 'the tendency of the dream-work to fuse into a single action all events of interest which occur simultaneously' and to Delboeuf (1885), who spoke of '*rapprochement forcé*' ['enforced convergence']; in the edition of 1909, Freud saw this as an instance of condensation, but omitted that remark after the 1922 edition (*ID* 179 n.). Freud's own contribution was his discovery that condensation produces in the manifest dream-content greater psychical intensities than those of the latent thoughts, and that it does so in order to escape censorship. Heading 11 can therefore be read at two levels. At the level of the manifest content, it explains the mechanism of condensation from a theoretical viewpoint, i.e. in terms of secondary psychical processes. At the level of the latent content, a wish is evoked which is common to all his own or his patients' dreams where analysis is taken as far as an interpretation of their latent meaning – the little boy's wish for the delights of the breast that feeds him, the young man's wish for the pleasures afforded by the female sex. This wish is described as 'dangerous', as a source of mental or physical illnesses resulting in a general paralysis of body and mind, in other words impotence.

Heading 12: Displacement (Verschiebung) (Chapter 6, Section B; *ID* 305–9). – This heading is very short: dreams displace psychical intensities, even to the point of reversing values. Freud returns to the dreams he discussed in the first part of the preceding heading – three of his own dreams, 'Uncle with the yellow beard', 'Botanical monograph', and 'Irma's injection', and two dreams by patients, 'Lovely dream' and 'May-beetle'. Freud had already expounded in detail the idea of the displacement of quantity both in dreams and in hysterical symptoms in 'Project for a Scientific Psychology' (1950*a*, 402–10); and the example he gave there was, precisely, the dream of 'Irma's injection'. This heading is almost entirely theoretical: it does not point up any new wish.

Heading 13: Representability (Chapter 6, Sections C and D; *ID* 310–49). – I have included under this heading the two sections where Freud examines successively *Darstellungsmittel* (the means of representation) and *Darstellbarkeit* (representability): dreams use distinctive formal characteristics to represent the abstract relationships between different thing-presentations (Section C) and between different word-presentations (Section D). The psychical apparatus takes into account representability, in other words it seeks out the mnemic, visual and auditory traces capable of representing the latent dream-thoughts. The writing of this heading took place in more or less chronological order: Section C, the longer of the two, which deals with thing-presentations, dates from the first version of the book; Section D, like all passages dealing with word-presentations, was probably added during the second version.[1] Freud's own dreams are quoted almost only in Section C.

Dreams represent:
– logical relations by simultaneity (no examples);
– an alternative by enumeration: the Irma dream;
– a succession of different thoughts by an alternative: the dreams of 'Villa Secerno' (April 1897) and 'Close the eyes' (October 1896), which show traces of hostile feelings towards Fliess and Freud's father;
– similarity by identification or by the formation of a composite figure: the dreams of 'Irma's injection' and 'Uncle with the yellow beard', and the

1. Section D was considerably enlarged in subsequent editions. The analogy between the manifest dream-content and hieroglyphic script was added in 1909 to Section D (*ID* 341) and in 1914 to Section C (*ID* 321).

fourth 'Rome' dream (January 1897), in which Prague represents Freud's wish to go to Rome with Fliess;
– contrast by reversal into the opposite: initial analysis of the dream of 'Goethe's attack on Herr M.' (April 1898), which does not mention Fliess by name, but ends by referring to 'the contemptuous implications of the idea of "turning one's back on something"', and in which the theme of general paralysis recurs;
– differences in intensity and clarity: the dream of 'Phantasies during sleep' (spring–summer 1898?), which contains not only further disguised criticism of Fliess but also a similarly disguised wish to appropriate his theory of bisexuality; it also illustrates the fact that the intensity of the manifest dream-images does not necessarily relate to the intensity of the latent dream-thoughts; and without naming his source Freud applies Nietzsche's phrase, the 'transvaluation of all psychical values', to dreams;
– a 'no' by the feeling of not being able to do something: the 'Hall with machines' dream (May 1898), which expresses a twofold fear – of being accused of dishonesty, and of death.

Section D contains a very brief reference to the Irma dream and, again, the 'Hall with machines' dream as examples of verbal ambiguity.

Heading 13 is completed by other dreams by patients and friends. In Section C: two examples of composite structures, the dream of the 'Bathing hut, outside closet and attic' (representing a scene of undressing), and the dream of 'Legs covered with caviare' (representing a sister's fear of 'contagion'); an example of contraries in 'Lovely dream' (already mentioned); and an example of how the feeling that a dream is indistinct and muddled can in fact represent a lack of clarity in its latent content, in the dream of 'Who is the baby's father?'. In Section D: the 'Wagner opera' dream (which represents the woman dreamer's secret love for the composer Hugo Wolf, who went insane: in this dream, each word used in the formulation of the wish is represented by a corresponding visual image); the dream of 'Carts with vegetables' (a literal representation of the expression *Kraut und Rüben*, literally 'cabbages and turnips', which means 'higgledy-piggledy' or 'disorder'). But the most important dream is 'Language of flowers', dreamt by a woman patient; it is revealed in successive fragments in Section C to illustrate:

a) the representation of causal relations by a reversal of temporal sequence (my life is what it is because of my humble origins);
b) the representation of opposite and contradictory elements (the blossoming branch held by the dreamer symbolises sexual innocence, but is covered with camellias, which symbolise sexual impurity);
c) the representation of similarity.

This dream is reported in full at the end of Section D. Freud then interprets it, but only in a series of eleven brief footnotes: the walk in the garden represents an exploration of the dreamer's own body, particularly her sexual organs; certain images are symbolic representations of sexual functions and activities: undressing, children's sexual games, exhibitionism, defloration, menstruation, masturbation, discovery of the male erection, and 'marriage precautions'; Freud restricts himself to the latter rather vague term, but we can gather from the dream that one garden is being replaced by another, i.e. vaginal intercourse is being replaced by anal intercourse. In 1899, Freud was still reluctant to refer to 'base' sexual desires. In 1909, however, he inserted a dream (without any reference as to the identity of the dreamer) which, he said, explicitly represented an attempt at *coitus a tergo* (*ID* 397). Just as the diachronic sequence in Part One of the book ended with an onrush of anxiety, guilt feelings, and fear of punishment after his formulation of the incestuous and parricidal Oedipal wish (i.e. with a resistance against recognising the castration complex), so the theoretical systemisation set forth at the beginning of Part Two (condensation, displacement, representability) was halted by a resistance against recognising pregenital infantile sexual theories. Freud's Irma dream was a programme-dream for the discovery of psychoanalysis that he was about to make; the woman patient's 'Language of flowers' dream was a programme-dream for the sexual symbolism which Freud systematised only in later editions of his book.

Freud's epistemological advance as regards scientific data on sexuality is shown in Table 5.

TABLE 5. *The various stages of Freud's gathering of scientific data on sexuality*

a) Data which resulted from the observation of patients and provoked an ever greater personal involvement on Freud's part:
- discovery of phantasies of pregnancy and childbirth in hysterics (1889–93);
- hypothesis that anxiety neurosis was caused by lack of sexual satisfaction resulting chiefly from contraceptive techniques (*coitus reservatus*, *coitus interruptus*) and from the prohibition of sexual relations before marriage (1892–93);
- discovery that children can be subject to sexual desires and acts on the part of adults (parents, servants) (1893–95);
- Freud's awareness of his need to exonerate himself for feeling a counter-transferential sexual attraction for young female hysterics (July 1895);
- discovery of copulation and defloration phantasies in hysterics (autumn 1895).

b) Data resulting from Freud's self-analysis, which enabled him to verify on himself suppositions he had drawn from the observation of patients, relatives, friends and

colleagues, and which led to his discovery of the existence of an autonomous infantile sexuality:
– discovery of the existence of anal and oral erotogenic zones; first intimations of sado-masochism (beginning of 1897);
– exhibitionist wishes (spring 1897);
– infantile wishes and phantasies concerning the sexual seduction of parents (September 1897);
– children's Oedipal wishes towards parents; the incestuous and fratricidal nature of children's games (October 1897);
– role of learning to be clean (October 1897);
– children's curiosity about the other sex (voyeurism) (October 1897);
– children's curiosity about parents' sexual relations (July–August 1898);
– connection between megalomaniac wishes and urethral pleasure (summer 1898);
– connection between ambivalence towards authority and anal pleasure (summer 1898);
– importance of infantile masturbation and the phantasies connected with it (this is the main idea which Freud intentionally censored out of his book; it is therefore difficult to date it accurately: it is probable that he gradually became aware of it during the winter of 1898–99; his paper on the disguised autobiographical screen memory (1899*a*) unobtrusively takes it for granted);
– discovery of the symbolism of the human body, of the genitals, and of sexual activities and functions (spring 1899?);
– first intimations that the anxiety connected with masturbation and with visual awareness of the difference between the sexes is castration anxiety (summer 1899).

c) Data resulting from further observation of patients:
– discovery of the *fellatio* phantasy (Dora case, autumn 1900);
– description of the polymorphous nature of pregenital infantile sexuality, i.e. of the representation of erotogenic zones as places where both sexual intercourse and childbirth occur (*Three Essays on the Theory of Sexuality*, 1905*d*);
– description of the sublimation of component instincts (*ibid.*);
– description of the castration 'complex' (*ibid.*).

In Heading 13 more than in any other, Freud illustrates his points with a mixture of his own dreams and those of his patients. His own include not only old dreams belonging to the diachrony of his discovery but dreams contemporaneous with the writing of this new, synchronic Part Two. Thus we find two dreams which preceded the discovery of the Oedipus complex, and which are here cited almost as the result of 'deferred action' – 'Villa Secerno', where for the first time he shows resentment towards Fliess (because he had gone to Italy without him and without letting him know his address), and 'Close the eyes', in connection with which Freud mentions, for the first time in his book, his father's death; like the Irma dream, it is a dream that attempts to exonerate him from criticism he has incurred. The diachronic sequence contained in Part One was unable, then, to exhaust the flood of wishes that were struggling to gain recognition in it. So when he came to write Part Two on the dream-work, Freud did so not only for theoretical and scientific reasons (which were perfectly valid), but to provide an outlet, in the guise of synchronic reflections, for unconscious motives which had not been taken into consideration in the earlier diachronic account. But this theoretical work which Freud undertook while writing the first version in the spring and early summer of 1898 did not rescue him from the maelstrom of phantasies into which his self-analysis had sucked him irreversibly; far from it, various forms of unknown unconscious wishes, exerting their inexorable dynamic, halted his theoretical work, appeared more and more insistently in new dreams, interrupted the first version of the book, and prevented him from resuming work on it until such time as, having managed better to 'heed' the nature of his own wishes and to understand their anxiety-generating repercussions on him, he was able to return to his theoretical work on a broader base.

When dreaming, in the 'Phantasies during sleep' dream, of a theory of bisexuality which – unlike Fliess's – would be clear, consistent and flawless, Freud recognised implicitly that his own theory of dreams and of the psychical apparatus still contained obscurities, contradictions and weaknesses. It was probably no coincidence that in 1911 he inserted, just after his own dream of 'Phantasies during sleep' and the woman patient's pointedly interrogative dream of 'Who is the baby's father?', a young man's dream which was punctuated by 'gaps' – on analysis, the 'gaps' turned out to be female genital apertures. Freud, then, still needed a few more years before he could fill the gaps in his theory by, precisely, devising a theory of gaps – namely a theory of castration anxiety and of the castration complex – and recognise that the 'gap' he believed to be in the nature of an intellectual judgment in secondary process thinking was in fact one of the most important thing-presentations in primary process thinking. It is easy, too, to see why the 'Hall with machines' dream, the last both to be dreamt and to be described, should have recorded a feeling of 'not being able to do something'.

When completing his heading with Section D during the second version of his book, Freud added two important theoretical ideas: a) that representability can also be applied to words; and b) that representations, whether they be of things or words, are not necessarily those of the individual subject: the body, its various parts, its functions, and in particular its sexual organs, as was shown by Scherner (one of the few authors who made any contribution to Freud's theory of dreams), are represented in the preconscious by a symbolism which, if it is not universal, is at least transindividual. At this point, instead of using one of his own dreams as an illustration (which would have been regarded as indiscreet, not to say indecent), Freud returned to the woman patient's 'Language of flowers' dream. Similarly, he preferred to publish separately (and attribute to a third party) the personal record that would have fitted quite naturally into this section, the screen memory of the 'Green meadow with yellow flowers snatched from Pauline', in which the female genitals are symbolised by a flower and in which a word-presentation – the very common vulgar term in German for masturbation, 'to pull one out' – is transcribed literally into images. This is confirmed by the fact that a few days after telling Fliess that he had analysed this screen memory (January 3, 1899) Freud wrote: 'A few other things of minor significance have yielded results as well – for instance, that hysterical headaches rest on an analogy in phantasy which equates the top with the bottom part of the body (hair in both places – cheeks [*Backen*] and buttocks [*Hinterbacken*; literally, "hindcheeks"] – lips [*Lippen*] and labia [*Schamlippen*; literally, "shamelips"] – mouth = vagina), so that an attack of migraine can be used to represent a forcible defloration, and yet the entire ailment once again represents a situation of wish-fulfilment. The necessary conditions of the sexual become clearer and clearer' (*F*, January 16, 1899, 340). But Freud also said the same thing indirectly in his book, through the woman patient's 'Language of flowers' dream, to which he returned at regular intervals throughout Heading 13 before giving a full description of it at the end. He probably included this dream while writing the second version and understood it only after elucidating his own screen memory.

Section E of Chapter 6, 'Representation by Symbols in Dreams – Some Further Typical Dreams', was first constituted in the edition of 1914. It took over most of the material that had been added in 1909 and 1911 to Subsection (γ), 'Other Typical Dreams', of Section D, 'Typical Dreams', of Chapter 5. Still more material was added to it in subsequent editions.

The following headings, 14, 15 and 16, examine specific cases of representability. There are two reasons for assuming that these headings date from the second version: first, all Freud's own dreams cited in them date from after the first version; secondly, what is studied in them is the way word-presentations are transformed by dreams.

Heading 14: Calculations and verbal expressions in dreams (Chapter 6, Section F; *ID* 405–25). – Dreams themselves do not calculate or speak; any calculations or speeches that may be found in them are borrowed from memory traces, in other words they reproduce numbers and words actually uttered or thought in real life.

First point: verbal expressions. Dreams can take them literally by transcribing them into images. This is illustrated by four dreams, the first three by other people, probably patients, and the last by Freud: 'Chimpanzee [*Schimpanse*] and gorilla-cat', in which a servant-girl hurls these two animals at the woman dreamer (= a transliteration of 'to hurl invective [*Schimpfworten*] at someone'); 'Child with deformed skull', in which a doctor talks of compression (= a transliteration of the abstract concept of 'impressions on children'); 'Wet weather at the Hilmteich' (= a transcription of the word 'superfluous', or *überflüssig*, via the adjective 'fluid', *flüssig*); and the first mention of a new dream of Freud's, 'Dissecting my own pelvis' (spring 1899?), in which the name of Stannius, an expert on the nervous system of fishes, is represented by silver-paper (stanniol).

Second point: calculations. This is illustrated by three patients' dreams containing numbers: 'Paying 3 florins 65 kreuzers' for something (a woman's wish to reduce the cost of both her psychoanalytic treatment and her daughter's school fees); 'Three theatre tickets for 1 florin 50 kreuzers' (a woman's regret at having been in a hurry both to book seats and to marry a man of such little 'worth'); and 'I was born in 1882' (a patient's wish to pay court to a young woman who used regularly to come after him in Freud's consulting room).

Third point: word-presentations again. Dreams can reproduce actual speeches textually. This is illustrated by a dream (not Freud's) of 'Dead bodies being burnt', in which a sentence from the previous day, 'I can't bear the sight of it', is reproduced, and by a new dream of Freud's, '*Non vixit*' (October 1898), in which these two words in the dream partly reproduce the inscription on the pedestal of a statue of Emperor Josef II. But Freud's analysis of the latter dream suddenly becomes much more than a mere illustration of a formal psychical process: ambivalence towards a rival and self-justification in the face of criticism are both expressed in it with great power – a power that derived from a scene in a play which the 14-year-old Sigismund (Brutus) and his older nephew John (Julius Caesar) acted out together, and which reproduced, in a transposed symbolic form, the fierce fights they had had as infants. Fliess, the current incarnation of the rival-cum-friend at whom the dream is overtly aimed, is not discussed at all at this point. Freud does so later on, when he returns to this dream at the end of Heading 17. Just as in Part One Freud only gradually introduced the notion of the Oedipus complex, so in Part Two, where one of the essential factors of its latent dynamic is the negative 'transference' on to Fliess, he shows his hand only gradually.

Heading 15: Absurdity in dreams (Chapter 6, Section G, first part; *ID* 426–45). – Dreams are only apparently absurd; and the presence in the manifest dream-content of a feeling of absurdity is due to ambivalent latent wishes. The heading begins with a series of dreams about dead fathers – a sign that the work of mourning which began in October 1896 was in the process of completion, and that the aggressive Oedipal wishes, which had been revived by the death of Freud's father, and which in the spring of 1898 caused the writing of the first version to grind to a halt, had at last undergone a working out as a result of a transferential-type relationship with Fliess. First, Freud cites another dream by a patient, 'Father in a railway accident' (a failure to distinguish a bust and a photograph from an actual person, long since dead; a transliteration of a common and ambiguous expression such as 'There's something wrong with Father, don't you think?'). It is followed by another of Freud's own dreams, 'Father on his death-bed like Garibaldi' (February–March 1899), which centres on a wish to behave irreverently towards the father (he who wanted to appear as 'great and unsullied' ended up base and dirty). Freud then further analyses one of his own dreams, 'Count Thun' (August 1898) (the impression of absurdity in dreams arises from the latent dream-thought: 'It is absurd to be proud of one's ancestry; it is better to be an ancestor oneself.'), and one dreamt by a woman patient, 'Wagner opera' (where the absurdity of the crazy performance means: 'We live in a crazy society; the person who deserves something doesn't get it, and the person who doesn't care about something *does* get it'). Three new dreams by Freud centre on an increasing wish to behave irreverently towards Fliess: '1851 and 1856' (summer 1899?), a dream of rebelling against former mentors on whom Freud used to be dependent, Breuer and Meynert; 'Goethe's attack on Herr M.' (April 1898) (first discussed in Heading 13), where the 'absurdity' of Fliess's ideas is denounced and Freud identifies with a general paralytic and with a patient who had emasculated himself in a fit of madness (a respectively clear and obscure representation of the two forms of punishment caused by sexual excesses); and the second part of the dream of 'My son, the Myops' (January 1898), in which the two neologisms, *Auf Geseres-Auf Ungeseres*, represent a criticism of Fliess's theory on the link between bilaterality and bisexuality: it is Fliess who is short-sighted.

After Heading 6, which dealt with infantile memories and wishes in dreams, this is the second time in *The Interpretation of Dreams* that so many of Freud's own dreams are to be found together in a single heading. But while Heading 6 was the turning-point of the first version of the book (the observation that wishes repressed since childhood do in fact survive served as an introduction to the Oedipus complex), Heading 15 is the nodal point of the second version. This is less because it partly lifts the veil on the consequences of the Oedipus complex that Freud will subsequently describe (the super-ego, castration anxiety) than because it contains an epistemological reversal. The originality of *Studies on Hysteria* was that it adopted the dynamic point of view. Part One of *The Interpretation of Dreams*, which is diachronic in form, basically deals with the repercussions of infantile sexuality on the psychical processes of adults – the genetic point of view. In Part Two, which is synchronic in form, Freud finally adopts, after many false starts and an earlier abortive essay ('Project for a Scientific Psychology' in the autumn of 1895), the economic point of view: we are driven not just by past wishes, long ago frustrated and now demanding to be satisfied in retrospect, but also – and more particularly – by present, universal, eternal and indestructible wishes, which are cathected in those around us and in the tasks of daily life, wishes with which we constantly have to negotiate compromises between discharge and defence.

Heading 15 ends with a veiled allusion to Fliess, an ideal friend, a narcissistic double, but also someone who was scientifically not very rigorous and psychologically not very receptive to the unconscious. The allusion is along the lines of the saying 'If the cap fits, wear it!': 'Dreams, then, are often most profound when they seem most crazy. In every epoch of history those who have had something to say but could not say it without peril have eagerly assumed a fool's cap' (*ID* 444).

Heading 16: Intellectual activity in dreams (Chapter 6, Section G, second part; *ID* 445–59). – Dreams do not pass judgment; judgments made on a dream in the course of dreaming or after waking are part of its latent content. Freud discusses two dreams by patients who were extremely reluctant to describe them: 'Who is the baby's father?' (this dream, already mentioned by Freud earlier on, is a visual representation of the common German phrase, *Nicht auf meinem eigenen Mist gewachsen*, literally 'not grown on my own manure', which means 'I am not responsible for that' or 'I didn't invent that'); and a new dream, 'I must tell the doctor that' (the dreamer, after waking, thinks he must describe this dream to Freud, thus contradicting and revealing a latent wish not to tell him about a *liaison* he has just started). Another of Freud's dreams, 'Frau Doni' (December 1898), conceals, beneath his feeling of great satisfaction on waking that he was going 'to discover from this analysis the meaning of "I've dreamt of that before"', the satisfaction that his marriage had brought him children. Freud then resumes analysis of several of his own dreams: 'Father on his death-bed like Garibaldi' (where the satisfaction he experienced on waking repeated his satisfaction at the birth of his second son, called Oliver after Oliver Cromwell); 'Goethe's attack on Herr M.' (where the two words 'improbable' and 'plausible' were those used by Freud in connection with the young man who had emasculated himself); and '1851 and 1856' (where the apparently 'logical conclusion' of the dream in fact conceals criticism of people – including Breuer, who is not mentioned by name, and probably also Fliess – who draw conclusions without sufficient evidence, and affirms Freud's confidence in his own ability, in the course of his therapeutic work and theoretical research, to draw conclusions).

The dream of 'Dissecting my own pelvis' (spring 1899?), which was touched upon in Heading 14, seemed 'strange' to the dreamer even while he was still asleep: an allusion to Rider Haggard's strange science-fiction novels and to the strange task that Freud was hesitating to carry out: the publication of his self-analysis. Lastly comes the 'Hollthurn' dream (July 1898), where the dreamer's supposed '*automatisme ambulatoire*' during sleep 'went back [. . .] to a scene of early childhood in which the child, probably driven by sexual curiosity, had forced his way into his parents' bedroom and been turned out of it by his father's orders.' This is the last point Freud makes in this heading. Thus, what he has explicitly revealed, under the guise of 'intellectual activity' (the name given by Freud to this heading), is the existence in young children of a primal scene phantasy. It was foreshadowed by the dream of 'Tutor and nurse in bed' (cf. Heading 6), dreamt by someone who attended his lectures.

Heading 17: Affects in dreams (Chapter 6, Section H; *ID* 460–87). – As latent affects in dreams cannot, like ideas, be repressed, they do not undergo the transformations (condensation, displacement, representability) to which ideas are liable. They are often kept as they are by the dream, in which case they appear in its manifest content. Conversely, an unexpected lack of affect in the manifest content of a dream where an affect would logically be expected is matched by a corresponding lack of that affect in the latent wish. This is illustrated by two female patients' dreams: 'Three lions in a desert' (the dreamer is no more afraid of the lions in her dream than she was, the day before, of an important man, a 'social lion' in the capital, who had lavished attentions on her during a visit); and the already cited 'Little Karl in his coffin' (the young girl's lack of sadness, in her dream, at the death of her nephew was due to a latent wish, which naturally had no overtones of sadness, to see the man she loved, who belonged to her sister's entourage, when he offered his condolences).

Affects are, however, liable to three modifications (which are not, truly speaking, transformations), all of which are illustrated exclusively by a wide selection of Freud's own dreams. First, the affect can, while remaining intact, be separated from the idea to which it was originally attached and come into contact with another idea in the dream. Thus, in a new dream by Freud, 'Castle by the sea' (May 1898), the dreamer's indifference to the governor's death replaces Freud's latent anxiety about the future of his family should he die prematurely. The anxiety does, on the other hand, break through into the manifest content with the mention of the 'breakfast-ship', despite the fact that the word 'breakfast-ship' recalls some particularly enjoyable latent memories of a trip to Italy.

Secondly, the latent affect can be neutralised. This is a second result of censorship, which 'represses' ideas and 'suppresses' affects; there is an important distinction to be made here between repression (*Verdrängung*), which is described in the first version of the book, and suppression (*Unterdrückung*), which appears only in the second version. So in the frequently cited dream of the 'Botanical monograph', 'a passionately agitated plea on behalf of my liberty to act as I chose to act' produces a dream with 'an indifferent ring about it', like 'the peace that has descended upon a battlefield'. So, too, in a new dream, the 'Open-air closet' (July–August 1898), the surprising lack of disgust at the sight of the closet conceals two contrary latent affects, disgust with oneself and megalomaniac ambitions.

Thirdly, an affect can be reversed into its opposite. Thus, in another frequently cited dream, 'Uncle with the yellow beard', the great affection in the dream for R. conceals a latent dream-thought which calls him a simpleton.

Freud then returns to two recently described dreams in order to show the complicated process governing the formation of affects in dreams. In the dream of 'Dissecting my own pelvis', there is no horror because the dream fulfils one of Freud's current latent wishes – to overcome the distress which the publication of his self-analysis is causing him, and which has unfortunately resulted in his postponing the printing of his manuscript. A single affect can be fed in a dream by several different affective sources; different affects can arise from a single affective source.

An example of this is to be found in the '*Non vixit*' dream, which contains a succession of two affects – a hostile and distressing affect when the opponent and friend is annihilated with the two words '*Non vixit*', and a delighted state of mind at the concluding idea that revenants can be eliminated by a mere wish. The succession of affects corresponds to the two mixed feelings with which Freud has just reacted to disturbing news about an operation undergone by Fliess: first, he feels concern for his friend's life, regret that because of an awkwardly placed boil he cannot visit him, and fear that he will arrive too late if the operation has a fatal outcome; but he also feels annoyed, offended and irritated at being suspected of indiscretion, because Fliess's Viennese parents-in-law have asked him to say nothing of the operation. In the dream the fear is carried into effect (the friend is dead) and the reproach is parried (those who during their lifetime directed reproaches at Freud – Brücke, Jacob Freud – are now dead and reduced to a state of nothingness). At the end of the heading, Freud rapidly discusses the question of anxiety dreams: the more the mood of the previous day is distressing, the more it can become the motive force of the dream, because it is all the more able to deceive censorship, thus providing an opportunity for the most strongly suppressed wishes to be fulfilled.

As can be seen from the dates of the dreams it contains, Heading 17 was added during the second version of the book. Its dominant personal theme is one of contradiction – the contradiction between one's wishes and censorship, between over-estimation of oneself and disgust with oneself, between horror and satisfaction at publishing the book, and, lastly, between love and hatred for one and the same person, Fliess.

Heading 18: Secondary revision (Chapter 6, Section I; *ID* 488–508). – This heading, unlike its predecessors, contains very few of Freud's own dreams. Secondary revision (*Sekundäre Bearbeitung*) is a process whereby the waking thinking (the preconscious) rearranges the dream-content so as to give it greater consistency. Freud then alludes to Heine's derisive dismissal of Hegel's system (without mentioning either man by name): '[Secondary revision] fills up the gaps in the dream-structure with shreds and patches' (*ID* 490).[1] This process also occurs during day-dreaming, when conscious phantasies are erected on the basis of unconscious phantasies (as in the example of the day-dreamer in Daudet's *Le Nabab*). It was in Draft L, which Freud sent to Fliess on May 2, 1897 – before the discovery of the Oedipus complex – that he stated for the first time that hysterical symptoms were not attached to actual memories but to unconscious phantasies (*Phantasie*) built on them. Certain dreams are merely reproductions of such day-time phantasies: Freud again mentions a dream by his son, 'Achilles and Diomede' (1897), and the second part of his own dream, '*Autodidasker*' (December 1898).

Secondary revision seeks to change a nocturnal dream into a day-dream. He gives the example of a patient's dream, 'Arrest in restaurant' (the fulfilment of a phantasy of marriage, accompanied, however, by a fear that

1. Heine's poem runs as follows:

> *Mit seinen Nachtmützen und Schlafrockfetzen*
> *Stopft er die Lücken des Weltenbaus.*
> [With his nightcaps and the tatters of his dressing-gown
> He patches up the gaps in the structure of the universe.]
> (*Die Heimkehr*, LVIII).

Freud quotes these lines in a letter to Martha of October 31, 1883 (JI, 214), and also in the last of his *New Introductory Lectures on Psycho-Analysis* (1933*a*).

marriage would cost him his freedom), and again discusses Maury's 'Guillotine' dream and the dream of the 'Crossing of Tagliamento'. Freud draws parallels with the deliberate distortion of texts as a joke and with the involuntary misinterpretation of unexpected events (for example, a man from the provinces attending a sitting of the French Chamber at which a bomb thrown by an anarchist exploded believed that it was customary to fire a shot as a tribute to a particularly good speech). This heading ends, as it began, with a philosophical reference (again without mentioning any names): the dream-work (condensation, displacement, representability and secondary revision) aims to evade censorship by making use of a displacement of psychical intensities, to the extent of producing a 'transvaluation of all psychical values' as described by Nietzsche.

It is hard to establish when this heading was written. An initial draft containing the notions of day-dreams and secondary revision probably dates from the first version. When writing the second version, Freud made a few additions – possibly the reference to *Le Nabab* and the quotation from Nietzsche, and certainly the further discussion of the '*Autodidasker*' dream. Of all the headings so far described, this is the most impersonal. It concludes Part Two, and is apparently intended to close the cycle of wishes. The theory of the dream-work is complete, clear and without gaps, like Hegel's system, and as new as Nietzsche's philosophy. For the time being, secondary process thinking is firmly in control of primary psychical activity. It is a case of 'peace on the battlefield'.

At the same time that Freud was dealing with secondary revision, he was putting the finishing touches to a theory which itself functioned for him as a kind of secondary revision designed to cast a veil over his own 'gaps'. For the moment, he still understood 'gap' only as a word-presentation, i.e. as a conceptual gap. He had yet to discover the underlying thing-presentation, in other words to allow himself and others to see and recognise the half-real, half-imaginary corporal gap without which his theory of the unconscious would remain complete.

PART THREE: A SYNCHRONIC ACCOUNT OF THE TOPOGRAPHY

Part Three of *The Interpretation of Dreams*, which corresponds to Chapter 7, is more rigorously synchronic than Part Two: the theory set forth in it – that of the psychical processes in general – is more comprehensive and more abstract than the theory of the dream-work. Thus, the two synchronic accounts put forward successively by Freud in his book correspond with different levels of symbolisation. The first account deals with the systems which transform word- and thing-presentations and the system which modifies affects: it corresponds with the first level of symbolisation.

The second account deals with the systems of the psychical apparatus which make possible such transformation and modification systems: this is the second level – the symbolisation of symbolisation. Freud had attempted to outline Part Three while writing the first version of the book; but he failed, with the result that the first version came to nothing. He resumed work on Part Three when nearing the end of the second version in late August and early September 1899, and completed it successfully after spending two weeks in an almost somnambulistic state of creative inspiration and mental concentration.

In Part One, Freud set out his discovery from the genetic point of view and chose a diachronic form suited to that content. In Part Two, he approached dreams from the economic point of view and adopted a synchronic form appropriate to that content. Here, in Part Three, he explains his discovery of the topographical point of view. Apart from his dream of 'My mother and the bird-beaked figures', which was dreamt in his childhood and therefore before self-analysis, all of Freud's own dreams cited in Part Three have already been described and analysed in Parts One and Two. The only new personal evidence produced by Freud is Monsieur Joyeuse's supposed day-dream – but even that is unintentional, since he wrongly attributes it to a character in *Le Nabab*.

On the other hand, Freud draws heavily on clinical evidence provided by his patients. It, too, consists as much of day-dreams and waking visions as of dreams proper. The dominant themes are masturbation and castration. In Freud's case, the corresponding latent thought was fear of impotence. That fear can be sensed lurking behind a remark he made just after discovering the Oedipus complex: 'Sexual excitement, too, is no longer of use for a person like me' (*F*, October 31, 1897, 276). It was only after he had analysed the screen memory of the 'Green meadow with yellow flowers' that Freud was able to recognise the importance of that fear in his patients. On January 16, 1899, he described three cases to Fliess – that of a woman hysteric who imagined she had *atresia hymenalis*, or an imperforate hymen (hence the idea that 'melancholia [is] fear of impotence'), a similar case of frigidity, and a completely different case of sexual hyper-arousal in a young woman, who was the mistress of a man old enough to be her father, and who fell into a parahypnotic state at the very first approach and had 'four to six orgasms during one coitus'.

Part Three begins with the horrible dream of the 'Burning child', which I have already mentioned. It enables Freud to recapitulate the various types of causes whose overdetermination instigates dreams: an external stimulus (light), the memory of words actually spoken by the child during his illness ('I'm burning', 'Father, don't you see?'), and the dreamer's wish that the child were still alive and able to speak to him. The dream, says Freud, 'raises no problem of interpretation'; its essential characteristics do, on the other hand, 'call for explanation'. Part One showed that dreams have a meaning and explained how to find it out. Part Two showed how a latent meaning is transformed to produce a manifest dream. Part Three leaves aside the question of the significance of a dream's meaning and addresses itself to the question of the origin of that meaning: what does the psychical apparatus consist of, and how does it work in order to produce meaning? But theoretical questions do not merely hinge on intersubjective scientific considerations; they also answer individual phantasy needs. Part One – what is wish-fulfilment? – is subtended by an Oedipal 'phantasmatic' which is revealed clearly at the end; Part Two – how do wishes evade censorship? – is subtended by a primal scene phantasy which is described more than once, but only fleetingly; and Part Three – is it possible to construct a 'gapless' theory of the psychical apparatus? – is a defence against castration anxiety, castration being of course a gap *par excellence*.

Heading 19: A plea in favour of his technique (Chapter 7, Section A; *ID* 512–32). – Freud calls this heading 'The Forgetting of Dreams', yet not much of it is devoted to that topic. A more apt title would be 'Objections Answered', or 'Problems of Interpretation'. Like Heading 2, it is a plea by Freud in favour of his technique, which rests on an assumption which may seem surprising at first sight: that credence may be given to the account a subject gives of his dream.

First objection: the account of the dream rearranges the dream. Answers:

a) Often it is rather inconspicuous and uncertain details which point to the right interpretation: that in itself is proof of their authenticity; e.g. the dreams of 'Irma's injection', '1851 and 1856', and '*Non vixit*';

b) distortions occur during the dream and not just when the subject reports it; they are due to secondary revision;

c) if you get a patient to repeat his account of a dream, its weak spots are revealed: they are the parts he describes in different terms;

d) a subject's doubt about the accuracy of his account of a dream is the result of a resistance.

Second objection: the dreamer partly forgets his dreams. Answers:

a) Forgetting is the result of censorship: e.g. the 'Hollthurn' dream, part of which (concerning a grammatical mistake) was forgotten for a time because it concealed a scatological indecency;

b) when a resistance is overcome by the analyst, the patient remembers his dream;

c) Freud succeeded in analysing many dreams – of his own, or his patients' – which were often very old and perfectly preserved.

The work of interpretation based on the dreamer's free associations provides a practical answer to such objections. It obeys three rules:
– The patient must be induced to abandon conscious purposive ideas so that his concealed purposive ideas can assume control of his associations of ideas (hence the rule of non-omission);
– superficial associations are substitutes by displacement for suppressed deeper ones (experimentalists succeeded in studying only the former, and did not connect them with the latter, which escaped their notice because they are subject to resistance and censorship; it is because sleep reduces the power of censorship that it allows the formation of dreams);
– another purposive idea, which is unsuspected by the patient, consists of the analyst himself (an allusion to transference, which is not here named as such).

The work of interpretation is long, difficult, complex, and essentially incomplete: this explains two things – first, the need for 'fractional' dream-interpretation, for 'over-interpretation' of a dream's over-determinations, and for interpreting together dreams dreamt during the same night, and secondly the existence of 'the dream's navel, the spot where it reaches down into the unknown'.

Heading 20: First picture of the psychical apparatus (Chapter 7, Section B; *ID* 533–49).[1] This heading, entitled 'Regression' by Freud, in fact draws a first picture of the systems making up the psychical apparatus.

Freud takes as his starting point one of the characteristics of dreams, dramatisation (he did not use the word until a year later, in *On Dreams*): in dreams, a wishful thought is represented as a scene. On the one hand, the scene is experienced by the dreamer as taking place in the present, for the present tense is the one in which wishes are represented as fulfilled (e.g. the dreams of the 'Burning child' and 'Irma's injection', and the day-dream attributed by Freud to Monsieur Joyeuse); on the other hand, the latent ideational content is not thought but transformed into sensory images which the dreamer thinks he is experiencing in real life, and which are often borrowed from real life (e.g. the '*Autodidasker*' dream). If that is so, and if, as Fechner contended (1889), the scene of action in dreams is different from that in waking ideational life (Freud referred to Fechner's theory in a letter to Fliess of February 9, 1898), it must mean that this purely psychical scene

1. The only part of this heading added after 1900 (the ante-penultimate and penultimate paragraphs) distinguishes between three kinds of regression (topographical, temporal and formal) and argues that dreams are an ontogenetic recapitulation of a phylogenetic childhood.

takes place in a 'psychical locality' (similar to the ideal points at which images come into being in a microscope or telescope), and that there exists a 'psychical apparatus' composed of 'agencies' or 'psychical systems'.

Freud then returns to part of the neuro-psychological 'schematic picture' he originally devised in 'Project for a Scientific Psychology' (which he wrote in the autumn of 1895) and later gave an increasingly psychological slant in various letters to Fliess, more particularly those of January 1, 1896, May 30, 1896, December 6, 1896 (which formulated the notion of the 'psychical apparatus' for the first time), May 2, 25, and 31, 1897, and November 14, 1897). The apparatus has two ends to it, a sensory end and a motor end; psychical processes, of which reflexes are the simplest form, proceed from the sensory to the motor end. But two differentiations have to be introduced into this schema. The first, at the sensory end, is intended to explain how perceptions are able to leave memory-traces in the psychical apparatus in view of the fact that the perception-consciousness system which receives sensations has no memory, but only passes on perceptual stimuli to consciousness. It has to be supposed that there is another system, or rather two other systems which transform the excitations of the first system into traces capable of retaining those excitations. One of them retains the associations according to simultaneity of occurrence or similarity; the traces can be feebly remembered, i.e. become conscious again, but they no longer possess the vividness that is characteristic of sensory qualities; it is in fact that lesser degree of vividness that enables human beings to distinguish between memories and perception. Another system remains essentially unconscious; it retains not the connections between traces but their content; that content consists chiefly of the impressions that left the greatest effect on us during our earliest youth and thus shaped our character: even if some such memories become conscious again, the effects they produce operate at an unconscious level.

The second differentiation is located at the motor end; evidence afforded by dreams helps us to understand it. The preconscious, censor of the unconscious (Freud later described this as the first censorship), is located just before the motor end. Behind it, and with no access to consciousness except via the preconscious, lies the unconscious, the seat of wishes. Dreams cannot be explained solely by the lowering of censorship during sleep (otherwise all our dreams would be in the nature of ideas, as in the case of the '*Autodidasker*' dream), but also by the regression of excitation from the motor end to the sensory end – a regression which is accompanied by a transfer of psychical intensities and results in a hallucination.

It should be stressed that for Freud regression did not originally have the chronological overtones of a return to an earlier state which he later gave it (cf. p. 490n.), and to which it has all too often been reduced by other writers since then: regression was first of all an economic and topographical process resulting in psychical energy being withdrawn from the normal and automatic channel of motor discharge and orientated towards the purely imaginary channel of a supposed perception, that is to say, of a belief (though Freud does not use the latter term). Regression causes the associative relations to disintegrate and retains only the content of the image. While regression obviously occurs in dreams, it can also take place in waking life, though to a lesser degree except in certain pathological states where it produces veritable waking visions of great intensity. As usual, Freud bases his theory on clinical observation: he cites the case of a 12-year-old hysterical boy, who was prevented from falling asleep by terrifying 'green faces with red eyes' (the vision represented for him the dangers of masturbation); in another case, a 40-year-old hysterical woman patient, on waking in the morning, saw her brother in the room (she knew he was in fact in an insane asylum) and, terrified that her small son would have a fright and fall into convulsions when he saw his uncle, she pulled the sheet over his face, whereupon the apparition vanished (it was a re-enaction of her nurse's story about how the patient's mother, who died very young, had suffered convulsions as a result of a fright caused by her brother – the uncle in question – who disguised himself as a ghost with a sheet over his head); the revival of the memory fuelled her fears that her child might follow in the footsteps of his uncle, whom he resembled); Freud also refers the reader to a case of hallucinatory paranoia he had described in 1896 (1896*b*). The unconscious memory does not remain passive; it attracts into regression the thoughts which are connected with it and which are suppressed by censorship. Thus, a dream might be described as 'a substitute for an infantile scene modified by being transferred on to a recent experience': in other words, it is a 'repetition' of that scene in the form of a phantasy. In the case of hysterical visions, such infantile scenes lose their hallucinatory force in the process of being reported.

The beauty of dream images derives from the day's residues, not from infantile memories. Thus the vivid colours in the dream of 'Castle by the sea' (May 10–11, 1898) were caused by a construction of toy bricks that Freud's children had got him to admire the previous day and by vivid and pleasant memories of a recent trip to Istria (Freud himself used the word 'vivid' in his enthusiastic letter describing the trip to Fliess in April 14, 1898). The 'regard for representability' which Freud stressed in his first version becomes here, in the second version, 'the selective attraction exercised by the visually recollected scenes touched upon by the dream-thoughts'.

Heading 20 begins to set forth an important theoretical discovery, that of the topography of the psychical apparatus. Freud's distinction between the three systems – consciousness, the preconscious, and the unconscious – was the first positive result of his work of mourning after Jacob's death; he told Fliess about it on December 6, 1896; he had deduced it from his analysis of neuroses; at that time his theory remained very general. It was after his analysis of the dream-work that he was able, in the course of the two successive versions of his book, to give his theory the degree of rigour, precision and consistency it needed. The phantasies that Freud decided to use to illustrate this theoretical discovery were scenes of threats: the threat of physical decline because of masturbation, and the threat that his own children would suffer mental disorders (the underlying idea being the fear that children may have to pay for the sins of their parents).

Heading 21: Wishes (Chapter 7, Section C; *ID* 550–72). – Freud entitles this heading 'Wish-fulfilment'. A more accurate title might be: 'Psychical Quantity in Search of Qualities Likely to Represent It', or 'From Needs to Wishes'. At first sight, Heading 21 seems merely to cover the same ground as Chapter 3 (Heading 3 in my arrangement), which is called 'A Dream Is the Fulfilment of a Wish'. But in reworking his material Freud transformed it considerably. Heading 3 and the first version in general were descriptive. Wishes fulfilled in dreams could fall into any of the following four categories:

a) Wishes of the previous day not satisfied for external reasons;
b) Wishes of the previous day not satisfied because suppressed;
c) Old, deep, suppressed wishes;
d) Wishful impulses arising in the body during the night (thirst, sexual needs) – J. Guillaumin (1973) has suggested that they should be called 'the night's residues' on the analogy of the day's residues.

These four kinds of wishes, which Freud recapitulates at the beginning of Heading 21, have up to now been treated on an equal footing. Heading 21 gives them an order and a hierarchy; instead of merely describing, it explains, and in order to do so draws on the theoretical discovery expounded in the previous heading, that of the topographical organisation of the psychical apparatus. Wishes of the first kind are localised in the preconscious: Freud recalls the dream of the 'Trip across Lake Aussee' and similar children's dreams. Wishes of the second kind have been driven out of the preconscious into the unconscious: the example here is a new dream by a woman patient, '*Dutzendmensch*' (she had dreamt the formula: '*In the case of repeat orders it is sufficient to quote the number*'; this fulfilled a repressed wish of the previous day to tell acquaintances what she really thought of a woman friend's fiancé – that he was a '*Dutzendmensch*', literally, a 'dozen man', a very commonplace person). Wishes of the third kind belong exclusively to the unconscious system; the book has already given many examples of them. And wishes of the fourth kind belong to the conscious system. This new grouping provided Freud with theoretical corroboration for a supposition which had gradually gained ground in his mind without his being able to justify it: a conscious or preconscious wish is insufficient, on its own, to produce a dream in the case of adults (it can do so only in the case of children, whose unsatisfied wishes of the previous day remain very strong); what is fulfilled in a dream is an unconscious wish, and a conscious or preconscious wish can become a dream-instigator only if it succeeds in awakening an unconscious wish.

This supposition proves particularly satisfying for Freud with regard to the rigour and fecundity of the hypothetical-deductive reasoning he uses in Part Three, as opposed to the inductive reasoning that sustained Parts One and Two.[1] The topographical hypothesis on the unconscious nature of wishes that are fulfilled in dreams prompts two corollary assertions, one of them genetic: 'A wish which is represented in a dream must be an infantile one' (*ID* 553), and the other economic: the sum of quantities of excitation (i.e. over-determination, a notion already used by Freud in *Studies on Hysteria* in 1895 to explain symptom formation, and here extended to dreams) is necessary for the dream-work to be able to get under way. But Freud does not cast his theoretical argument in such formal terms as these (had he done so, he would have had to adopt, as a compositional model, Spinoza's *Ethica*, which was *ordine geometrico demonstrata*); he uses a mythological analogy when reformulating his topographical/genetic/economic hypothesis that unconscious wishes are indestructible – 'They are only capable of annihilation in the same sense as the ghosts in the underworld of the Odyssey – ghosts which awoke to new life as soon as they tasted blood' (*ID* 553 n.) – whereas preconscious wishes, on which psychotherapy focusses, are destructible. Similarly, he says, unconscious wishes are of infantile origin, deeply buried, and ever on the alert, like 'the legendary Titans, weighed down since primaeval ages by the massive bulk of the mountains which were once hurled upon them by the victorious gods and which are still shaken from time to time by the convulsion of their limbs' (*ID* 553).

The second version of the book here resorts again to a technique, in the

1. Freud does not use the terms 'dynamic', 'economic', 'topographical' or 'genetic' in *The Interpretation of Dreams*. But in it he does implicitly differentiate between the ways of investigating the psychical apparatus that correspond to those terms. That is why, in the hope of better revealing the workings of Freud's scientific reasoning, I have taken it upon myself to use these terms.

exposition of a hypothesis, that Freud had already used in the first version when describing the Oedipus complex. The technique is two-faceted: it has a theoretical facet which aims to ensure that his discovery will find a place in the corpus of scientific knowledge being amassed during the nineteenth century, and more particularly that it will form the logical continuation of certain existing neuro-physiological and psychological theories; and it has a mythical/poetic facet which aims to ensure that discoveries made in the very specialised areas of pathology (neurosis) and subjectivity (dreams) will be seen as cultural phenomena springing from a common heritage and belonging to the fields of normality and intersubjectivity. The difference and complementarity of these two facets mirror the difference and complementarity of the scientific and popular attitudes to dreams, which Freud discusses in the very first two headings (and which serve as guidelines for the whole of *The Interpretation of Dreams*). For Freud, as indeed for any psychoanalyst, a hypothesis is true if it can be formulated both in the specialised and abstract language of science and in the figurative and concrete language of popular belief. These two forms of language naturally correspond to the work of consciousness and the work of the preconscious respectively. There exists, then, a fundamental coherence, which Freud is spontaneously seeking but has not yet formulated, between what he talks about and the way he talks about it. The psychical apparatus is the conjunction of the two ways in which consciousness and the preconscious, respectively, deal with the unconscious. Like it, *The Interpretation of Dreams* combines, in its very composition, an argument of a conscious type and an argument of a preconscious type about the psychical apparatus and its characteristic product, the dream.

From that overdetermination of wishes, which itself results from the threefold nature of the psychical topography, Freud made several deductions that tallied with observations which he had already made in random fashion and which could now be put in logical sequence. Dreams are, so to speak, out of centre: apparently only conscious (or preconscious) wishes are fulfilled in them; yet while the foreground of the stage is thus occupied, unconscious wishes concealed by displacement are satisfied in a direct representation, which has a particular sensory intensity, and which constitutes the true hub of the dream. The day's residues (and, I would add, the night's residues as well) make up the dream's raw material: anyone who can brush aside the worries of the previous day and does not dream is, like Napoleon, a good sleeper. The day's residues try to make their way into dreams even if they are not in the nature of wishes: for example, in one of Freud's own dreams already quoted, 'Otto was looking ill', the day's residue (fears for Otto's health) was obliged to find a connection with an infantile megalomaniac wish (to become a professor, like Professor R.) before it could penetrate the dream. An unconscious wish – the analogy is Freud's – is like a capitalist, who can afford the outlay for a project, whereas the preconscious day's residues correspond to the ideas put forward by the entrepreneur. Each needs the other; the day's residues seek an unconscious wish which can construct them into a dream; the unconscious wish, which is pure quantity (a 'motive force' [*Triebkraft*], *ID* 560–1), seeks an idea on to which it can 'transfer'[1] its intensity while at the same time getting itself 'covered' by it.

Preferably the idea should be indifferent so that it evades censorship, and recent so that it has not had time to set up strong and varied associative ties; that is why it tends to be found among the day's residues. But that is only a general pattern: it can happen, too, that the day's residue (the entrepreneur) makes a small contribution to the capital (a wish), that several capitalists (several wishes) combine to put up what is necessary for a single project, and so on. This provides an intelligible explanation for other phenomena already recorded by Freud or his predecessors: the day's residues disturb sleep, which the dream then protects by associating such disturbances with an unconscious wish that needs to find representation; moreover, dreams can solve problems that have been left unsolved the previous day, but only if the uncompleted thoughts succeed in finding an infantile wish which will take control of them until they reach completion. Freud regrets that he has no example of problem-solving in dreams. But surely his own discovery of psychoanalysis is itself a perfect illustration of such a process: if his self-analysis had not mobilised his memories and childhood wishes, Freud would never have had the dreams he had, nor been able to translate his deepest insights first into images and then into ideas and words.

At this point, Freud returns to the psychical apparatus, whose topographical organisation he has already described. He now outlines its genesis: it was originally a purely neuro-physiological reflex apparatus, designed to discharge any excitation along the motor path and obeying the constancy principle (this was one of the themes of 'Project for a Scientific Psychology'). With the appearance of major somatic needs (such as hunger), at a second stage, there emerges a mental activity described later on as 'primary': experience of the satisfaction of needs sets off a psychical impulse (*Regung*) which cathects the memory trace, i.e. the image of that

1. In *The Interpretation of Dreams*, Freud uses the same word, *Übertragung* (transference), sometimes in the psychoanalytic sense of transference on to the analyst, and sometimes, as here, in the more general psychological sense of a movement of psychical energy from one object to another.

satisfaction, and re-evokes the hallucinatory perception of the situation of original satisfaction. This is how a wish comes into being – it attaches itself, he says later, to a need (cf. anaclisis). At a third stage there appears the psychical activity, which is later called secondary, and which takes the wish on a roundabout path via the external world so that it achieves motor satisfaction which is no longer hallucinatory but connected with reality. Dreams are a survival from the second phase: during sleep, both perception of reality and the path to motricity are blocked; censorship can sleep, and forbidden wishes take advantage of that fact to satisfy themselves; the psychical apparatus grants itself that satisfaction, which is of no consequence since it is purely imaginary. A similar dynamic is at work in psychosis, with the difference that the weakening of the censorship between the unconscious and the preconscious occurs during a waking state, which is pathological, and results not in dreams but hallucinations, which can lead to unconscious wishes being fulfilled in real life by real acts. The fact remains that thought, before learning the roundabout path via reality, is by nature nothing but 'a substitute for a hallucinatory wish'.

Dreams are not the only way unconscious wishes achieve 'primary' fulfilment: symptoms are another. Hysterical symptoms require, like dreams, the joint fulfilment of an unconscious wish and of a preconscious wish, the latter being, for example, a wish for self-punishment (Freud improved his formula later when he said that symptoms fulfil both wishes and defences). Thus, in a woman patient, hysterical vomiting fulfilled a suppressed wish, dating from puberty, to be continuously pregnant and to be pregnant by many different men, and a preconscious wish to ruin her good looks as punishment for having the other wish. It does not occur to Freud to extend to dreams everything that is implied in the example of this symptom. But he does note the presence, in the often cited dream of 'Uncle with the yellow beard', of a mechanism of reaction-formation. On the other hand, returning in the last few lines of the heading to the topographical point of view, after embarking on this digression from a dynamic angle, Freud is able to complete his answer to the question: what is the function of dreams? Dreams protect sleep by fulfilling not only unconscious wishes in a figurative and displaced form, but also by satisfying a preconscious wish – simply the wish to sleep, an idea which he attributed (wrongly, as we have seen) to Liébeault (1889), and which he had recently communicated to Fliess, on June 9, 1899. The dream of the 'Burning child' demonstrates well the collusion between the father's repressed, unconscious wish that his son should still be alive, and the wish of the preconscious, which suggests he continue sleeping: 'Never mind! go on sleeping! after all it's only a dream.' This collusion, which occurs at the level of primary thought, is aimed at denying the obvious fact, which is part of secondary thought and is imposed by the night's residues, that the child's corpse is burning.

Heading 22: The first censorship; anxiety (Chapter 7, Section D; *ID* 573–87). – Freud's own title is more complicated and more accurate: 'Arousal by Dreams – The Function of Dreams – Anxiety-Dreams.' This heading begins with a precise, clear and concise outline of how dreams are formed, which summarises and complements what has been said in earlier headings. Phase 1: during waking life or sleep, an unconscious wish effects a transference on to the day's residues, or else a recent wish, having been suppressed, gains fresh life in the unconscious. Phase 2: to evade the censorship (*Zensur*) that exists between the unconscious and the preconscious (and which is later called the first censorship), the wish undergoes distortion; in a waking state this process would result in an obsessive idea or a delusion; the sleeping state of the preconscious, which is dominated by the wish to sleep, opens up to it a regressive path towards perception; the dream-process yields to the attraction exerted on it by visual memories and acquires through them the possibility of representation. Phase 3: now that its content has become perceptual, the dream-process draws the attention of the preconscious to itself (i.e. part of the latter's available cathectic energy), and causes the latter to carry out a secondary revision; at the same time, it can get itself noticed, as it is presented as a perception of consciousness; it is at this point that the psychical apparatus becomes aware of the dream.

Here, Freud introduces the elements of a theory of consciousness. The first two systems – the unconscious and the preconscious systems – operate on psychical quantities; they 'are lacking in any psychical quality and so cannot be objects of consciousness, except in so far as they bring pleasure or unpleasure to perception', resulting in a first type of automatic regulation of 'cathectic processes'. A second type of regulation, able to make more delicate adjustments, and not dependent on signs of unpleasure, came into being as a result of the preconscious being able, through a mnemic system of indications of speech (word-presentations are peculiar to the preconscious), to acquire new qualities of its own capable of attracting consciousness. Consciousness then had 'as it were, *two* sensory surfaces, one directed towards perception and the other towards the preconscious thought-processes'. During sleep, the latter surface becomes far less susceptible to excitation, while the former remains susceptible.

Analysis of these processes solves a number of questions previously debated by authors who had written about dreams – the duration of dreams, for instance (Freud explains that the dream-processes begin the day before, develop during a period of the night that may vary in length, and are perceived by consciousness either in the middle of the night like an exploding firework or only at the moment of waking), or the relationship between dreams and sleep (in Freud's view, the aim of dreams, like that of psychotherapy, is to bring free excitation under the control of the preconscious;[1] dreams then take on the guise of guardians of sleep: even if they wake us momentarily, we immediately fall asleep again, rid of the quantity of unconscious excitation that had accumulated in us).

On the question of the function of dreams, Freud combines two types of explanation, an economic one (an economy of energy results for consciousness if it allows a dream to take its course while expending detached attention on it during sleep rather than holding the unconscious as tightly under control at night as in the daytime), and a topographical one (the dream, like the symptom, is a compromise formation in the service of both systems, the unconscious, one or several of whose wishes are temporarily fulfilled and satisfied, and the preconscious, whose wish to sleep is preserved). A successful dream is one in which the economic equilibrium and the topographical equilibrium are in harmony. A failed dream, i.e. one which results in the dreamer waking up and being unable to get back to sleep quickly, arises from a conflict between economic requirements and topographical requirements. The latter case, which the theory provides for, is that of the anxiety-dream, which is well-known in real life but as yet unexplained. Like all safety valves, dreams can fail to work properly, or even prove dangerous: it can happen that the unconscious excitations trigger off affects which, as a result of earlier repression, are seen by consciousness as unpleasures and therefore cause anxiety. The psychical apparatus returns to the economic equilibrium of the waking state: the preconscious, rather than granting the unconscious a hallucinatory satisfaction, is forced to hold it tightly under control, which uses up much more energy and requires the dreamer to wake up.[2] The topographical compromise is then destroyed: fulfilment of the unconscious wish is no longer compatible with fulfilment of the preconscious wish to sleep.

Freud here brings off a tour de force in his use of evidence; he turns a serious objection into an argument in his favour, and that argument is not only conclusive for him but productive. At first sight, the existence of anxiety-dreams contradicts the key argument in Freud's dream theory –

1. To take Freud's idea here a little further, might it not be said that dreams are a form of self-therapy, and that analysis of one's own dreams continues, extends and consolidates that self-therapy?

2. This analysis results in something that D. Lagache (1949) was the first to point out: psychological consciousness is a consequence of moral consciousness, i.e. conscience; the state of wakefulness results from repression.

that dreams fulfil wishes. This can be seen as a contradiction only by someone who confuses the various points of view (dynamic, economic, genetic and topographical). To say that all dreams are wish-fulfilments is to argue from the dynamic point of view. But an exclusively dynamic hypothesis remains a pre-psychoanalytic argument – it had already been proposed by the Berlin psychiatrist Griesinger as an explanation of cases of delirium and extended by him to cover dreams as well. Wishes fulfilled in dreams are, moreover, overdetermined (the economic point of view); if a wish that is not satisfied the previous day is enough to produce a dream in a child, it is because of its strength (and, I would add, because of the low differentiation of the psychical apparatus in children), whereas in adults only the activation – either spontaneous or instigated by a daytime wish – of one or several repressed infantile wishes is enough to produce a dream (the genetic point of view). But the dream theory is not complete unless the fourth point of view (topographical) comes into play: daytime wishes are preconscious, adults' suppressed infantile wishes are unconscious, and the preconscious also has its own wish, which is to sleep at night.

The unconscious and the preconscious are systems for preserving, displacing and discharging psychical quantities; consciousness does not preserve, displace or discharge anything: it perceives psychical qualities directly (pleasure-unpleasure) or indirectly (through the preconscious system of indications of speech, a system not without quality). The validity of this fourfold theory is proved by the fact that it is possible to deduce from it all the types of dreams encountered in real life. The fecundity of this theory resides in the fact that it can be applied to psychical phenomena other than dreams: Freud explicitly mentions neurotic and even sometimes psychotic symptoms (for example, he shows that in agoraphobia the same type of compromise between unconscious discharge and preconscious control operates as in dreams); but another psychical phenomenon, which is implicitly present throughout his book, is implicitly explained by the same theoretical model: the creative process.

And it is precisely at the end of Heading 22 that a fresh surge in Freud's creative process may be observed, under the cloak of a clinical illustration of his theory. He describes another of his own dreams, the last such dream to be cited by him in the book. Unlike all those he has so far analysed, it dates not from the period of his self-analysis, but from his childhood. Dreamt during prepuberty, it completes the genetic point of view of his theory by explaining the transition between children's dreams, which are merely fulfilments of frustrated wishes (hunger, thirst, motricity), and adults' dreams, in which the fulfilment of repressed wishes is distorted because of censorship. The dream in question, which would today be called post-Oedipal, is an anxiety-dream, in other words a sexual dream. So far Freud's theory of the neuroses has been enriched by his dream theory. Here, the reverse process takes place: his dream theory is enriched by the theory of neuroses he elaborated between 1893 and 1895. 'Neurotic anxiety arises from sexual sources'; anxiety-dreams are those where the unconscious wish is at once sexual and strongly repressed; the appearance of anxiety-dreams in children marks the end of the period when 'sexual excitations directed towards a parent of the opposite sex have not yet met with repression and, as we have seen, are freely expressed' and the coming into being of censorship between the unconscious and the preconscious.

The dream concerned is 'My mother and the bird-beaked figures'. Secondary revision brings out the fear that his mother is dead. The dream is in fact a dual presentation – a thing- and a word-presentation – of sexual intercourse. Freud does not take his analysis any further, so let me attempt to complete it. The intercourse in question is that of his parents. The unconscious wish that is seeking fulfilment is sexual desire for the mother. The anxiety in question is that of the primal scene: the child notices that his mother has enjoyed another source of pleasure than himself; his incestuous wish then seems to him to be both impossible (he is too small) and prohibited (by the paternal rival and possessor of the mother). True, at the beginning of September 1899, when he was writing Part Three, Freud did not see the question in such clearcut, precise terms, though he was becoming increasingly convinced that he was on the right track.

The discovery of the Oedipus complex, which Freud made in October 1897 and described at the end of Part One as being a straightforward combination of an incestuous wish and a parricidal wish was, then, on the verge of being complemented by the revelation in children of two representations that are both structuring and pathogenic – that of parental intercourse, and that of the effect of threats from a rival. The closing pages of Heading 22 may justifiably be regarded both as Freud's complementary associations to his prepubertal dream and as evidence that those two representations were surfacing in his conscious and conceptual thought. The first representation can be observed in the case of one of Freud's patients (after having watched, at the age of nine, his parents make love and interpreted their act as violent and bloody, he had a recurrent anxiety-dream in early adolescence of being pursued by a man with a hatchet and being paralysed). The second representation comes from psychiatric literature: Debacker (1881) reported the case of a 13-year-old boy who suffered repeatedly from *pavor nocturnus*, during which the Devil shouted at him 'Now we've got you, now we've got you!', and which was clearly connected with the memory of threats of severe punishment for infantile masturbation (though Debacker preferred, primly and defensively, to explain the child's anxiety-dreams as having been caused by – of all things – cerebral anaemia due to puberty and possibly heredity). Freud quotes Debacker's conclusions to show how 'the blinkers of medical mythology can cause an observer to miss an understanding of such cases.' But, just before that, he repeats his assertion that anxiety appears when Oedipal wishes are repressed. The parallel with masturbation implies a conclusion which Freud does not yet state clearly, but which he had certainly grasped intuitively: behind the conscious and manifest prohibition of masturbation there lies an unconscious and latent prohibition governing Oedipal wishes, which are fulfilled, precisely, by masturbatory phantasies.

The closing section of Heading 22 is as rich in resonances as a dream. It apparently obeys two logical requirements of secondary process thinking: the need to make several theories hang together (the dream theory enriched by the theory of neuroses), and the need to adduce evidence (the supposition that anxiety-dreams fulfil Oedipal wishes after the latter have been affected by the prohibition of masturbation can be shown to be objectively true because of its universality: proof has been provided by three dreams, one by Freud himself, another by one of his patients, and a third taken from the scientific literature – the latter being all the more persuasive because it was reported by a doctor who was particularly unreceptive to the notion of the unconscious).

But behind these logical requirements, which are the equivalent, in their effect, of secondary revision in dreams, we can detect two present unconscious phantasies running through the three dreams reported by Freud (perhaps dreams belonging to a single passage in the text, like those dreamt in a single night, should be treated as one and the same dream . . .). One of them is explicitly described in Freud's analysis: it is the primal scene phantasy. The other concerns the effect of threats from a rival. It is not until Heading 24 (the last) that this phantasy is described for what it really is – a castration phantasy. Back in 1898, in a letter to Fliess of June 20, Freud had already said that 'the psychology' – the first version of Part Three of *The Interpretation of Dreams* – was 'composed as if in a dream': as regards this final version, that expression may be taken literally.

Heading 23: Psychical activity (Chapter 7, Section E; *ID* 588–609).[1] – This heading is appropriately entitled by Freud 'The Primary and Secondary

1. Only two sentences were added to this heading in 1909: a reference to Delage as a precursor as regards the theory of repression (*ID* 591), and the celebrated formula: 'The interpretation of dreams is the royal road to a knowledge of the unconscious activities of the mind' (*ID* 608).

Processes – Repression [*Verdrängung*]'. It deals with psychical activity as a whole and with the difference between normal and pathological psychical activity. Dreams provide an excellent subject for study in this respect since they contain both types: normal psychical activity continues during sleep and dreaming; at the same time, dreams are phenomena of a pathological nature (they are hallucinations), and the dream-work shows similarities with pathological psychical activity.

Freud begins by summarising – once again in the form of a plea on his own behalf – the explanation of dreams he gave in Parts One and Two: earlier theories had focussed on only one or other aspect of dreams; his own theory alone takes into account all the distinctive characteristics of dreams. Dreams are not caused by the day's residues or by external or internal nocturnal excitations: they 'interpret' them, and that 'interpretation is carried out in such a way that the object perceived shall not interrupt sleep and shall be usable for purposes of wish-fulfilment' (*ID* 589). A dream, then, is a spontaneous 'interpretation' in the service of unconscious infantile wishes and the preconscious wish to sleep. To complete the analogy, I should perhaps point out (since Freud does not do so) that the psychoanalytic interpretation of dreams is voluntary, and that it is in the service either of a conscious and unsuppressed epistemological wish (as in the case of Freud's self-analysis), or of preconscious wishes mobilised in the course of transference during treatment (the wish to please the analyst, etc.); whether spontaneous or voluntary, interpretation is always *work*. In my view, psychoanalytic interpretation is possible only because interpretation is specifically a dream process and more generally a characteristic of the psychical apparatus.

Freud then returns to, and enlarges upon, his conception of the topography of the mind. A train of thought can occur without the assistance of consciousness, either because of lack of attention on its part, or because of repression; it is the preconscious which is the seat of thought. Freud here returns – for the last time in all his works – to the notion of attention, which played such a vital role in his 'Project for a Scientific Psychology' in 1895. Attention (which as the previous heading showed is a preconscious process) gives a certain quantity of psychical energy to thoughts governed by conscious purposive ideas and by the associative paths selected by those ideas: it is therefore a process of 'hypercathexis' triggered off in the preconscious by consciousness (which itself does not have quantity). Thoughts which are neglected by consciousness and have become preconscious attract the attention of consciousness if they can find in the preconscious a cathexis greater than a high quantitative threshold. This is normal psychical activity. If thoughts have again become preconscious because they are repressed, the process is much more complex and typifies pathological psychical activity. Such thoughts need – it is a vital condition though not in itself sufficient – the transfer of energy they receive from an unconscious wish which cathects them. But as that wish is prohibited, it is not enough for them to have become intense in order to become conscious; they have to foil censorship, and to do so they need to undergo a specifically psychopathological variety of transformations.

Freud mentions four ways in which intensities can be transferred: a) condensation (or compression: the example of the word 'trimethylamin' in the Irma dream); b) the formation of compromise ideas (which can also be noted, Freud points out, in waking life, where they are known as 'slips of the tongue'; we know that he began studying these in the autumn of 1898); c) verbal associations, both phonematic and semantic (Freud became interested in them in connection with his dreams of the autumn of 1898; he mentions the '*Autodidasker*' dream as an example); and d) the juxtaposition of mutually contradictory thoughts whose intensities reinforce, but do not nullify, each other. Compared with Headings 11, 12 and 13 of the first version, which reduced the dream-work to condensation, displacement and representation, Heading 23 is based on a reclassification that is all the more significant because it heralds Freud's next two major works, *The Psychopathology of Everyday Life* and *Jokes and their Relation to the Unconscious*. His new classification is a direct result of his acceptance of the topographical point of view: if what occurs in dreams occurs not so much during sleep as in the preconscious, it must be possible, outside the field of the pathology of neuroses, to detect comparable preconscious processes during the waking state.

The aim of the transfer of intensities is to make the cathectic energy mobile and able to discharge itself (the constancy principle). Once again comparing dreams with hysterical symptoms (adducing evidence through a comparison of two different fields), Freud notes that transference operates in the same way in the formation of dreams as in symptom-formation: 'A normal train of thought is only submitted to abnormal psychical treatment of the sort we have been describing if an unconscious wish, derived from infancy and in a state of repression, has been transferred on to it' (*ID* 598). Repression is therefore the main process in these two types of formation. To explain what he means by repression, Freud returns to his 'fiction of a primitive psychical apparatus' – though it should be noted that he describes it in successive phases: rather than give a systematic and dogmatic account of it, he prefers to explain this or that section so as to give a more accurate picture of the whole, or to outline an overall view so that the individual sections can be seen better to hang together. In this way, his description maintains the creative momentum that enables him to pursue his discoveries.

Returning to an idea which he put forward in common with Breuer (who probably inspired it) in *Studies on Hysteria*, and later developed in 'Project for a Scientific Psychology', Freud establishes an economic difference between the unconscious and preconscious systems. The unconscious system allows a free discharge of the quantities of excitation, which is felt as unpleasure when it increases and as pleasure when it is discharged; it is automatically regulated by the perception of pleasure and unpleasure; it is characterised by the wish, which is 'first [. . .] a hallucinatory cathecting of the memory of satisfaction'; but in the long run hallucination cannot satisfy the need or bring about the true pleasure which only a real satisfaction of the need can provide. The second system inhibits that free discharge, transforms it into a quiescent cathexis, and then allows the excitation to be discharged in movement when perception of reality proves favourable to the obtention of satisfaction. The two systems, then, can be distinguished from one another by the principles that govern them – the unpleasure principle alone in the first case, and both the unpleasure principle and the reality principle in the second. Only the first principle is named as such by Freud, and restrictively at that, because his formulation is limited to unpleasure: 'the experience of an external fright' caused by unpleasure is, he says, more important than 'the experience of satisfaction' which causes pleasure. Later, he amended the wording of the first principle to 'the pleasure-unpleasure principle', and explicitly called the second principle the 'reality principle'.

The unconscious system cannot do anything but wish; it avoids both the perception and the recollection of anything painful or unpleasant; this averting (*Abwendung*) constitutes the first model of repression (which Freud later describes as 'primal'). The preconscious system avoids unpleasure by cathecting memories of unpleasure, i.e. experiences of fright, and by inhibiting the discharge of excitation which might cause that unpleasure to recur: it 'can only cathect an idea if it is in a position to inhibit any development of unpleasure that may proceed from it' (*ID* 601). Inhibition (*Hemmung*) is the first phase of secondary repression; it is a specific property of the preconscious.

The primary process strives to bring about an immediate discharge through a perceptual identity; it is characteristic of the unconscious system. The secondary process, which is characteristic of the preconscious system, aims to establish a thought identity; thought is a circuitous path to satisfaction; it needs to free itself from automatic regulation by the pleasure-unpleasure principle, which it can do by means of a 'further hypercathexis, brought about by consciousness'. But a 'gap' in the functional efficiency of the psychical apparatus makes it possible for 'thoughts, which represent themselves as products of the secondary thought-activity, to become subject to the primary psychical process'. This gap has two causes. First, as primary processes are innate and primal, they are stronger than the secondary processes, which develop gradually and mature late; the core of unconscious wishes remains inaccessible to the inhibitions of the preconscious.

Secondly, wish-fulfilments which contradict the purposive ideas of secondary thinking are transformed during infancy into affects of unpleasure (for instance, into disgust); but thoughts associated with repressed wishes and still alive tend to return into the preconscious; the latter tries to prevent them doing so (counter-cathexis), then effects a compromise with them (a dream, a symptom); it is because these secondary thoughts have been abandoned by the preconscious that they become subject to the primary psychical process, thus acquiring pathological characteristics: they become charged with the unihibited energy from the unconscious which is striving to find an outlet, and seek a motor or hallucinatory discharge; the linking of preconscious ideas to words may display the same displacements and confusions. Taking as his model (though he does not say so) Hughlings Jackson's concept of dissolution and liberation, Freud defines the primary process as being that of the psychical apparatus 'when freed from an inhibition'. He then shows, in a single sentence, the fecundity of his theory by using it to shed light on a new, and this time perfectly normal, phenomenon: in humour, the surplus of energy needed to inhibit these processes is discharged into laughter if we allow them to force their way through into consciousness.

Freud repeats what he said in the previous heading (but without any further proof), namely that it is sexual wishes that are subject to repression. But he says that he will wait till another occasion (*Three Essays on the Theory of Sexuality*) before examining the problems of the repression of sexuality in childhood, perversions, and bisexuality (his recognition that human beings are fundamentally bisexual had the effect of undermining his relationship with Fliess, from whom he derived the idea).

Freud's discovery of the duality of the primary and secondary processes, which he now defined in far greater detail than in 1895, led him to a conclusion that ran counter to the generally held view about the pathogeny of neuroses: hysteria is not due to the impact of a pathological disturbance on the mind; the psychical mechanisms of such a psychoneurosis are present already in the very structure of normal mental life. Neurosis does not destroy the psychical apparatus; it does not create fresh splits in its interior; it does no more than strengthen or weaken the various components in the interplay of forces that are common to the normal and the pathological, to dreams at night and to uncontrolled actions during the day (forgetting, screen memories, parapraxes, etc.). In other words, what Freud is getting at is this: the difference between the normal and the pathological is one of degree, not of essence. Repression is the key factor in this interplay of forces: what is repressed moves into another part of the mind, becomes unconscious, yet continues to be active and to have repercussions on the whole psychical apparatus and its productions (Freud later gave a name to this phenomenon: the return of the repressed). The line from the *Aeneid* which Freud used as a motto for his book and which he quotes again at this point – *Flectere si nequeo superos, Acheronta movebo* – describes that unconscious dynamic in mythical and poetic, rather than theoretical, terms: when the higher powers remain inflexible, the forces of hell – the repressed wishes – rage furiously.

Concerned as he is to put the normal and the pathological on an equal footing, Freud concludes this heading by suggesting that his theory of the two psychical processes may throw light not only on psychopathology but on normal psychology as well: 'The compounding of the apparatus out of two agencies makes it possible for the normal mind too to function with greater delicacy than would be possible with only one of them' (*ID* 608–9).

Heading 23 is the most theoretical in content of the whole book. It contains no concrete examples of dreams or symptoms. But in tone it is an impassioned glorification of the psychical apparatus, an awe-struck discovery of its workings, an exploration of its bountiful, ever-renewed potential. Freud, as a child, must have loved his mother's body in the same way.

Heading 24: The second censorship; consciousness (Chapter 7, Section F; *ID* 610–21). This is the final heading. Freud appropriately calls it 'The Unconscious and Consciousness – Reality'. The previous heading differentiated between the unconscious and the preconscious; this one differentiates between the unconscious and consciousness; censorship between the unconscious and the preconscious, which is what Freud has been referring to so far, becomes the first censorship, to which a second censorship between the preconscious and consciousness is now added.

Freud begins by cautioning against too literal an interpretation of the metaphors he uses to describe the psychical apparatus. Among other things, he issues a warning that seems to have escaped the notice of those who have attempted to rethink psychoanalysis in terms of linguistic structuralism: 'We may speak of an unconscious thought seeking to convey itself into the preconscious so as to be able then to force its way into consciousness. What we have in mind here is not the forming of a second thought situated in a new place, like a transcription which continues to exist alongside the original' (*ID* 610). However, so that readers can grasp the difference between consciousness and the unconscious, Freud sees fit to resort to an optical metaphor: 'Everything that can be an object of our internal perception is *virtual*, like the image produced in a telescope by the passage of light-rays. But we are justified in assuming the existence of the systems (which are not in any way psychical entities themselves and can never be accessible to our psychical perception) like the lenses of the telescope, which cast the image. And, if we pursue this analogy, we may compare the censorship between two systems to the refraction which takes place when a ray of light passes into a new medium' (*ID* 611).

Freud then compares his conception of the unconscious with that of Lipps and of Scherner (a hypothesis is given added validity by the convergence of findings by researchers working independently). Lipps (1897) is a precious ally, because he arrived at the same general conclusion at about the same time as Freud: traditional psychology's assumption that 'psychical' meant 'conscious' is wrong. 'It is essential to abandon the overvaluation of the property of being conscious before it becomes possible to form any correct view of the origin of what is mental. In Lipps's words, the unconscious must be assumed to be the general basis of psychical life. The unconscious is the larger sphere, which includes within it the smaller sphere of the conscious. Everything conscious has an unconscious preliminary stage; whereas what is unconscious may remain at that stage and nevertheless claim to be regarded as having the full value of a psychical process. The unconscious is the true psychical reality; *in its innermost nature it is as much unknown to us as the reality of the external world, and it is as incompletely presented by the data of consciousness as is the external world by the communications of our sense organs*' (*ID* 612–3).

It is this overvaluation of consciousness which has resulted, according to Freud, in a misunderstanding of not only dreams and symptoms, but the creative process as well: the latter is scarcely conscious at all. A sudden inspiration can produce a discovery or a work of art as an almost ready-made whole, whether during the day or, as in the case of Tartini's *Trillo del Diavolo*, in a dream. From this point of view, the respect paid by antiquity to dreams and the 'daemonic' power expressed in them – i.e. the unconscious – shows greater insight than the intellectualised theories of traditional psychology. As for Scherner (1861), he had realised, before Freud, that dreams make symbolic representations of the body: such representations, Freud adds, are the result of sexual phantasies.

However, the originality of Freud's conception of the mind as compared with that of Lipps or Scherner was that he held there to be not one but two kinds of unconscious – the unconscious proper and the preconscious, the former being able to reach consciousness only through the latter, which acts as both an intermediary and a screen. *The Interpretation of Dreams* began with a plea by Freud on behalf of his technique and his audacity in revealing himself in a published work. The book closes with a threefold paean of praise. Freud extols the preconscious, which does not merely play a role of censorship, but also controls access to the power of voluntary movement and has at its disposal for distribution a mobile cathectic energy, attention. He praises consciousness, which although no longer regarded as omnipotent cannot, either, be reduced to a mere epiphenomenon; it fulfils two important roles: that of a sense organ for the perception of psychical qualities (pleasure and unpleasure); and that of directing and distributing in expedient fashion the mobile quantities of cathexis by replacing automatic regulation according to the unpleasure principle by a second and more discriminating regulation which takes better account of external reality; this regulation is obtained when thought-processes, which initially are without quality, acquire the residues of quality which exist in verbal memories, i.e. word-presentations; it is this hypercathexis, creator of a new series of qualities, which constitutes the superiority of man over animals. Lastly, Freud praises psychotherapy, which increases psychological consciousness and internal freedom by subjecting whatever produces unpleasure to preconscious cathexis and to conscious working over, and by replacing the repression of memories by control over the perceptions.

At this point, Freud posits the existence of a second censorship, this time between the preconscious and consciousness, which comes into force only above a certain quantitative limit. This hypothesis is suggested to Freud by hysterical thought-processes, whereas the notion of the first censorship, between the unconscious and the preconscious, had been suggested by dreams. As an illustration of the 'intimate and reciprocal relations between censorship and consciousness', Freud cites the last two clinical examples in his book – examples whose relevance, all of a sudden, extends beyond this point of theory and even beyond the bounds of the book as a whole. The first case is that of a little girl who complained of having 'a feeling in her body as though there was something "stuck into it" which was "moving backwards and forwards" and was "shaking" her through and through'. The sexual connotations were obvious; but the girl described her symptoms so naively that the first censorship and the mother failed to notice this phantasy of sexual intercourse, which would normally have been preconscious and was in this case disguised merely as a complaint.

The second example is a waking vision (of draughts, a dagger, a sickle and a scythe) experienced at his first consultation by a 14-year-old boy. It, too, was a transposition of a sexual phantasy. He had been threatened by his father, a hard man, because he had played with his genitals (hence, in his vision, 'the playing at draughts; the forbidden moves; the dagger which could be used to kill'). His father had divorced and remarried, much to the boy's chagrin; hence the sickle, the one with which Zeus castrated his father Kronos, who was guilty of devouring his own children.[1] Freud, then, concluded his book with two discoveries which were to prove to be of considerable importance, but which he had not yet fully grasped: girls' penis need, and boys' castration anxiety. Because of the defensive protection afforded by his very coherent theory, Freud was able to hint, between the lines, at the dual phantasy which attempts to come to terms with the difference between the sexes. He had come a long way from the notion of bisexuality as postulated by Fliess. He could now finish his book: the cycle of discoveries that began with his insight into the Oedipus complex was now to all intents and purposes complete.

Freud signs off by pleading once again not guilty – a plea that is particularly significant coming as it does immediately after a reference to the threat of castration: people cannot be held guilty for what they dream. Freud even hesitates to attribute 'reality' to unconscious wishes! It was only in 1909 and 1914 that he added a passage drawing a distinction between 'psychical reality' and 'material reality'. He quotes one last philosopher, Plato, who held that 'the virtuous man is content to *dream* what a wicked man really *does*'. Freud argues that men should be judged by their actions, not their dreams. But 'it is in any case instructive to get to know the much trampled soil from which our virtues proudly spring': so he is quite prepared to assert, as he has just done in the case of psychology, that our 'morality' is 'antiquated'. After upbraiding his contemporaries, Freud begs to differ with the ancients: dreams give us knowledge of the past, not the future. And if a dream does foretell the future, it is because it pictures in advance our wishes as fulfilled; but those wishes derive from the past. In the final sentence of the book, Freud refers to, but does not name, the state of mind that occurs when childhood wishes achieve deferred fulfilment in adulthood; he mentioned it in a letter to Fliess of January 16,

1. As we have already seen, Freud mixed up two episodes in the myth: Kronos the son, castrating his father Uranus for not allowing his unborn children to leave the womb of his wife, Gaia (mother earth), and Kronos the father, devouring his children and later dethroned by his son Zeus, who had escaped that fate.

1898, and later discussed it in *Civilization and its Discontents* (1930*a*); it is the purpose, the goal and the dream of every man – happiness.

As we have seen, then, the composition of *The Interpretation of Dreams* is characterised by a constant interaction between diachrony and synchrony. The more or less chronological account that Freud gives of his discoveries is intended to be distinct from the purely synchronic description of his theory of mental processes. But both strands intertwine, because the theory of the dream-work, which remains at a primary level of abstraction in relation to the dream material, requires a theory of the psychical apparatus that is located at a secondary level of abstraction. The epistemological gulf between the two theories meant that an interval of time elapsed between their respective elaborations, during which Freud's self-analysis got going again and the diachronic sequence was reactivated. Throughout the book, there is a clear oscillation between the subject of the proposition (the man who one moment dreams and the next tries to understand his dreams in combination with those of his patients) and the subject of the utterance (the man who one moment writes a retrospective account of an internal adventure and the next pursues, but never completes, the systematisation of his theory). Thus, Freud brings into play four distinct characters – the dreamer, the interpreter, the narrator and the theorist – in the actual composition of his work (a composition which, as I pointed out at the start, displays both the diachronic pattern of the period of elaboration and the synchronic pattern of the articulation of parts in the completed whole). The illusion which sustained Freud while he was writing the two successive versions of his book was that the four characters might come together. But when two or three of them happened to do so, Freud felt paralysed and his writing ground to a halt. It was the tension between them – as long as it was kept to a tolerable level – which produced Freud's bursts of creativity.

So in this case diachrony cannot be reduced to mere chronology: it obeys the phenomenon of deferred action, which Freud not only realises, but understands better and better as his self-analysis progresses. This kind of composition – which sets out to explain a structure not only by a retrospective description of its genesis but also by inserting into it fragments of the genesis of that description, as long as the fragments, in their capacity as condensations, displacements or representations, are derivatives of that structure – has been much used by contemporary literature; it is to be found in perhaps its purest form in Michel Butor's *L'emploi du temps* (1956).

At the same time, the basic synchrony of the structure, at the very moment when the author believes he is grasping and communicating it, which is the moment when it is most likely to close in on itself and gag all living ideas, does however, under the pretext of providing clinical examples to back up the validity of the theory, open up the way for a renewed regressive impetus and for the revelation, in the form of a thinking in images, of a wish, phantasy or anxiety not yet identified by conceptual thinking.

The Interpretation of Dreams is as innovatory in its internal structure as it is in its ideas and examples. It tries to give an account of unconscious processes not only by what it says about them, but by the very way the text is organised. It might be likened to a screen memory, where events from different periods come together to form a significant wish scenario; or to a dream where the work of the representation of the wish is carried out by condensation, displacement and representation, as well as by dramatisation and reversal into the opposite, and where everything is reshuffled by secondary revision. So in *The Interpretation of Dreams* – the *fons et origo* of psychoanalysis – the work of composition, which forms an important part of the work of creation, both extends and represents the dream-work; in other words it reduplicates it. The junction between the two was made by another form of psychical work (which Freud erected into a theory only 18 years later), namely the work of mourning following his father's death in October 1896. During the summer of 1899, when he was writing Chapter 7 'as if in a dream', Freud gave the various forms of psychical work a psychical localisation, the preconscious. In its content, form and origins, the first book on psychoanalysis is very much a book on the preconscious.

A PSEUDO-PREMONITORY DREAM FULFILLED

The question of premonitory dreams, which Freud touched upon in the closing paragraph of *The Interpretation of Dreams*, cropped up again when the book came out. It was published on November 4, 1899, as Freud informed Fliess in a letter the following day. In the same letter he said he had discovered the meaning of premonitory dreams. On November 10, he wrote a short paper called 'A Premonitory Dream Fulfilled' (1941*c*, *SE* 5, 623–5). The dream in question, 'Meeting Dr. K. in the Kärntnerstrasse', had been dreamt by one of his women patients. The paper was not published until after Freud's death, but he included a substantial summary of it in Section D, devoted to prophetic dreams and the feeling of '*déjà vu*', of Chapter 12 in the second edition (1907) of *The Psychopathology of Everyday Life*. It runs as follows:

'A good example of a dream which may justly be called prophetic was once brought to me for detailed analysis by an intelligent and truthful woman patient. Her story was that she had once dreamt she met a former friend of hers and family doctor in front of a certain shop in a certain street; and that when next morning she went into the Inner Town she in fact met him at the very spot named in the dream. I may observe that no subsequent event proved the importance of this miraculous coincidence, which could not therefore be accounted for by what lay in the future.

'Careful questioning established that there was no evidence of her having had any recollection of the dream on the morning after she dreamt it – that is, until after her walk and the meeting. She could produce no objection to an account of what happened which robbed the episode of anything miraculous and left nothing but an interesting psychological problem. She was walking along the street in question one morning and met her old family doctor in front of a particular shop, and thereupon, on seeing him, she felt convinced that she had dreamt the night before of having this meeting at that precise spot. Analysis was then able to show with great probability how she arrived at this sense of conviction, which, according to general rules, cannot fairly be denied a certain right to be considered authentic. A meeting at a particular place, which has been expected beforehand, amounts in fact to a *rendezvous*. The old family doctor awakened her memory of former days, when meetings with a *third* person, also a friend of the doctor, had played a very important part in her life. Since then she had continued her relations with that gentleman and had waited for him in vain on the day before the dream was supposed to have taken place. If I were able to report the circumstances of the case in greater detail it would be easy for me to show that her illusion, when she saw her friend of former days, of having had a prophetic dream was equivalent to some such remark as this; "Ah! doctor – you remind me now of past times when I never had to wait in vain for N. if we'd arranged a meeting' (*PEL* 262–3). So what the woman in question had imagined to be an earlier prophetic nocturnal dream was in fact a present preconscious day-dream (but just as much a wish-fulfilment as a nocturnal dream).

Occasional self-analysis and continued work

THE WRITING OF *THE PSYCHOPATHOLOGY OF EVERYDAY LIFE* (NOVEMBER 1899–FEBRUARY 1901)

At the end of 1899, Freud wrote his own autobiographical note for J. L. Pagel's *Biographisches Lexicon hervorragender Ärzte des neunzehnten Jahrhunderts* (1901*c*), and above all thought about his future work: he planned a theory of sexuality, and a theory of repression and wish-fulfilment, which would serve as an introduction to a general psychology of neuro-psychoses and even to a metapsychology. Freud's hope was that knowledge of neuroses would eventually be admitted as a science. He continued to amass data for two more imminent and easier works, *The Psychopathology of Everday Life* (1901*b*) and *Jokes and their Relation to the Unconscious* (1905*c*), in which he extended his discoveries about dreams to related areas. It can happen, then, that the created work continues, after its publication, to produce creative activity in writers of genius. This final chapter of my book is devoted to a phenomenon which might be called 'the working of the work' ('*le travail de l'oeuvre*' in French),[1] i.e. to the development by Freud of ideas, affects and attitudes prompted by his work of self-analysis between 1897 and 1899, and crystallised for the first time in *The Interpretation of Dreams*.

He remained in a state of elation despite several external reasons for disgruntlement. He complained that his book had been virtually ignored, and that the few reviews which had appeared were rather unfavourable.[2] Yet again, his name failed to appear in the list of newly appointed professors at the end of September 1899. Finally, his practice was shrinking, and as a result he was in financial straits. He gloomily faced the prospect of having to make do with shorter summer holidays in 1900, to stop travelling, and to get a job, at least for the summer, at a hydrotherapeutic establishment. As in 1895, he took his family to Bellevue as an economy measure, but this time as early as the end of May because of an unbearable heat-wave in Vienna. But after a disappointing meeting with Fliess at Achensee in early August he did in fact go on another trip to Italy.

Freud's self-analysis now took on a different air. No longer did it amount to the calling into question of himself or the reconstitution of his past that had monopolised his energies from the winter of 1896–97 to the summer of 1899. It now focussed on fragmentary details as in the early days of 1895 and 1896 when he was still perfecting his technique and training himself to use it. By 1900 he was in total control of it and could ask it to come up with as many examples as he needed to illustrate subsequent works. This explains why *The Psychopathology of Everyday Life* is different in character from *The Interpretation of Dreams*: it marks a transition between works of an almost confessional nature and his more impersonal publications.

Ellenberger (E 495–6) outlines the existing literature on parapraxes before Freud tackled the subject. Already Goethe, Schopenhauer, and von

1. Chapter 6 of the original French edition of this book is entitled 'Le Travail de l'Oeuvre'.

2. As often when it came to social life, Freud's reaction was too one-sided and negative. True, his book was selling slowly, but it was a bulky and forbidding work. On the other hand, there were numerous reviews, most of them quite favourable (see Ellenberger's round-up of reactions to the book, E 783–4); from 1901 on, *The Interpretation of Dreams* was mentioned, in their bibliographies, by philosophers and psychiatrists dealing with topics connected with dreams (such as Bergson).

Hartmann had shown interest in slips of the tongue and pen, and described them as manifestations of the unconscious. In Freud's time, R. Meringer and C. Mayer had published a study of slips of the tongue, *Versprechen und Verlesen* (1895), but they were more concerned with pronunciation than with meanings. In the 1880s, Hans Gross, the celebrated criminologist of Graz, and founder of judicial psychology, had recorded slips of the tongue in the testimony of witnesses and accused persons. He described the case of a man who, replacing a genuine witness in order to give false testimony, inadvertently signed the statement with his real name. Theodor Vischer, in his novel *Auch Einer* (1879), made popular the term 'the malice of objects' to describe the misadventures that happened to some people whose everyday objects are continually being hidden, substituted or changing place. The significance of misprints which showed the true thoughts of the author was well-known, and Karl Kraus collected them in his journal *Die Fackel*. In his *Voyage au centre de la terre* (*Journey to the Centre of the Earth*) (1864), Jules Verne depicts an old professor deciphering a text written in an unknown language with the help of his nephew, who is secretly in love with the professor's daughter, Gräuben; the nephew thinks he has found the key and spells out the words: 'I am in love with Gräuben.' In *Vingt mille lieux sous les mers* (*Twenty Thousand Leagues under the Sea*) (1869), Professor Arronax is looking for pearls on the bottom of the sea, but has forgotten to warn his companions that the place is infested with sharks; he tells them he has found a giant oyster that contains 'no less than 150 sharks'.

Freud finished writing *The Psychopathology of Everday Life* in February 1901, and corrected the proofs in May. *Monatsschrift für Psychiatrie und Neurologie* published it in two lengthy instalments in July and August 1901. When it came out in book form in 1904, it incorporated parts of two papers which had already appeared on the forgetting of proper names and screen memories (1898*b* and 1899*a*), but did not include the disguised autobiographical fragment of the 'Green meadow with yellow flowers.' I have already discussed several passages from the book in connection with Freud's systematic self-analysis. To recapitulate, they are: the memory of the scene of his mother being 'boxed up', the forgetting of the name Signorelli, the 'Oedipal' slip in the medical treatment of the old lady, the mistake over Monsieur Joyeuse's day-dream, the slips concerning Marburg and Hasdrubal, and the figure 2,467.

In the course of dashing off the final pages of *The Interpretation of Dreams* in the country, away from his library, and hastily correcting proofs, Freud came across more material for his self-analysis. For instance, at a time when he was preoccupied about a rival book on dreams that was due to be published, he misread a caption in an illustrated weekly as 'A Wedding

Celebration in the Odyssey' (instead of 'A Wedding Celebration on the Ostsee [the Baltic]'): he was concerned over questions of priority in the interpretation of exhibitionist dreams of being naked (e.g. Odysseus appearing naked before Nausicaä, and the quotation from Gottfried Keller's *Der grüne Heinrich: ID* 246–7).

The day after *The Interpretation of Dreams* came out, Freud told Fliess he had mixed up Hasdrubal and Hamilcar (*F*, November 5, 1899, 382; cf. *PEL* 217–20, *ID* 197, and the fourth 'Rome' dream). Two other errors could be explained by Freud's embarrassment at revealing his complex feelings towards his father: his confusion over Marbach and Marburg (*F*, November 12, 1899, 385; *PEL* 217–19); and the 'Hollthurn' dream, *ID* 456); and his mistaking of generations (*ID* 256 and 619) in two passages on the subject of filial piety, where he says that Zeus castrated and overthrew his father Kronos, whereas in fact it was Kronos who subjected his own father, Uranus, to that fate (*PEL* 218 and 220). Freud sees in this last error the influence of a conversation with his brother Emanuel, who had sternly reminded Sigismund that as he was the child of a second marriage he belonged to the third generation in relation to his father. The parapraxis confirms that one of Freud's major problems was how to establish his position in such a complicated family tree: it must certainly have overdetermined his interest in any system that made it possible to decipher hidden structures (e.g. histology, archaeology, psychoanalysis).

Freud realised just how attached every individual is to all that is personal to him – his name, his style, his works. Proof of this he saw in his disagreeable feeling when a patient called Herr S. Freud turned up at his consulting room (*PEL* 25), and in his inability to remember the title of a book whose author had been referred to as follows by an acquaintance: 'His style reminds me very much of your own, and his way of thinking, too, is the same as yours' (*PEL* 139–40).

There are countless such examples taken from Freud's own experience in *The Psychopathology of Everyday Life*. Following Freud's classification, they may be divided into two broad categories, depending on whether they belong to the family 'circle of thoughts' or the professional 'circle of thoughts'.[1] In most cases, they involve feelings and attitudes towards other people, and confirm or clarify what we already know of Freud's relations with this or that person.

Freud's hostility towards Breuer was suggested by his inability to find a particular shop which sold strong-boxes – and was located near the latter's

1. Under Jung's influence, Freud changed 'circles of thought' to 'complexes' from 1907 (2nd ed.) on.

home (*PEL* 137–8). Two examples concerning Fliess are discussed on pp. 518 and 528–9.

In two examples of forgetting, Freud owns up to a mixture of consideration for, and annoyance at, Martha: he was quite unable to remember the subject of a conversation, overheard by Martha during their summer holidays in 1900, between some fellow table d'hôte diners, including one gentleman from Vienna with whom Freud did not wish to renew acquaintance (the incident appears in the dream of 'Company at table d'hôte'); on another occasion, described immediately afterwards, Freud wished to have a good laugh with a friend over a remark made by Martha a few hours before, and forgot what it was (*PEL* 136–7). Freud does not, on the other hand, say what caused him to forget the name of the street – Radetsky-Strasse – where Martha lived during their engagement (*PEL* 65).

Freud's brother, Alexander, was the cause of considerable concern to him. The prospect (revealed in August 1899) that he might become a professor before his elder brother caused something of a stir in the family, and their mother had expressed her surprise to Sigmund. He then made a revealing slip: he mistakenly read in a newspaper that someone was crossing Europe 'in a tub' (*im Fass*) instead of 'on foot' (*zu Fuss*). Alexander was an authority on matters to do with transport (*Beförderung*), and seemed likely to gain promotion (*Beförderung*) before Sigmund. Alexander the Great, after whom Alexander Freud was named, once admired Diogenes and his tub. The structure of the parapraxis is exactly the same as that of a dream or an act of forgetting. The word *Beförderung*, with its many meanings, is its symbolic key:

a) What a way to draw attention to oneself, using a means of transport like that (a tub)!

b) How curious that a person can appear in the newspaper on account of such stupidities – an allusion to a patient whose pathological ambition to see himself in print had been transformed into an anxiety about reading newspapers?

c) Alexander could not possibly be appointed professor of anything but a minor subject such as his, transport, which makes him a worthy rival of the eccentric Diogenes.

So the parapraxis did have a meaning: it fulfilled Sigmund's wish to minimise his brother's prospects (*PEL* 107–9).

Alexander's conduct was the source of other worries, which were discreetly alluded to by Freud's forgetting the first name of a patient whose elder sister was also treated by Freud and whose mother was also called Amalia. Freud had repressed the question: 'Would my brother in the same circumstances have behaved in a similar way, or would he have done the opposite?' Amalia and the two substitute names that had sprung to Freud's mind, Daniel and Franz, were all names from Schiller's play, *Die Räuber* (which, it will be remembered, played an important role in the '*Non vixit*' dream) (*PEL* 23–4).

Freud's impatience with his little daughter Anna, who had not been listening to him, caused him to make a slip of the tongue when quoting the following rhyme:

Der Affe gar possierlich ist,	[The ape's a very comic sight
Zumal wenn er vom Apfel frisst	When from an apple he takes a bite.]

In place of '*Affe*', Freud had used the non-existent '*Apfe*' – a compromise-formation (*PEL* 61–2).

Lastly, fear of the death of a relative or close friend, one of the most persistent themes of Freud's self-analysis, was responsible for his forgetting the name of a patient and friend, who revived memories (to do with blindness, injury and suicide) that caused Freud to fear the worst for a member of his family (*PEL* 24–5). The same fear was also responsible for Freud's misreading a letter which announced that '*der arme* [the poor] Dr. Wilhelm M.' was dying: he read '*die arme* Wilhelm M.' (the feminine form '*die*' implied that his wife was being referred to). In so doing, Freud's unconscious was trying to deny that the man could die, for 'another person in close contact with me' – obviously Wilhelm Fliess – was suffering from a similar illness (*PEL* 109–10).

The theme of death becomes more important when Freud deals with 'professional circles of thought'. When going through his medical engagement book, Freud saw that he had marked a patient he had treated six months earlier simply as 'M—l' and could not remember who it was. It turned out that the patient had been a 14-year-old hysterical girl, who greatly improved under treatment except for persistent abdominal pains; the pains were in fact symptoms of a sarcoma, which Freud, with all his attention concentrated on the hysteria, had overlooked, and which led to her death two months later (*PEL* 146 n.1) (cf. the Irma and '*Autodidasker*' dreams for the distinction between hysterical and organic symptoms).

On another occasion, a timely bungled action warned Freud in advance to be wary in making a similar differential diagnosis: he put a tuning fork into his pocket instead of a reflex hammer. The tuning fork had last been handled by an imbecile child. Freud's first association to 'hammer' ('*Hammer*') was '*Chamer*', the Hebrew for 'ass'. So the parapraxis meant: don't go making an imbecile and an ass of yourself this time (*PEL* 165–7).

The patient most often referred to in *The Psychopathology of Everyday Life* is the old lady whom Freud used to visit daily in order to give her treatment, and who played a role in the Irma dream and in the discovery of the Oedipus complex (she died in August 1901; cf. *F*, August 7, 1901, 446). On two occasions Freud kept on walking up the stairs when he got to the landing outside her flat, and ended up a floor too high. The first time, he was engrossed in a day-dream about his career, in which he was himself 'climbing ever higher and higher'; the second time, he had been irritated by a (phantasied) criticism that he was always 'going too far' (*PEL* 164–5). On another occasion, the cabman taking him to the old lady's address made a mistake, although he had often done the journey, and stopped in front of a house with the same number in a nearby street which ran parallel (*PEL* 256–7): 'If I were *superstitious* I should see an omen in the incident, the finger of fate announcing that this year would be the old lady's last.' Freud uses the example – thus further extending the field of applied psychoanalysis – to prove that superstition is 'nothing but psychology projected into the external world' (*PEL* 258).

Freud quotes other examples of the professional complex. He failed to spot the misprint Buckrhard, in a favourable review by him (1900*b*) of a book by an obstetrician called Burckhard: the contempt implied by the distortion of the name was in fact directed at another Burckhard, who had written an unintelligent review of *The Interpretation of Dreams* in *Die Zeit* of January 6 and 13, 1900 (*PEL* 117–18: *F*, January 8, 1900). A common parapraxis of Freud's, when visiting patients at their homes, was to take his own key out of his pocket as he arrived at their door. The meaning was: '"Here I feel I am at home", for it only occurred at places where I had taken a liking to the patient' (*PEL* 163).

On several occasions, financial considerations lay behind the parapraxis. Freud often forgot to return books he had borrowed, to pay for his cigars (*PEL* 157–8), and to make visits to impecunious patients or colleagues – because they were free (*PEL* 157). Once, after returning from his holidays and in need of patients, he even brought forward by a whole month in his diary the appointment that one of his women patients had suggested in a letter (*PEL* 116–17). He therefore adopted Darwin's 'golden rule' (Darwin put into writing any thoughts or published facts that contradicted his theory, because otherwise he tended to forget them), and jotted down in the morning all the visits he had to make during the day, so he would be sure not to forget the ones he did not want to make.

Two other self-analytic fragments involved, respectively, the art of eliciting a gift – he inadvertently broke the marble cover of his inkpot just after his sister had told him that it did not go with his desk (*PEL* 167) – and even sexual desire: he had found a certain girl attractive ever since an incident when they had both rushed to fetch a chair for her very old uncle, and in the course of helping her he had put his arms around her waist (*PEL* 175–6).

Freud could feel the influence of such occasional self-analysis on his memory and on his candour. As I have already pointed out, he found it increasingly difficult not to tell the truth. He stopped sending congratulations – usually white lies anyway – on occasions such as birthdays, anniversaries, weddings and promotions; he warned a friend who had asked him to send a congratulatory telegram on his behalf that he might forget to do so (*PEL* 154–5); he ended up not writing a promised review because deep down he did not want to (*PEL* 161). Freud took a firm stand against the hypocrisy of social conventions current at the time: 'It is due to painful experiences in the course of my life that I am unable to manifest sympathy on occasions where the expression of sympathy must necessarily be exaggerated, as an expression corresponding to the slight amount of my feeling would not be allowable. [. . .] Where my emotional activity no longer has anything to do with social duty, its expression is never inhibited by forgetting' (*PEL* 155).

As Freud got accustomed to submitting all his own acts of forgetting to psychological analysis and gradually liberated his unconscious, so his memory improved. In his youth, he had an extremely good memory, and could repeat almost verbatim a page he had read or a lecture he had heard: 'Since then the command that I have over my store of memories has steadily deteriorated; yet right up to the most recent times I have convinced myself over and over again that with the aid of a certain device I can remember far more than I would otherwise have believed possible. When, for instance, a patient in my consulting hour claims that I have seen him before and I can recall neither the fact nor the time, I help myself by guessing: that is to say, I quickly think of a number of years, counting back from the present. In cases where records or more definite information from the patient enable me to check what has come to my mind, they show that I have rarely been more than half a year out in ten. [. . .] In this way I extend my conscious memory by invoking my unconscious memory, which is in any case far more extensive' (*PEL* 135–6).

The second edition of *The Psychopathology of Everyday Life* in 1907 (in fact the third publication of the text, which had originally come out in the form of scientific papers between 1898 and 1901, and was then published as a book, with only minor changes, in 1904) contains among its numerous additions some further parapraxes and related phenomena connected with his self-analysis. I list them here because several of them probably, if not certainly, date from the period 1900–02:

– Freud's affection for Rosa, his favourite sister, which had been reinforced

by his visiting her an hour before, led him to forget, when booking a ticket at Reichenhall station, the name of the next main station: Rosenheim (literally, 'Rose-home') (*PEL* 23);
– he forgot the name of the place in Italy where he wanted to send a patient to a sanatorium: Nervi (literally, in Italian, 'nerves') (*PEL* 22);
– he forgot the name of an inn, the Hochwartner, because its name was 'only too similar' to that of a Viennese colleague (*PEL* 22–3);
– his love of antiques led him, when on holiday, to read every shop sign that resembled the word in any way as 'Antiken' (*PEL* 110);
– he explains how he succeeded in recalling the name Monaco after forgetting it (*PEL* 55), but it was only later, in *Introductory Lectures on Psycho-Analysis*, that he gave a (partial) explanation of why he forgot it in the first place: 'Monaco is also the Italian name for Munich; and it was that town which exerted the inhibitory influence' (*SE* 15, 111);
– his omission to get out some books on Venice that a patient who was going there had asked to borrow, followed by his mistake in lending him a book on the Medici, who have nothing to do with Venice, forced Freud to admit something he would have preferred to keep secret – disapproval of his patient's trip (*PEL* 220–21);
– his feeling of 'remarkable coincidence' when he unexpectedly met two people he had just been thinking about obeyed the same mechanism as the woman patient's pseudo-prophetic dream already discussed (pp. 512–13); they were a married couple who had turned down his offer to treat their little daughter because they thought he lacked experience: Freud, who had just been awarded the title of professor (March 1902), caught a glimpse of them unconsciously as he walked towards them in the street, but set the perception aside and immediately imagined, in phantasy, that, dazzled by his title, they had begged him to treat the child – which, out of revenge, he had refused to do. At that point, this phantasy was interrupted by their greeting: 'Good day to you, Professor!' (*PEL* 263–4).

THE END OF E.'S TREATMENT AND THE ELIMINATION OF FREUD'S 'TRANSFERENCE' ON TO FLIESS (DECEMBER 1899–AUGUST 1900)

Fliess saw Freud in Vienna in early December 1899, shortly before the birth of his third child, Conrad. As usual, their meeting acted as an intellectual stimulant for Freud, though less so than in the past. In a letter of December 9, he told Fliess he was abandoning one of the last surviving remnants of his old theory of traumatic seduction, namely the notion that the 'choice of neurosis' depended on the age at which the traumas occurred; he now related that choice to the stages of psychosexual development with regard to the object, and developed the idea of a primal 'auto-erotism', with 'allo-erotism' coming only later. This was the first hint of his subsequent theory of narcissism. But he did not follow up the idea: as often when he had a new insight (cf. the example of the family romance, p. 221), Freud related it to specific factors which restricted its import and prevented him, for quite some time, from spotting its more general significance.

The limiting factor here was the fact that he connected auto-erotism with paranoia alone, but not with hysteria or obsessional neurosis: 'The lowest of the sexual strata is auto-erotism, which dispenses with any psychosexual aim and seeks only locally gratifying sensations. It is then succeeded by allo-erotism (homo- and hetero-erotism), but certainly continues to exist as an undercurrent. Hysteria (and its variant, obsessional neurosis) is allo-erotic, since its main path is identification with the loved one. Paranoia again dissolves the identification, re-establishes all the loved ones of childhood who have been abandoned (compare the discussion of exhibitionist dreams), and dissolves the ego itself into extraneous persons. So I have come to regard paranoia as a forward surge of the auto-erotic current, as a return to a former state. The perversion formation corresponding to it would be the so-called idiopathic insanity. The special relations between auto-erotism and the original "ego" would throw a clear light on the nature of this neurosis. At this point the thread breaks off again" (*F*, December 9, 1899, 390). It is worth noting that this passage also contains two other future insights – children's identification with loved ones, and the splitting of the ego.

On December 21, Freud gave a fresh explanation of his railway phobia: 'My phobia, then, was a phantasy of impoverishment, or rather a hunger phobia, determined by my infantile greediness and evoked by my wife's lack of a dowry (of which I am so proud)' (*F* 392). This explanation, which, by the way, is aggressive towards Fliess, who married a rich woman, was suggested to him by one of his patients, the celebrated E. (cf. p. 190 n.1), who, to Freud's delight, had just recalled an authentic primal scene: 'You can well imagine how important this one persistent patient has become to me. It now appears that the dream will be fulfilled. I cautiously say "appears", but I am really quite certain. Buried deep beneath all his phantasies, we found a scene from his primal period (before twenty-two months) which meets all the requirements [. . .]. It is everything at the same time – sexual, innocent, natural, and the rest. I scarely dare believe it yet. It is as if Schliemann had once more excavated Troy, which had hitherto been deemed a fable. At the same time the fellow is doing outrageously well' (*F* 391–2). He gave further details on January 8, 1900:

'In E.'s case, the second genuine scene is coming up after years of preparation; and it is one which may *perhaps* be confirmed objectively by asking his elder sister. Behind it a third, long-suspected scene approaches' (*F* 395). E. was becoming more important to Freud than Fliess.

The first half of 1900 was one of the most remarkably empty periods in Freud's life. His financial situation, after worsening further, picked up before Easter thanks to a few more patients. Freud's publisher complained that *The Interpretation of Dreams* was not selling well. According to Jones (J I, 395), it took eight years in all to sell the 600 copies of the book that were printed, 123 going in the first six weeks, and 228 over the next two years. Freud's scientific and professional isolation had never been greater. But he did not despair, for he was certain that with his discoveries he was fifteen to twenty years ahead of his time. He shelved plans for other books. He took things easy, played chess, read novels: 'I vegetate harmlessly' (*F*, March 11, 1900, 404). This, then, was no lasting period of depression of the kind he had suffered on several previous occasions. He started reading, no doubt for the first time, 'Nietzsche, in whom I hope to find words for much that remains mute within me' (*F*, February 1, 1900, 398).

E.'s treatment was marked by similar ups and downs: once again, we find striking parallels between the way Freud was developing and the way E.'s case was going (this was to be so until treatment ended in April 1900). On January 26, Freud reported that neither patient nor analyst was making much headway: 'New ideas came slowly, but there never is total stillness. In the case of E., there is again a delay and a darker region, but the earlier findings still stand' (*F* 397). By March 11, Freud was assailed by doubts, disappointment and fear of failure: 'Prospects seemed most favourable in E.'s case – and that is where I was dealt the heaviest blow. Just when I believed I had the solution in my grasp, it eluded me and I found myself forced to turn everything around and put it together anew. [. . .] I could not stand the depression that followed. [. . .] When I am not cheerful and collected, every single one of my patients is my tormentor' (*F* 403–4).

It comes as no surprise to find the same ups and downs in Freud's relationship with Fliess. Freud's suggestion that his friend might help him with his next five books as he had done with *The Interpretation of Dreams* was met by a stony silence. Fliess, on the other hand, had hoped that Freud would in turn help him to finish his book on the causal relationship between the nose and the sexual organs and to write up his other discoveries (bisexuality, the periodicity theory). He began to write less frequently. Freud complained of this (*F*, March 11, 1900, 402), and reacted by trying to re-inject some warmth into their relationship. The same letter of March 11 contains a remarkable description of his mental state since the previous summer, and ends with an explanation of how he pulled out of the depression into which he had been plunged by the apparent failure of E.'s treatment: 'I found a way out by renouncing all conscious mental activity so as to grope blindly among my riddles. Since then I am working perhaps more skilfully than ever before, but I do not really know what I am doing. [. . .] In my spare time I take care not to reflect on it. I give myself over to my phantasies' (*F* 404). This passage reveals one of the side-effects of his self-analysis – greater flexibility in his working methods. After being trained by Brücke to use experimental methods based on a clinical, rational approach and on positivist rigour, Freud learned how to liberate his creative imagination. The study of dreams and memory revealed to him that man knows more than he thinks he knows. Increasingly, the practice of psychoanalysis was becoming for him the art of letting his own unconscious listen to the patient's unconscious.

Fliess responded to Freud's new, more confiding tone with a friendly gesture: he suggested they meet at Easter. Freud turned down the idea, and bluntly told him why: 'In fact it is more likely that I shall avoid you' (*F*, March 23, 1900, 405). He attempted to explain the 'accumulation of imponderables' which were weighing heavily on him. He had believed that the dream book would bring him the independence and happiness he so desired. 'I have had to demolish all my castles in the air, and I am just now mustering enough courage to start rebuilding them again. During the catastrophic collapse you would have been invaluable to me; in the present stage I would scarcely be able to make myself intelligible to you. I conquered my depression with the aid of a special diet of intellectual matters and now, thanks to the distraction, it is slowly healing. If I were with you I could not avoid trying to grasp everything consciously and describe it all to you; we would talk reason and science; your beautiful and positive biological discoveries would arouse my innermost (impersonal!) envy. The upshot would be that I would go on complaining to you for five days and return all upset and dissatisfied to my summer, for which I shall probably need all my composure. No one can help me in the least with what oppresses me; it is my cross, I must bear it; and God knows that in adapting to it, my back has become noticeably bent' (*F* 405–6). This letter marks the beginning of the process whereby Freud eliminated his 'transference'. His deeply emotional friendship for Fliess had helped him to develop internally; now he wanted to be left to his own devices. He told Fliess he was going to go on another trip to Italy with Alexander – just as he had done in 1898 after their disagreement over bilaterality. Freud had taken a first step towards intellectual independence by breaking first with

Meynert, then with Breuer. His self-analysis had made him psychologically independent of the father figure. He now saw that he needed to detach himself from the last symbol of his infantile and neurotic dependence, Fliess the revenant.

Twelve days later, on April 4, 1900, he was able to break the great news to Fliess: 'E. will terminate treatment at Easter, having benefited enormously, I hope' (*F* 408). He sent confirmation on April 16: 'E. at last concluded his career as a patient by coming to dinner at my house. His riddle is *almost* completely solved; he is in excellent shape, his personality entirely changed. At present a remnant of the symptoms is left. [. . .] The asymptotic conclusion of the treatment basically makes no difference to me, but is yet one more disappointment to outsiders. [. . .] Since he had to suffer through all my technical and theoretical errors, I actually think that a future case could be solved in half the time' (*F*, April 16, 1900, 409). At the same time, Freud began better to understand the phenomenon of transference: this was what had caused 'the apparent endlessness' of E.'s now completed treatment – if the cap fits, wear it (*ibid.*); he also had his first inkling of the homosexual basis of his attachment to Fliess: 'But no one can replace for me the relationship with the friend which a special – possibly feminine – side demands' (*F*, May 7, 1900, 412).

Freud was unquestionably perturbed about the relative failure of *The Interpretation of Dreams*. He had long dreamt of making a great invention that would bring him fame, affluence, and security for himself and his family. It seemed to him that he had once again missed the mark. It was not that he rejected his latest discoveries as worthless; he simply doubted that they would be recognised for what they were in his lifetime. 'Yes, I really am 44 now, an old, somewhat shabby Jew, as you will see for yourself in the summer or autumn. My family nevertheless wanted to celebrate the day. My own best consolation is that I have not deprived them of all future achievements' (*F* 412). Now Freud did not want Fliess to see him in that condition. So he turned down the proposed Easter meeting, and took steps to avoid one at Whitsun: 'I was afraid that you too might come to Vienna at Whitsun, because my eldest brother from Manchester wrote that he will visit us during this time' (*F*, May 20, 1900, 415).[1] Freud did not want to see Fliess again until the summer holidays, when, he said, he would be quite willing to go to Berlin to meet him. Yet he left Fliess out of his plans for a trip to Italy in the summer.

All these complications over the date and place of their next rendezvous

1. Van den Heide (1952) postulates that the visit to Vienna by Emanuel and John triggered off the elimination of Freud's transference on to Fliess. I would argue rather that it helped to speed it up.

could only have meant that Freud wanted to give it a new significance. Gone was the mythical 'congress' in Rome: 'If I closed with "Next Easter in Rome", I would feel like a pious Jew' (*F*, April 16, 1900, 409) – an allusion to the ritual of orthodox Jews, who say to each other 'next year in Jerusalem!' at the end of the Passover service. In my view, Freud now wanted to see Fliess again solely as an esteemed colleague with whom he could profitably exchange ideas. He no longer wanted him to be an object of passion, his only audience; he no longer wanted him as a transferential figure. Edith Buxbaum (1951) believes that Freud's personal problem was that he sought to establish priority, even when he was wrong, over his rivals – his brother Julius, his nephew John, his father Jacob; had he not done so, he would have had to admit himself to be the weaker and to accept the female role with respect to them. This problem, she argues, cropped up again with Fliess and would recur later on with others: the moment Freud recognised any feminine tendency in himself, he broke off his friendships, though always with some rationalisation as a pretext; in this sense, then, his self-analysis failed, for of course his transference on to Fliess could not be resolved in the absence of a true psychoanalyst.

I would suggest a different interpretation of Freud's letters to Fliess during this period: he was making a remarkable effort to avoid estrangement and to size up the situation lucidly. He believed that the only way he could get Fliess to accept the transformation of his (Freud's) friendship without spoiling his own (Fliess's) was to tell the truth – something which, precisely, he felt he had to do at all costs with his patients. So he simply explained how he was feeling at the time, and why, for the moment, he did not want to see him; he told him that he had become aware of a feminine need for friendship. In other words, he shook off his 'transference'. At the same time, Freud solicited letters, news, and future 'congresses'; he showed as much interest as he could in Fliess's work, gave him bibliographical information, and paid him measured compliments: in other words, he behaved as any ordinary friend would do. It seems to me that Freud was trying to save his friend from perdition, to protect Fliess the human being against the repercussions of the metamorphosis undergone by the phantasy figure he had represented for Freud during his self-analysis.

Although Freud's later life does not fall within the province of the present work, I would tend to think that the cause of his quarrels with Adler, Jung and others should be sought less in his own neurosis than in that of his ex-colleagues: it was the dissidents who quite clearly acted towards Freud as an object of 'transference'. Lastly, after his self-analysis, Freud's feminine side no longer sought male attachments, but was drawn to intellectually brilliant women with some masculine personality traits. Jones (J II, 469) draws up a list of them in chronological order: Minna Bernays, Emma Eckstein, Loe Kann, Lou Andreas-Salomé, Joan Rivière and Marie Bonaparte. The most likely hypothesis is that the break with Fliess was offset by the crystallisation of his affection for Martha's sister Minna, who lived with the Freuds and was at that time the only person in the family with the ability to follow Sigmund's work closely: available, intelligent, capable of deep empathy with her brother-in-law, responding internally to his secret incestuous desire, shielded from having to respond physically by her moral uprightness and attachment to her dead fiancé, and constantly present in the household, Minna gradually came to provide Sigmund with greater creative stimulation than Fliess – a fact which must certainly have helped Freud to withdraw from Fliess. Fifteen years later, in the autumn of 1913, after spending 'seventeen delicious days' in Rome with Minna (Freud was then 57), he wrote 'On Narcissism: An Introduction' (1914*c*; J II, 116 and 340–41) with the same feverish haste and enthusiasm with which he had written 'Project for a Scientific Psychology' in the autumn of 1895 and Chapter 7 of *The Interpretation of Dreams* in the summer of 1899; the subsequent *Beyond the Pleasure Principle* (1920*g*) was written by Freud in a similar state of elation. But no sooner had he finished with its 'difficult labour' (letter to Abraham, March 18, 1914; see J II, 340) than he found that this incestuous child bore 'all the marks of a corresponding deformation'.

On the first stage of his journey to Italy after spending July 1900 with his family at Bellevue, Freud finally saw Fliess at Achensee, near Innsbruck, at the beginning of August. Their 'congress' was a disaster. It is hard to establish exactly what happened, but we do know that it was to be their last meeting because of a parapraxis made by Freud. There are two versions of events. Freud's is to be found in *The Psychopathology of Everyday Life*: 'One day in the summer of 1900 I remarked to a friend with whom I used at that time to have a lively exchange of scientific ideas: "These problems of the neuroses are only to be solved if we base ourselves wholly and completely on the assumption of the original bisexuality of the individual." To which he replied: "That's what I told you two and a half years ago at Br. [Breslau] when we went for that evening walk. But you wouldn't hear of it then." It is painful to be requested in this way to surrender one's originality. I could not recall any such conversation or this pronouncement of my friend's. One of us must have been mistaken and on the "*cui prodest?*" [who benefits?] principle it must have been myself. Indeed, in the course of the next week I remembered the whole incident, which was just as my friend had tried to recall it to me; I even recollected the answer I had given him at the time: "I've not accepted that yet; I'm not inclined to go into the question"' (*PEL* 143–4).

Fliess gave his version of their meeting six years later when they had a public row: 'On that occasion [the summer of 1900] Freud showed a violence towards me which was at first unintelligible to me. The reason was that in a discussion of Freud's observations of his patients I claimed that periodic processes were unquestionably at work in the psyche, as elsewhere; and maintained in particular that they had an effect on those psychopathic phenomena on the analysis of which Freud was engaged for therapeutic purposes. Hence neither sudden deteriorations nor sudden improvements were to be attributed to the analysis and its influence alone. I supported my view with my own observations. During the rest of the discussion I thought I detected a personal animosity against me on Freud's part which sprang from envy. Freud had earlier said to me in Vienna: "It's just as well that we're friends. Otherwise I should burst with envy if I heard that anyone was making such discoveries in Berlin!"' (quoted in *The Origins of Psycho-Analysis* (1950*a*), July 10, 1900, 324 n.1).

The notion of a fundamental biological bisexuality was Fliess's own. It is more difficult to say whether its application to the psychology of neuroses and to general psychology was Freud's idea alone, or whether it was also suggested to him by Fliess. When, after the completion of *The Interpretation of Dreams*, Freud came to lay the foundations of what was to become *Three Essays on the Theory of Sexuality* (1905*d*), he was finally convinced of the notion of bisexuality (whose origins he had forgotten, but which, as we have seen, continued to feature in several of his dreams). He believed, however, that he had made the discovery himself – yet another example of Freud's frequent cryptomnesia.

Freud thought he could wipe the slate clean by admitting his mistake. But for Fliess their friendship was well and truly over: he decided never again to discuss his scientific findings with such an untrustworthy person as Freud and to restrict his correspondence with him to pure formalities. Freud immediately left with Martha and Minna for their planned trip to Carinthia, northern Italy (Stelvio, Adige) and Venice. But, as compensation for his disappointment at Achensee, he extended his holiday, first with Minna, to Trento, Lake Garda, Stresa, and Merano, where she remained for treatment of her tuberculosis, and then alone to Milan and Genoa. When he returned to Vienna in mid-September, he felt in excellent form to get back to work. He finished gathering material for *The Psychopathology of Everyday Life*, including the following significant act of forgetfulness: he kept on forgetting to buy the blotting-paper (*Löschpapier*) he needed, until he recalled that, while he normally *wrote Löschpapier*, in conversation he used another word for blotting-paper, *Fliesspapier* (*PEL* 159).

PREPARATION OF A SECOND BOOK ON DREAMS: *ÜBER DEN TRAUM* (*ON DREAMS*)

In October 1900 Freud broke off writing *The Psychopathology of Everyday Life* to work on something more urgent; he returned to it full-time at the end of January 1901 and, as I have said, completed it the following month. The more urgent task was a paper on dreams which he had promised Löwenfeld for a collective work on the frontier problems of psychology and neurology. Throughout the spring, he had been putting off writing his contribution because he did not feel like working. But later, when he forgot to send back the proofs of his paper, he realised there had been another reason for his slackness: he was afraid that the interests of the publisher of *The Interpretation of Dreams* would be harmed by his writing a more approachable summary of the book and getting it published by someone else (*PEL* 159–61). This parapraxis reminded him that Charcot had been displeased with him for adding notes to the German translation of his book (1892–1894), and that another publisher had raised difficulties when Freud wanted to reproduce, in his contribution to Nothnagel's *Specielle Pathologie und Therapie* (1897*a*), a few unaltered passages from his earlier monograph on cerebral paralyses in children (1893*b*). Freud's mind was obviously very keenly exercised by the problem of being tempted, or fearing, to trespass on someone else's intellectual property. In the present case, as soon as he understood the reason for his misgivings, he put them to the test by discussing the problem with Deuticke, the publisher of *The Interpretation of Dreams*, who eventually authorised Freud to publish his second work on dreams.

Freud first mentioned his promise to write *On Dreams* in a letter to Fliess of April 4, 1900, in answer to his friend's suggestion that he should produce an abridged version of *The Interpretation of Dreams*. On May 20, he told Fliess that he had found it impossible to get down to writing the pamphlet for Löwenfeld, and on July 10 that he had postponed it till October. It was probably during this incubation period, between April and October 1900, that Freud jotted down, for the record, three new dreams which he later added to Chapter 4 of *On Dreams* as examples of condensation.

DREAM OF THE '*TROTTOIR ROULANT*' (SPRING–SUMMER 1900)

'Thus, I dreamt on one occasion that I was sitting on a bench with one of my former University teachers, and that the bench, which was surrounded by other benches, was moving forward at a rapid pace. This was a combination of a lecture theatre and a *trottoir roulant*. I will not pursue this train of ideas further' (*OD* 651–2).

The *trottoir roulant* concerned was the celebrated moving roadway, or travelator, installed at the Paris Exposition Universelle of 1900 – which confirms that Freud had the dream that year. Freud offers no interpretation. The one that immediately springs to mind concerns his ambition (to be 'moving forward'), and his wish to be appointed professor.

DREAM OF THE 'GLASS TOP-HAT' (SPRING–SUMMER 1900)

This dream follows straight on from the '*Trottoir roulant*' dream in *On Dreams*:

'Another time I was sitting in a railway carriage and holding on my lap an object in the shape of a top-hat ['*Zylinderhut*', literally 'cylinder-hat'], which however was made of transparent glass. The situation made me think at once of the proverb: '*Mit dem Hute in der Hand kommt man durchs ganze Land*' ['If you go hat in hand, you can cross the whole land']. The glass cylinder led me by a short *détour* to think of an incandescent gas-mantle; and I soon saw that I should like to make a discovery which would make me as rich and independent as my fellow-countryman Dr Auer von Welsbach was made by his, and that I should like to travel instead of stopping in Vienna. In the dream I was travelling with my discovery, the hat in the shape of a glass cylinder – a discovery which, it is true, was not as yet of any great practical use' (*OD* 652).

This dream also expresses Freud's ambition, but in a different form: he wants to make a great discovery. The glass top-hat, 'not as yet of any great practical use', stands for the first book on dreams and the discovery of an interpretative method that makes them transparent – a book that is hardly selling at all, and a discovery that has not yet been recognised.

This dream probably dates from the spring of 1900: from May 1 on, Freud's financial situation worsened, and he feared that he could no more afford to travel during the summer than he could the previous summer. As we have seen, it turned out that he was able after all to visit Italy again from mid-August to mid-September 1900.

THE 'SWIMMING-POOL' DREAM (SUMMER 1900?)

'For instance, I once had a dream of a sort of swimming-pool, in which the bathers were scattering in all directions; at one point on the edge of the pool someone was standing and bending towards one of the people bathing, as though to help her out of the water. The situation was put together from the memory of an experience I had had at puberty and from two paintings, one of which I had seen shortly before the dream. One was a picture from

Schwind's series illustrating the legend of Mélusine, which showed the water-nymphs surprised in their pool (cf. the scattering bathers in the dream); the other was a picture of the Deluge by an Italian Master; while the little experience remembered from my puberty was of having seen my instructor at a swimming-pool helping a lady out of the water who had stopped in until after the time set aside for men bathers' (*OD* 648–9).

I would suggest that Freud had this dream at the end of August or beginning of September 1900, on the assumption that the second picture referred to had been seen by him during his trip to Italy at that date. The theme of the dream is the boy's curiosity about female nakedness and the dangers inherent in such curiosity.

THE DREAM OF 'COMPANY AT TABLE D'HÔTE' AND THE BEGINNING OF THE DORA CASE (OCTOBER 1900)

In early October, Freud at last took the plunge and began writing *Über den Traum* (*On Dreams*) (1901*a*). He informed Fliess of this on October 14, 1900. Also in early October, Freud began the treatment, which was to last three months, of a young hysteric, whom he later called Dora when writing up the case. Freud believed that she broke off her treatment prematurely because he had failed 'to look out in time for the transference'. The dream of 'Company at table d'hôte' – the parallel is to my mind obvious, though as far as I know it has never been drawn before – expressed, as its second motif, Freud's early counter-transference on to Dora, just as the Irma dream had expressed his counter-transference on to Irma. Later on we shall see the influence of another day's residue, which has been equally overlooked by commentators: the marriage of one of Breuer's daughters to a friend of Fliess's, and the serious illness of Fliess's mother-in-law, who was being given treatment by Breuer of which Freud disapproved.

The dream also uses a more immediate day's residue, which Freud does this time specifically mention. As usual, he had spent the Saturday evening with his friend, the oculist Leopold Königstein (who was about to be nominated for a professorship), and, no doubt, their usual tarot partners Oscar Rie and Ludwig Rosenberg (cf. 'Otto' and 'Leopold' in the Irma dream). The copious dinner was no doubt followed by the customary game of tarot. The atmosphere was lively. Freud asked his host for news of a woman patient whom he had sent on to him to have spectacles fitted. One of the guests took a cab and offered to take Freud home in it. During the ride, Freud made some witty remarks about the taximeter: the moment you get into a cab you already owe money because of the pick-up charge; it is like a table d'hôte, where the debt grows fast and one is afraid of getting the worst of the bargain; he then quoted a couple of lines with a double meaning from one of the Harp-player's songs in Goethe's *Wilhelm Meister*. The words are addressed to the Heavenly Powers:

Ihr führt ins Leben uns hinein,
Ihr lasst den Armen schuldig werden.

Freud quoted the lines again at the end of Chapter 7 of *Civilization and its Discontents* (1930*a*). Two of the words in the second line are ambiguous: '*Armen*', like 'poor', can mean either 'wretched' or 'impecunious', and '*schuldig*' can mean either 'guilty' or 'in debt'. So the lines can be translated in two ways:

You lead us into life,
You make the poor creatures guilty
or You make impecunious creatures indebted.

That night Freud had the following dream:

'Company at table or table d'hôte . . . spinach was being eaten . . . Frau E.L. was sitting beside me; she was turning her whole attention to me[1] and laid her hand on my knee in an intimate manner. I removed her hand unresponsively. She then said: "But you've always had such beautiful eyes." . . . I then had an indistinct picture of two eyes, as though it were a drawing or like the outline of a pair of spectacles . . .' (*OD* 636–7).

An initial passage containing Freud's description of the dream and his first associations is to be found in Chapter 2, which deals with the procedure of dream interpretation (*OD* 636–40). He discusses successively:

– the party the evening before, and the taximeter episode, with its references to the table d'hôte, debt, and the two lines from Goethe;
– a disagreement between Sigmund and his wife at a table d'hôte in the Tyrol (cf. p. 517), and a caress she had given him under the table-cloth when they were still secretly courting each other;
– the fact that Frau E.L. is the daughter of a man to whom Freud was once in debt, and that his friends always made him pay dearly for whatever advantages he had got from them;
– a gift from Freud to Königstein of an antique bowl known as an '*occhiale*', round which there were eyes painted;
– the fact that one of Freud's children – the one with the 'beautiful eyes' – hated spinach, and the second meaning of the quotation from Goethe;
– the double contrast between 'selfish' and 'unselfish' and between 'being in debt' and 'without paying for it' which lies behind the construction of the dream;
– his refusal for personal reasons to explain the dream's 'single nodal point'.

1. The German phrase '*wendet sich ganz mir zu*' means literally 'turned completely towards me' and figuratively 'gave me her complete attention'.

Chapter 4, which deals with condensation, returns to this dream on three occasions:
– it provides an example of wish-fulfilment by its opposite: the woman in the dream turns towards Freud, which is not what happened in real life; 'the bitter thought [was] revealed in the analysis that I had never had anything free of cost' (*OD* 648);
– the dream condenses memories of three scenes: a love scene (Martha's hand caressing his knee under the table); a scene of annoyance with his wife (she had paid too much attention to other people at table d'hôte in the Tyrol, in particular to a man Freud did not like), and, concealed behind this last scene, a serious row with Martha – of which no details are given – at the time of their engagement; and lastly, a scene where someone places a hand on his knee, which in turn was the starting-point of two separate sets of memories – whose description he intentionally censors (*OD* 649);
– the dream also provides an example of verbal condensation, here expressed by the double meaning of the German word '*Kosten*', which can mean both 'cost' and 'to taste'. Thus, the idea that Freud has to pay for whatever advantages he gets (whatever he is given will have 'cost' him something) is represented by the spinach, the kind of dish which children do not like, and which their mothers try to make them 'taste' (*OD* 650).

Chapter 5, which deals with displacement, refers twice to the dream:
– the manifest content (a woman makes advances to him) conceals the dreamer's latent wish to enjoy love that costs nothing, to be loved for the sake of his beautiful eyes (*OD* 655);
– the dream displaces on to an insignificant event (the free cab-drive offered by a friend) the significance of an important event: a considerable sum of money he had paid out on behalf of a member of his family of whom he was 'fond', who had accompanied him on several cab-drives, and whose gratitude would not therefore be 'free of cost' (*OD* 656–7).

A final mention of the dream comes in Chapter 8, which deals with repression and the disguise of dreams. Freud detects, behind the wish to experience love that costs nothing, an unconscious regret: 'I regret having made that expenditure'. Why? The answer 'is another and a far-reaching question'. Once again, Freud's voluntary censorship was at work (*OD* 672–3).

This is Freud's last recorded dream.[1] I therefore propose to analyse it in great detail.

1. I.e. the last recorded dream of this period, the period of Freud's work on dreams and of his self-analysis. There are many other dreams inserted into later editions of *The Interpretation of Dreams* dating from later – see pp. 555ff below and, e.g., *ID* 167. [Translator's note]

INTERPRETATION IN RELATION TO FREUD'S WORK

Freud had promised to write an abridged version of *The Interpretation of Dreams* for Löwenfeld. He was reluctant to do so for several reasons: nothing is more tedious than rewriting a book one has just completed; he was completely wrapped up in his next work, *The Psychopathology of Everyday Life*; he was also thinking, in vaguer terms, of a book on neuroses and sexuality (which ended up as *Three Essays on the Theory of Sexuality*); lastly, he feared that the second book on dreams might prejudice the sales of the first, whose commercial failure, now confirmed, greatly depressed him. The dream's double use of the notion of 'expenditure' (of money and effort) neatly summed up Freud's resistance to the task at hand. Moreover, he had few patients, with the result that both his income and his morale were low. He had postponed writing the essay until after the summer holidays. Feeling rested and more energetic, he finally got down to it in early October.

Even so, writing it was a joyless chore which he was carrying out as a duty: you have 'to eat spinach' even if you do not like it. *On Dreams* seemed to him like the kind of cheap, ordinary meal you eat with strangers at table d'hôte, unlike *The Interpretation of Dreams*, which might be compared to a carefully chosen menu, served à la carte and at separate tables. He had written a brief introductory chapter on the various theories of dreams (philosophical, medical, popular), and was looking for an example to illustrate his next chapter on procedure, just as in *The Interpretation of Dreams*, after a historical and bibliographical first chapter, he had devoted the subsequent chapter to the Irma dream. The following Saturday night, his expectations were faithfully answered by the dream of 'Company at table d'hôte', whose content he noted down and analysed the very next day, remarking that his most recent dream, the one he had had 'last night', would serve his purposes very well.

Similarly, the Irma dream, which occurred during the night of July 23–24, 1895, had already faithfully answered his expectations. What were they? By 1895, Freud, who had got all he could out of his collaboration with Breuer, was impatient to stand on his own two feet and to embark on the exploration of infantile sexuality – something which Breuer found repugnant. He was keen to leave for his holidays so he could verify from his own experience that, in both normal people and neurotics, dreams are wish-fulfilments. That was confirmed to him by the Irma dream.

In 1900, Freud's expectations mirrored to some extent those of 1895. He had got all he could out of his collaboration with Fliess and was keen to continue his elaboration of psychoanalytic theory without his friend, who in any case had not really understood *The Interpretation of Dreams*. In both cases, dreams provided evidence that the internal process of detaching himself from a close colleague had begun. By 1900, Freud's psychoanalytic technique had improved, but the results of his treatment remained unpredictable and gave him the same guilt feelings he had experienced five years earlier: accordingly, both the Irma dream and the dream of 'Company at table d'hôte' fulfilled the wish to exonerate himself.

Freud's associations to the second dream contain not only the same message, but also, to a great extent, the same structure and cast of characters as the first dream. In both cases, the characters include Freud's colleagues, Fliess, Breuer, Otto (Oscar Rie) and Leopold (Ludwig Rosenberg), as well as Martha his wife and, in Irma's place, the young Dora. In the second dream, however, two new characters play leading roles, the oculist Leopold Königstein, a friend he could count on, unlike so many disappointing teachers and friends, and Frau E.L., who, as we shall see, represents Minna Bernays, the sister-in-law to whom Sigmund was very attached, a woman who could be confided in and relied on.

As far as structure is concerned, the two dreams show the same sequence of tableaux:

– First of all, there is a representation of the preconscious thronged with latent thoughts: 'A large hall – numerous guests, whom we were receiving.'

– 'Company at table or table d'hôte.'

– Then a seduction scene where Freud is either the seducer or the seduced: he takes Irma 'on one side' and carries out a laryngeal-cum-gynaecological examination of her. – 'Frau E.L. was sitting beside me; she was turning her whole attention to me and laid her hand on my knee in an intimate manner.'

– After the wish, the defence: 'She showed signs of recalcitrance.' – 'I removed her hand unresponsively.'

– Between the wish and the defence, a compromise: seeing is allowed, touching is forbidden. 'I saw [. . .] some remarkable curly structures which were evidently modelled on the turbinal bones of the nose': an allusion to Fliess's speciality. – ' "But you've always had such beautiful eyes" ': an allusion to Königstein's speciality.

– The next scene in the first dream (where colleagues examine Irma and discuss the diagnosis) has no equivalent in the second; by then, Freud felt independent of them.

– Lastly, the explanation: 'Trimethylamin (and I saw before me the formula for this printed in heavy type).' – 'I then had an indistinct picture of two eyes, as though it were a drawing or like the outline of a pair of spectacles.' The explanation is ternary in the first case (anticipating the three systems of the psychical apparatus), and binary in the second (alluding to bisexuality). In both cases there is the idea that dreams are transcriptions, and that Freud knows how to read the formula or decipher the picture puzzle.

But that is as far as the similarities go. In 1895, Freud was setting out on an adventure which, he hoped, would lead to his discovering the meaning and processes of dreams. By 1900, his adventure was over, and his discovery made; he could do no more than recapitulate them, before setting out in search of other fields of enquiry. The dream of 'Company at table d'hôte' in itself has nothing original about it; it is a copy, designed for popular consumption, of the first specimen dream that was the starting point of Freud's creative impetus. This explains the emphasis, at the end of the second dream, on the notion of a 'copy': the 'beautiful eyes' – real, living, loved, clear-sighted – are replaced by 'a drawing', which itself gives way to 'a pair of spectacles'; even then, the spectacles are not real, for the dream ends with the words 'like the outline of a pair of spectacles'.

Freud's analysis of the 'Company at table d'hôte' dream, on the other hand, is peppered with references to parapraxes, mistakes, and acts of forgetting, none of which are to be found in his associations to the Irma dream, and which underline his new interest in the faulty functioning of normal mental processes.

After the commercial failure of *The Interpretation of Dreams*, after his disappointing meeting with Fliess in the summer, after waiting all spring for patients, Freud now gained new confidence in his own pioneering abilities: I have already made one discovery (represented by its metonymical substitute, the Irma dream); there is no reason why I should not make another (along the same lines, and represented by its metaphorical substitute, the dream of 'Company at table d'hôte').

INTERPRETATION IN RELATION TO INSTINCTUAL CATHEXES ON MEMBERS OF HIS CIRCLE

Freud had several reasons to feel bitter towards Fliess. It was Fliess who had suggested (*F*, April 4, 1900) that he write an abridged version of *The Interpretation of Dreams*; his failure to recognise the originality of the book had finally been revealed; his request for help in preparing his own book on the relationship between the nose and the sexual organs irritated Freud all the more because he was becoming increasingly aware of the dubiousness of his friend's theories. That bitterness can be sensed in Freud's letters during the spring of 1900, in which he puts off several plans for 'congresses' with Fliess (whereas before he could not get enough of them), and asks to be allowed to continue on his way alone. The dream of 'Company at table d'hôte' puts that bitterness on a more general plane by alluding to his friends' ungrateful and selfish behaviour.

Meanwhile, Freud's attitude towards Fliess's periodicity theory had become openly ironical. In his letters he embarked on calculations that made a mockery of it: he complained, for example, that Fliess had not written to him for a fortnight: 'December 24 to January 7 = 14 = 28/2' (*F*, January 8, 1900, 395). The news that Breuer's daughter planned to marry a Dr Schiff, who was very close to Fliess and Fliess's wife's family, irritated Freud: he predicted – correctly, as it turned out – that Breuer and his future son-in-law would become unquestioning supporters of the periodicity theory; in his letter of March 11, 1900, Freud denounced the impending 'Breuerisation' of his friend (*F* 402). The dream's concluding doublet – spectacles becoming a drawing of spectacles, then simply an outline of spectacles – could be an image for the new tandem of Fliess and Breuer and for Freud's increased sense of detachment from them.

But although Freud rejected Fliess's more debatable theories, he did appropriate the only interesting idea contributed by his friend (even to the point of forgetting that he had borrowed it from him): the idea of bisexuality. When they finally met at Achensee at the beginning of August, the misunderstanding came out into the open; it subsequently took on ever greater proportions and eventually caused their final break in 1905. I would suggest that bisexuality is represented in the dream by the uncertainty between 'table' and 'table d'hôte'. The 'table' is the one on which Sigmund Freud, Leopold Königstein, Oscar Rie and Ludwig Rosenberg had had dinner and played their traditional Saturday game of tarot the previous evening; this 'table' is, then, a metonymical substitute for the satisfaction of homosexual tendencies, whereas the 'table d'hôte' in the dream, with its colliding hands, knees and glances, is associated with heterosexual seduction.

In the dream, too, the drawing of two eyes recalls a dream of early 1898, 'My son, the Myops' (*Auf Geseres-auf Ungeseres*), in which Freud criticised one of Fliess's scientific ideas for the first time, accusing him of spoiling the interesting idea of bisexuality by attempting to base it on the bilaterality of the body.

The presence of spectacles is probably due to another overdetermination connected with Fliess. Ten months after the dream, Fliess made a cutting remark about the talent Freud thought he had acquired for the scientific interpretation of dreams and parapraxes. The remark says much about

Fliess's understanding of Freud's discovery: 'The reader of thoughts merely reads his own thoughts into other people.' Freud replied on August 7, 1901 (cf. pp. 551–2 for the complete quotation): 'In this you too have come to the limit of your perspicacity.' We may suppose that by October 1900 ideas about 'second sight' had already been unconsciously exchanged by the two men, and that it was only in August 1901 that they actually started using them for the purposes of mutual recrimination. The last sentence of the 'Company at table d'hôte' dream refers to the dreamer having 'a picture' of something. Freud is here making a clear assertion of his perceptiveness in comparison with Fliess's pseudo-scientific bilaterality theory (the *two* eyes) and in answer to his perfidious criticism (the outline of a pair of spectacles). But, according to the now familiar mechanism of reversal, 'clear' is disguised as its opposite, 'indistinct'. The answer to the objection is therefore: 'Of us two, *I* am the clear-sighted one.' The insight underlying the denouement of this dream might be formulated as follows: the psychoanalyst works neither with the two eyes that everyone has, nor with the spectacles of his theory, but with a third eye.

Let us now turn to Breuer. His daughter's marriage brought him closer to Fliess, with whom he already had connections because he had treated his wife, Ida. Who is the Frau E.L. of the 'Company at table d'hôte' dream? Freud says she is the daughter of someone who had once lent him money and whom he had not seen for some time. Seeing that Freud had received considerable financial support from Breuer and had broken off relations with him and, no doubt, his family in about 1896, I would put forward the supposition that Frau E.L. is one of his daughters, perhaps even the one who married a Hammerschlag son. Samuel Hammerschlag, who had taught Freud Hebrew, lived in the same block of flats as Breuer; I earlier suggested that his daughter Anna, Rudolf Lichtheim's widow, was the Irma of the Irma dream. What could have constituted a more powerful Oedipal revenge on Breuer than for Freud to dream that his former protector's daughter had tried to seduce him? The fact that another Breuer daughter, born during the treatment of Anna O. in 1882, was called Dora only serves to reinforce my hypothesis: Dora Breuer would have been 18 in 1900, i.e. the same age as the patient whom Freud was beginning to treat and to whom he gave the pseudonym Dora. It was probably Dora Breuer who had just got engaged to Fliess's friend, Dr Schiff.[1] Always supposing Frau E.L. is Breuer's daughter-in-law, she replaces her young sister-in-law Dora in the dream and establishes a link between Freud's new patient and

1. According to Hirschmüller (1978), it was Margarethe (Gretel) Breuer (b. 1872) who married Arthur Schiff, on May 27, 1900. See also *F* 404 n.2, 377, 381. [Translator's note]

his former patient, Irma, who, always supposing she is Anna Hammerschlag-Lichtheim, is another sister-in-law of Frau E.L.

On May 20, 1900, Freud told Fliess that he would love to break altogether with Breuer, but was unable to because of an old money debt. The debt amounted to the considerable sum of 2,300 florins (the figure estimated by Freud in his letter to Fliess of January 16, 1898, *F* 294). He tried in 1898 to repay part of his debt in instalments, but Breuer, who had probably regarded his 'loans' as gifts, refused to hear of such a thing and suggested to Freud, who always held it against him later, that he regarded the sum as payment for treatment which Freud was then giving to a member of Breuer's family, Fräulein N.N. The impossibility of settling his debt with Breuer (the debt was moral as well as financial, as Breuer had, up to 1895, supported him with advice, friendship, encouragement, and help in various delicate family matters) filled Freud with guilt feelings that were all the greater because he had lost such an invaluable friend for purely scientific reasons. This is expressed in the dream image of someone laying a hand on his knee in an intimate manner and his removing it unresponsively.

This also explains the charge of ingratitude which Freud, in his analysis of the dream, levels at his friends – apparently the projection of his own uncomfortable feeling of ingratitude towards some of them, like Breuer and Fliess, who long helped him and with whom he parted company successively. One of the meanings of the 'Company at table d'hôte' dream concerns the wish, already noted in the Irma dream, to exonerate himself vis-à-vis his professional colleagues: no, despite appearances, I am not guilty of ingratitude towards them; truth must prevail over sentiments, whether they be the confused sentiments of young, attractive and attracted women, or noble sentiments towards reliable friends; neither a financial debt nor a loyal friendship will be allowed, whatever the internal cost to me, to take precedence over candour or the achievement of scientific progress.

The metaphorical expression of that idea is to be found in the 'spinach' of the dream. Children in general do not like spinach (the young Freud and his own children were no exception to this rule), and they eat it only because they are forced to and want to please their mother. Anyone who makes a discovery has to break away from the norm, from the acceptance of *idées reçues*, has to stop saying that spinach is nice when he does not like it, has to be prepared to hurt people of whom he is fond and who are fond of him. Anyone who asserts his independence of thought faces the risk of losing the love of those whom he tells: I do not want to go on doing things for the sake of 'your beautiful eyes'. Paraphrasing Freud's play on the word *kosten*, we might have him saying: whatever tastes bad [*mauvais goût*], costs [*mauvais coût*].

But the dream of 'Company at table d'hôte' aims at more than a mere professional exoneration. It takes revenge – both professionally and Oedipally – on the two colleagues and friends who have become hostile rivals. In the dream, Breuer's daughter-in-law (whom Freud may still see occasionally in real life) makes advances to him: what a revenge on Breuer! But the dream also reflects an actual revenge which Freud took on both Breuer and Fliess, and which was revealed by Schur. Ida Fliess's mother was seriously ill and receiving treatment from Breuer. Freud did not agree with his treatment. The patient's state proved Freud right, as he learnt from Ida Fliess, who always got on very well with him and often visited him when she came to see her mother in Vienna: the scene in the dream where Frau E.L. makes advances to Freud was directly instigated by her visits (cf. letters to Fliess of October 23 and November 25, 1900, and January 1, 1901, in which Freud refers to the illnesses of Fliess's mother and mother-in-law). It should be noted, too, that Oscar Rie (Otto), who married Ida Fliess's sister, also disagreed with Breuer about the treatment he was giving his mother-in-law: Freud and Rie must certainly have discussed this problem when they met to play tarot on the evening before the dream. Schur believes that the illnesses of Fliess's mother and mother-in-law kept Freud's correspondence with him going during the first half of 1901, and quotes strong evidence in support of this (S 215–17).

Let us now turn to the connection between Frau E.L. and Freud's wife and sister-in-law. In his analysis of the dream, Freud says that Frau E.L. represents his wife Martha. During a trip to Austria and Italy the previous summer, possibly at the La Mendola pass, where they met an old medical friend who had emigrated to New York, Lustgarten, and other Viennese friends (*F*, September 14, 1900, 423), Martha, 'who had heard no more than his distinguished name, revealed too plainly that she was listening to his conversation with his neighbours, for from time to time she turned to me with questions that took up the thread of their discussion. I became impatient and finally irritated' (*PEL* 136).

This incident with Martha reminded Freud of a 'far more important scene from the time of our engagement, which estranged us for a whole day' (*OD* 649). If one refers to Sigmund's published letters to Martha and to additional fragments revealed by Jones, it emerges that they were on the brink of calling their marriage off on two occasions. They were engaged on June 17, 1882; by July, Freud was already demanding that she stop seeing someone for whom she felt great affection, Fritz Wahle, who, although engaged to her cousin Elise, was in fact in love with Martha. She resigned herself, with great reluctance, to the fact that an old and rewarding friendship had been brought to an end; and for several years after that Freud referred jealously to the spectre of his rival, Fritz. One sentence in the dream fulfils the deeper wish that she should '[turn] her whole attention to me.'

The second incident that nearly put an end to their relationship, in June 1886, three months before their wedding, had to do not with jealousy but with financial matters. Freud was poor: he scraped a living from a few lessons, the occasional consultation, and loans (or gifts) from Breuer, Hammerschlag (himself no rich man), Schwab (Hammerschlag's wealthy brother-in-law), other friends, and distant relations. In addition, as his father's business was doing badly, he had had to contribute to the cost of educating his youngest sisters and little brother, Alexander. Martha, whose father had died several years before, had no money: so Freud married her 'for the sake of her beautiful eyes'. As we have seen, the theme 'If I had followed my father's advice and married a wealthy woman' recurs several times in Freud's self-analysis and was explained by his analysis of the screen memory at the beginning of 1899. Martha's modest dowry would have made a vital contribution to their financially somewhat hazardous plans for marriage. But she had given half the amount to her brother Eli, who had gone into business and just married Anna, the eldest of Sigmund's sisters. Eli had invested the money and was unable to return it as soon as he was asked to by Freud, who, knowing nothing of the business world, wrongly suspected that Eli had used the money for himself. He threatened to break off his engagement to Martha because she had not wanted to put too much pressure on her brother, and demanded that Eli reimburse the amount. This he did. But relations between the two couples remained cool long after the incident. The quarrel was certainly exacerbated by the animosity that Sigmund had felt towards his first sister, Anna, ever since she was born, and by the jealousy aroused in him by Martha's attachment to her brother. They were slowly but surely reconciled. The dream of the 'Castle by the sea' echoed Freud's fears, during the Spanish-American War, for Eli and Anna Bernays, who lived in New York.

The central idea of the 'Company at table d'hôte' dream – that love is a costly business – applies to both incidents during the period of Freud's engagement, but in two different ways that reflect the ambiguity of the German verb 'to cost', as Freud emphasises in his associations. In the incident involving Fritz, the cost of love is an emotional risk – the risk of losing that love. In the incident involving Eli, the cost of love is debt, financial insecurity, and ill-treatment at the hands of businessmen.

But does Frau E.L. stand only for Martha? Freud's insistence on mentioning only his wife in his analysis must be regarded as suspect. But he gives us an obvious clue by referring to a member of his family whom he had accompanied not long before on several cab-drives and on whose behalf he had paid out a considerable amount of money. This is obviously Minna Bernays. In August 1900, after meeting Fliess near Innsbruck, Freud joined Martha and Minna and they together toured the Alps. Martha, who was easily tired, then returned home. Freud and Minna continued their travels, ending up in Merano, where Minna was to be treated for tuberculosis (which turned out not to be serious). As we have already seen, Minna had been living in the Freud household since October 1896 because she had been unwilling to start a new life and wished to alleviate Martha's task of bringing up six children. She had no private income and was entirely supported by Freud. On the occasion when Freud mistakenly drew out 438 kronen instead of 380 from his Post Office Savings Bank account with the intention of sending 300 kronen to 'an absent relative for purposes of medical treatment' (*PEL* 119), the recipient was probably Minna. Freud immediately spotted the meaning of his parapraxis, which was fear of ruining himself with such expenditure. When seen in the context of the 'Company at table d'hôte' dream, the meaning can be narrowed down to a fear of ruining himself for the sake of her beautiful eyes.

Minna was four years Martha's junior. She had not been worn out, like her sister, by household tasks and repeated pregnancies. She was more vivacious, wittier, and more intellectual. According to Jones (J I, 168), 'as a girl she had gone about her housework with a duster in one hand and a book in the other'. Sigmund found it easier to discuss his work with her than with his wife, easier to ask her to accompany him on his mountain excursions. Lastly, as she was unmarried and unattached, she must have been for Freud an available, desirable and prohibited libidinal object. Jones (*ibid.*) denies that there was any 'sexual attraction on either side' and denounces the 'malicious and entirely untrue legend that she displaced his wife in his affections.' Besides, if Frau E.L. is Breuer's daughter-in-law, she appears in the dream, as we have seen, in place of her young sister-in-law, Dora Breuer, who had just got engaged to Dr Schiff: the fact that a woman is replaced by her sister-in-law would then have to be interpreted as being indicative of a problematic situation in Freud's family.

Nevertheless, Freud never once mentions Minna in his associations despite the fact that she is manifestly involved in several of his dreams and that all other members of his family and close friends feature sooner or later in his analyses of dreams. Minna, then, is censored. That censorship materialises the incest taboo which must have operated between them throughout their lives: Jones is surely right on this point, and to suspect otherwise is to overlook Freud's upright, loyal and somewhat prim nature and the strict morals of the Jewish milieu in which he lived. But that did not stop him being aware of the sexual instinctual basis of his friendship and profound empathy with his sister-in-law, while at the same time remaining determined to keep the consequences of that awareness strictly to himself. Such sublimations suited Freud and his period perfectly, as he wrote much later in *Civilization and its Discontents* (1930*a*).

In 1900, then, Freud's sublimated homosexual friendship for Fliess was in its final phase, giving way, in his psychical economy, to a sublimated incestuous heterosexual friendship for Minna. This oscillation between a homosexual object and a heterosexual object reflects the notion of bisexuality which, in my view, underlies the dream of 'Company at table d'hôte' – a notion much cherished by Fliess, and now in the process of being appropriated, at his expense, by Freud.

INTERPRETATION IN RELATION TO COUNTER-TRANSFERENCE AND THE FORMULATION OF THE RULE OF ABSTINENCE

In his letter of October 14, 1900, Freud told Fliess not only that he had begun the new pamphlet on dreams, but that he had started treating a new woman patient, whom he later called Dora. My hypothesis is as follows: Frau E.L. in the dream represents Dora with the erotic transference with which she appeals to Freud; to defend himself against that transference, Freud remembers, so as not to fall into the same trap, Breuer's conscious blindness and unconscious connivance when faced with Anna O.'s erotic transference. This hypothesis enables the dream to be interpreted as follows:

– Frau E.L. was sitting beside me,
  = Dora was reclining before me (the position for psychoanalytic treatment);
– she was turning her whole attention to me,
  = her libido is on the move and is concentrated on me (transference);
– and laid her hand on my knee in an intimate manner,
  = as a daughter might do with her father (incestuous wish);
– I removed her hand unresponsively,
  = I did not respond to her attempt at seduction (rule of abstinence).

If my interpretation is correct, that final sentence contains all the ambiguity that was going to characterise Dora's treatment and resulted in her breaking it off. It expresses a counter-Oedipal defensive counter-transference: let us not allow ourselves to be led astray, like Breuer, by the incestuous wishes of a young and charming hysteric who has quite some experience in the matter: did she not seduce a friend of her father's, Herr K., a married man the same age as Freud? Was she not already familiar with erotic literature at the age of 18? Freud realised when writing up the case that his failure to detect an Oedipal transference was the reason why treatment failed. The dream of 'Company at table d'hôte' visualises at the same time a vital rule of psychoanalysis which Freud had not yet clearly formulated but which he was obviously in the process of realising – the rule of abstinence: the frustration with which the analyst responds to the patient's unconscious wish is the indispensable mainspring of treatment.

Let us go into further detail. Jones knew Dora's real name, but did not disclose it as her brother was a well-known Socialist leader (J I, 397 n.1). Freud had treated her father in 1894 for a syphilitic complaint of the nervous system. In June 1898, when she was 16, Dora was brought to Freud for the first time suffering from a cough and from hoarseness. Treatment was postponed by her parents, but when, in 1900, a letter was found in which she said she was going to commit suicide they decided to put her in Freud's hands. Treatment soon revealed the two traumas which had caused the fits of *tussis nervosa* and the suicidal depression respectively. When she was 14, a great friend of the family, Herr K., the husband of her father's supposed mistress, had kissed her on the mouth: hoarseness ensued. When she was 16, the same man, she alleged, made a proposal of marriage while they were walking by a lake and approached her in a way that terrified her and led her to demand that the very close relationship between her parents and the K. family should be broken off. Her father refused to do so, just as he refused to believe her story about what had happened by the lake – particularly when Herr K., on being questioned by him, denied everything and accused Dora of being interested in nothing but sexual matters and reading books on the subject which had made her 'over-excited'.

If I am right in assuming that the dream of 'Company at table d'hôte' preceded the letter to Fliess of October 14, Freud must have dreamt it while investigating these two traumatic scenes and the childhood memories connected with them. But it would seem to have occurred earlier than the two dreams which were to form the backbone of Freud's report of the case. In that report, he expressed surprise at Dora's disgusted reaction to Herr K.'s kiss and her horror at the same man's proposal, which was couched in very decent terms, by the side of the lake. He tried to get Dora to understand that she was unconsciously in love with the man and that his behaviour had been a rather natural response to the seduction she had been exerting on him. The dream of 'Company at table d'hôte' expresses Freud's need, when listening to Dora's account, to defend himself against identifying with Herr K. In order not to resemble Herr K., he dismisses the idea that he, too, is subject to Dora's sexual seduction. But this is a conscious notion of his (Frau E.L. in the dream said she was prepared to love him for the sake of his beautiful eyes) – a fact which enabled him to improve the patient's condition considerably, though incompletely.

Treatment centred on two of Dora's dreams, thus making the case history a direct continuation of *The Interpretation of Dreams*: Freud said as much in his letter to Fliess of January 25, 1901, in which he announced that he had finished his analysis of the case. The following letter, of January 30, described the two discoveries of general importance which the Dora case had enabled him to make.

The first was the concrete importance of the erotogenic zones, in this case, the mouth,[1] where the symptoms – *tussis nervosa* and aphonia – were located; the origins of the sexualisation of that zone could be traced back to thumb-sucking, in conjunction with an infantile sexual theory: she had imagined sexual intercourse taking place through the mouth (*fellatio*). This explained why in Dora's case sensual pleasure turned into disgust.

The second discovery was the concrete importance of bisexuality: there was a conflict between Dora's attraction to men and her attraction to women; there was also a conflict between her masculine identification with her father and her feminine identification with Frau K. as a person loved by her father. The notion of bisexuality had up to then been only of theoretical importance; this would seem to be the first major case where it was clinically applied and verified.

Let us return to the dream of 'Company at table d'hôte'. I have already indicated how in my view bisexuality is represented in it. Dora's disgust at kissing and *fellatio* is mirrored in it by the allusion to children's abhorrence of spinach.

INTERPRETATION IN RELATION TO CHILDHOOD MEMORIES

Sigismund was his mother's first-born and favourite child. She must have spoken to him lovingly of his beautiful eyes. His women patients must also

1. Freud first outlined the idea of erotogenic zones in December 1896; the notion of an oral sexual system appeared in letters to Fliess of January 3 and 11, 1897 (cf. p. 189). Then in 1898, his self-analysis explored the psychical repercussions of the anal and urethral zones in particular. It seems that his analysis of Dora led him to return to, and further investigate, the sexual characteristics of the oral zone.

have mentioned them. It is a fact that all those who met Freud found something fascinating in his gaze. His mother's incestuous-tending love developed a high degree of masochism in him. This is a frequent feature of the childhood of future creative geniuses, whose mothers often display what M. Besdine (1968) has rightly called a 'Jocasta complex'. The love of such mothers is not unselfish: their child is a libidinally hyper-cathected object which they strive to keep for themselves. They tend therefore to adopt an educational attitude designed to make the child feel guilty for his wish for autonomy, to obtain his unconditional obedience, and to reinforce his dependence. The dream echoes the sort of remark made by mothers with that attitude: 'If you don't eat up your spinach, you'll make mother cry!' Children tend not to like spinach, probably because its dark-green, acid, squidgy characteristics have repellent urethro-anal connotations. It is as if the mother asked the child, as proof of his love, to eat the faeces that come out of her body just as he came out of her body. The quotation from Goethe says the same thing in more abstract terms: the gods (= mothers) give us life in order to make us feel guilty and impose a debt on us that we shall not be able to repay in a whole lifetime.

Masochism was the price Freud had to pay for his mother's love. His relationship with her was something he tended to reactivate with other women. He married Martha solely for her beautiful eyes, as she had almost no dowry; he knew that her unselfish love had 'cost' something – his abandonment of a career as a scientific researcher, his mistake over the properties of cocaine, financial problems. More generally speaking, women have to be paid for. This is one of the essential themes of the dream of 'Company at table d'hôte'. There was a price, too, to be paid for Minna, his affectionate, intelligent, desirable, prohibited sister-in-law – financial sacrifices and sexual renunciations. Prostitutes procure pleasure, but they do not do their job for the sake of their customer's beautiful eyes: like à la carte meals or cabs with taximeters, each dish and each ride is paid for separately. Lastly, beautiful young women patients love their psychoanalyst via transference, i.e. for the sake of their beautiful eyes; but the price which has to be paid for that is respect for the rule of abstinence.

INTERPRETATION IN RELATION TO THE BODY IMAGE

It should be remembered that Freud himself never interpreted a dream from this angle; so what follows is purely my own hypothesis. The first image of the dream, a table at which spinach is being eaten, reminded Freud of meals taken collectively either at table d'hôte while on holiday or at home. The table is a symbolic representation of the suckling mother's breast. Two frustrations are indicated here, one of them implicitly – the obligation to share the breast with others – and the other explicitly – the obligation to eat something repellent (spinach) in order to please the mother, the latter obligation being a symmetrical reversal of that of cleanliness, which requires the child to retain something repellent in his body out of obedience to the mother.

The next image of the dream, a woman placing a hand on a knee, is the transposition of a sexual seduction scene in which the penis has been replaced by the knee. The underlying memories, although not specified by Freud, can easily be inferred: erotogenic hygiene administered by Monika Zajíc, the nurse who 'initiated' him; children's games of sexual fondling.

The end of the dream focusses on a sense organ whose role in Freud's instinctual economy we have already amply observed – the eyes, which have scarcely been absent from his dreams since the one he had following his father's death. The manifest content emphasises the declaration of love: 'You've always had such beautiful eyes'. Conversely, the latent content (the *occhiale*, with its painted eyes, given to an oculist) stresses what might be called a declaration of hatred: 'You have the evil eye.' The increasing importance of the evil eye can be sensed from a gradual deterioration in the representation of the beautiful eyes. Freud first says: 'I had an indistinct picture', a sign that his eyesight is not, or is no longer, good. Then he sees eyes which are not real, but drawn. Finally, the drawing no longer depicts eyes at all, but only the outline of a pair of spectacles. Geza Róheim has established the connection between orality and the eyes by studying the beliefs of primitive peoples in the evil eye and the rites they perform to ward it off.

For the infant, the mother is at once a breast that suckles, a mouth that speaks, and eyes that look: the dream of 'Company at table d'hôte' visualises those three functions successively. What lies behind that visualisation is the infant's resentment against his mother: she feeds him lovingly, but imposes her discipline on him; she speaks to him affectionately, but he is overwhelmed by the danger of responding to her incestuous approaches; he can see his own love and his own hatred reflected in the mirror of his mother's eyes. The reader will remember Freud's criticism of Fliess for being 'short-sighted' in the dream 'My son, the Myops' and Brücke's 'terrible blue eyes' which rebuked Freud for being late, and which the latter used, in the '*Non vixit*' dream, to get rid of the revenants: in those cases, the evil eye represented the wish to destroy a rival. Later, in his paper on 'The "Uncanny" ', Freud demonstrated that the apparition of an imaginary double embodies the terrible visitation on the subject of the destruction he wished on another. The dream of 'Company at table d'hôte' makes up the intermediate link between these two stages in Freud's theory.

Let me now draw a general conclusion from the dream of 'Company at table d'hôte'. Freud was unenthusiastically writing a second book on dreams which was but a pale and lifeless summary of the first – a drawing of a pair of spectacles, if you like, in comparison with a living eye. Nevertheless, so he could offer an example that was not already in the first book, he needed a dream that was as new, fresh and stimulating as the young Dora, whom he had just begun to treat. It was in that context that he had the dream of 'Company at table d'hôte'. It gave him the confidence to continue his self-analysis in a less systematic form, to go back to and continue his creative work, to reflect on his counter-transference, and to complete his discovery of psychoanalysis. Yes, he must have thought to himself, I am still capable of dreaming, and of finding; I can once again open my eyes and see clearly. He derived fresh impetus from the combination of narcissism and masochism which lies behind all creative work; but at the same time it was becoming increasingly obvious to him that it was his relationship with the mother and female figure which was being played out again. At a point in his scientific career when he was going to blaze a new trail, he regained control of that primal impetus which is provided by a mother's generous yet selfish love, and which turns a man into a conqueror at once happy and harrowed. Had he not written to Fliess on February 1, 1900, that he was a 'conquistador'? 'For I am actually not at all a man of science, not an observer, not an experimenter, not a thinker. I am by temperament nothing but a conquistador – an adventurer, if you want it translated – with all the curiosity, daring and tenacity characteristic of a man of this sort' (*F* 398).

PLAN OF *ON DREAMS*

Freud had finished *On Dreams* by December 1900 at the latest, for at the beginning of January 1901 he began writing up the case history of Dora, whose treatment had ended on December 31. It is a short book (53 pages in the *Standard Edition*, as compared with 621 pages for *The Interpretation of Dreams*), swiftly[1] and straightforwardly written, and without any table of contents or chapter titles. Here is its plan:

Chapter 1. The three misconceptions of dreams: romantic, materialist, and symbolic/popular.

Chapter 2. The psychoanalytic technique of free association. The example of the 'Company at table d'hôte' dream.

1. Unlike *The Interpretation of Dreams*, few additions were later made by Freud to *On Dreams* (see *Standard Edition*).

Chapter 3. Dramatisation:[1] a dream is the visualisation of an unsatisfied wish of the previous day. Examples of children's dreams already cited in *The Interpretation of Dreams*): 'Strawberries', 'Basket of cherries', 'Trip across Lake Aussee', 'Dachstein', 'Rohrer Hütte and the Hameau', and 'Achilles and Diomede'; and an adult's dream (already cited in *The Interpretation of Dreams*): 'Menstruation'; a new child's dream: 'Bed too small''.

Chapter 4. Example of visualisation of a wish: further analysis of the 'Company at table d'hôte' dream. The condensation of two scenes and two words in that dream. Three new dreams by Freud: 'Swimming-pool', '*Trottoir roulant*', and 'Glass top-hat'. A woman patient's dream (already cited in *The Interpretation of Dreams*)): 'Language of flowers'.

Chapter 5. Displacement: the 'Company at table d'hôte' dream again; example of the propyl injection in the Irma dream (already cited in *The Interpretation of Dreams*).

Chapter 6. Considerations of representability: example of Freud's dream (already cited in *The Interpretation of Dreams*): 'Goethe's attack on Herr M.'.

Chapter 7. Secondary revision. Three patients' dreams (already cited in *The Interpretation of Dreams*): 'Market dream', 'Paying 3 florins 65 kreuzers', 'Three theatre tickets for 1 florin 50 kreuzers'.

Chapter 8. Repression and distortion: further analysis of the dreams of 'Company at table d'hôte' and 'Three theatre tickets for 1 florin 50 kreuzers'.

Chapter 9. Anxiety in dreams. Its cause: dreams are disguised fulfilments of repressed wishes. Example of a woman patient's dream (already cited in *The Interpretation of Dreams*): 'Little Karl in his coffin'.

Chapter 10. Censorship between the unconscious and the preconscious.

Chapter 11. Dreams as the guardians of sleep: examples of one of Freud's dreams (already cited in *The Interpretation of Dreams*): 'Riding on a horse'; and of a new dream by a friend: 'Applause in theatre'.

[Chapter 12 on the sexual symbolism of dreams was added in 1911.]

Chapter 13. Conclusion.

This list shows the importance given by Freud to his own dreams. In this second book, he returns to several of his own and patients' dreams already cited in *The Interpretation of Dreams*. He adds six new dreams – four of his own, one of which is exhaustively analysed, one by a friend, which is described in only one sentence, and one by a child; there is no new patient's dream. In *The Interpretation of Dreams*, the proportion of his own dreams was smaller: it contained 43 such dreams (about three-quarters of which were interpreted at some length, and a dozen of which recurred several times in the book) and 62 dreams and three day-dreams by patients, friends and children (most of which were only briefly reported and analysed, and only

1. The concept of dramatisation is, however, formulated as such only in the last paragraph of Chapter 4 (in parentheses) and the first paragraph of Chapter 5. In Chapter 1 of *The Interpretation of Dreams*, Freud quoted Spitta's notion (1882) that dreams 'dramatise' an idea, but did not himself use that verb subsequently in the book. It was when he was writing *On Dreams* that the noun 'dramatisation' probably first occurred to him.

three of which – 'Language of flowers', 'Lovely dream', and 'Burning child' – were discussed several times in the book).[1]

FREUD IN 1901 AND 1902

The writing up of the Dora case took three weeks and was completed on January 24, 1901. On the 30, Freud told Fliess that the key to the case was psychical bisexuality: 'The principal issue in the conflicting thought processes is the contrast between an inclination toward men and an inclination toward women' (*F* 434). The manuscript, entitled 'Dreams and Hysteria', was accepted by the publisher, but for reasons of professional secrecy Freud delayed its publication. It finally came out in 1905 under another title, 'Fragment of an Analysis of a Case of Hysteria' (1905*e*). Freud explains his choice of the pseudonym Dora in *The Psychopathology of Everyday Life* (*PEL* 240–41). Dora was the name of the nursemaid who worked for his sister Rosa. The day before choosing the pseudonym, Freud had learnt that the nursemaid's real name was Rosa, like her employer's, and that, to avoid confusion, she was known in the household as Dora. It then turned out to be the only name he could think of to give his patient. But as we already know it was also the name of Breuer's daughter, who was born shortly before the unsuccessful termination of Anna O.'s treatment, and who had probably just married Fliess's friend, Dr Schiff. What is more, Dora Breuer and Dora the patient were both 18 years old in 1900.

Freud immediately started work again on *The Psychopathology of Everyday Life*. On January 30, 1901, it was 'half finished'; on February 15, he expected to finish it 'in a few days'; and by May 8, he had already begun correcting the proofs. The work, as we have seen, was published in two large instalments in July and August 1901.

From February to August 1901, Freud's correspondence with Fliess succeeded in striking a difficult balance. On the one hand, it continued and completed the elucidation of their relationship in its more emotional aspects; on the other, it strove to restrict their exchanges to intellectual and professional matters. I would differ with Buxbaum and argue that Fliess played the role of psychoanalyst for his friend: he gave him interpretations. But Fliess clearly lacked any psychoanalytic insight, and his interpre-

1. If we also take into account the premonitory dream of 'Meeting Dr K in the Kärntnerstrasse' (published posthumously), the two dreams by Dora, and the two new dreams (other than his own) published in *On Dreams*, we arrive at a total of 70 dreams and day-dreams by patients, friends and children recorded by Freud up until 1902. Freud also mentioned a total of 43 dreams from existing literature, most of which he could not interpret for lack of associative material.

One last remark: it is no coincidence that of Freud's many dreams in *The Interpretation of Dreams* only one is rediscussed in detail and subjected to complementary analysis in *On Dreams*, and that is a dream about, or rather against, Fliess, 'Goethe's attack on Herr M.' It marks the elimination of Freud's transference on to him.

tations were more than once inaccurate or laden with 'counter-transference'.

Fliess's first interpretation concerned the wish expressed by Freud to get to Rome at last during Easter (*F*, January 30, 1901, 435). In his next letter, Freud summed up Fliess's interpretation (which he had meanwhile received) as follows: the trip to Rome was a myth which had come into being during the time they were good friends; a 'congress' in Rome would have marked the apotheosis of their friendship; it was meaningless now that they were estranged from each other (*F*, February 15, 1901, 436). Perhaps because of this demystification, the journey to Rome now became a concrete possibility: Freud went there without Fliess in September 1901 with a feeling of triumph tempered by slight disappointment, due probably to the deep incestuous significance of his wish to possess the Mother City.

Fliess's second interpretation is also known to us from Freud's reply to it (*F*, August 7, 1901, 447) and has already been quoted: 'The reader of thoughts merely reads his own thoughts into other people.' That scathing remark jettisoned, at a stroke, the whole of psychoanalysis and *The Interpretation of Dreams*. It also proved that Fliess had misunderstood the most fundamental aspect of Freud's discovery. Freud replied as follows: 'In this you too have come to the limit of your perspicacity. [. . .] If that is what you think of me, just throw my *Everyday Life* unread into the wastepaper basket. It is full of references to you – manifest ones, for which you supplied the material, and concealed ones, for which the motivation goes back to you. The motto, too, was a gift from you.[1] Apart from anything that might remain of the content, you can take it as a testimonial to the role you have played for me up to now' (*ibid.*). The deeply emotional relationship between the two men was now well and truly dead. Two paragraphs from the same letter also quoted by Schur refer to the fact that in the end Fliess became deeply disappointed with the way Breuer was treating his sick mother-in-law. Far from exulting, Freud gave Fliess a lesson in moral dignity and psychological acumen by assessing his former teacher, helper and friend in a manner that showed not only no animosity but a great understanding of the nature of Breuer's friendships:

'So, too, in the judgment of Breuer. I no longer despise him and have not for some time; I have felt his strength. If he is dead as far as you are

1. The motto in question is another quotation from Goethe:

> *Nun ist die Luft von solchem Spuk so voll,*
> *Dass niemand weiss, wie er ihn meiden soll.*
> [Now fills the air so many a haunting shape,
> That no one know how best he may escape.]
> *Faust, Part II*, Act V, Scene 5

concerned, then he is still exerting his power posthumously. What is your wife doing other than working out in a dark compulsion the notion that Breuer once planted in her mind when he told her how lucky she was that I did not live in Berlin and could not interfere with her marriage? [. . .]

'As to Breuer, you are certainly quite right about *the* brother, but I do not share your contempt for friendship between men, probably because I am to a high degree party to it. In my life, as you know, woman has never replaced the comrade, the friend. If Breuer's male inclination were not so odd, so timid, so contradictory – like everything else in his mental and emotional make-up – it would provide a nice example of the accomplishments into which the androphilic current in men can be sublimated' (*ibid.*).

So Freud had gone one step further than his reference, in a letter to Fliess of May 7, 1900, to the 'feminine side' of his attachment to his friend, and was now aware of the 'androphilic' sublimation – in other words, latent homosexuality – that is peculiar to male friendships in general.

The question was: now that their friendship had lost its strong emotional quality, would Freud and Fliess be able to continue their scientific collaboration? For a time it seemed to them that it might be possible. Fliess suggested that Freud return the favour he had done him in correcting the proofs of *The Interpretation of Dreams* by reading the manuscript of his forthcoming book on the relationship between the nose and the sexual organs: on May 8, 1901, Freud agreed to do so. On July 4, at the end of a long and friendly letter full of news about his family, his practice and his books, he passed on to Fliess what may be regarded as the first insight into the psychoanalytic interpretation of totemism (he had just read a report of Sir Arthur Evans' excavations at Knossos): 'Have you read that the English excavated an old palace in Crete (Knossos), which they declare to be the real labyrinth of Minos? Zeus seems originally to have been a bull. Our old god, too, is said to have been worshipped as a bull prior to the sublimation imposed by the Persians. This is cause for all sorts of thoughts too premature to write down' (*F*, July 4, 1901, 445).

Encouraged, Freud made a proposal which was a veritable test: 'As far as I can see, my next work will be called 'Human Bisexuality' [. . .]. I shall need about six months to put the material together and hope to find that it is now possible to carry out the work. But then I must have a long and serious discussion with you. The idea itself is yours. [. . .] So perhaps I must borrow even more from you; perhaps my sense of honesty will force me to ask you to co-author the book with me' (*F*, August 7, 1901, 448). The test proved conclusive in the long term, as it was bisexuality that subsequently occasioned the public row between the two men. For the time being Fliess's reply (alluded to in *F*, September 19, 1901, 450) was that his views on bisexuality did not square very well with Freud's, and that Freud had been as unfair to his work (a reference to his periodicity theory) as he was accusing him (Fliess) of being to his own.

Apart from a few short polite missives exchanged between the two men, sometimes on the subject of patients, Freud was to write only two more long and personal letters to Fliess. On September 19, 1901, at the same time as he abandoned for good any idea of further collaboration with his friend, Freud gave his impressions of his trip to Rome with Alexander:

'It was overwhelming for me too and, as you know, the fulfilment of a long-cherished wish. As such fulfilments are if one has waited too long for them, this one was slightly diminished, yet a high point of my life. But while I was totally and undisturbedly absorbed in antiquity (I could have worshipped the abased and mutilated remnant of the Temple of Minerva near the forum of Nerva), I found I could not freely enjoy the second [the medieval, Christian] Rome; the atmosphere troubled me. I found it difficult to tolerate the lie concerning man's redemption, which raises its head to high heaven – for I could not cast off the thought of my own misery and all the other misery I know about.

"I found the third, the Italian, Rome full of promise and likeable (*F* 449).

While this lively and friendly letter was on its way to Berlin, Fliess sent Freud the manuscript of his next book, *Über den ursächlichen Zusammenhang von Nase und Geschlechtsorgan: Zugleich ein Beitrag zur Nervenphysiologie* (On the causal connection between the nose and the sexual organ, as well as a contribution to the physiology of the nervous system), which came out in 1902 with its title slightly changed at Freud's suggestion. Freud replied immediately: '*Tableau!* [Amazing!] Our letters crossed! [. . .] I [. . .] am glad to say you have never before produced anything so clear, so concise, and so rich in substance' (*F*, September 20, 1901, 451). Freud's enthusiasm was polite and inconsequential. His subsequent letters discussed Frau D., a patient who had been sent to him by Fliess, and noted the fact that they wrote to each other less and less often.

On March 11, 1902, three days after informing Fliess that he had been appointed professor, Freud sent his friend what was to be his last long personal letter. In it, he explained how he had obtained his long-awaited appointment: 'It was my doing, in fact. When I came back from Rome, my enjoyment of life and work was somewhat heightened and that of martyrdom somewhat diminished. I found my practice had almost melted away; I withdrew my last work from publication because just a little earlier I had lost my last audience in you. I could foresee that waiting for recognition might take up a good portion of my life and that in the meantime none of my fellowmen would bother about me. And I did want to see Rome again, take care of my patients, and keep my children in good spirits. So I made up my mind to break with strict virtue and take appropriate steps, as other humans do' (*F* 456).

It is far from certain, as was long believed, that anti-Semitism in Viennese government circles had been responsible for Freud's appointment coming so late. Budgetary restrictions and bureaucratic *vis inertiae* would seem to have been more important reasons. They worked against all the candidates: only those who could benefit from political influences or recommendations in high places were successful. Freud proved unable to secure his appointment for as long as he took no active interest in it. He got it the moment he resigned himself to take the 'appropriate steps'. The Minister of Education, Wilhelm von Hartel, was an open-minded man: he had publicly condemned anti-Semitism and been instrumental in getting a literary prize awarded to the Jewish writer, Arthur Schnitzler – thus causing an outcry in anti-Semite circles. Freud is wrong in claiming, in the same letter, that a woman patient (Baroness Marie von Ferstel) had intervened on his behalf by donating Böcklin's *The Ruined Castle* to the Modern Galerie in exchange for a promise that he would get his professorship, since the painting in question was not sold by its owners until 1948 and the only recorded gift by the baroness to the museum in 1902 was a picture of lesser value by Emil Orlik.[1]

This change of attitude, which began with his Rome trip, was the main personal benefit that Freud derived from his self-analysis, which was also, of course, very fertile from a scientific point of view. Up to then, he had been guided by a selfish ambition to become a great scientist, and was always ready to react intransigently and scornfully to those who questioned his discoveries. We now find someone more concerned with practical efficiency, ready to take the concrete realities of human life into account, and soon to turn his energies to the social organisation of psychoanalysis, its dissemination, its applications, and the training of its practitioners. He had dreamt of becoming an exceptional figure; he now accepted that he was just another man like any other.

He stopped writing to Fliess, thus losing what he called his 'last audience', but he reached a much larger one. He attracted his first followers (Alfred Adler, Max Kahane, Rudolf Reitler and Wilhelm Stekel), and in October 1902 founded the Psychological Wednesday Society, forerunner of the Vienna Psychoanalytical Society. He had

1. R. Gicklhorn (1958), J. and R. Gicklhorn (1960) and K. Eissler (1958, 1966), who have all investigated the details of Freud's appointment closely, reach partly divergent conclusions; H. E. Ellenberger (E 452–4) gives an accurate and clear summary of the question, which I have used as the basis for my remarks.

emerged from his isolation and was determined that his scientific work should continue to develop.

The epilogue in the relationship between Freud and Fliess was as follows. Freud mentioned bisexuality to a Viennese psychologist, Hermann Swoboda, whom he was treating. Swoboda passed on the idea to the writer Otto Weininger, who in 1902 published a sensational book called *Sex and Character* and made use of Fliess's theory without mentioning his name. In 1904, Swoboda published a monograph entitled *Die Periode des menschlichen Organismus in ihrer psychologischen und biologischen Bedeutung* (The periods of the human organism and their psychological and biological significance), which drew on Fliess's periodicity theory but explicitly acknowledged him. Fliess then engaged in a row over priority. He exchanged letters with Freud, who first tried to placate Fliess, then replied with typical bluntness: yes of course he must have wanted to pinch Fliess's discovery of bisexuality from him, but what a pity that Fliess found no time to write to him except over such a trivial matter. In 1905, Fliess got a friend to publish a pamphlet attacking Weininger, Swoboda and Freud, which provoked an immediate response from Swoboda and Freud. In 1906, Fliess published his 1904 correspondence with Freud, despite its very private nature (J I, 346–7). Freud later remained interested in bisexuality and periodicity, and always acknowledged Fliess (1905*d*; 1913*i*; 1920*g*). He encouraged the Berlin psychoanalyst Karl Abraham to get in touch with Fliess. As for Fliess himself, he struggled right up until his death in 1928, at the age of 70, to gain acceptance for his biological system – but with little success. He remained interested in psychoanalysis; and his son Robert, who was born only a few days after Anna Freud, became, like her, a professional psychoanalyst of repute.

SELF-ANALYSIS IN FREUD'S LATER LIFE AND WORK

Freud continued to practise self-analysis from time to time for the rest of his life, using new examples to enrich subsequent editions of his earlier works and to illustrate some of his later publications. Here is an inventory of such examples (which does not claim to be exhaustive; all the dreams that appear in it are, of course, Freud's own).

Subsequent editions of *The Interpretation of Dreams* contained the following dreams:

In 1909: 'Forgotten church-tower' (*ID* 14–15) and 'Restaurant garden at Padua' (*ID* 15), identifications of landscapes seen in dreams; and an interpretation of examination dreams (*ID* 275) as reassuring dreams: Freud dreamt only of examinations he had passed.

In 1911: 'Working in the laboratory' (*ID* 475–6), where he carries out the chemical analyses of his youth – a nostalgic dream by someone who has now succeeded in making other analyses, but who is growing old; and four dreams about Fliess. Three of them refute the periodicity theory: 'Savonarola's profile', 'Archimedes' statue', and 'Professor Oser's dietary' (*ID* 166 n.2). The fourth, 'Reconciliation with a friend' (*ID* 145 n.1), is a 'hypocritical dream' and disguises the real wish, which is the opposite: to treat the ex-friend as a stranger or an enemy.

In 1914: 'The Pope is dead' dream (*ID* 232; also referred to in 1916–17, *SE* 15, 94) is a fine example of the wish to sleep.

In 1919: In 'News of son from the front' (*ID* 558–60), he dreamt his son had died in battle; he interpreted it as expressing an old father's envy of his son's youth, and gave a more complete description of the accident in his infancy when he fell and hurt his jaw.

Subsequent editions of *The Psychopathology of Everyday Life* included new self-analytic fragments (1907 edition: *PEL* 169 and 180), and then name-forgettings and misreadings connected with the 1914–18 war (1917 edition: *PEL* 33–4, 113–14).

Two examples taken from his self-analysis were the subject of two later papers by Freud.

His 'Open letter to Romain Rolland on the Occasion of his Seventieth Brithday' (1936*a*) describes a disturbance of memory experienced by Freud on the Acropolis in 1904, which he had long been unable to explain and at last decided to analyse. He did so in a letter to Rolland because the latter had already experienced and written about a similar experience. The disturbance took the following form. During the summer of 1904, after much hesitation, he went on an unexpected visit to Athens with his brother Alexander. When he stood on the Acropolis, instead of being filled with admiration, as he had expected, he had a strange feeling of doubt. He was surprised that something he had learnt about at school could actually exist. He felt himself being divided into two persons, one who registered through his senses that he was in fact on the Acropolis, and the other who could not believe that this was so. The reason was that going to Athens, like going to Rome, was the object of a wish with overtones of guilt. Going to Athens meant going further than his father, who was too poor to travel and not cultured enough to be interested in the site. Climbing the Acropolis meant outstripping him definitively, something which children are prohibited from doing. To understand the meaning of the incident, Freud had first to reach the age of 80 and have become patriarch who found travelling impossible. And to publish it, he had to address it to someone who, like his travelling companion Alexander, was ten years his junior.

'The Subtleties of a Faulty Action' (1935*b*) contained a fine example of the ease with which one can content oneself with an incomplete piece of self-analysis. Wishing to give a woman friend a birthday present, Freud was about to send his jewellers a gem for insertion into a ring. On the note for the jewellers, he wrote: 'Voucher for the supply by Messrs. L., jewellers, of a gold ring *bis* for the attached stone etc.' The word *bis* (which means 'until' in German) was quite out of place, and he crossed it out. Analysis revealed an aesthetic explanation: *bis* in Latin and in French means 'for a second time', and was warning him against an awkward repetition of 'for' in the sentence; by crossing out the *bis*, he symbolically did away with the second, superfluous 'for'. But then his daughter, when consulted, came up with the real explanation: he had already given the same person a similar gem; that was the repetition which his unconscious was probably seeking to avoid. Do not all gifts cause a twinge of regret in the giver?

Later in his life, Freud lived in an atmosphere of permanent self-analysis. This was revealed when Jones (J II, Appendix) published numerous extracts from the correspondence between Freud and the pioneers of the psychoanalytic movement. They often exchanged psychoanalytic interpretations or passed on their own self-analytic thoughts. It even got to the point where some of them complained about this. Here are three examples out of many.

I have already referred to the first (cf. p. 428). In November 1912, during a meeting in Munich intended to iron out the first conflicts provoked by Jung, Freud took the discussion so personally that he passed out. When he revived, he murmured: 'How sweet it must be to die.' Not long afterwards, on December 8, he wrote to Jones: 'I saw Munich first when I visited Fliess during his illness and this town seems to have acquired a strong connection with my relation to that man. There is some piece of unruly homosexual feeling at the root of the matter. When Jung in his last letter again hinted at my "neurosis" I could find no better expedient than proposing that every analyst should attend to his own neurosis more than to the other's' (J I, 348).

The writing of *Totem and Taboo* (1912–13) shows a curious parallel with that of *The Interpretation of Dreams*: it took place in the spring of 1913 at the very time when the rivalry between Freud and Jung was becoming exacerbated; it was preceded by a preparatory period of two years which was characterised by internal unhappiness and increasing involvement in his work; and it was accompanied by a state of creative elation which Freud had already experienced when writing Chapter 7 of *The Interpretation of Dreams*. He had the feeling that this was his best work. But once he had finished the book he fell prey to the wildest doubts about its worth, and asked Jones and Ferenczi for their opinion. They explained that his doubts were a reaction against the fact that he had lived through, in his imagination, the exciting experience of killing and eating his father. Freud confirmed this in a conversation with Jones: '[In *The Interpretation of Dreams*] I described the wish to kill one's father, and now I have been describing the actual killing; after all it is a big step from a wish to a need' (J II, 397).[1]

Of all the leading figures of the psychoanalytic movement, Ferenczi was Freud's favourite. He suffered from considerable personal problems, such as hypochondria and fear of sibling rivalry. Freud discussed these constantly in his correspondence with him, encouraging him to carry out self-analysis and calling him 'My dear son'. He induced him to behave decently and cooperatively with his brothers and friends. He helped him to make up his mind, after eighteen years, to marry the lady of his choice. He devoted a significant footnote to him in *The Psychopathology of Everyday Life*: 'Ferenczi reports that he himself was once an "absent-minded person" [*ein "Zerstreuter"*]. [. . .] But, he says, the signs of this absent-mindedness have almost completely disappeared since he began treating patients by psychoanalysis and found himself obliged to turn his attention to the analysis of his own self as well' (*PEL*, 1910 edition, 156 n.2). This example shows how necessary it is for the psychoanalyst to resort to self-analysis in order to clarify his counter-transference.

For Freud, self-analysis was the best instrument there was for his own professional training. So it was only to be expected that he should urge his disciples to follow suit and advocate it as a method in all his published works, while at the same time remaining aware of its limitations. 'The interpretation of dreams is in fact the royal road to a knowledge of the unconscious. [. . .] If I am asked how one can become a psychoanalyst, I reply: "By studying one's own dreams"' (*Five Lectures on Psycho-Analysis*, 1910*a*, *SE* 11, 33).

'Some years ago I gave as an answer to the question of how one can become an analyst: "By analysing one's own dreams." This preparation is no doubt enough for many people, but not for everyone who wishes to learn analysis. Nor can everyone succeed in interpreting his own dreams without outside help. [. . .] Not only is one's aim of learning to know what is hidden in one's own mind far more rapidly attained and with less expense of affect, but impressions and convictions will be gained in relation to oneself which

1. Similar elation, followed by similar doubts, had occurred for the first time in the autumn of 1895 when Freud was writing 'Project for a Scientific Psychology'. The same syndrome repeated itself in the autumn of 1913 when he wrote 'On Narcissism: An Introduction'.

will be sought in vain from studying books and attending lectures. And lastly, we must not under-estimate the advantage to be derived from the lasting mental contact that is as a rule established between the student and his guide.

'An analysis such as this of someone who is practically healthy will, as may be imagined, remain incomplete. Anyone who can appreciate the high value of the self-knowledge and increase in self-control thus acquired will, when it is over, continue the analytic examination of his personality in the form of a self-analysis, and be content to realise that, within himself as well as in the external world, he must always expect to find something new' ('Recommendations to Physicians Practising Psycho-Analysis', 1912*e*, *SE* 12, 116–17). Self-analysis remained vital to the proper working of 'evenly suspended attention' and of the unconscious memory, which Freud now saw as the instrument with which the patient's unconscious could be grasped by the psychoanalyst's unconscious.

In 'A Note on the Prehistory of the Technique of Analysis' (1920*b*), Freud quoted three authors who were precursors of the free association technique: the physician, poet and Swedenborgian mystic Garth Wilkinson; Schiller, already referred to in this connection in a revised edition of *The Interpretation of Dreams*; and Ludwig Börne, author of an essay entitled 'The Art of Becoming an Original Writer in Three Days', of which Freud's discovery was probably an unconscious reminiscence. These are all examples of self-analysis carried out for literary purposes.

In a 'Forward to E. Pickworth Farrow's *A Practical Method of Self-Analysis*' (1926*c*), Freud remarks: '[Farrow] proceeded to make a systematic application of the procedure of self-analysis which I myself employed in the past for the analysis of my own dreams. His findings deserve attention precisely on account of the peculiar character of his personality and of his technique' (*SE* 20, 280).

Finally, Freud's paper 'Analysis Terminable and Interminable' (1937*c*) took his remarks of 1910 and 1912 one stage further. Psychoanalysis is not a process from which a subject can ever say to himself that he is discharged. In a sense, and despite practical criteria for what constitutes a cure, no patient can ever finish with analysis. 'Not only the therapeutic analysis of patients but [the analyst's] own analysis' is an interminable, not a terminable, task (*SE* 23, 249). Seen from that angle, the purpose of psychoanalysis is not just to remove symptoms or reform a personality, but to set in motion a process that will continue after the treatment has finished. Although Freud does not use the term here, he is obviously referring to self-analysis. For the psychoanalyst, that process is the best protection against the shortcomings of his training and the risks of his profession. 'This alone would not suffice for his instruction; but we reckon on the stimuli that he has received in his own analysis not ceasing when it ends and on the process of remodelling the ego continuing spontaneously in the analysed subject and making use of all subsequent experiences in this newly-acquired sense. This does in fact happen, and in so far as it happens it makes the analysed subject qualified to be an analyst himself' (*SE* 23, 248–9).

The dangers of analysis are two-edged. 'It would not be surprising if the effect of a constant preoccupation with all the repressed material which struggles for freedom in the human mind were to stir up in the analyst as well all the instinctual demands which he is otherwise able to keep under suppression. [. . .] Every analyst should periodically – at intervals of five years or so – submit himself to analysis once more, without feeling ashamed of taking this step' (*ibid.*). But this very porosity of the psychoanalyst to the treatment he gives is at the same time an invitation to self-analysis. While it is true that an artificial self-analysis which has no strong motivation is doomed to failure, there is surely no more powerful and more valid motivation than the internal repercussion on the analyst of his analytic relationship with his patients.

Conclusion

'La théorie, c'est bon, mais ça n'empêche pas d'exister.'
('Theory is all very well, but it doesn't prevent things from existing.')
(A verbal reply by Charcot to an objection by Freud when he was at La Salpêtrière during the winter of 1885–86; it was a favourite quotation of Freud's, first mentioned in his obituary of Charcot (1893*f*, *SE* 3, 13).)

Freud's achievement

Let us cast our minds back to the Freud of 1895. Like many married men in Jewish circles at the time, he was deeply involved in a nexus of frequent and satisfying relations with his parents, wife, brothers and sisters, children and family-in-law, the only exceptions to that rule being a bout of fierce jealousy concerning Martha at the beginning of their engagement, and a long period of resentment towards Martha's brother, Eli Bernays, who had married one of Freud's sisters. He was a medical specialist, first in neurology, then in psychiatry, with the coveted but virtually honorary title of *Privat-Dozent* of neuropathology at Vienna University; his practice earned him a barely adequate income. He was variously judged by his colleagues: some saw him as one of the great hopes of brain anatomopathology, others dismissed him as a nutty expert in hysteria and hypnosis. He formed close friendships, always with Jews, partly because of profound intellectual and ethical – but not religious – affinities with those who, like him, had espoused their cultural legacy, and partly because of a resurgence of anti-Semitism at that time; friends occupied an important place in his professional work and leisure time. He felt constricted by Vienna, and would have liked to get away more often. As a researcher, he was assiduous and obstinate rather than meticulous and well-organised, and wanted very badly to make a great discovery. He was a typical scientist, constricting his imagination because of an exclusive faith in determinism, reluctantly maintaining a practice, and dreaming passionately of extending to neurology and psychology the dynamic principles which had just laid the foundations of modern physiology as a science. He was dazzled by

Wilhelm Fliess, whose friendship he had won, and who, he imagined, would revolutionise biology. He was a man of considerable literary and historical learning, which he cultivated in his spare time. He had made a number of minor and often unremarked contributions first to natural science, then to psychopathology. His latest discovery had been a technique of free association that made it possible to replace hypnotic suggestion by 'psychical analysis' in the treatment of psychoneuroses.

Yet Freud, who was so talented, so intellectually and physically energetic, so apparently calm and reasonable, was gnawed by suffering. He easily gave in to resentment, remorse, self-doubt, and dependence on others. He was not easily discouraged, but became depressed. He tended to wallow in failure. He attributed his moodiness to the vicissitudes of life, and in particular to health problems following a recent and distressing cardiac episode. In fact Freud, then nearly 40, was simply in the throes of the mid-life crisis that ushers in maturity.

If we now examine the same man seven years later, in 1902, we are struck by a number of changes. Freud was more at ease with himself. He felt sure that he was right. He faced attacks on his work with determination and self-confidence. True, his phobias of taking trains or crossing the street, his fear of death, and his emotional ambivalence in human relationships had not disappeared but simply waned. He was more or less aware of their mechanisms, not too affected by their repercussions, and now capable of dealing with his internal problems through self-analysis or discussion with colleagues. Moreover, by 1902, he had unfettered his imagination as a scientist, and the discoveries he had just made were the result not of laborious effort but of flashes of insight. He had learned the very lesson he spelled out to his patients in 1895: let your preconscious do the talking. His cultural interests had taken a new turn: he loved reading about lost civilisations and began collecting antiques; he travelled a lot, climbed the Alps, visited the artistic treasures of northern Italy. In 1901, he even crossed his own Rubicon: he, a Jew and a product of Germanic civilisation, had gone to Rome. Having finally decided to take the appropriate steps and secure the necessary recommendations that would shake the Viennese administration out of its torpor, he had just obtained his appointment as a professor *extraordinarius* (i.e. an associate professorship, not the chair).

There had been only two major changes in his family life: he had taken permanently into the household his brilliant and devoted sister-in-law, Minna Bernays, who after her fiancé's death had given up the idea of marriage, and made her his confidante; at about the same time he lost his father and from that point on went through an intense work of mourning which fuelled his systematic self-analysis. Now that he was disillusioned with Fliess, he no longer had any friends working along the same lines as himself; but in 1902 he attracted his first followers and founded the Psychological Wednesday Society, forerunner of the Viennese Psychoanalytical Society. Otherwise he had kept all his other friends, with whom he spent his spare time or who like him worked to defend the status of Jews. His financial situation, although erratic, was often healthy, and he was reaching the point where in order to earn a decent living he did not need to concern himself with his reputation in Vienna. He had given up neurology and hypnosis for good. His practical work was exclusively focussed on psychopathology, his theoretical work on a pure form of general psychology which he called metapsychology. He had published a book of considerable importance, *The Interpretation of Dreams*, which had been well received by a small band of specialists, and, in two instalments, another major work, *The Psychopathology of Everyday Life*. He already had in his mind the material that would produce *Jokes and their Relation to the Unconscious* and *Three Essays on the Theory of Sexuality*. He had accepted the specificity of psychical processes and given up trying to explain them by their dependence on the brain. The only thing he retained from the science of physiology he had learned from Brücke and Helmholtz was a certain pattern of thinking. He had further improved the technique of treatment which he now called 'psychoanalysis'. He was much less emotionally perturbed – and less often caught off his intellectual guard – by his psychoneurotic patients. He knew how to treat not only hysteria, but obsessional neurosis and phobia as well. He was aware of what went into a successful course of treatment, thanks to the case of Herr E., the vicissitudes of which marked the various stages of Freud's self-analysis. And when he failed, he also knew why, thanks to the Dora case history which he wrote in 1901, but which came out only in 1905.

This was his first major case history since those he had contributed to *Studies on Hysteria*. That Freud had made immense strides between the two works can be seen by comparing them. He had completed, in decisive fashion, the discovery of psychoanalysis. He knew how to interpret dreams and elucidate the meaning of parapraxes. He was aware of the existence of infantile sexuality, one of whose keys he had identified as being the Oedipus complex, and whose other basic components – the primal scene, perverse sexual polymorphism, castration anxiety and auto-erotism – he had already guessed. He knew that psychical traumas are pathogenic through deferred action, i.e. through the forbidden wish they awaken, and not as a direct result of the event itself or its memory. He had elaborated a schema of the psychical apparatus consisting of three systems, which are at once systems of transformations of forces and of circulation of meaning – consciousness, the preconscious, and the unconscious, with two intermediate censorships. And he was about to formulate his theory of the libido and of the stages of its fixation on erotogenic zones.

TABLE 6. *Alphabetical list of psychoanalytic notions acquired by Freud during his self-analysis (1895–1901)*

Abortion phantasies
Abstinence, rule of (described but not formulated)
Activity and passivity
Actual neuroses
Agency (or psychical system)
Alteration of the ego
Ambivalence (described but not formulated)
Anal stage (described but not formulated)
Attention
Attention, evenly-suspended
Auto-erotism (as the opposite of allo-erotism) (a notion present in manuscript form but not yet published)

Bisexuality
Bungled actions, unconscious factors in

Castration (still embryonic)
Childhood memories, importance of
Choice of neurosis
Cleanliness, unconscious repercussions of learning
Clitoral erotogenic zone
Compromise-formation
Compulsion (still embryonic, present in manuscript form but not yet published)
Condensation
Condom phantasies
Copulation phantasies

Day's residues
Death wishes
Debasement in the sphere of love (still embryonic, present in manuscript form)
Deferred action
Defloration phantasies
Distortion of latent thoughts
Dramatisation
Dreams, unconscious factors in
Dream-work

Ego
Egoism
Erotogenic zones
Exhibitionistic wishes
Experience of pain
Experience of satisfaction

Facilitation
Family romance
Fellatio phantasies
Fixation (in the psychoanalytic sense) (a notion present only in manuscript form)
Forgetting, unconscious factors in
Free association, method of

Helplessness, state of (still embryonic, present in manuscript form but not yet published)
Hypercathexis

Identification
Identification with the lost object (described but not yet formulated)
Incest, horror of (present in manuscript form but not yet published)
Incestuous wishes
Infantile amnesia (described but not yet formulated)
Infantile sexuality
Instinctual impulses (still embryonic, and described as 'endogenous stimuli' or simply 'impulses')

Interminable analysis (present in manuscript form but not yet formulated or published)
Interpretation

Latency period (a biological notion of Fliess's, not yet applied by Freud to the psyche)
Latent content
Libidinal stage (described but not yet formulated)
Literary works, unconscious factors in
Locality, psychical
Lost object (still embryonic, present in manuscript form)

Manifest content
Metapsychology
Money = faeces (symbolic equivalence)
Moral factors, unconscious

Need for punishment
Negative therapeutic reaction (still embryonic, present in manuscript form)
Neuronal inertia, principle of

Object of wish (still embryonic, present in manuscript form)
Oedipus
Oral sexual system
Over-determination
Over-interpretation

Parapraxes, unconscious factors in
Perception-consciousness system
Perceptual identity
Perversion, neurosis as the negative of
Phallus (as a symbol) (described but not yet formulated)
Picture-puzzle, dream as a
Pleasure-unpleasure principle
Preconscious
Pregnancy phantasies
Presentations, word-, thing-
Primal scene
Primary processes
Protective shield
Psychical apparatus
Psychoanalysis
Psychology, clinical (formulated in manuscript form)
Purposive ideas

Reaction-formation (described but not formulated)
Reality-testing (described but not completely formulated)
Regression
Repetition (still embryonic, present in manuscript form)
Representability
Reversal of an affect into its opposite

Screen memory
Secondary gain
Secondary processes
Secondary revision
Self-analysis
Self-reproach
Sibling rivalry
Somatic compliance
Specific action
Sublimation (still embryonic)
Suppression of affects
Symbolism
Symptom-formation (analogous with dream-work)

Threats of punishment for masturbation
Totemism, psychoanalytic interpretation of (still embryonic, present in manuscript form)

Unconscious (in the psychoanalytic sense)
Unconscious phantasies
Urethral stage (described but not yet formulated)

Verbal associations, the pole of

Wish-fulfilment

The man of talent had become a genius. Two phrases sum up his approach. One of them he quoted to Fliess (*F*, May 8, 1901, 441) and used as an epigraph for the paper (1914*d*) he wrote in response to the secession of Adler and Jung:

Fluctuat nec mergitur!
[It floats and does not sink]

In memory of Charcot, Freud the Viennese adopted the motto on the Paris coat of arms as his own, and later made it the watchword for psychoanalytic orthodoxy. The second phrase was often on his lips when he wished to pass on the best of his experience to other people: let your unconscious do the talking. 'When making a decision of minor importance, I have always found it advantageous to consider all the pros and cons. In vital matters, however, such as the choice of a mate or a profession, the decision should come from the unconscious, from somewhere within ourselves' (quoted in Reik, 1948, p. vii).

What, then, had occurred between 1895 and 1902? He had achieved the extraordinary feat of subjecting himself to the psychoanalysis he was in the process of discovering from his patients. It would be quite wrong to see his self-analysis as an almost mechanical or intellectual application of a new technique. Its effectiveness stemmed from the fact that it called into question the whole man in his relationship with his family, his patients, his work and his body. In its manner of execution, it should be regarded, I think, as the successful effort of one man, who was not very different from his fellows as regards his psychical organisation, not only to find his true place in his family, his work, the world of science and human society, but also, and much more, to invent a procedure and a system that would enable him to listen to his wishes, transcribe his phantasies and understand his anxieties while at the same time holding them at arm's length and looking them straight in the face.

If we turn from Freud's personal development to the enrichment of his conceptual thinking, we can see that it was considerable. Table 6 shows the 'Psychoanalytic notions acquired by Freud during his self-analysis (1895–1901.' There are twice as many notions as those used by Freud in 1895 (cf. Table 2, p. 125) just before his creative surge. The vast majority of them, apart from one or two suggestions by Fliess, are the result of Freud's inventive genius alone, whereas about half of his conceptual vocabulary in 1895 was that of Helmholtz, Herbart, Charcot, Breuer and contemporary psychiatrists and psychologists. Many of these new notions were still only brief insights that had not been conceptualised or published; Freud stored them away for future use, and over the twenty years that followed drew on this reserve to elaborate the whole of his first theory of psychoanalysis. Only very few of them were left by the wayside or dropped for good. Then in the twenties, during the crisis of entering old age, Freud went through a further and equally productive period of creative renewal, which resulted in his second theory of the psychical apparatus (the id, the ego and the super-ego) and his second theory of the instincts (life instincts and death instincts).

The most important scientific insights are always those with the simplest formulations. Freud's genius – which, as we have seen, consisted precisely of making a direct transition from seeing to writing, in other words from thing-presentations to the code – distinguished itself between 1895 and 1902 by producing a long string of such formulae: dreams are wish-fulfilments; perversions are the negative of neuroses; money is a symbolic equivalent of faeces; superstition and mythology are psychologies projected into the external world; happiness is the achievement in maturity of a childhood wish; we forget what we find unpleasant; dreams are picture puzzles, and also fulfilments of the wish to sleep; we identify with a lost object in order to keep it; pathogenic memories are reconstructed through deferred action; death wishes are directed against loved ones; phantasies reproduce seen, heard or imagined primal scenes; symptoms, dreams, and screen memories are compromises between wishes and defences; undischarged libido turns into anxiety; threats of punishment for masturbation are the cause of *pavor nocturnus* and nightmares; unconscious motives determine morality, works of art, jokes, and so on.

At the same time Freud gave names for the first time to notions that are now widespread, such as regression, psychical locality, reality-testing, somatic compliance, horror of incest, family romance, and sexual systems (oral, anal, urethral, phallic). Hypotheses often occurred to him in the form of pairs of opposites: psychical quantity/quality, thing-/word-presentation, latent/manifest content, primary/secondary processes, experience of satisfaction/pain, displacement/condensation, primary/secondary gain from illness, first/second censorship, hallucination/discharge (or again: perception/motricity), auto-erotism/allo-erotism, activity/passivity, and masculinity/femininity (opposites inherent in the notion of bisexuality), to mention only the most important. The basic rules of treatment, free association, abstinence, and evenly-suspended attention had become increasingly clear to him. Several years of metapsychological reflection on dreams had led him to another discovery – a new point of view as regards the functioning of the psychical apparatus: the topographical point of view. Freud now knew that any psychoanalytic explanation of a phenomenon had to approach the question from four different points of view, the dynamic, economic, genetic and topographical, though he did not yet call them that. Lastly, he had implicitly formulated the criteria for adducing proof: any hypothesis that attempts to explain unconscious psychical phenomena requires threefold verification on patients (clinical data), on oneself (self-analytic data), and on cultural products (mythological or literary data). For is it not true that all psychical events need to be perceived from both within and without, from both a scientific and a poetic angle, and according both to individual evidence and to collective products, which societies of every age have supplied?

THE FUTURE

Can self-analysis be regarded as a generally valid technique of investigation and treatment? Obviously, Freud's own self-analysis was a quite exceptional event in that it coincided with the very discovery of psychoanalysis itself. It is in that sense that O. Mannoni (1967) dubbed it 'the primal analysis'. There was an efficacious self-therapeutic dimension to it, but it took second place to Freud's fundamental scientific need to verify on himself the existence and nature of unconscious processes he had observed or glimpsed in his patients. Looked at from a subjective point of view, self-analysis and the discovery of psychoanalysis were the only way for him to live through and resolve his mid-life crisis; he became a creator by working over the depressive phase that is normally exacerbated by that crisis. Many precocious geniuses, on the other hand, fail to overcome their mid-life crisis and are then doomed to sterility, decline and spiritual death.

Many of Freud's imitators tried to solve their own problems through self-analysis alone – and failed. There is nothing surprising in that, since they took a narcissistic view of self-analysis as something that would promote self-knowledge, as a kind of retreat from the outside world and from life, as a resistance to internal change, as a form of introspective self-indulgence. There was certainly a large narcissistic element in Freud's self-analysis, but it never became its only element. It resulted in his experiencing moments of regression which were very far-reaching but always under the control of the ego. In all the aspects I have just mentioned, his self-analysis proceeded in exactly the opposite way to that attempted by his imitators. His main aim was knowledge not so much of the self as of general, normal psychical processes. There can be no denying that Freud withdrew into himself – though subsequently, as we have seen, he greatly exaggerated the extent of his isolation: scientifically he was indeed isolated, but socially, professionally and emotionally he was not.

Freud's self-analysis was a constant dialogue with Fliess, to whom he was bound by great complicity in phantasy and by latent homosexuality, and on to whom he experienced a kind of Oedipal and ambivalent 'transference'. There can be no proper self-analysis unless it is communicated to someone else: that is something which seems to me indisputable, to judge from the very evidence of this book. When Fliess ceased to play the role of Freud's 'only audience', Minna became the person to whom he opened his thoughts. For Freud self-analysis involved three things at the same time – a constant dialogue with his patients, sensitivity to the chords struck within him by their transference (i.e. by their desire for him), and awareness of counter-transferential movements in their direction (i.e. his desire for them).

Thus, Freud's self-analysis began and ended with two parallel dreams, one about Irma, the other about Dora (the dream of 'Company at table d'hôte') – both patients of his. Published near the beginning of two different works, *The Interpretation of Dreams* (1900*a*) and *On Dreams* (1901*a*), they are shot through with more or less conscious sexual phantasies aroused in Freud by an overchaste widow in his circle (Irma), and by a perverse young *ingénue* (Dora), who had already shown her ability to seduce a man of mature years, just as Anna O. had Breuer. But unlike Breuer Freud was able both to experience his phantasies in his head and to renounce them in real life. Besides, he was not solely interested in women patients or hysterics. The final stage of Freud's discovery of the Oedipus complex was prompted by the incestuous dream of an obsessional young man, who was being treated for phobia of homicidal impulses. Freud's self-analysis more or less covered the five years he needed to complete successfully his treatment of Herr E., whom he regarded as a case of male hysteria. Often mentioned in letters to Fliess, the ups and downs of that case helped Freud, by interacting with his self-analysis, to achieve a more accurate assessment of himself. He agreed to stop giving treatment even though the symptoms had been only partly cured: this meant that he accepted the limitations of his therapeutic powers and was willing to abandon the infantile wish for omnipotence whose imaginary fulfilment and indirect, implicit elucidation marked successive stages of his self-analysis.

If it is carried out in an interrelational context of this kind, self-analysis is feasible. Indeed, it is necessary for those who, like psychoanalysts for example, are faced with a situation where the people they treat or teach subject them to intense instinctual cathexes and phantasied projections, which can be anything from fascinating to wearing. In any case, one of the results, if not one of the aims, of successful psychoanalytic training is to incite in the subject an introjective identification with the psychoanalyst in the form of an ego capable of self-analysis, and to make the psychoanalyst more likely to find his own self-analysis in the lives of people to whom he can talk freely, and even to go into inter-analysis with those who share the same aims. It is surely wrong to contend, as Mannoni does in the paper I have already referred to (1967), that the only successful self-analysis ever was Freud's, on the grounds that as there was no one to teach him psychoanalysis he had to invent it – like Adam, he had no navel – and that since its invention it has only been possible to hand it on through someone else. Mannoni's argument was sharply, and I think rightly, refuted by Stein (1968*b*).

Every psychoanalyst has, to some degree, to reinvent psychoanalysis for his own purposes; and self-analysis forms an indispensable complement to and natural extension of his own psychoanalysis – at least when the self-analysis has the interrelational characteristics I have described. Surely one of the aims of psychoanalytic societies is to provide each practitioner with a range of possible interlocutors, who, by what they say about their clinical experience, can trigger off in the listener a rewarding sequence of self-reflexive regression, or who, conversely, because of their attentive and receptive attitude, facilitate the setting in motion or explanation of self-analytic processes in a colleague. Self-analysis is evaded or dreaded only in groups whose *raison d'être* is loyalty to the words or the power of a single person. For Freud's successors, it remained what it had been for him: a permanent act of personal appropriation of psychoanalysis.

These remarks call for one rider, which I should perhaps now indicate, and which follows on from what I have just been saying: profitable self-analysis is possible only for those subjects who, in the course of their development, have reached the Oedipal phase in the organisation of the psyche; self-analysis does not work in narcissistic or psychotic organisations. This perhaps calls for another rider. As we have seen, Freud's self-analysis revealed to him his Oedipal problem and his pregenital fixations; it enlightened him about his ambivalence towards his father; it prolonged the work of mourning and facilitated the struggle against depressive anxiety. On the other hand, it enabled him only to half-glimpse the infant's dual relationship with the mother, the formidable importance of the imago of the phallic mother, and identification with the breast as an idealised omnipotent object. For Freud it was the father who devoured his children, like Kronos; the mother was threatening only insofar as she was desirable and prohibited; he treated fragmentation and persecution anxieties with cocaine or tobacco, not with psychical analysis.

How much credit is due, in the discovery of psychoanalysis, to Freud and how much to the period he lived in? There are two common oversimplified – and contradictory – views on this question. Some argue that Freud was the prototype of the genius who set out to defy the prejudice and ignorance of his time, and that he was the sole progenitor of all his discoveries. Others – who sometimes also belong to the first group – contend that Freud, with his petty bourgeois and puritanical morals, general classical culture, and theoretical model of the psychical apparatus borrowed from a now obsolete form of neurophysiology, was very much a prisoner of his age, and that today, at the end of the twentieth century, he has dated terribly.

It is true that the discovery of psychoanalysis was in the air in 1895. There had been increasing interest since 1850 in dreams, hypnosis and dual personality, and since 1880 in infantile sexuality and adult sexual perversions. The Victorian moralism and hypocrisy of late nineteenth-century Europe was being buffeted by a flood of sexual literature – scientific, fictional and sometimes pornographic. After the romantic period, philosophy, psychology and psychiatry relied increasingly, from a dynamic point of view, on the notion of the subconscious. Surely every great discovery depends on a felicitous conjunction of circumstances and genius?

It is nonetheless a fact that Freud found himself quite alone when, despite all the obstacles, he decided to push ahead along avenues which, in the view of the few people who took an interest in his work, would take him either too far or nowhere at all. Where did they lead him? To the Oedipus complex; to the phantasies of the primal scene, of castration, of penis need; earlier on, to an interpretation of dreams which, although by no means a popular dream book, remained close to the popular beliefs on the subject that had been dismissed as superstitions by the materialist scientists of the day (later on, symptoms, parapraxes, jokes and works of art turned out to be open to interpretation, like dreams); to a 'psychical apparatus' which was conceived not just according to the dynamic and economic model of the neurophysiologists, nor indeed along more modern evolutionist lines, but from a topographical point of view; to the demythologisation of the subconscious, which was no longer an entity, no longer a romantic imago of the all-engulfing mother, but something well delimited and defined as having two parts, the unconscious proper, with its primary processes and thing-presentations, and the preconscious, with its secondary processes and word-presentations.

That took quite some doing, as the expression goes. Not only did it mean – as other common clichés have it – that to progress he had to transgress a number of scientific taboos, that to produce he had to identify with the fertile and, in phantasy, omnipotent mother, that to leave something of value behind him he had to deny the inevitability of his own death. It also meant above all that he had to find those ideas, formulate them clearly and distinctly, and organise them into a coherent whole. As I have attempted to show throughout this book, ideas presented themselves to Freud in three strands – experience of psychoneuroses, experience of himself, and experience of the unconscious with which various civilisations have invested their cultural products; it was the interweaving of those three strands which gave rise to his discovery, and their unravelling which provided him with proof.

Freud relied on several different kinds of processes to provide him with new ideas. A common such process, as we have seen, was for a future idea to be anticipated in the form of a dream image – a case of figurative thought preparing the way for operative thought. Notions discovered in this way include the preconscious, seduction phantasies, and exhibitionistic wishes. A second process involved Freud borrowing a clinical notion from a colleague, because of its validity (Charcot's hysterogenic zones, for example), and then giving it a new psychoanalytic twist, again through a dream image (the erotogenic zones, prefigured by the third 'Rome' dream, and indeed already by the Irma dream).

A third process came into play in his recognition of the Oedipus complex. Several elements led up to it – the dreams of the 'One-eyed doctor and schoolmaster' and the 'Sheep's-head', and more especially Freud's recollection of childhood memories during the previous weeks and discussion of them with his mother. The formulation was supplied by a cultural reference, the memory of Sophocles' celebrated tragedy (a passage of which Freud had to translate for his end-of-school examinations). But the actual substance of his discovery was supplied to him by two patients, to whom he was giving psychical and organic treatment respectively: one of them was a man whose obsessional neurosis, it emerged, was based on a wish to kill his father – a wish that amounted to eliminating a rival for the incestuous possession of the mother; the other was an old lady whom Freud had been visiting daily for years to give her morphine injections and collyrium eye-drops: one day, he was so wrapped up in his thoughts about the other patient that he mistakenly put morphine into her eye, and almost gave her a collyrium injection (which would have been fatal) before realising the danger in time and grasping the significance of his mistake in the form of the following conscious thought: 'doing violence to the old woman'. Thus, the injection given to Irma in a dream was followed by the bungled injection given to a substitute for Monika Zajíc, the old nurse who had surfaced from his childhood a little earlier, in the dream of 'Running up stairs undressed': they were two 'criminal' injections. Irma was the prototype of the female patients with whom sexual fulfilment was prohibited by morality and professional ethics, and the nurse a double of his mother, with whom incest was prohibited. Freud probably hit upon the Oedipus complex on his way down the stairs from the old lady's flat, when he realised that he, too, like his patients, had experienced an incestuous desire for his mother, and that it had caused the wish to kill his father, which he had re-experienced with ever greater intensity during the work of mourning after Jacob's death in October 1896. He also realised that these two wishes are felt to be criminal by children. The three familiar references designed to guarantee the objectivity of his knowledge of the unconscious – the clinical reference to the patient, the cultural reference to human legend, and the subjective verification on himself – were thus combined in this single act of creative thought.

As for the castration complex, which is no more than hinted at by Freud at the end of *The Interpretation of Dreams*, a fourth process came into play – the transition to thing-presentations via word-presentations. In the dream of 'Phantasies during sleep', he dreamt that he had at last found a clear, coherent and '*gapless*' theory – that of Fliess's favourite notion of bisexuality! Freud probably had the dream while writing the first version of the dream book in the spring of 1898. It echoed his satisfaction at having found an explanation for the dream-work in condensation, displacement, representability and secondary revision. But he was already entering the phase where he would find it impossible to make any headway or construct a clear, coherent and 'gapless' theory of the functioning of the psychical apparatus in general. He ended up by abandoning the first version of his book: the presence of this 'gap', this 'nothingness', in his thinking brought his work to nothing. The process was accompanied by a subjective experience of general paralysis and impotence.

Freud's decisive achievement came in September 1899 when he was writing the last chapter of *The Interpretation of Dreams*. He was on the brink of fulfilling his dream – the dream of a metapsychology of dreams, the dream of a clear, coherent and 'gapless' theory of the psychical apparatus. All he needed now was an illustration of the last point that would make his theory complete and self-contained, namely that in addition to the first censorship between the unconscious and the preconscious there also exists a second censorship between the preconscious and consciousness. If latent thoughts run up against the first censorship, they are distorted (displaced, condensed, and represented by mental images associated or not, as the case may be, with word-presentations); if, on the other hand, after evading the first censorship, the thoughts have to undergo only the effects of the second censorship, they are not distorted but clearly enunciated in consciousness, in which case the psychotherapist has to take literally whatever the patient says about his anxiety or symptom. The action of the second censorship is confined to isolating the patient's discourse, which is kept intact and made conscious, from its meaning, which is kept unconscious, and to releasing the anxiety associated with that meaning. The action of the first censorship produces dreams, whereas the action of the second censorship alone produces a waking phantasy.

Thus, a 14-year-old boy, at his very first session, had a waking vision of a draughts-board, a dagger, a sickle and a scythe. What the boy subsequently said about his situation and the books he had read shed light on the meaning of the vision. When he was small, he had been forbidden to masturbate (the game of draughts) by his father, a hard and violent man, who had threatened to take revenge on his genitals (the dagger which could be used to kill, the scythe). Later, his father, after divorcing the boy's mother, imposed the presence of a much-detested step-mother on him. After reading about Greek mythology, the boy had imagined himself as the young Kronos springing from his hiding-place and castrating his father Uranus with a sickle – a retaliatory measure reciprocating the earlier threat. So just as Freud, adopting a second level of symbolisation (i.e. symbolising an apparatus whose function is to symbolise), was completing his theory of the psychical apparatus and presenting it as 'gapless', a gap suddenly appeared in his system as a result of a case history – a gap which needed to be understood, at an initial symbolic level, as the lack of male genitals after the subject had experienced in phantasy the threatened punishment. Freud was here describing, though not yet naming, castration anxiety. The guilt feelings that inevitably accompany any discovery prompted Freud to make a mistake: he mixed up the generations, and in his book wrote that the castration was carried out not by Kronos on Uranus, but by Zeus on Kronos. *The Interpretation of Dreams* began with the explicit notion of wish-fulfilment; it ended with the implicit notion of threat-fulfilment.

Freud ended up, as so often with admirable lucidity, by elucidating the very process of his discovery. A subsequent patient, we are told in a later edition of *The Interpretation of Dreams*, complained of a 'gap' in the account of the dream he was giving Freud. Analysis showed that the gap in question was a repetition, in speech, of a forgotten childhood memory where he watched little girls urinating and had seen, with horror, the female genitals – genitals distinguished by a gap, i.e. the lack of a penis. Thus in 1898 the gap as a word-presentation imposed itself on Freud in his dream of 'Phantasies during sleep' in order to represent and conceal the gap as a thing-presentation. We can see that the dreamer's insistence on the negation of the first gap (he wanted to construct a 'gapless' theory) was a transposition of an infantile negation of the second gap (women have penises, so castration does not exist). We can also see how thoroughly, and indeed doubly, right he was in his qualms that there might be a gap in his theory: without the notion of the castration complex, psychoanalytic theory would have been incomplete – it was no coincidence that the first version of his book ground to a halt; but with the castration phantasy, his own body was marked in the flesh by an irreparable gap – it was no coincidence that he then fell victim to a general feeling of impotence.

This process of reduplication between words and things, between the scientific theories of maturity and infantile sexual theories, between the symbolic and the phantasied, defines both the activity of the preconscious and Freud's creative mechanisms. Through the gaps in his theory, which was intended to be 'gapless', Freud came to recognise, between 1895 and 1900, virtually every phantasy that exists – at least all those in the Oedipal cycle and a good number of pregenital phantasies as well. They were able to express themselves because his theory had not foreseen them, and because, once they appeared, it did not attempt to assimilate them. At the same time, in order to express themselves, they used various pathways whose existence and formal functioning were explained by the theory, without it saying anything about the contents likely to move along those pathways.

The work of theoretical elaboration was, then, a useful defence mechanism for Freud: by mobilising the conscious attention and fixing secondary thinking processes on the abstract representation of psychical transformation systems, it gave the primary processes greater freedom to burst into consciousness with less need for distortion; when they did so, Freud's ego, protected by its sound theoretical footing, was then able to record the concrete forms of phantasy in which the primary processes manifested themselves and to attempt a transcription of their meaning.

Thus, in the autumn of 1895, after his first trip to northern Italy and a stimulating 'congress' with Fliess in Berlin, Freud elatedly wrote his first theoretical schema, which was posthumously published under the title of 'Project for a Scientific Psychology'. With the feeling that the schema somehow guaranteed his scientific objectivity, he was able, after his father's death in 1896, to experience fully the work of mourning and at the same time to become aware of the depressive scenario at work in it: he had destroyed the man he loved. So he reorganised his schema (a dialectical interaction of theoretical and clinical material was a constant feature of Freud's method), changed the name of what he and his teachers had hitherto called 'the nervous system' to the 'psychical apparatus', and arranged it into three systems of 'transcription', the unconscious, the preconscious, and consciousness. He was then able to enter into another regressive phase, recollect his earliest childhood memories, re-experience his erotic desire for his mother and his nurse, and discover the Oedipus complex: 'I cannot convey to you any idea of the intellectual beauty of this work,' he wrote to Fliess.

On two other occasions during the period under consideration here, his theory was again outmanoeuvred, so to speak, by phantasies that had slipped through its interstices. In the spring of 1898, Freud set to work writing the first version of his dream book; no sooner had he composed, 'as if in a dream', the schema of the dream-work than his thoughts became confused and the book began to 'drag'. Shielded by that schema, he was then able to dream the series of 'excrement' dreams in June, July and August 1898 which led to the discovery of the primal scene phantasy. In September 1899, Freud was on the point of finishing the second and final version of his book; he had just reorganised his conception of the psychical apparatus by taking into account regression, the topographical point of view, and the two censorships; his theory – or so he thought – was as complete as it could be. The elation which was characteristic of his mood at such moments had reached its peak: Anna Freud later recalled that her father seemed to be sleep-walking. When he reached the penultimate page of his book, two case histories involving children, not adults, and waking phantasies, not dreams (the second of which I have just mentioned), enabled him to describe clearly, without yet giving any intellectual formulation, penis need in girls and castration anxiety in boys. 'On Narcissism: An Introduction', *Totem and Taboo*, and *The Ego and the Id* all came into being as a result of similar internal processes. It could be, too, that Freud's discovery, when treating Dora in the autumn of 1900, of strong bisexual identifications and of a phantasy that children are produced as a result of *fellatio* had arisen in counterpoint to the writing of the second dream book, *On Dreams*, in which Freud strove both to simplify his theory and to systematise it as much as possible.

This brings me to another question: who other than Freud could have invented psychoanalysis? The discovery was, as I have said, very much in the air. If Freud had not existed, someone else would have made it – someone who would necessarily have shared certain creative characteristics with Freud, but who would have put a different personal stamp on the discovery because of differences in personality.

The use of theory as a convenient defence to keep phantasies at a respectable distance – far enough away to escape their effects, and close enough for the subject to be able, at his leisure, to examine and analyse them – is symptomatic of a hysterophobic mental structure where the threatening object is kept permanently under the control of consciousness. We know, moreover, that this was the essence of Freud's own psychopathology, and explains his railway phobia, anxiety about the effects of heavy smoking on the heart, and anxiety about crossing the street. A hysteric, as Fliess probably was, would have been too absorbed by the corporal experiencing of phantasies to achieve what Freud did; someone with an obsessional personality like Breuer or Charcot would have been too prone to conceptual oversystematisation and prevarication; a pre-psychotic, like Tausk or Reich, would have been, by turns, too subjective and too abstract.

Throughout the systematic self-analysis which was set in motion by the death of his father, Freud used theory as a defence against depression. Freudian psychoanalytic theory was the product of a working over of the depressive position, whereas Kleinian psychoanalytic theory was the product of a working over of the schizo-paranoid position. In this, Freud anticipated structuralism, the great defence of presentday intellectuals against the depressive anxiety engendered by modern civilisation and education. In diagram form, the formula for trimethylamin which concludes the specimen dream of 'Irma's injection':

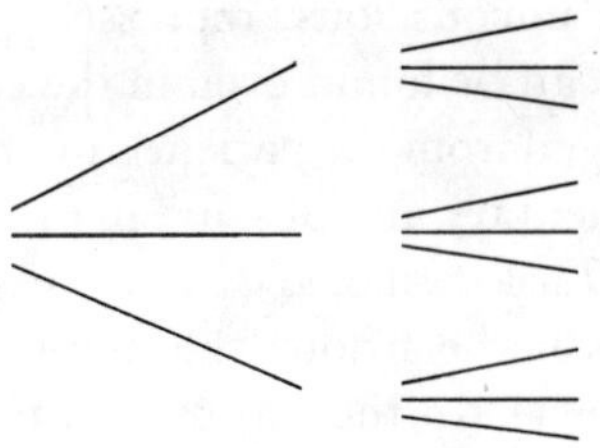

prefigures not only the ternary structure of Freud's two theories of the psychical apparatus, but also the basic structures of kinship according to Lévi-Strauss, Chomsky's trees of generative grammar, and, more generally, the diagrams now commonly used in the human sciences.

But there existed in Freud much more than the mere ability to focus on data, in the strictly optical sense of the word, much more than a reparation of himself after being destroyed in the course of the destruction of his internalised love-objects. True, where others propounded theories with their eyes closed, he would simply observe; and where others were happy to see, he looked around or behind. But once he saw what he saw, he was not content merely to report it – a process which can be interminable (Janet did little else all his life) and which exempts the researcher from the need to think – but immediately homed in on the code that would account for it. This, it seems to me, is the essence of Freud's genius: his ability, when awake, to make an immediate transition from the thing seen to the written word (his self-analysis was a written self-analysis); and his ability, when dreaming, to shift from a landscape to onomastics, toponymy, an inscription, a combinative, a poster, a placard, a proverb, or a double meaning, to move from a herbarium to systematics, from an illustration to a text, from facts to a formula. I have already mentioned, in passing, Lacan's error of interpretation when, basing his argument on passages such as these in Freud, he makes the supposition that the unconscious is structured like a language and that it is a kind of writing: Lacan took for a characteristic of the unconscious what was in fact a feature of Freud's own creative genius. Derrida (1967) has suggested, more sensibly, that there was a 'writing scene' in the development of Freud's theory of the psychical apparatus.[1] The inventor of psychoanalysis had the gift, which he probably derived from rich exchanges, first sensual then linguistic, with his mother, of bypassing the first level of symbolisation when dealing with psychical material and going directly to the second – that of the symbolisation of symbolisation. That was the difference between Freud and his patients. When he applied the technique of psychoanalysis not to himself but to his patients, he hoped to get them to function on the first level, in other words to get them to verbalise unconscious, repressed and pathogenic thing-presentations. This idea can be found even in the early *Studies on Hysteria*: 'Once a picture has emerged from the patient's memory, we may hear him say that it becomes fragmentary and obscure in proportion as he proceeds with his description of it. *The patient is, as it were, getting rid of it by turning it into words*. [. . .] As soon as this has been done, the picture *vanishes, like a ghost* that has been laid' (*SE* 2, 280–1). In their approach to Freud's dream interpretation, most commentators and followers of Freud, in particular the Surrealists, have emphasised the *figurative* aspect of the dream thoughts, which use images (picture puzzles) to express the subject's wishes, whereas Freud himself was much more interested in the *operative* aspect of the transformations which are undergone by thing-presentations, word-presentations, and affects in dreams, symptoms, parapraxes and jokes (the dream-work, the prototype of any psychical process). Freud never

1. Derrida does, however, go along with the common fallacy (which I have pointed out on p. 331) that from the very first edition of *The Interpretation of Dreams* in 1900 Freud used hieroglyphics as a model for his theory of the psychical apparatus, whereas he introduced the metaphor of hieroglyphs only in later editions.

separated the figurative from the operative and never isolated the operative from the figurative, any more than he separated synchrony from diachrony.

This brings me to one last consideration – the traces left on psychoanalysis by the very characteristics of its discovery.

Psychoanalysis could have been invented only by someone, like Freud, in whom the three psychical systems – the unconscious, the preconscious, and consciousness – were sharply differentiated, in whom the two censorships were strong enough to separate those systems and flexible enough to allow a large-scale circulation of instinctual representatives between them, and in whom associations of thing-presentations and word-presentations, depending on internal or external circumstances, were formed, broke up, varied, ramified, became stronger, or, as André Breton later put it, came and 'knocked on the window'. In these characteristics of his preconscious, Freud was a typical product of the education and culture of his period, when the considerable freedom accorded to children in many respects contrasted with the strictness of the taboos and threats directed at infantile and adolescent sexuality, and when access to culture and the wish to learn were valorised, and incentives to acquire new manual or mental aptitudes encouraged.

I have in passing drawn brief portraits of several of Freud's contemporaries, who like him played a creative role in science or the arts. In almost all of them we find a blend of orderliness and whimsicality, of conformism in one department and originality in another. In his social and family relations, Freud led a settled existence, but he was also a man of wit; intellectually, he was a glutton for work, but also a revolutionary. An education and a culture in which discipline carries a certain weight within well-defined limits provide the individual with sturdy internal censorships without which the distinction between psychical systems remains blurred. The encouragement given by the family to learning, and a high-level secondary education that placed equal emphasis on science and arts subjects, were both factors that must have helped an active and fertile preconscious to develop. On top of that, the *joie de vivre*, wit, lighthearted spontaneity and all the other typical features of Viennese society towards the end of the nineteenth century are evidence that alongside the taboos, the hypocrisy and the perversions there existed vast areas of instinctual freedom. Freud's theory of the psychical apparatus in general not only was modelled on his own, but reflected the mental structures engendered in his milieu by contemporary European civilisation, which was at its apogee. It was a civilisation whose internal contradictions helped to produce the various kinds of psychical conflict whose mechanisms Freud elucidated. But by raising, almost a century later, his analyses of those mechanisms to the status of dogma, we run the risk of deluding ourselves about the new kinds of conflict now caused by the evolution of culture and its contradictions.

Freud's self-analysis contains, as we have seen, direct evidence of what he called, towards the end of his life, 'civilization and its discontents' – some of whose aspects he experienced very fully during his childhood and youth: the transition from the extended family in Freiberg (the primal horde) to the restricted family in Vienna; the emergence of the Jews from their ghetto, and their access to civil rights, classical European culture, and liberal, political and intellectual professions; an increasing sense of injustice at the way masturbation was commonly the subject of castigation, adolescent sexuality prohibited, and a veil drawn over love-making techniques and contraceptive methods; and faith in the value of science and in a future founded on the primacy of science.

The hysterophobic structure of Freud the man was responsible for the introduction of one very particular aspect of psychoanalytic technique: the patient is placed at just the right distance from the psychoanalyst, who can see but not touch him; he reclines, with his back to the therapist, in other words he has been made harmless; moreover, during the period covered by this book, the patient was also recommended to close his eyes. As Pontalis (1974) has correctly pointed out, Freud's organisation of space was at opposite poles from the crowded, theatrical, voyeuristic space which Charcot favoured as a setting for his hysterical seances. But, in turn, the Freudian arrangement of psychoanalytic space, while it may be beneficial in many cases of psychoneurosis, has the effect of restricting the conduct of treatment and the choice of patients by making any failure to adjust to such a set-up a contraindication to psychoanalysis. There is still a great deal of resistance to the idea that psychoanalytic treatment can be given lying down, sitting, or standing, alone in the analyst's consulting room, in a group, or wherever the patient happens to live or work.

There is no room here to review systematically all the features which modern psychoanalysis has inevitably inherited from the very manner of its invention, and which were the result partly of Freud's own preoccupations and partly of the cultural crisis of his time. Here are a few examples. The traditional psychoanalytic technique of free verbalisation presupposes the existence of an unconscious phantasy life that spontaneously becomes preconscious if the right conditions (benevolent neutrality, evenly-suspended attention) are created: this was true for Freud and for his patients (at least those he kept), but no longer holds for about half the number of people who today ask for analysis: the preconscious has become impoverished. Another point: Freud's innate confidence in the superiority of life instincts over death instincts made his self-analysis possible and helped him to act as a psychotherapist with his patients. That confidence, however, was where he differed from Nietzsche, for whom self-destruction was undoubtedly the stronger, both in his thought and in his life. But Freud at no point referred to this divergence of views (just as at the end of his life, in 'Analysis Terminable and Interminable', he expressed surprise at negative therapeutic reactions), preferring to emphasise the (real) similarity of their respective views on most other characteristics of the unconscious. In this sense, our era is more Nietzschean than Freudian: predominant social and family attitudes to children now reinforce self-destructive tendencies in them as well as in our civilisation as a whole. Psychoanalysts have had to revise their conception of treatment situations and of techniques: significant examples of this new approach have been provided by Kohut in the United States and Winnicott in Great Britain.

Lastly, I have demonstrated at length that Freud undertook his self-analysis to fight against his depressive tendencies, and that his elaboration of psychoanalytic theory, particularly in its dynamic and economic aspects, corresponded to a setting up of obsessional defences against depressive anxiety. Throughout the history of the psychoanalytic movement, analysts whose personal problems tended to be of a schizo-paranoid nature found great difficulty in getting accepted: the most brilliant of them, first Victor Tausk, then Wilhelm Reich, were rejected, and their colleagues proved unable to come up with a therapeutic attitude appropriate to their mental structure which might have checked them on their perhaps inevitable course towards suicide or madness. Tausk was the first, in 1919, to draw attention to the fact that, in the psychopathological belief in an influencing machine, the decisive factor is not genital or pregenital sexuality, but the subject's ante-sexual dissociation from the unifying image of his own body. Wishes and sexual problems arise only if the subject feels that he inhabits his body with a minimum of security, i.e. if he feels self-confident in his being. The contra-phobic and anti-depressive conception of psychoanalysis is not only ineffectual but even to be discouraged in the case of fragmentation and persecutory anxiety. Like all discoveries, psychoanalysis has tended to be satisfied with only part truths. If we wish to remain faithful to Freud's spirit and genius, we should take into account the historical circumstances that handicap its conception of treatment, its inherent limitations, and the power it can still exert as long as the psychoanalyst, like Freud, shows concern for the patient without too great an emotional bias and exercises his intelligence without too great a theoretical bias.

Like the great majority of his fellow human beings, Freud led a fairly ordinary life. Like those who realised themselves to be ordinary people, he sought what could qualify him as ordinary. Until about the age of 41, he sought a number of attributes that normally secure that status – love, fatherhood, laboratory work, a practice. Like Musil's hero (Musil admired Freud, incidentally), Freud was for a time a man without qualities; but thanks to his reading of Sophocles he eventually, in October 1897, found two qualities – the longing for an impossible incest and the temptation of parricide (or fratricide), two characteristics whose combination he saw, with modesty and scientific genius, as embodying *the* human quality par excellence, that is to say the most ordinary quality, at least in his period and milieu. Although, like most moderately neurotic people, he was more or less resigned to his ordinariness and indeed quite happy with it, he made a great discovery and was proud of it. His discovery remains a great one even today, but more as an example to follow – in its tremendous freedom of approach and analytical precision – than for the conclusions he arrived at, some of which are no longer valid. There have, for instance, been considerable changes in culture, education and the psychical apparatus itself. Fewer and fewer people today recognise themselves in Freud's descriptions; and those who do not are quick to question, often stridently, a theory that no longer means anything to them and to call for an overhaul of what they see as fossilised practices. Indeed, such is precisely the new and urgent task facing psychoanalysts today.

But while his critics continue to fire their poorly aimed broadsides, and his sterile epigoni keep the sacred flame burning, there are a number of psychoanalysts, like myself, for whom Freud means much more than a father figure to be toppled or worshipped. He did not merely reduce the apparent richness and multifaceted polysemy of symptoms and symbols to a return of the repressed, which is universal and very impoverished. He discovered something even more unknown and more useful: the mechanisms of the dream-work, the work of mourning, the work of treatment, the work of creation. In order to do that, he took great care – a rare quality – to verify on himself and on such collective products of the human mind as art, religion, mythology and ideology, the various registers of mental processes that he was learning to analyse in other people. He was an ordinary man, but a man of great presence; he was marked by his era but remained attentive to the psychical conflicts of his time; he was a man of considerable instinctual energy, but took several decades to realise that he was struggling against self-destruction.

The new scientific and industrial era in the West has ushered in a society of popularisation and tolerance, a consumer society. Morals have changed, sex has become freer, families have shrunk, education has been liberalised, the incest taboo has been called into question as a fundamental force of social organisation. Nothing is prohibited, yet at the same time prohibition is creeping into society; that society is regarded as permissive, yet fewer and fewer things are possible. Distinctions are becoming blurred, and no one really knows where to put the dividing line between the individual and the world, the individual and other people, or the ego and the rest of the psychical apparatus. Moreover, mankind has no grand schemes for its future, and threats are coming from a different quarter: nature has been mastered and no longer needs to be struggled against. But the whole of mankind is facing new dangers – the population explosion, nuclear war, overcrowding, pollution from waste, and the destruction of the balance of nature. What the scientific age produced and believed to be beneficial has now turned against it and become a threat. More generally speaking, there is more invested in economic life than in human relations. People tend increasingly to exchange manufactured objects or empty words rather than feelings.

Modern man is not at ease in his body. He feels stifled by education, language, mass communications, institutions. He is distressed by discord between couples and between groups. He does not understand the meaning of death. In this context, children tend to be one moment too well understood and, in both senses of the word, spoilt, and the next treated with indifference or discarded as nuisances, as trash, as objects at the disposal of their parents' vain dreams of omnipotence or at the mercy of their affective thirst that life has failed to satisfy, as depositories of all the evil which parents can no longer project on to the external natural world and which they are forced to locate in what they have themselves produced. That explains why we now find new forms of thinking and feeling, new conceptions of intellectual and emotional maturity, mental health and social justice. That explains why there is an increasing yearning to free human life from the tyranny of economic realities. That explains the increasing frequency of narcissistic excesses and deficiencies, of depression. That also explains the general mood of moroseness and, even more, puzzlement, flagging energies, allergy to education, to technology, to the division of tasks. That explains the call for total care by the state, the renaissance of egalitarian Utopias, the fashion of continuing education which dishes out illusions of individual eternity, the resurgence and increase of delinquency.

In more strictly psychoanalytic terminology, the two censorships, the super-ego, the differentiation of systems within the psychical apparatus, the articulation of word-presentations and thing-presentations in the preconscious, genital primacy over the component instincts, the balance of power in favour of life instincts over death instincts – all this has changed since Freud's time, or, to be more precise, all these elements do not function in human beings today in quite the same way as Freud observed them functioning in most of the people he treated or found confirmation in himself. The narcissistic problem has become more important and more widespread today than the Oedipal problem. As a result, the post-Oedipal super-ego is no more than half-formed, thus leaving the field clear for the archaic, persecutory and destructive super-ego.

Henri-Irénée Marrou, the French authority on the origins of Christianity, used to say that it was no coincidence that he had studied Saint Augustine, who witnessed the final decline of the Roman empire, and who in his *Confessions* shows himself to be perhaps the first modern man. When trying to find an answer to the state of utter confusion into which the world was plunged at about the time of the Second World War, Marrou turned for an answer to the man who had seen the ancient world crumble and Europe's first steps into an era that was to become the Middle Ages, a thinker cast in the mould of traditional culture, open to new realities, living out his faith with intelligence and passion, fighting heresies with determination, resolved to pass on what he had to say, and having succeeded in talking in a new way of the inner man. The crisis of modern civilisation is today more marked, more acute and more widespread than during the last war. A new mental life seems to have come into being in many people, and it is one which those who continue to think with the old mentality have difficulty in understanding, and towards which they feel defenceless or hostile.

I have turned to Freud for an answer, because he strove to investigate and understand the repercussions of the crisis in European culture at the end of the nineteenth century on education, private life, and internal conflicts. I have done so in order that I may better understand, and that others with me may better understand, by following his example, the repercussions that the world crisis is having at the end of the twentieth century on the nature and forms of psychical activity, on the sensibility and imagination of human beings, on the art of exploiting their resources and on the manner in which their pathology is treated. I have done so, too, to bear witness to the fact that there was a time and place where human beings did function as Freud described and as he recognised in himself; to contribute possibly to the hope that what happened then, which no doubt did not happen for the first time, may one day happen again in more or less the same form; and lastly to accept that Freud was what he was and that we are who we are.

Freud Bibliography

(1877*a*) 'Über den Ursprung der hinteren Nervenwurzeln im Rückenmarke von Ammocoetes (Petromyzon Planeri)', *S.B. Akad. Wiss. Wien* (Math.-Naturwiss. Kl.), III Abt., **75**, 15.

(1877*b*) 'Beobachtungen über Gestaltung und feineren Bau der als Hoden beschriebenen Lappenorgane des Aals', *S.B. Akad. Wiss. Wien* (Math.-Naturwiss. Kl.), I Abt., **75**, 419.

(1878*a*) 'Über Spinalganglien und Rückenmark des Petromyzon', *S.B. Akad. Wiss. Wien* (Math.-Naturwiss. Kl.), III Abt., **78**, 81.

(1879*a*) 'Notiz über eine Methode zur anatomischen Präparation des Nervensystems', *Zbl. med. Wiss.*, **17**, Nr. 26, 468.

(1880*a*) Translations of J. S. Mill's 'Enfranchisement of Women' (1851); review of Grote's *Plato and the Other Companions of Sokrates* (1866); 'Thornton on Labour and its Claims' (1869); 'Chapters on Socialism' (1879), under the titles 'Über Frauenemancipation'; 'Plato'; 'Die Arbeiterfrage'; 'Der Sozialismus', in Mill's *Gesammelte Werke*, **12** (ed. Gomperz), Leipzig.

(1882*a*) 'Über den Bau der Nervenfasern und Nervenzellen beim Flusskrebs', *S.B. Akad. Wiss. Wien* (Math.-Naturwiss. Kl.), III Abt., **85**, 9.

(1884*a*) 'Ein Fall von Hirnblutung mit indirekten basalen Herdsymptomen bei Scorbut', *Wien. med. Wschr.*, **34**, Nr. 9, 244, and 10, 276.

(1884*b*) 'Eine neue Methode zum Studium des Faserverlaufes im Centralnervensystem', *Zbl. med. Wiss.*, **22**, Nr. 11, 161.

(1884*c*) 'A New Histological Method for the Study of Nerve-Tracts in the Brain and Spinal Cord' [in English], *Brain*, **7**, 86.

(1884*d*) 'Eine neue Methode zum Studium des Faserverlaufes im Centralnervensystem', *Arch. Anat. Physiol., Lpz.*, Anat. Abt., 453.

(1884*e*) 'On Coca', in S. Freud's *The Cocaine Papers*, Vienna and Zurich, 1963.

(1885*a*) 'Contribution to the knowledge of the Effect of Cocaine', in S. Freud's *The Cocaine Papers*, Vienna and Zurich, 1963.

(1885*b*) 'On the General Effect of Cocaine', in S. Freud's *The Cocaine Papers*, Vienna and Zurich, 1963.

(1885*c*) 'Ein Fall von Muskelatrophie mit ausgebreiteten Sensibilitätsstörungen (Syringomyelie)', *Wien. med. Wschr.*, **35**, Nr. 13, 389, and 14, 425.

(1885*d*) 'Zur Kenntnis der Olivenzwischenschicht', *Neurol. Zbl.*, **4**, Nr. 12, 268.

(1885*e*) 'Opinion on Parke's Cocaine', in S. Freud's *The Cocaine Papers*, Vienna and Zurich, 1963.

(1886*a*) 'Akute multiple Neuritis der spinalen und Hirnnerven', *Wien. med. Wschr.*, **36**, Nr. 6, 168.

(1886*b*) With Darkschewitsch, L. O. von, 'Über die Beziehung des Strickkörpers zum Hinterstrang und Hinterstrangskern nebst Bemerkungen über zwei Felder der Oblongata', *Neurol. Zbl.*, **5**, Nr. 6, 121.

(1886*c*) 'Über den Ursprung des Nervus acusticus', *Mschr. Ohrenheilk.*, Neue Folge **20**, Nr. 8, 245, and 9, 277.
(1886*d*) 'Observation of a Severe Case of Hemi-Anaesthesia in a Hysterical Male', *SE* 1, 25.
(1886*f*) Preface to the Translation of Charcot's *Lectures on the Diseases of the Nervous System*, *SE* 1, 19.
(1887*a*) Review of Averbeck's 'Die akute Neurasthenie', *SE* 1, 35.
(1887*b*) Review of Weir Mitchell's *Die Behandlung gewisser Formen von Neurasthenie und Hysterie* (trans. G. Klemperer), *SE* 1, 36.
(1887*c*) Review of Adamkiewicz's 'Monoplegia anaesthetica', *Neurol. Zbl.*, **6**, Nr. 6, 131.
(1887*d*) 'Craving for and Fear of Cocaine', in S. Freud's *The Cocaine Papers*, Vienna and Zurich, 1963.
(1887*e*) Review of H. Obersteiner's *Anleitung beim Studium des Baues der nervösen Centralorgane im gesunden und kranken Zustande*, *Wien. med. Wschr.*, **37**, Nr. 50, 1642.
(1887*f*) 'Das Nervensystem', Abschnitt V of *Ärztliche Versicherungsdiagnostik*, ed. Buchheim.
(1887*g*) Review of J. Pal's 'Ein Beitrag zur Nervenfärbetechnik', *Neurol. Zbl.*, **6**, Nr. 3, 53.
(1887*h*) Review of Al. Borgherini's 'Beiträge zur Kenntniss der Leitungsbahnen im Rückenmarke', *Neurol. Zbl.*, **6**, Nr. 4, 79.
(1887*i*) Review of J. Nussbaum's 'Über die wechselseitigen Beziehungen zwischen den centralen Ursprungsgebieten der Augenmuskelnerven', *Neurol. Zbl.*, **6**, Nr. 23, 543.
(1888*a*) 'Über Hemianopsie im frühesten Kindesalter', *Wien. med. Wschr.*, **38**, Nr. 32, 1081, and 33, 1116.
(1888*b*) 'Hysteria' and 'Hystero-Epilepsy' in Villaret's *Handwörterbuch der gesamten Medizin*, *SE* 1, 39 and 58. (Unsigned, authorship uncertain.)
(1888–89) Preface to the Translation of Bernheim's *Suggestion*, *SE* 1, 73.
(1889*a*) Review of August Forel's *Hypnotism*, *SE* 1, 91.
(1891*a*) With Rie, O., *Klinische Studie über die halbseitige Cerebrallähmung der Kinder*, Heft III of *Beiträge zur Kinderheilkunde*, ed. Kassowitz, Vienna.
(1891*b*) *On Aphasia*, London and New York, 1953.
(1891*c*) 'Kinderlähmung' and 'Lähmung' in Villaret's *Handwörterbuch der gesamten Medizin*, **2**, Stuttgart. (Unsigned, authorship uncertain.)
(1892*a*) Translation of H. Bernheim's *Hypnotisme, suggestion et psychothérapie: études nouvelles*, Paris 1891, under the title *Neue Studien über Hypnotismus, Suggestion und Psychotherapie*, Vienna.
(1892–93) 'A Case of Successful Treatment by Hypnotism', *SE* 1, 117.
(1892–94) Preface and Footnotes to the Translation of Charcot's *Tuesday Lectures*, *SE* 1, 131.
(1893*a*) With Breuer, J., 'On the Psychical Mechanism of Hysterical Phenomena: Preliminary Communication', *SE* 2, 3.
(1893*b*) *Zur Kenntniss der cerebralen Diplegien des Kindesalters (im Anschluss an die Little'sche Krankheit)*, Heft III, Neue Folge, of *Beiträge zur Kinderheilkunde*, ed. Kassowitz, Vienna.
(1893*c*) 'Some Points for a Comparative Study of Organic and Hysterical Motor Paralyses', *SE* 1, 157.
(1893*d*) 'Über familiäre Formen von cerebralen Diplegien', *Neurol. Zbl.*, **12**, Nr. 15, 512, and 16, 542.
(1893*e*) 'Les diplégies cérébrales infantiles' [in French], *Rev. neurol.*, **1**, No. 8, 177.

(1893*f*) 'Charcot', *SE* 3, 9.
(1893*g*) 'Über ein Symptom, das häufig die Enuresis nocturna der Kinder begleitet', *Neurol. Zbl.*, **12**, Nr. 21, 735.
(1893*h*) Lecture 'On the Psychical Mechanism of Hysterical Phenomena', *SE*, 3, 27.
(1894*a*) 'The Neuro-Psychoses of Defence, *SE* 3, 43.
(1895*b* [1894]) 'On the Grounds for Detaching a Particular Syndrome from Neurasthenia under the Description "Anxiety Neurosis" ', *SE* 3, 87.
(1895*c* [1894]) 'Obsessions and Phobias', *SE* 3, 71.
(1895*d*) With Breuer, J., *Studies on Hysteria*, *SE* 2.
(1895*e*) 'Über die Bernhardt'sche Sensibilitätsstörung am Oberschenkel', *Neurol. Zbl.*, **14**, Nr. 11, 491.
(1895*f*) 'A Reply to Criticisms of my Paper on Anxiety Neurosis', *SE* 3, 121.
(1896*a*) 'Heredity and the Aetiology of the Neuroses', *SE* 3, 143.
(1896*b*) 'Further Remarks on the Neuro-Psychoses of Defence', *SE* 3, 159.
(1896*c*) 'The Aetiology of Hysteria', *SE* 3, 189.
(1897*a*) *Infantile Cerebral Paralysis*, translated by Lester A. Russin, University of Miami Press, 1968.
(1897*b*) *Abstracts of the Scientific Writings of Dr. Sigmund Freud (1877–1897)*, *SE* 3, 225.
(1898*a*) 'Sexuality in the Aetiology of the Neuroses', *SE* 3, 261.
(1898*b*) 'The Psychical Mechanism of Forgetfulness', *SE* 3, 289.
(1898*c*) 'Cerebrale Kinderlähmung [I]' (32 reviews and abstracts), *Jbr. Leist. Neurol.*, **1** (1897), 613.
(1899*a*) 'Screen Memories', *SE* 3, 301.
(1899*b*) 'Cerebrale Kinderlähmung [II]' (29 reviews and abstracts), *Jbr. Leist. Neurol.*, **2** (1898), 632.
(1900*a*) *The Interpretation of Dreams*, *SE* 4–5.
(1900*b*) 'Cerebrale Kinderlähmung [III]' (22 reviews and abstracts), *Jbr. Leist. Neurol.*, **3** (1899), 611.
(1901*a*) *On Dreams*, *SE* 5, 633.
(1901*b*) *The Psychopathology of Everyday Life*, *SE* 6.
(1901*c*) [1899]) Autobiographical Note, in J. L. Pagel's *Biographisches Lexicon hervorragender Ärzte des neunzehnten Jahrhunderts*, Berlin, *SE* 3, 325.
(1904*a*) 'Freud's Psycho-Analytic Procedure', *SE* 7, 249.
(1905*c*) *Jokes and their Relation to the Unconscious*, *SE* 8.
(1905*d*) *Three Essays on the Theory of Sexuality*, *SE* 7, 125.
(1905*e* [1901]) 'Fragment of an Analysis of a Case of Hysteria', *SE* 7, 3.
(1906*c*) 'Psycho-Analysis and the Establishment of the Facts in Legal Proceedings', *SE* 9, 99.
(1907*a*) *Delusions and Dreams in Jensen's 'Gradiva'*, *SE* 9, 3.
(1908*b*) 'Character and Anal Erotism', *SE* 9, 169.
(1908*c*) 'On the Sexual Theories of Children', *SE* 9, 207.
(1909*a* [1908]) 'Some General Remarks on Hysterical Attacks', *SE* 9, 229.
(1909*b*) 'Analysis of a Phobia in a Five-Year-Old Boy', *SE* 10, 3.
(1909*d*) 'Notes upon a Case of Obsessional Neurosis', *SE* 10, 155.
(1910*a* [1909]) 'Five Lectures on Psycho-Analysis', *SE* 11, 3.
(1910*c*) *Leonardo da Vinci and a Memory of his Childhood*, *SE* 11, 59.
(1910*d*) 'The Future Prospects of Psycho-Analytic Therapy', *SE* 11, 141.
(1910*h*) 'A Special Type of Choice of Object made by Men', *SE* 11, 165.
(1912*e*) 'Recommendations to Physicians Practising Psycho-Analysis', *SE* 12, 111.

(1912–13) *Totem and Taboo*, *SE* 13, 1.
(1913*f*) 'The Theme of the Three Caskets', *SE* 12, 291.
(1913*i*) 'The Disposition to Obsessional Neurosis', *SE* 12, 313.
(1914*c*) 'On Narcissism: an Introduction', *SE* 14, 69.
(1914*d*) 'On the History of the Psycho-Analytic Movement', *SE* 14, 3.
(1916*d*) 'Some Character-Types Met with in Psycho-Analytic Work', *SE* 14, 311.
(1916–17) *Introductory Lectures on Psycho-Analysis*, *SE* 15–16.
(1917*b*) 'A Childhood Recollection from *Dichtung und Wahrheit*', *SE* 17, 147.
(1917*e* [1915]) 'Mourning and Melancholia', *SE* 14, 239.
(1919*e*) '"A Child is Being Beaten"', *SE* 17, 177.
(1919*h*) 'The "Uncanny"', *SE* 17, 219.
(1920*b*) 'A Note on the Prehistory of the Technique of Analysis', *SE* 18, 263.
(1920*d*) 'Associations of a Four-Year-Old Child', *SE* 18, 266.
(1920*g*) *Beyond the Pleasure Principle*, *SE* 18, 7.
(1923*a* [1922]) 'Two Encyclopaedia Articles', *SE* 18, 255.
(1925*a* [1924]) 'A Note upon the "Mystic Writing-Pad"', *SE* 19, 227.
(1925*d* [1924]) *An Autobiographical Study*, *SE* 20, 3.
(1926*c*) 'Foreword' to E. Pickworth Farrow's *A Practical Method of Self-Analysis*, *SE* 20, 280.
(1926*d* [1925]) *Inhibitions, Symptoms and Anxiety*, *SE* 20, 77.
(1927*a*) 'Postscript to *The Question of Lay Analysis*', *SE* 20, 251.
(1928*b*) 'Dostoevsky and Parricide', *SE* 21, 175.
(1930*a*) *Civilization and its Discontents*, *SE* 21, 59.
(1930*e*) Address delivered in the Goethe House at Frankfurt, *SE* 21, 208.
(1932*a*) 'The Acquisition and Control of Fire', *SE* 22, 185.
(1933*b* [1932]) *Why War?*, *SE* 22, 197.
(1935*b*) 'The Subtleties of a Faulty Action', *SE* 22, 233.
(1936*a*) 'A Disturbance of Memory on the Acropolis', *SE* 22, 239.
(1937*c*) 'Analysis Terminable and Interminable', *SE* 23, 211.
(1939*a* [1937–39]) *Moses and Monotheism*, *SE* 23, 3.
(1940*c* [1922]) 'Medusa's Head', *SE* 18, 273.
(1940*d* [1892]) With Breuer, J., 'On the Theory of Hysterical Attacks', *SE* 1, 151.
(1941*a* [1892]) Letter to Josef Breuer, *SE* 1, 147.
(1941*b* [1892]) 'III', *SE* 1, 149.
(1941*c* [1899]) 'A Premonitory Dream Fulfilled', *SE* 5, 623.
(1950*a* [1887–1902]) *The Origins of Psycho-Analysis: Letters to Wilhelm Fliess, Drafts and Notes, 1887–1902, by Sigmund Freud.* Edited by Marie Bonaparte, Anna Freud and Ernst Kris; translated by Eric Mosbacher and James Strachey, London and New York, Basic Books and Imago, 1954.
(1950*a* [1895]) 'Project for a Scientific Psychology', *SE* 1, 283.
(1956*a* [1886]) 'Report on my Studies in Paris and Berlin, on a Travelling Bursary Granted from the University Jubilee Fund, 1885–6', *SE* 1, 3.
(1961) *Letters of Sigmund Freud, 1873–1939*, edited by Ernst L. Freud, translated by Tania Stern and James Stern, London, Hogarth Press.
(1980) *Sigmund Freud. Briefe, 1873–1939*, new and enlarged edition (1st ed., 1960), Frankfurt, Fischer Verlag.
(1985) *The Complete Letters of Sigmund Freud to Wilhelm Fliess, 1887–1904*, translated and edited by Jeffrey Moussaieff Masson, Cambridge (Massachusetts) and London, The Belknap Press of Harvard University Press.

Bibliography Excluding Freud

Abbott, J. A. (1966) 'A Note on Freud's Dandelion Memory', *American Imago*, **23**, 208–9.

Abraham, N. (1972) 'Le temps, le rythme et l'inconscient', *Revue française de Psychanalyse*, **36**, No. 4, 557–83.

Adams, L. (1953) 'A New Look at Freud's Dream: "The Breakfast Ship" ', *American Journal of Psychiatry*, **110**, No. 5, 381–4.

Alexandrian, S. (1974) *Le surréalisme et le rêve*, Paris, Gallimard.

Amacher, P. (1965) 'Freud's Neurological Education and Its Influence on Psychoanalytic Theory', *Psychological Issues*, **4**, No. 4, Monograph 16, New York, International Universities Press.

Andersson, O. (1962) *Studies in the Prehistory of Psychoanalysis. The Etiology of Psychoneuroses and Some Related Themes in Sigmund Freud's Scientific Writings and Letters 1886–1896*, Stockholm, Svenska Bokförlaget.

Anzieu, D. (1953) Preface to *L'Auto-analyse*, the French translation of Horney (1942), Paris, Stock.

Anzieu, D. (1956*a*) 'Introduction aux études freudiennes', *Bulletin de la Faculté de Lettres de Strasbourg*, **34**, No. 7, 301–26.

Anzieu, D. (1956*b*) 'Biographie de Freud', *Bulletin de Psychologie*, **9**, Nos. 11–12, 605–16.

Anzieu, D. (1956*c*) *Le psychodrame analytique chez l'enfant*, Paris, Presses Universitaires de France.

Anzieu, D. (1956*d*) 'Note sur Freud philosophe', *Revue Philosophique*, No. 4, 538–9.

Anzieu, D. (1956*e*) 'Quelques explications de la découverte de la psychanalyse', *Etudes philosophiques*, **11**, No. 4, 637–45.

Anzieu, D. (1959) *L'auto-analyse. Son rôle dans la découverte de la psychanalyse par Freud. Sa fonction en psychanalyse*, Paris, Presses Universitaires de France.

Anzieu, D. (1960) Introduction to the Tourneur-Anzieu edition of Pascal's *Pensées*, Paris, Armand Colin.

Anzieu, D. (1971*a*) 'Le corps et le code dans les contes de Borges', *Nouvelle Revue de Psychanalyse*, No. 3, 177–210.

Anzieu, D. (1971*b*) 'Paralysie et créativité: naissance d'un concept freudien', *Sciences de l'Art, Scientific Aesthetics*, **8**, No. 1, 3–8.

Anzieu, D. (1972) 'Etude littérale d'un rêve de Freud: la mère endormie et les personnages aux becs d'oiseaux', *Nouvelle Revue de Psychanalyse*, No. 5, 83–99.

Anzieu, D. (1973) 'La bisexualité dans l'auto-analyse de Freud: le rêve "Mon fils, le myope" ', *Nouvelle Revue de Psychanalyse*, No. 7, 179–91.

Anzieu, D., Béjarano, A., Kaës, R., Missenard, A., and Pontalis, J.-B. (1972) *Le travail psychanalytique dans les groupes*, Paris, Dunod.

Anzieu, D., Mathieu, M., Besdine, M., Guillaumin, J., and Jaques, E. (1974) *Psychanalyse du génie créateur*, Paris, Dunod.

Aron, W. (1956–57) 'Notes on Sigmund Freud's Ancestry and Jewish Contacts', *Yivo Annal of Jewish Social Sciences*, **11**, 286–95.

Bachelard, G. (1938) *La formation de l'esprit scientifique: contribution à une psychanalyse de la connaissance objective*, Paris, Vrin.

Bakan, D. (1958) *Sigmund Freud and the Jewish Mystical Tradition*, New York, Van Nostrand.

Benedikt, M. (1868) *Elektrotherapie*, Vienna, Tendler.

Benveniste, E. (1956) 'Remarques sur la fonction du langage dans la découverte freudienne', *La Psychanalyse*, **1**, 3–16, Paris, Presses Universitaires de France.

Berenstein, I. (1974) 'Sobre el contenido manifiesto de los sueños', *Revista de Psicoanalisis* (Buenos Aires), **31**, 915–52.

Bernfeld, S. (1944) 'Freud's Earliest Theories and the School of Helmholtz', *Psychoanalytic Quarterly*, **13**, No. 3, 341–62.

Bernfeld, S. (1946) 'An Unknown Autobiographical Fragment by Freud', *American Imago*, **4**, No. 1, 3–19.

Bernfeld, S. (1949) 'Freud's Scientific Beginnings', *American Imago*, **6**, No. 3, 165–96.

Bernfeld, S. (1951) 'S. Freud, M.D., 1882–1885', *International Journal of Psycho-Analysis*, **32**, No. 3, 204–17.

Bernfeld, S. (1953) 'Freud's Studies on Cocaine, 1884–1887', *Journal of the American Psychoanalytic Association*, **1**, No. 4, 581–613.

Bernfeld, S., and Bernfeld, S. C. (1944) 'Freud's Early Childhood', *Bulletin of the Menninger Clinic*, **8**, 107–15.

Bernfeld, S., and Bernfeld, S. C. (1952) 'Freud's First Year in Practice (1886–1887)', *Bulletin of the Menninger Clinic*, **16**, No. 2, 57–65.

Bernfeld, S. C. (1951) 'Freud and Archaeology', *American Imago*, **8**, No. 2, 107–28.

Bernfeld, S. C. (1952) 'Discussion of Buxbaum, Freud's Dream Interpretation in the Light of his Letters to Fliess', *Bulletin of the Menninger Clinic*, **16**, No. 2, 70–72.

Besdine, M. (1968) 'The Jocasta Complex, Mothering and Genius', *Psychoanalytic Review*, **55**, No. 2, 259–77 and No. 3, 574–600.

Binswanger, L. (1957) *Sigmund Freud: Reminiscences of a Friendship*, New York, Grune & Stratton.

Brome, V. (1967) *Freud and his Early Circle*, London, Heinemann.

Brun, R. (1936) 'Sigmund Freuds Leistungen auf dem Gebiet der organischen Neurologie', *Schweizer Archiv für Neurologie und Psychiatrie*, **37**, No. 2, 200–7.

Buxbaum, E. (1951) 'Freud's Dream Interpretation in the Light of his Letters to Fliess', *Bulletin of the Menninger Clinic*, **15**, No. 6, 197–212.

Chertok, L. (1961) 'On the Discovery of the Cathartic Method', *International Journal of Psycho-Analysis*, **42**, 284–7.

Chertok, L. (1968) 'The Discovery of the Transference', *International Journal of Psycho-Analysis*, **49**, 560–76.

Chertok, L. (1970) 'Freud in Paris: a crucial stage', *International Journal of Psycho-Analysis*, **51**, 511–20.

Chertok, L., and Saussure, R. de (1973) *Naissance du psychanalyste. De Mesmer à Freud*, Paris, Payot.

Cixous, H. (1968) *L'exil de James Joyce*, Paris, Grasset.

Clark, R. W. (1980) *Freud: the Man and the Cause*, London, Weidenfeld.

Dalma, J. (1963) 'La catarsis en Aristoteles, Bernays y Freud', *Revista de psiquiatría y psicología medical* (Tucumán), **6**, 253–69.

Delboeuf, J. (1885) *Le sommeil et les rêves*, Paris.

Deleuze, G. and Guattari, F. (1977) *Anti-Oedipus, Capitalism and Schizophrenia*, New York, Richard Seaver Books.

Derrida, J. (1967) *L'écriture et la différence*, Chap. 7, 'Freud et la scène de l'écriture', Paris, Seuil.

Dorer, M. (1932) *Historische Grundlagen der Psychoanalyse*, Leipzig, F. Meiner.

Dufresne, R. (1971) 'Pour introduire la lecture française de Freud', *Interprétation*, **5**, No. 1, 41–97.

Dufresne, R. (1973) *Bibliographie des écrits de Freud*, Paris, Payot.

Edinger, D. (1963) *Bertha Pappenheim, Leben und Schriften*, Frankfurt, Ner-Tamid-Verlag.

Eissler, K. R. (1951) 'An Unknown Autobiographical Letter by Freud and a Short Comment', *International Journal of Psycho-Analysis*, **32**, No. 4, 319–24.

Eissler, K. R. (1958) 'Kritische Bemerkungen zu Renée Gicklhorns Beitrag "Eine mysteriöse Bildaffäre" ', *Wiener Geschichtsblätter*, **13**, 55–60.

Eissler, K. R. (1966) *Sigmund Freud und die Wiener Universität*, Bern, Hans Huber.

Ellenberger, H. F. (1956) 'Fechner and Freud', *Bulletin of the Menninger Clinic*, **20**, No. 4, 201–14.

Ellenberger, H. F. (1964) 'La maladie créatrice', *Dialogue, Canadian Philosophical Review*, **3**, 25–41.

Ellenberger, H. F. (1970) *The Discovery of the Unconscious*, New York, Basic Books.

Erikson, E. H. (1954) 'The Dream Specimen of Psychoanalysis', *Journal of the American Psychoanalytic Association*, **2**, 5–56.

Erikson, E. H. (1964) *Insight and Responsibility. Lectures on the Ethical Implications of Psychoanalytic Insight*, New York, Norton.

Fechner, G. T. (1889) *Elemente der Psychophysik*, 2 vols., Leipzig.

Fenichel, O. (1946) 'Some Remarks on Freud's Place in the History of Science', *Psychoanalytic Quarterly*, **15**, No. 3, 279–84.

Fliess, R. (1942) 'The Metapsychology of the Analyst', *Psychoanalytic Quarterly*, **11**, 211–27.

Freud, M. (1957) *Glory Reflected*, London, Angus and Robertson.

Freud-Bernays, A. (1940) 'My Brother Sigmund Freud', *American Mercury*, **51**, No. 203, 335–42.

Fromm, E. (1951) *The Forgotten Language*, New York, Harper.

Fromm, E. (1959) *Sigmund Freud's Mission: An Analysis of His Personality and Influence*, New York, Harper.

Gardner, M. (1966) 'Mathematical Games: Freud's Friend Wilhelm Fliess and His Theory of Male and Female Life Cycles', *Scientific American*, **215**, No. 1, 108–13; No. 2, 99.

Garnier, A. (1872) *Traité des facultés de l'âme, contenant l'histoire des principales théories psychologiques*, 3 vols., Paris.

Gicklhorn, J., and Gicklhorn, R. (1960) *Sigmund Freuds akademische Laufbahn im Lichte der Dokumente*, Vienna, Urban & Schwarzenberg.

Gicklhorn, N., Kalivoda, F., and Sajner, J. (1967) 'Nové archívní nálezy o dětství Sigmunda Freuda v Příboře', *Československa Psychiatria*, **43**, 131–6.

Gicklhorn, R. (1958) 'Eine mysteriöse Bildaffäre', *Wiener Geschichtsblätter*, **13**, 14–17.

Gicklhorn, R. (1959) 'Das erste öffentliche Kinder-Kranken-Institut in Wien', *Unsere Heimat*, **30**, 146–57.

Gicklhorn, R. (1965) 'Eine Episode aus Sigmund Freuds Mittelschulzeit', *Unsere Heimat*, **36**, 18–24.

Gicklhorn, R., and Sajner, J. (1969) 'The Freiberg Period of the Freud Family', *Journal of the History of Medicine*, **24**, 37–43.

Goldmann, L. (1955) *Le dieu caché. Etude sur la vision tragique dans les 'Pensées' de Pascal et dans le théâtre de Racine*, Paris, Gallimard.

Green, A. (1972) 'De l'*Esquisse* à *L'interprétation des rêves*: coupure et clôture', *Nouvelle Revue de Psychanalyse*, No. 5, 155–80.

Greenacre, P. (1952) *Trauma, Growth, and Personality*, New York, Norton.

Grinstein, A. (1980) *Sigmund Freud's Dreams*, New York, International Universities Press.

Grotjahn, M. (1956) 'A Letter by Sigmund Freud with Recollections of His Adolescence', *Journal of the American Psychoanalytic Association*, **4**, 644–52.

Grotjahn, M. (1967) 'Freud's Tragic Conflicts as Presented in His Dreams', *Newsletter, South California Psychoanalytic Society and Institute*, November.

Grotjahn, M. (1969) 'Sigmund Freud as a Dreamer, Writer and Friend', *Voices*, **5**, (2), 70–73.

Guillaumin, J. (1973) 'Le rêveur et son rêve', *Revue française de Psychanalyse*, **37**, No. 1–2, 5–48.

Hervey de Saint-Denis, Marquis d' (1867) *Les rêves et les moyens de les diriger*, Paris (published anonymously).

Hildebrandt, F. W. (1875) *Der Traum und seine Verwertung für's Leben*, Leipzig.

Hirschmuller, A. (1978) *Physiologie und Psychoanalyse im Leben und Werk Josef Breuers*, Bern, Hans Huber.

Horney, K. (1942) *Self-Analysis*, London, Routledge & Kegan Paul.

Jackson, J. Hughlings (1958) *Selected Writings*, two vols., New York, Basic Books.

Jaques, E. (1965) 'Death and the Mid-Life Crisis', *International Journal of Psycho-Analysis*, **46**, 502–514.

Jelliffe, S. E. (1937) 'Sigmund Freud as a Neurologist', *Journal of Nervous and Mental Disease*, **85**, 696–711.

Jessen, P. (1855) *Versuch einer wissenschaftlichen Begründung der Psychologie*, Berlin.

Jones, E. (1952) Letter on Van der Heide, *Bulletin of the Menninger Clinic*, **16**, No. 5, 192.

Jones E. (1953) *Sigmund Freud: Life and Work. Vol. I: the Young Freud, 1856–1900*, London, Hogarth Press.

Jones, E. (1955) *Sigmund Freud: Life and Work. Vol. II: Years of Maturity, 1901–1919*, London, Hogarth Press.

Jones, E. (1956) *Sigmund Freud: Four Centenary Addresses*, New York, Basic Books.

Jones, E. (1957) *Sigmund Freud: Life and Work. Vol. III: the Last Phase, 1919–1939*, London, Hogarth Press.

Khan, M. Masud R. (1970) 'The Catalytic Role of Crucial Friendship in the Epistemology of Self-Experience in Montaigne, Rousseau and Freud', *Dynamische Psychiatrie* (Berlin), **3**, No. 3, 168–78.

Kligerman, C. (1972) 'Panel on "Creativity"' (27th International Psycho-Analytic Congress, Vienna, July 29, 1971), *International Journal of Psycho-Analysis*, **53**, No. 1, 21–30.

Krafft-Ebing, R. von (1889) 'Über Neurosen und Psychosen durch sexuelle Abstinenz', *Jahrbuch für Psychiatrie*, **8**.

Kris, E. (1950) 'The Significance of Freud's Earliest Discoveries', *International Journal of Psycho-Analysis*, **31**, Nos. 1–2, 108–16.

Lagache, D. (1949) 'Les rapports de l'angoisse et de la conscience', *Revue Philosophique*, **139**, Nos. 1–3, 60–66.

Lagache, D. (1961) 'La psychanalyse et la structure de la personnalité', *La Psychanalyse*, No. 6, 5–54.
Laplanche, J. (1970) *Vie et mort en psychanalyse*, Paris, Flammarion.
Laplanche, J., and Pontalis, J.-B. (1973) *The Language of Psycho-Analysis*, London, Hogarth Press.
Leavitt, H. C. (1956) 'A Biographical and Teleological Study of Irma's Injection Dream', *Psychoanalytic Review*, **43**, 440–47.
Leclaire, S. (1966) 'Fantasme et théorie', *Cahiers pour l'analyse*, Nos. 1–2, 59–65.
Leclaire, S. (1968) *Psychanalyser*, Paris, Seuil.
Lefort, C. (1972) *Le travail de l'oeuvre. Machiavel*, Paris, Gallimard.
Lehmann, H. (1966) 'Two Dreams and a Childhood Memory of Freud', *Journal of the American Psychoanalytic Association*, **14**, No. 2, 388–405.
Liébeault, A.-A. (1889) *Le sommeil provoqué et les états analogues*, Paris.
Lipps, T. (1897) 'Der Begriff des Unbewussten in der Psychologie', *Records of the Third International Congress of Psychology*, Munich.
Mann, T. (1936) *Freud und die Zukunft*, Vienna, Bermann Fischer (English translation in *Essays of Three Decades*, New York, Knopf, 1947).
Mannoni, O. (1967) 'L'analyse originelle', *Temps modernes*, **22**, No. 253, 2136–51.
Maury, L. F. A. (1878) *Le sommeil et les rêves*, Paris.
Maylan, C. (1930) *Freuds tragischer Komplex*, Munich, Ernst Reinhardt.
Merlan, P. (1945) 'Brentano and Freud', *Journal of the History of Ideas*, **6**, No. 3, 375–77.
Merlan, P. (1949) 'Brentano and Freud', *Journal of the History of Ideas*, **10**, 451.
Painter, G. D. (1959–1965) *Marcel Proust*, 2 vols. London, Chatto & Windus.
Pascal, B. (1960) *Pensées*, edited by Tourneur and Anzieu, Paris, Armand Colin.
Peto, A. (1969) 'Terrifying Eyes', *The Psychoanalytic Study of the Child*, **24**, 197–212.
Politzer, G. (1928) *Critique des fondements de la psychologie*, Paris, Presses Universitaires de France.
Pollock, G. H. (1958) 'The Possible Significance of Childhood Object Loss in the Joseph Breuer-Bertha Pappenheim (Anna O.)-Sigmund Freud Relationship', *Journal of the American Psychoanalytic Association*, **16**, 711–39.
Pontalis, J.-B. (1972) 'La pénétration du rêve', *Nouvelle Revue de Psychanalyse*, No. 5, 257–71.
Pontalis, J.-B. (1974) 'Freud in Paris', *International Journal of Psycho-Analysis*, **55**, 455–58 (reprinted as 'Between Freud and Charcot: from One Scene to the Other', in *Frontiers in Psychoanalysis*, London, Hogarth Press, 1981, 17–22).
Radestock, P. (1879) *Schlaf und Traum*, Leipzig.
Reik, T. (1940) *From Thirty Years with Freud*, New York, Farrar & Rinehart.
Reik, T. (1948) *The Inner Experience of a Psychoanalyst*, London, George Allen & Unwin.
Ribeiro Hawelka, E. (1974) Introduction to the critical edition of Freud, S., *'L'Homme aux rats'. Journal d'une analyse*, Paris, Presses Universitaires de France.
Ricoeur, P. (1965) *De l'interprétation. Essai sur Freud*, Paris, Seuil.
Ritvo, L. B. (1965) 'Darwin as the Source of Freud's Neo-Lamarckianism', *Journal of the American Psychoanalytic Association*, **13**, 499–517.
Roazen, P. (1969) *Brother Animal*, New York, Knopf.
Robert M. (1964) *La révolution psychanalytique. La vie et l'oeuvre de Sigmund Freud*, 2 vols., Paris, Payot.
Robert, W. (1886) *Der Traum als Naturnotwendigkeit erklärt*, Hamburg.
Rosenfeld, E. M. (1956) 'Dreams and Vision. Some Remarks on Freud's Egyptian Bird

Dream', *International Journal of Psycho-Analysis*, **37**, No. 1, 97–105.

Rosenfeld, H. (1960) 'On drug addiction', *International Journal of Psycho-Analysis*, **41**, 467–75.

Rosenblum, E. (1973) 'Le premier parcours psychanalytique d'un homme, relaté par Freud: apport à son auto-analyse', *Etudes psychothérapeutiques*, juin-septembre, 51–8.

Rosolato, G. (1969), *Essais sur le symbolique*, Paris, Gallimard.

Sachs, H. (1944) *Freud: Master and Friend*, Cambridge, Harvard University Press.

Sajner, J. (1968) 'Sigmund Freuds Beziehungen zu seinem Geburtsort Freiberg (Příbor) und zu Mähren', *Clio Medica*, **3**, 167–80.

Scherner, K. A. (1861) *Das Leben des Traumes*, Berlin.

Schick, A. (1968–69) 'The Vienna of Sigmund Freud', *Psychoanalytic Review*, **55**, No. 4, 529–51.

Schoenwald, R. (1954) 'A Turning-Point in Freud's Life: "Zur Auffassung der Aphasien"', *Osiris*, **11**, 119–26.

Schoenwald, R. (1955) 'Recent Studies of the Young Freud', *Bulletin of the History of Medicine*, **29**, 261–8.

Schönau, W. (1968) *Sigmund Freuds Prosa. Literarische Elemente seines Stils*, Stuttgart, J. B. Metzler.

Schur, M. (1966) 'Some Additional "Day Residues" of the "Specimen Dream of Psychoanalysis"', in *Psychoanalysis – A General Psychology: Essays in Honor of Heinz Hartmann*, ed. R. M. Loewenstein, L. M. Newman, M. Schur, and A. J. Solnit, New York, International Universities Press, 45–85.

Schur, M. (1972) *Freud: Living and Dying*, London, Hogarth Press.

Simon, P.-M. (1888) *Le monde des rêves*, Paris.

Spehlmann, R. (1953) *Sigmund Freuds Neurologische Schriften. Eine Untersuchung zur Vorgeschichte der Psychoanalyse*, Berlin, Springer.

Spitta, H. (1882) *Die Schlaf- und Traumzustände der menschlichen Seele*, Tübingen.

Starobinski, J. (1970) *La relation critique*, Paris, Gallimard.

Starobinski, J. (1985) 'Recettes éprouvées pour chasser la mélancolie', *Nouvelle Revue de Psychanalyse*, No. 32.

Stein, C. (1967) 'Rome imaginaire. Fragment d'un commentaire de "L'interprétation des rêves" de Sigmund Freud', *L'Inconscient*, No. 1, 1–30.

Stein, C. (1968*a*) 'Le père mortel et le père immortel', *L'Inconscient*, No. 5, 59–100.

Stein, C. (1968*b*) 'L'identification à Freud dans l'auto-analyse', *L'Inconscient*, No. 7, 99–114.

Stengel, E. (1954) 'A Re-evaluation of Freud's Book "On Aphasia". Its Significance for Psychoanalysis', *International Journal of Psycho-Analysis*, **35**, 85–9.

Strümpell, L. (1877) *Die Natur und Entstehung der Träume*, Leipzig.

Ticho, E. A., and Ticho, G. R. (1972) 'Freud and the Viennese', *International Journal of Psycho-Analysis*, **53**, 301–6.

Tyson, A., and Strachey, J. (1956) 'A Chronological Hand-List of Freud's Works', *International Journal of Psycho-Analysis*, **37**, No. 1, 19–33.

Valabrega, J.-P. (1962) *La relation thérapeutique médecin et malade*, Paris, Flammarion.

Vandendriessche, G. (1972) 'La relation entre la pulsion et la fonction cognitive dans le rêve de la monographie botanique et le souvenir-écran de la scène dans la prairie', *Revue française de Psychanalyse*, **36**, No. 5–6, 987–98.

Van der Heide, C. (1952) 'Discussion of Buxbaum (1951)', *Bulletin of the Menninger Clinic*, **16**, No. 2, 66–9.

Velikovsky, I. (1941) 'The Dreams Freud Dreamed', *Psychoanalytic Review*, **30**, 487–511.

Veszy-Wagner, L. (1969) 'Freud's "Dissection Dream" and "The Idol with the Feet of Clay"', *Scientific Bulletin of the British Psychoanalytic Society*, **32**, 19–32.

Volkelt, J. (1875) *Die Traum-Phantasie*, Stuttgart.

Wittels, F. (1924) *Sigmund Freud: his Personality, his Teaching, and his School*, translated from the German by Eden and Cedar Paul, London, Allen & Unwin.

Wittels, F. (1931) *Freud and His Time*, translated from the German by Louise Brink, New York, Liveright.

Zilboorg, G. (1952) 'Some Sidelights on Free Associations', *International Journal of Psycho-Analysis*, **33**, No. 4, 489–95.

Zweig, S. (1931) *Die Heilung durch den Geist: Franz Anton Mesmer, Mary Baker Eddy, Sigmund Freud*, Leipzig, Insel Verlag.

Name Index

Compiled by Peter Graham

A la recherche du temps perdu, 4, 120, 456
Abraham, Karl, 26, 211, 527, 555
Abraham, Nicolas, 207n.
Acropolis, 146
  disturbance of memory on, 46, 428, 440, 556
Adam Bede, 402
Adams, L., 315
Adler, Alfred, 526, 554, 566
Adler, Fritz, 20
Adler, Viktor, 20, 343
Aeneas, 116, 177–8, 189, 194, 203, 426, 457
Aeneid, 21, 177, 189, 457, 507
Albahary, Regina, 401–3
Alexander the Great, 18, 517
Alexandrian, S., 5, 129n.(2)
Alice in Wonderland, 457
Amacher, Peter, 160n.
Andersen, Hans Christian, 102, 226, 467
Andersson, O., 48n., 56n., 60, 75n., 156n.
Andreas Hofer, 358
Andreas-Salomé, Lou, 91, 527
Antarctic, 355n.
Anzieu, Annie, 207
Anzieu, Didier, ix–xiv
Apologie de la religion chrétienne, 4
Aquileia, 272, 316–17, 430
Aragon, Louis, 87
Ariosto, Ludovico, 21
Aristotle, 32, 70, 119
Arnim, Achim von, 119
Artemidorus of Daldis, 368, 464
Atlantide, L', 422
Augustine, Saint, 76, 119, 371, 426, 584
Aussee, Lake, 167–8, 188, 233, 276, 324, 333, 336–8
Austro-Hungarian Empire, 7, 9, 27, 196, 338, 359, 413
Avariés, Les, 90

Babinski, François, 46
Bachelard, Gaston, 110–11, 232, 352
Bachofen, Johann Jakob, 90
Baginsky, Adolf, 45n., 52
Bakan, David, 96
Baldwin, James Mark, 101, 249
Balint, Michael, 3
Balzac, Honoré de, 85, 204
Bánffy, Deszo, 413–14
Beard, George, 125
Beaumarchais, Pierre, 101, 339, 348
Bebel, August, 90
Bechterew, Vladimir, 87, 389–90
Beckett, Samuel, 352
Beethoven, Ludwig van, 102
Belle Hélène, La, 102
Bellevue, 120, 144–5, 337, 514, 527
Benedikt, Moritz, 48, 56, 76, 87, 94, 97
Benoît, Pierre, 422
Berchtesgaden, 114, 432, 434–6
Berenstein, I., 137–8, 145
Berge, André, 141
Bergson, Henri, 86, 128, 514n.(2)
Bernays, Anna Freud (Freud's sister), 11–14, 16, 18, 21, 134, 238–40, 248, 262, 285–94 *passim*, 300, 315, 410, 541, 561
Bernays, Berman (Freud's father-in-law), 26
Bernays, Edward (Anna and Eli Bernays' son), 18, 315
Bernays, Eli (Freud's brother-in-law), 18, 21–3, 25, 134, 314, 317, 541, 561
Bernays, Emmeline (Freud's mother-in-law), 23, 52, 102, 168, 354
Bernays, Isaac (Berman Bernays' father), 26
Bernays, Jakob (Berman Bernays' brother), 26, 71
Bernays, Judith (Anna and Eli Bernays' daughter), 18, 315
Bernays, Lucia (Anna and Eli Bernays' daughter), 18, 315
Bernays, Martha, *see* Freud, Martha Bernays
Bernays, Michaël (Berman Bernays' brother), 26–7
Bernays, Minna (Freud's sister-in-law), 15, 21, 23, 31n., 346, 403–4, 432, 540–3
  Freud's relationship with, 119, 261, 328, 337, 427, 527, 535, 546, 569
  Freud's trips with, 324, 328, 336–8, 354, 360, 528
Bernfeld, Siegfried, xvi, 34–5, 216, 256, 405
Bernfeld, Suzanne Cassirer, xvi, 183, 232
Bernhardt, Dr., 54
Bernhardt, Sarah, 24
Bernheim, Hippolyte, 53, 61, 64, 80–1, 83, 87, 104

Besançon, Alain, xix, 28, 192
Besdine, M., 204, 546
Bible (*see also* Philippson brothers), 2, 8, 17, 96, 186, 214, 217, 280, 289, 295, 299–305, 320, 427, 430
Binet, Alfred, 85, 93, 101
Binswanger, Ludwig, 150n.
Bion, W. R., 307
Bizet, Georges, 102
Bleuler, Eugen, 87
B'nai B'rith, 95, 163, 254
Böcklin, Arnold, 102, 220, 452, 554
Bölsche, Wilhelm, 91
Boltraffio, 360
Bonaparte, Princess Marie, 31n., 527
Bondy, Ida, *see* Fliess, Ida Bondy
Bondy, Pauline (Fliess's mother-in-law), 531, 540, 551
Borges, Jorge Luis, 6, 97, 209
Borgia, Lucrezia, 347
Borne, Karl Ludwig, 107, 559
Bosnia, 359–60, 362
Botticelli, Sandro, 360
Bourgeau, Hélène, xix
Bourget, Paul, 86–7, 101
Braid, James, 86
Brandes, Georg, 245
Brasch, Lucie (Lux), *see* Freud, Lucie (Lux) Brasch
Braun, Heinrich, 20
Braun-Vogelstein, Julie, 20
Brave New World, 42
Brentano, Bettina, 119
Brentano, Clemens, 84, 119
Brentano, Franz, 32, 100, 103–4, 119
Breslau, 198, 252–6, 264–5, 268, 369, 397, 399, 410, 527
Breton, André, 87
Breuer, Dora (Breuer's daughter), 57–8, 538, 542, 550
Breuer, Josef, 12, 23–5, 29–30, 36–7, 43, 51, 54, 75, 77–8, 81–2, 87, 91, 103, 109, 113–14, 118, 126, 134–55 *passim*, 164n.(1), 208, 377, 394, 399, 544, 551–2, 566, 577
  advises Freud, 24, 37, 395
  and Anna O., 40, 56–9, 569
  Freud's collaboration with, 59–71, 122–5, 267, 505
  Freud's financial debt to, 382–3, 437, 538–9, 541
  Freud's rupture with, 110, 131, 162, 267, 329, 381, 387, 425, 437–8, 482, 516, 525, 539
  theories of, 78–9, 157, 180, 351
Breuer, Margarethe (Gretel) (Breuer's daughter), 531, 537–8
Breuer, Mathilde (Breuer's wife), 30, 57, 134
Bride of Dreams, The, 130
Briquet, Paul, 94
British Psycho-Analytical Society, xiii
Browning, Robert, 85
Brücke, Ernst, 24, 30, 32–6, 44–5, 50–1, 56, 103, 106, 118, 146, 160n., 185, 354, 367, 376, 381–2, 395, 399, 420–1, 425, 433, 486, 524, 547, 563
Brühl, Carl, 98
Brun, R., 34n.
Brutus, 195, 384–6, 481
Burckhard, Max, 519
Burckhardt, J. L., 412, 420
Bürger, Gottfried, 100
Busch, Wilhelm, 100
Butor, Michel, 511
Buxbaum, Edith, xvi, 171n(1), 216, 231–4, 255–7, 263, 317, 526

Cagliostro, Alessandro di, 85
Callot, Jacques, 102, 416, 418
Candide, 101
Carmen, 102
Cassius, 384–5
Castle in Ruins, A, 102
Cauquil, Guy, xix
Cervantes, Miguel de, 20–1
Cézanne, Paul, 398
Champollion, François, 201–2
Charcot, Jean-Baptiste, 103
Charcot, Jean-Martin, 23, 30, 37, 45–56 *passim*, 64–6, 74, 87, 93, 103–4, 118, 146, 192, 264, 447, 529, 559, 566, 577
  Freud's assessment of, 47
  influence on Freud, 45–56 *passim*, 59, 185
  methods used by, 46–8, 94, 580
  views on the origins of nervous disorders, 47, 61–2, 72, 124, 351, 572
Chertok, L., 46, 49, 58n.(1), 63, 98n.
Chevreul, Michel, 86
Chomsky, Noam, 577
Chopin, Frédéric, 115
Chrobak, Rudolf, 72, 148
Cimetière marin, Le, 111
Cixous, Hélène, 4
Claretie, Jules, 87
Clark, Ronald W., xi–xii
Claus, Carl, 32
Clerk-Maxwell, James, 325–7
Coleridge, Samuel Taylor, 5
Columbus, Christopher, 178
'Committee, the', 26
Confessions (Saint Augustine), 584
Confessions (Rousseau), 92, 101, 111–12
Conrad, Joseph, 111
Consulate and Empire, 19
Contes cruels, 86
Conversations with Goethe, 238
Count of Monte Cristo, The, 84

Cromwell, Oliver, 19, 30, 415, 417–18, 483
Cyclops, 242, 258, 292–3

Dahn, Felix, 348
Dalma, Juan, 71
Dame aux camélias, La, 101
Dante, 21, 189, 320
Darwin, Charles, 32, 101, 122
Darwin, Erasmus, 91
Daudet, Alphonse, 87, 90, 101, 310, 312, 320, 369, 445–7, 486
Daudet, Léon, 87
David, Jakob Julius, 100, 394–6
David, King, 8, 303
Death of Wallenstein, The, 329
Debacker, F., 295, 302, 501–2
Defoe, Daniel, 457
Dekker, Edward Doyweac, 99n.
Delage, Y., 474, 502n.
Delboeuf, Joseph, 127, 474
Delcourt, Marie, 195
Deleuze, Gilles, 212
Démoniaques dans l'art, Les, 87
Denker, Henry, 64n.(2)
Derrida, Jacques, 179, 578
Des Indes à la planète Mars, 86
Deuteronomy, 186, 301, 304
Deuticke, Franz, 279, 310, 420, 455, 529
Devil's Elixir, The, 85
Dichter?, Ein, 394–6
Dichtung und Wahrheit, 119, 370–1
Difformes et les malades dans l'art, Les, 87
Diogenes, 517
Divine Comedy, The, 21
Docteur Pascal, Le, 99
Doctor Brodie's Report, 6
Doll's House, A, 391
Don Giovanni, 102, 166
Don Quixote, 21, 24, 102, 457
Donato, Alfred, 87
Dora, *see under* case histories *in* SUBJECT INDEX
Doré, Gustave, 102
Dorer, Maria, 35n.
Dostoevsky, Fedor, xii, 85, 101, 204
Double, The, 85
Dreyfus, Alfred, 260–1, 265, 453
Drucker, Esti, *see* Freud, Esti Drucker
Du Bois-Reymond, Emil, 34, 122
Du Maurier, George, 88, 130
Du Prel, C., 474
Dumas, Alexandre (*père*), 84–5
Dumas, Alexandre (*fils*), 101
Dupanloup, Félix-Antoine, Bishop of Orleans, 92

E., Herr, *see under* case histories *in* SUBJECT INDEX
Eckermann, Johann, 238
Eckstein, Emma (*see also under* case histories *in* SUBJECT INDEX), 137, 141–4, 146, 164, 527
Eckstein, Fritz, 98
Edinger, Dora, 58n.(2)
Egyptian gods, 17, 129, 295–309 *passim*, 317, 430
Ehrlich, Paul, 90
Einstein, Albert, 72
Eissler, Kurt, 554n.
Elective Affinities, 119
Eliot, George, 101, 402
Ellenberger, Henri F., 9, 34n., 46n., 57–8, 71, 76, 79, 89, 105, 232, 432, 514, 554n.
Ellis, Havelock, 93, 405
Emma, *see under* case histories *in* SUBJECT INDEX
Emmerich, 'Saint' Anna Katharina, 66n., 84–5
Emperor's New Clothes, The, 467
Emploi du temps, L', 511
Enemy of the People, An, 95n.
England, 15, 328, 408
  Freud's love of, 327, 417
  Freud's move to, 31n.
  as haven for the Jews, 262, 417
Enriquez-Coupère, Nicole, xix
Epheyre, Charles, 85
Erikson, Erik H., 137, 146, 363
Eros, 12, 203
Essays (Macaulay), 99
Essays (Montaigne), 111–12
Ethica, 494
Etruscan civilisation, 183, 316, 361, 426–7, 430, 430–1
Evans, Sir Arthur, 552
Eve future, L', 90
Exner, Sigmund Ritter von, 36, 125, 156, 160n., 376, 382

Facts in the Case of Mr. Valdemar, The, 85
Faria, Abbé, 84
Farrow, E. Pickworth, 559
Farthest North, 355
Faust, 98, 120, 294
  Freud quotes from, 176n.(6), 250, 255, 290, 365, 375, 387, 425, 428–9, 551n.
Fechner, Gustav Theodor, 34–5, 39, 75, 265, 462, 490
Fécondité, 99
Féré, Charles, 93
Ferenczi, Sándor, x, 428, 558
Fichtl, Paula, x, 31n.
Fidelio, 102
Fiesco, 320–2, 330
Finnegans Wake, 4
Flammarion, Camille, 86
Flechsig, Paul, 39

Fleischl von Marxow, Ernst, 24, 36, 40–1, 47, 97, 135, 138–9, 142, 367, 376–83, 399
Fliess, Conrad (Fliess's son), 521
Fliess, Ida Bondy (Fliess's wife), 109, 113, 134, 141, 144–6, 198, 219, 236, 265–7, 272–3, 278, 358, 538, 540
Fliess, Pauline (Fliess's daughter), 273, 277, 357–8, 377
Fliess, Pauline (Fliess's sister), 236, 358, 377–80
Fliess, Robert (Fliess's son), 163, 236, 377, 442, 470, 555
Fliess, Wilhelm (*see also under* ambivalence; bilaterality; bisexuality; homosexuality; nose and sexual organs; periodicity; superstition; transference *in* SUBJECT INDEX), 47, 51, 62, 65, 71–8, 91, 100, 108–14, 126, 131–55 *passim*, 169–71, 175–6, 188–90, 193–4, 198, 210, 212–22 *passim*, 226–7, 233–43 *passim*, 249–51, 271–9, 281, 284, 287–93, 328, 333–4, 346, 357–9, 366–9, 372–5, 390–5, 403–4, 442–5, 453–5, 457, 459, 476, 479, 482–3, 534–43 *passim*, 557, 562–3, 577
  Freud's 'congresses' with, 109, 143; in Achensee, 514, 527; in Berchtesgaden, 114, 434; in Berlin, 109, 575; in Breslau, 252–6, 258, 268, 276, 464, 527; in Dresden, 163; in Innsbruck, 419; in Munich, 109, 428; in Nuremberg, 218, 229; in Salzburg, 109, 163; in Vienna, 109; their effect on Freud, 163, 235, 404, 419, 428, 434, 575
  Freud's correspondence with: complete, xiv, xvi, 283n.(2); selected, xiii
  Freud's relationship with: builds up, 53, 160–7; deteriorates, 252–67 *passim*, 310–14, 317, 320, 375–88 *passim*, 399, 425, 433–41 *passim*, 475, 478, 481, 486, 506, 521–9, 547, 550, 552–4; is broken off, 257, 313, 323, 554–5, 563, 569
Florence, 168, 233
Flournoy, Théodore, 86
Flushing, 389–90
Fluss, Alfred, 13, 22, 25, 407n.
Fluss, Emil, xi, 13, 21–2, 25, 407n.
Fluss, Gisela, 13
  Freud's love for, 22, 189, 197, 205, 358, 407–8
Fluss, Richard, 13, 22, 25, 407n.
Fontane, Theodor, 100
Ford, Ford Madox, 111
Forel, Auguste, 79, 87
Fourier, Charles, 92
Fox, John, 86
France, Anatole, 99, 101, 120
Frankl-Hochwart, L., 213
Franz Josef I, Emperor, 336n., 338–40, 346
Freiberg (Příbor) (Freud's birthplace), 7–15, 146, 173, 201, 206, 340n.(7), 341n.(2)
  Freud family moves from, 1, 193, 196–7, 211, 236n.(1), 238, 255, 262, 357, 383, 399–400
  Freud returns to, 407
  Freud's memories of, 53, 189, 199, 217–18, 235, 285, 299, 304, 316, 345, 357, 377, 386
Freischütz, Der, 102
Freud, Adolfine (Freud's sister), 18, 248
Freud, Alexander (Schani) (Freud's brother), 10, 17–18, 30, 248, 346, 394, 397, 444, 517, 541
  Freud's trips with, 156, 168, 182, 272, 309, 316–18, 337, 341n.(3), 342, 360, 524, 553, 556
Freud, Amalie Nathansohn (Freud's mother) (*see also under* Zajíc, Monika), 7–19, 21, 58, 146, 235, 238–43, 248, 253, 262, 265, 294–309 *passim*, 338, 363, 365, 371, 384, 386, 400, 403, 410, 441, 465, 517, 545, 572–3, 576
  character of, 1, 21
Freud, Anna (Freud's daughter), xiii, 15, 31n., 134, 148, 163, 168, 240, 283, 377, 401–3, 443, 445, 518, 555, 557, 576
Freud, Anna (Freud's sister), *see* Bernays, Anna Freud
Freud, Anton Walter (Jean Martin Freud's son), 31n.
Freud, Berta (Freud's niece), 12–13, 15, 248, 262, 408
Freud, Clemens (Clement) Raphael (Ernst Freud's son), 31n.
Freud, Emanuel (Freud's half-brother), 1, 10–15, 24, 146, 149, 152, 198, 210, 235–6, 247–8, 262, 298, 312–13, 324, 328, 357, 383, 408, 441, 453, 516, 525
Freud, Ernst (Freud's son), 15, 30, 31n.
Freud, Esti Drucker (Jean Martin Freud's wife), 31n., 283n.(1)
Freud, Eva Mathilde (Oliver Freud's daughter), 31n.
Freud, Harry (Alexander Freud's son), 18
Freud, Henny Fuchs (Oliver Freud's wife), 31n.
Freud, Jacob (Freud's father) (*see also under* ambivalence; guilt feelings; work of mourning *in* SUBJECT INDEX), 1, 7–19, 58, 146, 196, 203, 235, 240, 247–8, 262, 286, 298–301, 305, 326, 344–6, 387, 394, 408, 410, 447–9, 466, 475, 516, 526, 570
  character of, 95–7, 198, 300
  death of, 169–74, 210–11, 226, 308, 369, 378, 401, 414–19, 427, 429, 436–41, 482, 486, 493, 512, 573, 575
  operation for glaucoma, 41, 291, 346, 370

Freud, Jean Martin (Martin) (Freud's son), 15, 30, 261, 355, 395, 401–3
Freud, John (Freud's nephew), 12–15, 199, 209–10, 218, 235–6, 248, 255, 262, 285, 304, 324, 328, 374, 379–80, 383–7, 405–8, 481, 525n., 526
Freud, Joseph (Freud's uncle), 19, 214–18
Freud, Julius (Freud's brother), 11–12, 14, 45, 51, 236, 239, 248, 261, 322, 336, 358–9, 377, 380, 384–5, 394, 403, 410, 526
Freud, Lilly (Maria (Mitzi) Freud's daughter), 18
Freud, Lucian Michael (Ernst Freud's son), 31n.
Freud, Lucie (Lux) Brasch (Ernst Freud's wife), 31n.
Freud, Margarethe (Maria (Mitzi) Freud's daughter), 18
Freud, Maria (Emanuel Freud's wife), 12, 15, 146, 247, 262
Freud, Maria (Mitzi) (Freud's sister), 18, 248
Freud, Martha (Mitzi Freud's daughter), 18
Freud, Martha Bernays (Freud's wife), 116, 135, 138–54 *passim*, 168, 185–6, 224, 236–7, 240, 261, 265–7, 281–3, 288, 290, 317, 337, 354, 365–6, 394–6, 401, 403–4, 408, 411, 444, 517, 522, 532–3, 535, 540–2, 546
  character of, 21, 23
  engagement to Freud, 36, 437, 540–1, 561
  first meets Freud, 21
  Freud's correspondence with, xiii, 16n., 22–30, 57, 109, 126
  Freud's trips with, 233, 277, 359–60, 528, 542
  marriage to Freud, 52
  menopause of, 282–3
Freud, Martin, *see* Freud, Jean Martin
Freud, Mathilde (Freud's daughter), 15, 30, 138–9, 151, 153, 167, 222–3, 354
Freud, Miriam Sophie (Jean Martin Freud's daughter), 31n.
Freud, Moritz (Maria (Mitzi) Freud's husband), 18
Freud, Oliver (Freud's son), 15, 30, 168, 414–15, 417, 483
Freud, Pauline (Freud's niece), 12–15, 235–6, 248, 262, 285–8, 304, 318, 328, 357–8, 374, 384, 405–6, 408, 410–11
Freud, Pauline (Pauli) (Freud's sister), 18, 248
Freud, Philipp (Freud's half-brother), 1, 10–15, 24, 198, 248, 262, 298–9, 305, 357, 441
Freud, Rebekka (Jacob Freud's second wife), 10–11, 441
Freud, Regine (Rosa) (Freud's sister), 18, 248, 278, 377, 520, 550
Freud, Sally Kanner (Jacob Freud's first wife), 1, 10, 248, 312–13, 441
Freud, Schlomo (Freud's paternal grandfather), 8, 45, 297
Freud, Sophie (Freud's daughter), 15, 30, 168, 376, 381, 401–3
Freud, Stefan (Stephen) Gabriel (Ernst Freud's son), 31n.
Fromm, Erich, 216, 226, 281–2
Fulda, Ludwig, 100

Galicia, 7–9, 11, 95
Galician Story, A, 9
Galton, Francis, 36, 101, 106, 215
Gargantua, 101, 333–5, 393
Gargantua et Pantagruel, 348
Garibaldi, Giuseppe, 414–19
Garnier, A., 467
Garnier, Jules, 101–2, 333, 335–6
Gärtner, Gustav, 41, 279–80, 286
Gellert, Christian Fürchtegott, 100
Germinal, 343, 348
Ghosts, 90, 392
Gicklhorn, J., 20, 554n.
Gicklhorn, Renée, 7, 16, 20, 554n.
Gide, André, 193
Gleichenberg, 184–6
Goethe, Hermann Jakob, 371
Goethe, Johann Wolfgang von, 19, 30, 34, 45, 98–9, 107, 177, 222, 237–8, 255, 293–4, 309–14, 319, 367, 370–1, 380, 423, 425n., 435, 514
  essay on Nature attributed to, 98, 227
  Freud's identification with, 20, 118–20, 146, 399
  quoted by Freud, 100, 176n.(2)(4) and (6), 184, 228, 250, 255, 288, 290, 364–5, 375, 387, 416, 418, 532, 546, 551n.
Goldmann, L., 115
Goldstein, Dr., 54
Gombaud, Antoine, chevalier de Méré, 4
Gomperz, Theodore, 99, 104, 458
Goncourt, Edmond and Jules, 87
Gotz von Berlichingen, 119–20
Gourmont, Rémy de, 92
Gozlan, Léon, 85
Gracq, Julien, 5
Gradiva, 333
Graf, Dr Heinrich, 18
Graham, Peter, xiv
Grashey, Dr., 55
Graz, 341
Greek Thinkers, 99, 458
Green, André, 160n.
Greenacre, Phyllis, 8
Gribinski, Michel, xix
Griesinger, Wilhelm, 36, 38–9, 51, 126, 463, 500
Grillparzer, Franz, 100, 348

Grimm, Jakob and Wilhelm, 100
Grinstein, Alexander, xvi–xvii, 11, 137, 183, 200, 217, 224–5, 227, 258, 280, 286–8, 295, 297, 301–4, 310–12, 320–2, 326–7, 330, 332–5, 342, 349, 363, 370, 380, 382–3, 385–6, 391, 394, 396, 401–3, 415, 418, 422–5
Gross, Hans, 515
Grotefend, Georg, 202
Grün, Anastasius, 100
Grundtatsachen des Seelenlebens, 358
Grüne Heinrich, Der, 226, 516
Guattari, Felix, 212
Guillaumin, J., 493
Gulliver, 333–6
Gulliver's Travels, 101

Haeckel, Ernst, 32, 122
Haggard, Henry Rider, 90, 101, 422–6, 484
Halberstadt, Ernst (Sophie Freud's son), 31
Halberstadt, Heinz-Rudolf (Sophie Freud's son), 31
Halberstadt, Max (Sophie Freud's husband), 31
Hamilcar Barca, 200, 203, 516
Hamlet, ix, 234, 245–6, 263, 469
Hamlet, xi–xii, 245, 249, 269, 287, 333, 469
Hammerschlag, Albert, 20
Hammerschlag, Anna, *see* Lichtheim, Anna Hammerschlag
Hammerschlag, Bertha, 135
Hammerschlag, Frau, 20, 30
Hammerschlag, Samuel, 20, 30, 95, 538, 541
Hannibal, 199–201, 203, 233, 254–5, 263
  Freud's identification with, 19, 198, 205, 254, 429
Hansen, Carl, 56, 86
Hariri, al-, 102
Hartel, Wilhelm von, 554
Hartmann, Eduard von, 100, 105, 514
Hartmann, H., 209
Hasdrubal, 199–200, 515–16
Hauffe, Friedericke, 84–5
Heart of the World, 422–6
Hegel, Georg, 101, 115, 486–7
Heidegger, Martin, 27
Heilige, Der, 401
Heimkehr, Die, 380, 486n.
Heine, Heinrich, 100–1, 107, 192, 204, 379–80, 486
Helmholtz, Hermann, 34, 36, 46, 118, 439, 563, 566
  his school of thought, 34, 38, 59, 70, 78, 106, 110, 122
Henri, V. and C., 406n.
Henriade, La, 5
Henry IV Part 1, 365
Henry IV Part 2, 383
Henry VI Part 3, 343
Heraclitus, 176n.(1)
Herbart, Johann Friedrich, 34–6, 38, 88, 105, 122, 566
Hercules, 333–4
Herder, Johann von, xi, 100, 370, 380
Hervey de Saint-Denis, Marie-Jean-Léon, 127, 129–30
Herzegovina, 359–60, 362
Herzl, Theodor, 100, 260
Herzlieb, Minna, 119
Hildebrand, F., 279n.(2)
Hildebrandt, F. W., 127, 130, 462
Hippolytus, 11
Hirschmüller, Albrecht, 538
Histoires insolites, 86
Hitopadesa, 102
Hobbes, Thomas, 101
Hoffman, Ernst, 85
Holbein, Hans, 102
Hollitscher, Robert (Mathilde Freud's husband), 31n.
Homer, 21
Horla, Le, 87–8
Horus, 303
Hugo, Victor, 86
Husserl, Edmund, 103, 196
Hutten, Ulrich von, 349
Hutten's Last Days, 99, 401
Huxley, Aldous, 42
Huysmans, Joris Karl, 87
Hymn to Joy, 102
Hypatia, 363

Ibsen, Henrik, 90, 95, 102, 391–3
Ihm, H., 92
Ilios, 420
Imperial Society of Physicians (Vienna), 49
Institute for Children's Diseases (Vienna), 52–3, 135, 151, 266
Institute of Physiology (Vienna), 24, 30, 32
International Psycho-Analytical Library, xii–xiii
Iphigenie auf Tauris, 364, 370
Irréparable, L', 86
Isis, 300, 303
Island of the Dead, 452n.
Istria, 272, 276, 309, 316, 337, 492

Jackson, J. Hughlings, 38–9, 54, 70, 206, 506
Jacobsen, Peter, 102
James, William, 101
Janet, Pierre, 46n., 59, 62, 71, 78–9, 86, 91, 105, 128, 293, 578
Jaques, Elliott, 4, 114–16, 211
Jardin secret, Le, 86
Jelliffe, S. E., 34n.
Jensen, Wilhelm, 333

Jerusalem, W., 105
Jessen, P., 461
Jocasta (*see also* Jocasta complex *in* SUBJECT INDEX), 223, 243, 301
Jones, Ernest, xiii, xv, xvi, 10, 15–16, 21–2, 34n., 35n., 43, 46, 49, 55, 57–8, 107, 114, 126, 254, 256–7, 297, 301, 305, 328, 441, 445, 543–4, 557–8
Josef II, Emperor, 381–2, 384, 481
Joseph
biblical, 14, 289, 300, 377, 381, 464
significance of name for Freud, 14, 19, 214, 300, 387, 418n.
Journal (Goncourt brothers), 87
Joyce, James, 4, 86
Joyeuse, Monsieur (character in *Le Nabab*), 369, 445–6, 488, 490, 515
Julius Caesar, 384–6, 481
Julius Caesar, 384–5
Jung, Carl, 80, 87, 150, 210, 243, 428, 516n., 526, 557, 566
Jungle Book, The, 99
Jurgens, Curt, 64n.(2)
Justine ou les infortunes de la vertu, 457

Kaan, Henricus, 93
Kafka, Franz, 103, 196
Kahane, Max, 554
Kann, Loe, 527
Kanner, Sally, *see* Freud, Sally Kanner
Kant, Immanuel, 35, 100
Kardec, Allan, 86
Karlsbad (Karlovy Vary), 188, 191, 193
Kassowitz, Max (*see also* Institute for Children's Diseases), 37, 52–3, 97, 135, 138, 151, 266
Kästner, Lotte, 230
Kaufmann, Rudolf, 126–7, 168
Kekulé von Stradonitz, Friedrich, 5–6, 150–1, 196
Keller, Gottfried, 99–100, 226, 516
Kepler, Johan, 276, 432–3
Kerner, Justinus, 84
Khan, M. Masud R., xix, 111–12
Kingsley, Charles, 101, 363
Kipling, Rudyard, 99, 101
Klecksographien, 84
Klein, Melanie, 3–4, 111, 114, 211, 577
Kleist, Heinrich von, 100, 450
Kligerman, C., 111
Knossos, 552
Köhler, Wolfgang, 106
Kohut, Heinz, 581
Koller, Carl, 40–1, 194, 279, 285, 291–2
Komik und Humor, 358
Königstein, Leopold, 40–1, 49, 135–40, 149, 153–4, 213–14, 216, 279–80, 288, 290–1, 399, 531–2, 535, 537
Körner, Karl Theodor, 106
Kortum, Karl, 100
Krafft-Ebing, Richard, 76, 87, 91–4, 103, 181, 213
Kraus, Karl, 515
Krauss, Friedrich, 92
Kris, Ernst, 209, 230
Kronos, 448–9, 468, 510, 516, 570, 574
Kubla Khan, 5
Kundt, August, 439

La Boétie, Etienne de, 111
Lacan, Jacques, 149n., 203, 244, 578
Laertes, 245
Lafontaine, Charles, 86
Lagache, Daniel, xv, 186, 499n.(2)
Laing, R. D., 232
Laius, 243, 249, 287, 301
Laplanche, Jean, xiii, 34n., 160n.
Laromiguière, Pierre, 88
Lasker, Eduard, 27, 90, 396–7, 399–400
Lassalle, Ferdinand, 27, 396–7, 399–400
Last Judgment, The, 360–1
Le Bon, Gustave, 87
Leavitt, H. G., 137
Lecher, Dr., 419
Leclaire, Serge, 355, 357
Lehmann, H., 355
Leibniz, Gottfried, 105
Leiden eines Knaben, Die, 333, 349
Lemberg (Lvov), 8–9
Lenau, Nicolaus, 100
Leonardo da Vinci, xii, 18, 204, 294n., 301, 372
Leonardo da Vinci, 100
Lessing, Gotthold, 100
Leute von Seldwyla, Die, 99
Leviathan, 101
Lévi-Strauss, Claude, 247, 577
Lewin, Bertram, 184
Lichtenberg, Georg, 100
Lichtheim, Anna Hammerschlag, 20, 134–5, 140, 153, 538
Lichtheim, Dr., 54–5, 134n.
Lichtheim, Rudolf, 20, 134, 153, 538–9
Liébeault, Ambroise, 61, 87, 432, 497
Lied von der Glocke, 416
Liguori, Alfonso de, 92
Lindau, Paul, 85
Lindner, Gustaf Adolf, 35
Lindner, S., 92
Lipps, Theodor, 277, 358, 472, 508–9
Lipschutz, Louis S., 288
Livy, 195
Louis Lambert, 85
Love Council, The, 90, 349–51
Löwenfeld, L., 529, 534
Löwenstein, Rudolph M., 209

Löwy, Emanuel, 249, 254
Lübeck, 184–5, 187
Ludwig, Karl, 34, 39
Lueger, Karl, 109, 163
Lustgarten, Sigmund, 39, 540
Lvov, *see* Lemberg

Macaulay, Thomas, 99
Madonna, 102
Magic Flute, The, 102
Magnan, Valentin, 93–4
Magnétiseur, Le, 85
Malade imaginaire, Le, 101, 326–7
Malleus Maleficarum, 182
Malraux, André, 72
Man without Qualities, A, 50n.
Manchester, 15, 17
Mann, Thomas, 244
Mannoni, O., 164n.(1), 568, 570
Mantegazza, Paolo, 91
Maqāmāt, 102
Marbach, 326, 329, 516
Marburg, 325–6, 328–9, 360, 515, 516
Maria Theresa, Empress of Austria, 200, 382, 416
Mariage de Figaro, Le (Beaumarchais), 101, 348, 349n.
Mariage forcé, Le, 101
Marie, Pierre, 46, 54
Marriage of Figaro, The (Mozart), 102, 339
Marrou, Henri-Irénée, 584
Marshall, H. R., 454
Marx, Karl, 72, 101
Masaryk, Thomas, 103
Masséna, André, 200–1, 429
  Freud's identification with, 19, 205
Masson, Jeffrey Moussaieff, xiv, xvi, 283
Matter and Motion, 325–7
Matthew (*Gospel according to Saint*), 427
Maundy Money, 102
Maupassant, Guy de, 87–8, 90–1, 101, 187
Maury, Alfred, 127–9, 367, 461–3, 487
Max Havelaar, 99n.
Mayer, C., 514
Maylan, Charles, 261n.
Médecin de Pecq, Le, 85
Medusa, 228, 371
Meistersinger von Nürnberg, Die, 102
Mémoires d'un médecin, Joseph Balsamo, 85
Mémorial, 4
Mendelssohn, Moses, 300
Mephistopheles, 290, 294, 425n.
Merezhkovsky, Dmitri, 100
Meringer, R., 514
Merlan, P., 104
Mesmer, Franz Anton, 48, 84
Mesmerism, 85
Meyer, B. C., 111
Meyer, Conrad Ferdinand, 99–100, 271, 274, 324, 333, 335, 349, 354, 401–2
Meynert, Theodor, 35–9, 46–7, 49, 55, 93, 103, 118, 126, 146, 160n., 181, 399, 438, 482, 525
Meysenbug, Malwida von, 91
Michelangelo, 204, 361
Michelet, Jules, 90, 92
Mill, John Stuart, 18, 24, 36, 101, 104
Milton, John, 101
Mintorn, William, 85
Miseries of War, 102
Mitchell, Silas Weir, 85
Moebius, Paul, 125
Molière, 101, 326
Moll, Albert, 48, 76, 87
Montaigne, Michel de, 111–12, 456
Moravia, Alberto, 194
Moravia (province), 7, 9, 95, 195
Morel, Bénédict-Augustin, 93
Morticoles, Les, 87
Moses, xii, 17, 166, 186, 203–4, 300, 301, 304, 327, 358, 457
Mozart, Wolfgang Amadeus, 102, 115, 166
Müller, Max, 101–2
Multatuli, 99
Munich, 109, 133, 147, 152, 336, 391, 428, 521, 557
Munthe, Axel, 87
Musil, Robert, 50n., 582
Myers, Frederick, 85

Nabab, Le, 369, 445–7, 486–8
Nancy, 49, 61
Nansen, Fridtjof, 102, 178, 354–7
Naples, 120, 183, 193
Napoleon, 200–2
Narayana, 102
Narcissus, 203
Nathansohn, Jacob (Freud's maternal grandfather), 297–9, 306
National Liberal Party (German), 27
Nausicaa, 226, 516
Nebuchadnezzar, 427
Neu-Titschein (Nový-Jičín), 7, 345
New Ghetto, The, 260
'New Melusina, The', 30
Nibelungenlied, 100
Nietzsche, Friedrich, 28, 72, 88–91, 100–1, 320, 476, 487, 523, 581
Norris, Edwin, 202
Nos fils, 92
Nothnagel, Hermann, 23, 37, 54, 162, 175, 213, 394–6, 399, 529
Notre-Dame de Paris, 333, 335, 393
Notre-Dame de Paris, 101
Novalis, 100
Nový-Jičín, *see* Neu-Titschein

Nozze di Figaro, Le, see Marriage of Figaro, The
Nuremberg, 198, 218–20, 229, 258, 369

O., Anna, *see under* case histories *in* SUBJECT INDEX
Obersteiner, Heinrich, 37
Odin's Consolation, 348
Odysseus, 226–7, 390, 516
Odyssey, 460, 494, 515
Oedipe, 193
Oedipus (see also Oedipus complex in SUBJECT INDEX), 70, 175, 193, 195, 203, 243–9, 264, 269, 287, 309, 335, 468–9
Oedipus Rex, 21, 175, 243–4, 246, 249, 269, 287, 469
Oeuvre, L', 397–8
Offenbach, Jacques, 102
Oneirocritica, 368
Orlando Furioso, 21, 102
Orlik, Emil, 554
Orvieto, 233, 360–1, 426, 428, 430
Osiris, 300, 303
Other, The, 85

Pagel, J. L., 513
Painter, G. D., 4
Paneth, Joseph, 30–1, 153, 376, 379–84
Panizza, Oskar, 90, 100, 349–52
Panurge, 336
Pappenheim, Bertha (*see also* Anna O. *under* case histories *in* SUBJECT INDEX), 24, 56–9, 134, 148
Paris, 188, 393
  Freud adopts motto of, 185, 190, 566, 728
  Freud's stay in, 37, 45–9, 101, 192–3, 333, 446
Pascal, Blaise, 4, 18, 101, 352, 456
Pascal, Etienne, 17
Paul, Jean, 100
Pavlov, Ivan, 389
Pensées, Les, 4, 456
Penthesilea, 450
Pescara, see Tempting of Pescara, The
Pestalozzi, Johann, 86, 394
Peter Ibbetson, 130
Peto, A., 425
Peyer, Alexander, 94
Phaedra, 11
Philippson brothers (publishers of *Bible*), 17, 95, 280, 289, 300–5, 309, 320, 430
Piccolomini, 329
Picture of Dorian Gray, The, 85
Pinel, Philippe, 47
Pirandello, Luigi, 86–7
Plato, 27, 104, 250, 387, 463, 510
Plutarch, 384
Poe, Edgar Allan, 85
Poetics, 70
Poirot-Delpech, Poirot, 14
Politzer, G., 399
Pompeii, 183, 193, 220
Pontalis, J.-B., xiii, 48, 155, 580
Prague, 183, 187–8, 190, 195–6, 198, 218, 254, 255, 476
Précieuses ridicules, Les, 101
Prévost, Marcel, 86
Příbor, *see* Freiberg
Prince, Morton, 85, 87
Propylaea (Munich), 147, 152, 391
Proust, Marcel, 4, 86–7, 120, 146, 204, 456
Provinciales, Les, 4
Proverbs, book of, 8
Pur, Josef (one-eyed doctor), 14, 217, 241–2
Purcell, Henry, 115
Puységur, Amand-Marie-Jacques, Marquis de, 84

Rabelais, François, 101, 333–6, 348, 349n.
Racine, Jean, 115
Radestock, P., 463
Rank, Otto, 106, 195, 243, 375
Raphael, 115
Räuber, Die, 385–6, 517–18
Ravenna, 168, 187–90
Rawlinson, Henry, 202
Red Thread, The, 64n.(2)
Reich, Wilhelm, 212, 577, 581
Reik, Theodor, xi, 256, 366, 566
Reitler, Rudolf, 554
Restif de la Bretonne, Nicolas, 92–3
Reuter, Fritz, 100, 137
Rhine Gold, The, 5
Ribeiro-Hawelka, E., xix, 339n.(1), 375
Ribot, Théodule, 85, 94
Richer, Paul, 87
Richet, Charles, 85, 87
Richterin, Die, 274, 333
Rickman, John, xiii
Rie, Oscar ('Otto'), 46, 53, 132, 135–40, 145, 149, 152–4, 240, 266–7, 387, 399, 495, 531, 535, 537, 540
Riklin, Franz, 428
Rilke, Rainer Maria, 91
Rimbaud, Arthur, 115
Rivail, Hippolyte, 86
Rivière, Joan, 527
Roazen, Paul, 282–4
Robbe-Grillet, Alain, 5
Robert, W., 130, 472
Robinson Crusoe, 457
Roheim, Geza, 547
Rolland, Romain, x, 556
Roman Villa, The, 102, 452n.
Rome (*see also under* anti-Semitism; dreams dreamt by Freud *in* SUBJECT INDEX), xi, 177, 182–212 *passim*, 223, 257, 260, 418, 436,

Rome – *cont.*
457, 526
Freud longs to visit, 12, 120, 180, 183, 182–212 *passim*, 249, 254–5, 277, 372, 412–13, 476, 551, 556
Freud visits, 527, 553–5, 562
Rorschach, Hermann, 84, 87
Rosenberg, Ludwig ('Leopold'), 135–40, 149, 153–4, 531, 535, 537
Rosenblum, Eva, xviii, xix, 8, 153–4, 161, 185–6, 191–2, 194, 292–3, 314, 338, 347, 362, 393, 400, 401n.
Rosenfeld, Eva, 295, 297, 301
Rosenfeld, Herbert, 45
Rosolato, G., 7
Rousseau, Jean-Jacques, 92–3, 101, 111, 119, 266
Ruined Castle, The, 554

Sacher-Masoch, Leopold Ritter von, 9, 93
Sachs, Hanns, 256
Sade, Marquis de, 93, 457
Sajner, J., 7, 10, 12n., 13–14, 217, 441
Salpêtrière, La, 45–9, 53, 59, 87, 561
Samuel, 301–3
Sanchez, Thomas, 92
Sandoz, Pierre, 397–8
Sant' Angelo, Ponte, 183–4, 187, 205
Sappho, 312, 320
Sardou, Victorien, 24, 101
Sartre, Jean-Paul, 204, 352
Saul, 301, 303
Saussure, R. de, 49, 58n.(1)
Scheffel, Joseph von, 100
Schelling, Friedrich von, 19, 34, 100
Scherner, Karl Albert, 127, 129, 316, 404, 462–3, 479, 508–9
Schiff, Arthur, 537, 542, 550
Schiller, Johann, 119, 325–6, 329–30, 399, 418, 559
quoted, 77, 100, 106, 320, 385, 409, 416, 433, 517
Schliemann, Heinrich, 420, 522
Schneider, Louis, 100
Schnitzler, Arthur, 100, 554
Scholz, Franz, 37
Schönberg, Ignaz (Minna Bernays' fiancé), 21, 23–5, 117, 153, 185–6, 562
Schöne Müllerin, Die, 102
Schopenhauer, Arthur, 91, 100, 105, 514
Schubert, Franz, 102
Schur, Max, xiii, 31, 43, 96, 113, 137, 143–4, 164–6, 268n., 273–4, 276, 372, 392, 422, 428, 432, 437, 441, 540
Schwab, Sophie, 30, 153, 376, 380
Schwind, Moritz von, 531
Seeress of Prevorst, The, 84
Sex and Character, 555
Shakespeare, William (*see also* individual plays), ix, 2, 17, 101, 204, 208, 245–6, 343, 365, 383–5, 399
She, 422–4, 426
Sherrington, Charles, 156
Sh'lōmōh, King, 8
Sibyl, 177
Siegfried, 8
Sieglinde, 8
Siena, 233, 257, 261
Signorelli, Luca, 233, 235, 359–62, 365–6, 393, 399, 430, 515
Silberer, Herbert, 343
Silberstein, Eduard, 20
Simmel, Ernst, 256
Simon, P. M., 127, 462
Sketches, 99
Smith, Adam, 101, 326–7
Smith, Helen, 86
Social Democratic Movement (German), 27
Soeur Marthe, 85
Somnambule, Le, 85
Sophocles, 21, 70, 175, 287, 469, 572, 582
Soulié, Frédéric, 85
Spehlmann, R., 34n.
Spencer, Herbert, 101
Spinoza, Baruch, 35, 494
Spitta, H., 462–3, 549n.
Spring Awakening, The, 91
Stannius, H., 421, 426, 481
Starobinski, Jean, xii, 234n., 244–6
Stein, Conrad, 155, 172, 210, 212, 320n., 417–18, 570
Steiner, Rudolf, 103
Stekel, Wilhelm, 243–4, 428, 471, 554
Stevenson, Robert Louis, 5, 85, 130
Story of San Michele, The, 87
Strachey, Alix, xiii
Strachey, James, xii–xiii, 159–60
Strange Case of Dr. Jekyll and Mr. Hyde, The, 85, 130
Stricker, Salomon, 39, 41, 97, 279, 280
Strümpell, Adolf, 128
Super Flumina Babylonis, 260
Sur la pierre blanche, 99
Svevo, Italo, 86
Swift, Jonathan, 101
Swinburne, Algernon, 101, 260
Swoboda, Hermann, 555
Széll, Koloman, 413–14, 416

Taaffe, Count, 338, 340
Taine, Hippolyte, 101
Tannhäuser, 102
Tartini, Giuseppe, 5, 508
Tartuffe, 101
Tausk, Victor, 212, 282, 577, 581
Tempting of Pescara, The, 401–3

Tennyson, Alfred Lord, 101
Terence, 102
Terre, La, 348
Théodora, 24, 101
Thiers, Adolphe, 19, 101
Thun, Count (*see also under* dreams dreamt by Freud in SUBJECT INDEX), 196, 337–40, 344, 346
Thoth, 300
Tiber, River, 183–4, 187–8, 457
Tilgner, Victor, 165–6
Titian, 102
Titus, 197, 260
Tobler, G. C., 98
Trasimeno, Lake, 198, 200, 233, 254
Trieste, 32, 51, 120, 316, 362
Trilby, 88
Twain, Mark, 99
Tysmenitz (Tysmenica), 8–9
Uhland, Johann Ludwig, 100
Ulysses, 4
Uranus, 449, 510n., 516, 574
Ursule Mirouet, 85
Ut mine Stromtid, 137

Valéry, Paul, 111
Van der Heide, C., xvi, 525
Van Dyck, Anthony, 102
Vandendriessche, G., 279n.(2), 280, 294n.
Vasari, Giorgio, 102
Vatican, 184–5, 188, 190
Venice, 156, 168, 218–19, 233, 238, 316, 521, 528
Venus in Furs, 9
Verne, Jules, 515
Veronese, Paolo, 102
Veszy-Wagner, Lilla, 427
Vienna (*see also under* anti-Semitism *in* SUBJECT INDEX)
  Freud family moves to, 15, 417
  Freud's dislike of, 2, 27, 210, 212, 262, 359, 372, 561
Vienna Psychoanalytical Society, 555, 563
Vienna University, 2, 23, 27, 51, 93, 97, 134, 343, 375–6, 560
Villaret, A., 53
Villiers de L'Isle-Adam, Auguste, 86, 90
Vinci, Leonardo da, *see* Leonardo da Vinci
Vingt mille lieux sous les mers, 515
Virgil, 20–1, 176n.(3), 177, 189
Vischer, Robert, 129n.(1)
Vischer, Theodor, 100, 129n.(1), 515
Vlissingen, 389–90
Volkelt, Johannes, 127–8, 404
Voltaire, 5, 101
Voyage au centre de la terre, 515
Voyage to Italy, 120

Wagner, Richard, 5, 8, 91, 102
Wagner-Jauregg, Julius von, 90
Wahle, Emil, 25
Wahle, Fritz, 25, 540–1
Wahle, Richard, 25
Waldeyer, W., 33
Wallenstein's Camp, 329
Wandsbek, 21–3, 31, 41, 45n.
Watteau, Antoine, 115
Waves of the Sea and of Love, The, 348–9
Wealth of Nations, The, 101, 325–7
Weber, Carl Maria von, 102
Wedekind, Frank, 91
Wednesday Society, 375, 554–5, 563
Weininger, Otto, 91, 555
Weiss, Nathan, 24, 37
Welsbach, Dr. Auer von, 530
Weltweisen, Die, 409, 432
Wernicke, Carl, 55, 134n., 359
Werther, 119–20, 222, 230, 333
Wilbrandt, Adolf, 100
Wild Duck, The, 391–2
Wilde, Oscar, 85
Wilhelm Meister, 30, 119, 146, 532
Wilhelm II, Kaiser, 109
Wilkinson, Garth, 559
William Wilson, 85
Winckelmann, Johann, 100, 200, 205, 254, 429
Winnicott, D. W., 112, 581
Winternitz, Valentin, 18
Wisdom, book of, 8
Wittels, Fritz, xi, 20, 61, 381
Wolf, Hugo, 476
Woolf, Virginia, 86

Zahme Xenien, 176n.(4)
Zajíc family, 12, 146, 173, 236, 238, 341n.(2)
Zajíc, Johann, 12–13
Zajíc, Monika (Freud's Czech nurse), 11, 13, 146, 199, 235, 247, 298, 341n.(1) and (2), 344, 406, 547, 572
  dishonesty of, 238–40, 261–2, 304, 320, 335, 386
  as double of Freud's mother, 9, 265, 357, 371, 410, 573, 576
  influence on Freud, 12, 227–8, 237–41, 320, 384, 399–400, 404
Zeus, 448–9, 468, 510, 516, 552, 574
Ziehen, Theodor, 359
Zilboorg, Gregory, 36, 106
Zola, Emile, 87, 99, 101, 265, 343, 348, 349n., 397–8, 400
Zuckerkandl, Emil, 97, 194
Zuckerkandl, Otto, 97, 194
Zweig, Arnold, xi
Zweig, Stefan, 89

Subject Index

Compiled by Peter Graham

abreaction, 75, 122, 125, 180
  Freud's first use of term, 70, 79
abstinence, rule of, 375, 543–4, 546, 564, 567
absurdity in dreams, *see under* dreams
activity, 564, 567
actual neurosis, 110, 116, 123, 307
aetiology of neuroses, sexual, *see* sexual aetiology of neuroses, Freud's theory of the
affects (*see also* quota of affect), 125
  displacement of, 75
  in dreams, Freud's theory of, 484–6, 578
  exchange of, 75
  suppression of, 280, 316, 421, 485, 565
  transformation of, 75, 385, 506
agency, 564
agoraphobia, 181, 186, 342, 500
allo-erotism, 522, 564, 567
alteration of the ego, 564
ambivalence, 374, 385, 411, 478, 481, 564, 562
  discovery of, 45
  Freud's, towards Fliess, 141, 218, 263, 388, 459
  Freud's, towards his father, xviii, 4, 19, 172, 209, 216, 218, 242, 374, 415, 570
anal erotism, 326, 478
anal material (*see also* faeces), 253, 328, 332, 348, 393, 414–17, 477
anal sexual system, 567
anal stage, 252, 336, 343, 345, 466, 564
  regression to, 250
anal zone, 189–191, 251, 478, 545n.
analysis (*see also* psychical analysis; psychoanalysis), 125
  interminable, 353, 559–60, 564, 581
anti-Semitism, 191, 199, 203, 205, 213, 215–16, 254, 260–3, 266, 335, 338, 393, 397, 453
  Freud resists, 26, 343
  of Roman Catholic church, 12, 184
  in Vienna, 27, 97–8, 109, 162–3, 212, 417, 554, 561
anxiety, 125, 158, 307–9, 498, 567
  castration, xix, 166, 263–4, 318, 351–4, 423, 430, 447–50, 478–9, 489, 510, 563, 574, 576
  about death, 362, 385, 388, 429, 518
    working over of, 362
  depressive, 45, 212, 371, 570, 581
  fragmentation, 430
  object-loss, 357, 430
  persecutory, 45, 570, 581
  punishment, 423–5, 471, 477
  separation, 173, 186, 256, 357
anxiety dreams, *see under* dreams
anxiety hysteria, 263
anxiety neurosis, 72n., 73–5, 82, 123, 125, 477
aphasia, 54–5, 118
archaeology, 200, 300
  Freud's interest in, 178, 420, 516
  compared to psychoanalysis, 179, 183, 208
artichoke, 281, 285, 287, 291, 348
attention, 564
  evenly-suspended, 559, 564, 567, 580
auto-erotism (*see also* masturbation), 44, 399–400, 563–4, 567

bed-wetting, *see* enuresis
benzene, structure of, 5
bilaterality, Fliess's theory of, 256–61, 268, 275, 291–2, 322, 328, 369, 482, 524, 538
bilingualism, 196, 201
biographers, Freud's attitude to, xi, 1
bisexuality, 90, 221, 393, 447, 479, 536–7, 550, 564, 567
  Dora's, 545, 576
  Fliess's theory of, 181, 229, 256–60, 264–5, 268, 275, 291–2, 322–4, 367–9, 436, 438, 440, 482, 510, 523, 543, 573
  factor in Freud's estrangement from Fliess, 91, 210, 434, 506, 527–8, 552–3, 555
body image, xix
  as element of dreams, 152–5, 172, 187, 198, 204, 225, 318, 346, 366, 404, 458, 546–8
brother horde, 386
bungled actions, unconscious factors in (*see also* parapraxes), 564

cardiac symptoms, Freud's (*see also under* hypochondria; smoking), xii, 43–4, 77, 113, 117, 136–7, 140, 142, 154–5, 165, 171–2, 226, 250, 274, 372, 439
case histories:
  Dora, 70, 80–1, 91, 152, 374, 478, 531, 535, 543–5, 548, 550, 563, 569, 576
  Herr E., 161, 181, 190, 223, 231, 253–4,

413, 437–8, 440, 521–5, 563, 569
Emma (*see also* Eckstein, Emma, *in* NAME INDEX), 137, 141–6, 158
Fräulein Rosalia H., 68
Irma (*see also under* dreams dreamt by Freud), 73, 132–4, 281, 531, 535, 538–9, 569, 573
Katharina, 66–7, 76, 78
Little Hans, 80
Frau Cäcilie M., 68–9, 82
Frau Emmy von N., 59–61, 66, 78, 83, 127
Anna O. (*see also* Pappenheim, Bertha, *in* NAME INDEX), 24, 40, 56–9, 70–1, 78, 123, 134–5, 140, 148, 152, 208, 217, 538, 543, 550, 569
Fräulein Elisabeth von R., 64–7, 78, 83
Fräulein Lucy R., 64–6, 78
Rat Man, 80, 375, 407n.
castration, notion of, 564, 571
castration anxiety, xix, 166, 263–4, 318, 351–4, 423, 430, 447–50, 478–9, 489, 510, 563, 574, 576
castration complex, 351, 449, 459, 477–9, 573, 574
castration phantasy, 233, 311, 350–2, 425, 460, 502, 574
catharsis, 60, 69–71, 122, 180
cathartic method, 58–9, 70, 104, 125, 208
cathexis, 122, 125
Freud's first use of term, 60, 63, 83
cerebral paralysis of children, 46, 53–4
censorship, 67, 79, 83, 125, 215, 253, 290, 414, 485–509 *passim*, 543
first, Freud's theory of (between the unconscious and the preconscious), 35, 498–502, 549, 566–7, 573–4, 576, 579, 584
Freud's first use of term, 465
second, Freud's theory of (between consciousness and the preconscious), 35, 68, 447, 450, 507–9, 566–7, 573–4, 576, 579, 584
cerebral paralysis of children, 46, 53–4
childhood memories, *see* infantile memories
childhood wishes, *see* infantile wishes
children's dreams, *see under* dreams
'chimney sweeping' (*see also* 'talking cure'), 57, 60
choice of neurosis, *see under* neurosis
cleanliness, learning of, 227, 237, 320, 478, 547, 564
clitoral zone, 251, 564
cocaine, 39, 51, 53, 56, 118, 139
anaesthetising properties of, 27, 40–2, 110, 133, 142, 194, 279, 285, 288, 290–2, 350, 367, 376, 392, 546
cases of addiction to, 31, 41, 44, 135, 367
Freud takes, 29, 40, 570
coitus interruptus, 94, 116, 223, 477
coitus reservatus, 74, 116, 477
colt's foot, 340, 346–8, 357
complex (*see also* castration complex; family complex; Jocasta complex; Oedipus complex; professional complex)
of ideas, 80, 123
Jung's use of term, 80, 243
component instincts, 3, 478, 584
compromise
dream as, 567
screen memory as, 567
symptom as, 162, 567
compromise-formation, 160–1, 210, 219, 409
Freud's notion of, 412, 499, 504, 564
compulsion, 564
condensation, 130, 151, 214, 275, 281, 299, 306, 308, 341, 344, 347, 398, 442, 453, 504, 511, 529, 533, 567, 573
Freud's theory of, 473–5, 549, 564
condom phantasies, 218
'congresses', *see under* Fliess, Wilhelm *in* NAME INDEX
consciousness (*see also under* censorship; preconscious; unconscious), 151, 156
Freud's theory of the preconscious, the unconscious and, 151, 179–80, 182, 202, 207, 277, 491–509 *passim*, 563, 565, 576, 579
splitting of, 63
constancy, principle of, 35, 63, 75, 81, 125, 156, 504
content, *see* latent content; manifest content
contraceptive techniques (*see also coitus interruptus*; *coitus reservatus*), 74, 90–1, 113, 116, 136, 141, 145–6, 282–3, 366, 477, 580
conversion, 83, 123, 125
conversion hysteria, 69, 75, 125, 263
copulation phantasies, 136, 140, 145–8, 288–90, 297, 305, 329, 423–5, 450, 477, 508, 564
counter-suggestion, 47, 59–60, 251
counter-transference, 216, 251, 452, 548, 553, 558
discovery of, 28
Freud's, on to female patients, xviii, 139–40, 223, 374, 477, 531, 543, 548, 569
cryptomnesia, 86
Freud's, 259, 528
cyclamen, 279–81, 286, 288, 292–3, 348
Czech language, 7, 196–7, 199, 201, 204, 235, 338

dandelion, 287, 340, 346–8, 357, 405
day-dreams, xvii, 6, 70, 291, 445–7, 486–8, 513
Freud's: 'Stopping a runaway horse', xvii, 445–7
'Revenge when "coincidentally" meeting parents who had not had confidence in his

day-dreams – *cont.*
professional capacities', xvii, 521
day's residues, 564
appearance of, in dreams, 280, 492, 495–6
relevance of, in understanding dreams, xvii, 152, 214, 225, 290, 452, 465
and wishes, 266, 281, 294
death
anxiety about, 362, 385, 388, 429, 518
connection with sexuality, 362, 365
Freud's fear of, 139, 165, 167, 263, 273, 278, 317–18, 562
death instincts, notion of, 567, 581, 584
death wishes, 221, 428, 564, 567
against Fliess, 317, 366
against parents of the same sex, 231, 247, 307, 317, 321, 366
debasement, 564
defence (*see also* neuro-psychoses of defence), 72, 78–9, 82–3, 105, 125, 131, 147, 162, 180, 257, 409, 567, 577, 581
defence hysteria, 75, 79, 125
deferred action, 66, 125, 158, 405, 409, 511, 563, 564, 567
defloration phantasies, 147, 304, 318, 404, 413, 564
degeneracy, as cause of hysteria, 19, 47, 61–2, 74–5, 351
depressive anxiety, 45, 212, 371, 570, 581
depressive position, 211
working over (through) of, 4, 45, 114, 212, 429, 577
depressive tendencies, Freud's, 29, 231–2, 523–4, 562, 577
deviations, sexual, 92–4
difference between the sexes, *see* sexual difference
dismemberment, 425, 427, 430
displacement, 123, 125, 130, 151–2, 214, 275, 280, 291, 409, 442, 487, 490, 511–512, 533, 567, 573
of affects, 75
Freud's theory of, 475, 549
of Oedipal object, 3
distortion, 152, 214–15, 290, 489
Freud's theory of, 465, 549, 564, 573
double, theme of, 85, 547
double personality, 57, 85–6, 571
dramatisation, 151, 462, 490, 512
Freud's theory of, 549, 564
dream, Freud's lost, 436, 444
dreams (*see also* interpretation of dreams; somatic sources of dreams *and under* compromise; faeces; jokes)
absurdity in, 263, 275, 310–13, 342, 414–15, 434, 442
anxiety, 17, 271, 294–6, 299, 309, 356, 436, 471, 486, 498–502, 549
of awakening, 167–8
children's, 167–8, 442–3, 450
compared to
hieroglyphs, 202n., 331, 475n.
picture-puzzles, 208, 300, 305, 306–7, 330–1, 459–60, 473, 565, 567, 578
screen memories, 567
symptoms, 158, 567
of compliance, 222
of convenience, 214, 431
and creativity, 5–6
examination, 193, 241, 470–1
of flying, 470–1
of hunger, 442–3
of nakedness, 226, 272, 366, 467–8, 522
punishment, 294
scientific literature on, 127–31, 460–3
of thirst, 167–8
unconscious factors in, 564
as wish-fulfilments, 126, 131, 140, 144, 158, 167, 212, 215, 221–2, 224, 226, 243, 258, 260, 268, 271, 281, 334, 373, 461, 463, 465, 468, 503, 567
dreams dreamt by Freud:
'Archimedes' statue', 556
'*Autodidasker*', 27, 261, 389, 394–400, 474, 486–7, 490–1, 504, 518
'Awake, being', 168
'Botanical monograph', 203, 268, 275, 278–95, 300, 335, 348, 356–7, 376, 466, 469
'Breakfast-ship', *see* 'Castle by the sea'
'Brücke and silver paper', *see* 'Dissecting my own pelvis'
'Castle by the sea' ('Breakfast-ship'), 273, 275, 314–18, 333, 430, 484–5, 492, 541
'Church-tower, the forgotten', 555
'Cliff in Böcklin style', xviii, 452, 465
'Close the eyes', 64, 128n., 169–74, 253, 275, 341n.(7), 378, 475, 478
'Closet, open-air', 277, 332–6, 342, 348, 356, 393, 485
'Count Thun' ('Revolutionary dream'), 277, 295, 297, 299, 310, 336–51, 354, 356–7, 369, 393, 414, 437, 466–7, 482
'Dishonesty', *see* 'Hall with machines'
'Dissecting my own pelvis' ('Brücke and silver paper', 'Self-dissection'), 417, 419–31, 433, 437, 447, 449, 481, 484–5
'1851 and 1856', 216, 310, 421, 433–41, 482–4, 489
'Etruscan cinerary urn', 430–1, 464
'Famous speakers', 419, 470
'Father on his death-bed like Garibaldi', 128n., 207, 310, 411–21, 426, 437, 482–3
'Frau Doni and the three children', 261, 400–4, 406, 414, 421, 437, 483
'Funeral oration by young doctor', xviii, 453, 465

'Glass top-hat', xvii, 530, 549
'Goethe's attack on Herr M.', 238, 272, 275, 309–14, 319–20, 348, 351, 388, 391, 393, 402, 414, 421, 437, 476, 482–3, 549, 550n.
'Grey horse', *see* 'Riding on a horse'
'Hall with machines' ('Dishonesty', 'Sanatorium'), 273, 275, 318–22, 476, 479
'Hearsing', 367, 388–90, 394, 396, 474
'Hella', xvii, 213, 221–4, 226, 234
'Hollthurn', 231, 277, 324–32, 336n., 337, 339, 345n., 348, 396, 402, 421, 484, 489, 516
'Irma's injection', 13, 41, 53, 120, 131–56, 158, 167, 171, 173, 175, 187, 194, 203, 207, 212, 214, 217–18, 221, 238–40, 263, 266–7, 270, 281, 287–9, 292, 294, 296–7, 309, 311, 340n.(1), 376, 391, 436, 438, 463–4, 469, 473, 475, 478, 489–90, 504, 518–19, 531, 534–6, 538–9, 549, 569, 572–3, 577
'Keeping a woman waiting', xviii, 452, 465
'Mother and daughter', xviii, 452, 465
'My mother and the bird-beaked figures', 13, 17, 271, 294–309, 317–18, 320, 332, 345n., 356–7, 407, 430, 462, 488, 501
'My son, the Myops', 41, 242, 257–67, 275, 292, 310, 313, 340n.(6), 341n.(1) and (7), 369, 388, 414, 437, 470, 482, 537, 547
'Nansen's sciatica', 354–8, 466
'*Non vixit*', 214, 217, 224, 278, 369, 372, 375–88, 434, 438, 481, 485, 489, 518, 547
'*Norekdal*', 389–94, 396, 474
'One-eyed doctor and schoolmaster', 217, 241–3, 572
'Otto was looking ill', 216, 265–7, 470, 495–6
'Padua, Restaurant Garden at', 555
'Periodical for 20 florins', 465
'Phantasies during sleep', 320, 322–4, 447, 476, 479, 573–5
'Pope is dead, the', 556
'Professor Oser's dietary', 556
'Professorship', 265
'Reconciliation with a friend', 556
'Revolutionary dream', *see* 'Count Thun'
'Riding on a horse' ('Grey horse'), 278, 372–5, 385, 467, 549
'Rome' series, 46, 166, 203–13, 215, 227, 251, 275, 318, 385, 429, 464, 466, 469
  first and second dreams, 183–7
  third dream, 181, 183, 187–95, 572
  fourth dream, 183, 195–213, 255, 476, 516
'Sanatorium', *see* 'Hall with machines'
'Savonarola's profile', 556
'Self-dissection', *see* 'Dissecting my own pelvis'
'Sheep's head', xvii, 119, 235–9, 241, 253, 465, 572
'Sixth form, being in the', xvii, 431–2
'Social Democrats, communication from', xvii–xviii, 452, 465
'Son, news of, from the front', 556
'Swimming-pool', xvii, 530–1, 549
'Table d'hôte, company at', xvii, 22, 517, 531–49
'Three Fates', 265, 277, 362–71, 380, 445, 466–7
'*Trottoir roulant*', xvii, 529–30, 549
'Uncle with the yellow beard', 213–18, 242, 266, 270, 309, 377, 385, 387, 425n., 464–6, 469, 473, 475, 485, 497
'Undressed, running up stairs', 213, 221, 224–9, 234, 237, 369, 464, 467–9, 572–3
'Villa Secerno', 213, 218–222, 230, 275, 369, 452n., 475, 478
'Working in the laboratory', 555–6
'Yellow lion', 215, 217, 354–8, 406, 466
dreams dreamt by others:
  'Achilles and Diomede', 464, 486, 549
  'Applause in theatre', 549
  'Arrest in restaurant', 486–7
  'Arrested for child-murder, being', *see* 'Infanticide, arrest for'
  '*Asplenium* and the lizards', 461
  'Attending a religious ceremony with an uncovered head', 461
  'Aussee, trip across Lake', 168, 464, 493, 549
  'Barrister's lost cases', 465
  'Bathing hut, outside closet and attic', 476
  'Bed too small', 549
  'Big dish with big joint', 470
  'Book with very small type', 462
  'Box packed with books', 466
  'Boys struggling', 466
  'Boys, two rows of', 467
  'Burning child', 460, 488–90, 497–8, 550
  'Cairo, shop in', 461
  'Candle and candlestick', 466
  'Carriage accident', 461
  'Carts with vegetables', 476
  'Caviare, legs covered with', 476
  '*Chauffeurs* of La Vendée', 461
  'Cherries, basket of', 465, 549
  'Child with deformed skull', 481
  'Children grew wings', 468
  'Chimpanzee and gorilla-cat', 481
  'Chocolate, bars of', 167–8, 464
  'Church bells', 461
  'Coffin, little Karl in his', 465–6, 468, 484, 549
  'Cooling apparatus', 467
  'Crockery, broken', 462
  'Dachstein', 168, 464, 549
  'Dead bodies being burnt', 481
  'Dead daughter in case', 465, 468
  'Dragged through a stream, being', 461

dreams dreamt by others – *cont.*
'Drawers, two rows of', 467
'*Dutzendmensch*', 493–4
'Explorers' dreams', 355n.
'Falling from a high wall', 461
'Father had died but did not know it', 538
'Father in a railway accident', 482
'Fire-alarm', 461
'*Gen-Italien*', 374
'Giants at table', 462
'Graben, falling down in the', 466
'Grotesque figures with strange coiffures', 462
'Guillotine', 461, 487
'Hanged, being', 461
'Hotel bedroom, mistaken number of', 425
'I must tell the doctor that', 483
'"I was born in 1882"', 481
'Income-tax return, false', 465
'Infanticide, arrest for' ('Arrested for child-murder, being'), 223, 465
'Kilometres', 367
'*Kontuszówka* Liqueur', 461
'Language of flowers', 407, 476–7, 480, 549–50
'Lovely dream' ('Up and down', '*Sappho*'), 310, 474–6, 550
'Lynx or fox', 468
'*Maistollmütz*, 391, 474
'Market dream', 466, 549
'Mask of pitch', 461
'May-beetle dream', 450, 474–5
'Medical student and hospital' ('Pepi's dream'), 127, 464, 467
'Meeting Dr. K. in the Kärntnerstrasse', 512, 550n.
'Menstruation', 464, 549
'Milk stains on vest', 464
'Montbrison, childhood at', 461, 466
'Mount Etna, climbing', 461
'Mussidan in Dordogne', 461
'Mustard plaster', 461
'Napoleon and the wine merchant', 461
'Napoleon's dream', *see* 'Tagliamento, crossing of'
'Orthopaedic institute', 466
'Orvieto wine', 461
'Pains in jaw', 464
'Party with Daudet, Bourget and Prévost', 464
'Paying 3 florins 65 kreuzers for something', 481, 549
'Pepi's dream', *see* 'Medical student and hospital'
'Piano a disgusting old box', 466
'Revolution of 1848', 461
'Rohrer Hütte and the Hameau', 464, 466, 549
'*Sappho*', *see* 'Lovely dream'
'Scalped, being', 461
'Schoolboy exposed in bed', 466
'Seven kine', 464
'Sleigh bells', 461
'Smoked salmon, supper of', 465
'Stake between the toes', 461
'Storm in the Channel', 461
'Strawberries', 168, 442–3, 464, 549
'Summer holidays with mother-in-law', 465
'Tagliamento, crossing of' ('Napoleon's dream'), 461, 467, 487
'Tartini's dream', 5, 508
'Three lions in a desert', 484
'Three theatre tickets for 1 florin 50 kreuzers', 481, 549
'Tortured by the Inquisition, being', 461
'Travelling at night with cold knees', 461
'Trilport, childhood at', 461
'*Tutelrein*', 391, 474
'Tutor and nurse in bed', 466, 484
'Up and down', *see* 'Lovely dream'
'Violent rush', 466
'Wagner opera', 476, 482
'Well-spread table', 462
'Wet weather at the Hilmteich', 481
'Who is the baby's father?', 476, 479, 483
'Winter overcoat', 466
dream-work, 130, 182
Freud's theory of, 444, 465, 472–3, 487, 564, 582
dual personality, *see* double personality
dynamic point of view (of mental processes), 36, 105, 122, 483, 500, 568, 571

economic point of view (of mental processes), 36, 63, 105, 122, 483, 494, 500, 568
ego, 226, 522, 564, 571
alteration of, 564
Freud's ego, 51–2
Freud's notion of, 156, 158–9, 162, 567
primary ego, 39
regression under control of, ix, 209, 568
secondary ego, 39
splitting of, 522
ego-ideal, 171
its relationship with super-ego in Freud, 51, 171, 304, 308–9, 438
ego-instincts, 366
egoism, 564
electrotherapy, 40, 56, 62, 94, 357
energy (free, bound), 125, 157
English language, 201
Freud's love of, 17, 20
enuresis, 54, 297, 299, 345–6, 350, 367, 393
Eros, 12, 203
erotism, *see* allo-erotism; anal erotism; hetero-erotism; homo-erotism; oral erotism;

urethral erotism
erotogenic zones (*see also* anal zone; clitoral zone; oral zone; urethral zone), 65, 93, 180–1, 187, 189, 218, 400, 545, 564, 566, 572
'eternal feminine, the', 423, 425, 428
excitation, *see* sexual excitation; summation of excitation; sum of excitation
excrement, *see* faeces
exhibitionism (*see also* dreams of nakedness), 92–3, 224, 467–8
exhibitionistic wishes, 224, 564, 572
experience of pain, 564, 567
experience of satisfaction, 157, 505, 564, 567

facilitation, 327, 563
faeces (*see also* anal material), 546
  equated with a gift, 334
  equated with money, 82, 189–90, 253, 327, 565, 567
  theme of, in dreams, 277, 325–36 *passim*, 342–6, 414–17, 420, 466, 576
fainting attacks, Freud's, 428, 557
family circle of thoughts, 516
family complex, 80, 516n.
family romance, 274, 458, 522, 564, 567
  Freud's first use of term, 221, 229
fellatio, 545
  phantasies, 576
fetishism, 93
filiation, Freud's Oedipal, 11, 206–7, 247–9, 298, 344, 440–1, 516
fixation, 81, 125, 229, 564, 566
flight into illness, 83
flight into psychosis, 123, 125
forgetfulness, forgetting, xvii, 152, 507, 517, 520, 528–9, 536
  caused by censorship, 489
  caused by repression, 177, 279, 358–60
  of names, 267, 278, 353, 358–62, 515, 518, 556
  unconscious factors in, 564
fragmentation, 570, 581
  anxiety, 430
free association(s), 60, 106–8, 126, 131, 148, 225, 360, 374–5, 490, 548, 562, 564, 567
French language, Freud's understanding of, 20, 46, 192, 201
Freud(e), die (German word for "joy"), 11n., 193, 388, 390, 446
  cause of jokes about Freud's name, 16, 164n., 369, 371, 389, 445
fright, 69, 122, 125, 505
frigidity, 74, 77

genetic point of view (of mental processes), 483, 494, 500, 568
German language, 7, 9, 16–17, 95, 195–8, 201, 203–8, 300
Greek language, 20, 201
guilt feelings (*see also* self-reproach), 88, 413, 429, 449, 471
  Freud's, towards his father, 19, 175

Hebrew, 8–9, 17, 20, 30, 95–7, 197, 201, 300–1, 440, 518
helplessness, notion of, 564
hetero-erotism, 522
hieroglyphs
  decipherment of, 201–3
  dreams compared to, 202n., 331, 475n.
  hysterical symptoms compared to, 67
holothurians, 325–6, 328, 348, 360
homo-erotism, 522
homosexuality, 230, 314, 367, 428, 440, 466, 537, 557
  disapproval of, in 19th century, 90, 93
  element of, in Freud's relationship with Fliess, 109, 165, 239, 243, 259, 292, 312, 393, 525–6, 543, 552, 569
hypercathexis, 503, 506, 509, 564
hypnoid state, 62–3, 70, 78–9, 125
hypnosis, 47–9, 72, 79, 84–8, 104–5, 251, 357, 563, 571
hypnotherapy, 56–71 *passim*
hypnotism, *see* hypnosis
hypochondria, 125, 558
  Freud's (*see also* cardiac symptoms), 42–3, 52, 132, 164
hysteria (*see also* anxiety hysteria; conversion hysteria; defence hysteria; retention hysteria; symbolisation, hysterical; symptoms, hysterical), 46–7, 79–83, 108, 161, 221, 283, 409
  allo-erotic, 522
  causes of (*see also* degeneracy), 47, 50n., 72, 75, 79, 94, 162, 182, 351, 356, 506
  male, 49, 55, 94, 161, 232, 438, 569
  perversion the negative of, 181
  and primal scenes, 218
  therapy of, 56–71 *passim*
hysterical symptoms, *see* symptoms, hysterical
hysterogenic zone, 64–5, 125

id, 88, 159, 567
identification(s), 151–2, 221, 564
  Freud's (*see also under* Goethe; Hannibal; Masséna *in* NAME INDEX)
    feminine, 239, 259, 427
    heroic, 2, 201, 205, 320, 334–5
    heroic-masochistic, 396, 400, 429
  with lost object, 222, 564
  with victim, 200, 223, 335, 385
imago
  maternal, 88, 430
  paternal, 88

impotence, 74
impulses, 564
hostile, 221
instinctual, 564
perverse, 219
incest, 8, 50n., 67, 177, 223, 225, 230, 247, 274, 318, 350, 423–4, 564, 567
incest taboo, 254–5, 298, 307, 327–8, 398, 543, 573, 582–3
incestuous phantasies, 240
incestuous wishes, 205, 234, 242, 245, 264, 285, 303, 317, 364, 468–9, 501, 564, 572
inertia, principle of, 81, 156, 158, 327, 565
infantile amnesia, 564
infantile memories (*see also* screen memories), xvii–xviii, 7, 173, 189, 198, 218, 227, 235–6, 285, 356, 383, 466, 545–6, 572, 576
infantile omnipotence, 212
infantile sexual theories, 90, 152, 264, 313, 335, 477, 545, 575
infantile sexuality, 91, 158, 161, 175, 226, 282, 286, 324, 327, 351, 466, 478, 483, 534, 563, 564, 571
infantile wishes, 145–6, 172–3, 189, 225, 244, 252, 258, 467
and day's residues, 280–1, 294, 495–6
Oedipal, 317–18, 423
for omnipotence, 212, 417, 447, 449, 569
inhibition, 74, 77, 88, 156, 224–8, 284, 374, 505–6
innervation, 125
instincts (*see also* death instincts; life instincts)
Freud's first theory of, 366
Freud's second theory of, 12, 567
Nietzsche on, 88
sexual, 366
instinctual impulses, 563
interminable analysis, 565
interpretation of dreams, notion of, 450–2, 489–90, 503, 530, 565
isolation, Freud's scientific, ix, xii, 28, 51, 54, 98, 110–11, 162–4, 212, 398, 453, 457–8, 523, 555, 568–9

Jew, Wandering, 8, 177, 457
Jewish background, Freud's (*see also under* anti-Semitism; jokes), 1, 7–10, 15, 20, 25–7, 94–8, 109, 134, 138, 190, 247, 282, 286, 342n., 365, 440, 543, 561
Jews (*see also under* England *in* NAME INDEX), 59, 400, 417, 580
superstition of, 96–7, 273, 400
Jocasta complex, 546
jokes (*see also under* Freud(e), die), 362, 487, 563
in dreams, 171, 229, 391, 435, 453–4, 578
Jewish, 96, 188, 190, 194, 229
and the unconscious,358, 567

latency period, 162, 565
latent content, notion of, 472–80, 565, 567
Latin language, 20, 196–7, 207
libidinal stage, 565
libido, 94, 125
Freud's first use of term, 75–6, 83
Freud's theory of, 229, 251, 307, 566–7
life instincts, notion of, 567, 581, 584
locality, psychical, 491, 565, 567
lost object, notion of, 565, 567

magnetism, 79, 84–6
manifest content, notion of, 472–80, 565, 567
masochism, 93
Freud's (*see also under* identification(s)), 546, 548
masturbation, 73–4, 77, 283, 302, 347, 407, 493
19th-century attitudes to, 92–4, 308, 365, 471, 580
phantasies, 219, 288, 307, 318, 406, 459, 502
'primary addiction', 44, 252, 287
threat of punishment for, 501–2, 565, 567, 574
megalomania, 333–5, 343, 485
infantile, 393, 496
melancholia, 75, 77, 211, 221–2, 488
memories, *see* infantile memories; screen memories
memory, *see* return of the memory
menopause
Martha Freud's, 282–3
male, 284
mental concentration, 64–5, 72, 106
mesmerism, 48
metapsychology, 163, 353, 358, 436, 456, 514, 565
mid-life crisis, 4
Freud's, xii, 3, 44, 114–21 *passim*, 211–12, 284, 376, 417, 422, 568
mourning, 77, 163
Freud's work of, 169, 175, 177, 182, 186, 210–11, 232, 234, 308, 317, 369, 378, 562, 570, 575
myths, 567
Freud's interest in, 21, 552
referred to by Freud, 70, 176–8, 189, 194, 203, 211, 222–3, 228, 258, 320, 468–9, 494, 516, 568, 574, 582
as wish-fulfilments, 243

narcissism, 203, 522
Freud's, ix, 2, 109, 205, 548, 568
narcissistic regression, 5, 211, 293
Nature, Freud's interest in the philosophy of, 19, 34, 98–9, 118, 227, 294, 311, 313
need for punishment, 565
negation, 69, 124–5

negative therapeutic reaction, 111, 565, 581
nervous system, Freud's theory of the, 33, 38
neurological research, Freud's, 33, 36–9, 52–6, 563
neurone theory, Freud's, 33, 156–61, 167, 180
neuropathic family, 62, 74, 124–5
neuro-psychoses of defence, 123, 125, 131
neuroses, sexual aetiology of, *see* sexual aetiology of neuroses, Freud's theory of the
neurosis
  actual, 110, 116,123, 307
  anxiety, 72n., 73–5, 82, 123, 125, 477
  choice of, 251, 521
  Freud's neurosis, xviii, 240, 257, 261n., 526, 557
  Freud's 'transference neurosis', xviii, 231–4
  as negative of perversion, 565, 567
  obsessional, 123–5, 161–3, 180, 219, 473, 522, 563, 572
night's residues, 493, 495, 498
nose and sexual organs, Fliess's theory of the connection between, 110, 113, 133, 136, 141, 163, 256, 272, 292–3, 310, 411, 440, 523, 536, 552–3

object of wish, 565
object-loss anxiety, 357, 430
obsessional neurosis, 123–5, 161–3, 180, 219, 473, 522, 563, 572
Oedipal filiation, Freud's, 11, 206–7, 247–9, 298, 344, 440–1, 516
Oedipus complex (*see also* Oedipus *in* NAME INDEX), 137, 154, 324, 495, 563
  Freud's discovery of, 117, 132, 140, 172, 175, 198–9, 240–50, 264, 297, 301, 377, 450–1, 469, 473, 481–2, 488, 501, 519, 572–3, 576
  Freud's first use of term, 80
omnipotence
  infantile wishes for, 212, 417, 449, 569
  phantasied, 385
ontogeny, 32, 38
oral erotism, 44, 92, 136, 204, 478, 545
oral sadism, 449
oral sexual system, 545, 565, 567
oral stage, 466
oral zone, 189, 251, 478, 545
over-determination, 69, 125, 290, 299, 327–9, 360, 467, 488, 490, 494–5, 500, 565
over-interpretation, 565

paralysis,
  cerebral, of children, 46, 53–4
  Freud's intellectual, 228, 232–3, 242, 267, 274, 277–9, 311–14, 350–4, 372, 411, 449, 511, 573
  general (general paresis) (*see also* syphilis), 90, 311–14, 348–53, 370, 372, 392–3, 396–400, 427, 474–6
paranoia, 77, 123, 125–6, 163, 180, 219, 221, 522
parapraxes
  cases of, 258, 296, 507, 514–21, 527
  as material for self-analysis, xv, 151, 515–21, 536–7, 542, 563, 571, 578
  unconscious factors in, 565
paresis, general, *see* paralysis, general
parricidal wishes, 468, 477, 572–3
parricide, 33, 172, 264, 303, 350, 449, 469, 501, 582
passivity, 564, 567
penis need, 450, 510, 571, 576
perception-consciousness (perceptual-conscious) system, 6, 157, 179–80, 491, 565
perceptual identity, 159, 565
periodicity
  Fliess's theory of, 109–10, 133, 141, 163–6, 256n., 273, 284, 292, 311, 322, 369, 377, 391, 438–40, 523, 537, 553, 555–6
  Freud's theory of, 77
persecution anxiety, 45, 570, 581
perversion (*see also* sexual deviations)
  Freud's theory of, 176n.(6), 180–1, 224, 368–9, 522
  hysteria (neurosis) as negative of, 181, 565, 567
  origin of, 93
phallic phase, 351
phallic sexual system, 567
phallus as symbol, 565
phantasies
  condom, 218
  copulation, 136, 140, 145–8, 288–90, 297, 305, 329, 423–5, 450, 477, 508, 564
  fellatio, 576
  incestuous, 240
  masturbation, 219, 288, 307, 318, 406, 459, 502
  pregnancy, 125, 140, 477, 565
  resonance of, 112–13
  unconscious, 565
  as wish-fulfilments, 243
phantasy, Freud's notion of (*see also* primal phantasy), 68, 151, 179, 405, 567, 575
phobia (*see also agoraphobia*; *railway phobia*), 181
phylogeny, 32, 38
picture-puzzles, dreams compared to, *see under* dreams
pleasure principle, 104, 159
pleasure-unpleasure principle, 36, 156, 454, 500, 505, 565
preconscious, the (*see also under* censorship; consciousness; unconscious), 105
  Freud's theory of, 147, 486, 505, 512, 565, 571, 572, 575

preconscious – *cont.*
Freud's theory of the unconscious, consciousness and, 151, 179–80, 182, 207, 277, 491–509 *passim*, 563, 565, 576, 579
thing-presentations and, 584
and the unconscious, 6
word-presentations and, 187, 202, 498, 571, 584
pregnancy phantasies, 125, 140, 477, 565
pregnancy, phantom, 57–8, 134, 148
presentations, *see* thing-presentations; word-presentations
primal horde, 1, 12–13, 207, 580
primal period, 14
primal phantasy, 351, 356, 406, 450, 484, 489, 502, 571, 576
primal scene, 68, 108, 148, 212, 218–19, 285, 298–9, 318, 329, 332–3, 342–6, 355–6, 362, 393, 501, 522, 563, 565, 567
primary gain, 567
primary processes, 151, 157–8, 396, 479, 502–3, 506, 565, 567, 571
professional complex, 80, 516, 518–19
professorship (*see also under* dreams dreamt by Freud)
Freud aspires to, 36, 93, 183, 194, 213, 216, 265–6, 269–70, 321, 335, 340n.(5), 343, 440, 454, 530
Freud obtains, 452n., 521, 553–4, 562
projection, 77, 83, 125
prostitutes, 90, 286, 369–70, 381, 389, 399, 546
protective fictions, 219, 229
protective shield, 565
psychical analysis, 64–5, 80, 124, 147, 562
psychical apparatus, Freud's theory (topography) of,
first, xviii, 6, 48, 147, 175–82 *passim*, 187, 220, 464, 472, 479, 487–511 *passim*, 536, 563, 565, 571, 573–9
second, 12, 212, 567, 577
psychical conflict, 35, 125
psychical locality, 565, 567
psychical system, 564, 579–80
psychical working out, 124–5
psychoanalysis
applied to literary works, 222, 230, 333, 401, 467
compared to archaeology, 179, 183, 208
discovery of, xvi, 2–3, 48, 108, 247, 571
Fliess's contribution to, 114
first use of term, 80, 162
today, 3, 251
psychoanalytic technique, 2, 48, 64, 172, 235, 251, 374–5, 390, 420, 437, 548, 580
psychology, clinical, 565
psychoneuroses of defence, *see* neuro-psychoses of defence

punishment,
anxiety, 423–5, 471, 477
need for, 565
threat of, 362
for masturbation, 501–2, 565, 567, 574
purposive ideas, 490, 565

quota of affect, 60, 80–1, 83, 122, 125

railway phobia, Freud's, 15, 114, 171, 178, 185, 233, 255–6, 263, 342, 434, 522, 562, 577
reaction-formation, 497, 565
reality-testing, 156, 565, 567
regression
to anal stage, 250
under control of ego, ix, 209, 568
examples of, 153, 232, 340n.(1), 429
Freud's theory of, 38, 67, 125, 151, 222, 396, 490–2, 565, 567, 576
narcissistic, 5, 211, 293
repetition, 492, 565
representability, 475–7, 479, 484, 487, 492, 549, 565, 573
representation, 340, 353
Freud's theory of, 105, 152, 214, 275, 421, 442, 472, 476, 479, 495–6, 498, 504, 511–12
symbolic, xvii
repression (*see also* return of the repressed), 88, 176n.(3), 177, 499n.(2), 502n.
as cause of forgetfulness, 177, 279, 358–60
Freud's theory of, 35, 63, 65, 69–70, 81–3, 123, 125, 151, 162, 180–1, 221, 230, 250–1, 253, 409, 468, 474, 485, 503–7, 513, 549
resistance, 148, 214, 234, 477
in creativity, 110–11
Freud's theory of, 61, 79, 83, 124–5, 176, 251, 489–90
resonance of phantasies, 112–13
retention hysteria, 125
return of the memory, *see* return of the repressed
return of the repressed, 35, 63, 82, 123, 507, 582
revenants, theme of, 228, 376–88 *passim*, 417, 485, 525
reversal into the opposite, 194, 214–15, 217, 310–14, 476, 485, 512, 538, 565
revision, *see* secondary revision
Romanticism, 34–5, 50–1, 84, 88, 90, 105, 115, 128–9

sado-masochism, 478
scientific literature on dreams, *see under* dreams
screen memories, xvi, 74, 267, 278, 353
Freud's:
'Green meadow with yellow flowers',

xvii, 10, 14, 189, 199, 217, 242, 262, 286–7, 304, 316, 328, 341n.(2), 355, 357–8, 377, 404–12, 478, 480, 488, 515
'Injury to his face with a lasting scar', xvii
'Tearing up book', 285–7, 290–1
'Wardrobe', 239–40, 305
Freud's theory of, 409, 515, 565, 567
secondary ego, 39
secondary gain, 250, 565, 567
secondary processes, 157–9, 396, 479, 487, 506, 565, 567, 571
secondary revision, 6, 296, 306, 396, 473, 486–7, 489, 498, 501–2, 512, 549, 565, 573
seduction, Freud's theory of childhood,
phantasised, 67, 356, 366, 478, 572
real, 50n., 67, 92, 123, 125, 140, 161–2, 181–2, 218, 220, 222–3, 229, 234–5, 359, 366, 409, 477, 521
self-analysis
Freud's, continues throughout his life, ix, 121, 428–9, 555–60
interruptions in Freud's, x, 249, 265, 268, 278, 283
notion of, 216, 419–30 *passim*, 565
period of Freud's systematic, 212, 231–3, 297, 457, 514, 562–3, 577
technique of, 450–2, 463–4, 566, 568–70
self-doubt, Freud's, xii, 289, 420, 426, 562
self-exoneration, 219, 224, 320, 335, 471, 478, 539
self-reproach, 163, 170, 221, 384, 565
separation anxiety, 173, 186, 256, 357
sex life, Freud's, 52, 107, 116, 282–4, 366, 445
sexual aetiology of neuroses, Freud's theory of the (*see also* seduction, Freud's theory of childhood), 57–79 *passim*, 123, 137, 141, 148, 158–63, 217, 234, 251, 269, 311, 366, 381, 395, 400
sexual chemistry, Fliess's theory of, 133, 136, 151, 158, 167
sexual deviations, 92–4
sexual difference, 264, 289, 314, 323, 327–9, 336, 478, 510
suppression of, 165
sexual instincts, 366
sexual organs and nose, *see* nose and sexual organs
sexual symbolism
of wardrobe, 239
of hat, 322
sexuality (*see also* infantile sexual theories; infantile sexuality), 105, 113, 454, 477, 513
attitude of Freud's contemporaries to, 49–50, 89–94 *passim*
connection with death, 362, 365
Freud's attitude to, 51, 116–17, 282, 368
sibling rivalry, notion of, 468, 565
smoking, Freud's, 43–4, 77, 113–14, 142, 144, 165, 167, 171–2, 226, 263, 284, 288, 439, 577
somatic compliance, 35, 565, 567
somatic conversion, 65
somatic sources of dreams, 271–2, 309, 342, 363, 462, 467–8
specific action, notion of, 565
splitting, 124
of the ego, 125, 522
of consciousness, 63
of the personality, 85–6
sublimation, 52, 88, 219, 250, 294n., 565
of component instincts, 3, 478
substitute-formation, 125
suggestion, 125
sum of excitation, 62, 81–2, 123, 125
summation, 82, 125, 176
summation of excitation(s), 39, 77
super-ego, 88, 346, 482, 567, 584
relationship with ego-ideal, in Freud, 51–2, 171, 304, 308–9, 438
superstition, 519, 567
about numbers
Fliess's, 377
Freud's, 96, 273
suppression of affects, 280, 316, 421, 485, 565
surrealists, 5–6, 87, 129n.
symbol equated with symptom, 69, 82
symbolisation, 317, 463, 574
Freud's theory of, 74, 82, 487–8, 578
hysterical, 69, 123, 125
symbolism, 459, 478, 565
sexual, 244, 477–8, 549
of wardrobe, 239
of hat, 322
symptom equated with symbol, 69, 82
symptom-formation, 176, 504, 565
symptoms
appearance of, 62
compared to dreams, 158, 567
curability of, 47
Freud's theory of, 69, 80–1, 161–2, 499, 567, 571, 578, 584
hysterical, 56–75 *passim*, 82, 148, 150, 345, 486
'join in the conversation', 65, 226
as wish-fulfilments, 222, 229, 268
syphilis, 73, 90–1, 260, 266, 286
as cause of general paralysis, 90, 312, 348–53, 370, 392, 396, 399, 449, 474

'talking cure', 57, 70, 208
Thanatos, 12
thing-presentations, 324, 330, 472–5, 487, 565, 567, 573, 575, 578–9
and preconscious, 584
and unconscious, 187, 202, 435, 571, 584

threat of punishment, *see* punishment, threat of
topographical point of view (*see also* psychical apparatus, Freud's theory (topography) of), 122–3, 488, 499–500, 504, 567, 576
topography, *see* psychical apparatus, Freud's theory (topography) of
totemism, 301, 552, 565
transference (*see also under* neurosis), 58, 79, 84, 124–5, 490, 496, 503, 543–4, 546
  Freud's, on to Fliess, xviii, 141–2, 209–10, 220, 231–4, 242, 245, 258–9, 264, 267, 291, 353, 385, 393, 425, 459, 481–2, 521–9, 550n.(2), 569
  Freud's, on to others, 346
transformation of affects, 75, 385, 506
'transvaluation of all psychical values', 320, 476, 487
trauma
  as cause of hysterical symptoms, 47, 57–79 *passim*, 122, 125, 158, 162, 181, 544, 563
traumatic hysteria, 125
trimethylamin, 133–42 *passim*, 146–50, 153, 167, 428, 504
  formula of, 13, 146, 158, 201, 263, 289, 535–6, 577

uncanny, the, 427, 547
unconscious, the (*see also under* censorship; consciousness; preconscious), 38, 105, 221, 309, 457, 567
  compared to a foreign language, 12
  Freud's theory of the preconscious, consciousness and, 151, 179–80, 182, 202, 207, 277, 491–509 *passim*, 563, 565, 576, 579
  and the preconscious, 6
  thing-presentations and, 187, 202, 435
  word-presentations and, 435
unconscious phantasies, 565
unconscious wishes, xvii, 565
unpleasure principle, 39, 159, 454n.
urethral erotism, 478
urethral sexual system, 567
urethral stage, 336
urethral zone, 189, 333–5, 343–8, 545n.

vacancy of consciousness, 62
venereal disease (*see also* syphilis), 73, 90–1, 260, 266, 365
verbal associations, pole of, 565

wishes
  exhibitionistic, 224, 564, 572
  incestuous, 205, 234, 242, 245, 264, 285, 303, 317, 364, 468–9, 501, 564, 572
  infantile, 145–6, 172–3, 189, 225, 244, 252, 258, 467
  parricidal, 468, 477, 572–3
  unconscious, 565
wish-fulfilment, 222, 269, 412–13, 435–6, 457, 489, 493–8, 506, 513, 565, 574
  in day-dreams, 513
  in dreams, 126, 131, 140, 144, 158, 167, 212, 215, 221–2, 224, 226, 243, 258, 260, 268, 271, 281, 334, 373, 461, 463, 465, 468, 503, 567
  Griesinger on, 39
  in myths, 243, 309
  in phantasies, 243
  in symptoms, 222, 229, 268, 412
witchcraft, 181–2, 458
word-presentations, 161, 324, 330, 405, 472–5, 480–1, 487, 565, 567, 573–4, 578–9
  and the preconscious, 187, 202, 498, 571, 584
  and the unconscious, 435
working out, psychical, 124–5

Yiddish, 7, 95, 192, 197, 201